PHILIP'S

STREET ATLAS
Wiltshire
and Swindon

www.philips-maps.co.uk

First published in 2002 by

Philip's, a division of
Octopus Publishing Group Ltd
www.octopusbooks.co.uk
2-4 Heron Quays, London E14 4JP
An Hachette Livre UK Company

Second edition 2006
Second impression 2008
WILBA

ISBN-10   0-540-08770-X (spiral)
ISBN-13   978-0-540-08770-9 (spiral)

© Philip's 2006

Ordnance Survey®

This product includes mapping data licensed
from Ordnance Survey® with the permission of
the Controller of Her Majesty's Stationery Office.
© Crown copyright 2006. All rights reserved.
Licence number 100011710.

Contents

III   **Key to map symbols**

IV   **Key to map pages**

VI   **Route planning**

X   **Administrative and Postcode boundaries**

1   **Street maps** at 3½ inches to 1 mile

163   **Street maps** at 1¾ inches to 1 mile

213   **Street maps** at 3½ inches to 1 mile

218   **Town maps** of Andover and Frome

219   **Index** of towns and villages

222   **Index** of streets, hospitals, industrial estates, railway
stations, schools, shopping centres, universities
and places of interest

Digital Data

The exceptionally high-quality mapping found in this atlas is available as digital data in TIFF format, which is easily convertible to other bitmapped (raster) image formats.

The index is also available in digital form as a standard database table. It contains all the details found in the printed index together with the National Grid reference for the map square in which each entry is named.

For further information and to discuss your requirements, please contact james.mann@philips-maps.co.uk

Key to map symbols

Motorway with junction number	**Ambulance station**
Primary route – dual/single carriageway	**Coastguard station**
A road – dual/single carriageway	**Fire station**
B road – dual/single carriageway	**Police station**
Minor road – dual/single carriageway	**Accident and Emergency entrance to hospital**
Other minor road – dual/single carriageway	**Hospital**
Road under construction	**Place of worship**
Tunnel, covered road	**Information Centre** (open all year)
Rural track, private road or narrow road in urban area	**Shopping Centre**
Gate or obstruction to traffic (restrictions may not apply at all times or to all vehicles)	**Parking, Park and Ride**
Path, bridleway, byway open to all traffic, road used as a public path	**Post Office**
Pedestrianised area	**Camping site**
Postcode boundaries DY7	**Caravan site**
County and unitary authority boundaries	**Golf course**
Railway, tunnel, railway under construction	**Picnic site**
Tramway, tramway under construction	**Important buildings, schools, colleges, universities and hospitals** — Prim Sch
Miniature railway	**Built up area**
Railway station Walsall	**Woods**
Private railway station	**Tidal water, water name** — River Ouse
Metro station South Shields	**Non-tidal water** – lake, river, canal or stream
Tram stop, tram stop under construction	**Lock, weir, tunnel**
Bus, coach station	**Non-Roman antiquity** Church

Acad	**Academy**	Inst	**Institute**	Recn Gd	**Recreation Ground**
Allot Gdns	**Allotments**	Ct	**Law Court**		
Cemy	**Cemetery**	L Ctr	**Leisure Centre**	Resr	**Reservoir**
C Ctr	**Civic Centre**	LC	**Level Crossing**	Ret Pk	**Retail Park**
CH	**Club House**	Liby	**Library**	Sch	**School**
Coll	**College**	Mkt	**Market**	Sh Ctr	**Shopping Centre**
Crem	**Crematorium**	Meml	**Memorial**	TH	**Town Hall/House**
Ent	**Enterprise**	Mon	**Monument**	Trad Est	**Trading Estate**
Ex H	**Exhibition Hall**	Mus	**Museum**	Univ	**University**
Ind Est	**Industrial Estate**	Obsy	**Observatory**	W Twr	**Water Tower**
IRB Sta	**Inshore Rescue Boat Station**	Pal	**Royal Palace**	Wks	**Works**
		PH	**Public House**	YH	**Youth Hostel**

Roman antiquity ROMAN FORT

67 **Adjoining page indicators and overlap bands**

168 The colour of the arrow and the band indicates the scale of the adjoining or overlapping page (see scales below)

■ The small numbers around the edges of the maps identify the 1 kilometre National Grid lines

■ The dark grey border on the inside edge of some pages indicates that the mapping does not continue onto the adjacent page

The scale of the maps on the pages numbered in blue is 5.52 cm to 1 km • 3½ inches to 1 mile • 1: 18103

0 ¼ ½ ¾ 1 mile
0 250 m 500 m 750 m 1 kilometre

The scale of the maps on pages numbered in green is 2.76 cm to 1 km • 1¾ inches to 1 mile • 1: 36206

0 ¼ ½ ¾ 1 mile
0 250m 500m 750m 1 kilometre

III

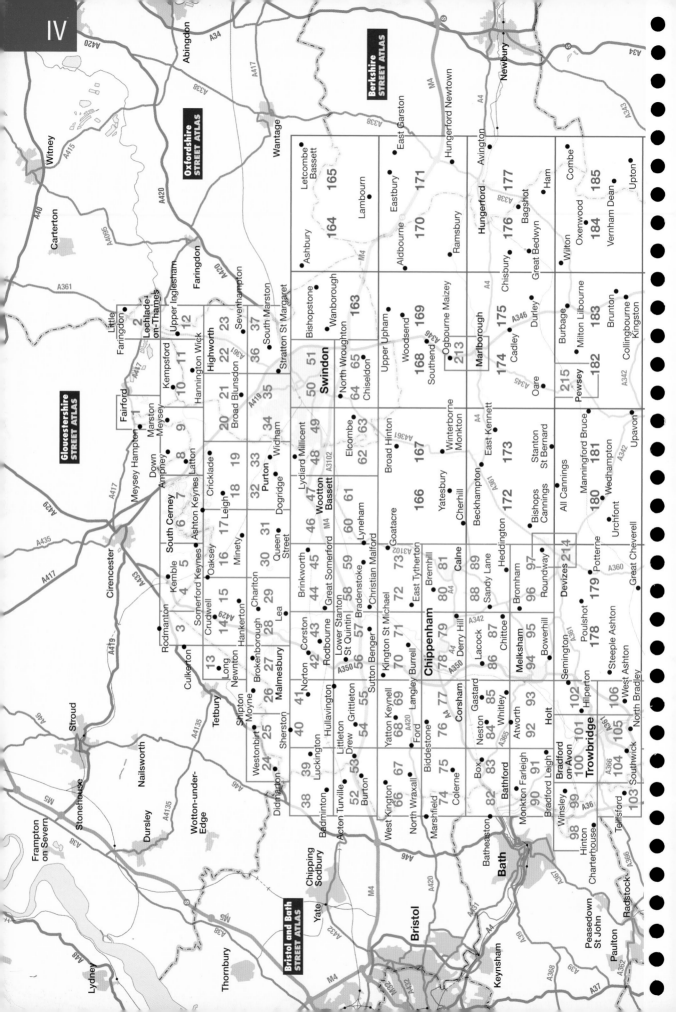

IV

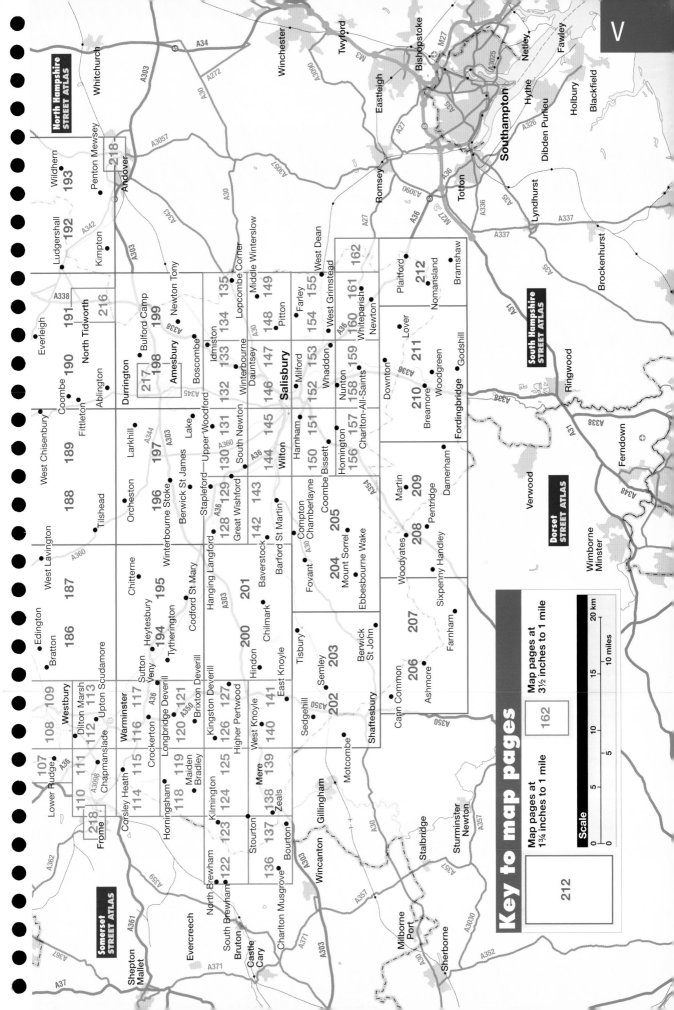

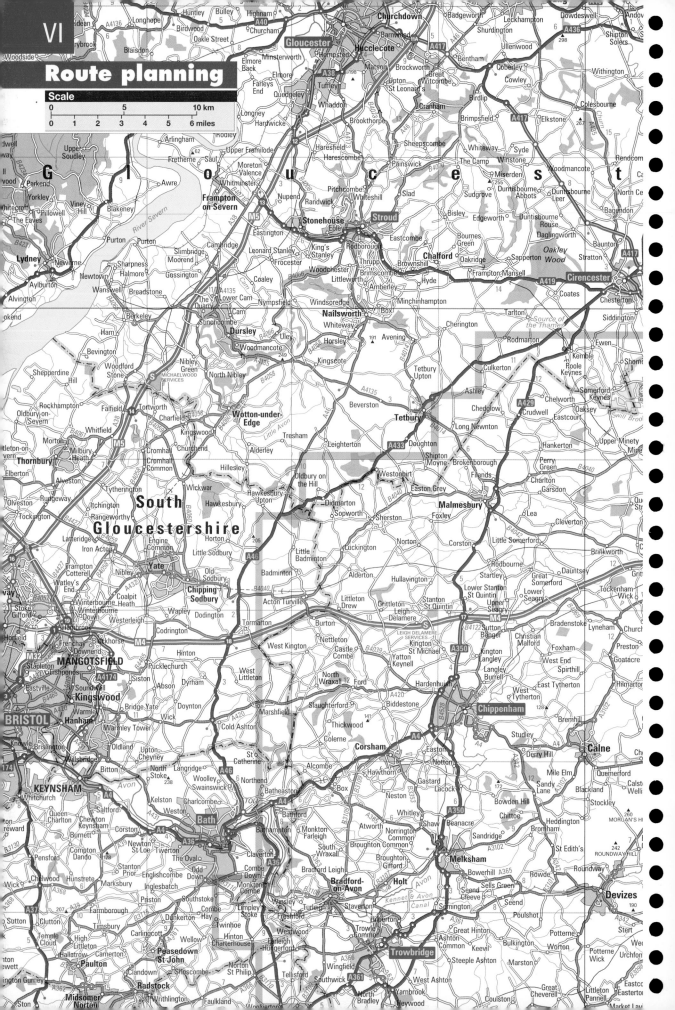

Scale

0 .... 5 .... 10 km
0 .. 1 .. 2 .. 3 .. 4 .. 5 .. 6 miles

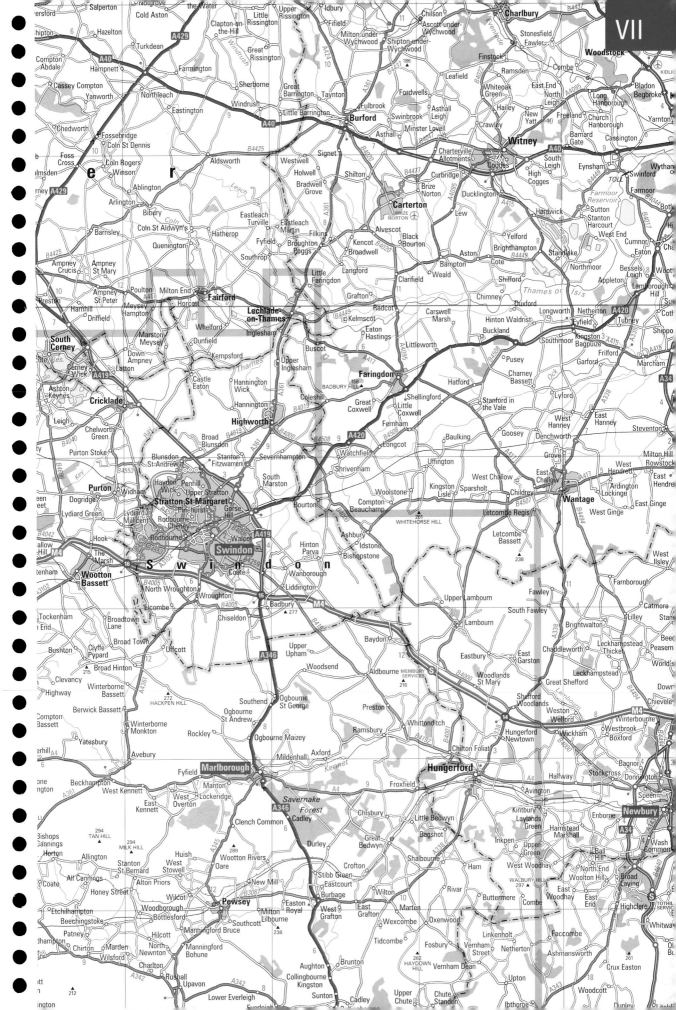

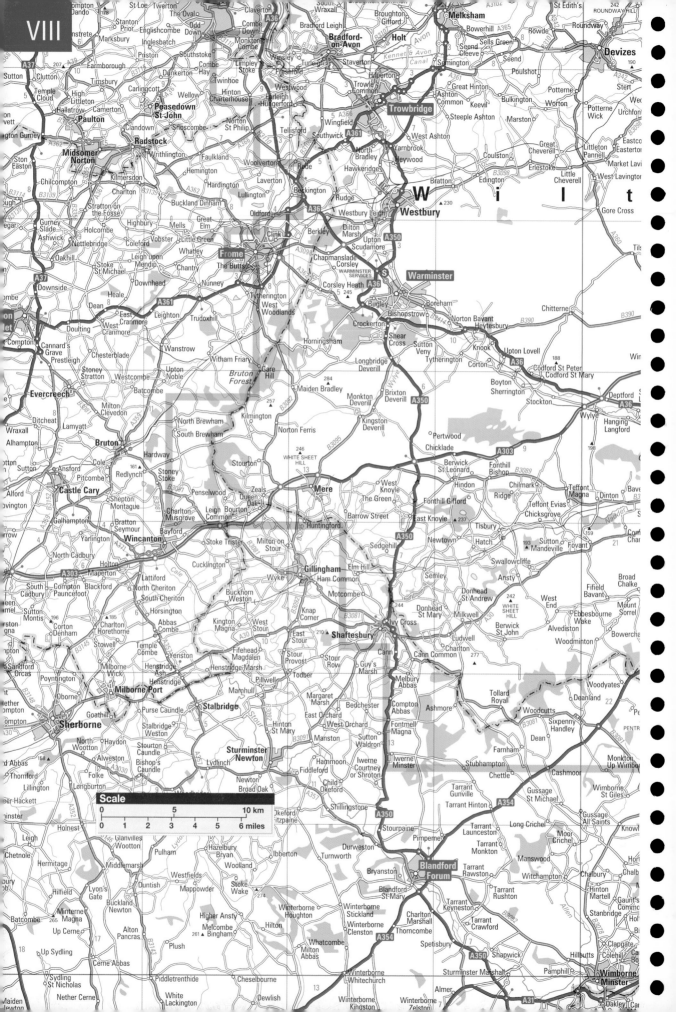

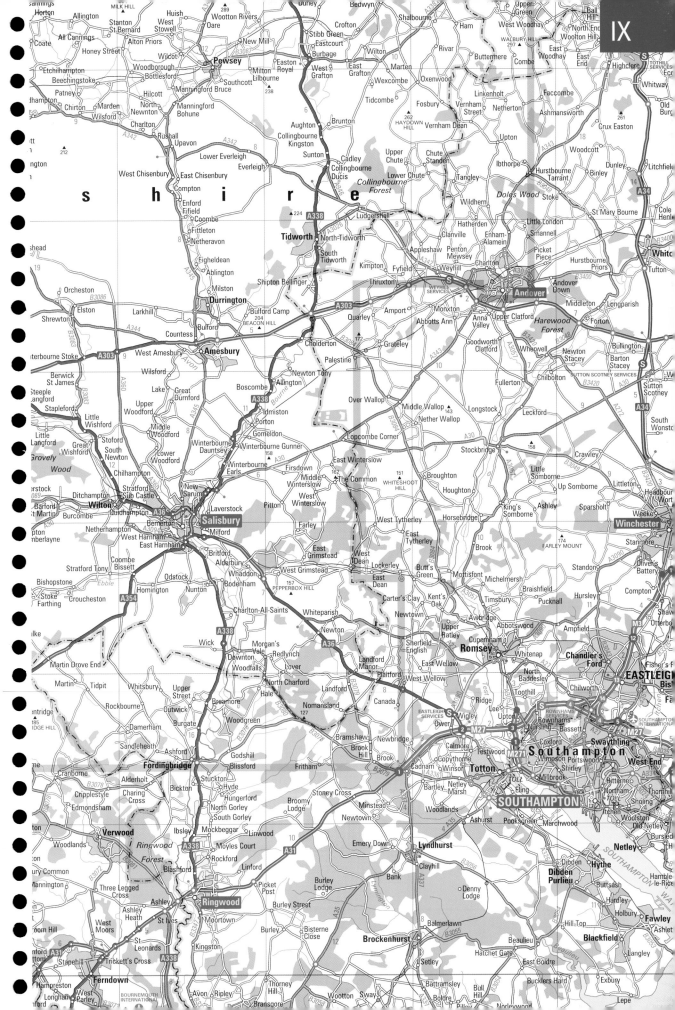

Gloucestershire

Oxfordshire

South Gloucestershire

Bath & North East Somerset

Somerset

Dorset

West Berkshire

Hampshire

North Wiltshire

West Wiltshire

Kennet

Wiltshire

Salisbury

Swindon

County and unitary authority boundaries
District boundaries
Postcode boundaries
Area covered by this atlas

Scale

0   5   10   15   20   25   30km

0   5   10   15   20 miles

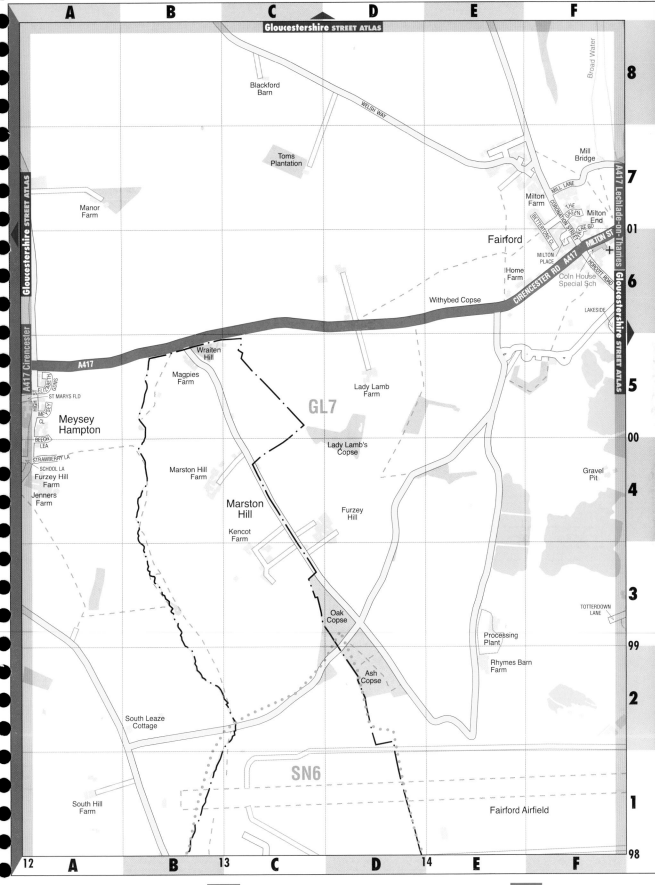

Broad Water

8

Mill Bridge

7

MILL LANE

Milton Farm

CORONATION STREET

THE GREEN

Milton End

01

BETTERTONS CL

Fairford

MILTON ST

Milton Place

MILTON PLACE

CIRENCESTER RD A417

HORCOTT ROAD

Coln House Special Sch

6

Home Farm

Withybed Copse

LAKESIDE

A417 Lechlade-on-Thames Gloucestershire STREET ATLAS

Manor Farm

Blackford Barn

WELSH WAY

Toms Plantation

Gloucestershire STREET ATLAS

A417 Cirencester

A417

Wraiten Hill

Magpies Farm

Lady Lamb Farm

GL7

5

ST MARYS FLD

BETH GDNS

ELIT

SEY

HIGH ST

ME

CL

Meysey Hampton

BEECH LEA

STRAWBERRY LA

SCHOOL LA

Furzey Hill Farm

Jenners Farm

Marston Hill Farm

Lady Lamb's Copse

00

Gravel Pit

4

Marston Hill

Kencot Farm

Furzey Hill

3

TOTTERDOWN LANE

Oak Copse

Processing Plant

99

Rhymes Barn Farm

Ash Copse

2

South Leaze Cottage

SN6

South Hill Farm

Fairford Airfield

1

98

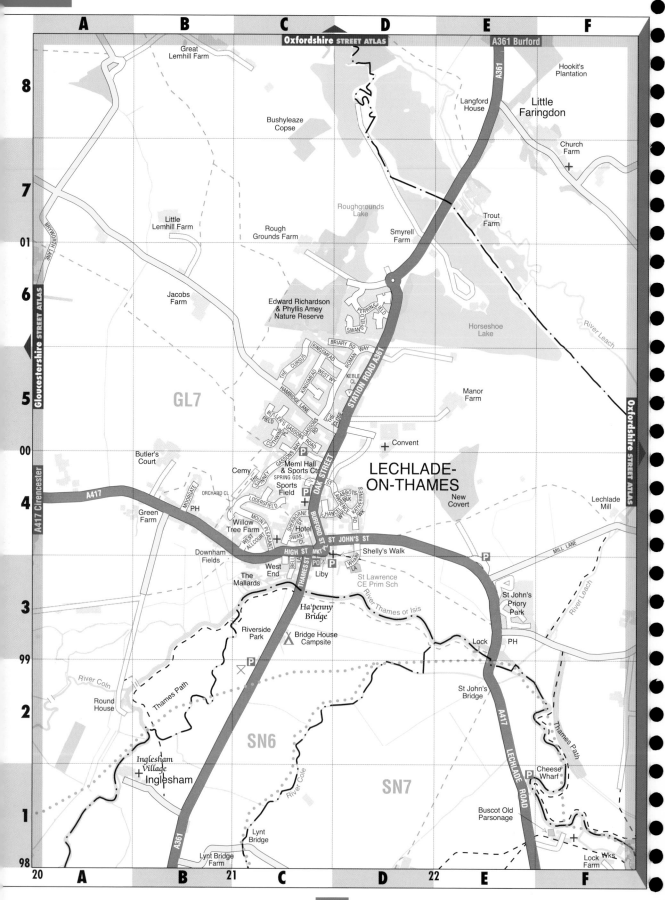

A361 Burford

Great Lemhill Farm

Hookit's Plantation

Little Faringdon

Langford House

Church Farm

Bushyleaze Copse

Roughgrounds Lake

Little Lemhill Farm

Rough Grounds Farm

Smyrell Farm

Trout Farm

Jacobs Farm

Edward Richardson & Phyllis Amey Nature Reserve

Horseshoe Lake

River Leach

GL7

BRIARY RD

ROMAN WAY

KINGSMEAD

THE CURSUS

HAMBIDGE LANE

KINGSMEAD WEST WY

KEBLE CL

STATION ROAD A361

THE CLOSE

Manor Farm

Butler's Court

BUTLER'S FIELD

STHWAITE PL

SASSONS WAY

GASSONS RD

Convent

LECHLADE-ON-THAMES

Cemy

THE SPINNEY

Meml Hall & Sports Ctr

SPRING GDS

Sports Field

GASSONS WAY

OAK STREET

ST JOHN'S ST

ABBOTS WK

ST LAWRENCE WK

CHANCERY WK

ST KATHERINE'S WK

New Covert

Lechlade Mill

ORCHARD CL

LOADERSFIELD

PH

Green Farm

Willow Tree Farm

MOUNT PLEASANT

WEST ALLCOURT

SHERBORNE

SWAN CL

BURFORD ST

MOORGATE

Hotel

Downham Fields

HIGH ST

THAMES ST

BELL LA

MKT PL

PO

WHARF LA

ST JOHN'S ST

Shelly's Walk

MILL LANE

West End

The Mallards

Liby

St Lawrence CE Prim Sch

River Thames or Isis

St John's Priory Park

Ha'penny Bridge

Riverside Park

Bridge House Campsite

PH

Lock

River Leach

River Coln

Thames Path

Round House

St John's Bridge

A417

Thames Path

SN6

SN7

Cheese Wharf

LECHLADE ROAD

Inglesham Village

Inglesham

River Cole

River Cole

Buscot Old Parsonage

Lynt Bridge

A361

Lynt Bridge Farm

Lock Farm

Wks

BRIWORTH LANE

A417 Cirencester

A417

Oxfordshire STREET ATLAS

20   01   00   99   98

8   7   6   5   4   3   2   1

A   B   C   D   E   F

21   22

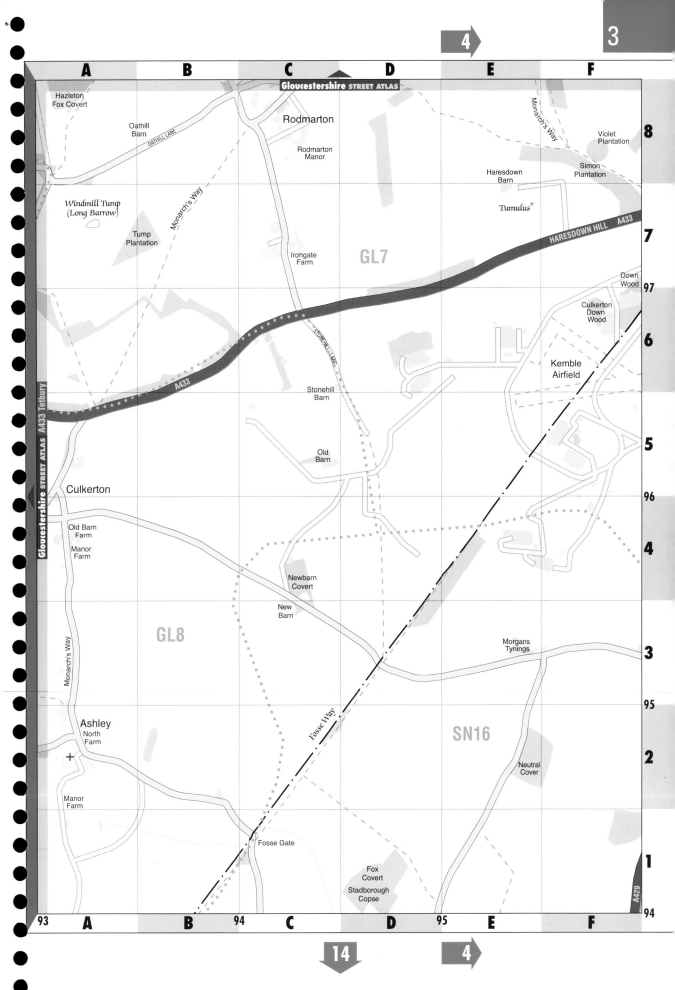

Gloucestershire STREET ATLAS

A   B   C   D   E   F

Hazleton
Fox Covert

Oathill
Barn

OATHILL LANE

Rodmarton

Rodmarton
Manor

Monarch's Way

Violet
Plantation

8

Haresdown
Barn

Simon
Plantation

Windmill Tump
(Long Barrow)

Tump
Plantation

Tumulus

HARESDOWN HILL A433

7

Monarch's Way

Irongate
Farm

GL7

Down
Wood

97

Culkerton
Down
Wood

STONEHILL LANE

A433

Kemble
Airfield

6

Stonehill
Barn

5

Old
Barn

Culkerton

96

Old Barn
Farm

Manor
Farm

4

Newbarn
Covert

GL8

New
Barn

Morgans
Tynings

3

Monarch's Way

Fosse Way

95

Ashley

North
Farm

SN16

2

+

Neutral
Cover

Manor
Farm

Fosse Gate

Fox
Covert

1

Stadborough
Copse

A429

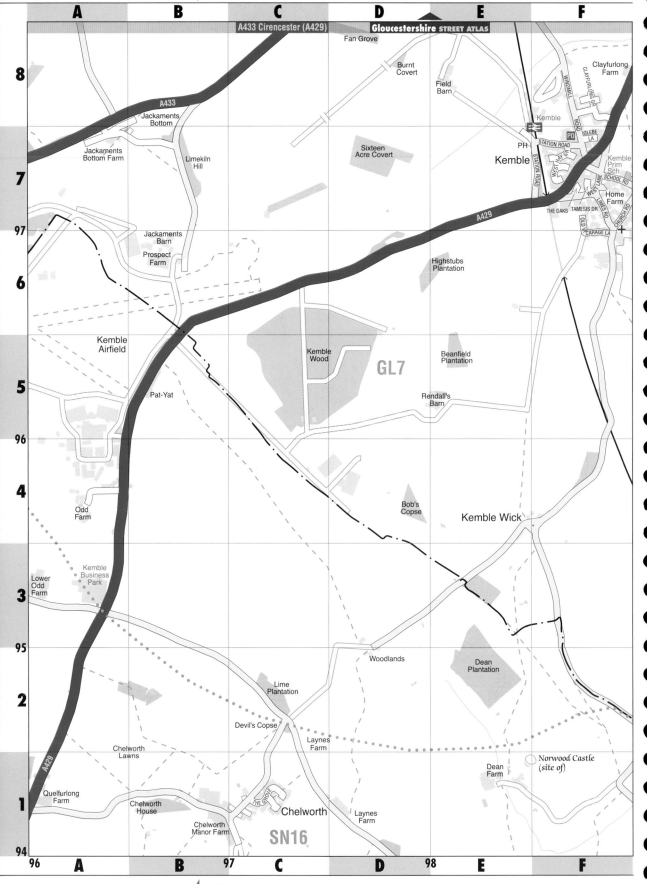

A433 Cirencester (A429)

Gloucestershire STREET ATLAS

Fan Grove

Burnt Covert

Field Barn

Clayfurlong Farm

Kemble

WINDMILL ROAD

CLAYFURLONG GR

PO

GLEBE LA

STATION ROAD

Kemble Prim Sch

Kemble

WEST WAY GR

SCHOOL RD

STATION ROAD

WEST LANE

Home Farm

THE OAKS

TAMESIS DR

LIMES RD

CHURCH RD

OLD/ CARAGE LA

PH

A433

Jackaments Bottom

Jackaments Bottom Farm

Limekiln Hill

Sixteen Acre Covert

Jackaments Barn

Prospect Farm

A429

Highstubs Plantation

Kemble Airfield

Kemble Wood

GL7

Beanfield Plantation

Pat-Yat

Rendall's Barn

Odd Farm

Bob's Copse

Kemble Wick

Lower Odd Farm

Kemble Business Park

Woodlands

Dean Plantation

Lime Plantation

Devil's Copse

Laynes Farm

Norwood Castle (site of)

Dean Farm

Chelworth Lawns

A429

Quelfurlong Farm

Chelworth House

THE GROVE

Chelworth

Laynes Farm

Chelworth Manor Farm

SN16

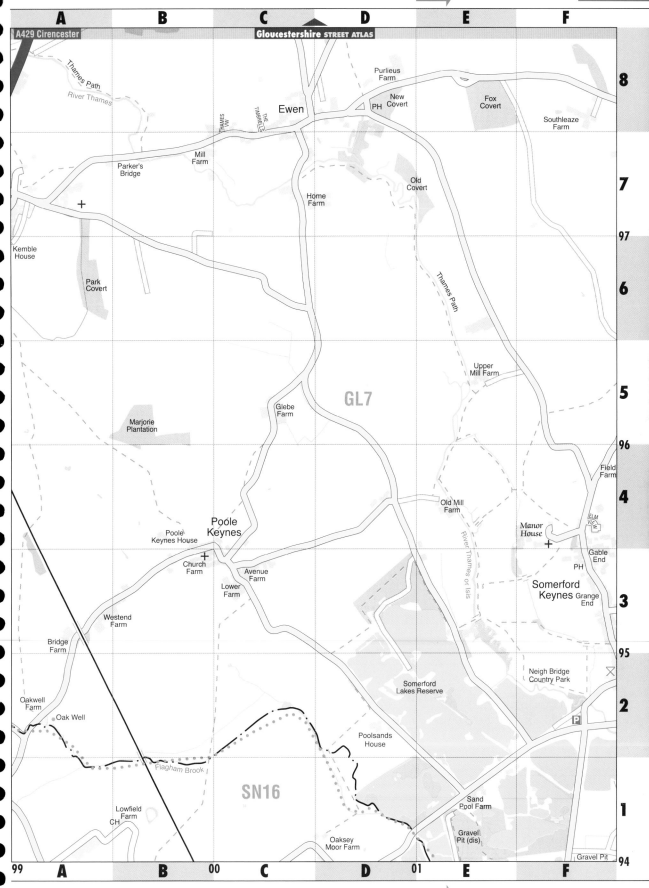

A B C D E F

8

7

97

6

5

96

4

3

95

2

1

94

Thames Path

River Thames

Ewen

Purlieus
Farm

PH

New
Covert

Fox
Covert

Southleaze
Farm

THE TIMBELLS

THAMES VW

Mill
Farm

Parker's
Bridge

Home
Farm

Old
Covert

Thames Path

Kemble
House

Park
Covert

Upper
Mill Farm

GL7

Glebe
Farm

Marjorie
Plantation

Field
Farm

Old Mill
Farm

Manor
House

ELM
VW

Poole
Keynes

Poole
Keynes House

Gable
End

PH

Church
Farm

Avenue
Farm

River Thames or Isis

Somerford
Keynes

Grange
End

Lower
Farm

Westend
Farm

Neigh Bridge
Country Park

Bridge
Farm

Oakwell
Farm

Oak Well

Somerford
Lakes Reserve

Poolsands
House

P

Sand
Pool Farm

Flagham Brook

SN16

Lowfield
Farm

CH

Oaksey
Moor Farm

Gravel
Pit (dis)

Gravel Pit

Gloucestershire STREET ATLAS

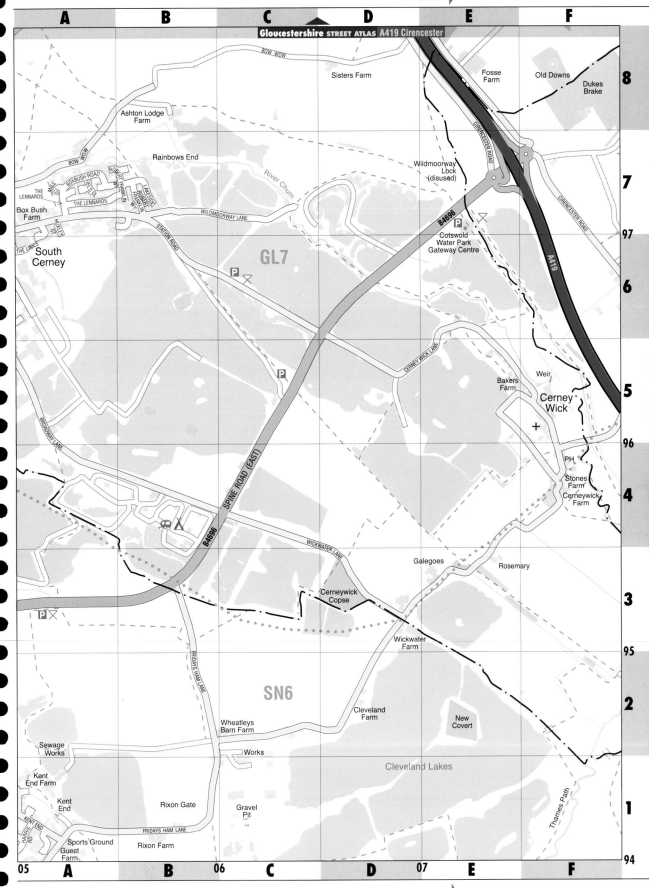

Gloucestershire STREET ATLAS A419 Cirencester

A | B | C | D | E | F

8
7
97
6
5
96
4
3
95
2
1
94

Bow Wow

Sisters Farm

Fosse Farm

Old Downs

Dukes Brake

Ashton Lodge Farm

Rainbows End

River Churn

Wildmoorway Lock (disused)

Cirencester Road

THE LENNARDS

BOXBUSH ROAD

ROBERT FRANKLIN W'Y

MILL CL

THE LENNARDS

LAKESIDE

ROBERT FRANKLIN

HUXLEY CT

Box Bush Farm

THE LIMES

South Cerney

STATION ROAD

WILDMOORWAY LANE

GL7

B4696

Cotswold Water Park Gateway Centre

A419

Cirencester Road

BROADWAY LANE

SPINE ROAD (EAST)

B4696

Cerney Wick Lane

Bakers Farm

Weir

Cerney Wick

PH

Stones Farm

Cerneywick Farm

WICKWATER LANE

Galegoes

Rosemary

Cerneywick Copse

Wickwater Farm

SN6

FRIDAYS HAM LANE

Cleveland Farm

New Covert

Wheatleys Barn Farm

Works

Sewage Works

Kent End Farm

KENT END

HARRIS RD

Kent End

Sports Ground

Guest Farm

Rixon Farm

Rixon Gate

FRIDAYS HAM LANE

Gravel Pit

Cleveland Lakes

Thames Path

05 | A | B | 06 | C | D | 07 | E | F

18

8

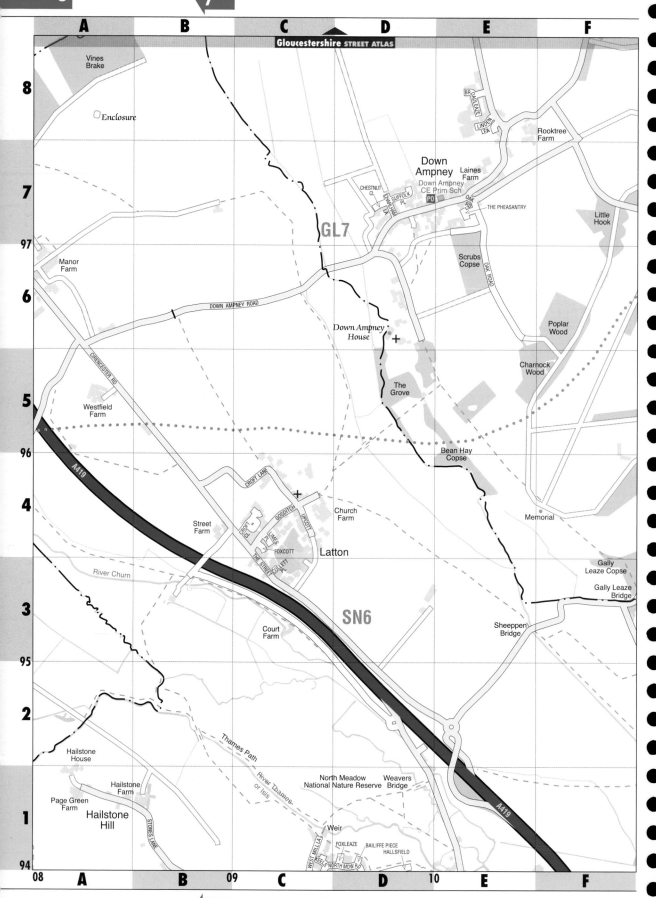

Gloucestershire STREET ATLAS

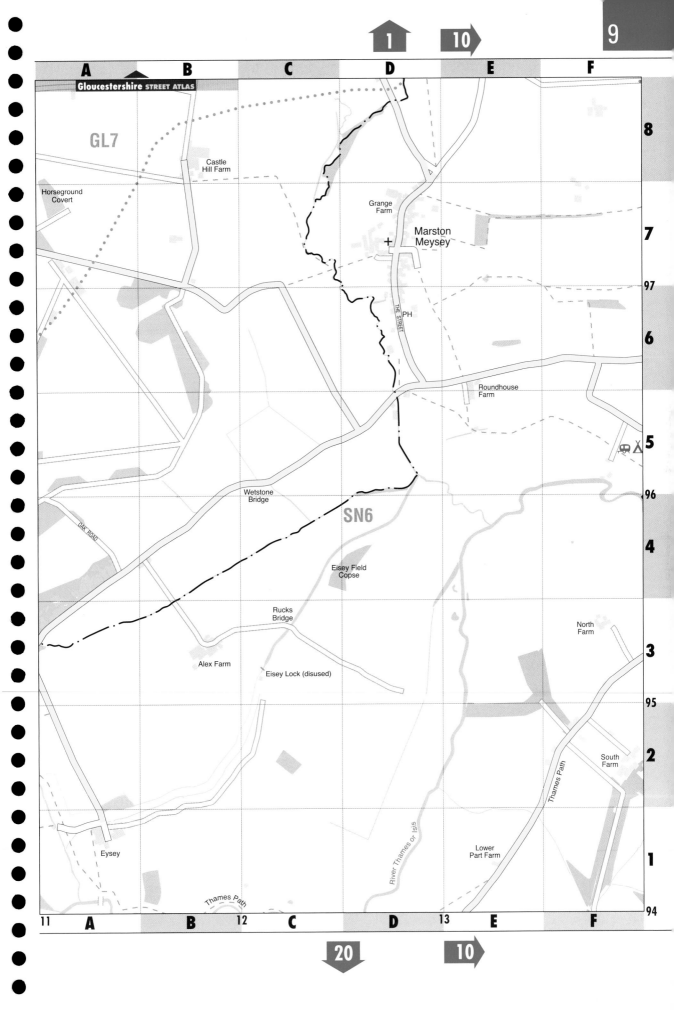

GL7

Horseground
Covert

Castle
Hill Farm

Grange
Farm

Marston
Meysey

THE STREET

PH

Roundhouse
Farm

Wetstone
Bridge

SN6

OAK ROAD

Eisey Field
Copse

Rucks
Bridge

North
Farm

Alex Farm

Eisey Lock (disused)

South
Farm

Thames Path

Eysey

Lower
Part Farm

River Thames or Isis

Thames Path

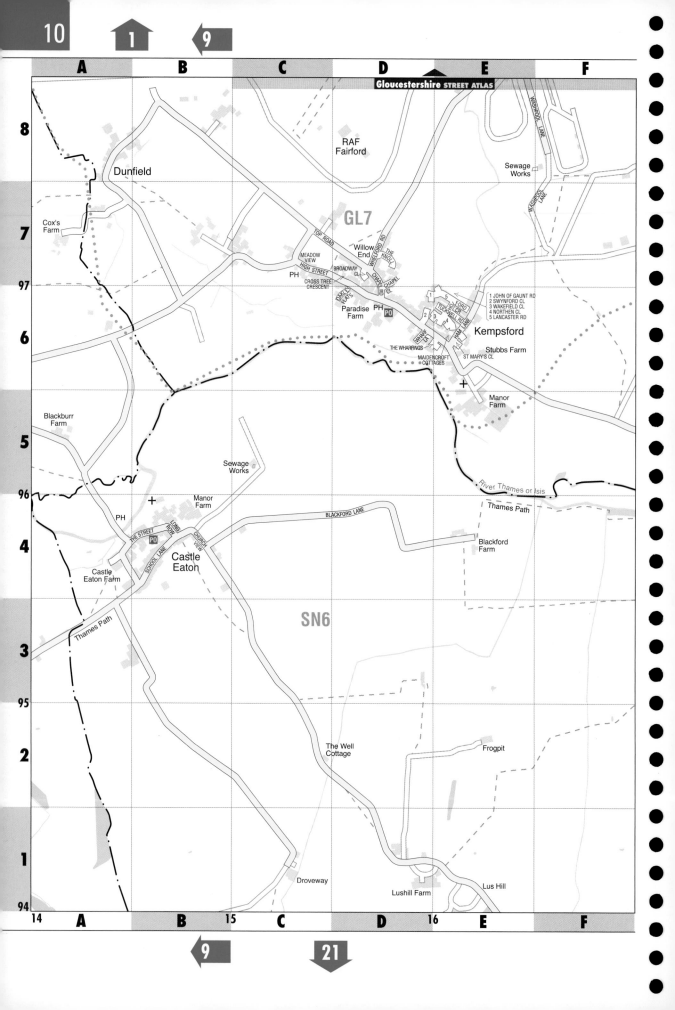

12

A
B
C
D
E
F
Gloucestershire STREET ATLAS
8
7
97
6
5
96
4
3
95
2
1
94
17
18
19
Ham Barn
GL7
Enclosure
Brazen Church Hill
River Thames or Isis
Manor House Barn
Thames Path
Strets Farm
Hannington Bridge
Bridge Farm
Thames Path
SN6
Enclosure
Hannington Wick
Yew Tree Farm
Sycamore Farm
North Leaze Farm
Enclosure
Enclosure
Manor Farm
Cherry Tree Farm
Pond Farm
Little Crouch Hill
Enclosure
Little Crouch Plantation
Box Hedge Farm
Pentylands Farm
Crouch Farm
Crouch Hill

22
12

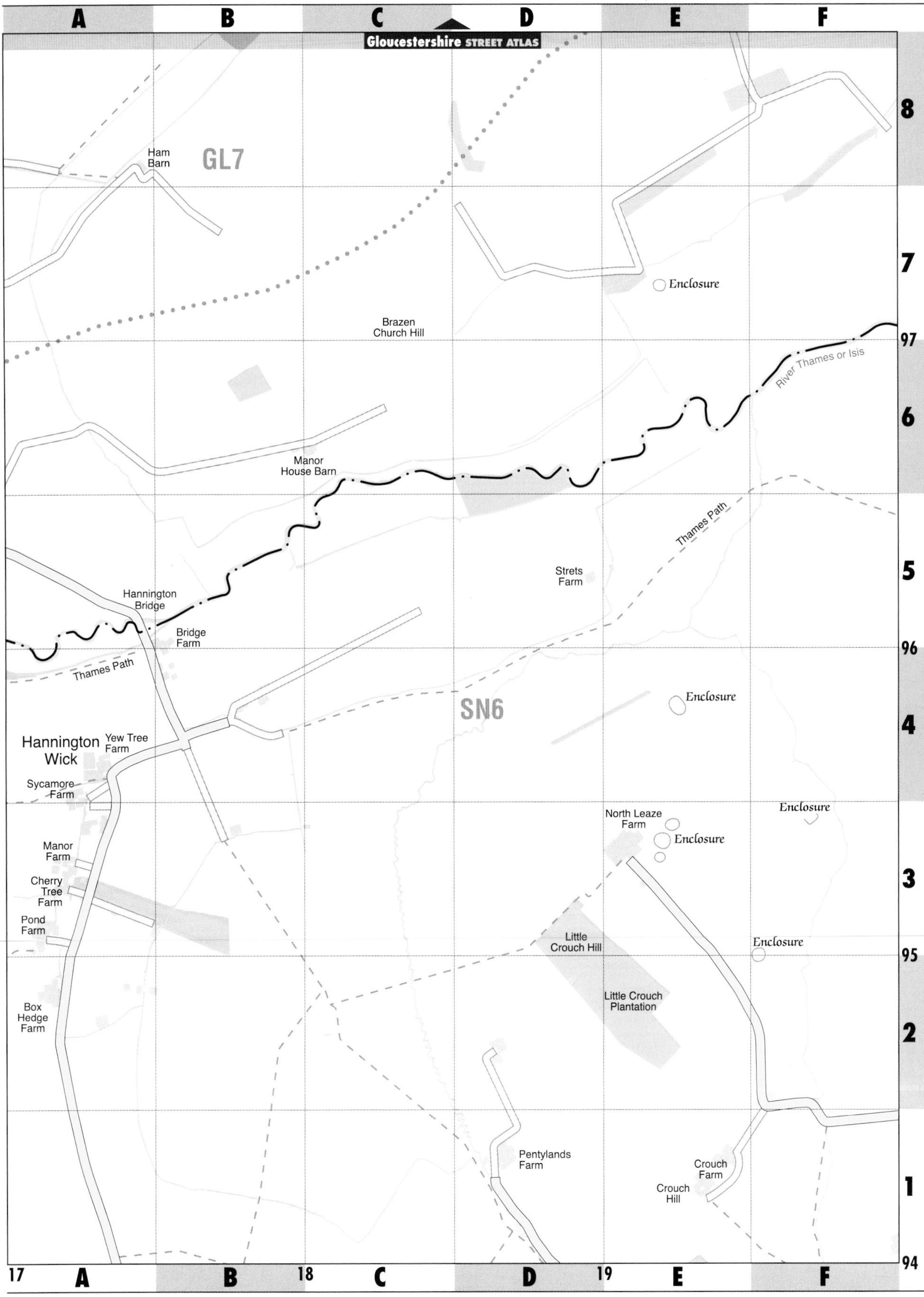

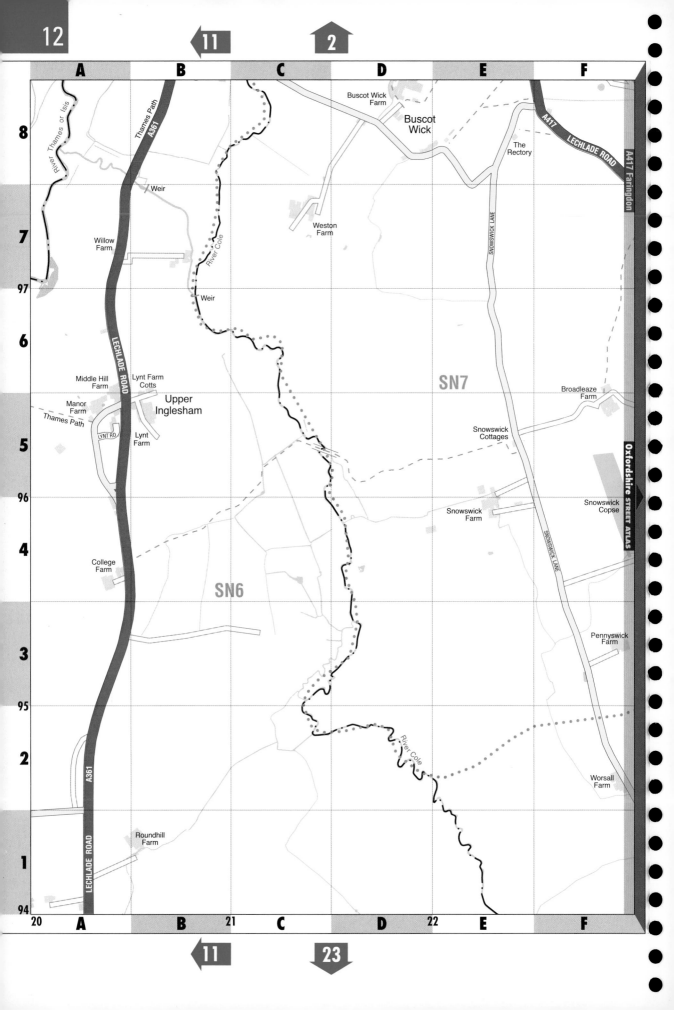

A B C D E F

8

7

97

6

5

96

4

3

95

2

1

94

20 21 22

A B C D E F

River Thames or Isis

Thames Path

A361

Weir

Willow Farm

River Cole

Weir

LECHLADE ROAD

Middle Hill Farm

Lynt Farm Cotts

Upper Inglesham

Manor Farm

Thames Path

LYNT RD

Lynt Farm

College Farm

SN6

A361

Roundhill Farm

LECHLADE ROAD

Buscot Wick Farm

Buscot Wick

Weston Farm

The Rectory

A417 LECHLADE ROAD

A417 Faringdon

SNOWSWICK LANE

SN7

Broadleaze Farm

Snowswick Cottages

Snowswick Farm

Snowswick Copse

SNOWSWICK LANE

Oxfordshire STREET ATLAS

Pennyswick Farm

River Cole

River Cole

Worsall Farm

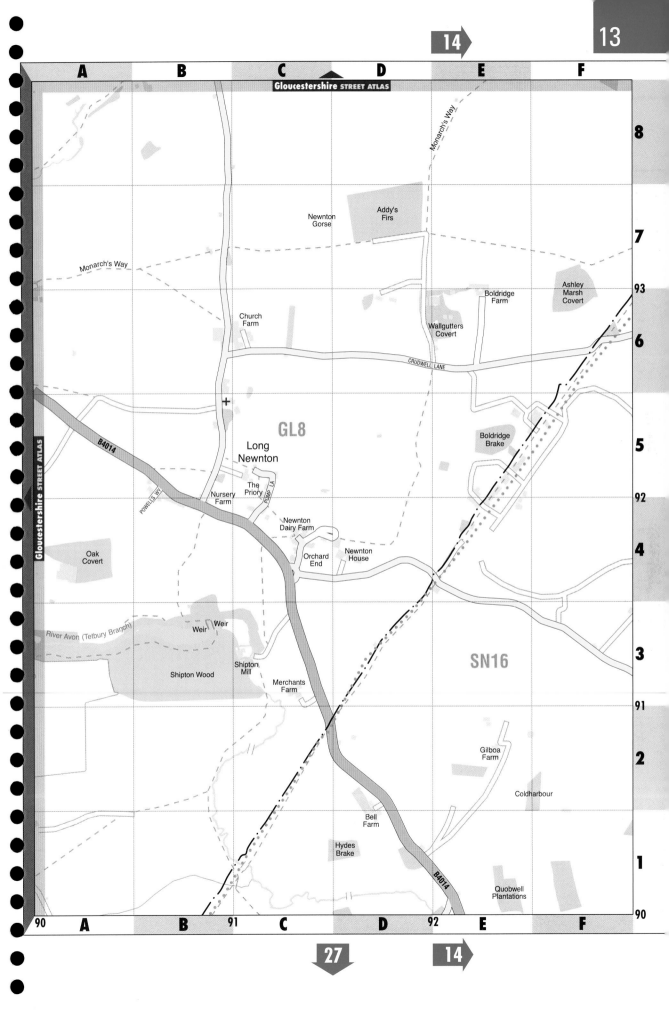

Gloucestershire STREET ATLAS

Gloucestershire STREET ATLAS

Monarch's Way

Newnton Gorse

Addy's Firs

Boldridge Farm

Ashley Marsh Covert

Monarch's Way

Wallgutters Covert

Church Farm

CRUDWELL LANE

GL8

Boldridge Brake

Long Newnton

Nursery Farm

The Priory

PUMP LA

POWELLS WY

B4014

Newnton Dairy Farm

Orchard End

Newnton House

Oak Covert

River Avon (Tetbury Branch)

Weir

Weir

SN16

Shipton Wood

Shipton Mill

Merchants Farm

Gilboa Farm

Coldharbour

Bell Farm

Hydes Brake

B4014

Quobwell Plantations

8
7
93
6
5
92
4
3
91
2
1
90

A B C D E F

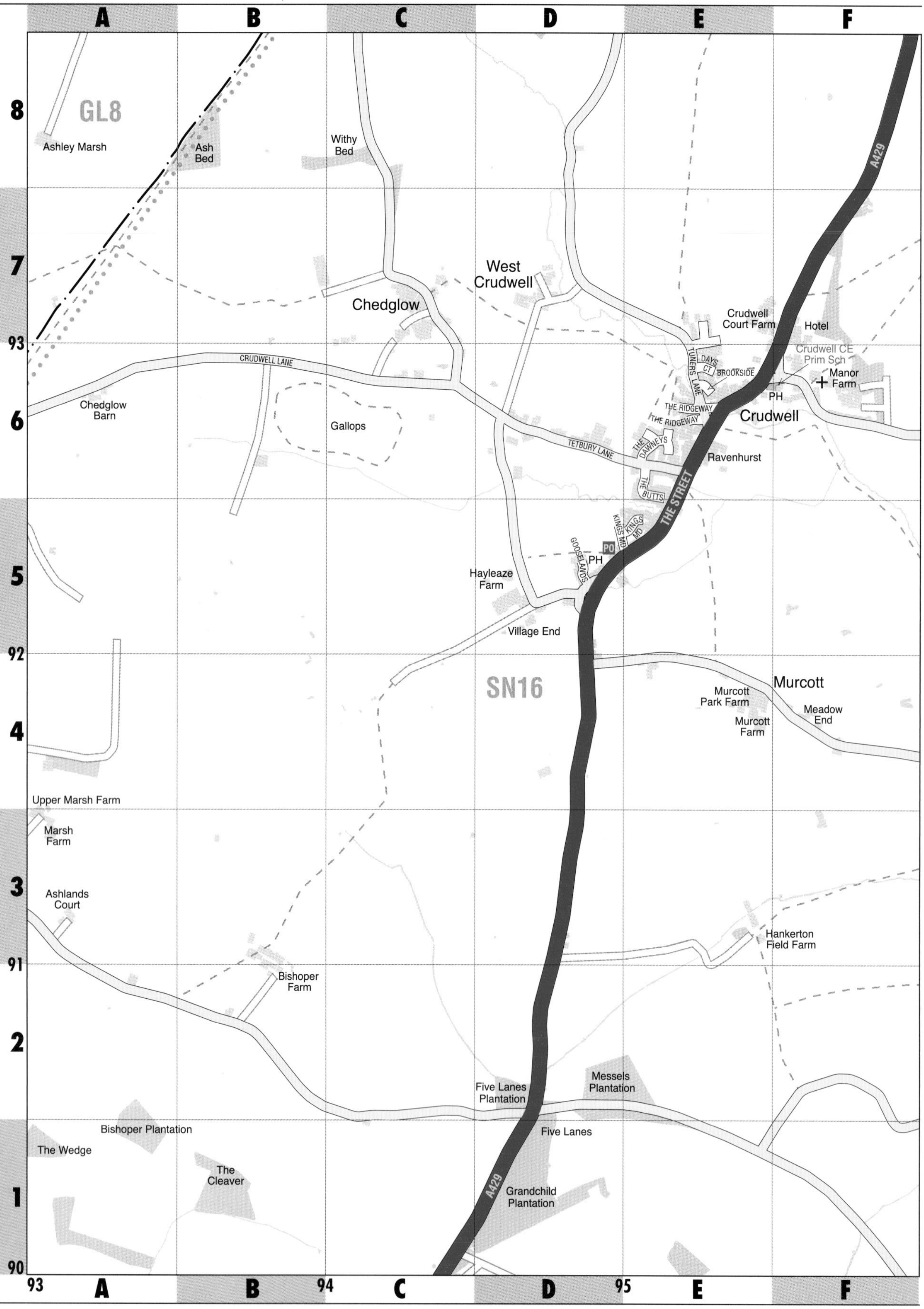

8

GL8

Ashley Marsh

Ash Bed

Withy Bed

7

West Crudwell

Chedglow

93

Crudwell Court Farm

Hotel

Crudwell CE Prim Sch

CRUDWELL LANE

DAYS CT BROOKSIDE

TUNERS LANE

Manor Farm

6

Chedglow Barn

Gallops

THE RIDGEWAY

THE RIDGEWAY

Crudwell

PH

TETBURY LANE

THE DAWNEYS

Ravenhurst

THE BUTTS

THE STREET

5

Hayleaze Farm

GOOSELANDS

KINGS MD

OLD KINGS MD

PO

PH

92

Village End

SN16

Murcott Park Farm

Murcott

4

Murcott Farm

Meadow End

Upper Marsh Farm

Marsh Farm

3

Ashlands Court

Hankerton Field Farm

91

Bishoper Farm

2

Five Lanes Plantation

Messels Plantation

Bishoper Plantation

Five Lanes

The Wedge

The Cleaver

1

A429

Grandchild Plantation

90

93 A B 94 C D 95 E F

A429

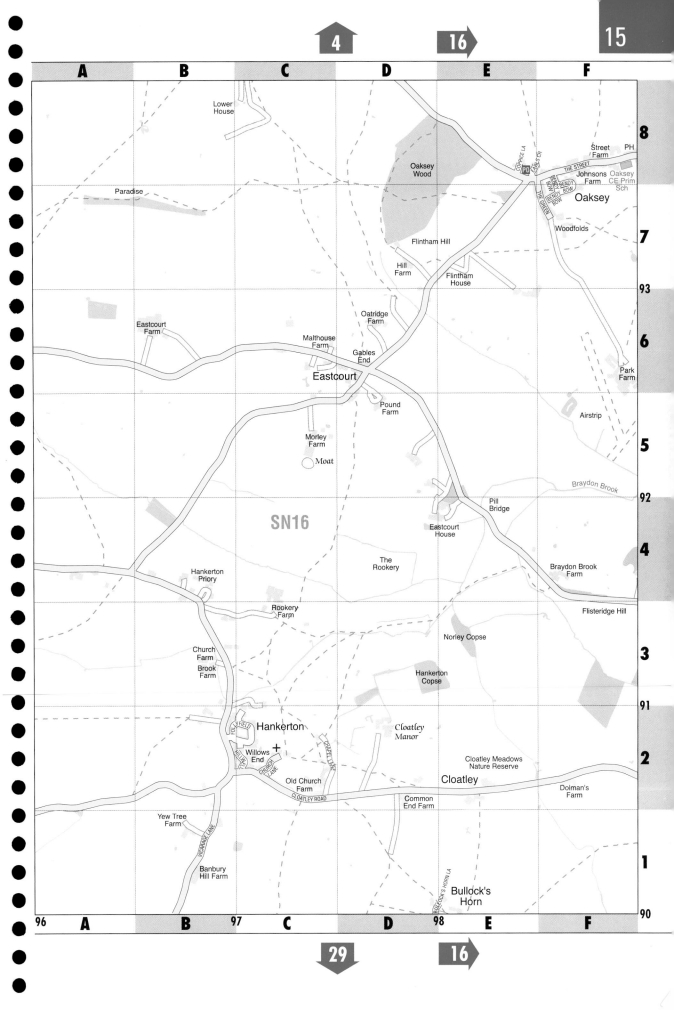

A   B   C   D   E   F

8

Lower
Moor Farm

Gravel
Pit

Gravel
Pit

PH
WHEATSHEAF
LA
Oaksey
THE STREET
WICK ROAD

Oaksey
Bridge

THE STREET

COURT
FARM
Court
Farm

Mallard
Lake

Swillbrook Lakes
Nature Reserve

7

MINETY LANE

Clattinger Farm
Nature Reserve

Clattinger
Farm

Swillbrook
Bridge

Lower
Swillbrook
Farm

93

6

Oaksey
Ford Bridge

Swill Brook

Park
Farm

Stert
Farm

Cooles
Farm

Airstrip

Barn Cooles
Farm

RIGSBY'S LA

5

Lyngrove
Farm

TIDLING
CORNER

92

SN16

Brandiers
Farm

LC

Ash Bed

Oaksey
Nursery

Upper
Lyngrove

Field End

4

Flisteridge
Wood

OAKSEY ROAD

Oakwood
Farm

Row Ash
Farm

Maskelyne's
Copse

Flistridge
Farm

Mansells
Farm

Upper
Minety

3

FLISTERIDGE ROAD

TELLINGS OR
ST LEONARD'S

PH
ST LEONARD'S

Osbourne
Farm

Cowleaze
Farm

91

PO
Thistledown

Home
Farm

Wellfield
Farm

Mill
Farm

The
Elms

Cockrode
Farm

2

Laurel
Farm

Alsperes
Farm

Cloatley End
Farm

HANKERTON ROAD

Brookside
Farm

Elms
Farm

Buxwell Farm

Cloatley
End

Fairholme
Farm

DOG TRAP LANE

Brownockhill
Plantation

1

Emmett Hill
Meadows
Nature Reserve

Woodward
Farm

90

99   A   B   00   C   D   01   E   F

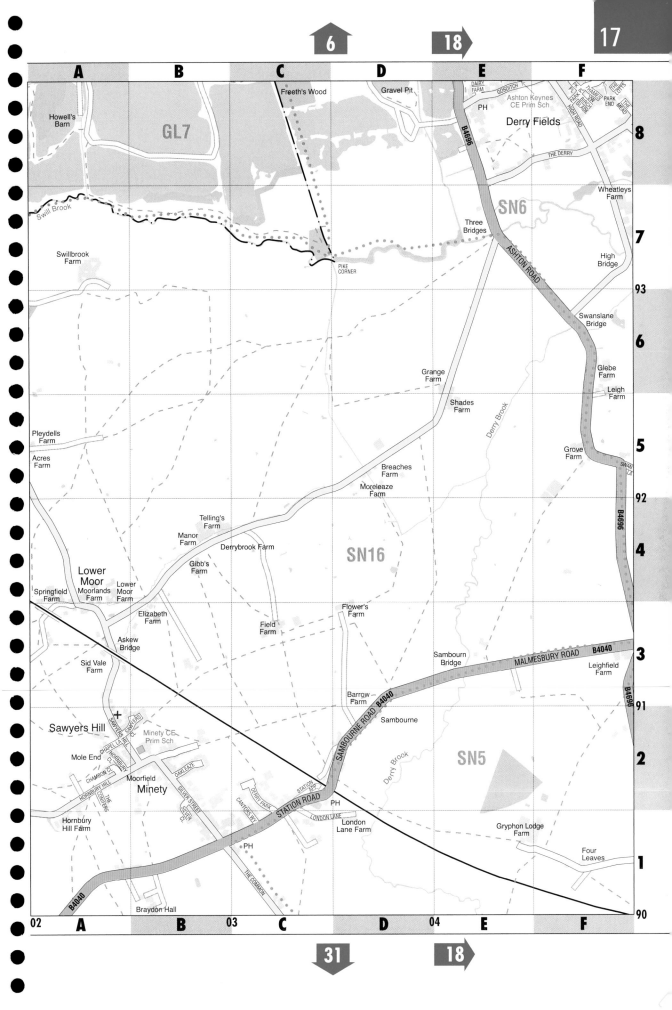

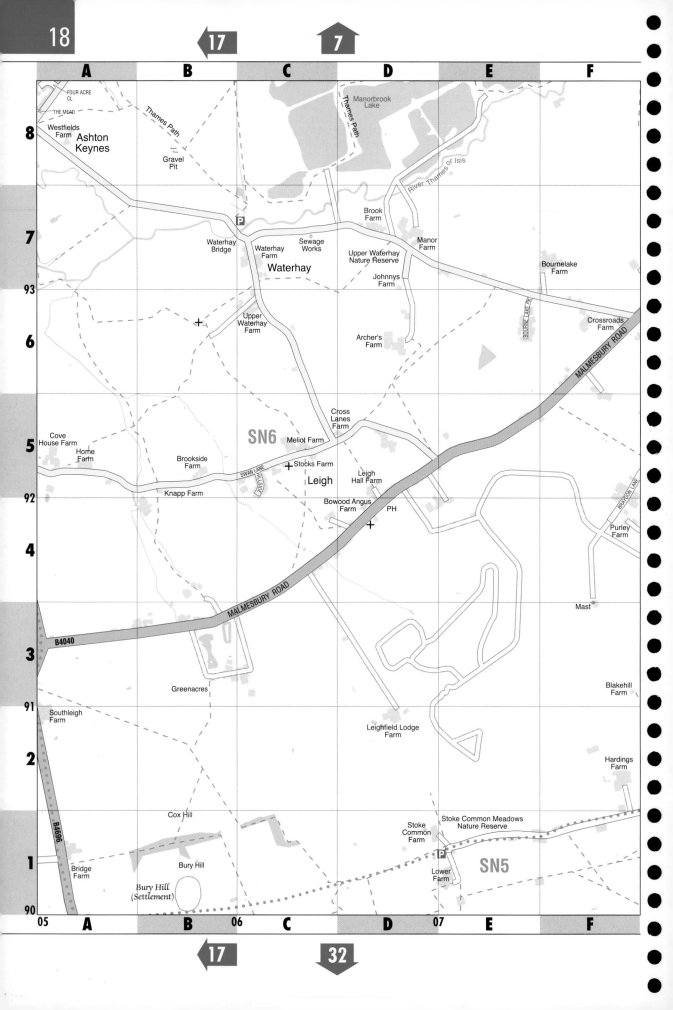

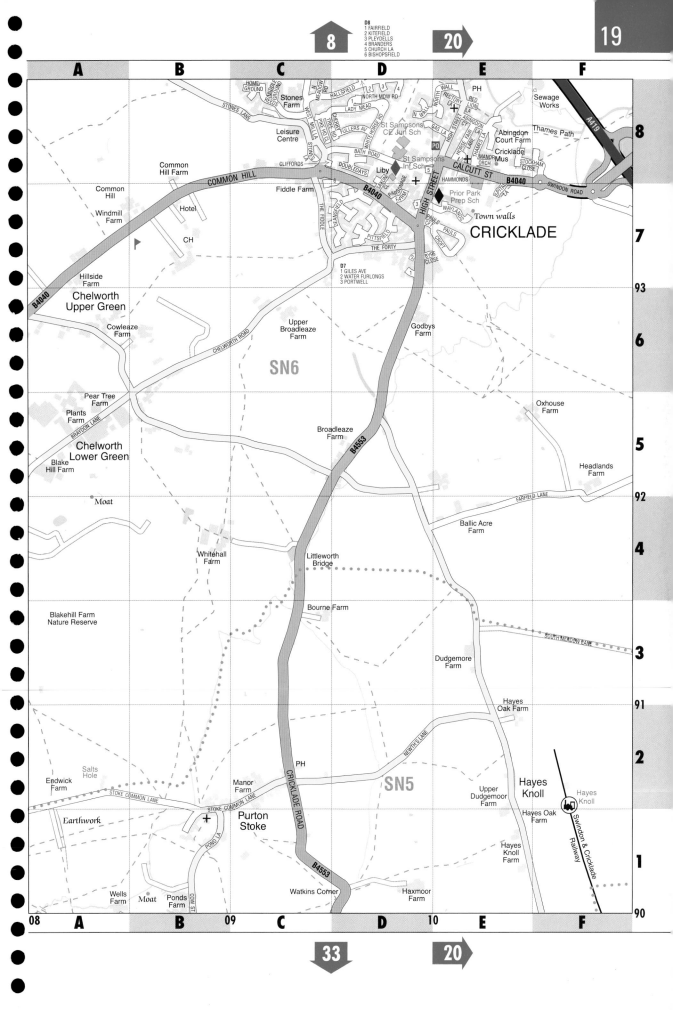

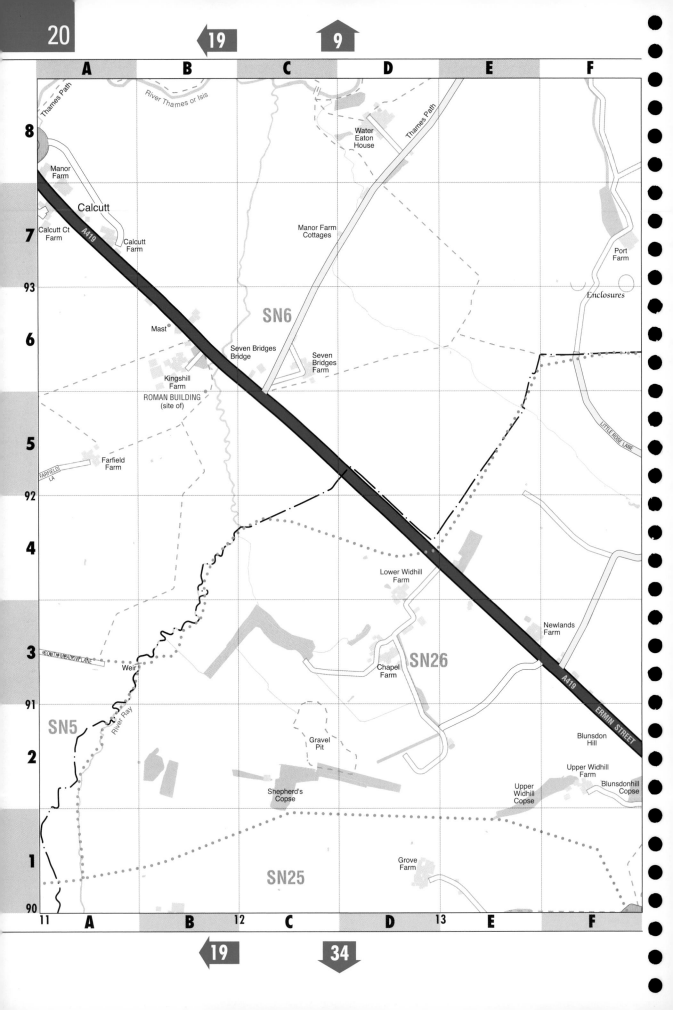

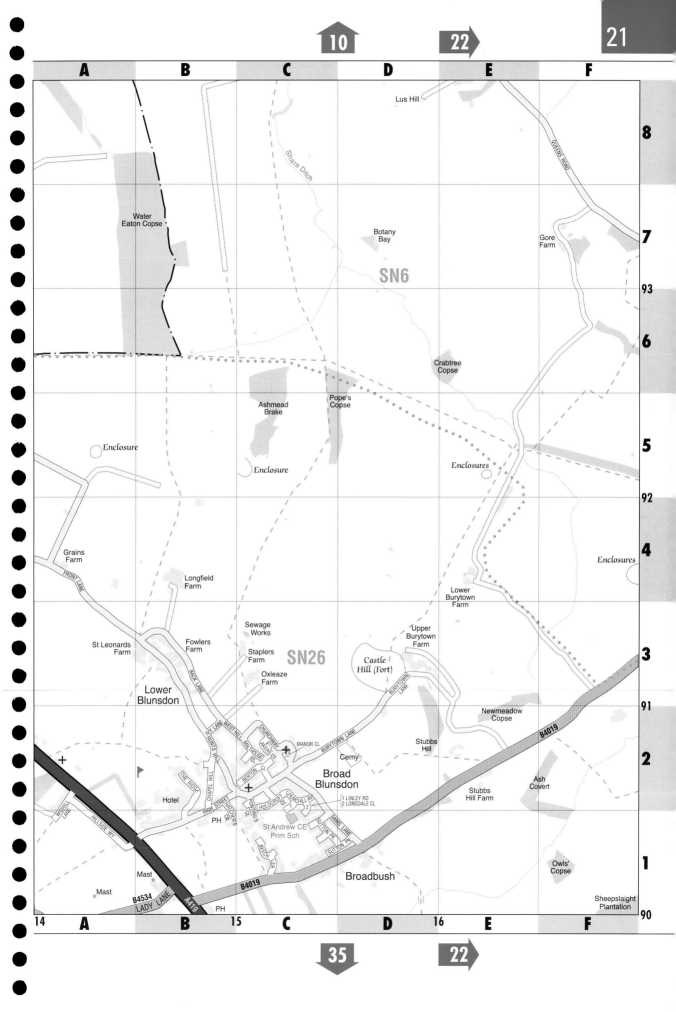

A B C D E F

8
7
93
6
5
92
4
3
91
2
1
90

Lus Hill

Share Ditch

Water
Eaton Copse

Botany
Bay

Gore
Farm

QUEENS ROAD

SN6

Crabtree
Copse

Ashmead
Brake

Pope's
Copse

Enclosure

Enclosure

Enclosures

Enclosures

Grains
Farm

Longfield
Farm

Lower
Burytown
Farm

FRONT LANE

St Leonards
Farm

Fowlers
Farm

Sewage
Works

Staplers
Farm

Oxleaze
Farm

SN26

Upper
Burytown
Farm

Castle
Hill (Fort)

Newmeadow
Copse

Lower
Blunsdon

BACK LANE

BURYTOWN LANE

Stubbs
Hill

B4019

IVY LANE WEST HILL HUNTS HILL

CHURCHWAY

MALTHOUSE

MANOR CL

ACRES CL

BURYTOWN LANE

Cemy

Ash
Covert

Hotel

CHAPEL HILL

THE RIDGE

HIGH STREET

THATCHER'S CR

BERTON CL

HOLDCROFT

CHURCHILL AVE

1 2

Broad
Blunsdon

Stubbs
Hill Farm

PH

POTTING'S

1 LINLEY RD
2 LONSDALE CL

SUTTON PK

SAMS LANE

St Andrew CE
Prim Sch

BEECH LA

SUTTON PK

Owls'
Copse

Mast

Mast

WROUGHILL LANE

HILLSIDE WY

B4534

LADY LANE

A419

B4019

PH

Broadbush

Sheepslaight
Plantation

14 A B 15 C D 16 E F

A B C D E F

8

Nell Farm

Lower Farm

Sewage Works

7

Hannington

NELL HILL

QUEENS ROAD

Manor Farm

PH

SKINNER'S CL

Hall

Florence Copse

Quarters Copse

Bydemill Farm

93

Bydemill Bridge

Bydemill Brook

BLACKWORTH

Sewage Works

PENTYLANDS CL

SKYE RD

KILDA RD

KILDA ROAD

STROMA WY

LISMORE RD

ST MICHAEL'S AVE

BUTE CL

ISLAY

GROVE

ORCHARD

POUND ROAD

BROOKFIELD

Westrop Prim Sch

BARRA CL

BARRA CL

HOMEFARM

HOME FARM

RIVERS WY

NEWBURGH

ST MICHAEL'S AV

THE RETREAT

QUARRY

STATION RD

6

SN6

Bydemill Copse

WINDRUSH

WINDRUSH

WINDRUSH

WINDRUSH

NORTH VW

STAPLETON

THE ARCHERS

OAK LTD

Hampton Hill

Hampton

5

Jubilee Copse

Hampton Farm

Hampton Copse

Cemy

BYDEMILL GDNS

B4019

BOTANY

ROMAN WY

WADE HILL

CRICKLADE ROAD

BEECH GR

COPPER BEECHES

THE ELMS

WESTHILL CL

Highworth Rec Ctr

THE GREEN

Botany Farm

CH

92

Snell Bridge

4

PH

Swanborough

Highworth Golf Club

Redlands

3

B4019

Stanton Water Bridge

Oxleaze Farm

TRENCHARD ROAD

Red Down

Red Down Farm

SWINDON ROAD

91

Red Down Hill

Enclosures

2

SN26

Red Down

Pickett's Copse

MILL LA

Mill Copse

Stanton Fitzwarren

TRENCHARD ROAD

HOSSIL LA

THE AVENUE

A361

HIGHWORTH ROAD

1

Queenlaines Farm

Maranatha Christian School

Sheepslaight Plantation

Hotel

90

17 A 18 B C D 19 E F

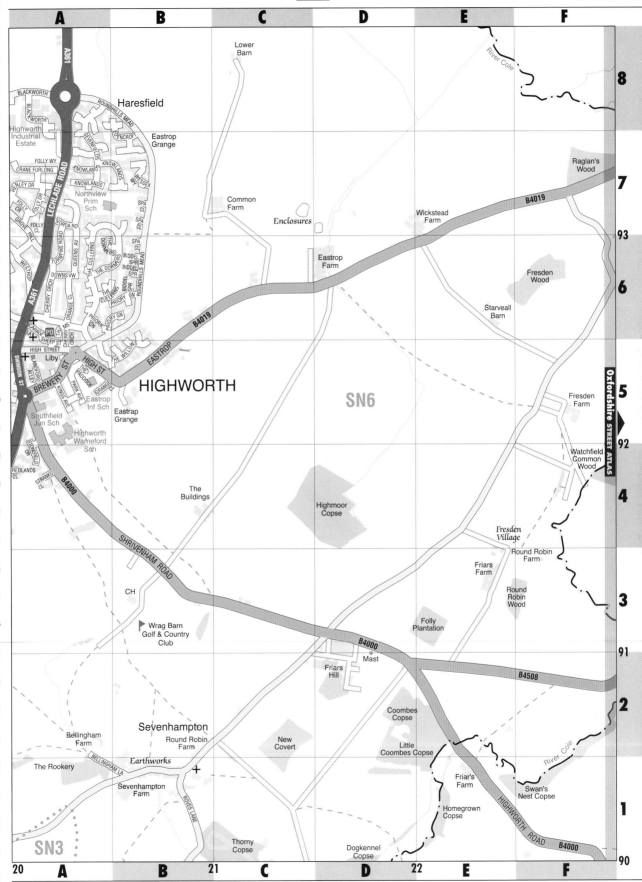

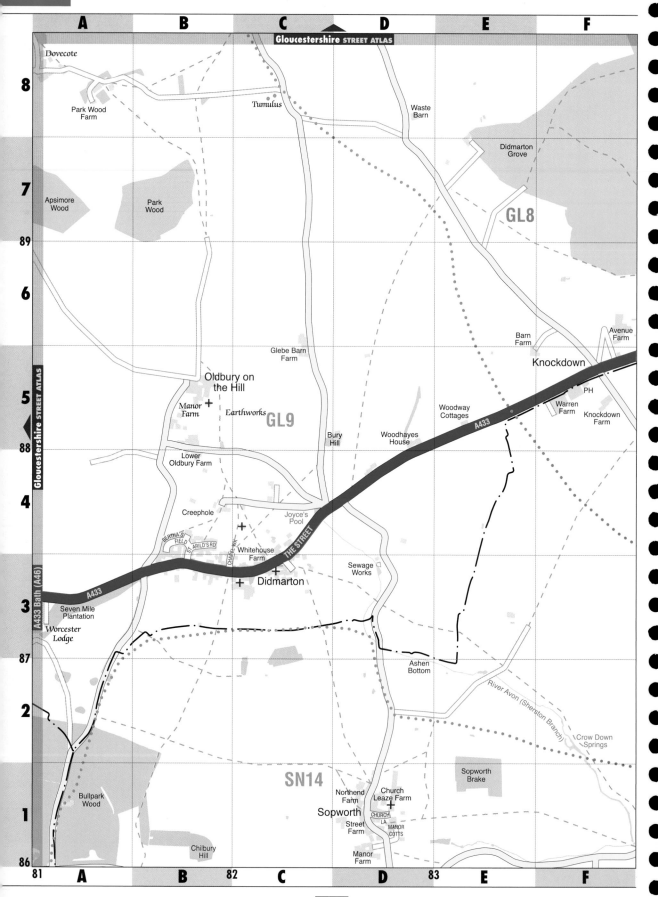

GL8

Didmarton Grove

Barn Farm

Avenue Farm

Knockdown

PH

Warren Farm

Knockdown Farm

A433

Woodway Cottages

Woodhayes House

Glebe Barn Farm

Oldbury on the Hill

Manor Farm

Earthworks

GL9

Bury Hill

Lower Oldbury Farm

Creephole

Joyce's Pool

BERTHA'S FIELD

ST ARILD'S RD

CHAPEL WY

Whitehouse Farm

THE STREET

Didmarton

Sewage Works

A433

A433 Bath (A46)

Seven Mile Plantation

Worcester Lodge

Ashen Bottom

River Avon (Sherston Branch)

Crow Down Springs

SN14

Bullpark Wood

Northend Farm

Church Leaze Farm

Sopworth Brake

Sopworth

CHURCH

LA

MANOR COTTS

Street Farm

Manor Farm

Chilbury Hill

Dovecote

Park Wood Farm

Tumulus

Waste Barn

Apsimore Wood

Park Wood

39

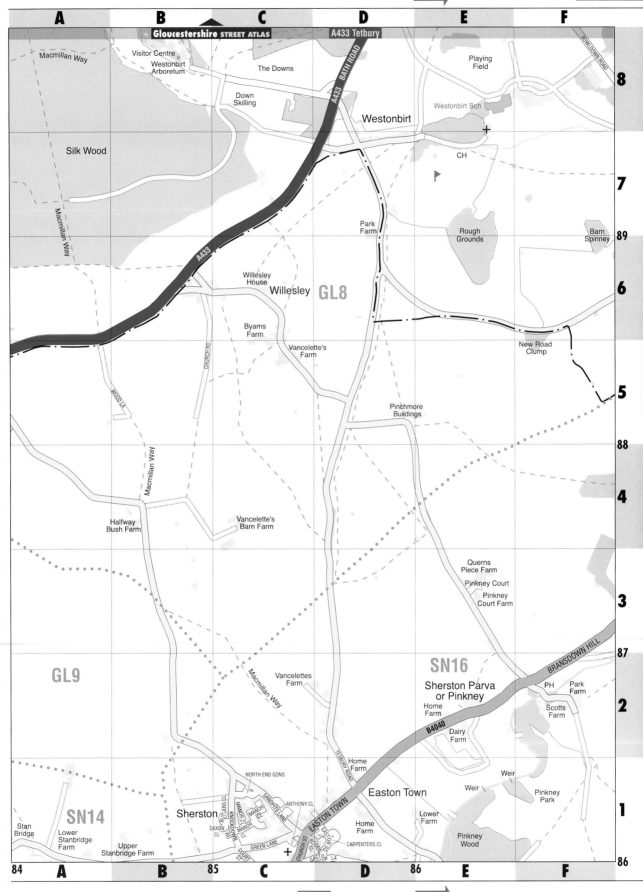

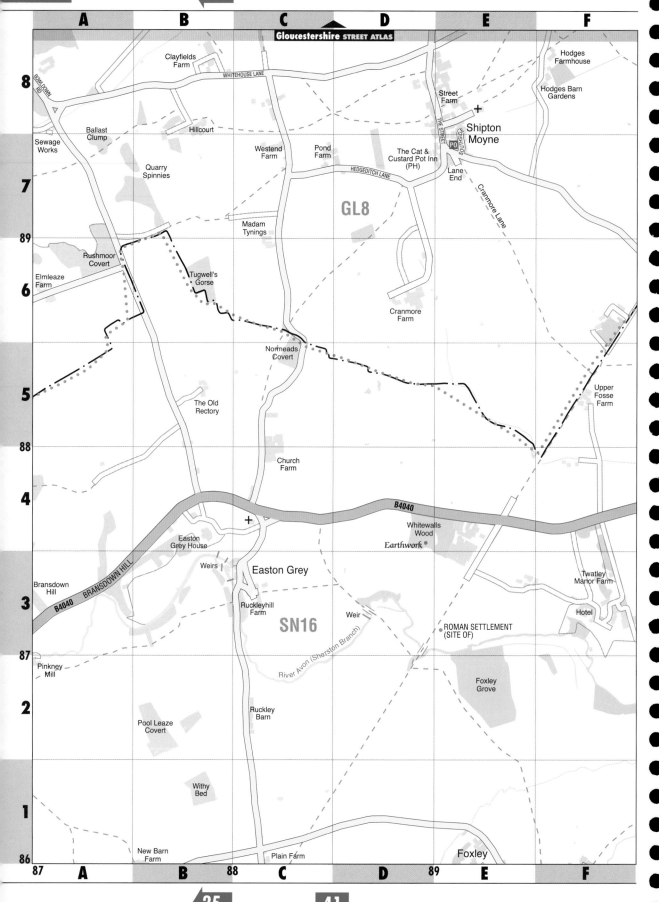

Gloucestershire STREET ATLAS

Clayfields Farm

WHITEHOUSE LANE

Hodges Farmhouse

Street Farm

Hodges Barn Gardens

8

BOWLDOWN RD

Ballast Clump

Hillcourt

Westend Farm

Pond Farm

The Cat & Custard Pot Inn (PH)

Shipton Moyne

THE STREET

Sewage Works

Quarry Spinnies

HEDGEDITCH LANE

Lane End

SOUTHSIDE

PO

GL8

7

Madam Tynings

Cranmore Lane

89

Rushmoor Covert

Tugwell's Gorse

Elmleaze Farm

Cranmore Farm

6

Normeads Covert

Upper Fosse Farm

The Old Rectory

5

88

Church Farm

B4040

Whitewalls Wood

4

Easton Grey House

Earthwork

Weirs

Easton Grey

Twatley Manor Farm

Bransdown Hill

BRANSDOWN HILL

Ruckleyhill Farm

SN16

Weir

Hotel

3

B4040

ROMAN SETTLEMENT (SITE OF)

87

Pinkney Mill

River Avon (Sherston Branch)

Foxley Grove

2

Pool Leaze Covert

Ruckley Barn

Withy Bed

1

86

New Barn Farm

Plain Farm

Foxley

87

A

B

88

C

D

89

E

F

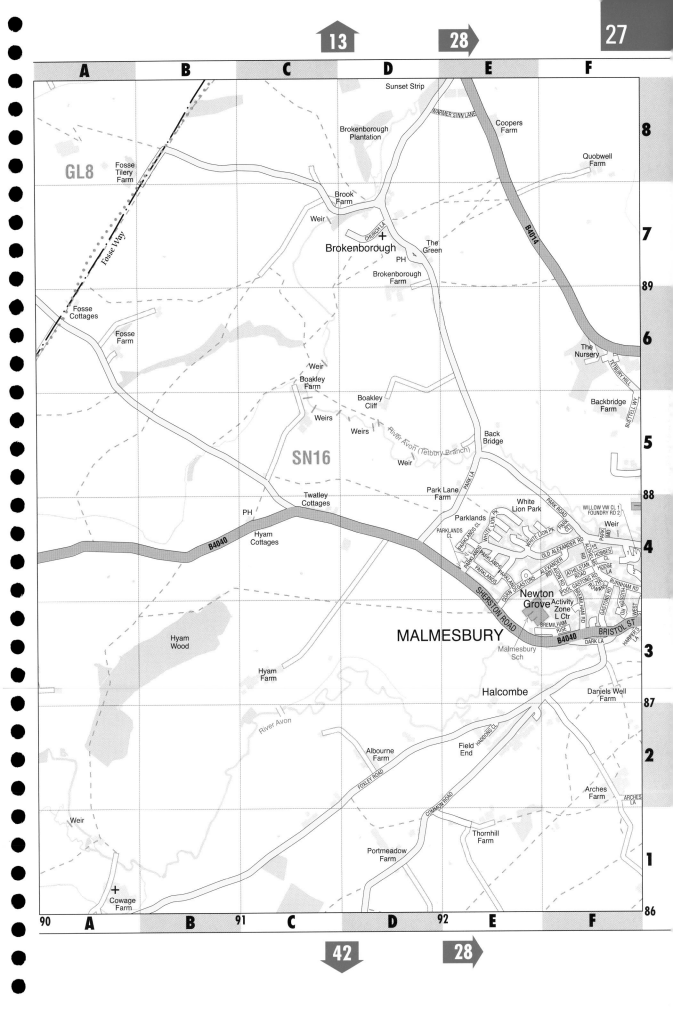

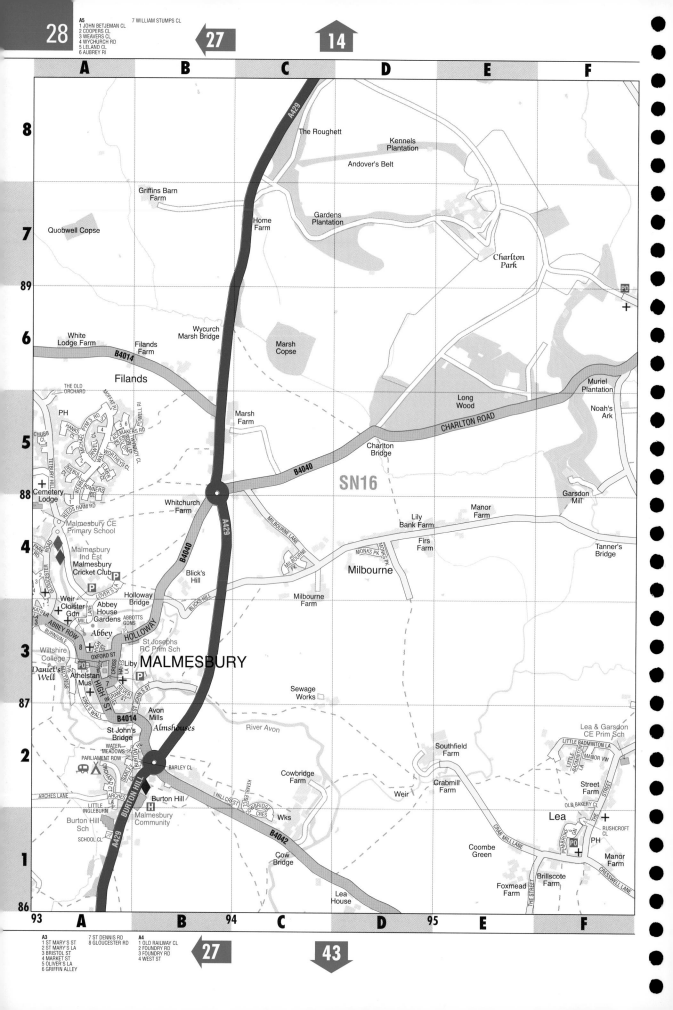

28

A5
1 JOHN BETJEMAN CL
2 COOPERS CL
3 WEAVERS CL
4 WYCHURCH RD
5 LELAND CL
6 AUBREY RI

7 WILLIAM STUMPS CL

27   14

A   B   C   D   E   F

8

The Roughett

Kennels
Plantation

Andover's Belt

Griffins Barn
Farm

Home
Farm

Gardens
Plantation

Charlton
Park

7

Quobwell Copse

89

White
Lodge Farm

Filands
Farm

Wycurch
Marsh Bridge

Marsh
Copse

Muriel
Plantation

6

B4014

Filands

THE OLD
ORCHARD

Marsh
Farm

Long
Wood

CHARLTON ROAD

Noah's
Ark

PH

CHUBB
CL

Charlton
Bridge

Garsdon
Mill

5

Cemetery
Lodge

LACEMAKERS RD

MOFFAT RI

POWELL RI

B4040

SN16

88

Malmesbury CE
Primary School

Whitchurch
Farm

MILBOURNE LANE

Lily
Bank Farm

Manor
Farm

4

Malmesbury
Ind Est
Malmesbury
Cricket Club

A4040

A429

Blick's
Hill

MILBOURNE PK

MONKS PK

MONKS PK

Firs
Farm

Milbourne

Tanner's
Bridge

Weir
Cloister
Gdn

Abbey
House
Gardens

Holloway
Bridge

BLICKS HILL

ABBOTTS
GDNS

Milbourne
Farm

Abbey

HOLLOWAY

St Josephs
RC Prim Sch

3

Wiltshire
College

OXFORD ST

Daniel's
Well

HIGH ST

MALMESBURY

Liby

Sewage
Works

Lea & Garsdon
CE Prim Sch

Athelstan
Mus

KING'S WALL

P

87

Avon
Mills

B4014

St John's
Bridge

Almshouses

River Avon

Southfield
Farm

LITTLE BADMINTON LA

MANOR VW

Street
Farm

2

WATER
MEADOWS

Parliament Row

BURTON HILL

BARLEY CL

Cowbridge
Farm

Crabmill
Farm

Weir

OLD BAKERY CL

ARCHES LANE

ARCHES
LA

LITTLE
INGLEBURN

Burton Hill

HILL CREST

KEMBLE CL

COWBRIDGE
CRES

Wks

Lea

CRAB MILL LANE

PEMBROKE

RUSHCROFT
CL

PH

Manor
Farm

Burton Hill
Sch

SCHOOL CL

Malmesbury
Community

B4042

Coombe
Green

THE STREET

CRESSWELL LANE

1

Cow
Bridge

Foxmead
Farm

Brillscote
Farm

86

93   A   B   94   C   D   95   E   F

A3
1 ST MARY'S ST
2 ST MARY'S LA
3 BRISTOL ST
4 MARKET ST
5 OLIVER'S LA
6 GRIFFIN ALLEY

7 ST DENNIS RD
8 GLOUCESTER RD

A4
1 OLD RAILWAY CL
2 FOUNDRY RD
3 FOUNDRY RD
4 WEST ST

27   43

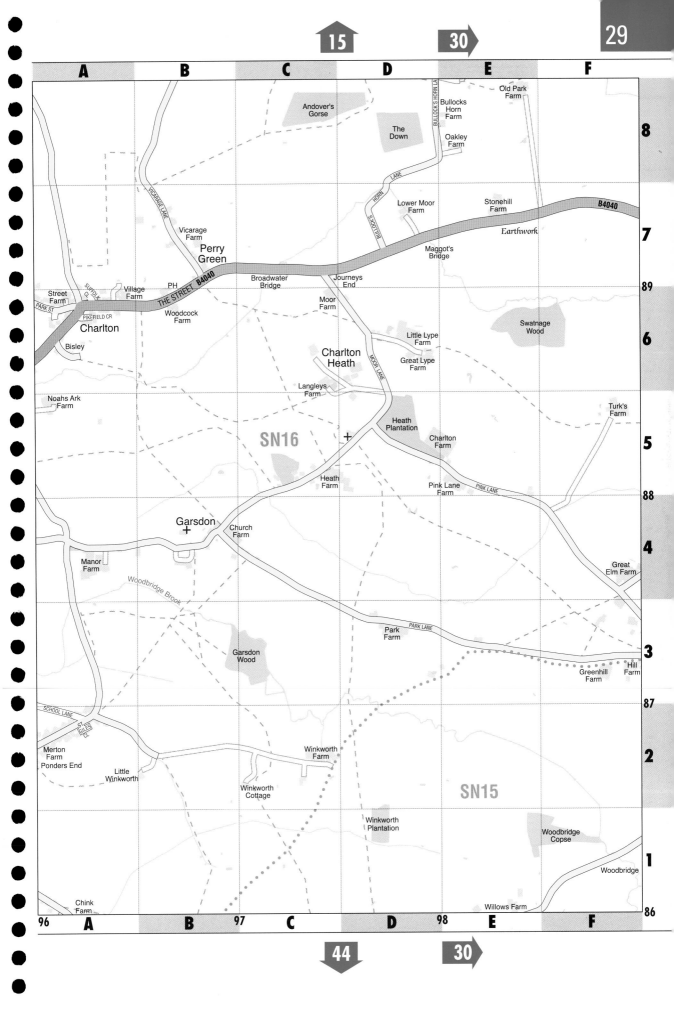

A   **B**   **C**   **D**   **E**   **F**

Andover's Gorse

The Down

Bullocks Horn Farm

Old Park Farm

Oakley Farm

8

BULLOCKS HORN LANE

Lower Moor Farm

Stonehill Farm

Earthwork

B4040

7

Vicarage Farm

Perry Green

Maggot's Bridge

Broadwater Bridge

Journeys End

89

PH

THE STREET **B4040**

Street Farm

SUFFOLK CL

Village Farm

Woodcock Farm

Moor Farm

Swatnage Wood

PARK ST

PIKEFIELD CR

Charlton

Bisley

Little Lype Farm

Charlton Heath

Great Lype Farm

MOOR LANE

6

Noahs Ark Farm

Langleys Farm

Heath Plantation

Charlton Farm

Turk's Farm

SN16

+

Pink Lane Farm

PINK LANE

5

Heath Farm

88

Garsdon
+

Church Farm

Manor Farm

Great Elm Farm

4

Woodbridge Brook

Garsdon Wood

Park Farm

PARK LANE

Greenhill Farm

Hill Farm

3

SCHOOL LANE

87

ST GILES CL

Merton Farm Ponders End

Little Winkworth

Winkworth Farm

SN15

2

Winkworth Cottage

Winkworth Plantation

Woodbridge Copse

Woodbridge

1

Chink Farm

Willows Farm

86

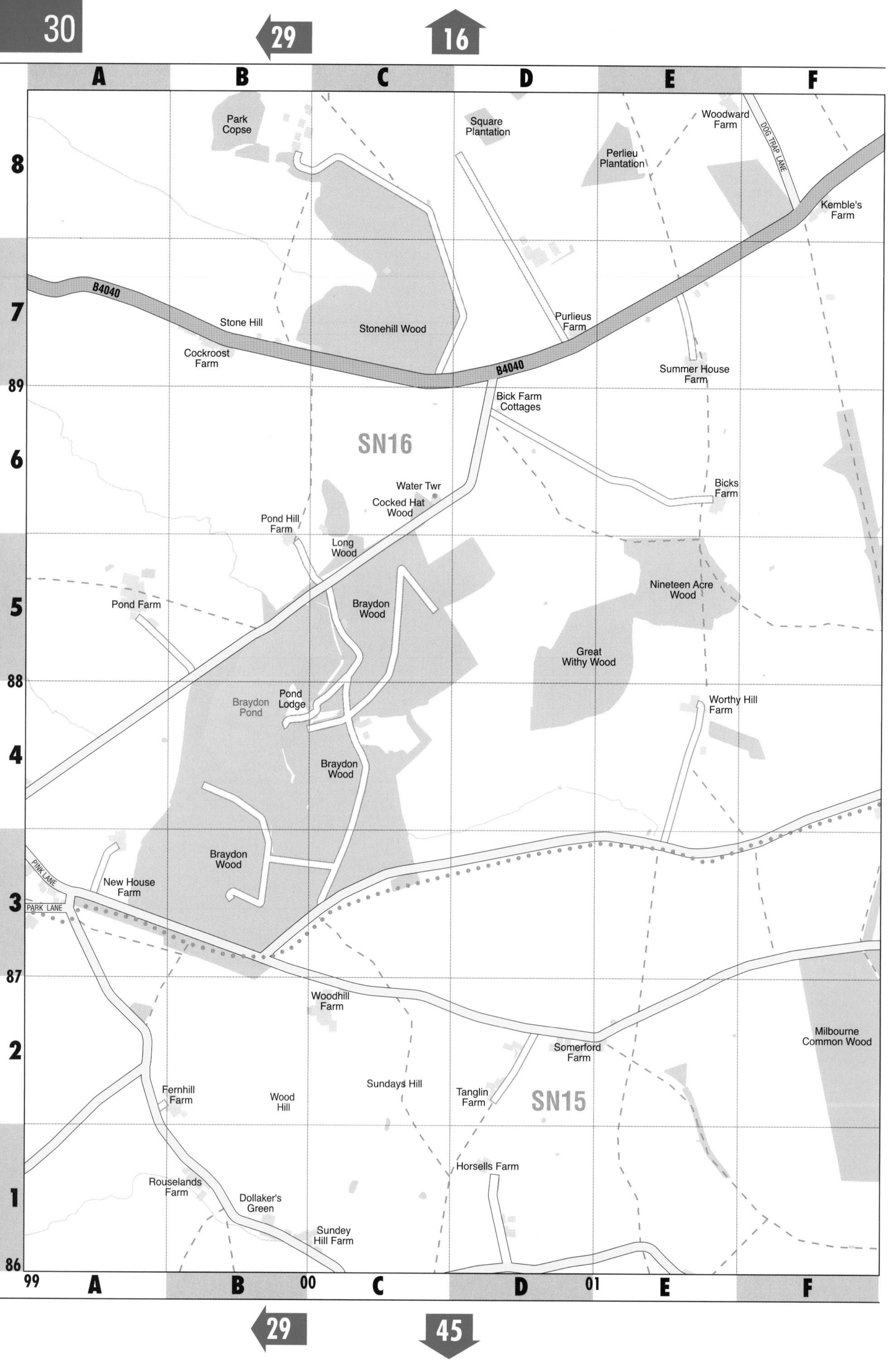

A   B   C   D   E   F

8

Park
Copse

Square
Plantation

Woodward
Farm

DOG TRAP LANE

Perlieu
Plantation

Kemble's
Farm

B4040

7

Stone Hill

Stonehill Wood

Purlieus
Farm

B4040

Cockroost
Farm

89

Bick Farm
Cottages

SN16

Summer House
Farm

6

Water Twr

Cocked Hat
Wood

Bicks
Farm

Pond Hill
Farm

Long
Wood

5

Pond Farm

Braydon
Wood

Nineteen Acre
Wood

Braydon
Pond

Pond
Lodge

Great
Withy Wood

88

Braydon
Wood

Worthy Hill
Farm

4

Braydon
Wood

PINK LANE

New House
Farm

3

PARK LANE

Woodhill
Farm

87

Milbourne
Common Wood

2

Somerford
Farm

Fernhill
Farm

Wood
Hill

Sundays Hill

Tanglin
Farm

SN15

Horsells Farm

1

Rouselands
Farm

Dollaker's
Green

Sundey
Hill Farm

86

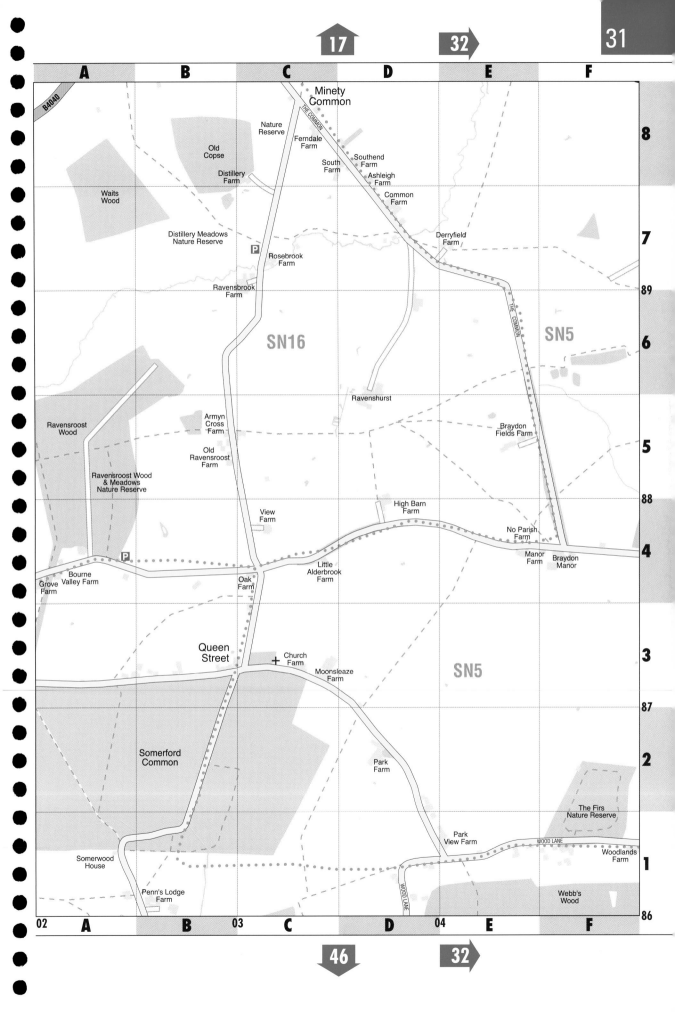

31
18

A   B   C   D   E   F

8

Black Dog
Bridge

Buryhill
Farm

Lower Buryhill
Farm

Elfins
Wood

White Lodge

B4696

White Lodge
Farm

Coxhill Farm

Pound
Copse

7

Square
Copse

River Key

89

Redlodge
Plantation

Pound
Farm

6

Gospel Oak
Farm

Oak
Copse

Red
Lodge

Parkgate
Farm

Maplesale
Farm

Red Lodge
Farm

+

Upper
Pavenhill
Farm

SN5

5

Battlelake
Plantation

Battle
Lake

88

Maple
Sale Copse

Brickkiln
Copse

Battlelake
Farm

Old Dairy
Upper Pavenhill
Farm

UPPER PAVENHILL

PH

4

Greenacres Farm

Woodside
Farm

South
Pavenhill
Farm

RESTROP VW

RINGSBURY CL

3

Braydon Green
Farm

Common
Farm

RINGSBURY CL

Dogridge

87

Ringsbury
Camp

2

Brockhurst Wood

Restrop
Farm

Ashbed
Copse

Brockhurst
Farm

Parley
Copse

Oxleaze
Copse

Matthew's
Copse

Drill Farm

Plain
Farm

WOOD LANE

Green
Hill

1

SN15

B4696

Brickkiln
Copse

SN4

Webb's Wood

Lydiard
Plain

Hill Farm

86

05   A   B   06   C   D   07   E   F

31
47

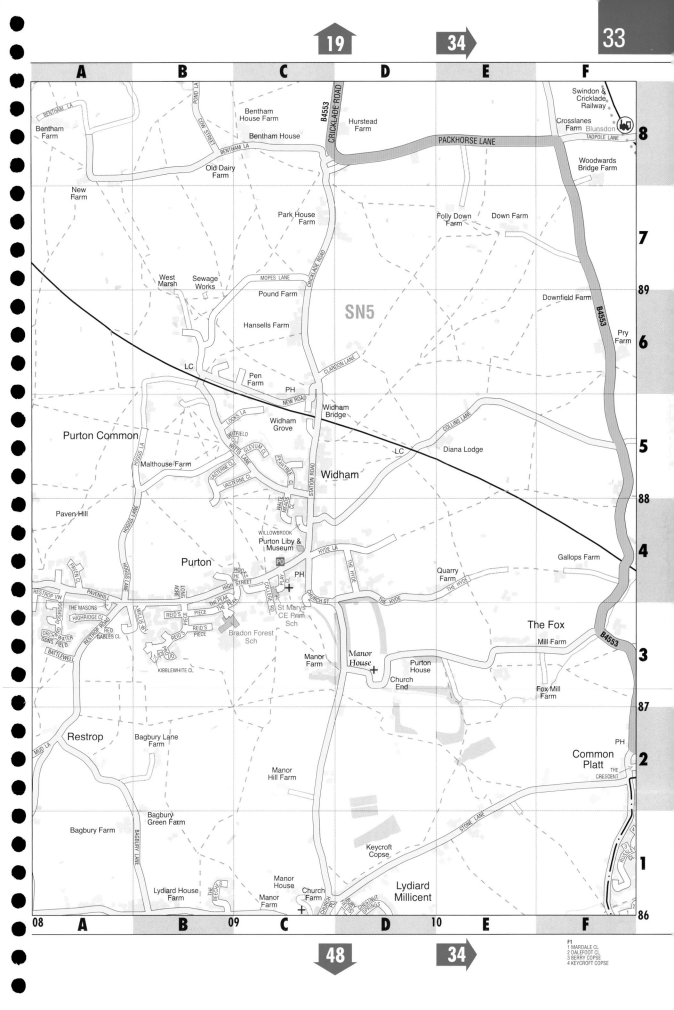

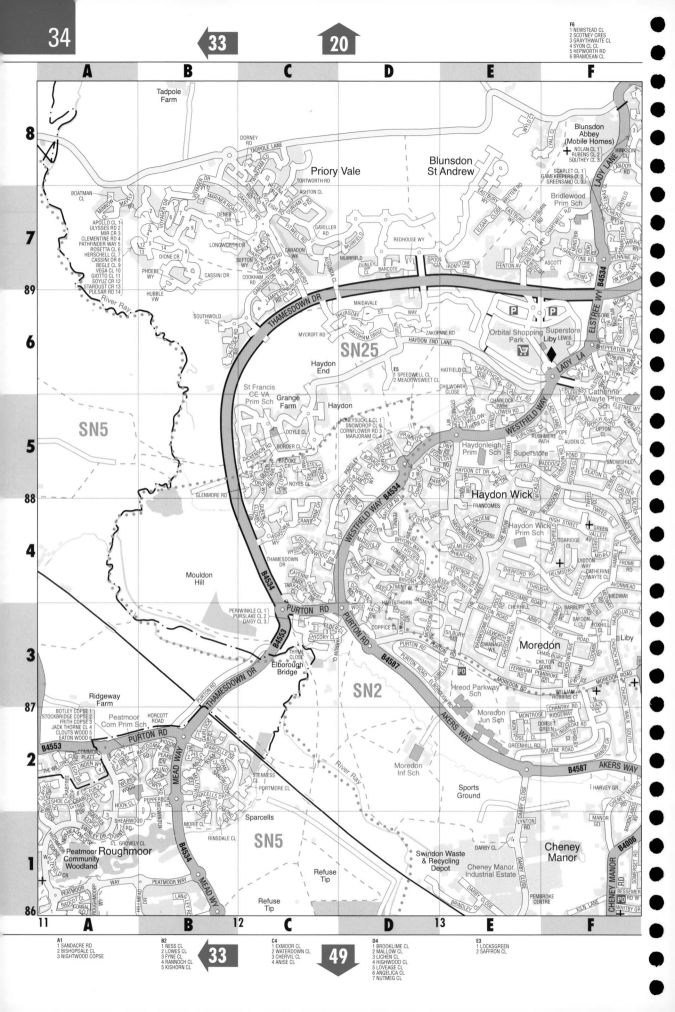

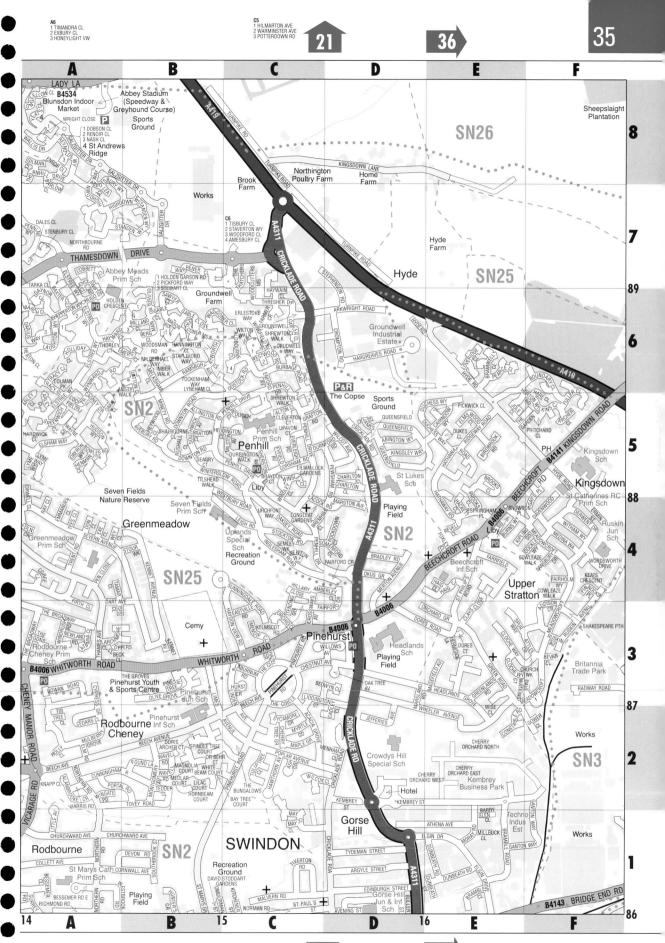

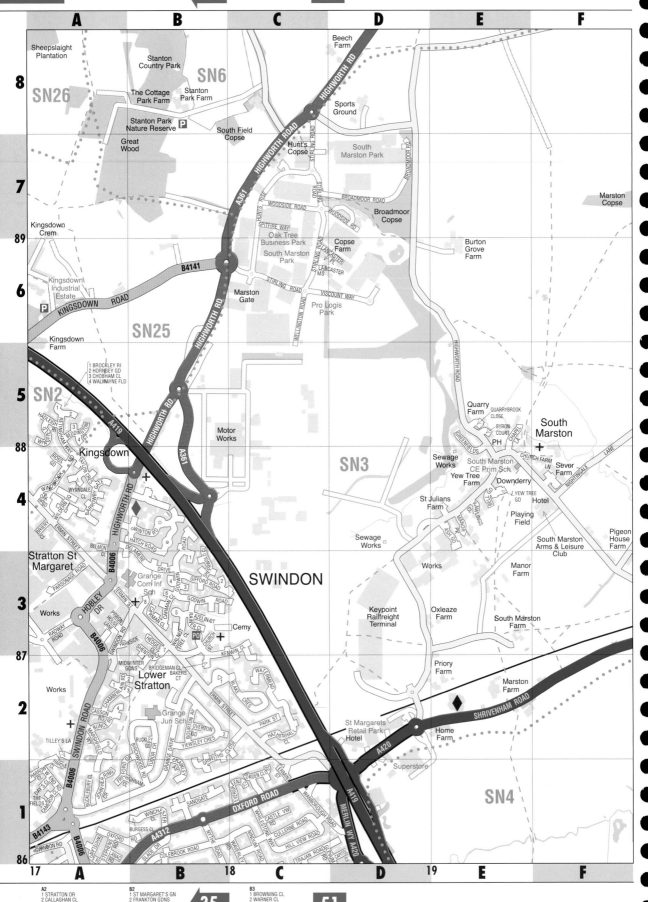

A2
1 STRATTON DR
2 CALLAGHAN CL
3 GOULDING CL
4 SHAPLANDS
5 THE PADDOCKS

B2
1 ST MARGARET'S GN
2 FRANKTON GDNS

B3
1 BROWNING CL
2 WARNER CL
3 COTTARS CL
4 BARON CL
5 BOWMAN CL
6 CRISPIN CL
7 CHURCH WAY
8 FRANK WARMAN CT

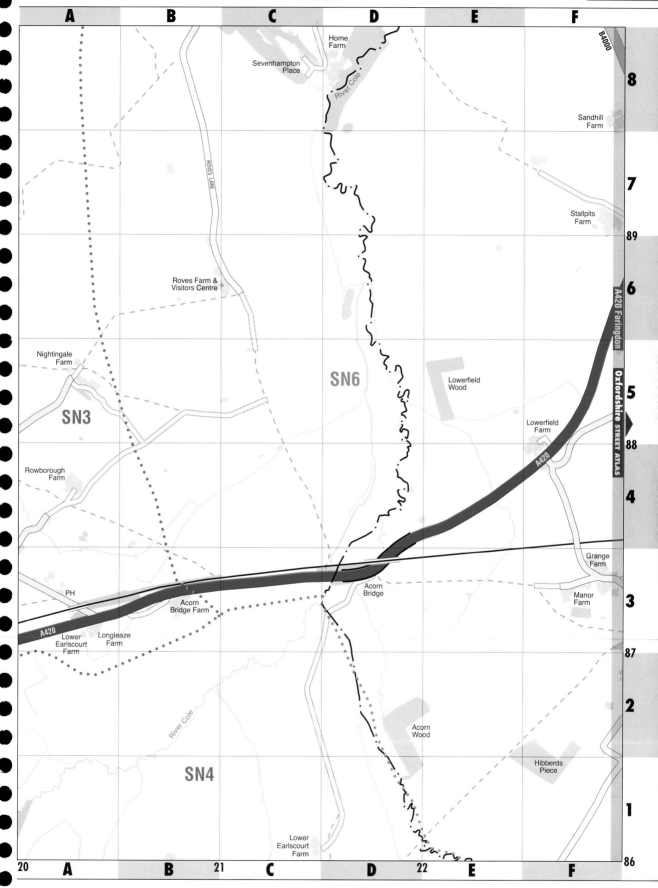

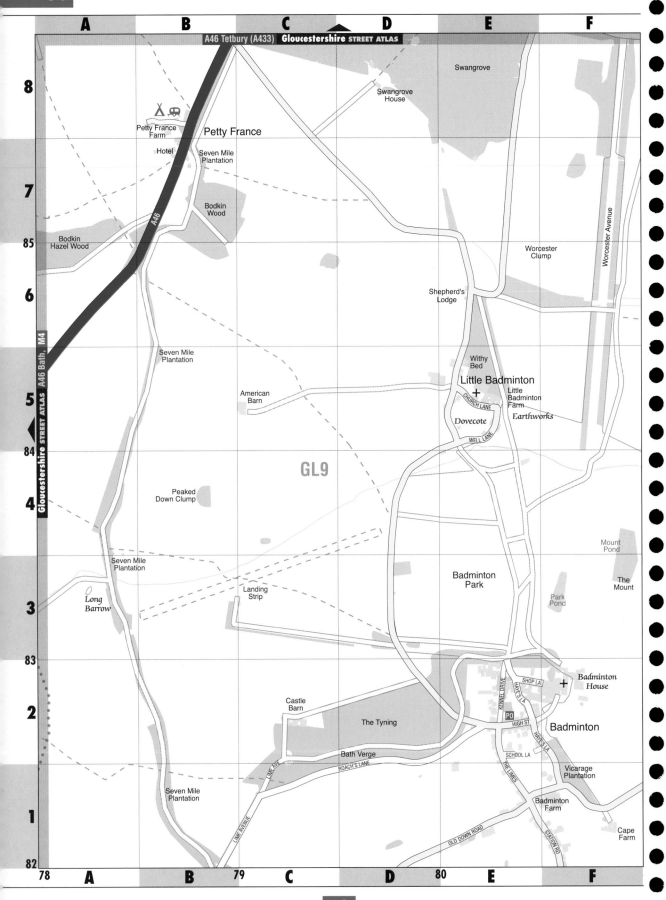

Gloucestershire STREET ATLAS

A46 Bath, M4

Swangrove

Swangrove
House

Petty France
Farm

Petty France

Hotel

Seven Mile
Plantation

Worcester Avenue

Bodkin
Wood

A46

Bodkin
Hazel Wood

Worcester
Clump

Shepherd's
Lodge

Seven Mile
Plantation

Withy
Bed

Little Badminton

American
Barn

CHURCH LANE

Little
Badminton
Farm

Earthworks

Dovecote

WELL LANE

GL9

Peaked
Down Clump

Mount
Pond

The
Mount

Seven Mile
Plantation

Badminton
Park

Park
Pond

Landing
Strip

Long
Barrow

Badminton
House

Castle
Barn

KENNEL DRIVE

SHOP LA

HAFE'S LA

The Tyning

PO

HIGH ST

Badminton

Bath Verge

LIME AVE

ROACH'S LANE

SCHOOL LA

HAFE'S LA

THE LIMES

Vicarage
Plantation

Seven Mile
Plantation

LIME AVENUE

Badminton
Farm

OLD DOWN ROAD

STATION RD

Cape
Farm

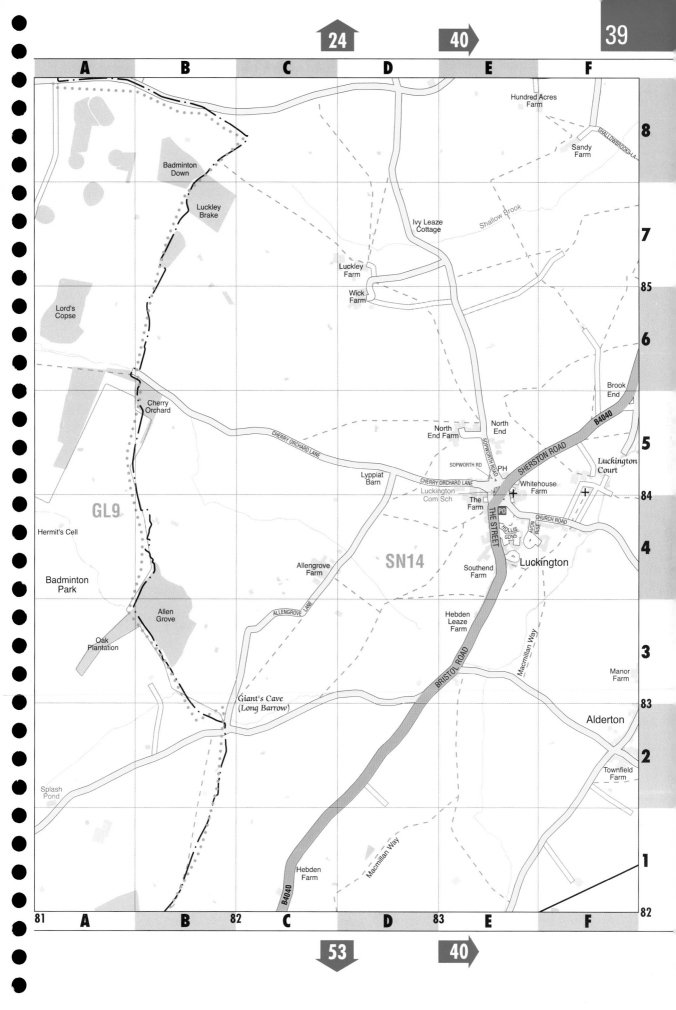

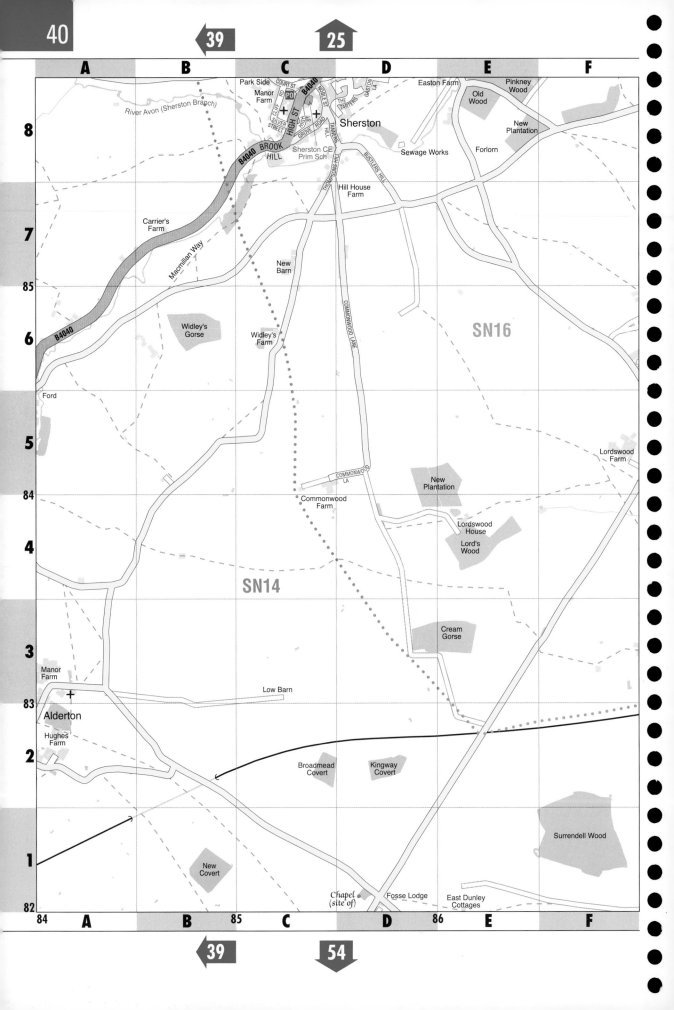

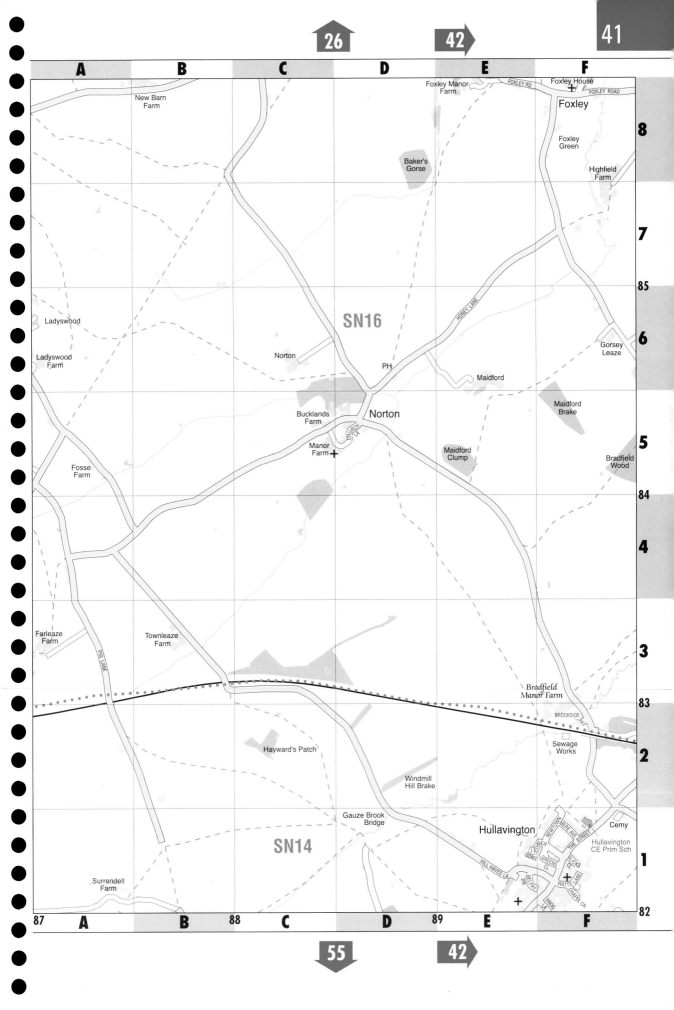

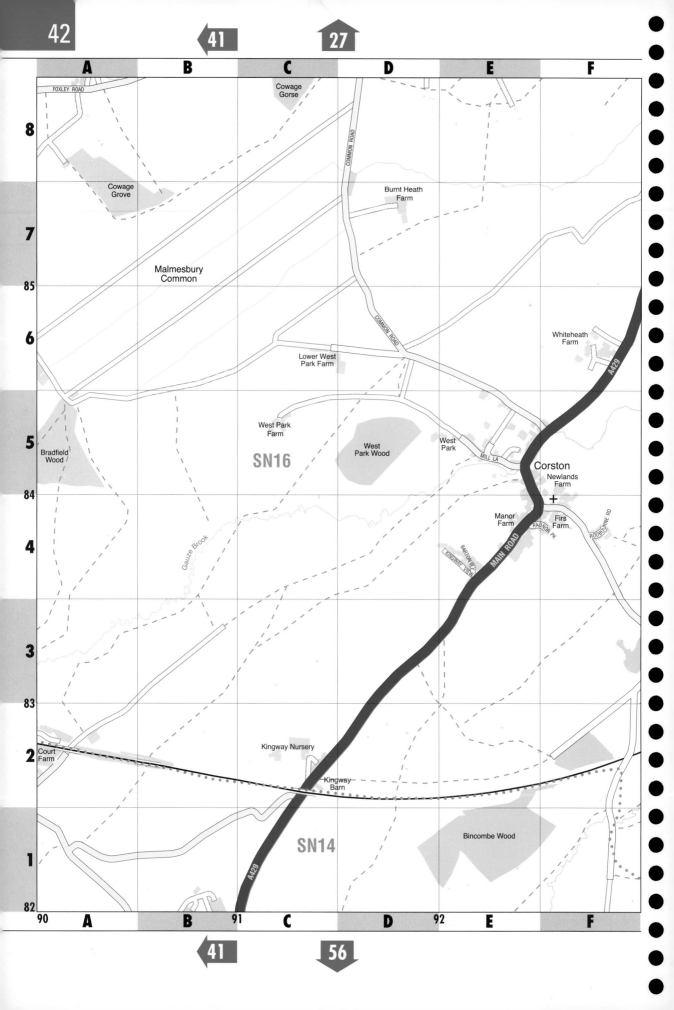

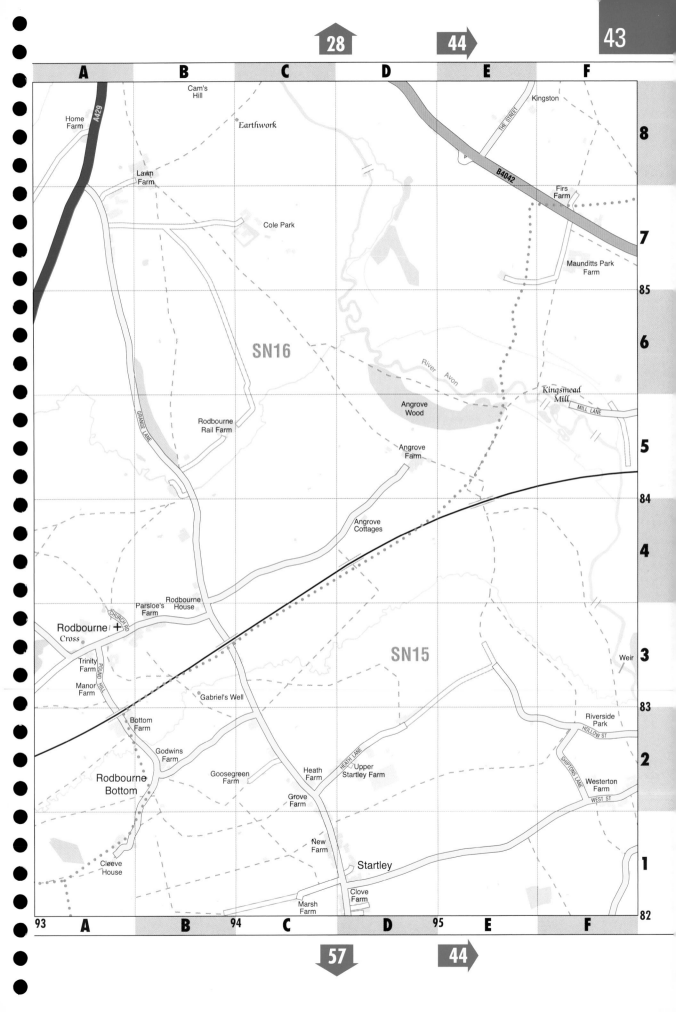

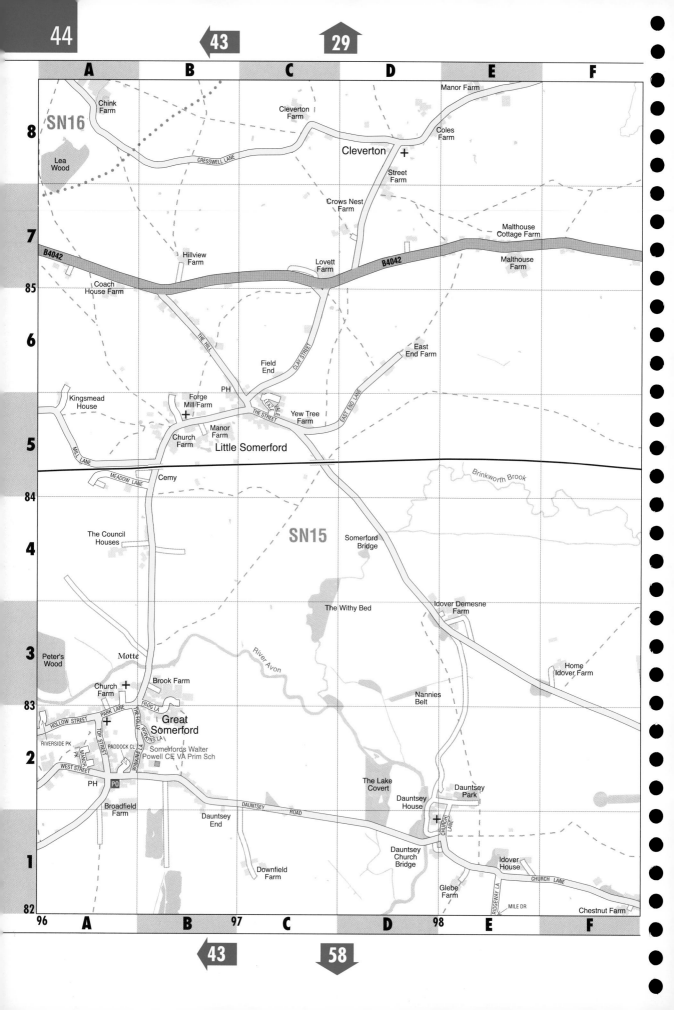

43
29

A · B · C · D · E · F

SN16

8

Chink Farm

Cleverton Farm

Manor Farm

Cleverton

Coles Farm

Lea Wood

CRESSWELL LANE

Street Farm

Crows Nest Farm

7

Hillview Farm

Lovett Farm

B4042

Malthouse Cottage Farm

85

B4042

Coach House Farm

Malthouse Farm

THE HILL

6

CLAY STREET

Field End

East End Farm

PH

Kingsmead House

Forge Mill Farm

THE STREET

LAKE

Yew Tree Farm

EAST END LANE

Manor Farm

5

Church Farm

Little Somerford

MILL LANE

MEADOW LANE

Cemy

Brinkworth Brook

84

The Council Houses

SN15

Somerford Bridge

4

The Withy Bed

Idover Demesne Farm

3

Peter's Wood

Motte

River Avon

Home Idover Farm

Brook Farm

Church Farm

FROG LA

Nannies Belt

83

HOLLOW STREET

PARK LANE

THE FOLLY

WILKINS LA

Great Somerford

RIVERSIDE PK

MANOR PK

TOP STREET

PADDOCK CL

WILKINS LA

Somerfords Walter Powell CE VA Prim Sch

2

WEST STREET

The Lake Covert

Dauntsey Park

PH

PO

Dauntsey House

CHURCH LANE

Broadfield Farm

DAUNTSEY ROAD

Dauntsey End

Dauntsey Church Bridge

1

Downfield Farm

Glebe Farm

Idover House

RIDGEWAY LA

CHURCH LANE

MILE DR

Chestnut Farm

82

96 · A · B · 97 · C · D · 98 · E · F

43
58

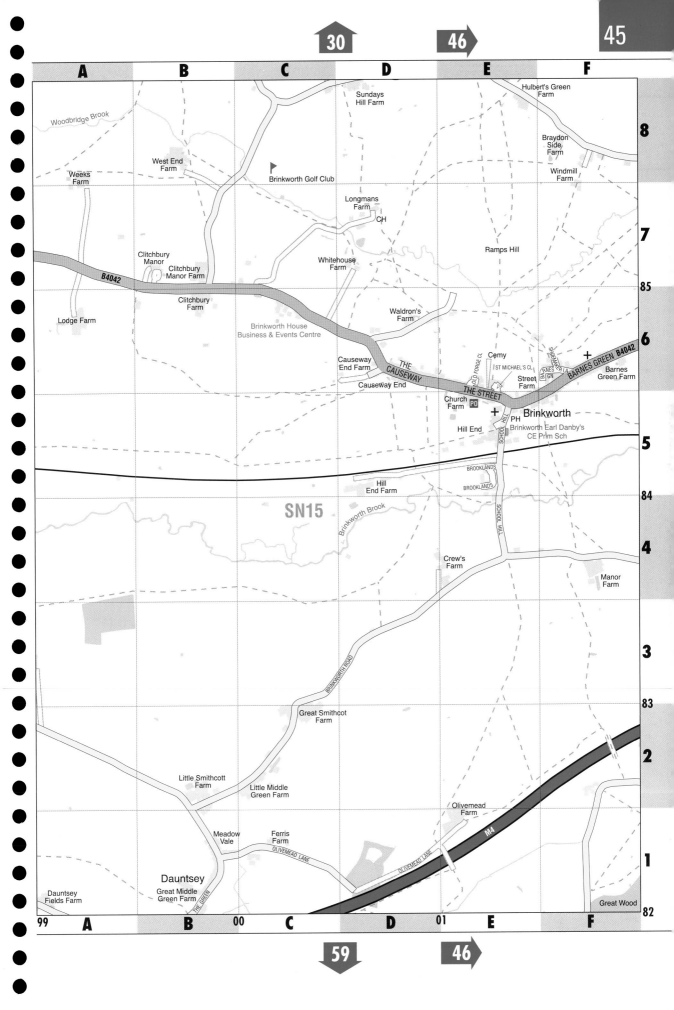

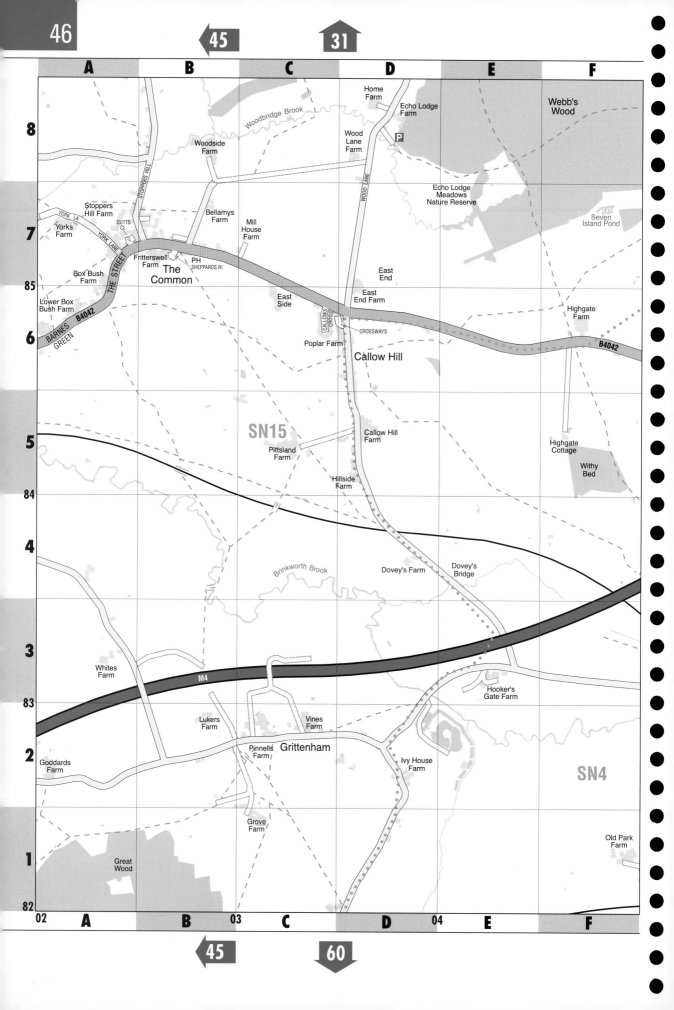

A   **B**   **C**   **D**   **E**   **F**

Woodbridge Brook

Webb's Wood

8

Home Farm

Echo Lodge Farm

Woodside Farm

Wood Lane Farm

Seven Island Pond

Echo Lodge Meadows Nature Reserve

STOPPERS HILL

Stoppers Hill Farm

Bellamys Farm

7

YORK LA

CUTTS CL

Yorks Farm

YORK LANE

Mill House Farm

WOOD LANE

Box Bush Farm

THE STREET

Fritterswell Farm

PH
SHEPPARDS RI

East End

85

The Common

East Side

East End Farm

Highgate Farm

Lower Box Bush Farm

B4042

CALLOWS CROSS

CROSSWAYS

6

BARNES GREEN

Poplar Farm

Callow Hill

B4042

SN15

Callow Hill Farm

Highgate Cottage

5

Pittsland Farm

Highgate Cottage

Hillside Farm

Withy Bed

84

4

Brinkworth Brook

Dovey's Farm

Dovey's Bridge

3

Whites Farm

M4

Hooker's Gate Farm

83

Lukers Farm

Vines Farm

2

Pinnells Farm

Grittenham

Ivy House Farm

SN4

Goddards Farm

Grove Farm

Old Park Farm

1

Great Wood

82

02   **A**   **B**   **03**   **C**   **D**   **04**   **E**   **F**

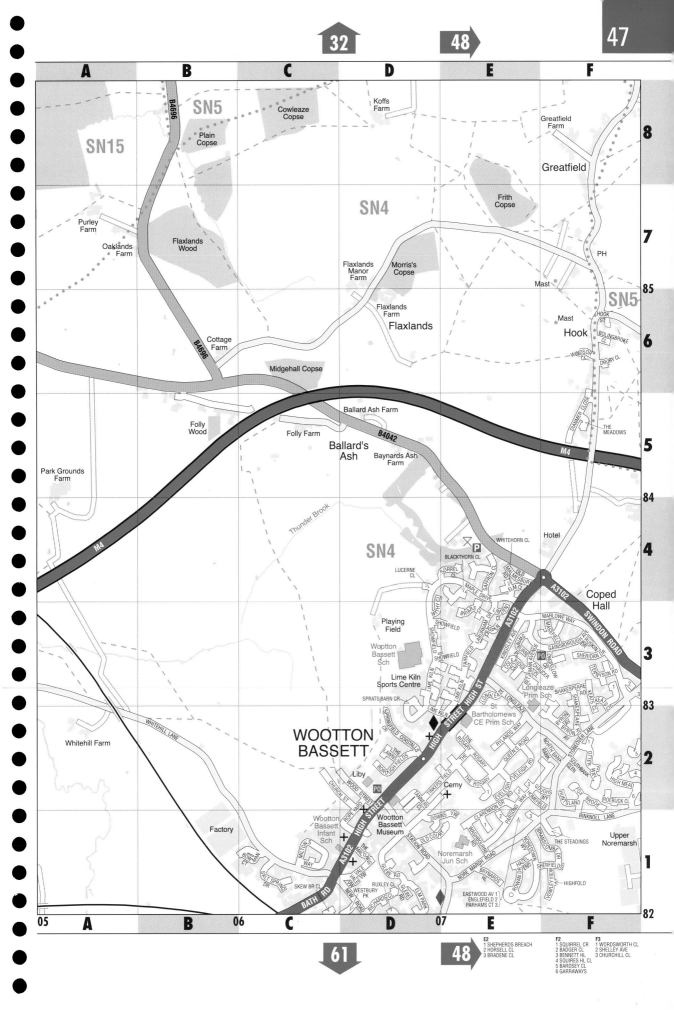

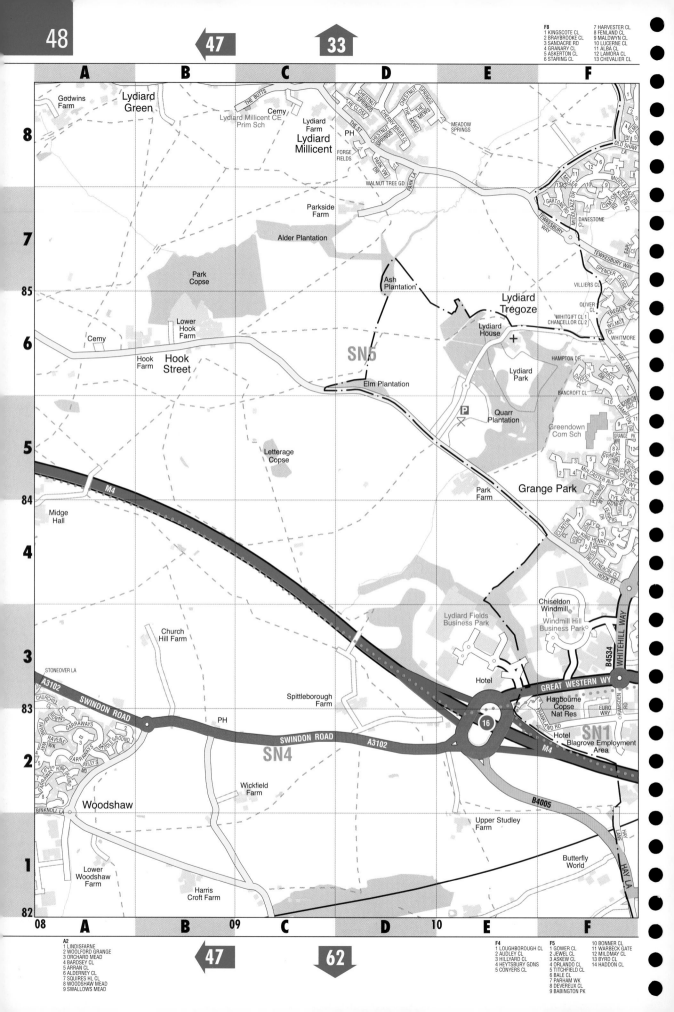

F8
1 KINGSCOTE CL
2 BRAYBROOKE CL
3 SANDACRE RD
4 GRANARY CL
5 ASKERTON CL
6 STARING CL
7 HARVESTER CL
8 FENLAND CL
9 MALDWYN CL
10 LUCERNE CL
11 ALBA CL
12 LAMORA CL
13 CHEVALIER CL

Godwins Farm

Lydiard Green

THE BUTTS

Cemy

Lydiard Millicent CE Prim Sch

Lydiard Farm

Lydiard Millicent

CHESTNUT SPRINGS

CHESTNUT SPRINGS

CHERRY BRIER

THE MEWS

THE CLOSE

PH

THE ST

CHESTNUT SPRINGS

MEADOW SPRINGS

FORGE FIELDS

PARK VW

PARK LA

WALNUT TREE GD

Parkside Farm

Alder Plantation

OLD SHAW LA

THE ELMS

MILLER

MIDDLELEAZE DR

GARTONS RD

CARTON

KIERAN CT

DANESTONE CL

TEWKESBURY WAY

TEWKESBURY WAY

EARL CL

SPENCER CLOSE

VILLIERS CL

Park Copse

Ash Plantation

Lydiard Tregoze

OLIVER CL

WHITGIFT CL 1

CHANCELLOR CL 2

TREGOZE WAY

WILMOT

WHITMORE CL

Lower Hook Farm

Cemy

Lydiard House

+

Hook Farm

Hook Street

SN5

Elm Plantation

HAMPTON DR

HAY LANE

Lydiard Park

D'ARCY CL

CABOT DR

BANCROFT CL

Lydiard Park

Quarr Plantation

HAMPTON DR

Letterage Copse

P
✕

Greendown Com Sch

GRANGE PK

CHAMPION

M4

Park Farm

Grange Park

MULCASTER AVE

GRINDALE DR

SUMMERLEAZE

ELBORTH

CUNHILL

PRYTHING

TYE CL

Midge Hall

CLINTON

SIDLEY

KING HENRY DR

LEAZERS

LINEACRE CL

HOOK ST

Church Hill Farm

Lydiard Fields Business Park

Chiseldon Windmill

Windmill Hill Business Park

WHITEHILL WY

B4534

STONEOVER LA

A3102

SWINDON ROAD

PH

Spittleborough Farm

Hotel

GREAT WESTERN WY

Hagbourne Copse Nat Res

EURO WAY

RAMSDEN RD

SN1

CHURCHILL CL

FARNE WAY

PROBYN

GARRAWAYS

COLE GROUND

RAVENS WK

GARRAWAYS MD

HOME GROUND

BAILEY'S

SWINDON ROAD

A3102

SN4

16

Hotel

FRANKLAND RD

M4

Blagrove Employment Area

BINKNOLL LA

Woodshaw

Wickfield Farm

Upper Studley Farm

B4005

HAY LA

HAY LANE

Lower Woodshaw Farm

Harris Croft Farm

Butterfly World

A2
1 LINDISFARNE
2 WOOLFORD GRANGE
3 ORCHARD MEAD
4 BARDSEY CL
5 ARRAN CL
6 ALDERNEY CL
7 SQUIRES HL CL
8 WOODSHAW MEAD
9 SWALLOWS MEAD

F4
1 LOUGHBOROUGH CL
2 AUDLEY CL
3 HILLYARD CL
4 HEYTSBURY GDNS
5 CONYERS CL

F5
1 GOWER CL
2 JEWEL CL
3 ASKEW CL
4 ORLANDO CL
5 TITCHFIELD CL
6 BALE CL
7 PARHAM WK
8 DEVEREUX CL
9 BABINGTON PK
10 BONNER CL
11 WARBECK GATE
12 MILDMAY CL
13 BYRD CL
14 HADDON CL

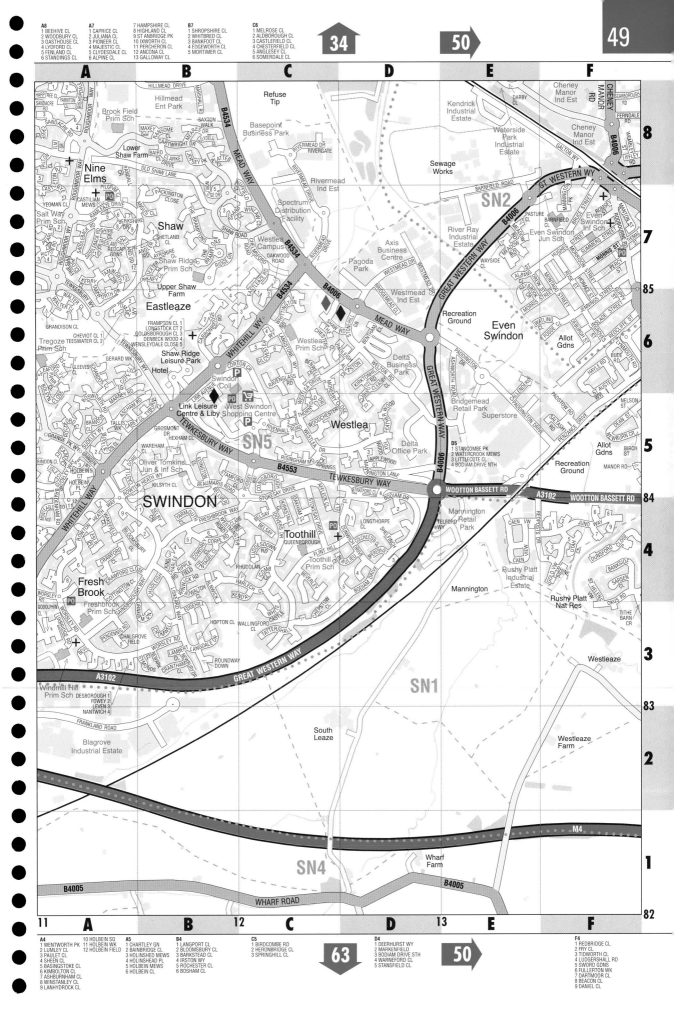

49

35

49

64

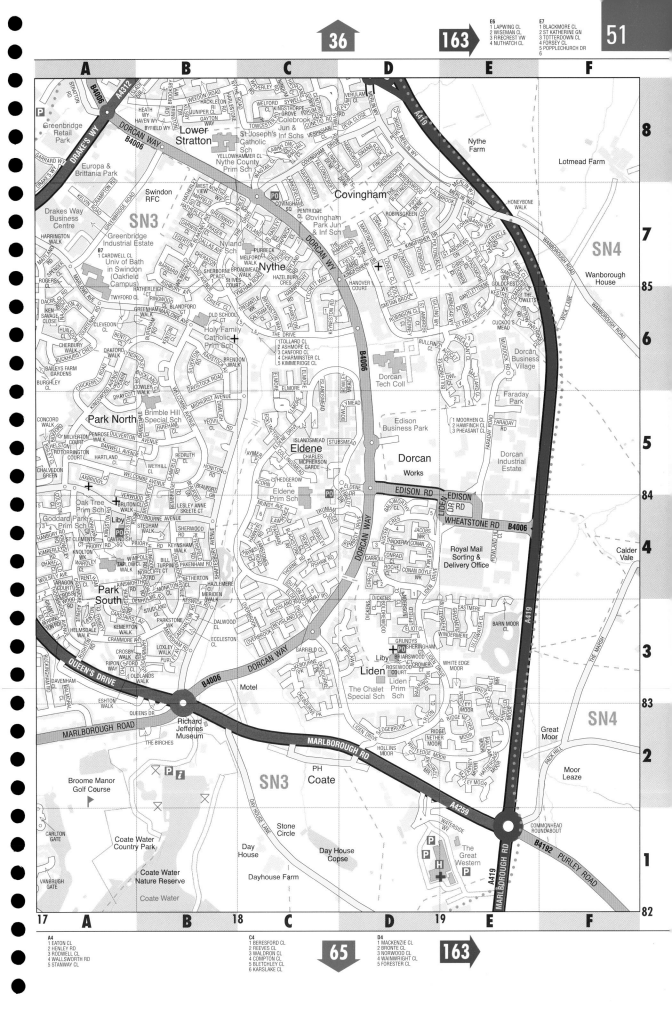

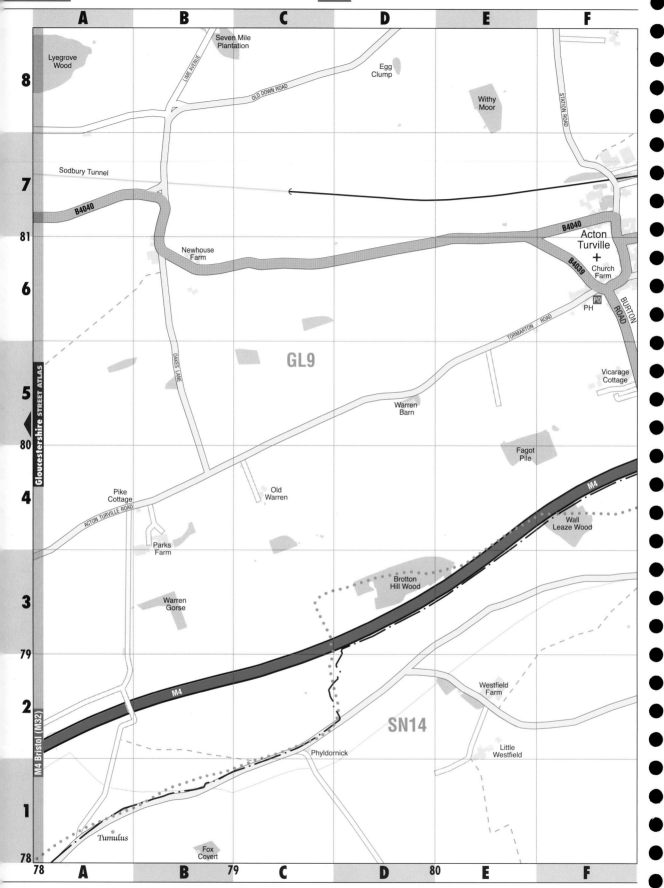

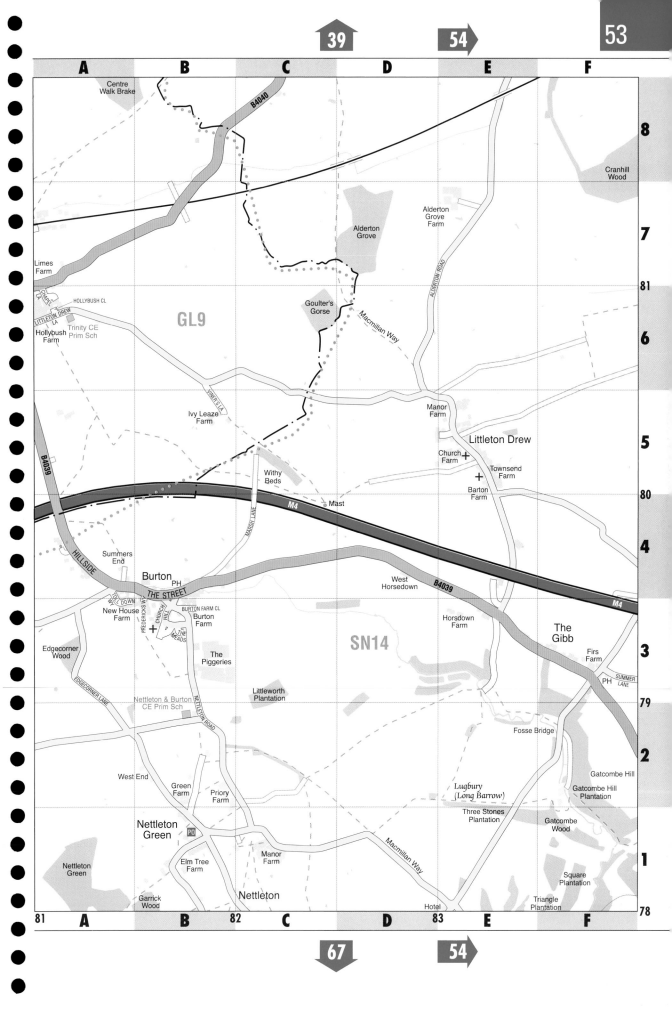

A   B   C   D   E   F

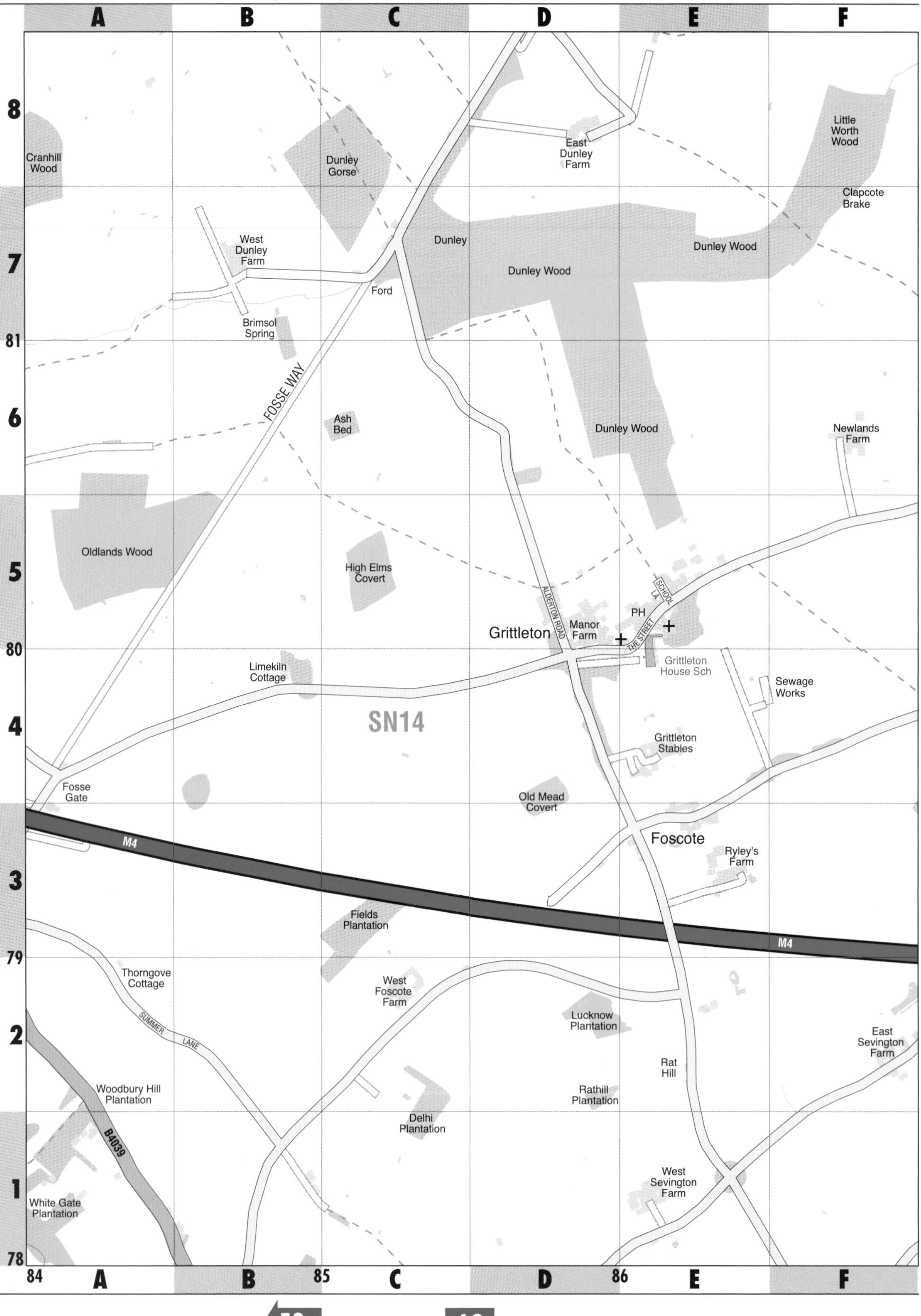

8

Cranhill
Wood

Dunley
Gorse

East
Dunley
Farm

Little
Worth
Wood

Clapcote
Brake

7

West
Dunley
Farm

Dunley

Dunley Wood

Dunley Wood

Ford

Dunley Wood

Brimsol
Spring

81

FOSSE WAY

6

Ash
Bed

Dunley Wood

Newlands
Farm

Oldlands Wood

5

High Elms
Covert

ALBERTON ROAD

SCHOOL LA

80

Grittleton

Manor
Farm

PH

THE STREET

+

+

Limekiln
Cottage

Grittleton
House Sch

Sewage
Works

4

SN14

Grittleton
Stables

Fosse
Gate

Old Mead
Covert

Foscote

Ryley's
Farm

M4

3

Fields
Plantation

M4

79

Thorngove
Cottage

West
Foscote
Farm

Lucknow
Plantation

East
Sevington
Farm

2

SUMMER   LANE

Woodbury Hill
Plantation

Rat
Hill

B4039

Delhi
Plantation

Rathill
Plantation

1

White Gate
Plantation

West
Sevington
Farm

78

84   A   B   85   C   D   86   E   F

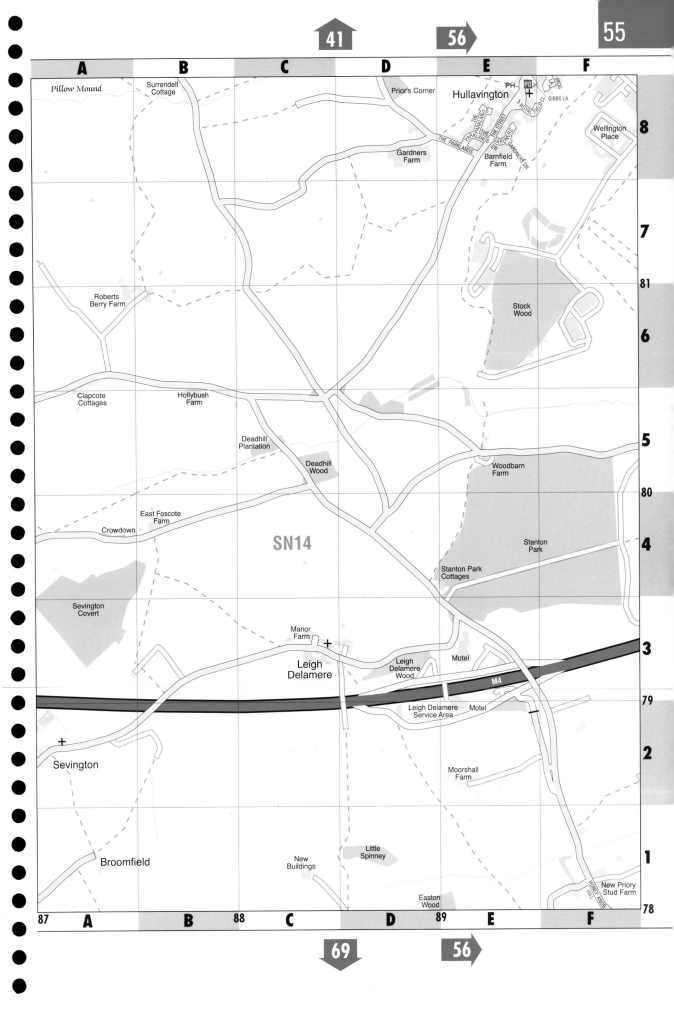

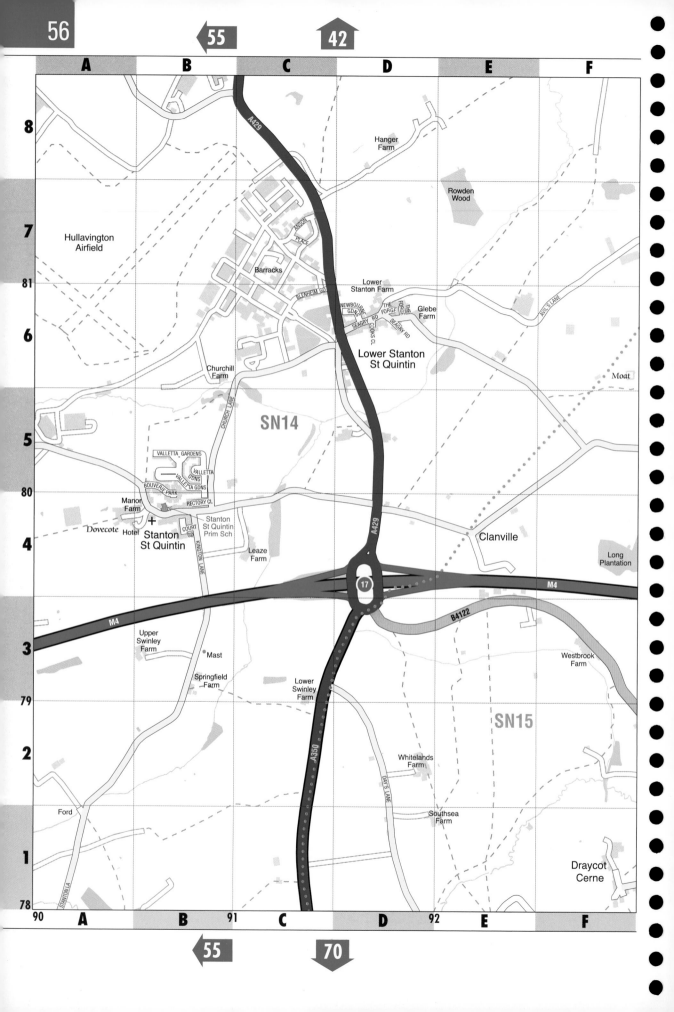

A B C D E F

8

7

81

6

5

80

4

3

79

2

1

78

90 A B 91 C D 92 E F

Hullavington
Airfield

Barracks

ANSON PLACE

BLENHEIM GD

Hanger
Farm

Rowden
Wood

Lower
Stanton Farm

NEWBOURNE
GD

SEAGRY RD

CONS CL

THE FORGE

THE FORGE

SEAGRY RD

Glebe
Farm

AVIL'S LANE

Moat

Lower Stanton
St Quintin

Churchill
Farm

CHURCH LANE

SN14

VALLETTA GARDENS

VALLETTA
GDNS

VALLETTA GDNS

BOUVERIE PARK

RECTORY CL

Manor
Farm

Dovecote

Hotel

COURT GD

Stanton
St Quintin

KINGTON LANE

Stanton
St Quintin
Prim Sch

Leaze
Farm

Clanville

Long
Plantation

A429

17

M4

M4

B4122

Westbrook
Farm

Upper
Swinley
Farm

Mast

Springfield
Farm

Lower
Swinley
Farm

A350

SN15

Whitelands
Farm

DAY'S LANE

Southsea
Farm

Ford

STANTON LA

Draycot
Cerne

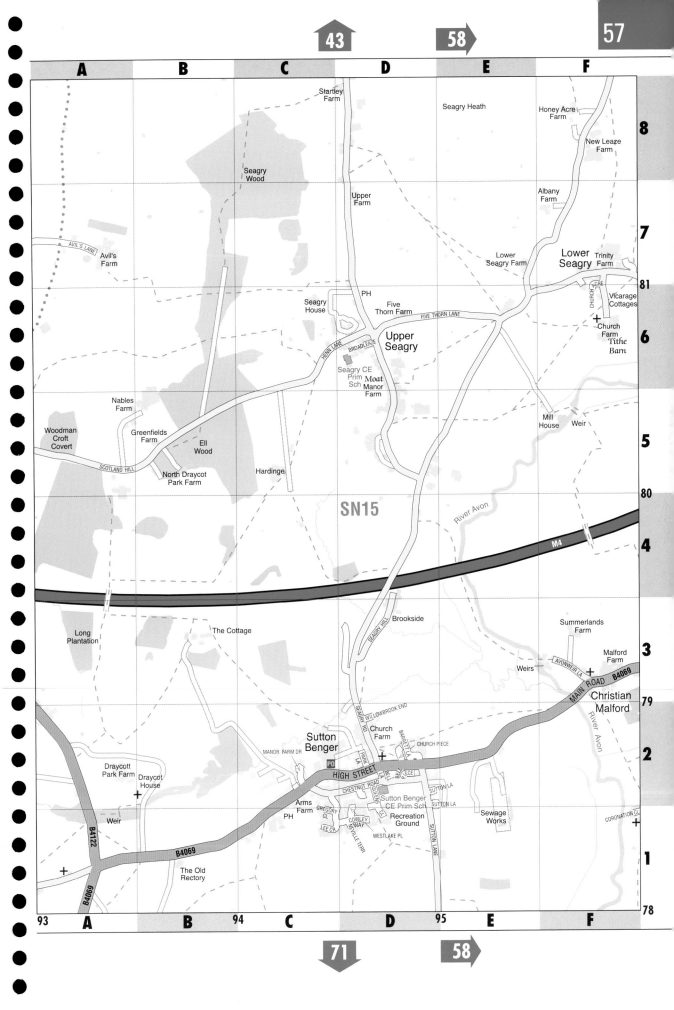

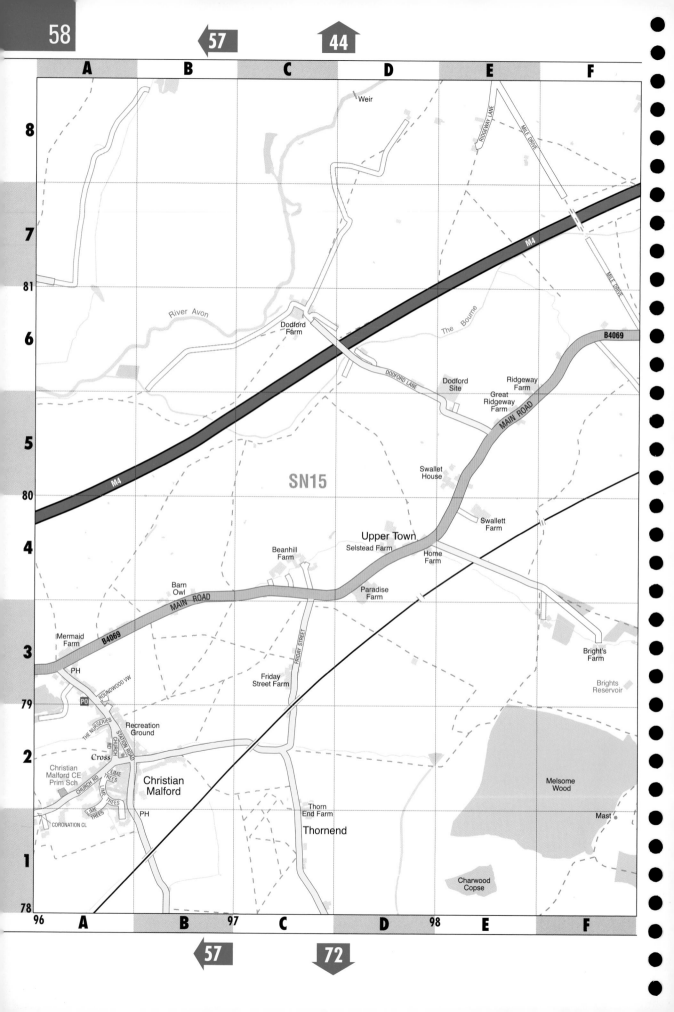

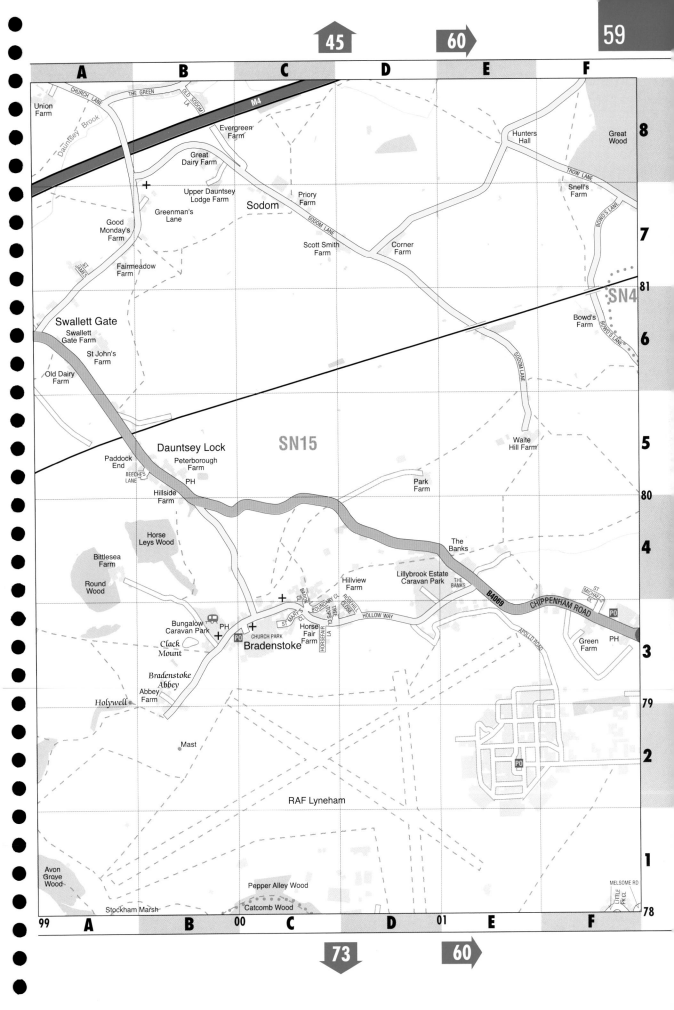

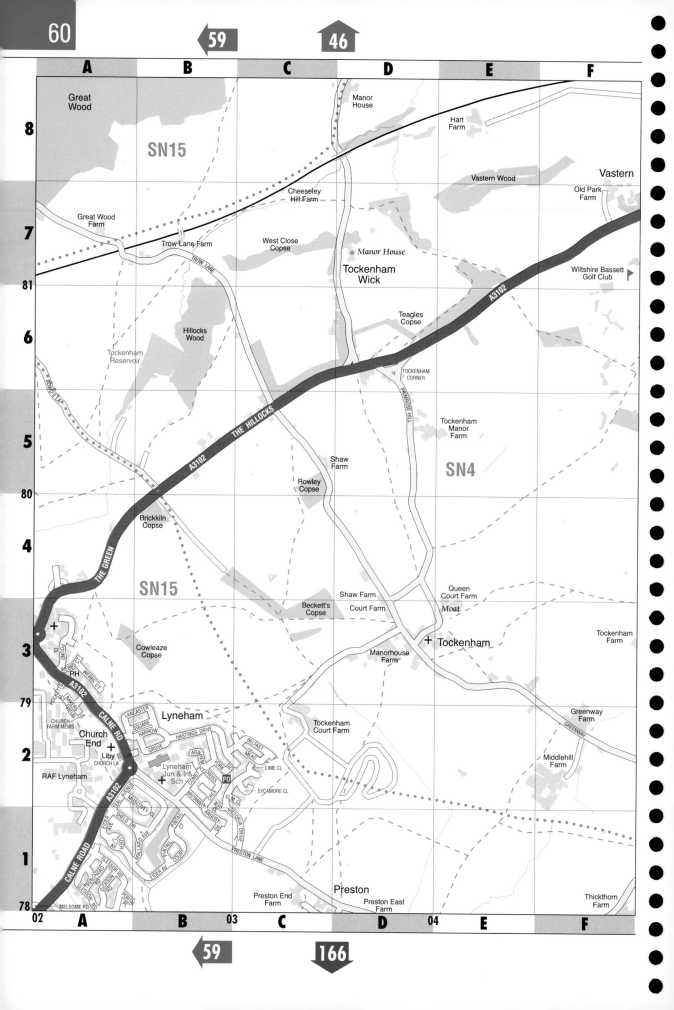

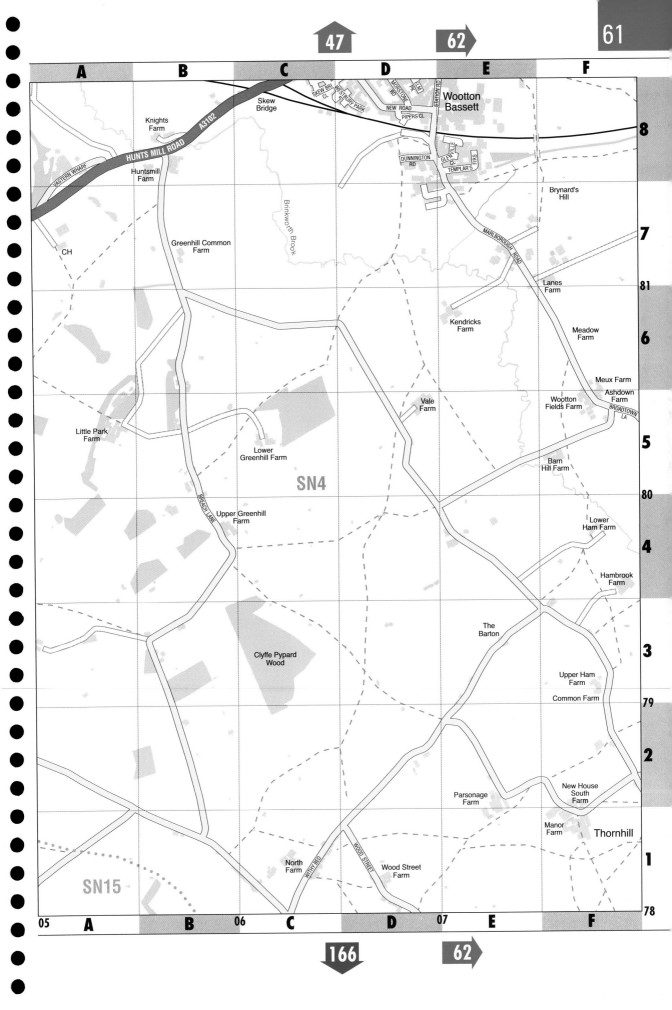

A B C D E F

SKEW BRI CL
WESTBURY PARK
MORSTONE RD
ELM PK
STATION RD
NEW ROAD
PIPERS CL
Skew Bridge
Wootton Bassett
Knights Farm
A3102
HUNTS MILL ROAD
VASTERN WHARF
Huntsmill Farm
DUNNINGTON RD
GLENVILLE CL
FIRS
TEMPLAR'S
Brynard's Hill
CH
Greenhill Common Farm
Brinkworth Brook
MARLBOROUGH ROAD
Lanes Farm
Kendricks Farm
Meadow Farm
Meux Farm
Ashdown Farm
Wootton Fields Farm
BROADTOWN LA
Vale Farm
Little Park Farm
Lower Greenhill Farm
SN4
Barn Hill Farm
Upper Greenhill Farm
BREACH LANE
Lower Ham Farm
Hambrook Farm
Clyffe Pypard Wood
The Barton
Upper Ham Farm
Common Farm
New House South Farm
Parsonage Farm
Manor Farm
Thornhill
North Farm
WITHY BED
WOOD STREET
Wood Street Farm
SN15

05 06 07
78 79 80 81
1 2 3 4 5 6 7 8

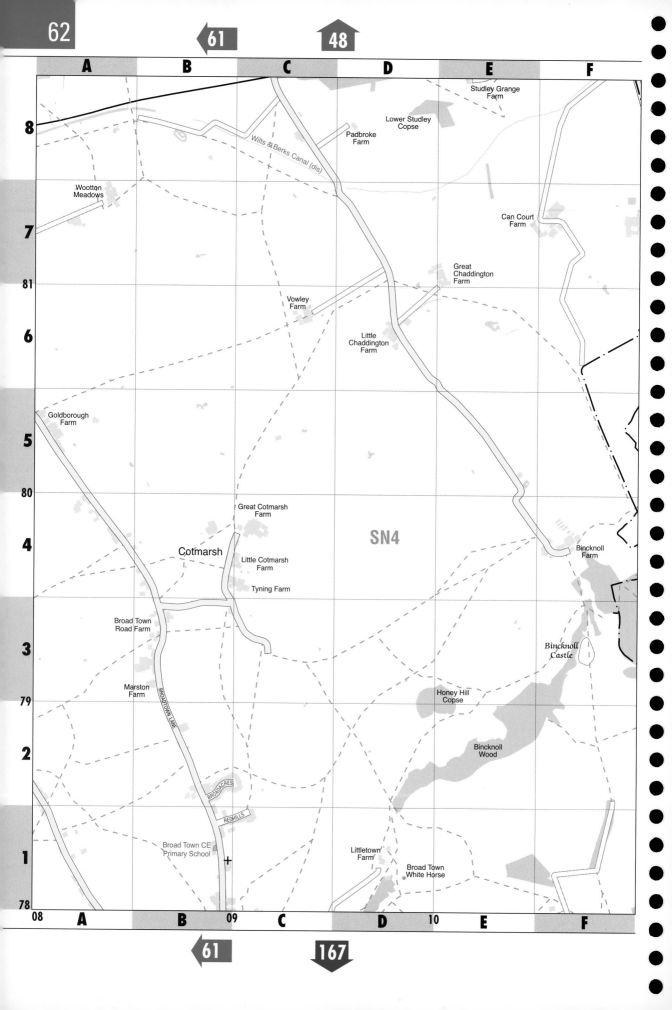

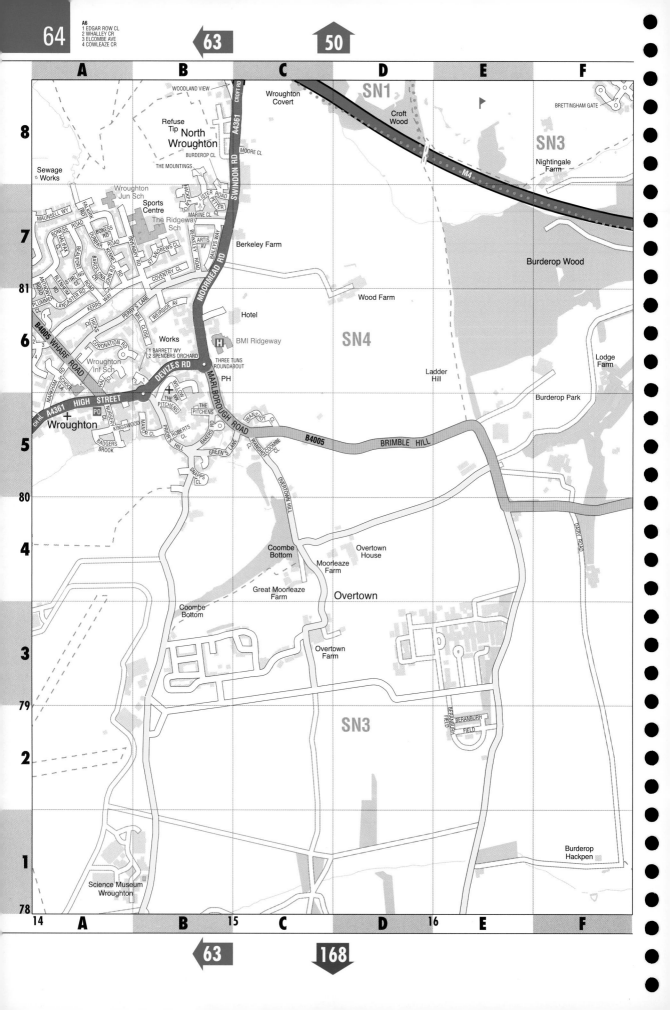

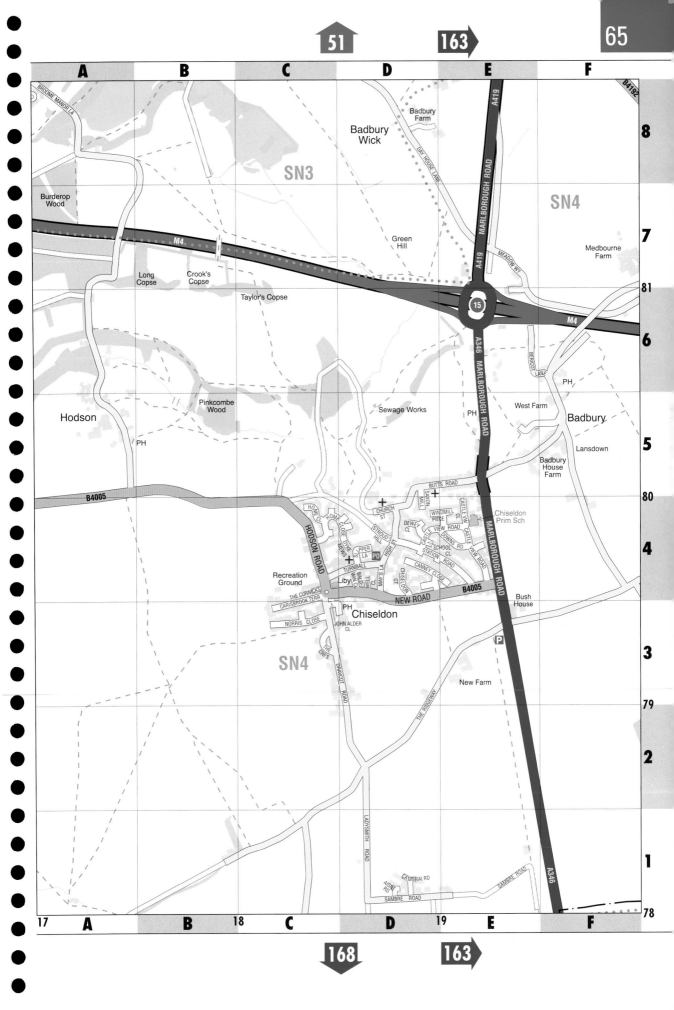

A B C D E F

BROOME MANOR LA

8

Badbury
Farm

Badbury
Wick

B4192

SN3

Burderop
Wood

SN4

DAY HOUSE LANE

MARLBOROUGH ROAD

A419

7

M4

Green
Hill

Medbourne
Farm

Long
Copse

Crook's
Copse

Taylor's Copse

A419

MEADOW WY

81

15

M4

6

A346

Pinkcombe
Wood

Sewage Works

MARLBOROUGH ROAD

BERCOT LANE

PH

Hodson

PH

West Farm

Badbury

PH

Lansdown

5

B4005

Badbury
House
Farm

BUTTIS ROAD

SAXON

80

CHURCH
ST

WINDMILL
PIECE

Chiseldon
Prim Sch

HODSON ROAD

HOME CL

HOME CLOSE

DEWEY
CL

CASTLE VW

CASTLE VIEW ROAD

DYKE

MEWS

ISTROUD ST

HILL

HIGH ST

STATION

E. VIEW
ROAD

DOWNS RD

SCHOOL
CL

CASTLE CL

MARLBOROUGH ROAD

4

UPPER
LA

PO

CANNEY CLOSE

Recreation
Ground

TURNBALL

BALD WIN CL

MAY'S LA

CHISELDON
CT

B4005

Liby

THE CURNICKS

CARISBROOK TERR

PH

NEW ROAD

Bush
House

NORRIS CLOSE

Chiseldon

JOHN ALDER
CL

P

3

SN4

THE CRES

DRAYCOT ROAD

New Farm

79

LADYSMITH ROAD

THE RIDGEWAY

2

A346

1

CAMBRAI RD

AISNE
RD

SAMBRE ROAD

SAMBRE ROAD

78

17 A B 18 C D 19 E F

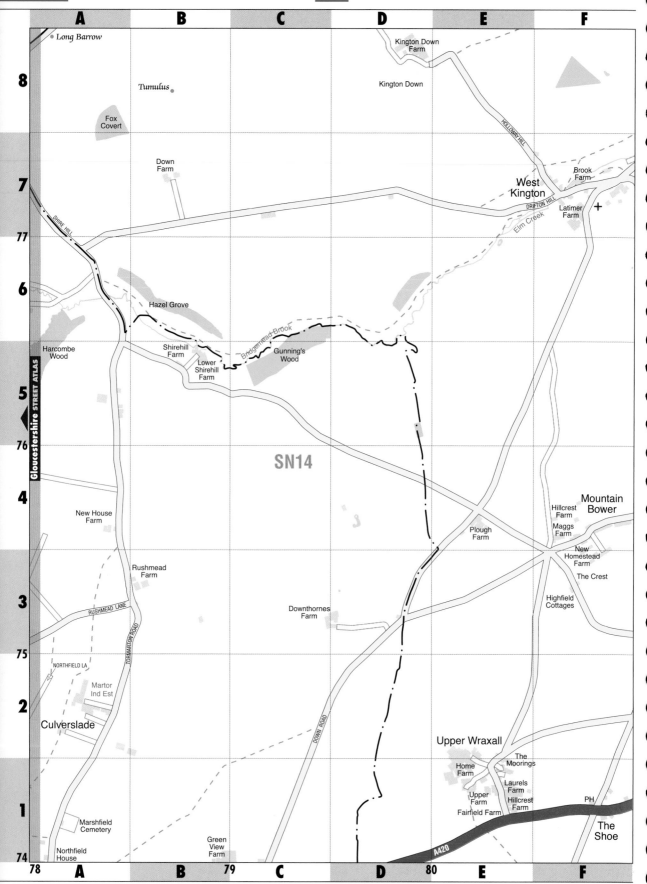

Long Barrow

Tumulus

Fox Covert

Kington Down Farm

Kington Down

HOLLOWAY HILL

Down Farm

West Kington

Brook Farm

DRIFTON HILL

Latimer Farm

SHIRE HILL

Elm Creek

Hazel Grove

Harcombe Wood

Bridgemead Brook

Shirehill Farm

Lower Shirehill Farm

Gunning's Wood

New House Farm

SN14

Mountain Bower

Hillcrest Farm

Maggs Farm

Plough Farm

New Homestead Farm

The Crest

Rushmead Farm

RUSHMEAD LANE

TORMARTON ROAD

Downthornes Farm

Highfield Cottages

NORTHFIELD LA

Martor Ind Est

Culverslade

DOWN ROAD

Upper Wraxall

The Moorings

Home Farm

Laurels Farm

Upper Farm

Hillcrest Farm

Fairfield Farm

PH

The Shoe

Marshfield Cemetery

Northfield House

Green View Farm

A420

Gloucestershire STREET ATLAS

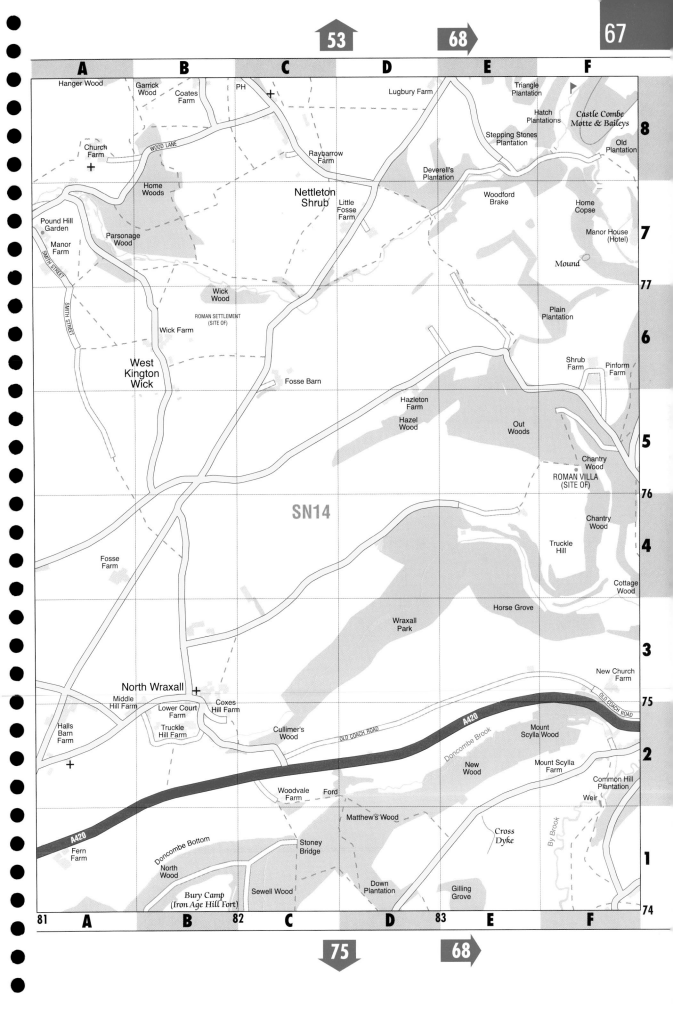

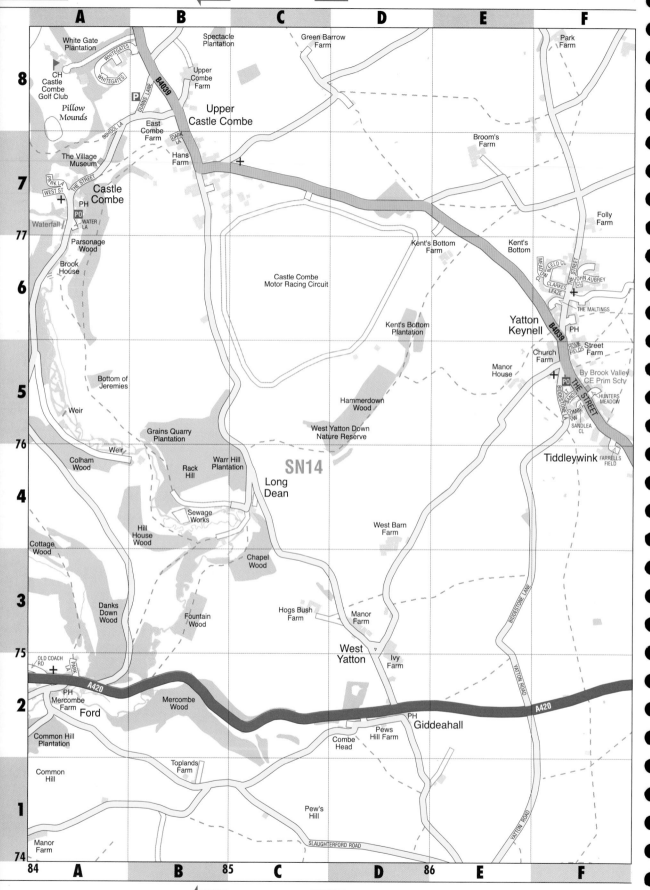

SN14

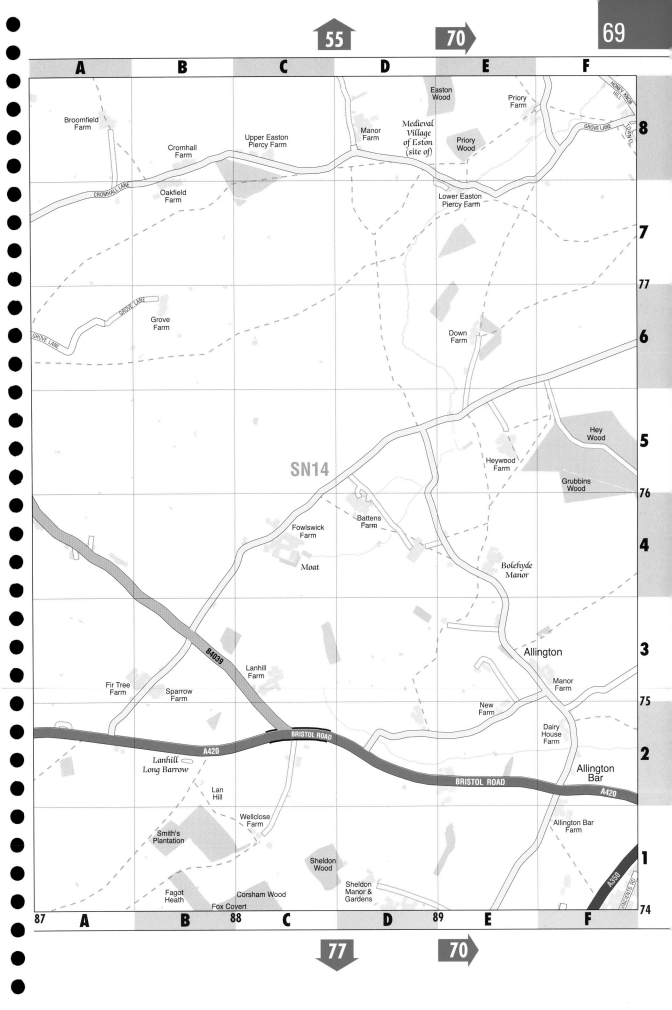

A B C D E F

8

Kington
St Michael

Tradewinds Farm

Hillside
Farm

Lypgate
Farm

Westbrook
Farm

Bowldown

Kington St Michaels
CE Prim Sch

PADDOCK END

Manor
Farm
Almshouses

PH

PO

7

NEWLANDS CL

WAYSIDE CL

DOVEY'S TERRACE

Kington
Langley
PH

SWINDON RD

Courtfield
Farm

77

Tor
Hill

Bright
Side

Church
Farm

Langley Fitzurse
CE Prim Sch

Limetree
Farm

PARKERS
LA

THE COMMON

CHURCH LANE

CHURCH ROAD

FAIRLEIGH
RISE

B4069

Tor Farm

6

The Moors

PH

PLOUGH LANE

PLOUGH LA

MOORS

Steinbrook
Farm

Lodge
Farm

P

Nature
Reserve

SWINDON ROAD

5

Hey
Wood

A350

JACKSOM'S LANE

76

White Wood

SN14

SN15

Marsh
Farm

Langley
House

Jackson's
Farm

4

Chippenham
Golf Club

Bird's
Marsh

Dog Kennel
Plantation

CH

A350

MALMESBURY RD

PH

WEST CEPEN WAY

3

Superstore

Barrow
Farm

BUTTERCUP CL 1
SORREL DR 2
BLUEBELL DR 3
PRIMROSE WY 4
HARES PATCH 5
PARTRIDGE CL 6
ROBINS CL 7
WOODPECKER MEWS 8
HARNISH WY 9

WEST CEPEN WAY

A350

COWSLIP

STAINERS WAY

HARDENHUISH
LA

Wiltshire Ambulance
Service NHS Trust HQ

CHIPPENHAM

B4158 MALMESBURY ROAD

St Pauls
Prim Sch

BIRDS MARSH
VW

75

SANDPIPER GDNS

BARNES

CHEVRAL
CL

RIDINGS

BELLINGER CT

Hill Corner Road

HEATHFIELD

HEATHFIELD

MADOX LA

PARSONAGE WAY

2

HARDENHUISH LANE

B4528

LANES HEAD

CHURCH
VW

BROOKWELL
CL

LONG RIDINGS

Hardenhuish
School

OAKLANDS
THE
OAKS

GREENWAY LA

GREENWAY
CT

GREENWAY LANE

BARROW

NORTH

HILL RI RISE

PEW HILL

Parsonage Way
Industrial Estate

HOLLYBUSH CL

A420

BRISTOL RD

STAINERS

BROOMFIELD

OAKLANDS

St Nicholas
School

DEANSWAY

ASHE CRESCENT

ELMWOOD
CT

CEDAR
LANGDOWN

PARSONAGE WAY

O DONNELL CL

COCKERILL LANE

1

MOUNT
PLEASANT

Bumpers Farm
Ind Est

HUNGERDOWN

BRISTOL ROAD A420

Sheldon
School

Hardenhuish
Park

B4158

MALMESBURY ROAD

PORTAL
CLOSE

GREENWAY GD

GREENWAY
AV

BIRCH GROVE

MURRAYFIELD

LANGLEY RD

B4069 MAUD HEATH'S CW

MAUD HEATH'S CAUSEWAY

LANGLEY
PARK

Works

Westpoint
Business
Park

ALLINGTON WAY

BYTHEBROOK

VINCIENTS RD

JASMINE CL

OLD HARDENHUISH
LA

Sports
Ground

HARDENHUISH AV

YEWSTOCK CR

EAST TINSTOCK CR

HUNGERFORD

WEDMORE
AV

ASHFIELD
RD

THE
HAMLET

GREENWAY LA

HAWTHORN RD

HAMLET CT

CLIFT
AV

TWICKENHAM WY

FOUNDRY CL

74

90 A 91 B C 92 D E F

A1
1 LONGSTONE RD
2 ALLINGTON WY
3 THE BATTENS
4 BARKEN RD
5 PIPSMORE RD

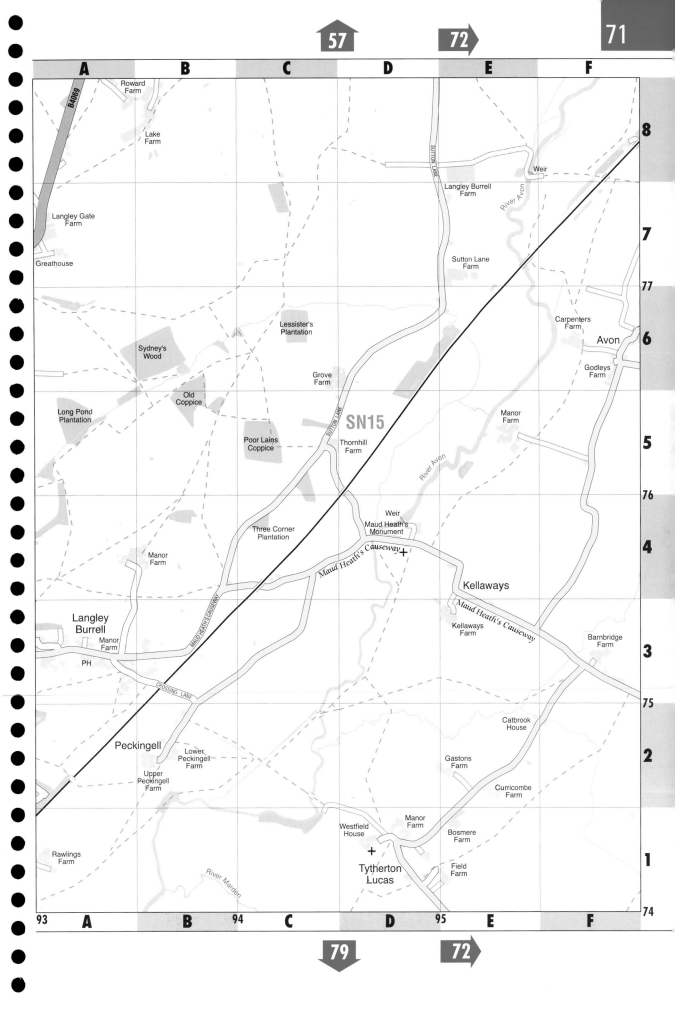

A   B   C   D   E   F

8

7

77

6

5

76

4

3

75

2

1

74

B4069

Roward Farm

Lake Farm

Langley Gate Farm

Greathouse

Langley Burrell Farm

Weir

SUTTON LANE

River Avon

Sutton Lane Farm

Lessister's Plantation

Carpenters Farm

Avon

Sydney's Wood

Grove Farm

Godleys Farm

Old Coppice

SUTTON LANE

SN15

Manor Farm

Long Pond Plantation

Poor Lains Coppice

Thornhill Farm

River Avon

Three Corner Plantation

Weir

Maud Heath's Monument

Manor Farm

Maud Heath's Causeway

Kellaways

MAUD HEATH'S CAUSEWAY

Maud Heath's Causeway

Langley Burrell

Manor Farm

Kellaways Farm

Barnbridge Farm

PH

CROSSING LANE

Catbrook House

Peckingell

Lower Peckingell Farm

Gastons Farm

Curricombe Farm

Upper Peckingell Farm

Westfield House

Manor Farm

Bosmere Farm

Rawlings Farm

River Marden

Tytherton Lucas

Field Farm

	A	B	C	D	E	F

8

Christian Farm

Brook Farm

Barn Farm

Heathercote

Park Farm

Foxham Farm

Elm Farm

Godsell Farm

7

West End Farm

West End

Summerleaze Farm

Gate Farm

PH

Foxham

PO

Lock Farm

SN15

Cadenham Park Farm

77

Cadenham Manor

6

Teal Farm

HARE STREET

Old Canal

5

Hare Street Farm

76

4

SN15

Wagon House Farm

Charlcutt Farm

Charlcutt

Tucks Farm

3

The Farm

Pinnigers Farm

Chestermans Farm

Bremhill /Grove Farm

Charlcutt Hill

75

Maud Heath Prim Sch

East Tytherton

Bremhill Grove Bridge

SN11

2

Wick Bridge

Bremhill Grove

Honeybed Wood

1

Wick Bridge Farm

Bremhill Wick

Field Farm

Hanger Park Farm

Wick Farm

Hill Top Farm

TURF HOUSE LANE

74

96	A	B	97	C	D	98	E	F

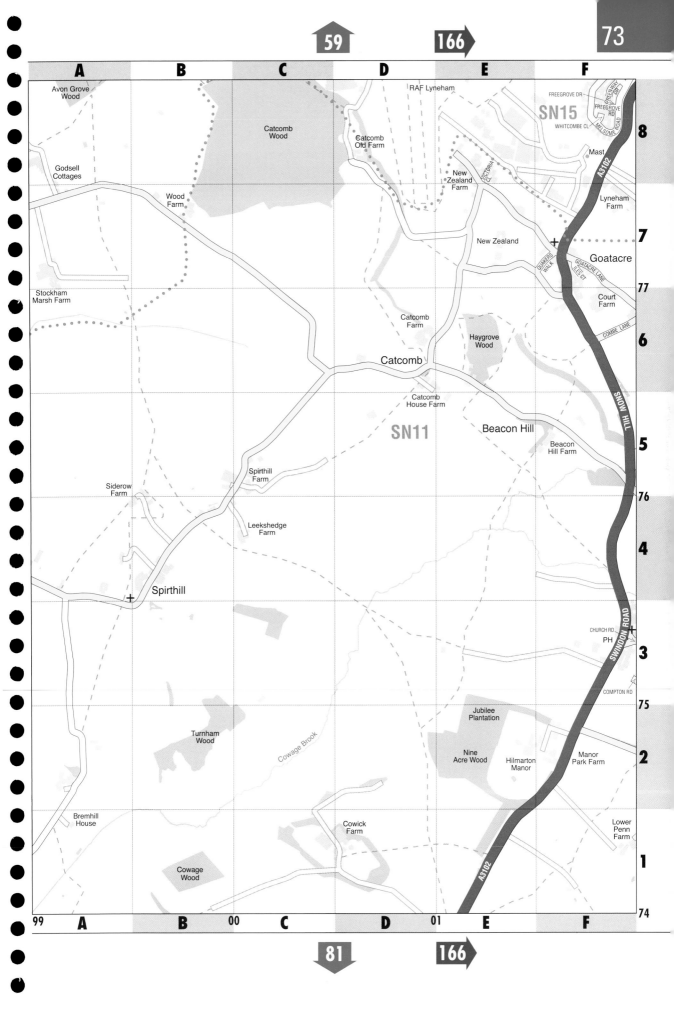

Gloucestershire STREET ATLAS

A420 Bristol

Marshfield

CHIPPENHAM RD

A420

DOWN ROAD

HAYFIELD
HAYFIELD
CHIPPENHAM ROAD
HAY STREET
MKT PL
DORMATON RD
BARN END
WITHYMEAD CL
FAIRFIELD CL
Marshfield VC CE Prim Sch

Garston Farm

Star Farm

STAR LA

Bond's Wood

WEIR
MARKET PLACE
CHURCH LA
WITHYMEAD RD

East End

Pitt Farm

Newleaze Wood

Woodlands Farm

8

Ringswell

Sewage Works

DONCOMBE HILL

Doncombe Scrubs

PINEWOOD WAY
PINEWOOD WAY
PINEWOOD WAY

Northwood Farm

7

Cloud Wood

73

Henleyhill Barn

Henley Hill

Marshfield Wood

WALNUT DR
FIR
LINDEN CL
HOLLY DR
CYPRESS WLK
LARCH RD
LAUREL DRIVE
ASPEN CL
OAK

6

Henleyhill Plantation

Raizes Wood

FOSS WAY

SN14

Raizes Plantation

5

The Raizes

Barracks

72

West Lodge

Ashwicke Grange

Ashwick Hall International Sch of Choueifat

4

Grange Plantation

Centre Plantation

Colerne Airfield

Motcombe Farm

Ashwicke Home Farm

ASHWICKE ROAD

East Lodge

3

Clift Wood

Diamond Wood

Colerne Rugby Football Club

BATH ROAD

71

Cherry Wood

Ranch House Farm

Longley Wood

Motcombe Wood

OAKFORD LANE

Bandywell Wood

Lictum Spring

2

Dicknick Wood

Rocky Wood

The Rocks

Hunters Hall

Breach Wood

BA1

Orchard Wood

Abbotscombe Wood

Ryder's Wood

Fewells Wood

Draught Wood

1

Moonshine Wood

Brokenboro Wood

ROAD HILL

Westwood Farm

West Wood

SN13

Oakford Farm

Rodney Wood

Three Shire Stones

70

78   **A**   **B**   **79**   **C**   **D**   **80**   **E**   **F**

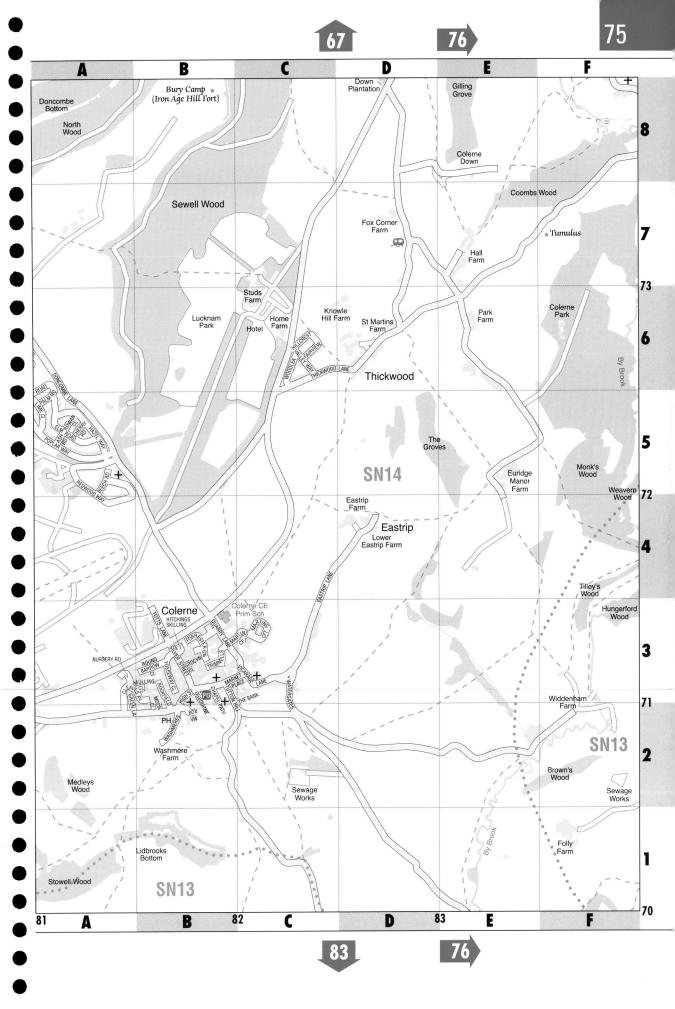

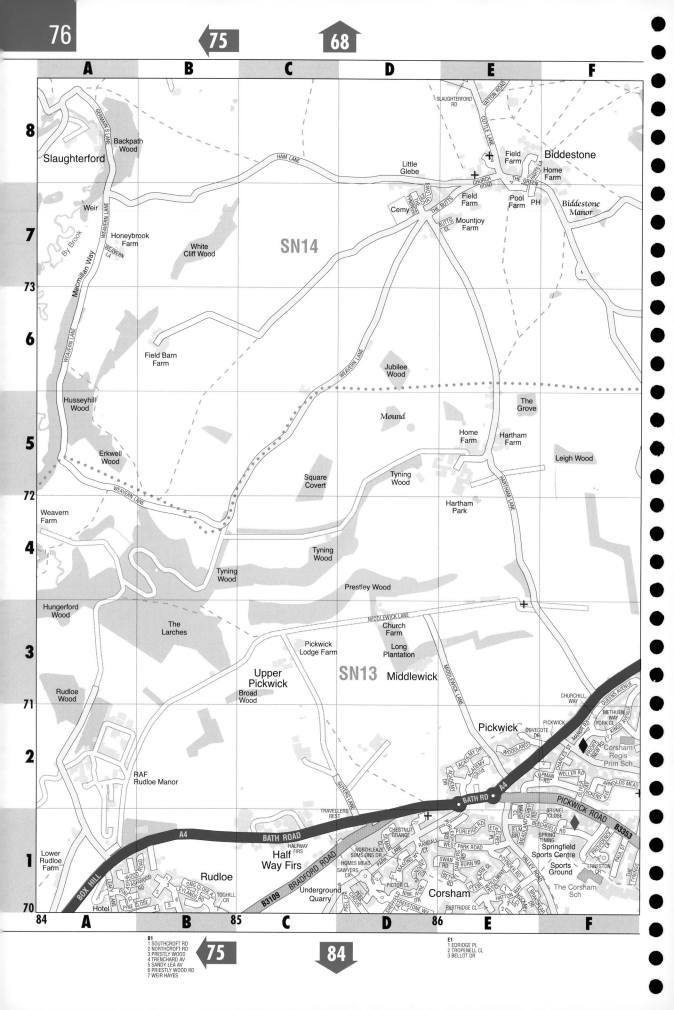

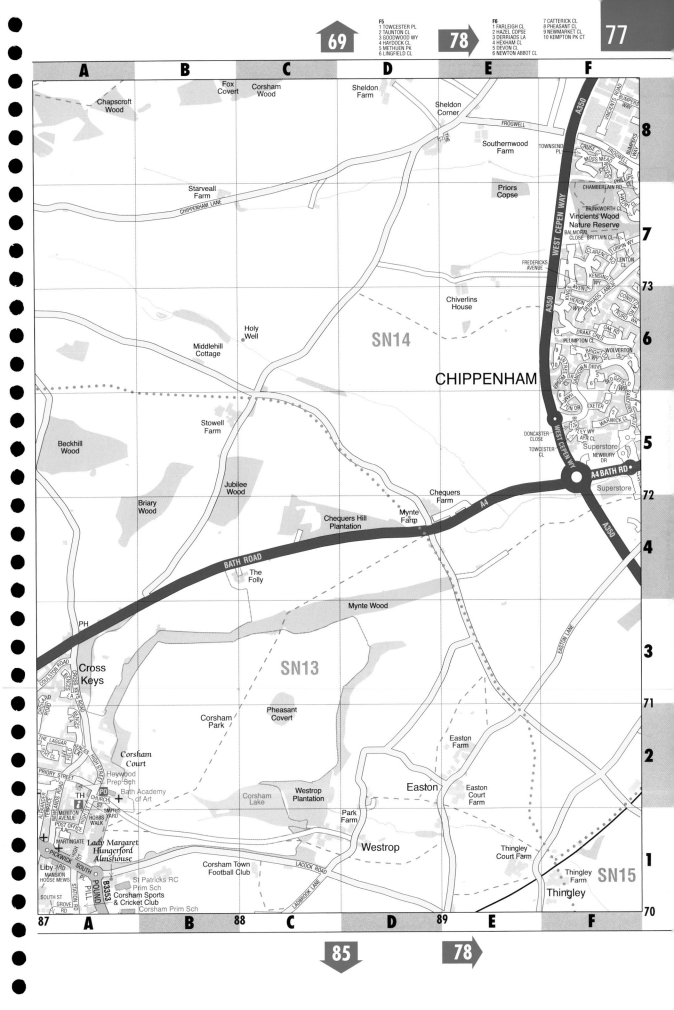

CHIPPENHAM

SN14

SN15

Major roads and places (selected labels):

BRISTOL ROAD A420, MARSHFIELD ROAD, PARK LANE, NEW ROAD, BATH ROAD A4, HUNGERDOWN LANE, SALTERSFORD LANE, WEST CEPEN WAY, PEWSHAM WY, A350, B4528, ROWDEN HILL, AVENUE LA FLECHE A4, IVY LA

Places: Frogwell Park, St Peters CE Prim Sch, Frogwell Prim Sch, Queens Crescent Sch, Redland Prim Sch, Hathaway Retail Park, Wiltshire College, Council Offices, Olympiad Leisure Centre, Monkton Park Prim Sch, Chippenham Mus & Heritage Cen, Monkton Park, Market Pl, Liby, Borough Parade, St Marys RC Prim Sch, St Francis Av, Chippenham Community, Rowden Hill, Sports Ground, Magistrates Court, Charter Prim Sch, Englands, Pheasant Business Park, Herman Miller Ind Est, Hunters Moon Farm, Taffswell Farm, Patterdown Farm, Milbourne Farm, Elm Tree Farm, Rowden Manor, Moat, Patterdown Rifle Range, Nursery, Showell Farm, Thingley Junction, Sewage Works, Lower Lodge Farm, Plucking Grove, The Barn, River Avon, Lackham Country Park, North Wood, Wiltshire College, Lackham Mus

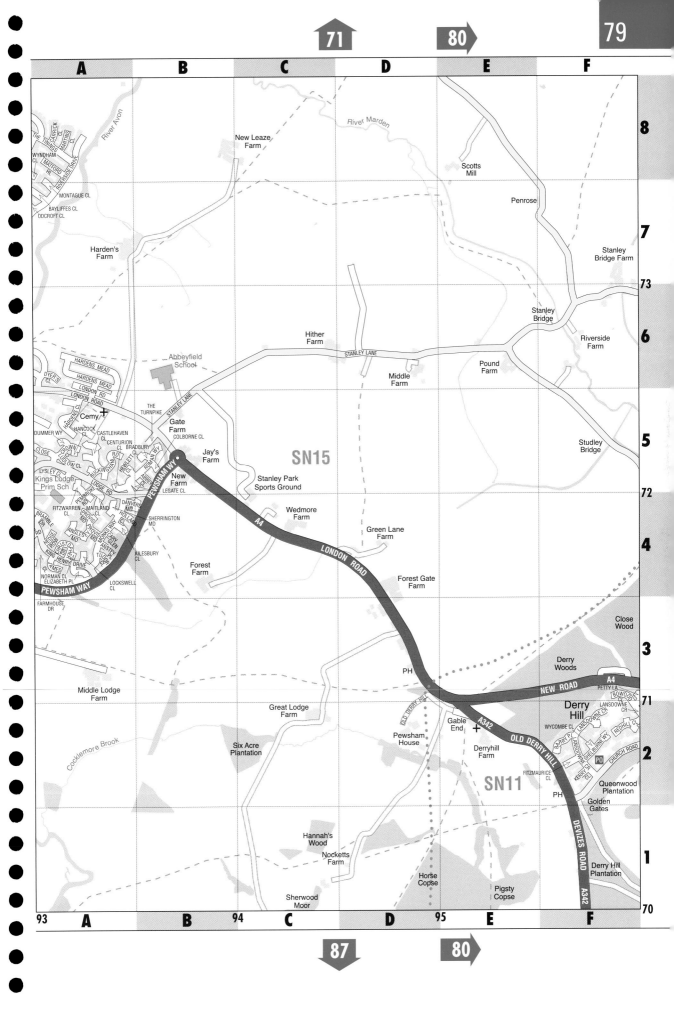

A   B   C   D   E   F

8

Old Canal

Maud Heath's Monument

Wick Hill

Monument Farm

Bremhill House

TURF HOUSE LANE

Low Bridge

Maud Heath's Stone

Bencroft Plantation

TURF HOUSE LANE

7

Bencroft Hill

Bencroft Farm

LODGWICKS

Tom-Len Grove

Glebe Farm

73

Stanley

Bencroft Hill Farm

TURF HOUSE LANE

Bremhill

SN11

Lower Whitley Farm

6

SN15

New Plantation

PH

Dumb Post Hill

Cowage Brook

River Marden

Hazeland Farm

5

Old Abbey Farm

Abbey (site of)

Hazeland Bridge

Ratford

Stanley Abbey Farm

Great Bodnage Copse

Ratford Bridge

Ratford Bridge Farm

72

Studley House Farm

Hazeland Wood

4

Top Farm

STUDLEY HILL

Crab Tree Copse

Swerves Farm

Sewage Works

A3102

HONEYSUCKLE

POPPY CL   HONEYSUCKLE

NEWBURY   CARPENTER CL

Close Wood

NORLEY LANE

Searchers Wood

Conigre Farm

WATERLILY WAY

FRESSIA   WINTER GR(N)

WOODSAGE   SAFRON (N3)

PENNY ROYAL GR

GREENACRES WAY

3

Studley

Sports Ground

PH

WALTER SUTTON CL

CHILVESTER HILL

A4

71

Lansdowne Hall

Derry Hill CE Prim Sch

A4   NEW ROAD

Rumsey Farm

Studley Brook Farm

Berhills Farm

PETTY LA

LANSDOWNE CR

CHURCH ROAD

OLD ROAD

Rumsey House

BLACK DOG HILL

2

Queenwood Plantation

SN11

Buck Hill

Bassett's Moor

1

Queenwood

Harrison's Coppice

Brick Kiln Wood

The Osprey

Adventure Playground

Waterfall

Bowood Lake

Dunn's Lane Wood

Moat

Deer Mead Pond

Pinhills Farm

70

96   A   B   97   C   D   98   E   F

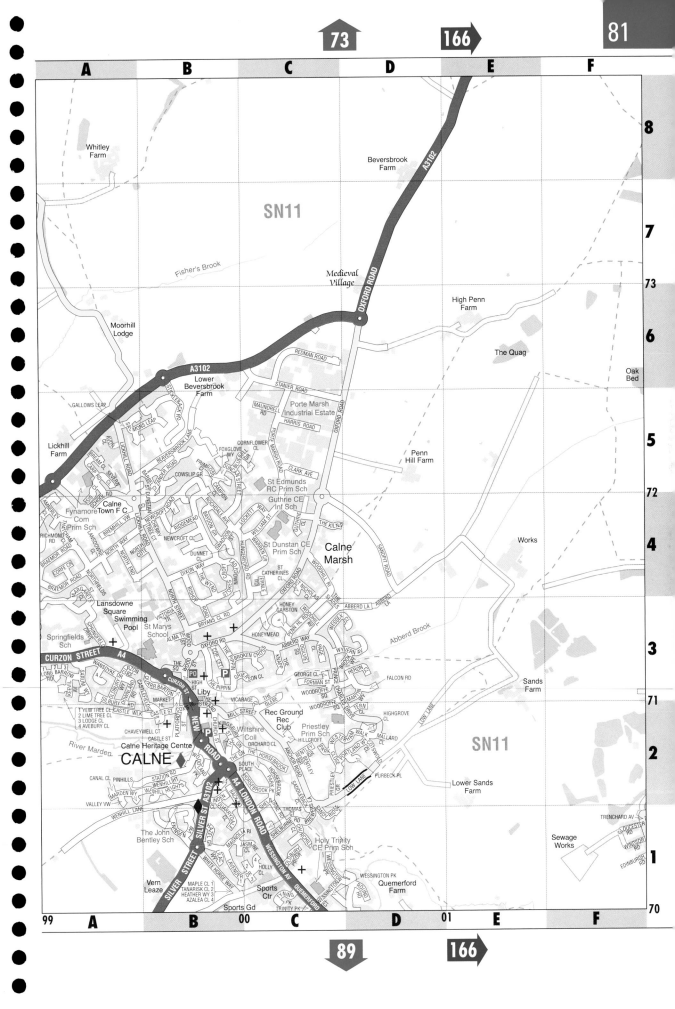

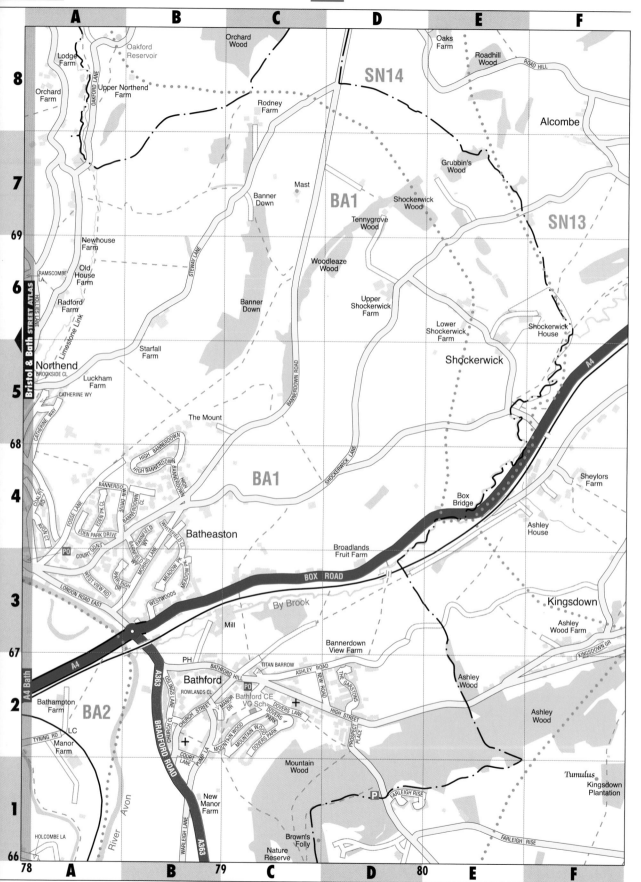

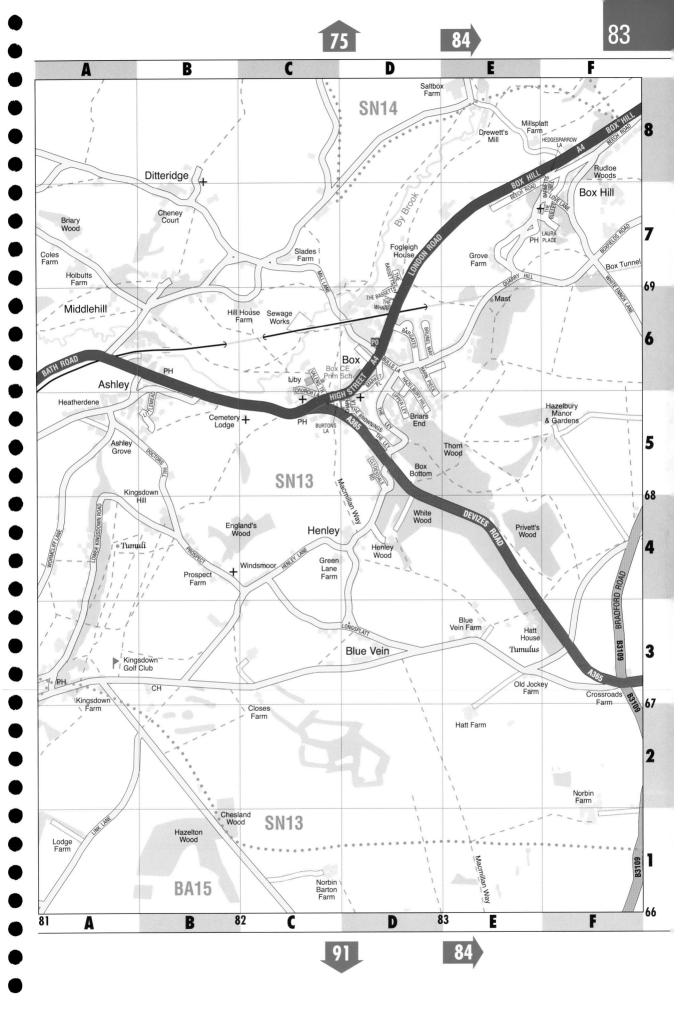

A   B   C   D   E   F

8

A4 BOX HILL
TRENCHARD AV
PARK AVENUE
TEDDER RD
PORTAL AVE
KIDSTON WY
HIGHLANDS CL
WESTWOOD RD
BROADWOOD AV
TOGHI CR
DOWDING AV
B3109
LEYLANDS RD
WATERS BANK RD
BANKWATERS ROAD
Box Highlands Primary School
ALLEN ROAD
PEEL CIR
BARBARA'S RD
HUDSWELL LANE
PARK LANE
SPRING LA
PADDOCK LA
SHEFFIELD LA
FREESTONE WAY
BELLOTT DRIVE
ASKER CT
BELLOTT DR
SYON CL
COTTLE CT
ANER CL
SPACKMAN CL
FULLER LN
VALLEY ROAD
LEIGH RD
HARDHAM CT
FURZEHILL
BRAKSPEAR DR
CRESWELLS
CHARLWOOD
SOUTHERN CL
RD
MATHILLS
HITHER
THE KNOWLE
POUND MEAD
WASTFIELD
TELGRO CT

Rudloe   Hudswell
Pockeredge Farm
POCKEREDGE DRIVE
POCKEREDGE ROAD
POTLEY LANE
Potley Farm

BOXFIELDS ROAD
Hawthorn
THE LINGS
SPRINGFIELD CL
CLIFT AV
BRADFORD ROAD
TROUT LANE
BASIL HILL ROAD
SPRING LANE
UPPER POTLEY
POTLEY LANE
LEAFIELD WY
EDINBURGH WY

7

PO
WESTWELLS ROAD
OLD SHAFT
SHEARWATER WY
CURL CROFT RD
Leafield

Box Tunnel
Ennox Wood
RAF Rudloe Manor
Westwells
WESTWELLS
GREENHILL
SHEPHERDS
Leafield Ind Est
LEAFIELD WY
LEAFIELD WAY
ELLEY GREEN
Great Lypiatt Farm
LYPIATT ROAD
New Grove Farm
Lypiatt Prim Sch

69

WHITE ENNOX LA
WEST ENNOX LANE
Corsham Media Park
MOOR PK
MOOR PK
DUKE'S PK
MOOR BARTON
NESTON CR
LEAFIELD ROAD
FLEETWOOD
POOL GREEN

6

B3109
BRADFORD ROAD
Round Wood
Sands Farm
Moor Green
Overmoor Farm
NETHERMORE
Neston
PH

5

Kingsmoor Wood
HMS Royal Arthur
SN13
JAGGARDS LANE
CHURCH RD
PITTS CFT
Neston Primary School
ROUGH STREET

68

Chapel Plaister
Wadswick Farm
Manor Farm
Wadswick
LOCKS CROSS
DAIRY LN
BROOKLEAZE
BAKERS CORNER
CHAPEL LANE
ATWORTH LANE

4

Gallop End
WADSWICK LANE

WADSWICK LANE

3

A365
Wormwood Farm
New Wood
Neston Park

67

Park Farm
Beech Plantation
Botleaze Wood

2

B3109
Cottles Wood
BATH ROAD
Denleys Farm
Parsonage Coppice
A365

1

Grove Mead Plantation
SN12
Atworth
GOODLINS
MEAD PK

66

Hobbs Bottom Farm
PO

84   A   85   B   C   D   86   E   F

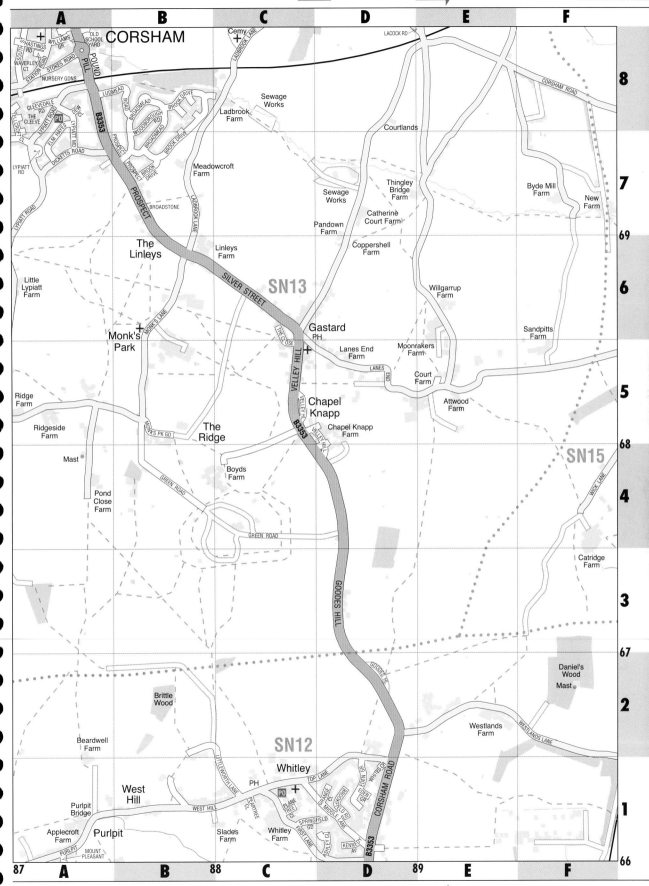

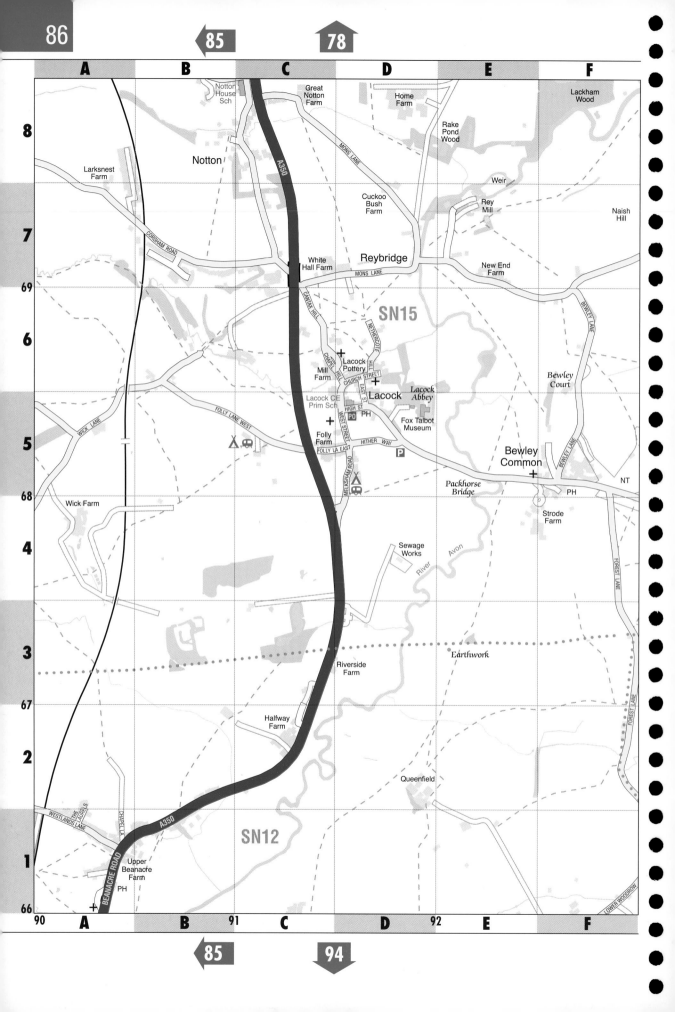

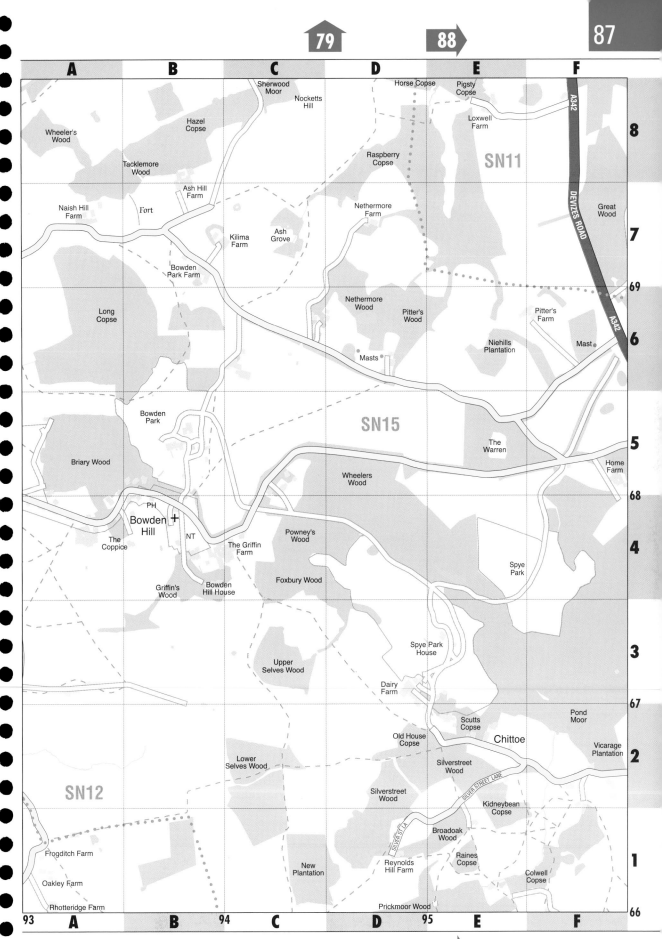

87
80

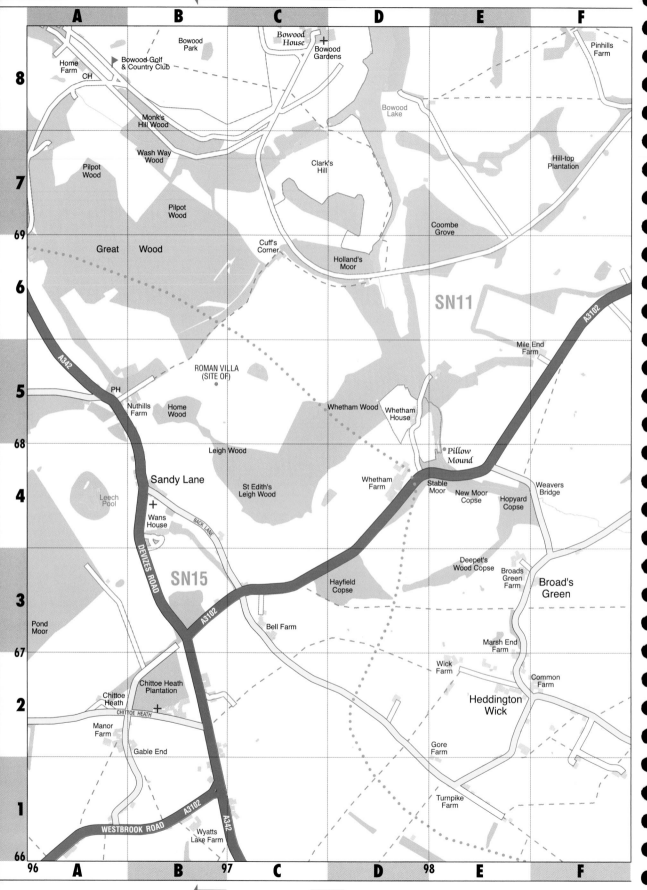

87
96

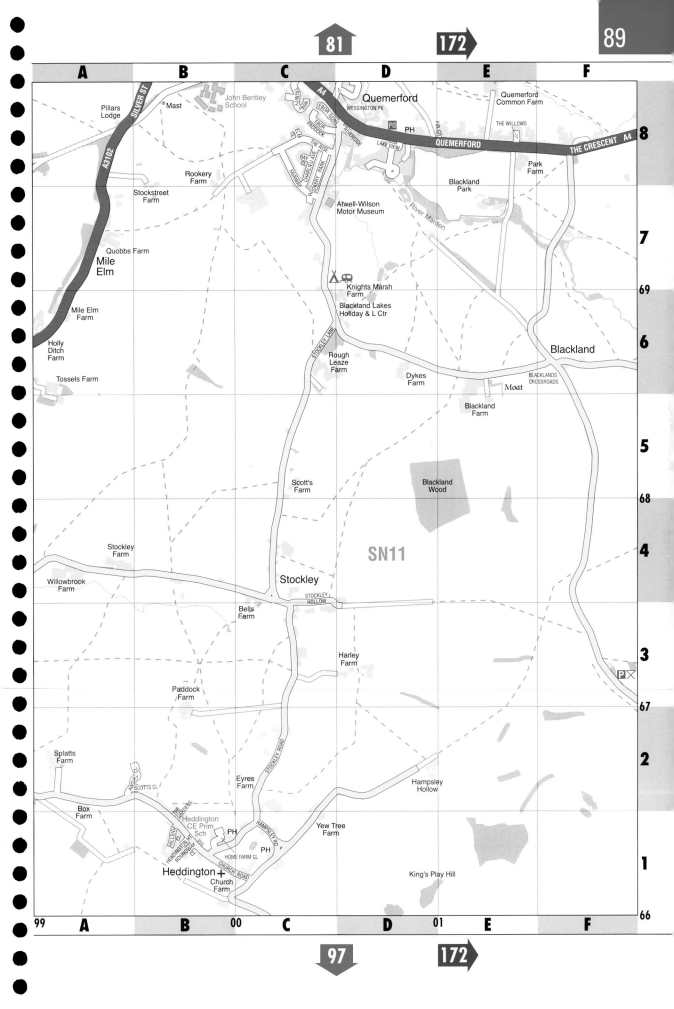

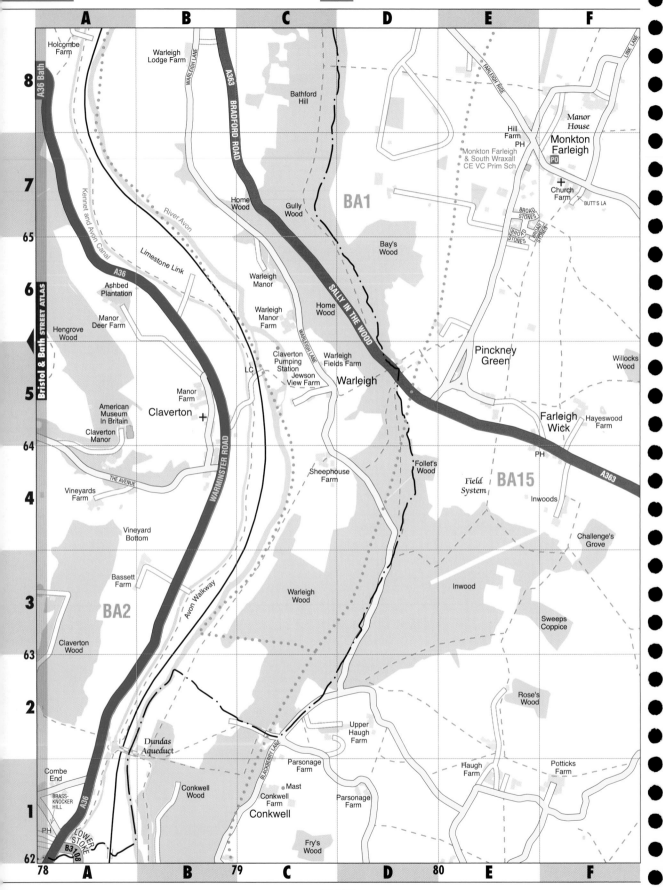

A36 Bath

Bristol & Bath STREET ATLAS

8

7

65

6

64

5

4

3

63

2

1

62

A B C D E F

78 79 80

Holcombe Farm

Warleigh Lodge Farm

Bathford Hill

Manor House

Hill Farm PH

Monkton Farleigh & South Wraxall CE VC Prim Sch

Monkton Farleigh

PO

LINK LANE

FARLEIGH RISE

Church Farm

BUTT'S LA

BROAD STONES

BROAD STONES

BROAD STONES

Kennet and Avon Canal

River Avon

A363

BRADFORD ROAD

Home Wood

Gully Wood

BA1

Bay's Wood

SALLY IN THE WOOD

Limestone Link

Ashbed Plantation

A36

Warleigh Manor

Warleigh Manor Farm

Home Wood

Warleigh Fields Farm

Pinckney Green

Willocks Wood

Hengrove Wood

Manor Deer Farm

Claverton Pumping Station

Jewson View Farm

Warleigh

LC

Manor Farm

American Museum In Britain

Claverton

Claverton Manor

Farleigh Wick

Hayeswood Farm

PH

A363

THE AVENUE

Vineyards Farm

Sheephouse Farm

Follet's Wood

Field System

BA15

Inwoods

Vineyard Bottom

Challenge's Grove

WARMINSTER ROAD

Bassett Farm

Avon Walkway

Warleigh Wood

Inwood

Sweeps Coppice

BA2

Claverton Wood

Rose's Wood

Dundas Aqueduct

Upper Haugh Farm

BLACKBERRY LANE

Parsonage Farm

Mast

Potticks Farm

Combe End

BRASS-KNOCKER HILL

Conkwell Wood

Conkwell Farm

Parsonage Farm

Haugh Farm

A36

PH

LOWER STOKE

B3108

Conkwell

Fry's Wood

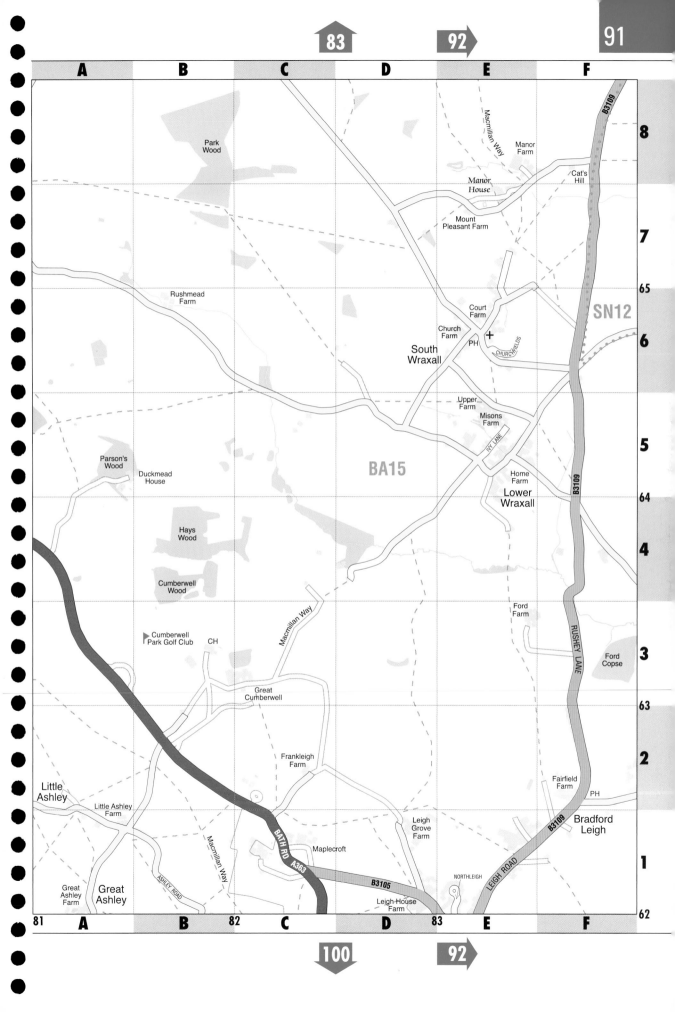

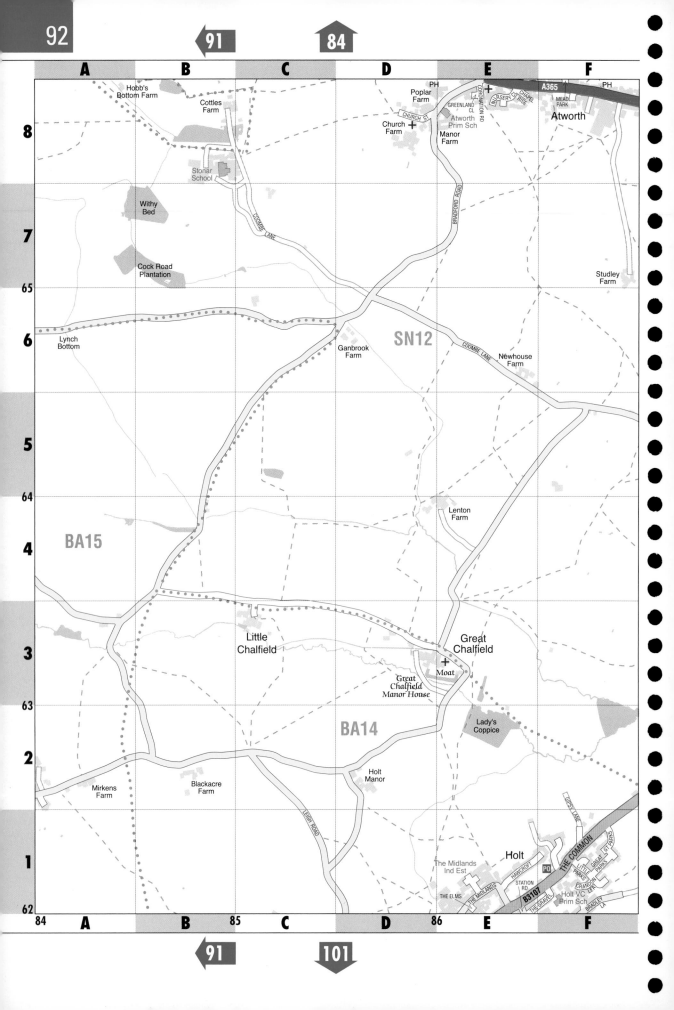

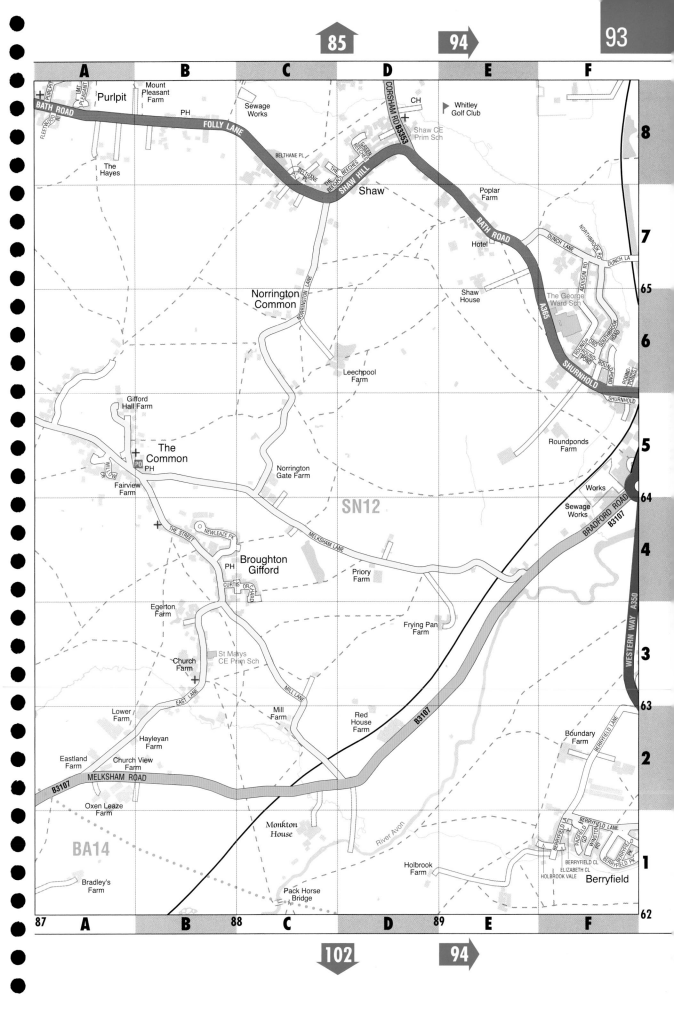

A B C D E F

8

7

65

6

5

64

4

63

2

1

62

Purlpit

BATH ROAD
FLEETWOOD RD
PURLPIT
MT PLEASANT

Mount Pleasant Farm

PH

FOLLY LANE

Sewage Works

The Hayes

BELTHANE PL

Belthane PL

THE BEECHES

GREEN BEECHES

SHAW HILL

Shaw

CORSHAM RD B3353

CH

Shaw CE Prim Sch

Whitley Golf Club

Poplar Farm

BATH ROAD

Hotel

DUNCH LANE

NORTHBROOK RD

ADDISON RD

DUNCH LA

Norrington Common

NORRINGTON LANE

Shaw House

A365

The George Ward Sch

SOUTHBROOK ROAD

ROUND POND

ROUND POND

SHURNHOLD

Leechpool Farm

ROUND PONDS

SHURNHOLD

Gifford Hall Farm

Roundponds Farm

The Common

WILL CM

PD

PH

Norrington Gate Farm

SN12

Works

Fairview Farm

Sewage Works

BRADFORD ROAD

B3107

THE STREET

NEWLEAZE PK

MELKSHAM LANE

Broughton Gifford

PH

Priory Farm

WESTERN WAY A350

CURTIS OR CHARD

Egerton Farm

Frying Pan Farm

Church Farm

St Marys CE Prim Sch

EAST LANE

MILL LANE

Lower Farm

Mill Farm

Red House Farm

B3107

Boundary Farm

BERRYFIELD LANE

Hayleyan Farm

Church View Farm

Eastland Farm

B3107

MELKSHAM ROAD

Oxen Leaze Farm

Monkton House

River Avon

Holbrook Farm

BERRYFIELD LA

BERRYFIELD LANE

PADFIELD GD

WINSTON RD

BERRYFIELD CL

ELIZABETH CL

HOLBROOK VALE

BERRYFIELD PK

Berryfield

BA14

Bradley's Farm

Pack Horse Bridge

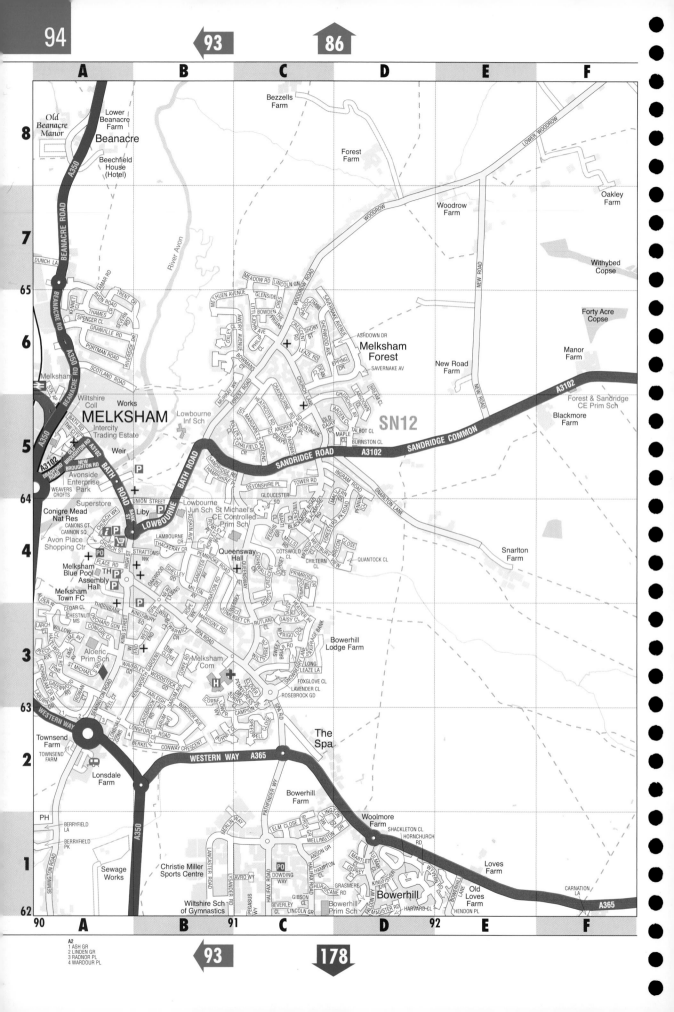

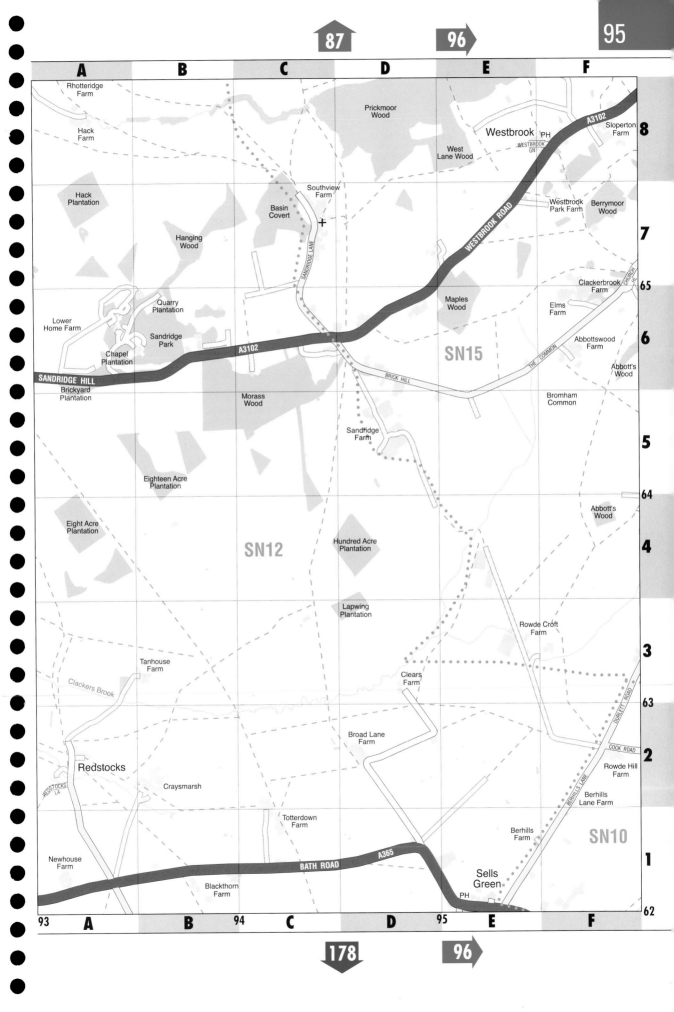

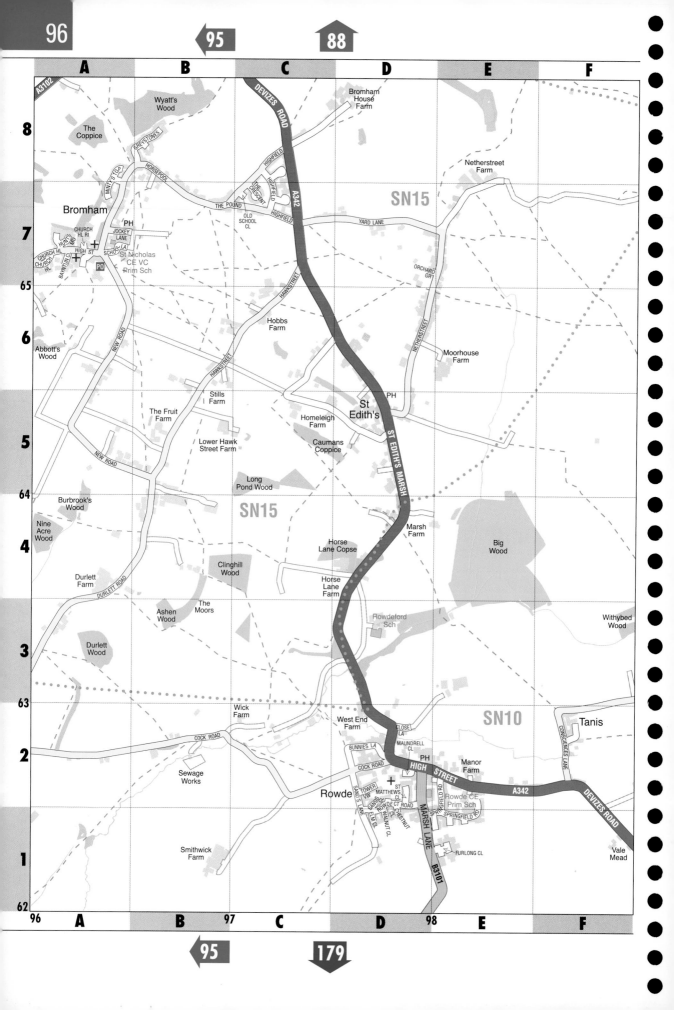

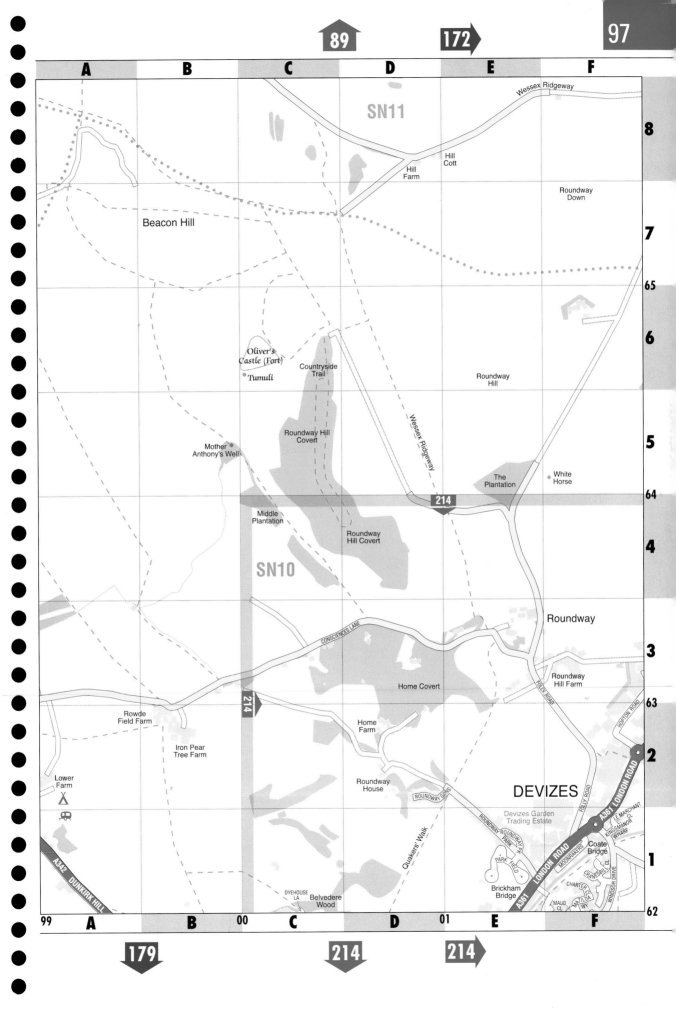

89 172

A B C D E F

SN11

Wessex Ridgeway

8

Hill Farm
Hill Cott

Roundway Down

7

Beacon Hill

65

6

Oliver's Castle (Fort)
• Tumuli

Countryside Trail

Roundway Hill

Wessex Ridgeway

Roundway Hill Covert

5

Mother Anthony's Well

The Plantation
• White Horse

64

Middle Plantation

214

Roundway Hill Covert

SN10

4

Roundway

Home Covert

3

CONSCIENCES LANE

Roundway Hill Farm

FOLLY ROAD

63

214

Rowde Field Farm

Home Farm

Iron Pear Tree Farm

2

Lower Farm

Roundway House

HOPTON ROAD

KINGSMANOR

A361 LONDON ROAD

ROUNDWAY GDNS

DEVIZES

Devizes Garden Trading Estate

LE MARCHANT CL
WHARF

ROUNDWAY PARK
ROUNDWAY PK

FOLLY ROAD

MOONRAKERS

Coate Bridge

1

A342 DUNKIRK HILL

Quakers' Walk

PARK FIELD

LONDON ROAD

CRANESBILL DRIVE

WINDSOR DRIVE

CHARTER CL
CL A

Brickham Bridge

DYEHOUSE LA
Belvedere Wood

A361

MAUD CL
MATILDA WY

62

99 A B 00 C D 01 E F

179 214 214

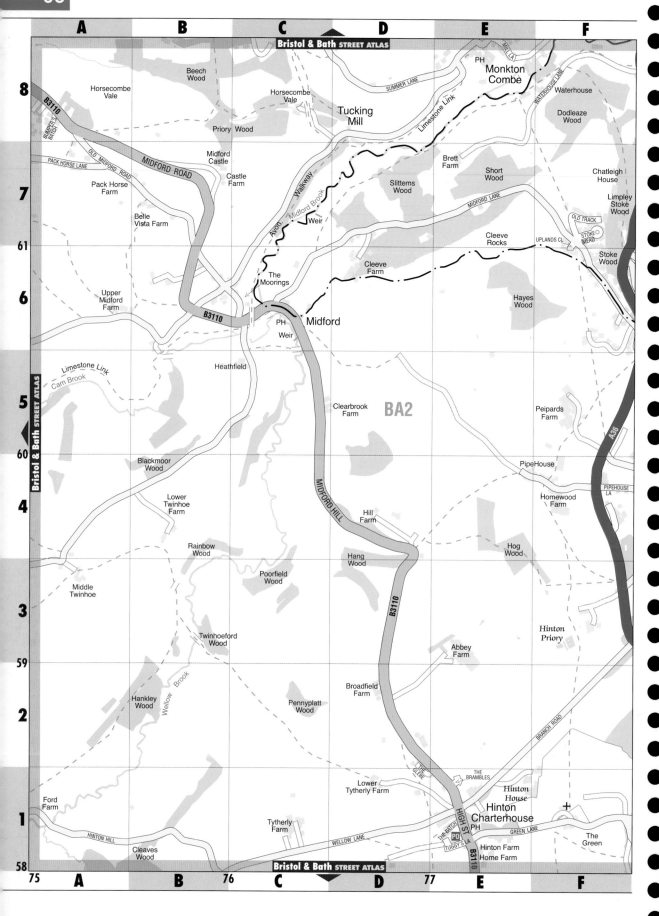

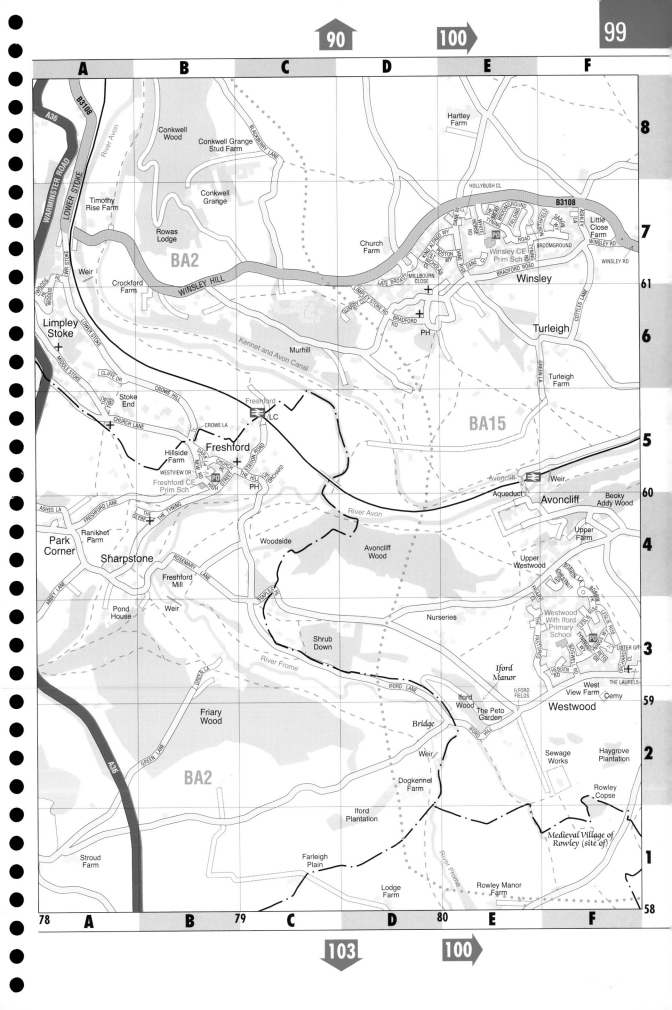

A B C D E F

8

7

61

6

5

60

4

3

59

2

1

58

81 A B 82 C D 83 E F

BATH ROAD
A363
Woolley Green
Woolley Barn Farm
B3105
NORTHLEIGH
Hotel
LEIGH RD
B3109
SLADESBROOK
Woolley Grange Farm
Lower Bearfield Farm
ASHLEY ROAD
Macmillan Way
PH
LEIGH PK RD
LEIGH PARK RD
Bradford-on-Avon Community
H
Christchurch CE Prim Sch
WOOLLEY STREET
THE OLD BATCH
THE ELMS
ASHLEY ROAD
Recreation Ground
BERRYFIELD RD
CHRISTCHURCH RD
CHRISTCHURCH
BANCROFT
BAINTON
GRANGE VW
WOOLLEY DRIVE
Wiltshire Music Centre
HUNTINGDON RISE
BEARFIELD BLDGS
CHURCH ACRE
WINSLEY RD
B3109 NEW ROAD
St Laurence Sch
BEAR CL
CHURCHES
ELMFIELD
HUNTINGDON
PRIORY CLOSE
MASON ST
IVY TERR
MOUNT PLEASANT
WHITEHILL
WOOLLEY STREET
HIGHFIELD
WOOLLEY ST
Woolley
MAGNON ROAD
BUDBURY
HUNTINGDON PL
PRIORY PARK
WHITEHEADS LA
IVY TERR
WOOLLEY TR
CHURCHES
PO
Huntingdon
THE WILDERNESS
KINGSFIELD
WOOLLEY ST
WESTFIELD
DOWNS VW
BUDBURY
NEWTOWN
SPRINGFIELD
KINGSFIELD GRANGE RD
B3108
WINSLEY ROAD
DOWNS
TYNING
BRIDGE
COPPICE HILL
SILVER STREET
B3107 HOLT ROAD
Cemy
MEADOWFIELD
BARTON ORCHARD
COAST RD
SANDY LEAZE
WINE STREET
BULL PIT
CHURCH ST
PO
KINGSTON RD
BRADFORD-ON-AVON
Cemy
RICKFIELD
GROVE RD
KNAPP
Swimming Pool
i
Liby & Mus
1 ST MARGARET'S HILL
2 ST MARGARET'S PL
3 ST MARGARET'S VILLAS
Belcombe Court
FROME RD
A363
LC
UPR REGENTS PK
BRIDGE ST
Weir
River Avon
P
Bradford-on-Avon
GREENLAND VW
CH
Bradford-on-Avon Golf Club
BELCOMBE ROAD
POUND LANE
Barton Farm
REGENTS PK
AVON
DOWNAVON
Barton Packhorse Bridge
Tithe Barn
FITZMAURICE PL
FROME RD
LAURENCE RD
KINGSTON AVE
MYTTERN MOW
Grip Wood
FROME RD
CULVERS
ST ALDHELM RD
SOUTHVILLE ROAD
WIDBROOK VIEW
Grip Wood Farm
Fitzmaurice Prim Sch
POULTON
CULVER CL
AVONFIELD AVE
TROWBRIDGE ROAD
Sewage Works
SOUTHLEIGH
KENNET GDNS
POULTON
LODDON WAY
BA15
JONES HILL
SPENCERS ORCHARD
POULTON LA
Becky Addy Wood
Barton Farm Country Park
ELMS CROSS DR
BAILEY'S BARN
POPLAR GROUND
WIDBROOK
B3109
60
Lye Green Farm
Mast
CATTERICK CL
SOUTHWAY RD
FOLLYFIELD
HOBBOUSE
DEVERELL CL
JOHN RENNIE CL
PH
Lye Green
TROWDEN LANE
BASSETTS PASTURE
BEDDOE CL
METHUEN CL
MOULTON DRIVE
Old Farm
HORTON CL
Rowden Farm
Widbrook
FROME ROAD
Vineyard
Hotel
A363
THE LAURELS
LINLEY CL
Hudds Farm
Westwood Manor House
WESTWOOD ROAD
BA14
Trowle Common
Manor Farm
Midway Manor
Oxstall Farm
Manor Court Farm
SHERBORNE PL
CYPRESS PL
LEAFIELD ROAD
B3109
Trowle Wood
SHORT ST
KINGSLEY PL

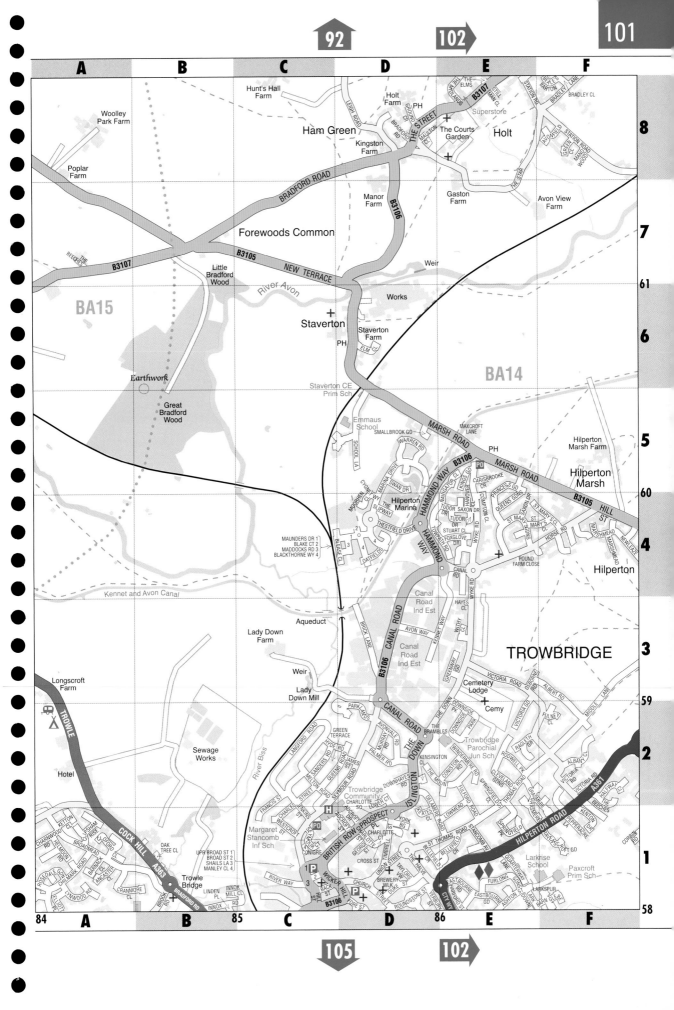

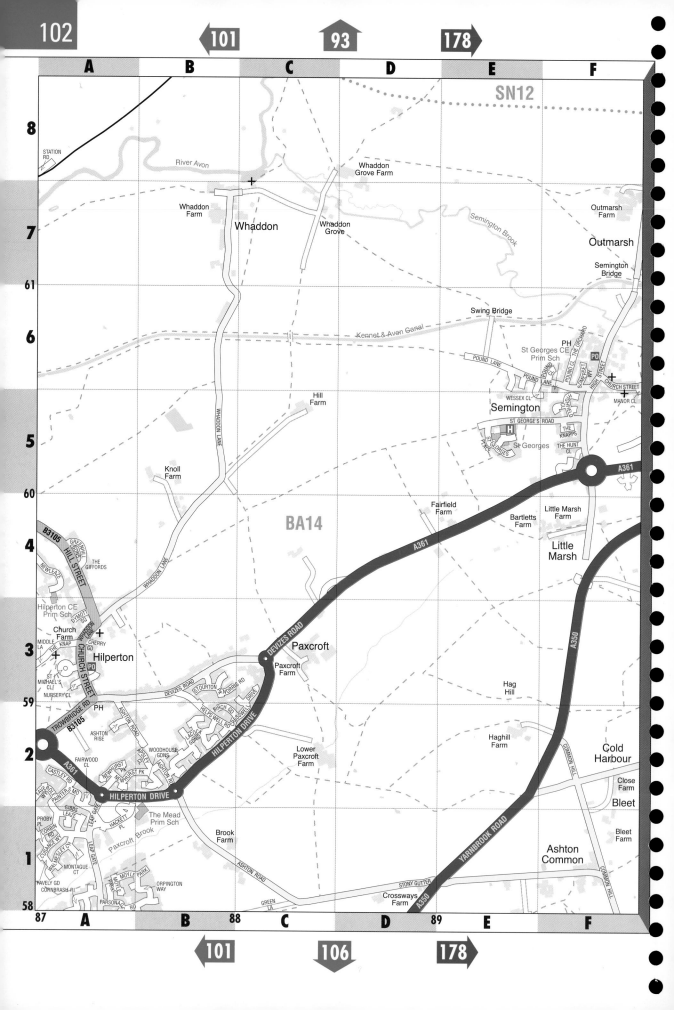

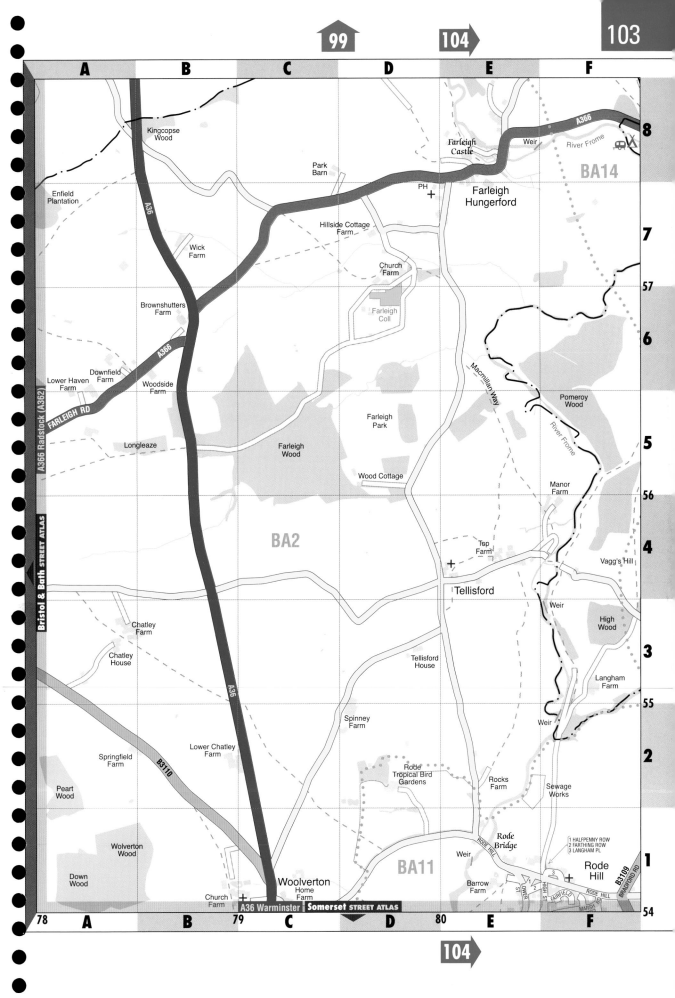

A B C D E F

8
7
57
6
5
56
4
3
55
2
1
54

Bristol & Bath STREET ATLAS

Kingcopse Wood

Enfield Plantation

A36

Wick Farm

Brownshutters Farm

A366

Downfield Farm

Lower Haven Farm

Woodside Farm

FARLEIGH RD

A366 Radstock (A362)

Longleaze

Chatley Farm

Chatley House

Springfield Farm

B3110

Peart Wood

Down Wood

Wolverton Wood

Lower Chatley Farm

A36

Church Farm

Woolverton Home Farm

Woolverton

A36 Warminster Somerset STREET ATLAS

Park Barn

Hillside Cottage Farm

PH

Church Farm

Farleigh Coll

Farleigh Park

Farleigh Wood

BA2

Wood Cottage

Farleigh Castle

Weir

River Frome

Farleigh Hungerford

BA14

Macmillan Way

River Frome

Pomeroy Wood

Manor Farm

Vagg's Hill

Top Farm

Tellisford

High Wood

Weir

Tellisford House

Langham Farm

Weir

Spinney Farm

Rode Tropical Bird Gardens

Rocks Farm

Sewage Works

Weir

Rode Hill

Rode Bridge

Barrow Farm

BA11

1 HALFPENNY ROW
2 FARTHING ROW
3 LANGHAM PL

Rode Hill

LOWER ST

HIGH ST

FAIRFIELD

RODE HILL

MARSH

B3109 BRADFORD RD

78   79   80

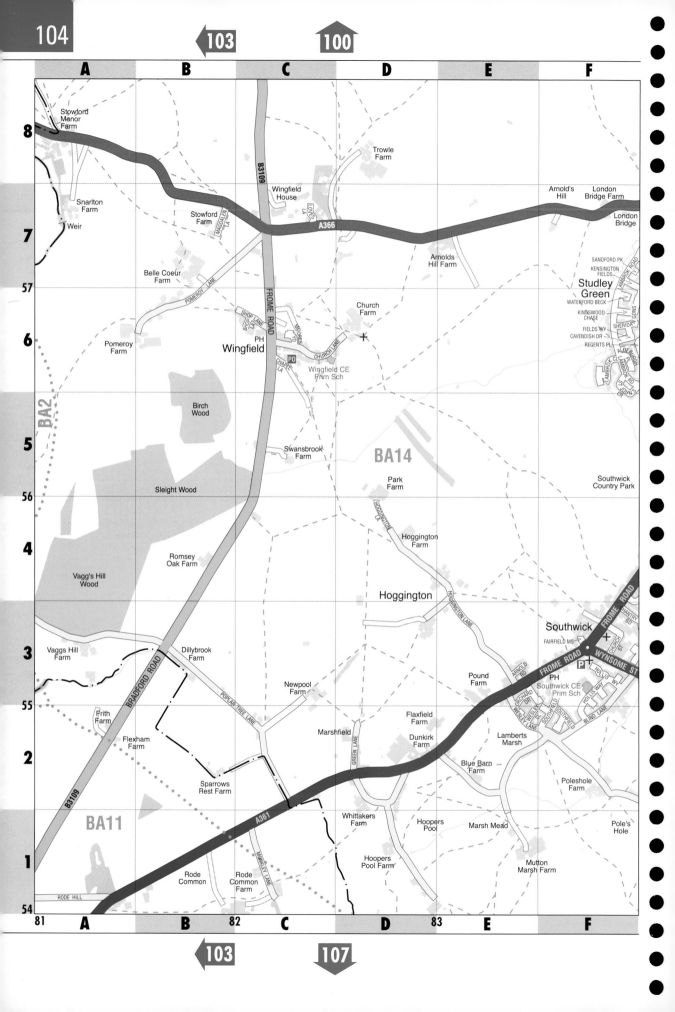

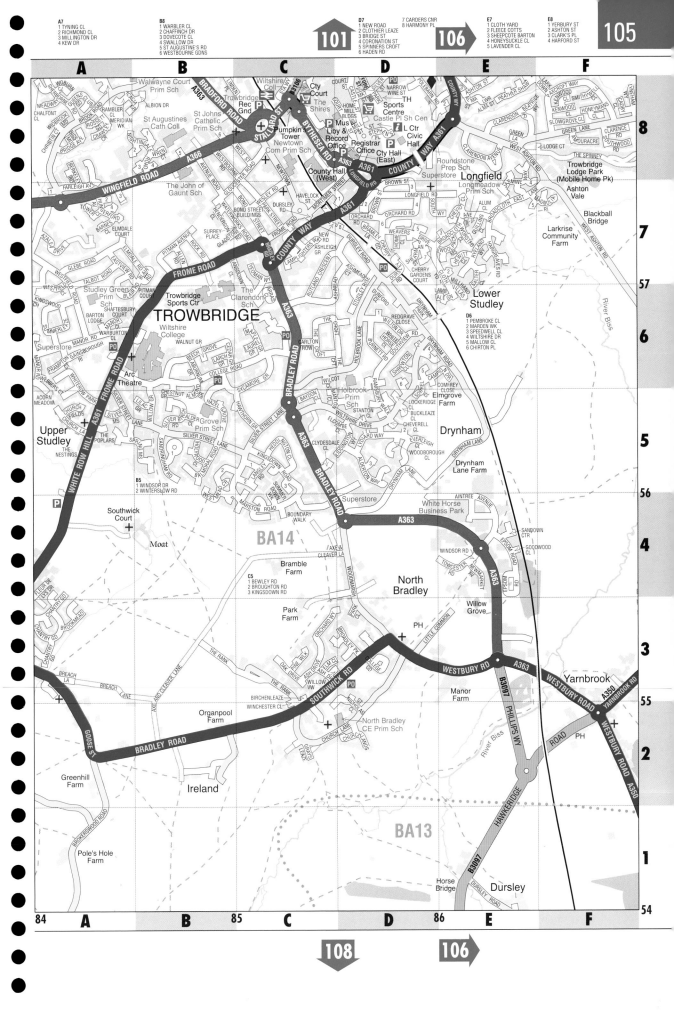

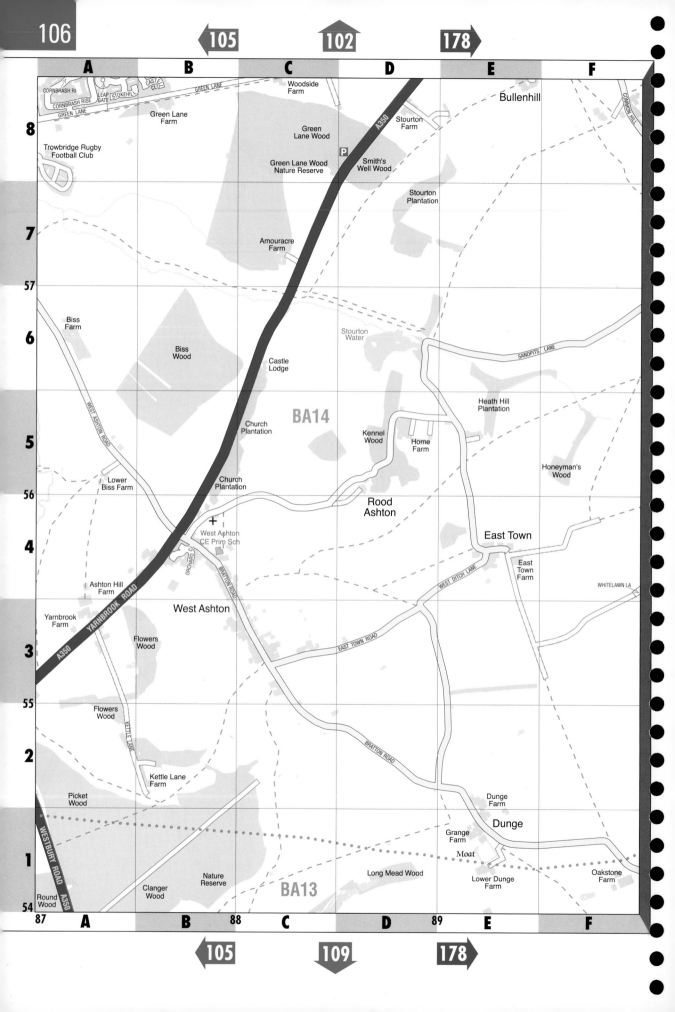

A · B · C · D · E · F

8

Cornbrash Ri
Cornbrash Rise
Green Lane
Leap Gate · Stokehill
Castle Cl
Green Lane
Green Lane Farm
Woodside Farm
Green Lane Wood
A350
Stourton Farm
Bullenhill
Common Hill

Trowbridge Rugby Football Club
Green Lane Wood Nature Reserve
P
Smith's Well Wood
Stourton Plantation

7

Amouracre Farm
Stourton Plantation

57

Biss Farm

6

Biss Wood
Castle Lodge
Stourton Water
Sandpits Lane
Heath Hill Plantation

BA14

West Ashton Road

5

Church Plantation
Kennel Wood
Home Farm
Honeyman's Wood

56

Lower Biss Farm
Church Plantation
Rood Ashton
East Town

4

West Ashton CE Prim Sch
Orchard Cl
Bratton Road
West Ditch Lane
East Town Farm
Whitelawn La

Ashton Hill Farm
Yarnbrook Road
West Ashton

3

Yarnbrook Farm
A350
Flowers Wood
East Town Road
Bratton Road

55

Flowers Wood
Kettle Lane

2

Kettle Lane Farm
Bratton Road
Dunge Farm

Picket Wood
Dunge
Grange Farm
Moat

1

Westbury Road
Nature Reserve
Long Mead Wood
Lower Dunge Farm
Oakstone Farm

54

Round Wood
A350
Clanger Wood
BA13

87 · A · B · 88 · C · D · 89 · E · F

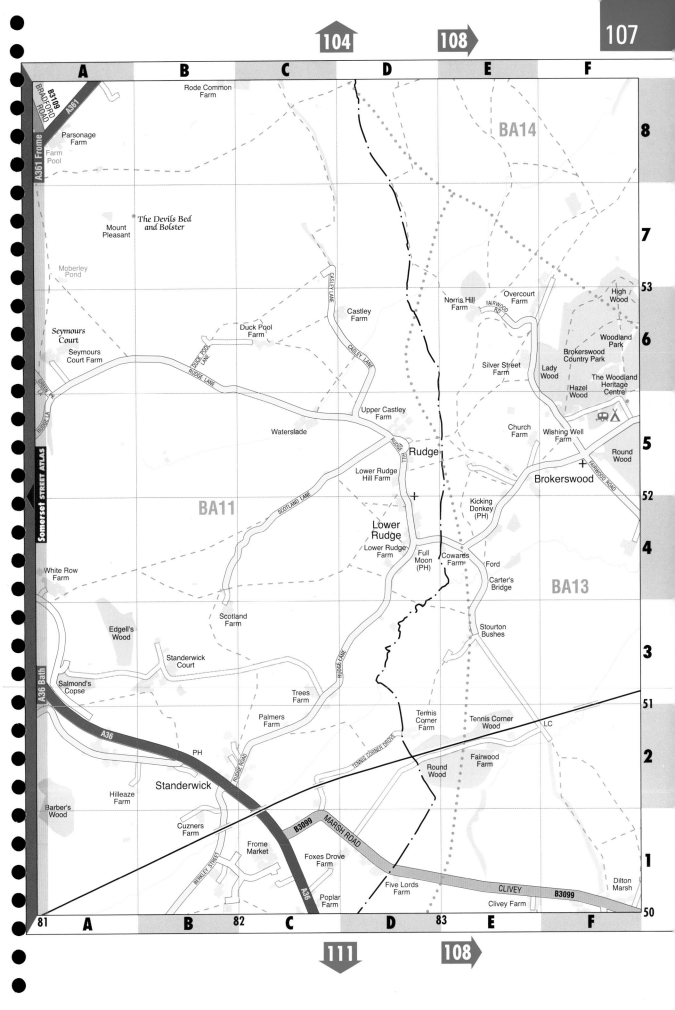

A   B   C   D   E   F

Somerset STREET ATLAS

B3109 BRADFORD ROAD
A361
A361 Frome

GREEN LA
RUDGE LA

A36 Bath

Rode Common Farm

Parsonage Farm
Farm Pool

The Devils Bed and Bolster

Mount Pleasant

Moberley Pond

Seymours Court
Seymours Court Farm

RUDGE LANE
DUCK POOL LANE

Duck Pool Farm

CASLEY LANE

Castley Farm

CASLEY LANE

Castley Farm

BA14

Norris Hill Farm

FAIRWOOD RD

Overcourt Farm

High Wood

Woodland Park

Brokerswood Country Park

The Woodland Heritage Centre

Silver Street Farm

Lady Wood

Hazel Wood

Upper Castley Farm

RUDGE HILL

Waterslade

Rudge

Church Farm

Wishing Well Farm

Round Wood

SCOTLAND LANE

Lower Rudge Hill Farm

BA11

Kicking Donkey (PH)

Brokerswood

FAIRWOOD ROAD

Lower Rudge

Lower Rudge Farm

Full Moon (PH)

Cowards Farm

Ford

Carter's Bridge

BA13

White Row Farm

Scotland Farm

RUDGE LANE

Stourton Bushes

Edgell's Wood

Standerwick Court

Salmond's Copse

A36

Trees Farm

Palmers Farm

Tennis Corner Farm

Tennis Corner Wood

LC

PH

RUDGE ROAD

TENNIS CORNER DROVE

Round Wood

Fairwood Farm

Standerwick

Hilleaze Farm

Barber's Wood

Cuzners Farm

BERKLEY STREET

B3099

MARSH ROAD

Frome Market

Foxes Drove Farm

A36

Poplar Farm

Five Lords Farm

CLIVEY

B3099

Dilton Marsh

Clivey Farm

81   82   83

A   B   C   D   E   F

8
7
53
6
5
52
4
3
51
2
1
50

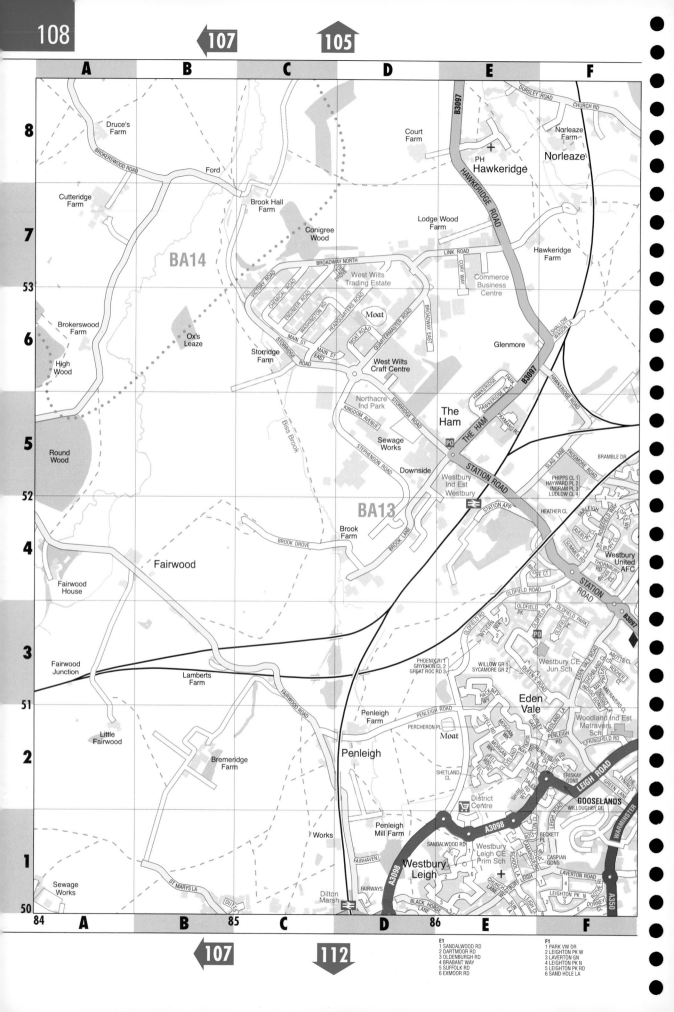

A B C D E F

8

7

53

6

5

52

4

3

51

2

1

50

84 A B 85 C D 86 E F

BA14

Druce's Farm

Cutteridge Farm

Brokerswood Farm

High Wood

Round Wood

Fairwood

Fairwood House

Fairwood Junction

Little Fairwood

Sewage Works

BROKERSWOOD ROAD

Ford

Brook Hall Farm

Conigree Wood

Ox's Leaze

Storridge Farm

Storridge Road

Biss Brook

BROOK DROVE

Lamberts Farm

FAIRWOOD ROAD

Bremeridge Farm

ST MARYS LA

Court Farm

PH
Hawkeridge

HAWKERIDGE ROAD

B3097

DURSLEY ROAD

CHURCH RD

Norleaze Farm

Norleaze

Lodge Wood Farm

LINK ROAD

Hawkeridge Farm

BROADWAY NORTH

West Wilts Trading Estate

Moat

CORY WAY

Commerce Business Centre

SHALLOW WAGON LA

VICTORY ROAD

CHEMICAL ROAD

ENGINEER ROAD

WASHINGTON RD

HEADQUARTERS ROAD

MOAT ROAD

QUARTERMASTER ROAD

BROADWAY EAST

Glenmore

HAWKERIDGE PK

B3097

HAWKERIDGE ROAD

MAIN ST

MAIN ST EAST

Storridge Farm

West Wilts Craft Centre

Northacre Ind Park

KINGDOM AVENUE

STORRIDGE ROAD

The Ham

THE HAM

PAXMANS RD

PO

Sewage Works

STEPHENSON ROAD

Downside

Westbury Ind Est
Westbury

STATION ROAD

SLAG LANE

FROGMORE ROAD

BRAMBLE DR

PHIPPS CL 1
HAYWARD PL 2
INGRAM PL 3
LUDLOW CL 4

HEATHER CL

EARLEIGH

ROSEFIELD WAY

AVERY RD

SILBURY RD

SUMMER RD

STATION APP

BA13

Brook Farm

Brook Drove

BROOK LANE

Westbury United AFC

THORNBURY RD

BRIAR CL

BRIDGE CT

OLDFIELD ROAD

STATION ROAD

B3097

OLDFIELD PK

OLDFIELD PARK

OLDFIELD PK

WYVERN

PO

AROTTS CL

Westbury CE Jun Sch

EDEN VALE ROAD

SCOTLAND RD

ROCHER CL

MATRAVERS CL

PHOENIX RI 1
GRYBHON CL 2
GREAT ROC RD 3

WILLOW GR 1
SYCAMORE GR 2

QUEEN'S ROAD

HACKNEY WY

Eden Vale

Woodland Ind Est Matravers Sch

SPRINGFIELD RD

PENLEIGH ROAD

Penleigh Farm

PERCHERON PL

Moat

SHETLAND CL

SHIRE GATE

MORGAN CL

PENLEIGH RD

REDLAND LA

HUNTERS GATE

ERISKAY GDNS

LEIGH ROAD

GREEN LANE

THE TYNINGS

Penleigh

District Centre

Works

Penleigh Mill Farm

SANDALWOOD RD

FAIRHAVEN

FAIRWAYS

DILTON MARSH

Dilton Marsh

Westbury Leigh

GOOSELANDS

WILLOUGHBY CL

A3098

BECKETT PL

CASPIAN GDNS

Westbury Leigh CE Prim Sch

BLACK HOUSE LANE

WESTBURY LEIGH

LAVERTON ROAD

WARMINSTER

A350

A3098

E1
1 SANDALWOOD RD
2 DARTMOOR RD
3 OLDENBURGH RD
4 BRABANT WAY
5 SUFFOLK RD
6 EXMOOR RD

F1
1 PARK VW DR
2 LEIGHTON PK W
3 LAVERTON GN
4 LEIGHTON PK N
5 LEIGHTON PK RD
6 SAND HOLE LA

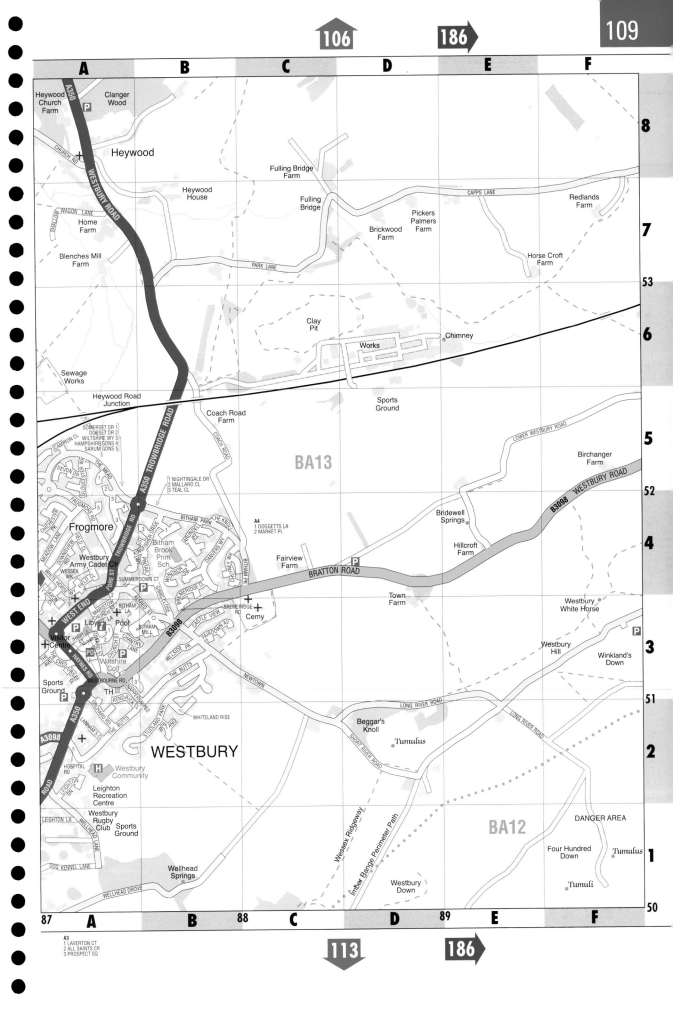

A350
Heywood Church Farm
Clanger Wood
Heywood
Heywood House
CHURCH RD
WESTBURY ROAD
Fulling Bridge Farm
Fulling Bridge
CAPPS LANE
Redlands Farm
SHALLOW WAGON LANE
Home Farm
Pickers Palmers Farm
Brickwood Farm
Horse Croft Farm
Blenches Mill Farm
PARK LANE
Clay Pit
Chimney
Works
Sewage Works
Heywood Road Junction
A350 TROWBRIDGE ROAD
Coach Road Farm
COACH ROAD
Sports Ground
BA13
SOMERSET DR 1
DORSET DR 2
WILTSHIRE WY 3
HAMPSHIRE GDNS 4
SARUM GDNS 5
CAMPION CL
THE MEAD
DEVON DR
1 NIGHTINGALE DR
2 MALLARD CL
3 TEAL CL
FROGMORE RD
FIELD CL
A4
1 DOGGETTS LA
2 MARKET PL
BITHAM PARK
HE KNOLL
CHICHESTER PK
MEADOW LANE
DOWNSVIEW RD
Frogmore
KINGFISHER DRIVE
ARUNDELL PL
DANVERS WY
LOWER WESTBURY ROAD
Birchanger Farm
B3098 WESTBURY ROAD
Bridewell Springs
Hillcroft Farm
Fairview Farm
Bitham Brook Prim Sch
WINDSOR DR
CHENEY WY
BITHAM PK
WESSEX WK
WHITE HORSE WY
FORE ST
SUMMERDOWN CT
BREMERIDGE CT
BRATTON ROAD
Town Farm
Westbury White Horse
Westbury Army Cadet Ctr
MARISTON
ALFRED ST
GIBBS CLOSE
CASTLE VIEW
BREMERIDGE RD
Cemy
WEST END
CHURCH LA
BITHAM LA
Liby
Pool
BITHAM MILL
FAIRDOWN AV
Westbury Hill
Visitor Centre
THE
HIGH ST
CHURCH ST
B3098
HILLSIDE PK
THE BUTTS
NEWTOWN
Winkland's Down
HAYNES RD
PO
CHANTRY LANE
EDWARD ST
Wiltshire Coll
WESTBOURNE RD
TH
KENDRICK CL
THE BUTTS
WHITELAND RISE
LONG RIVER ROAD
Sports Ground
A3098
ORCHARD RD
LANHAM'S CL
STUDLAND PARK
UPLAND
Beggar's Knoll
Tumulus
LONG RIVER ROAD
WESTBURY
HOSPITAL RD
H Westbury Community
Leighton Recreation Centre
SHORT RIVER ROAD
BA12
DANGER AREA
LEIGHTON GN
Westbury Rugby Club
Sports Ground
Wessex Ridgeway
Imber Range Perimeter Path
Four Hundred Down
Tumulus
LEIGHTON LA
WELLHEAD LANE
DOG KENNEL LANE
Wellhead Springs
Tumuli
WELLHEAD DROVE
Westbury Down

8
7
53
6
5
52
4
3
51
2
1
50

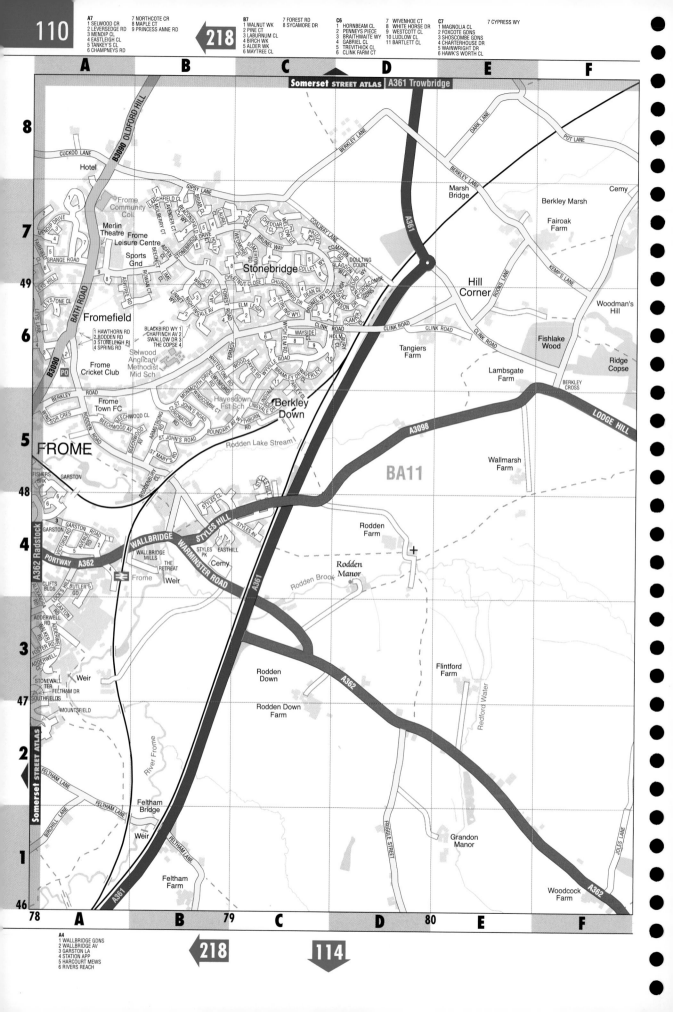

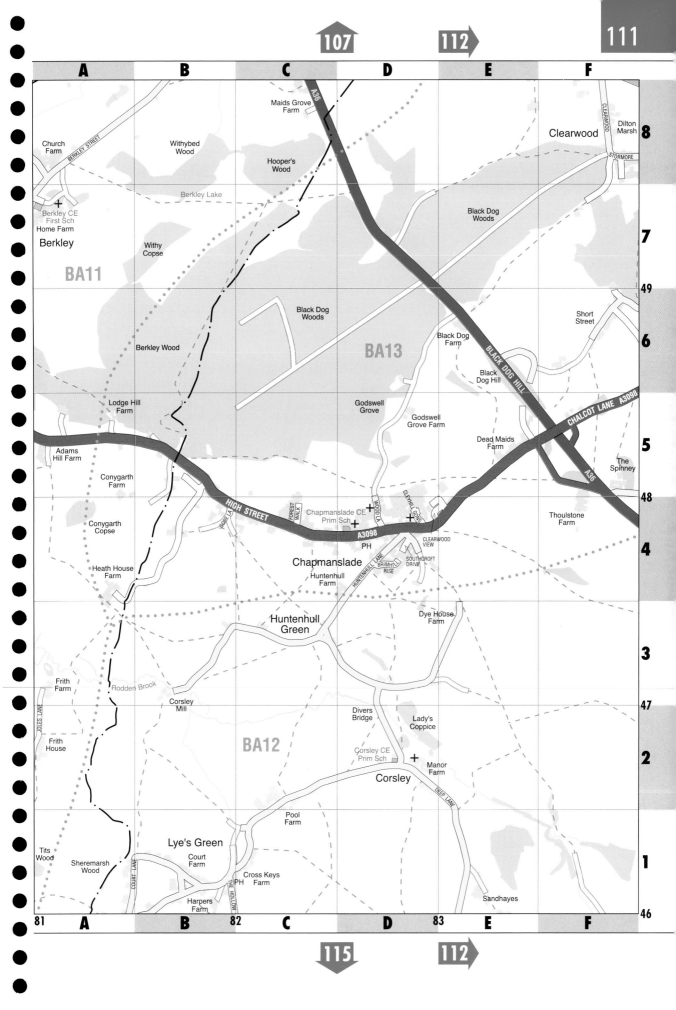

A   B   C   D   E   F

Maids Grove Farm

A36

Withybed Wood

Hooper's Wood

Church Farm

BERKLEY STREET

Berkley Lake

Black Dog Woods

8

Clearwood

CLEARWOOD

Dilton Marsh

STORMORE

Berkley CE First Sch
Home Farm

Berkley

7

BA11

Withy Copse

Black Dog Woods

49

Berkley Wood

Black Dog Woods

BA13

Black Dog Farm

Short Street

6

Lodge Hill Farm

Godswell Grove

Godswell Grove Farm

Black Dog Hill

BLACK DOG HILL

CHALCOT LANE

A3098

Adams Hill Farm

Dead Maids Farm

A36

5

Conygarth Farm

HIGH STREET

FOREST WALK

Chapmanslade CE Prim Sch

WOOD LA

CLEYHILL GDNS

The Spinney

48

Conygarth Copse

A3098

PH

CLEARWOOD VIEW

Thoulstone Farm

4

Heath House Farm

Chapmanslade

Huntenhull Farm

HUNTENHULL LANE

BRIMHILL RISE

SOUTHCROFT DRIVE

Dye House Farm

Huntenhull Green

3

Frith Farm

Rodden Brook

Corsley Mill

Divers Bridge

Lady's Coppice

47

JOLES LANE

Frith House

BA12

Corsley CE Prim Sch

Manor Farm

2

COURT LANE

Corsley

DEEP LANE

Pool Farm

Tits Wood

Lye's Green

Sheremarsh Wood

Court Farm

THE HOLLOW

PH

Cross Keys Farm

1

Harpers Farm

Sandhayes

46

A   B   C   D   E   F

8

CLIVEY
B3099
Dilton Marsh Farm
SHEPHERDS MEAD
Dilton Marsh
ATYEO CL
ST MARIS LA
HIGH STREET
B3099
SILVER ST
PO
PARK RD
THE AVENUE
ATYEO CL
WOODLAND
VW
ALAN POWELL CK
LYES GR
ORCHARD CL
WHITECROFT
PH
Dilton Marsh CE Prim Sch
PETTICOAT LANE
FRIARS CL
CLAY CLOSE
A3098
WESTBURY LEIGH
SAND HOLE LANE
Penknap
SAND HOLE LANE
WARMINSTER ROAD
A350

RED PIT
STORMORE
B3099
GREENACRES
+ Stormore

TOWER HILL
HONEY LANE
MILL LANE

Titford Farm

7

Chalcot Wood

Chalcot Park

Chalcot Park Farm

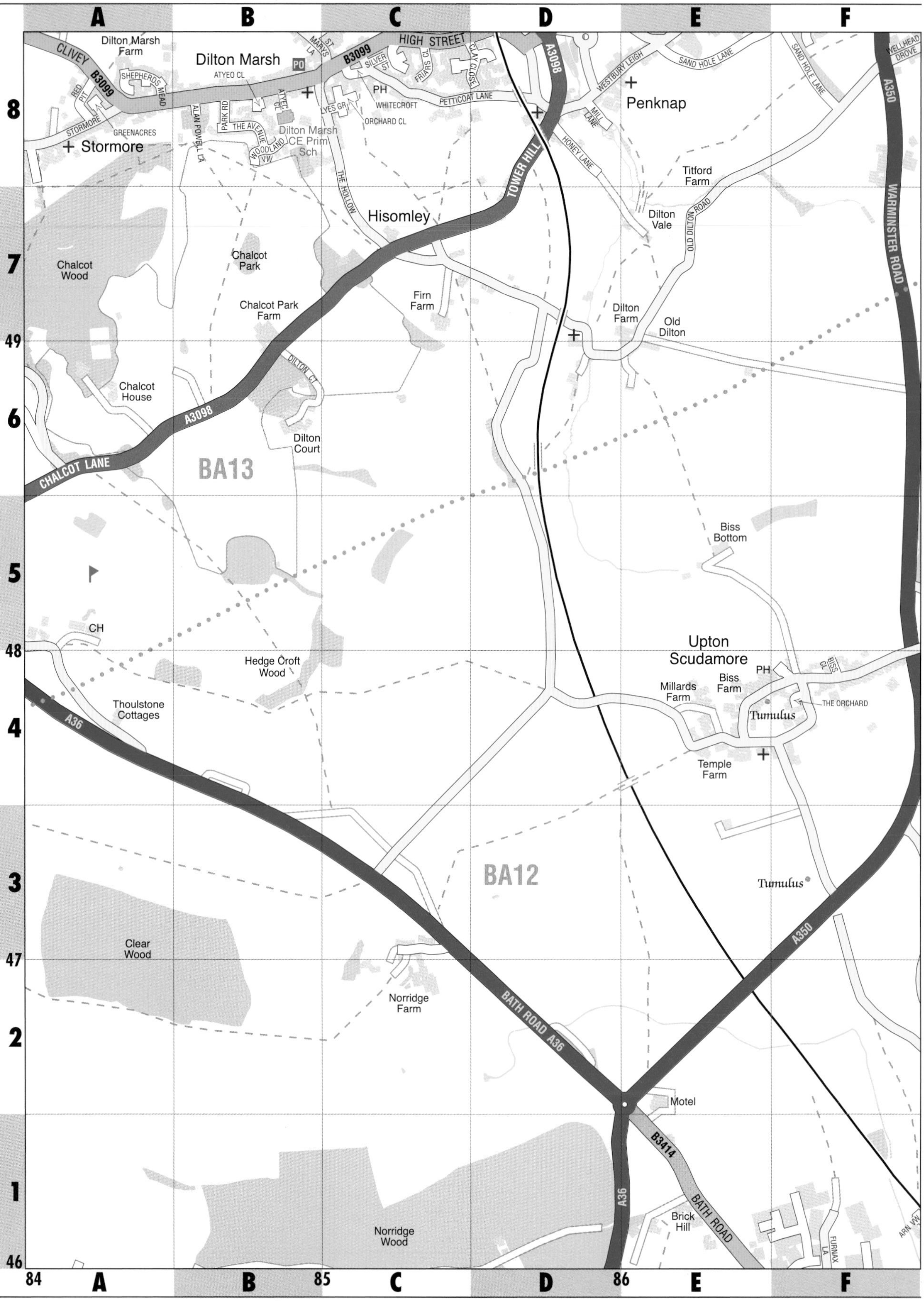

THE HOLLOW

Hisomley

Firn Farm

Dilton Vale

Dilton Farm

Old Dilton

49

DILTON CT

6

Chalcot House

A3098

Dilton Court

Dilton Court

BA13

CHALCOT LANE

OLD DILTON ROAD

5

Biss Bottom

48

CH

Hedge Croft Wood

Upton Scudamore

4

A36

Thoulstone Cottages

Millards Farm

Biss Farm

PH

BISS CL

THE ORCHARD

Tumulus

Temple Farm

+

BA12

Tumulus

A350

3

Clear Wood

47

Norridge Farm

BATH ROAD A36

2

Motel

B3414

BATH ROAD

1

Norridge Wood

A36

Brick Hill

FURNAX LA

ARN VW

46

84   A   85   B   C   86   D   E   F

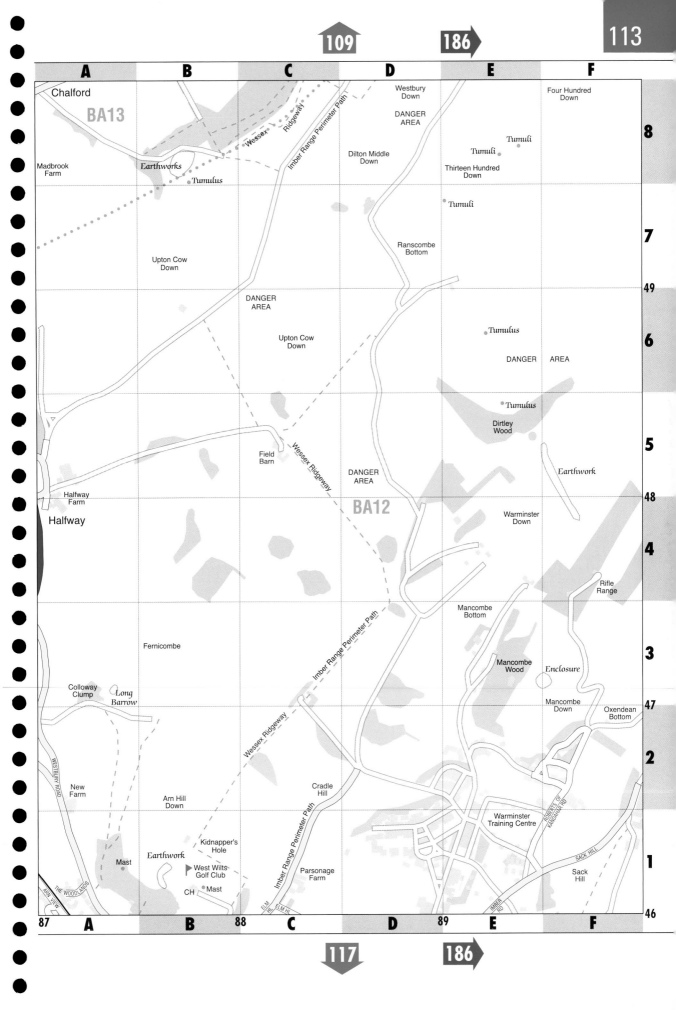

A B C D E F

8

Chalford

BA13

Madbrook Farm

Wessex Ridgeway

Imber Range Perimeter Path

Earthworks

Tumulus

Westbury Down

DANGER AREA

Dilton Middle Down

Four Hundred Down

Tumuli

Tumuli

Thirteen Hundred Down

7

Upton Cow Down

Ranscombe Bottom

Tumuli

49

DANGER AREA

6

Upton Cow Down

Tumulus

DANGER   AREA

Tumulus

5

Field Barn

Wessex Ridgeway

DANGER AREA

Dirtley Wood

Earthwork

Halfway Farm

BA12

48

Halfway

Warminster Down

4

Rifle Range

Imber Range Perimeter Path

Mancombe Bottom

3

Fernicombe

Mancombe Wood

Enclosure

Colloway Clump

Long Barrow

Mancombe Down

47

Oxendean Bottom

Wessex Ridgeway

2

WESTBURY ROAD

New Farm

Arn Hill Down

Cradle Hill

Warminster Training Centre

ROBERTS OF KANDAHAR RD

Imber Range Perimeter Path

ELM HL

Mast

Earthwork

Kidnapper's Hole

West Wilts Golf Club

CH   Mast

Parsonage Farm

IMBER RD

SACK HILL

Sack Hill

1

ARN VIEW

THE WOODLANDS

46

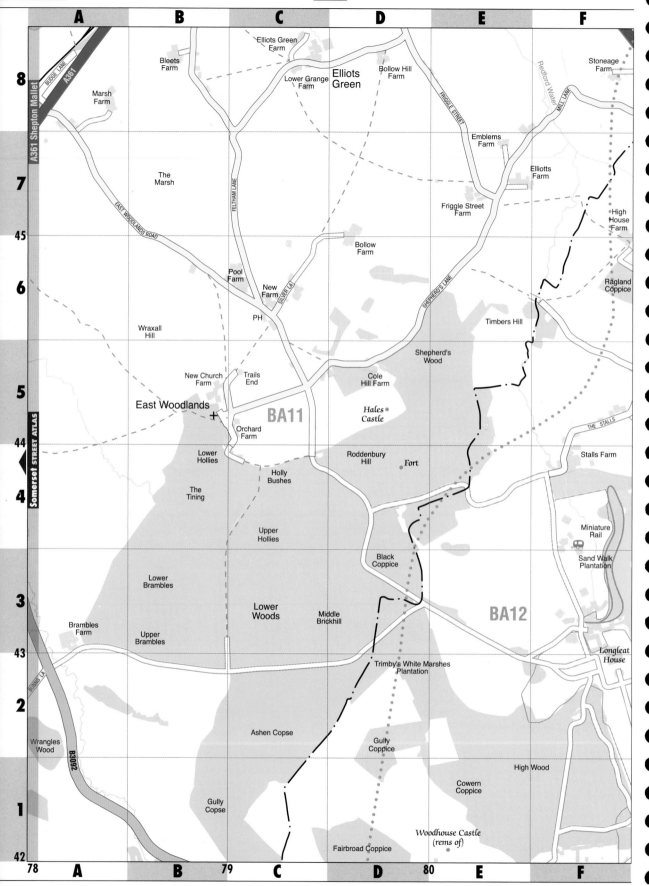

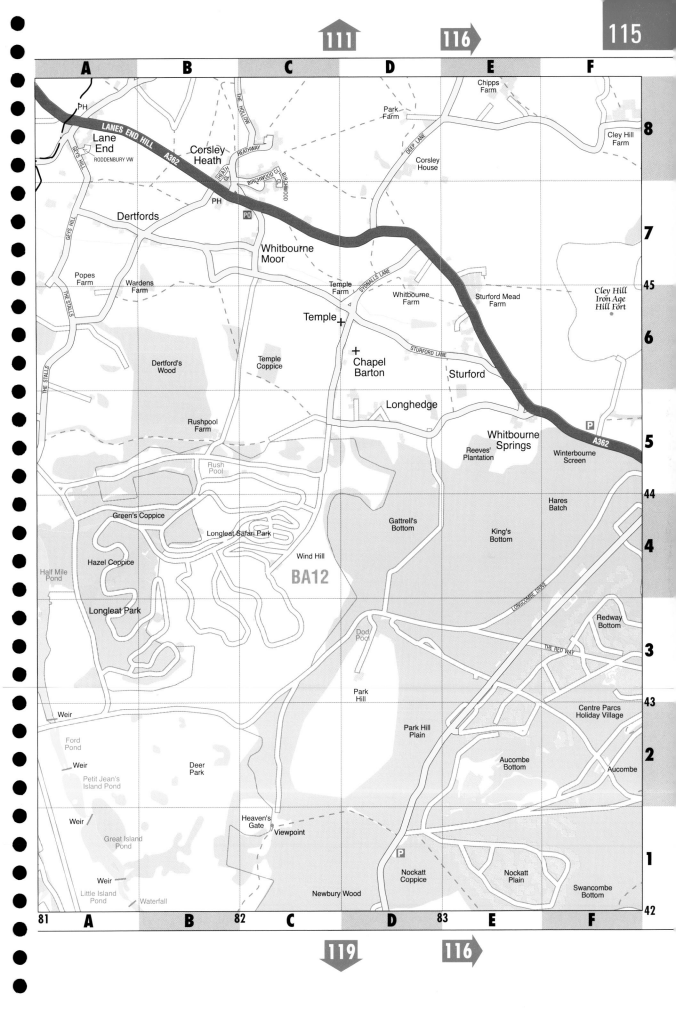

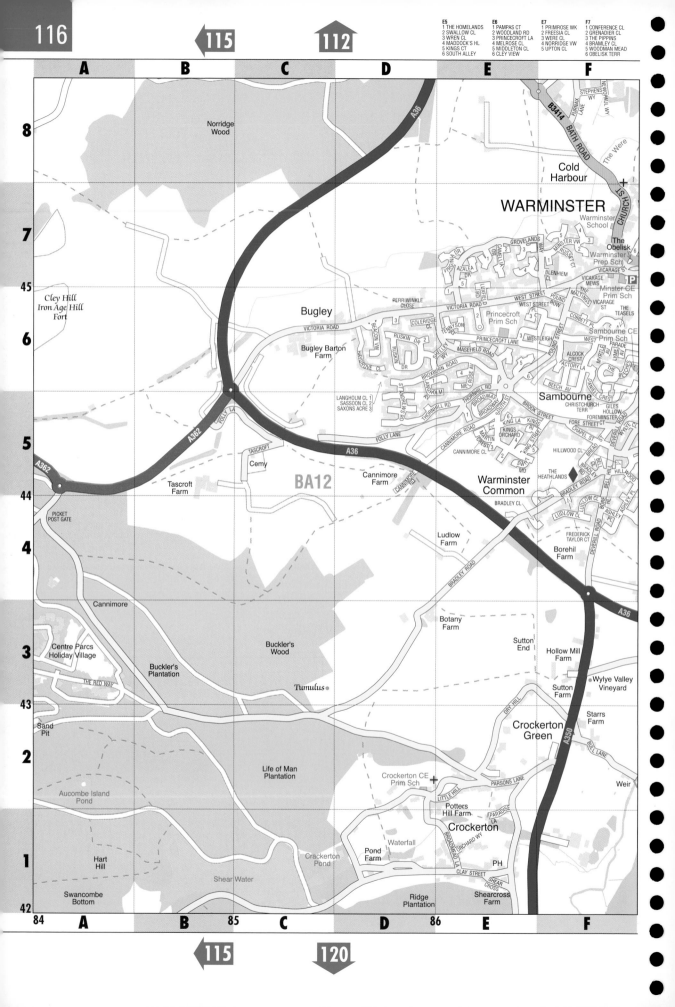

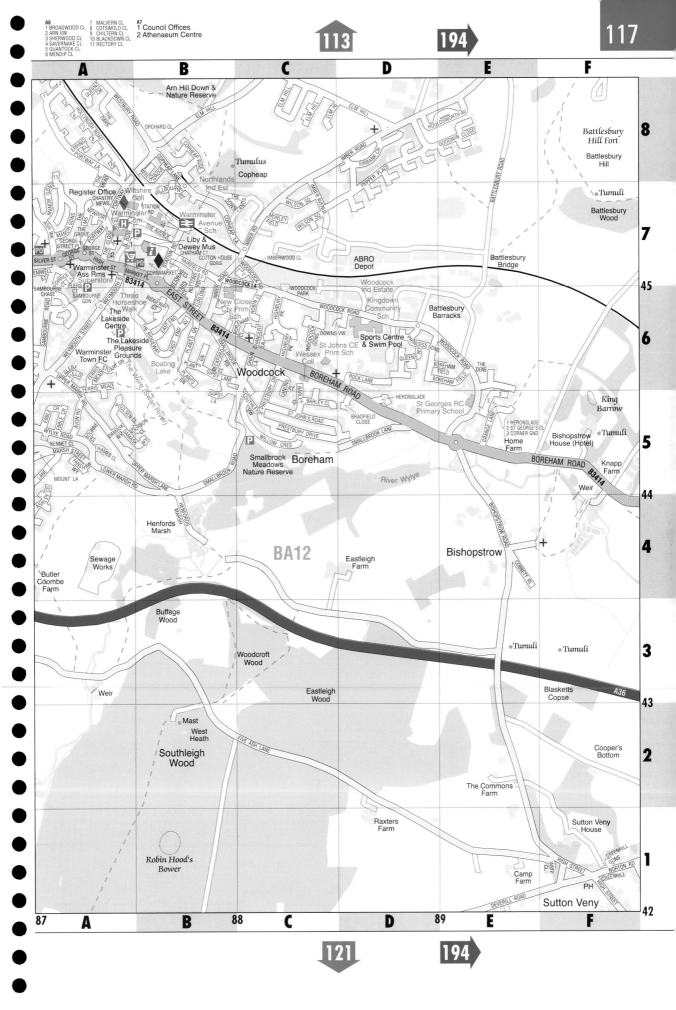

114

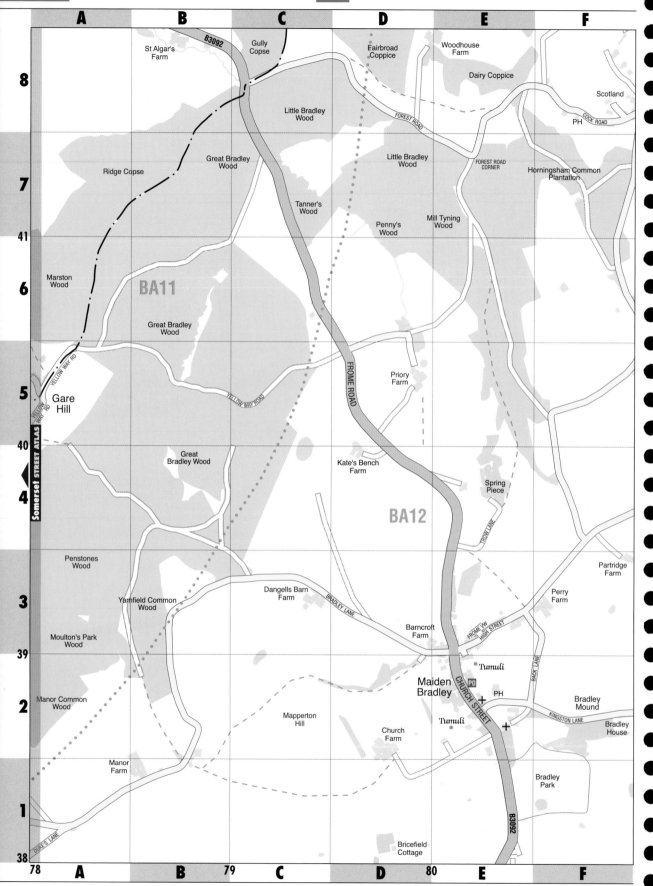

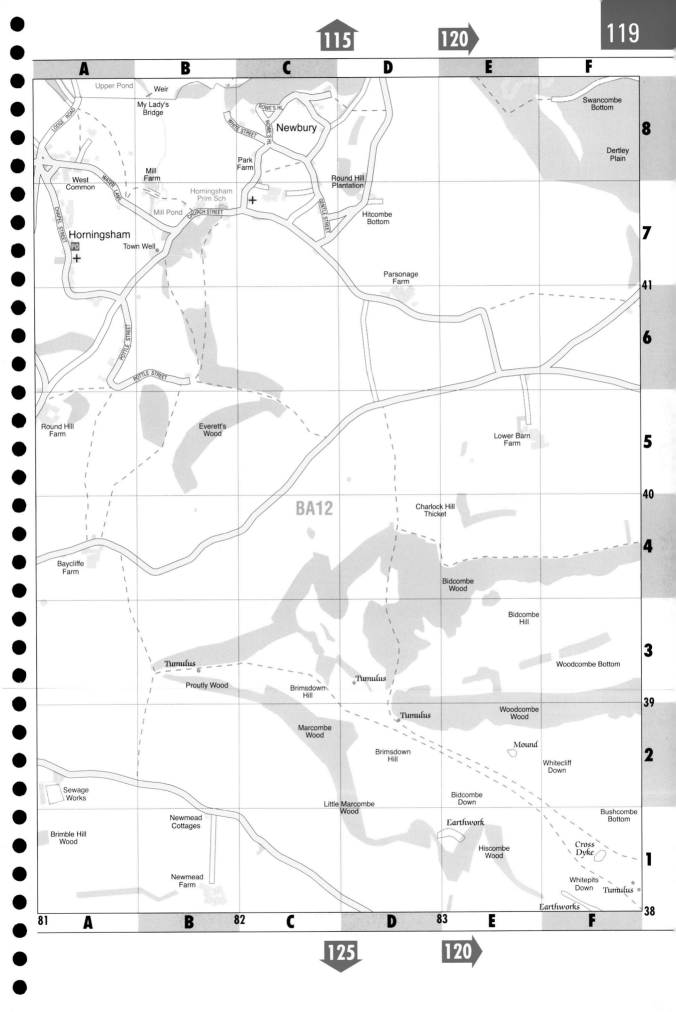

A   B   C   D   E   F

8   Swancombe
    Bottom

    Manswood

    Swancombe
    Cottage

    Ridge Plantation

    P

    Foxholes
    Plantation

    Fox
    Holes

    River Wylye

    Weir

7   Manswood
    Cottage

    Shute
    Farm

    Almshouses

    CHURCH STREET

    A350

41

    Longbridge
    Deverill

    PO

    HOMEFIELDS

6   Broomclose
    Farm

    Church
    Farm

    Rye Hill
    Cottages

    Wing
    Farm

    Hill Deverill

    MILL

    Mill
    Farm

5   Rye Hill
    Farm

    Medieval Village of
    Hill Deverill (site of)

    Hill
    Deverill
    Manor

    B3095

    The
    Manor

40

    BA12

    Marriages
    Farm

4   Bidcombe
    Wood

    Whitley
    Copse

3   Woodcombe
    Farm

    Brims Down

    Woodcombe
    Farm

    River Wylye

39 Woodcombe
    Wood

    Cross
    Dyke

    Drove End

    Brixton
    Deverill

2   Bushcombe
    Bottom

    Cross Dyke

    Manor
    Farm

    Long
    Barrow

    Cross Dyke

    Whitecliff
    Farm

1   Cold
    Kitchen Hill

    Tumulus

    Boar's
    Bottom

    B3095

38 Whitepits
    Down

    Cross Dyke

    Tumulus

    Summerslade
    Down

    84   A   B   85   C   D   86   E   F

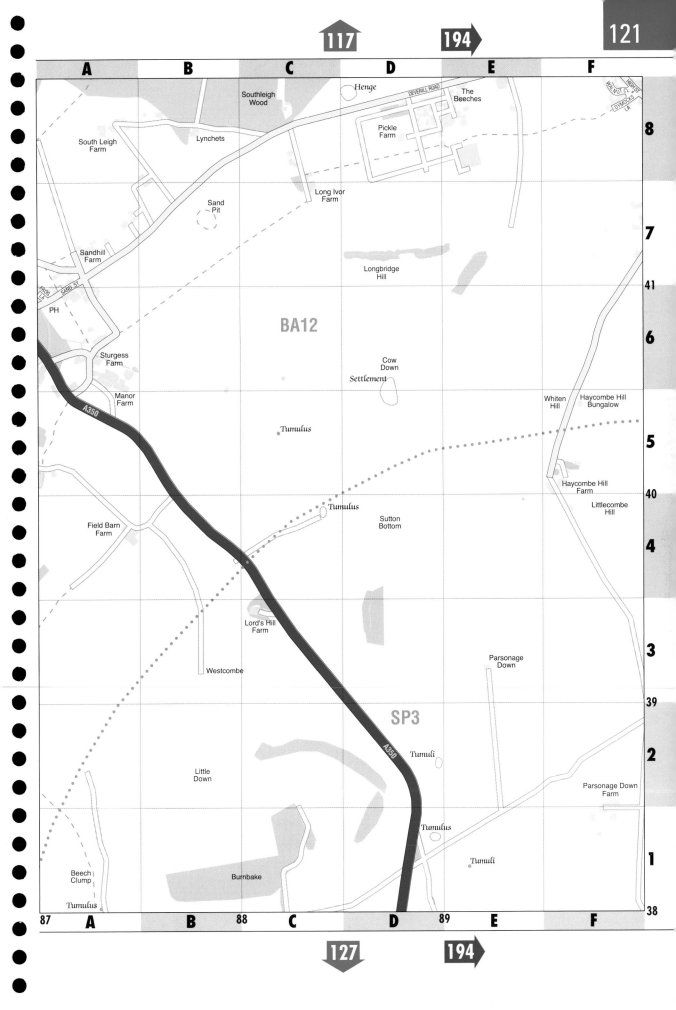

A B C D E F

8
7
41
6
5
40
4
3
39
2
1
38

Henge
DEVERILL ROAD
The Beeches
Southleigh Wood
Pickle Farm
WALNUT CL.
DYMOCKS LA.
Lynchets
South Leigh Farm
Sand Pit
Long Ivor Farm
Sandhill Farm
Longbridge Hill
SAND ST
FROG LA
PH
BA12
Cow Down
Settlement
Sturgess Farm
Whiten Hill
Haycombe Hill Bungalow
A350
Manor Farm
Tumulus
Haycombe Hill Farm
Littlecombe Hill
Field Barn Farm
Tumulus
Sutton Bottom
Lord's Hill Farm
Parsonage Down
Westcombe
SP3
A350
Tumuli
Little Down
Parsonage Down Farm
Tumulus
Tumuli
Beech Clump
Burnbake
Tumulus

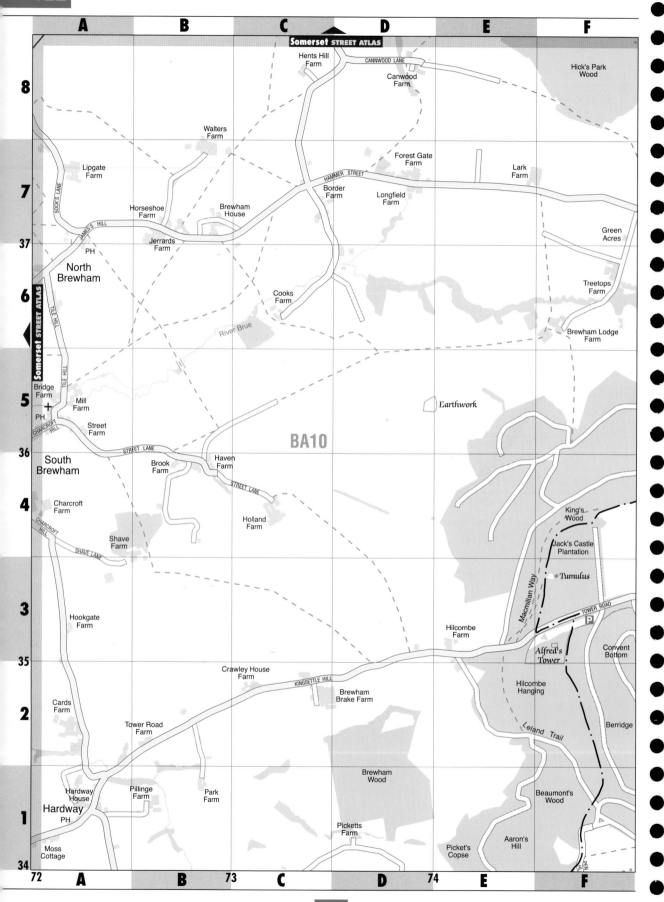

8

Hick's Park
Wood

Hents Hill
Farm

CANNWOOD LANE

Canwood
Farm

Walters
Farm

Forest Gate
Farm

Lipgate
Farm

HAMMER STREET

Lark
Farm

7

SOCK'S LANE

Horseshoe
Farm

Brewham
House

Border
Farm

Longfield
Farm

37

JAMES'S HILL

Jerrards
Farm

Green
Acres

PH

North
Brewham

Treetops
Farm

6

TILE HILL

Cooks
Farm

Brewham Lodge
Farm

River Brue

Earthwork

5

TILE HILL

Bridge
Farm

Mill
Farm

PH

Street
Farm

CHARCROFT HILL

BA10

STREET LANE

36

South
Brewham

Brook
Farm

Haven
Farm

STREET LANE

King's
Wood

4

Charcroft
Farm

Holland
Farm

Jack's Castle
Plantation

CHARCROFT HILL

Macmillan Way

• Tumulus

Shave
Farm

SHAVE LANE

3

Hookgate
Farm

Hilcombe
Farm

TOWER ROAD

P

Alfred's
Tower

Convent
Bottom

35

Crawley House
Farm

KINGSETTLE HILL

Hilcombe
Hanging

2

Cards
Farm

Brewham
Brake Farm

Leland Trail

Berridge

Tower Road
Farm

Pillinge
Farm

Park
Farm

Brewham
Wood

Beaumont's
Wood

1

Hardway
House

Hardway

PH

Pickett's
Farm

Aaron's
Hill

Moss
Cottage

Picket's
Copse

PEN

34

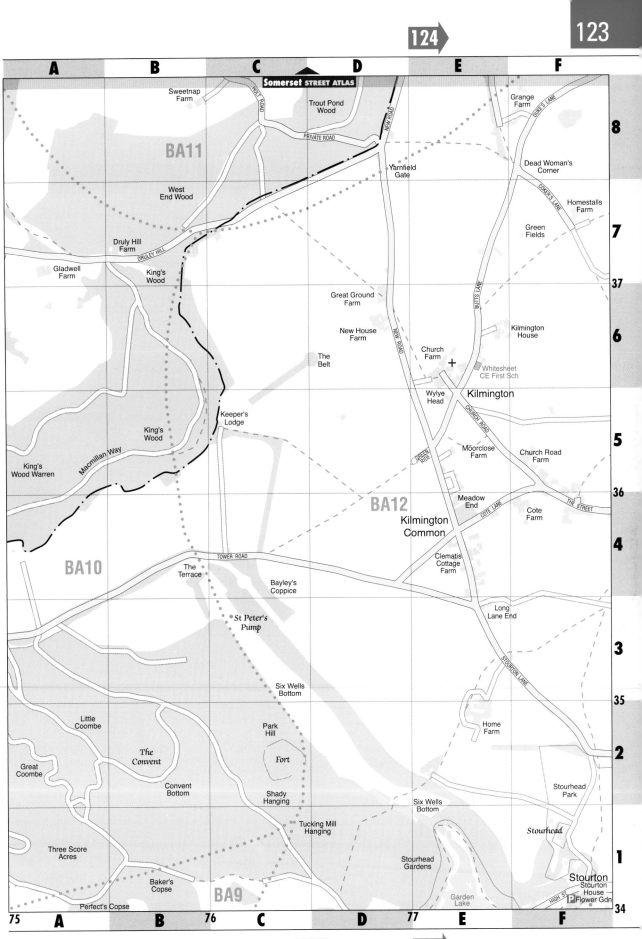

A   B   C   D   E   F

Sweetnap Farm

Trout Pond Wood

HOLT ROAD

PRIVATE ROAD

NEW ROAD

Grange Farm

DUKE'S LANE

8

BA11

Yarnfield Gate

Dead Woman's Corner

COKER'S LANE

West End Wood

Homestalls Farm

Green Fields

7

Druly Hill Farm

DRULEY HILL

King's Wood

37

Gladwell Farm

Great Ground Farm

BUTTS LANE

New House Farm

NEW ROAD

Church Farm

Kilmington House

6

The Belt

Whitesheet CE First Sch

King's Wood

Keeper's Lodge

Wylye Head

Kilmington

King's Wood

Moorclose Farm

Church Road Farm

5

King's Wood Warren

Macmillan Way

GREEN RIDE

CHURCH ROAD

BA12

Meadow End

Cote Farm

THE STREET

36

Kilmington Common

COTE LANE

BA10

The Terrace

TOWER ROAD

Bayley's Coppice

Clematis Cottage Farm

4

Long Lane End

St Peter's Pump

STOURTON LANE

3

Six Wells Bottom

35

Little Coombe

Park Hill

Home Farm

The Convent

Fort

2

Great Coombe

Convent Bottom

Shady Hanging

Stourhead Park

Tucking Mill Hanging

Six Wells Bottom

Stourhead

Three Score Acres

Stourhead Gardens

Stourton

1

Baker's Copse

BA9

Stourton House Flower Gdn

HIGH ST

Perfect's Copse

Garden Lake

P

34

A **B** **C** **D** **E** **F**

8

Long Knoll
Wood

Rag
Wood

Little Knoll
Wood

Little Knoll

Tumulus

Long
Knoll

B3092

7

37

Milbury
Coppice

Knoll
Farm

6

Elm
Farm

Manor
Farm

Norton
Ferris

COOMBE BARN LANE

5

Norton Ferris
Farm

Coombe Barn
Farm

COOMBE BARN LA

36

Street
Farm

Berkeley
Farm

BA12

THE STREET

4

Manor
Farm

White Sheet Downs

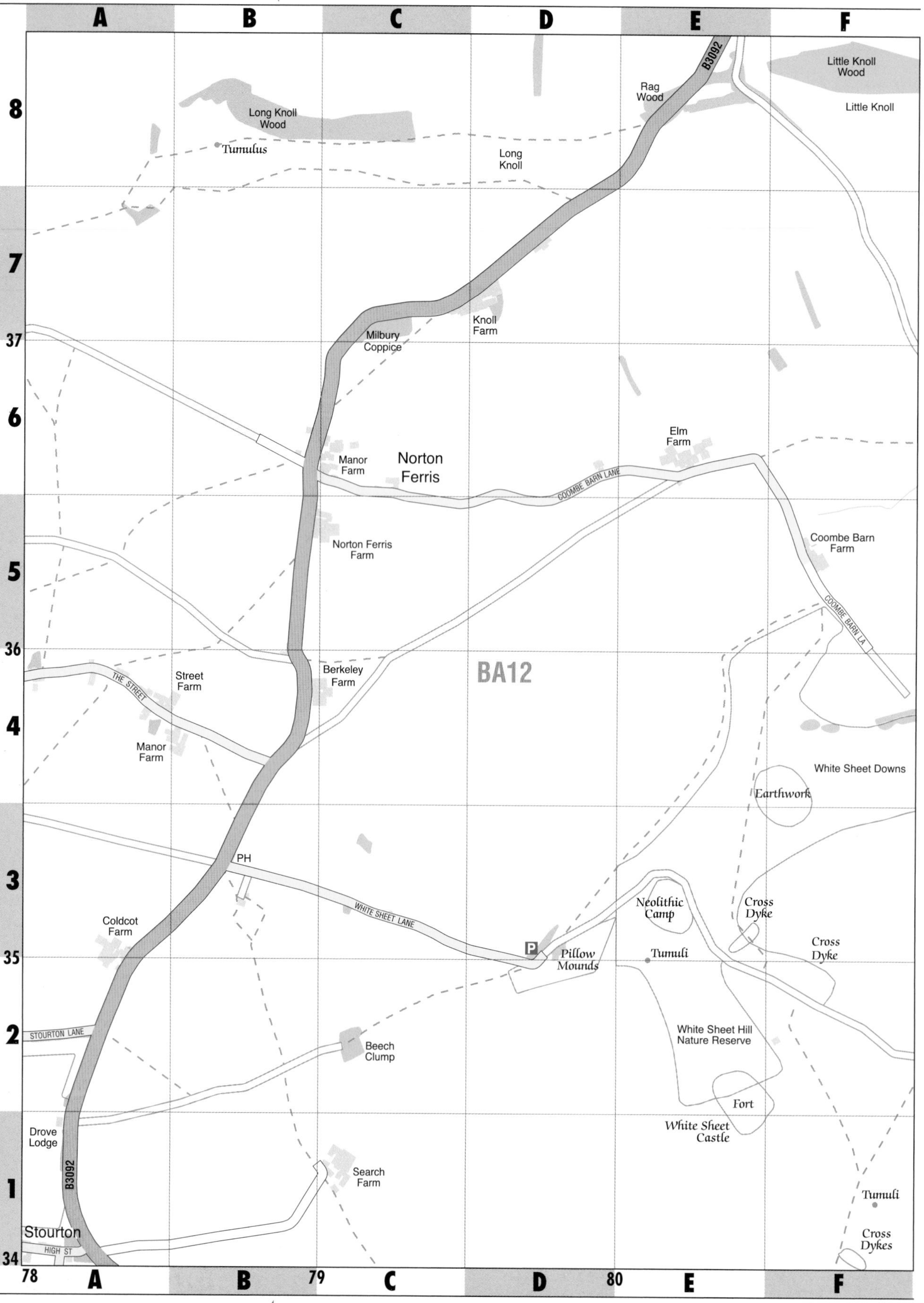

Earthwork

3

PH

WHITE SHEET LANE

Neolithic
Camp

Cross
Dyke

Cross
Dyke

Coldcot
Farm

35

P

Pillow
Mounds

Tumuli

2

STOURTON LANE

Beech
Clump

White Sheet Hill
Nature Reserve

Fort

Drove
Lodge

White Sheet
Castle

1

B3092

Search
Farm

Tumuli

Stourton

Cross
Dykes

34

HIGH ST

78 **A** **B** 79 **C** **D** 80 **E** **F**

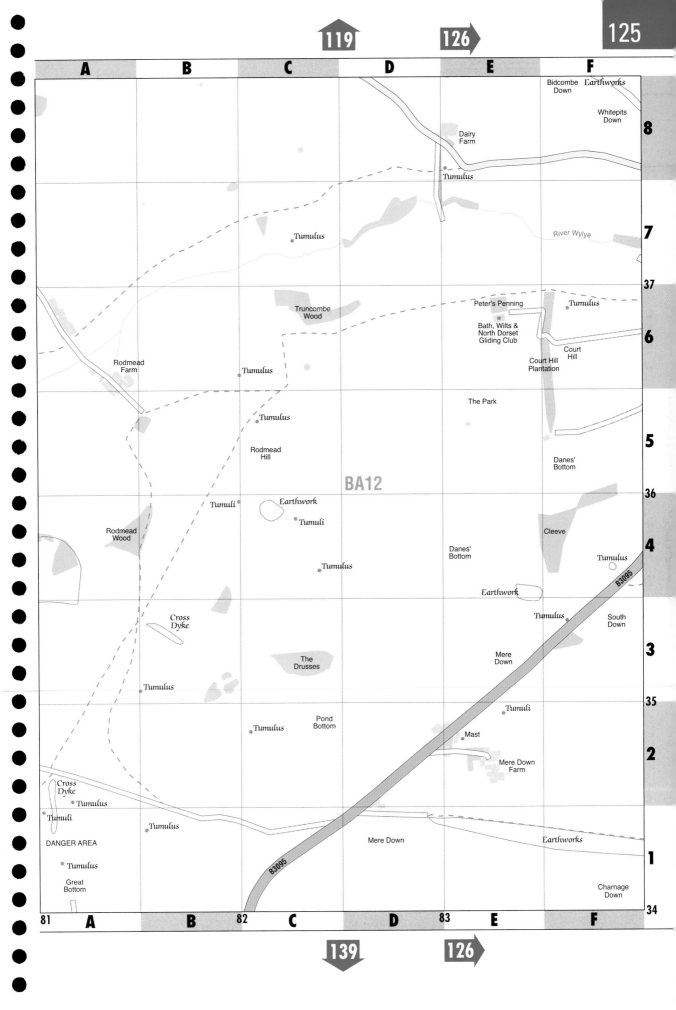

125
120

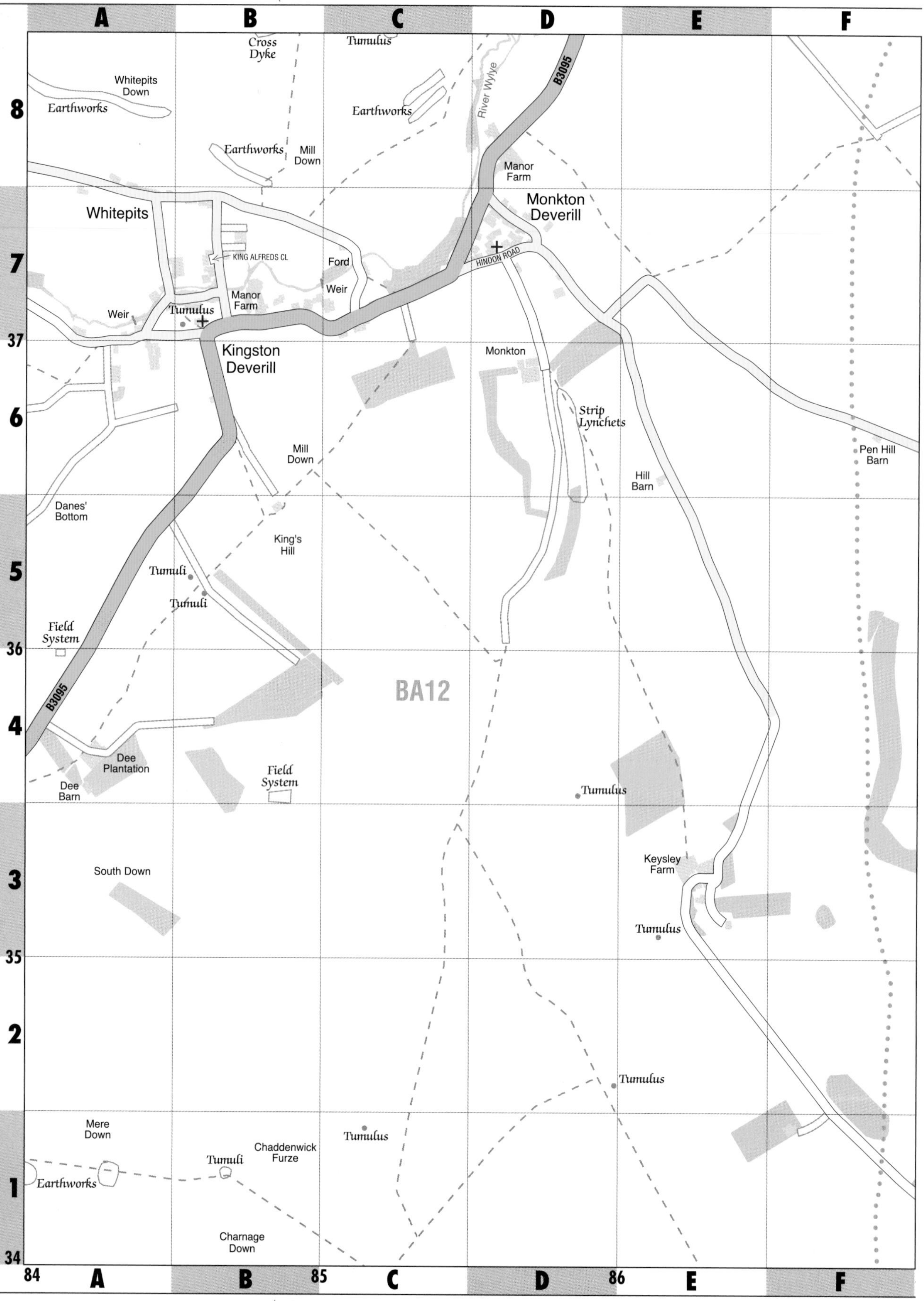

A B C D E F

8

Whitepits
Down

Earthworks

*Cross
Dyke*

Tumulus

Earthworks

River Wylye

B3095

Earthworks

Earthworks

*Mill
Down*

Manor
Farm

Monkton
Deverill

7

Whitepits

KING ALFREDS CL

Ford

Weir

Manor
Farm

HINDON ROAD

Weir

Tumulus

37

Weir

Kingston
Deverill

Monkton

Strip
Lynchets

6

*Mill
Down*

Hill
Barn

Pen Hill
Barn

*Danes'
Bottom*

*King's
Hill*

5

Tumuli

Tumuli

*Field
System*

36

BA12

4

B3095

*Dee
Plantation*

*Field
System*

*Dee
Barn*

Tumulus

3

South Down

Keysley
Farm

Tumulus

35

Tumulus

2

Tumulus

*Mere
Down*

Tumulus

Tumuli

*Chaddenwick
Furze*

1

Earthworks

*Charnage
Down*

34

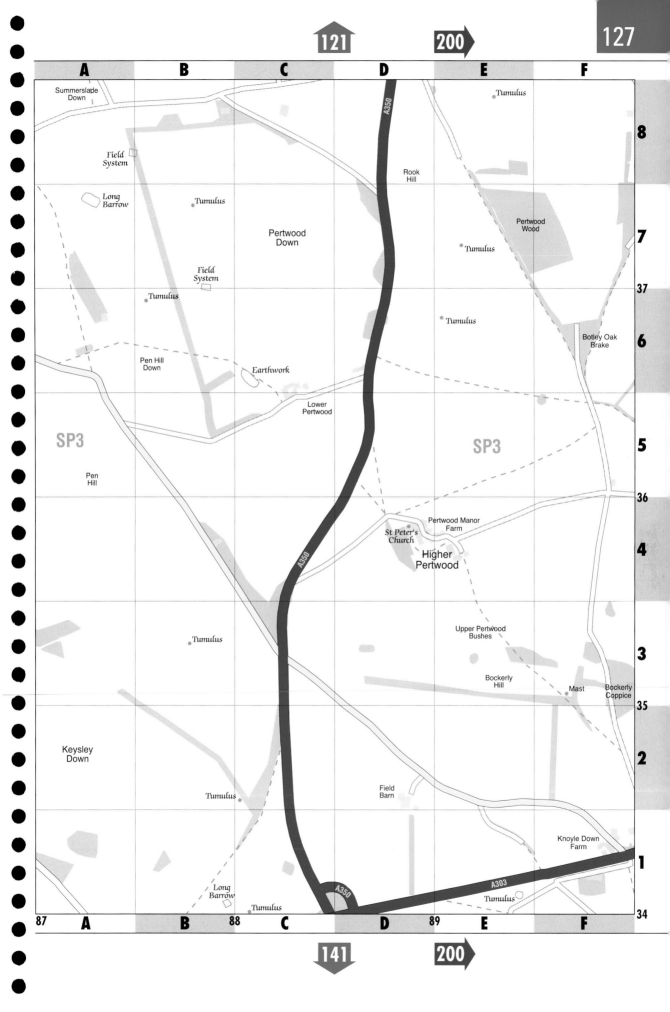

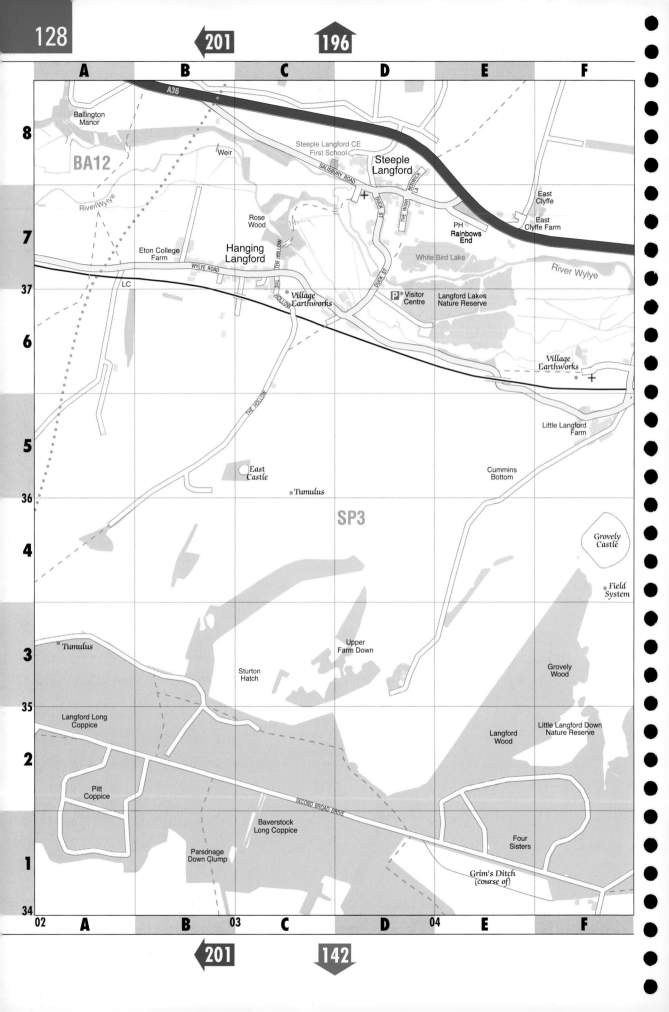

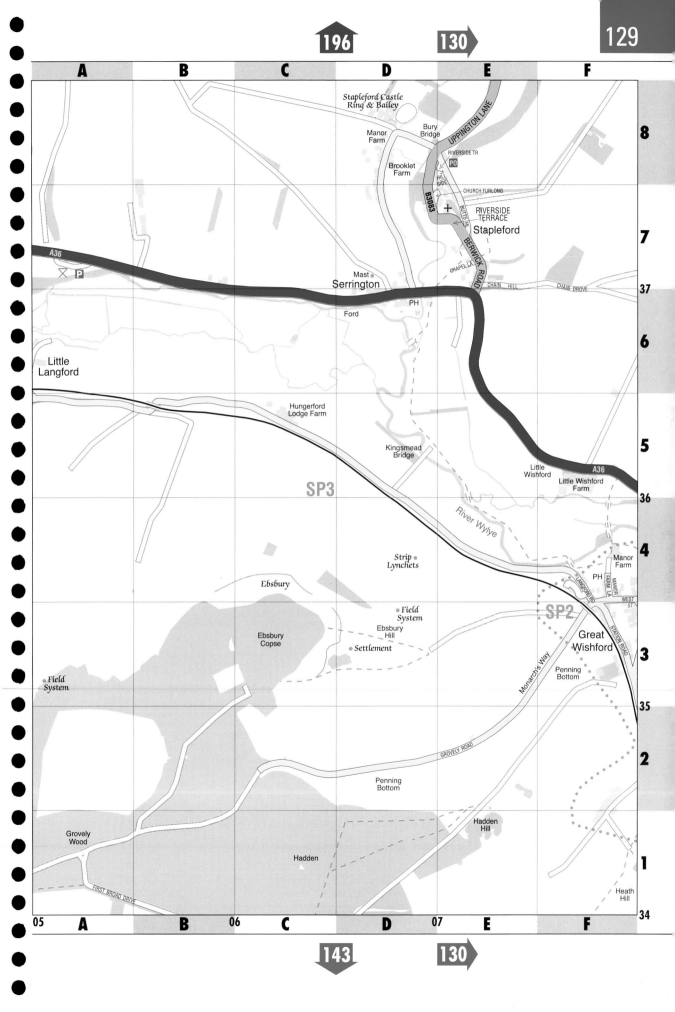

129
197

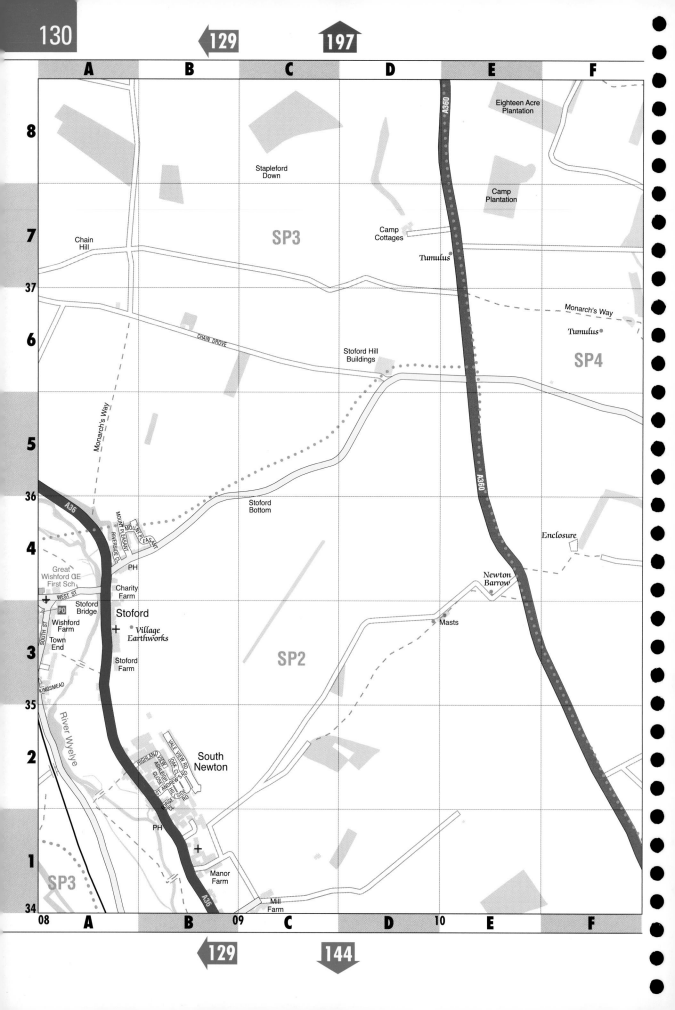

A | B | C | D | E | F

8

Stapleford
Down

Eighteen Acre
Plantation

7

Chain
Hill

SP3

Camp
Plantation

Camp
Cottages

Tumulus

37

Monarch's Way

6

CHAIN DROVE

Stoford Hill
Buildings

SP4

Tumulus

Monarch's Way

5

Monarch's Way

A360

36

A36

Stoford
Bottom

Enclosure

4

MOUNT PLEASANT

RIVERSIDE CL

MOUNT PLEASANT

PH

Newton
Barrow

Great
Wishford CE
First Sch

Charity
Farm

Masts

WEST ST

PO

Stoford
Bridge

Stoford

SP2

3

SOUTH ST

Wishford
Farm

Town
End

*Village
Earthworks*

Stoford
Farm

KINGSMEAD

35

River Wylye

2

HIGHLAND

VALE VIEW RD

TRENT

OAK CL

ASHE RD

ST ANDREW'S RD

CLOSE

THE

FORGE

CL

SIDE

RD

South
Newton

PH

1

SP3

Manor
Farm

Mill
Farm

A36

34

08 | A | B | 09 | C | D | 10 | E | F

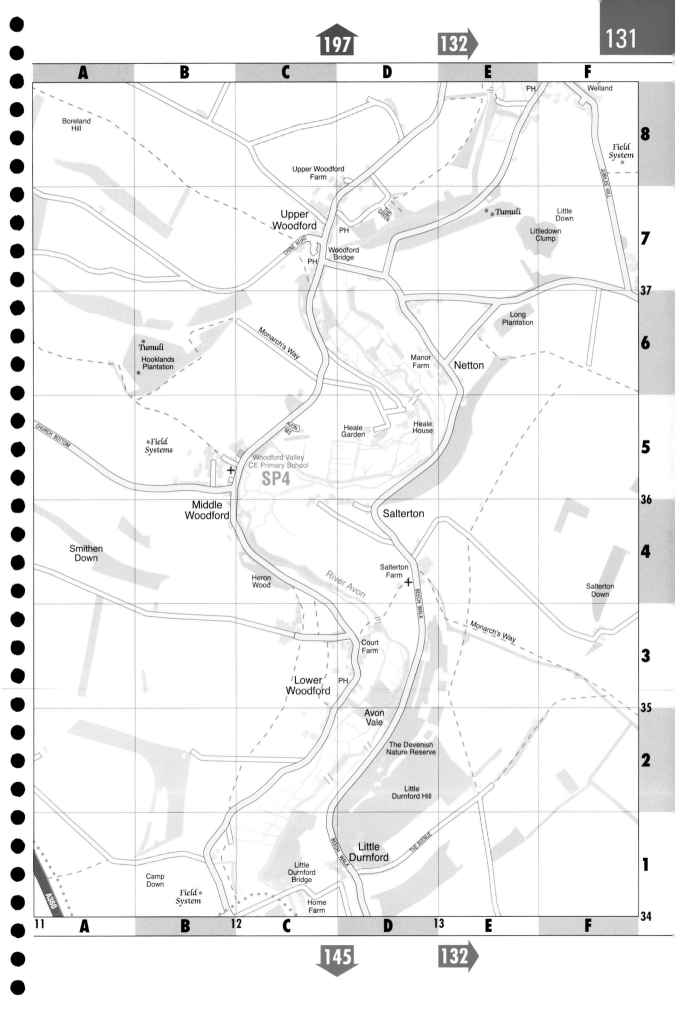

131
198

A B C D E F

8

Burnstack
Plantation

South
Farm

7

Cusse's
Gorse

37

Factory

High Post
Golf Club

6

DOWN BARN ROAD

Enclosure

Hotel   High
Post

Coffee
Farm

CH

SP4

5

Downbarn
West

36

Salterton
Down

FOURMILE HILL

4

Crabtree
Cottages

3

35

Hurdcott Farm

Monarch's Way

2

Monarch's Way

GREAT DROVE

Longhedge
Farm

A345

1

PORTWAY

Longhedge
Cottages

Tumuli

34

14   A   15   B   C   15   D   16   E   F

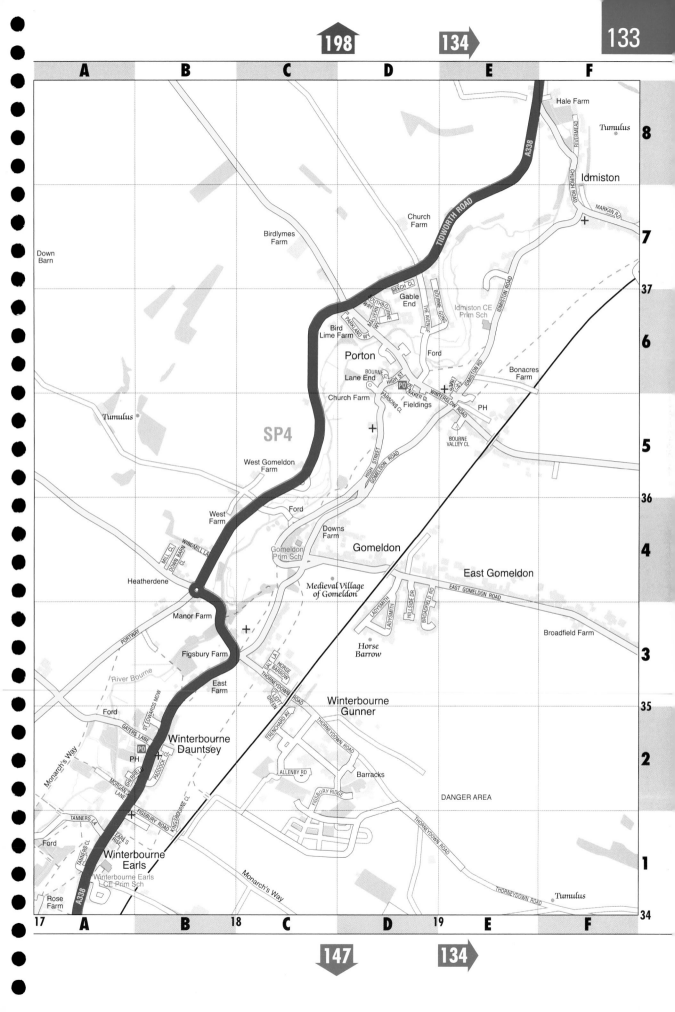

133
199

	A	B	C	D	E	F

8

CHURCH RD

7

CHURCH RD

SOUTHWAY

NORTHWAY

Tumuli

DANGER AREA

37

Sports Ground

6

Tumuli

Earthwork

Idmiston Down

BLACKGARN ROAD

DANGER AREA

Tumuli

5

Manor Farm

Tumuli

Enclosure

SP4

36

Tumulus

4

DANGER AREA

Porton Down

Tumuli

3

EAST GOMELDON RD

Tumuli

Winter Slow Firs

35

Tumuli

2

Battery Hill

DANGER AREA

1

Thorny Down

Refuse Tip

A30

SP5

34

20	A		B	21	C		D	22	E		F

133
148

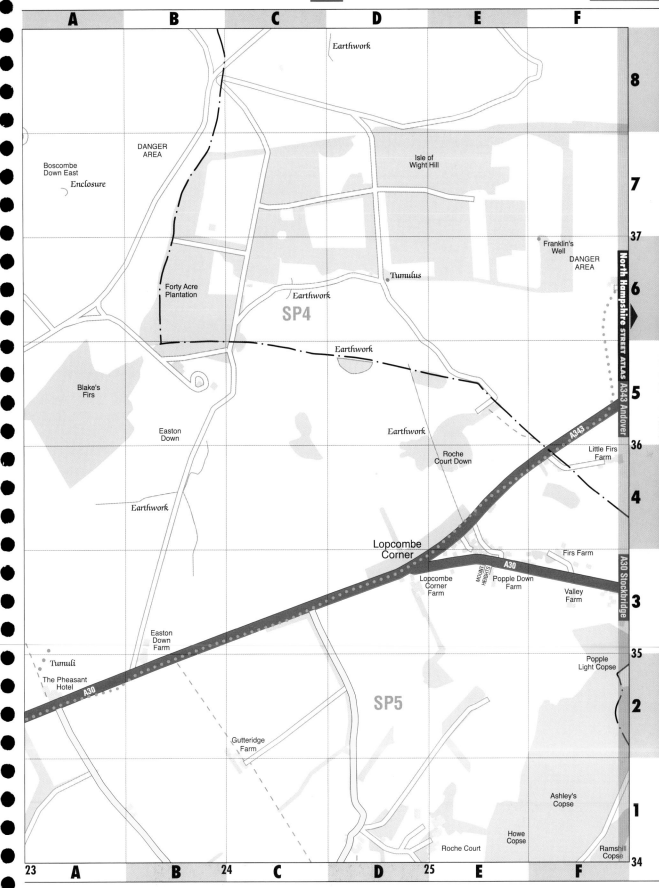

Earthwork

DANGER AREA

Boscombe Down East

Enclosure

Isle of Wight Hill

Franklin's Well

DANGER AREA

Forty Acre Plantation

Tumulus

Earthwork

SP4

Earthwork

Blake's Firs

Earthwork

Easton Down

Earthwork

Roche Court Down

Little Firs Farm

Earthwork

Lopcombe Corner

Firs Farm

Lopcombe Corner Farm

MOUNT HEIGHTS

Popple Down Farm

A30

Valley Farm

Easton Down Farm

Popple Light Copse

Tumuli

The Pheasant Hotel

A30

SP5

Gutteridge Farm

Ashley's Copse

Howe Copse

Roche Court

Ramshill Copse

North Hampshire STREET ATLAS A343 Andover

A343

A30 Stockbridge

122

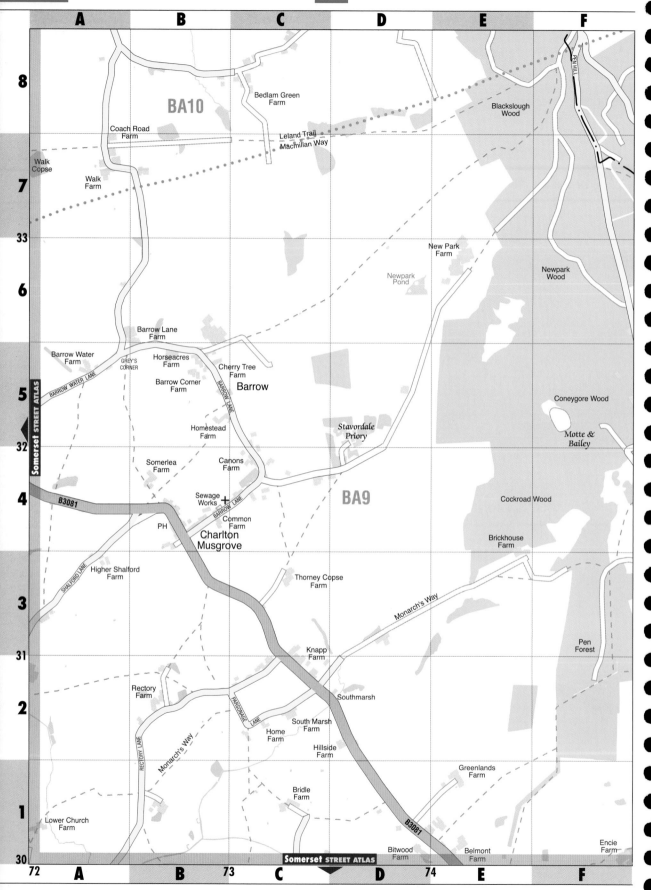

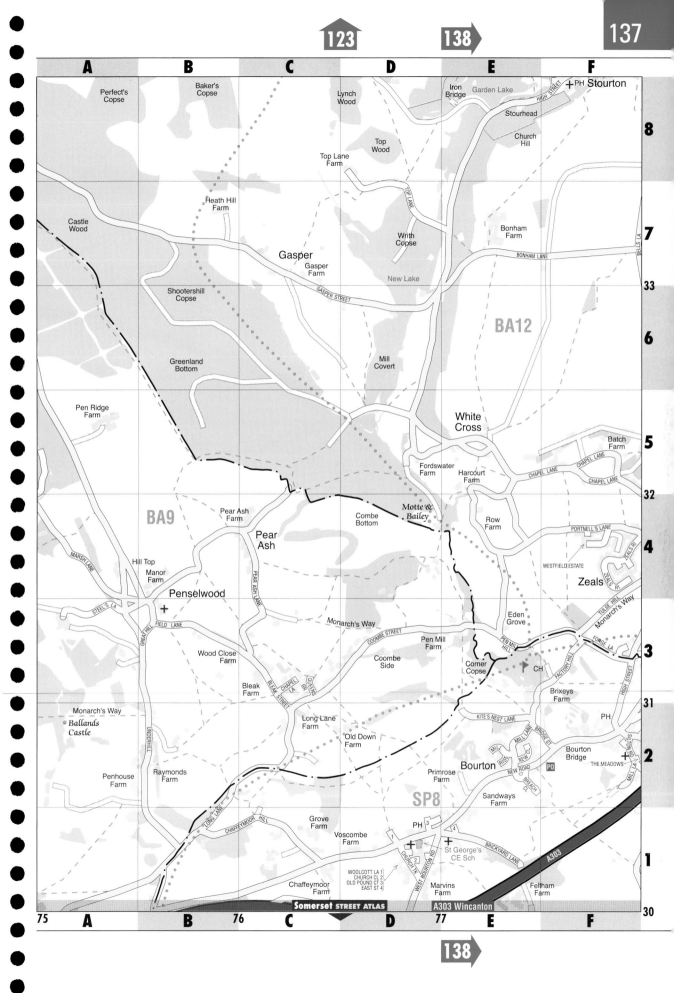

A B C D E F

8
7
33
6
5
32
4
31
2
1
30

Perfect's Copse

Baker's Copse

Lynch Wood

Iron Bridge

Garden Lake

PH Stourton

Stourhead

HIGH STREET

Church Hill

Top Wood

Top Lane Farm

TOP LANE

Writh Copse

Bonham Farm

BONHAM LANE

BELLS LA

Castle Wood

Heath Hill Farm

Gasper

Gasper Farm

GASPER STREET

New Lake

BA12

Shootershill Copse

Greenland Bottom

Mill Covert

White Cross

Pen Ridge Farm

Fordswater Farm

Harcourt Farm

Batch Farm

CHAPEL LANE

CHAPEL LANE

CHAPEL LANE

BA9

Pear Ash Farm

Pear Ash

Combe Bottom

Motte & Bailey

Row Farm

PORTNELL'S LANE

ZEALS RI

Westfield Estate

ZEALS RI

Zeals

Hill Top Manor Farm

Penselwood

PEAR ASH LANE

Monarch's Way

COOMBE STREET

Pen Mill Farm

Eden Grove

TULSE HILL

Monarch's Way

MARSH LANE

STEEL'S LA

GREAT HILL

FIELD LANE

Wood Close Farm

Coombe Side

PEN MILL HILL

Corner Copse

CH

FORGE LA

HIGH STREET

Bleak Farm

CHAPEL LA

BLEAK STREET

QUEENS GR

FACTORY HILL

Brixeys Farm

PH

Monarch's Way

Ballands Castle

UNDERHILL

Long Lane Farm

Old Down Farm

KITE'S NEST LANE

MILL LANE

BRIDGE ST

Bourton Bridge

MILL LA

TULSE HILL

THE MEADOWS

Penhouse Farm

Raymonds Farm

LONG LANE

Grove Farm

Voscombe Farm

SP8

Primrose Farm

Bourton

MILL RISE

NEW ROAD

BREACH CL

PO

Sandways Farm

BRICKYARD LANE

A303

CHAFFEYMOOR HILL

Chaffeymoor Farm

PH

WEST BOURTON RD

CHURCH TK

St George's CE Sch

Marvins Farm

Feltham Farm

WOOLCOTT LA 1
CHURCH CL 2
OLD POUND CT 3
EAST ST 4

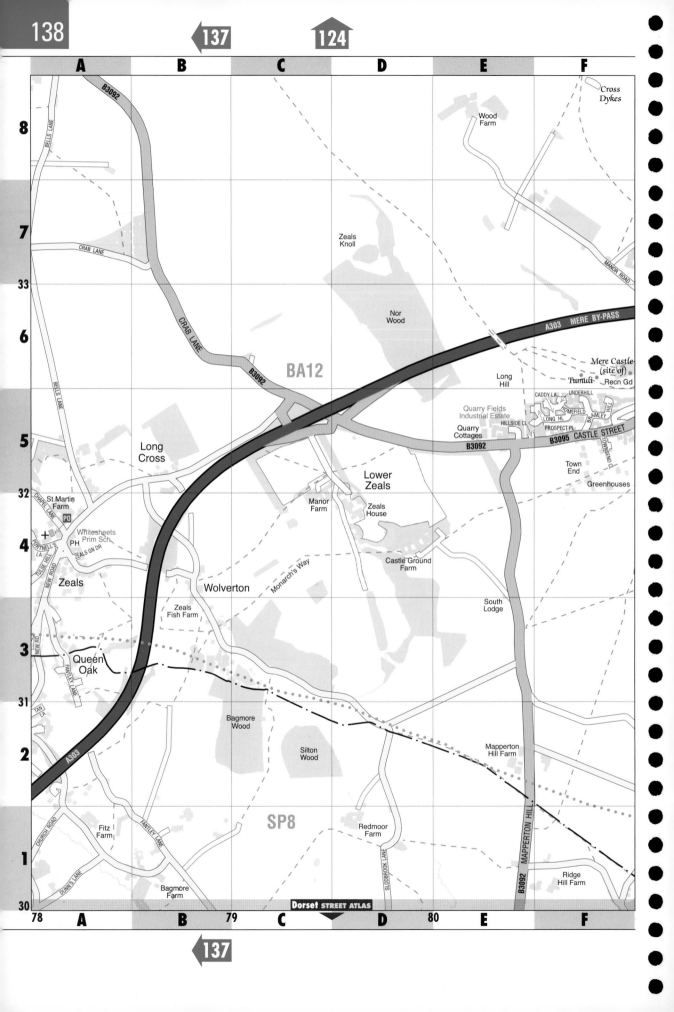

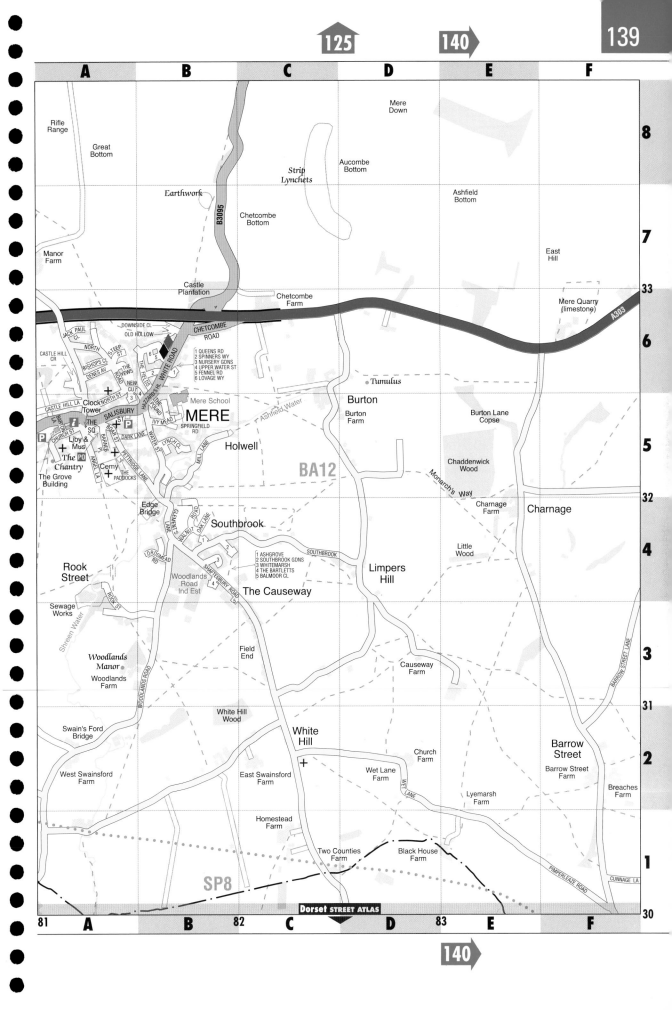

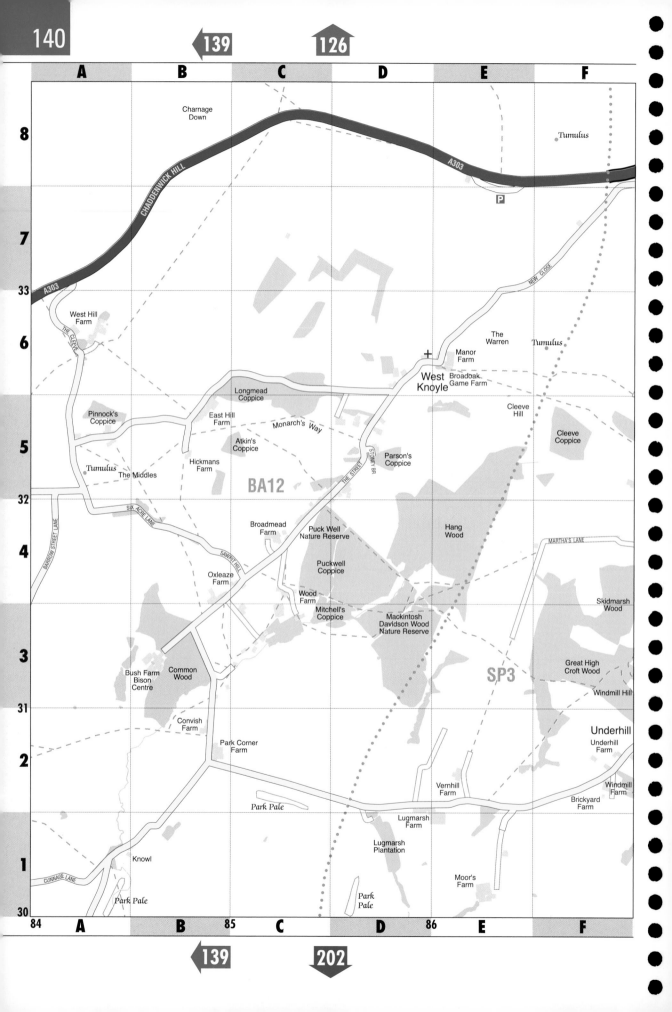

139
126

A   B   C   D   E   F

8

Charnage
Down

Tumulus

A303

7

CHADDENWICK HILL

33

A303

West Hill
Farm

6

THE CLEEVE

The
Warren

Tumulus

Manor
Farm

West
Knoyle

Broadoak
Game Farm

Cleeve
Hill

NEW CLOSE

Longmead
Coppice

Cleeve
Coppice

Pinnock's
Coppice

East Hill
Farm

Monarch's Way

5

Atkin's
Coppice

Parson's
Coppice

Tumulus

Hickmans
Farm

The Middles

STONEY BR

THE STREET

BA12

32

SIX ACRE LANE

BARROW STREET LANE

Broadmead
Farm

Puck Well
Nature Reserve

Hang
Wood

MARTHA'S LANE

4

SAWPIT HILL

Puckwell
Coppice

Oxleaze
Farm

Wood
Farm

Skidmarsh
Wood

Mitchell's
Coppice

Mackintosh
Davidson Wood
Nature Reserve

Great High
Croft Wood

3

SP3

Common
Wood

Bush Farm
Bison
Centre

Windmill Hill

31

Convish
Farm

Underhill

Park Corner
Farm

Underhill
Farm

2

Vernhill
Farm

Windmill
Farm

Park Pale

Brickyard
Farm

Lugmarsh
Farm

Lugmarsh
Plantation

Knowl

1

Moor's
Farm

CUNNAGE LANE

30

Park Pale

Park
Pale

84   A   B   85   C   D   86   E   F

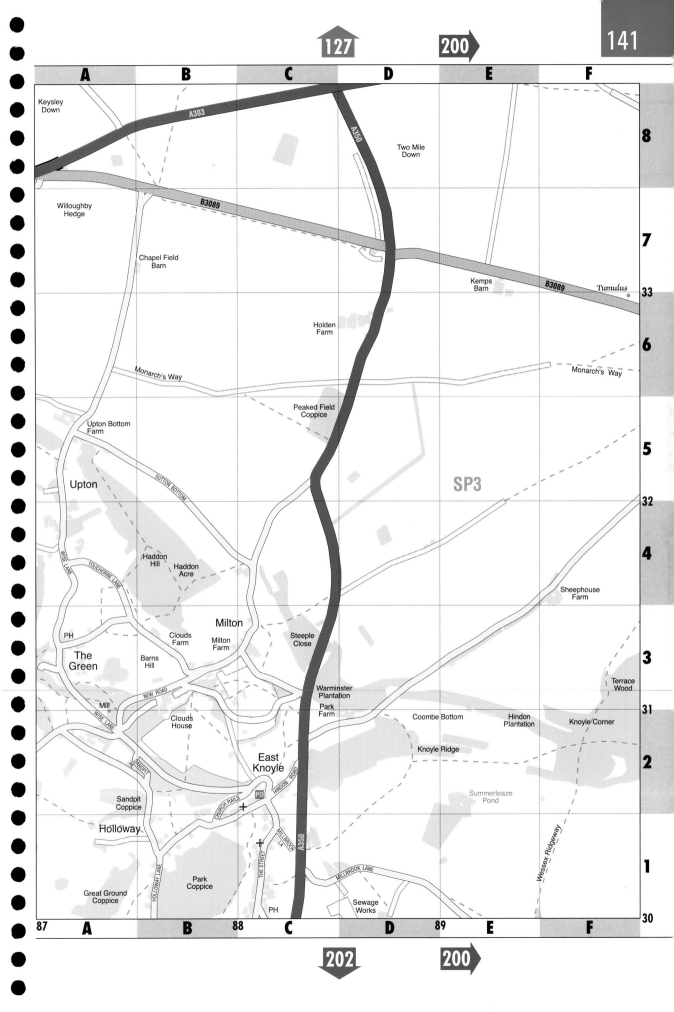

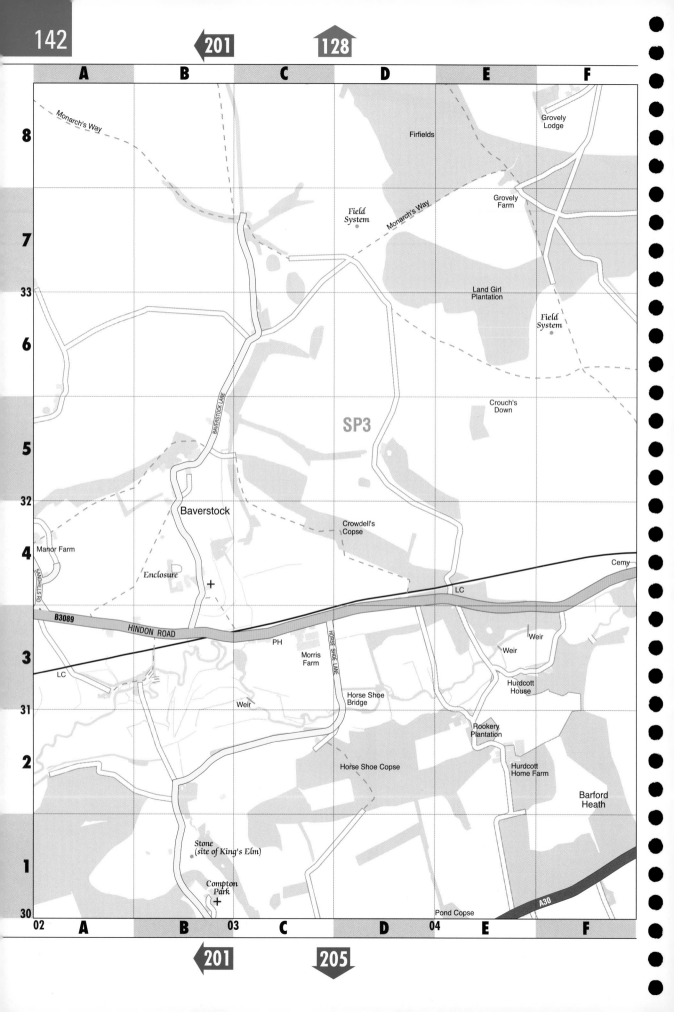

A   B   C   D   E   F

8

Monarch's Way

Grovely
Lodge

Firfields

Field
System

Monarch's Way

7

Grovely
Farm

33

Land Girl
Plantation

6

Field
System

Crouch's
Down

BAVERSTOCK LANE

SP3

5

32

Baverstock

Crowdell's
Copse

Manor Farm

4

Cemy

SANDHILLS RD

Enclosure

LC

B3089   HINDON ROAD

PH

Weir

Weir

Morris
Farm

HORSE SHOE LANE

Hurdcott
House

3

LC

Weir

Horse Shoe
Bridge

31

Rookery
Plantation

2

Horse Shoe Copse

Hurdcott
Home Farm

Barford
Heath

Stone
(site of King's Elm)

1

Compton
Park

A30

30

Pond Copse

02   A   B   03   C   D   04   E   F

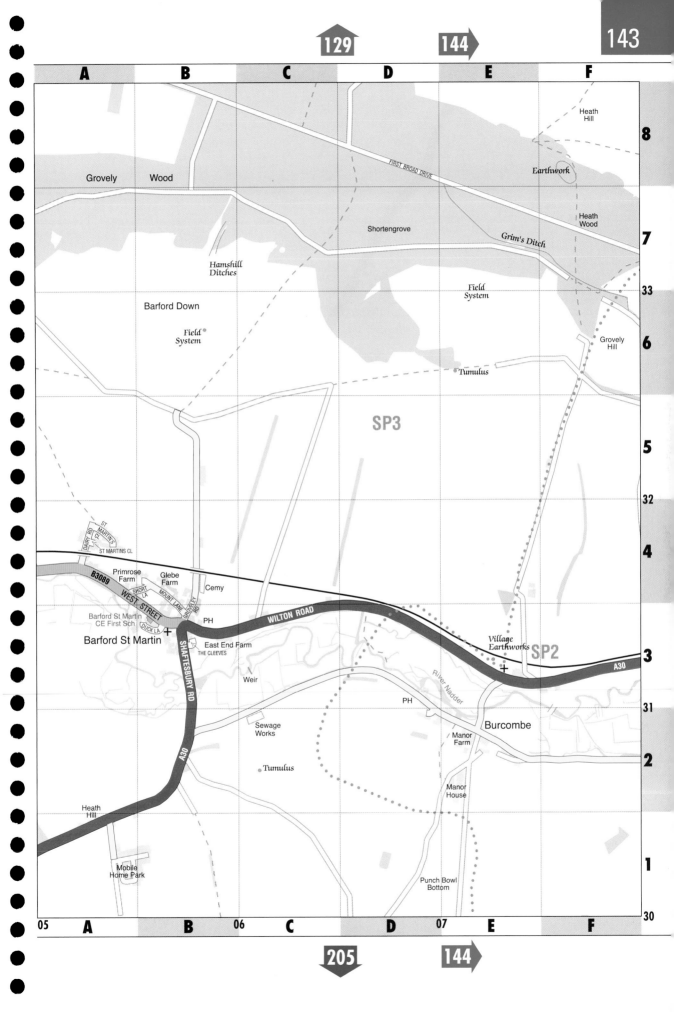

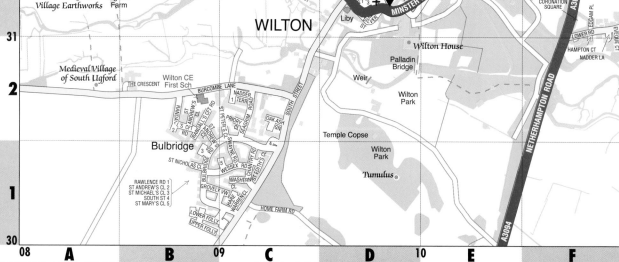

A   B   C   D   E   F

8
Heath
Hill
Custom
Bottom

SP3

7
Heath
Wood
FIRST BROAD
DR
Sewage
Works

33
Grovely
Down

Grim's
Ditch

6
Grovely
Hill

Folly
Farm

Field
System

Chilhampton
Farm

River Wylye

5
Pelly
Farm

Elizabeth
RD
OLIVER RD
PHILIP
RD
WISHFORD RD

Ford's Folly

The Avenue

32
SP2

Kingsway

P&R

MARCHMENT CL
THORNTON CR

4
Ditchampton

Wilton CE
Middle Sch

THE HOLLOWS
WATER DITCHAMPTON

ST JOHN'S CT
VICTORIA ROAD
VICTORIA CL

Burdens
Ball
Farm
PRIMROSE HL
KINGS GATE
FAIR
VW RD
KINGS GATE

Bridge
End

Erskine Barracks

Fugglestone
St Peter

FUGGLESTONE
MAPLE CR

Wilton
Carpet
Factory

Weir

WILEY TR

WARMINSTER RD
QUEEN ST
KING STREET

A36

3
Ugford

A30
SHORTLANDS
Cemy

SHAFTESBURY ROAD
SADDLERS MEAD

WEST ST
River Nadder

PO
RUSSELL ST
CASTLE ST
NORTH STREET
CHURCHILL CT
RIVERSIDE
Wilton
Sh Village
First
Bridge
MINSTER ST
A30

SALISBURY ROAD

WILTON RD

CORONATION
SQUARE

EDGAM PL
LOWER RD
HAMPTON CT
NADDER LA

ELY QUE CT

A3094

Ugford
Farm

Village Earthworks

WILTON

Liby
SILVER ST

Wilton House

Palladin
Bridge

Wilton
Park

NETHERHAMPTON ROAD

31
Medieval Village
of South Ugford

THE CRESCENT

Wilton CE
First Sch

BURCOMBE LANE
NADDER
TERR
RANDALL'S CFT RD
ST PETER'S CL
PRIORY CL
SEAGRIM RD
CL

OAK ASH
GM

SOUTH STREET

Weir

Wilton
Park

2

RANDALL'S CFT
RD
ST ANDREW'S CL
ST MICHAEL'S CL

ST NICHOLAS CL
BILBRIDGE
WESSEX CL
GROVELY VW
WASHERN CL
WASHERN
CHANTRY RD
ST EDITH'S CL

LOWER FOLLY
UPPER FOLLY

HOME FARM RD

Temple Copse

Wilton
Park

Tumulus

1
Bulbridge

RAWLENCE RD 1
ST ANDREW'S CL 2
ST MICHAEL'S CL 3
SOUTH ST 4
ST MARY'S CL 5

30

08   A   B   09   C   D   10   E   F

D3
1 GREYHOUND LA
2 PENNY'S LA
3 KINGSBURY SQ
4 CASTLE KEEP

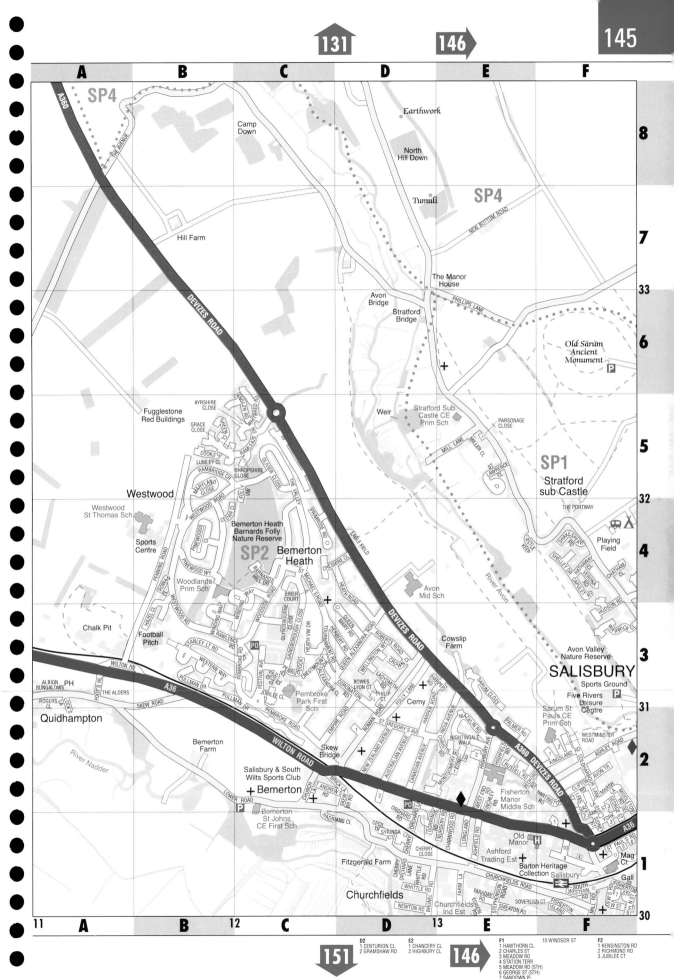

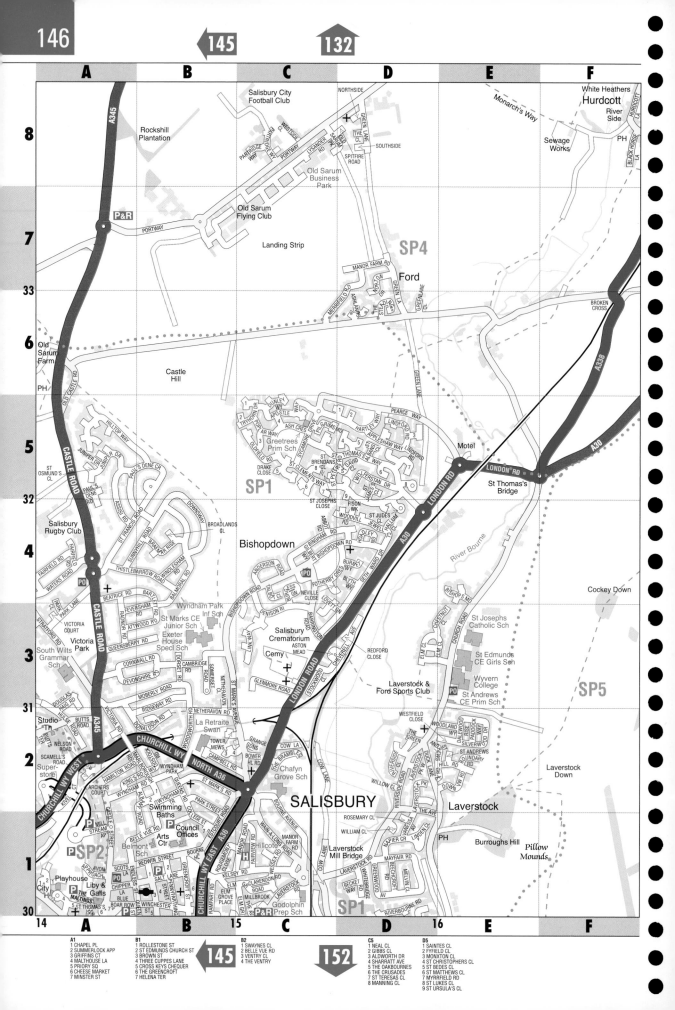

145
132

A1
1 CHAPEL PL
2 SUMMERLOCK APP
3 GRIFFINS CT
4 MALTHOUSE LA
5 PRIORY SQ
6 CHEESE MARKET
7 MINSTER ST

B1
1 ROLLESTONE ST
2 ST EDMUNDS CHURCH ST
3 BROWN ST
4 THREE CUPPES LANE
5 CROSS KEYS CHEQUER
6 THE GREENCROFT
7 HELENA TER

B2
1 SWAYNES CL
2 BELLE VUE RD
3 VENTRY CL
4 THE VENTRY

C5
1 NEAL CL
2 GIBBS CL
3 ALDWORTH DR
4 SHARRATT AVE
5 THE OAKBOURNES
6 THE CRUSADES
7 ST TERESAS CL
8 MANNING CL

D5
1 SAINTES CL
2 FYFIELD CL
3 MONXTON CL
4 ST CHRISTOPHERS CL
5 ST BEDES CL
6 ST MATTHEWS CL
7 MYRRFIELD RD
8 ST LUKES CL
9 ST URSULA'S CL

145
152

A B C D E F

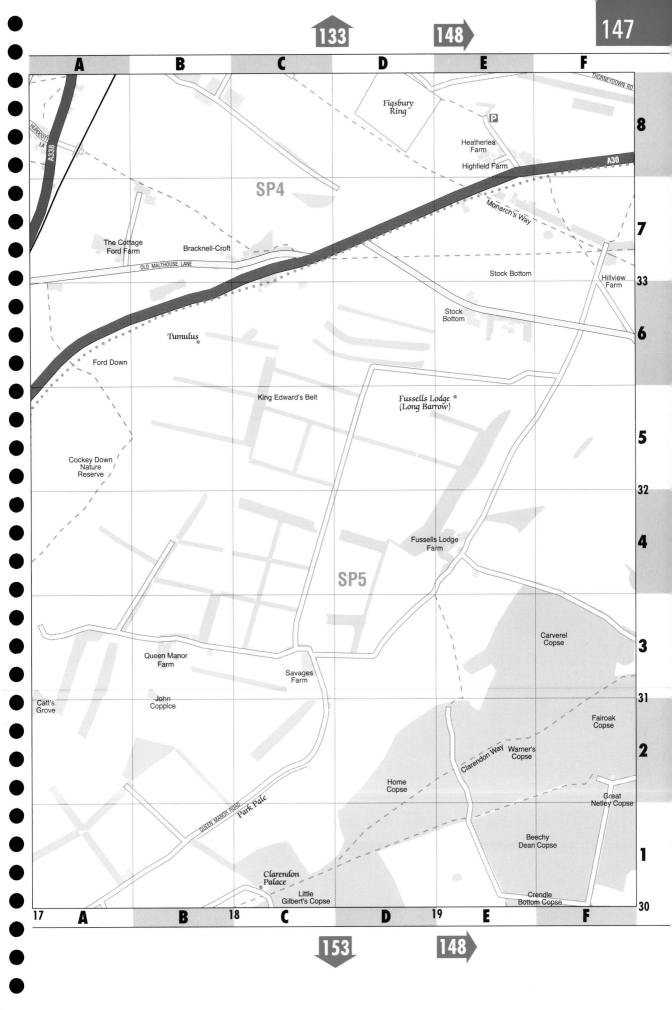

THORNEYDOWN RD.

Figsbury
Ring

8

P

Heatherlea
Farm

Highfield Farm

A30

SP4

7

The Cottage
Ford Farm

Bracknell-Croft

Monarch's Way

OLD MALTHOUSE LANE

Stock Bottom

Hillview
Farm

33

HURCOTT LA

A338

Stock
Bottom

6

Tumulus

Ford Down

King Edward's Belt

Fussells Lodge
(Long Barrow)

5

Cockey Down
Nature
Reserve

32

Fussells Lodge
Farm

4

SP5

Carverel
Copse

3

Queen Manor
Farm

Savages
Farm

Catt's
Grove

John
Coppice

31

Fairoak
Copse

Clarendon Way

Warner's
Copse

2

Home
Copse

Great
Netley Copse

QUEEN MANOR ROAD

Park Pale

Beechy
Dean Copse

1

Clarendon
Palace

Little
Gilbert's Copse

Crendle
Bottom Copse

30

17 A B 18 C D 19 E F

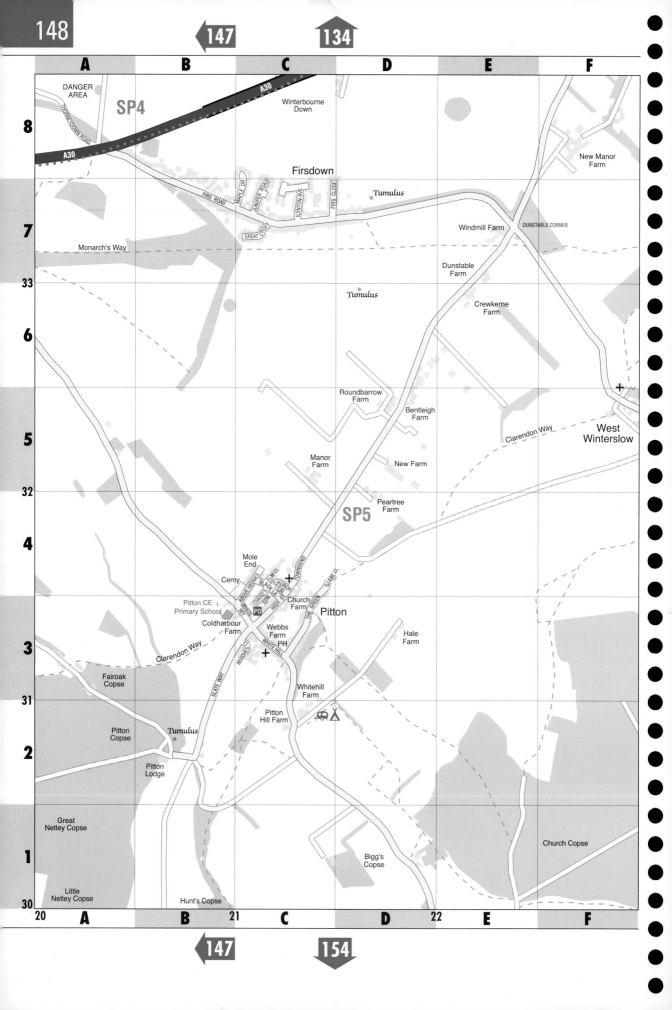

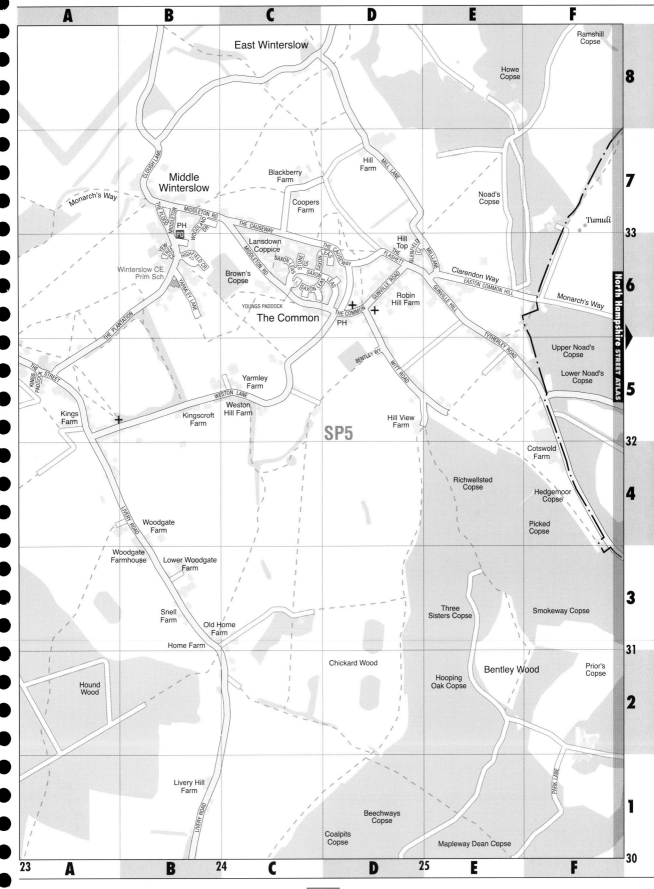

East Winterslow

Ramshill
Copse

Howe
Copse

Middle
Winterslow

Blackberry
Farm

Hill
Farm

MILL LANE

Noad's
Copse

Monarch's Way

CLOUGH LANE

Coopers
Farm

MIDDLETON RD

THE FLOOD

THE CAUSEWAY

PH

YEW TREE CL

PO

HIGHFIELD CR

WOODLAND DR

Lansdown
Coppice

THE CAUSEWAY

THE LEAS

Hill
Top

Tumuli

Winterslow CE
Prim Sch

MIDDLETON RD

Brown's
Copse

SAXON LEAS

STONE CL

SAXON LEAS

THE FLASHETT

GLENFIELD

MILL LANE

Clarendon Way

YARMLEY LANE

YOUNGS PADDOCK

SAXON LEAS

THE COMMON

GUNVILLE ROAD

Robin
Hill Farm

Easton Common Hill

GUNVILLE HILL

Monarch's Way

The Common

PH

Upper Noad's
Copse

THE PLANTATION

Yarmley
Farm

BENTLEY WY

WITT ROAD

TYTHERLEY ROAD

Lower Noad's
Copse

KINGS PADDOCK

THE STREET

Weston
Hill Farm

WESTON LANE

Hill View
Farm

Kings
Farm

Kingscroft
Farm

SP5

Cotswold
Farm

Richwellsted
Copse

Hedgemoor
Copse

LIVERY ROAD

Woodgate
Farm

Picked
Copse

Woodgate
Farmhouse

Lower Woodgate
Farm

Snell
Farm

Old Home
Farm

Chickard Wood

Three
Sisters Copse

Smokeway Copse

Prior's
Copse

Home Farm

Bentley Wood

Hound
Wood

Hooping
Oak Copse

PARK LANE

Livery Hill
Farm

LIVERY ROAD

Beechways
Copse

Mapleway Dean Copse

Coalpits
Copse

8
7
33
6
5
32
4
31
3
2
1
30

23   A   B   24   C   D   25   E   F

205
144
151

| | A | B | C | D | E | F |

8

Home Farm
HOME FARM ROAD
South Hills Sch
The Kennels

A3094
NETHERHAMPTON ROAD
PH

Warren Down

SP2

7

29

Hare Warren

Neale's Barrow

6

OLD SHAFTESBURY DROVE

Netherhampton Down

Tumuli

Salisbury Racecourse

5

28

Down Barn

North Down

4

PORTFIELD ROAD

DROVE LANE

SP5

3

Manor Farm

27

2

Coombe Farm

STRATFORD TONY ROAD

DROVE CL

A354

MARSH LA

Manor Farm

Manor Farm

Stratford Tony

Coombe Bridge
PH
PO

1

MILL LANE

Throope Manor House

Cranbourne Farm

OLD BLANDFORD RD

THORNE HOMINGTON RD

Coombe Bissett

Ragland's Hill

CHURCH LANE

BLANDFORD RD

Coombe Bissett CE Prim Sch

26

| 08 | A | | B | 09 | C | | D | 10 | E | | F |

205
156

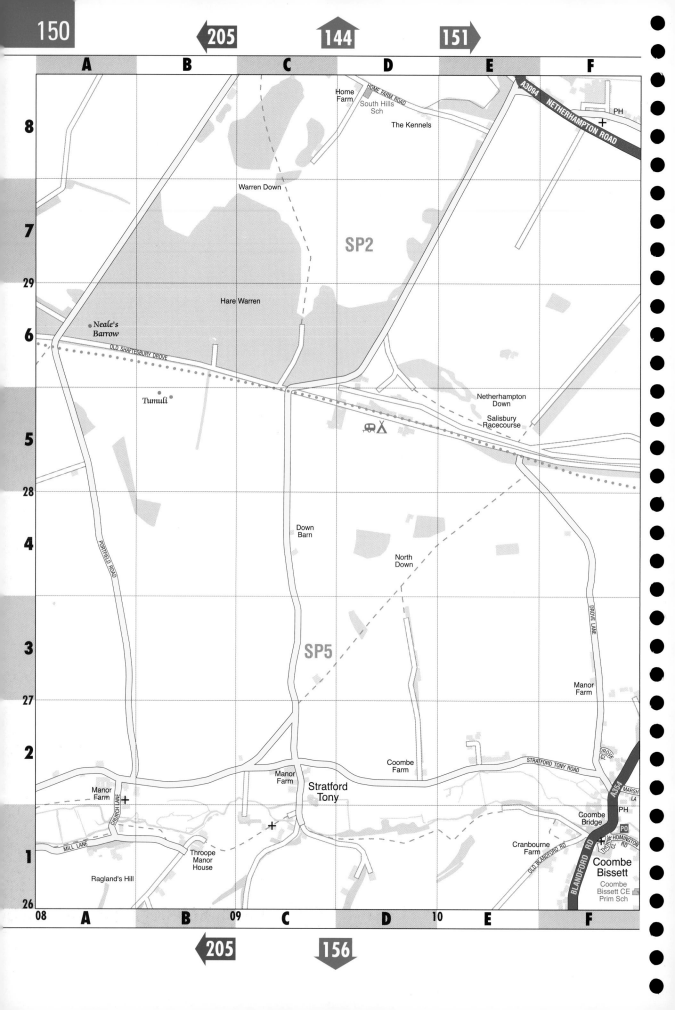

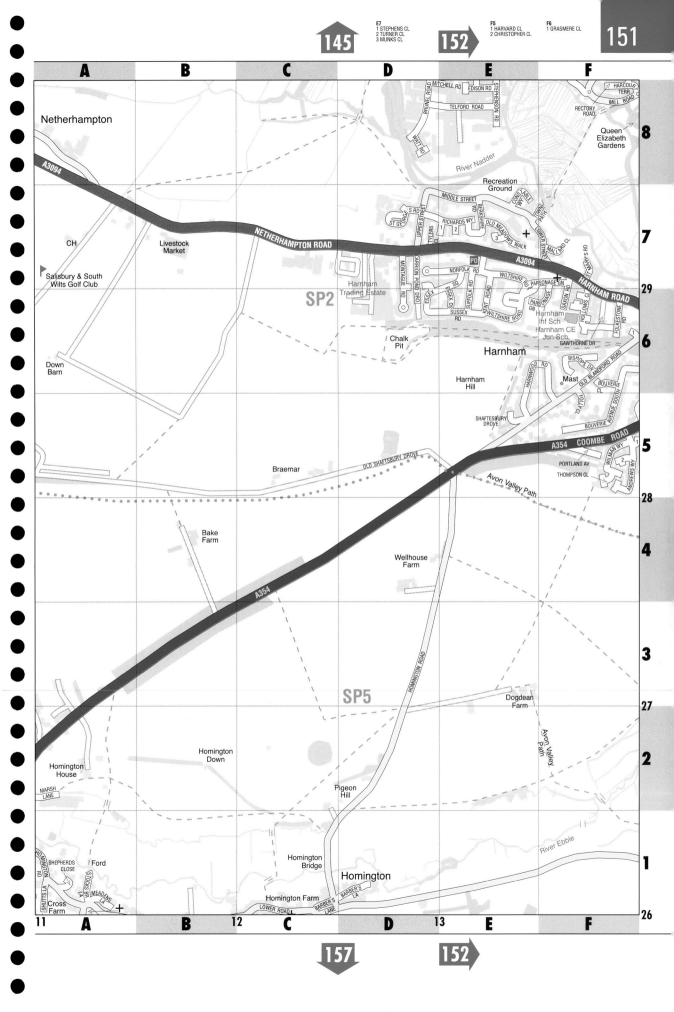

145

E7
1 STEPHENS CL
2 TURNER CL
3 MUNKS CL

152

F5
1 HARVARD CL
2 CHRISTOPHER CL

F6
1 GRASMERE CL

151

A   **B**   **C**   **D**   **E**   **F**

HARCOURT TERR
MILL ROAD
MITCHELL RD
EDISON RD
BRUNEL ROAD
TELFORD ROAD
STEPHENSON RD
RECTORY ROAD

Netherhampton

8

WATT RD

River Nadder

Queen Elizabeth Gardens

A3094

Recreation Ground

MIDDLE STREET

CONSTABLE WY

TOWN PATH

7

CH

Livestock Market

NETHERHAMPTON ROAD

S RD
S GEORGE
SPEAR STREET
TYLERS
RICHARDS WY
1 2
BERKSHIRE RD
OLD MEADOWS WALK
3
LOWER STREET
LRD CL

Salisbury & South Wilts Golf Club

A3094

HARNHAM ROAD
ST MARY'S RD

29

SP2

Harnham Trading Estate

PO
NORFOLK RD
WILTSHIRE RD
PARSONAGE GN
SAXON RD
HOLLOWS CL
FOLKESTONE

MONTAGUE RD
CARRION POND DRO
ESSEX RD
ESSEX SQ
SUFFOLK RD
KENT RD
WILTSHIRE ROAD
PARSONAGE GN
SUSSEX RD

Harnham Inf Sch
Harnham CE Jun Sch

6

Down Barn

Chalk Pit

Harnham

GAWTHORNE DR

Harnham Hill

HARNWOOD RD
BISHOPS DR
OLD BLANDFORD ROAD
Mast

BOUVERIE CL

SHAFTESBURY DROVE

TO ATTLE
BOUVERIE AVENUE SOUTH

A354 COOMBE ROAD

5

Braemar

OLD SHAFTSBURY DROVE

Avon Valley Path

WILMAN WY
1 2
ANDREWS WY

PORTLAND AV
THOMPSON CL

28

Bake Farm

4

A354

Wellhouse Farm

HOMINGTON ROAD

3

SP5

Dogdean Farm

27

Avon Valley Path

Homington Down

2

Homington House

MARSH LANE

Pigeon Hill

River Ebble

1

HOMINGTON RD
SHEPHERDS CLOSE
Ford
STOCKS BR LA
MEADENS LA
SHUTTS LA

Homington Bridge

Homington

Cross Farm

Homington Farm
LOWER ROAD
BARBER'S LANE
BARBER'S LA

26

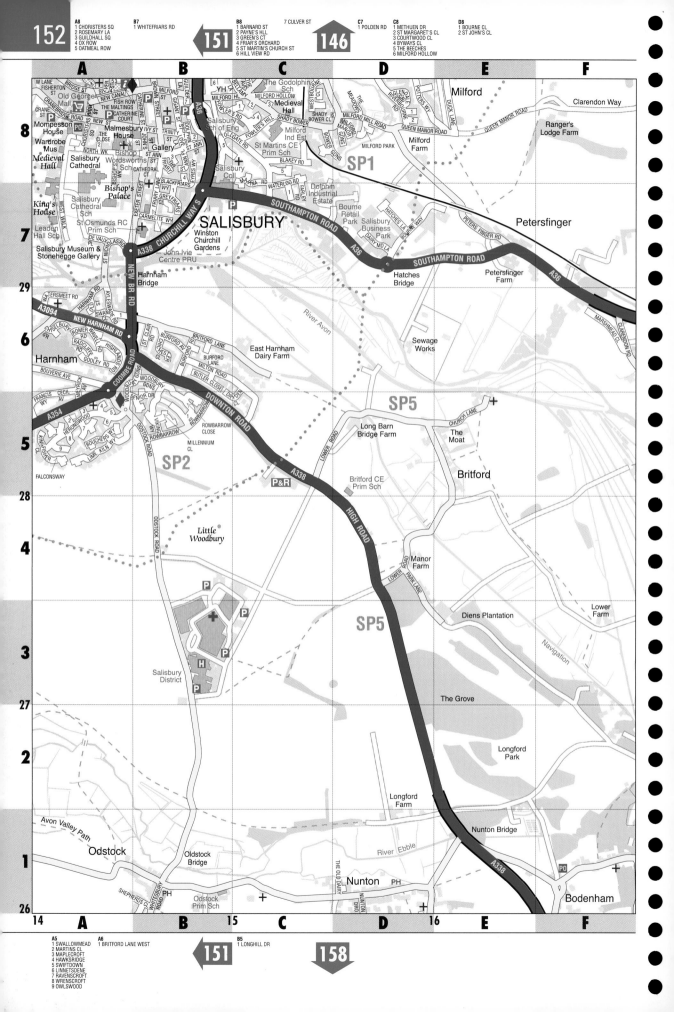

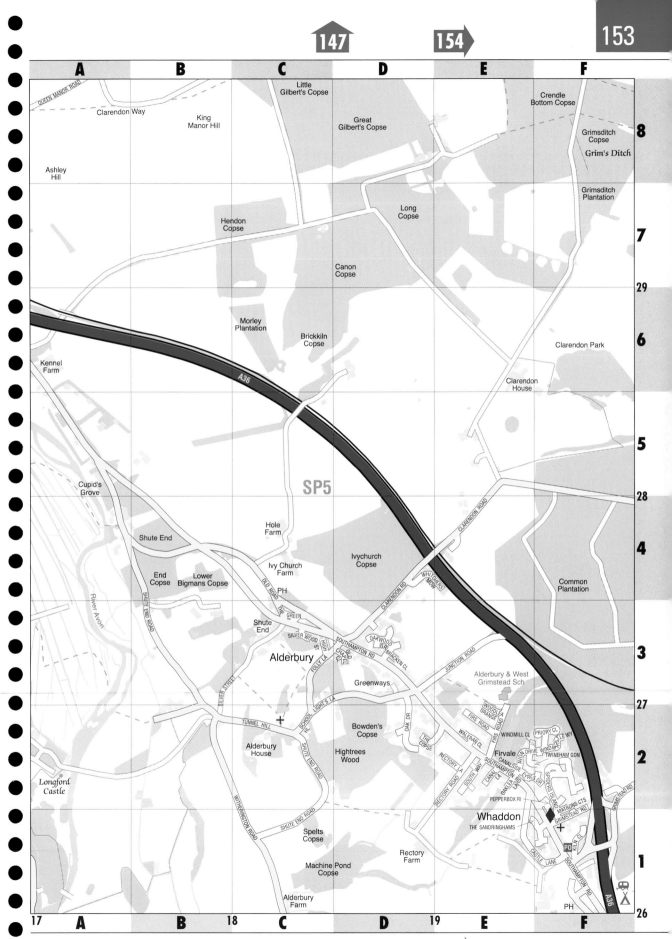

A   B   C   D   E   F

8
7
29
6
5
28
4
3
27
2
1
26

QUEEN MANOR ROAD
Clarendon Way
King Manor Hill
Little Gilbert's Copse
Great Gilbert's Copse
Crendle Bottom Copse
Grimsditch Copse
Grim's Ditch
Ashley Hill
Grimsditch Plantation
Hendon Copse
Long Copse
Canon Copse
Clarendon Park
Morley Plantation
Brickkiln Copse
Kennel Farm
A36
Clarendon House
Clarendon Road
SP5
Cupid's Grove
Hole Farm
Ivychurch Copse
Common Plantation
Shute End
End Copse
Lower Bigmans Copse
Ivy Church Farm
OLD ROAD
PH
THE GREEN
Shute End
River Avon
SHUTE END ROAD
SILVER WOOD ST
HIGH
FOLLY LA
Alderbury
SOUTHAMPTON RD
CHAPEL LA
CL
OAKWOOD GRI
BRACKEN CL
WHITCHERS MDW
Clarendon Road
JUNCTION ROAD
Alderbury & West Grimstead Sch
SILVER STREET
Greenways
OAK DR
THE COPSE
WOODLEA GRANGE
FIRS ROAD
FIRS ROAD
WINDMILL CL
PRIORY CL
LE WY
TUNNEL HILL
SCHOOL
LIGHT'S LA
SHUTE END ROAD
Bowden's Copse
Firvale
AVON DRIVE
TWINEHAM GDN
WINDM
Alderbury House
Hightrees Wood
WALERAN CL
CANALSIDE
EYRES DR
RECTORY LA
SOUTHAMPTON
CANAL LA
OAKLEA
SPIDERS ISLAND
MATRONS CTS
GRIMSTEAD RD
WITHERINGTON ROAD
RECTORY ROAD
SOUTH WAY
Whaddon
THE SANDRINGHAMS
PEPPERBOX RI
PO
CASTLE LANE
GRIMSTEAD RD
KILN CL
SOUTHAMPTON RD
Longford Castle
Spelts Copse
Rectory Farm
Machine Pond Copse
Alderbury Farm
PH
A36

153
148

A **B** **C** **D** **E** **F**

Little
Netley Copse

Crendle
Bottom

Grimsditch
Copse

8

Hunt's
Copse

Bests
Farm

Farley

All Saints
CE Prim Sch

PITTON ROAD

PARSONAGE HILL

CHURCH ROAD

PH

THE STREET

OAK CL

PENNY'S LA

BEN LANE

7

LUCEWOOD LANE

Knightwood Farm

Woodfields
Farm

29

Farley
Copse

March
Farm

Bracken
Farm

Adams Mere
Farm

6

The
Plantation

Nightwood Copse

Pitchers
Farm

Brown's
Copse

GRIMSTEAD ROAD

Hazel Hill Wood

5

Upper Brickwood
Farm

Old Brickwood
Farm

SP5

Hazel Hill
Farm

Lyvers
Farm

Meadow
End

Pope's Bottom

CLARENDON ROAD

Furzy Close Copse

Whitehouse
Farm

Drove
End

Horse
Close Copse

Dairy
Farm

Whitehouse
Farm

East
Grimstead

28

4

LONG DROVE

GREEN DROVE

Pucks Hill
Farm

Walden
House

Walden
Farm

BUTTER FURLONG ROAD

Manor
Farm

3

West Common
Plantation

Nursery
Farm

27

Crockford
Copse

CROCKFORD ROAD

CHAPEL HILL

GREENFIELDS

Whaddon
Common

GRIMSTEAD ROAD

Emmotts
Farm

Hill
Top

Hedge
End

West
Grimstead

CHURCH STREET

Thicket
Copse

Redlynch
Plantation

2

Oakridge
Copse

WINDWHISTLE LANE

Broadmead
Farm

Gallows Hayes
Copse

GRIMSTEAD ROAD

1

26

20 **A** **B** **21** **C** **D** **22** **E** **F**

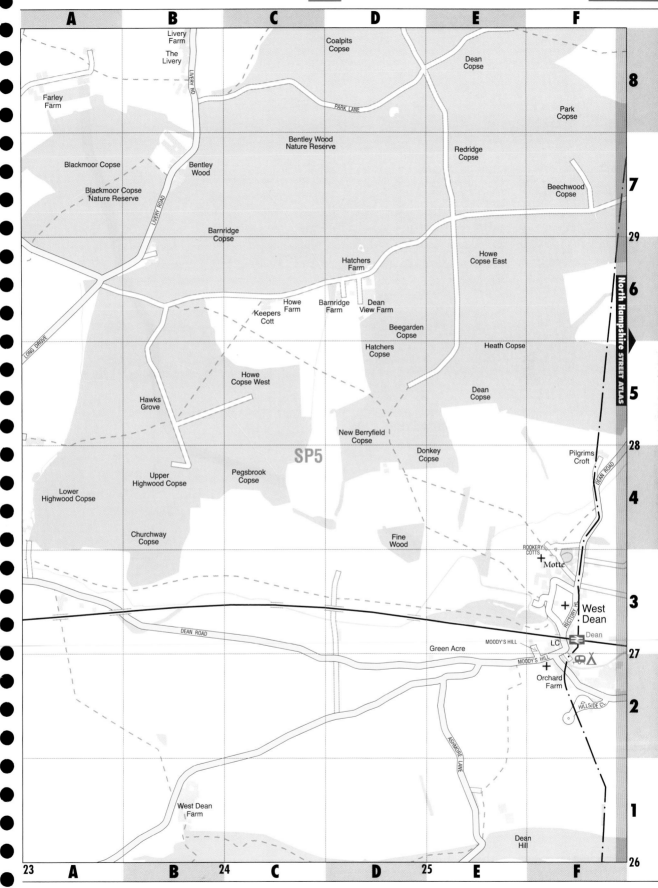

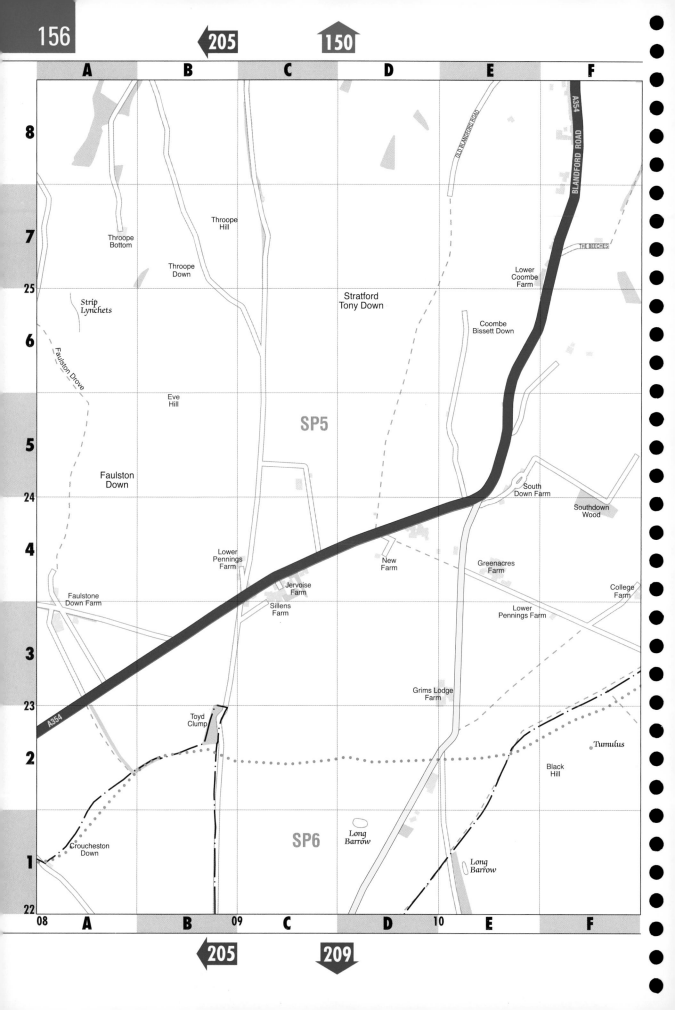

205 150

	A	B	C	D	E	F

8

7

Throope Hill

Throope Bottom

25

Throope Down

Strip Lynchets

6

Faulston Drove

Eve Hill

SP5

5

Faulston Down

24

4

Lower Pennings Farm

Jervoise Farm

New Farm

Sillens Farm

Faulstone Down Farm

3

A354

23

Toyd Clump

Grims Lodge Farm

Black Hill

Tumulus

2

Croucheston Down

SP6

Long Barrow

Long Barrow

1

22

OLD BLANDFORD ROAD

BLANDFORD ROAD

A354

THE BEECHES

Lower Coombe Farm

Stratford Tony Down

Coombe Bissett Down

South Down Farm

Southdown Wood

Greenacres Farm

Lower Pennings Farm

College Farm

205 209

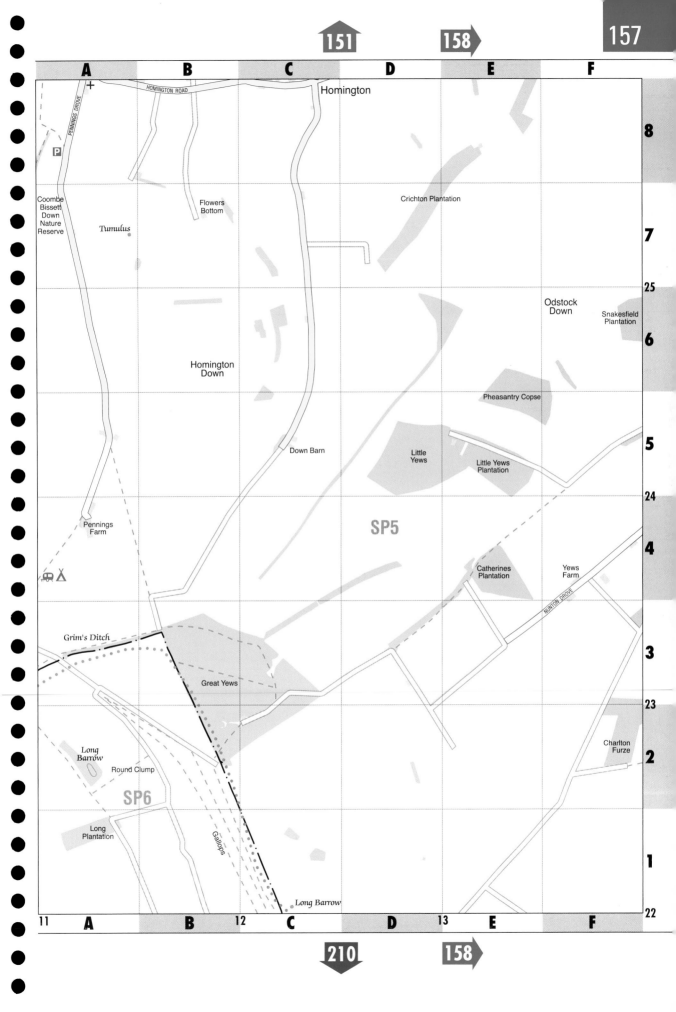

151
158

A **B** **C** **D** **E** **F**

Homington

HOMINGTON ROAD

PENNINGS DROVE

P

8

Coombe
Bissett
Down
Nature
Reserve

Flowers
Bottom

Crichton Plantation

Tumulus

7

25

Odstock
Down

Snakesfield
Plantation

6

Homington
Down

Pheasantry Copse

Down Barn

Little
Yews

Little Yews
Plantation

5

24

SP5

Pennings
Farm

4

Catherines
Plantation

Yews
Farm

NUNTON DROVE

Grim's Ditch

3

Great Yews

23

Charlton
Furze

Long
Barrow

2

Round Clump

SP6

Long
Plantation

Gallops

1

Long Barrow

22

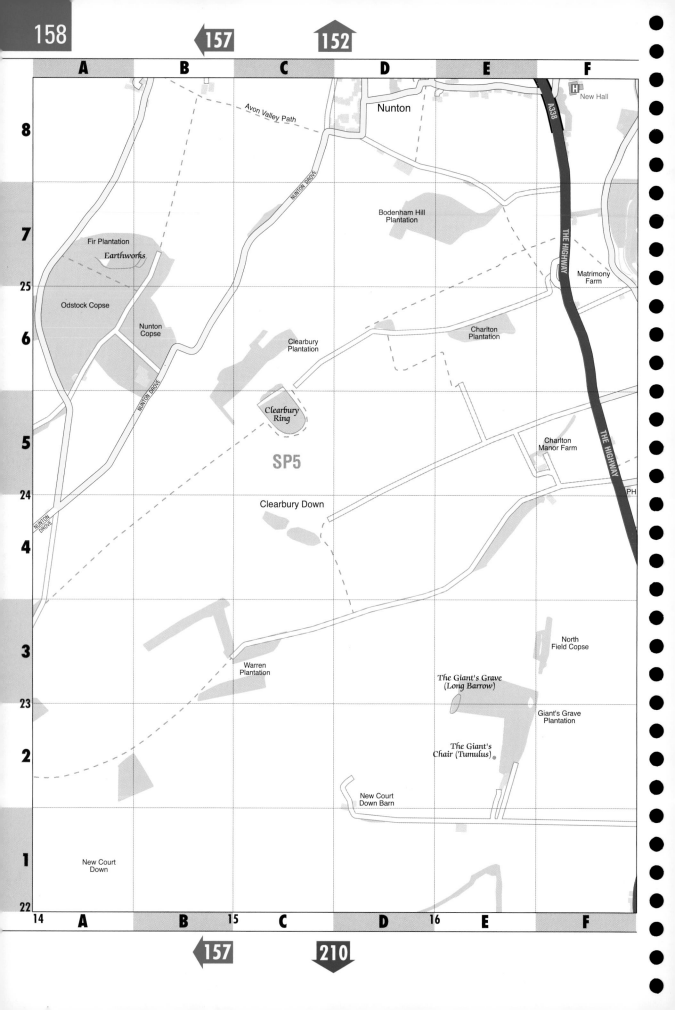

A   B   C   D   E   F

8

Nunton

New Hall

Avon Valley Path

NUNTON DROVE

A338

THE HIGHWAY

7

Fir Plantation

Earthworks

Bodenham Hill
Plantation

Matrimony
Farm

25

Odstock Copse

Nunton
Copse

Charlton
Plantation

6

Clearbury
Plantation

NUNTON DROVE

Clearbury
Ring

5

Charlton
Manor Farm

SP5

24

Clearbury Down

PH

4

NUNTON
DROVE

North
Field Copse

3

Warren
Plantation

The Giant's Grave
(Long Barrow)

Giant's Grave
Plantation

23

2

The Giant's
Chair (Tumulus)

New Court
Down Barn

1

New Court
Down

22

14   A   B   15   C   D   16   E   F

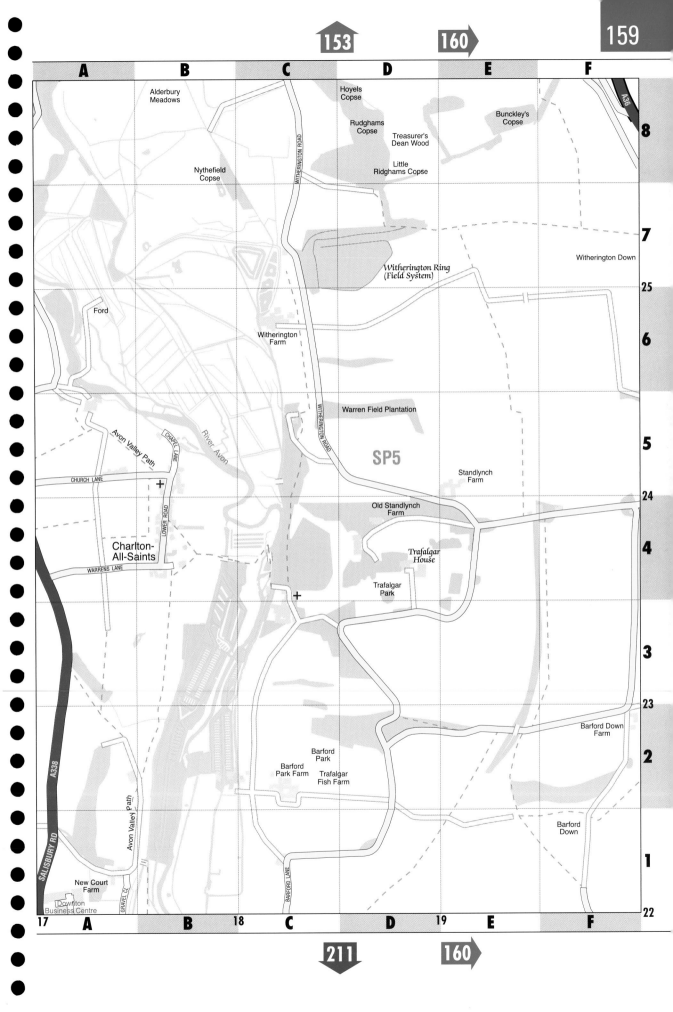

A B C D E F

8 7 25 6 5 24 4 3 23 2 1 22

Alderbury
Meadows

Hoyels
Copse

Rudghams
Copse

Treasurer's
Dean Wood

Bunckley's
Copse

Nythefield
Copse

Little
Ridghams Copse

A36

WITHERINGTON ROAD

Witherington Down

Witherington Ring
(Field System)

Ford

Witherington
Farm

Warren Field Plantation

SP5

Standlynch
Farm

Avon Valley Path

CHAPEL LANE

River Avon

LOWER ROAD

CHURCH LANE

Old Standlynch
Farm

Charlton-
All-Saints

WARRENS LANE

Trafalgar
House

Trafalgar
Park

Barford
Park

Barford Down
Farm

Barford
Park Farm

Trafalgar
Fish Farm

Barford
Down

A338

SALISBURY RD

Avon Valley Path

GRAVEL CL

BARFORD LANE

New Court
Farm

Downton
Business Centre

17 18 19 22

159
154

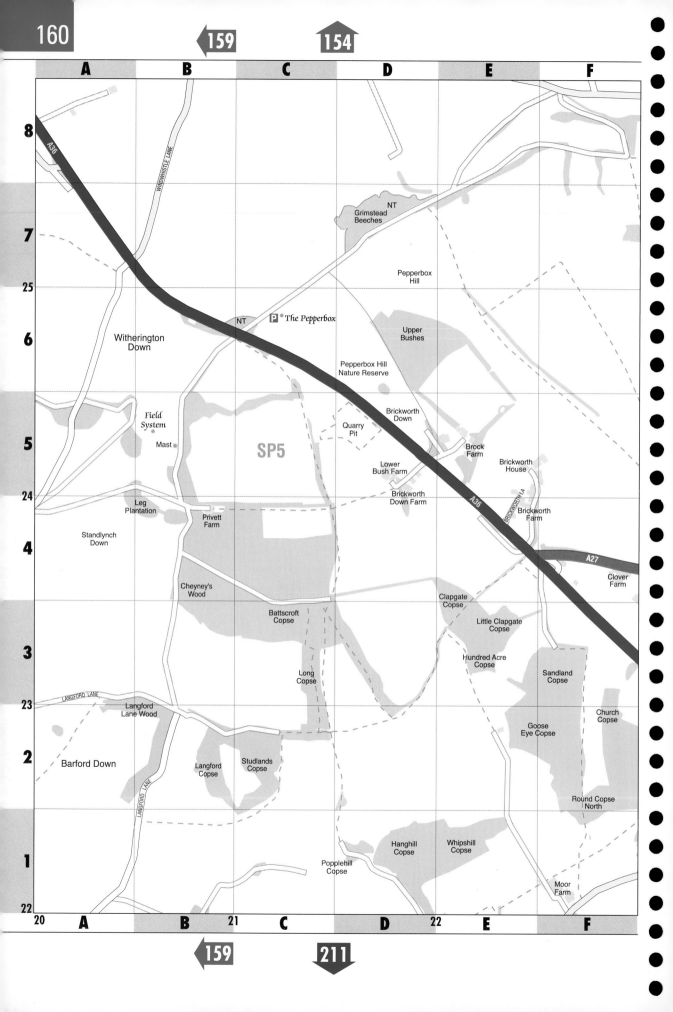

159
211

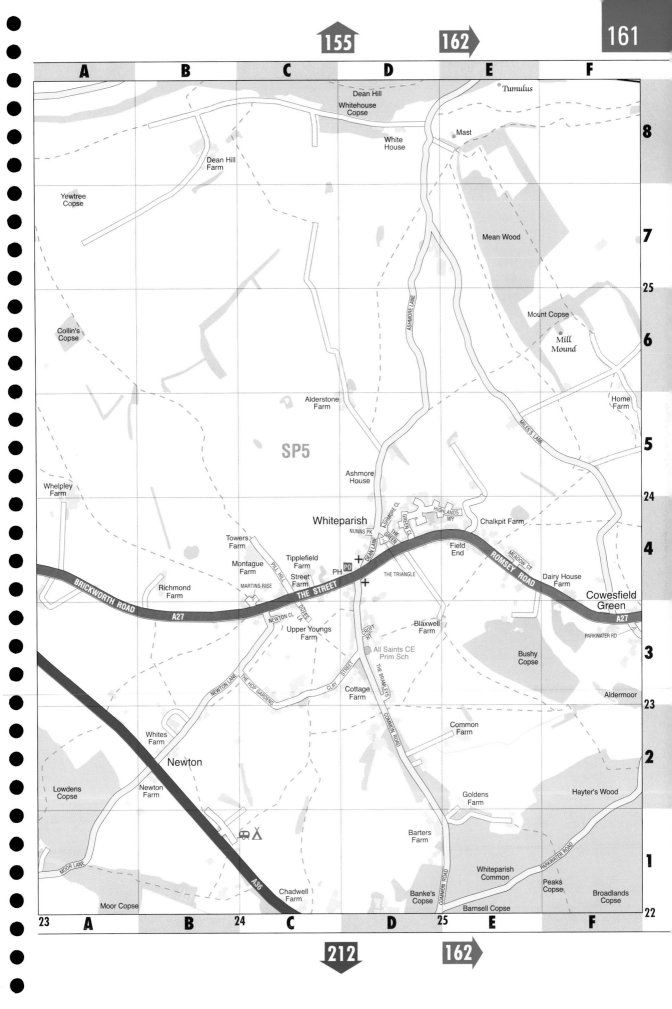

161

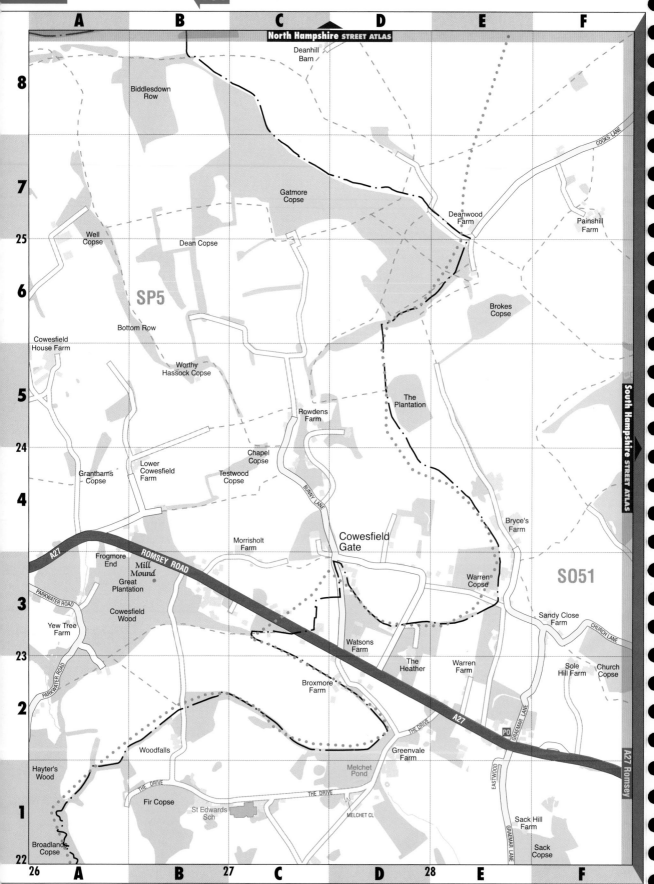

North Hampshire STREET ATLAS

South Hampshire STREET ATLAS

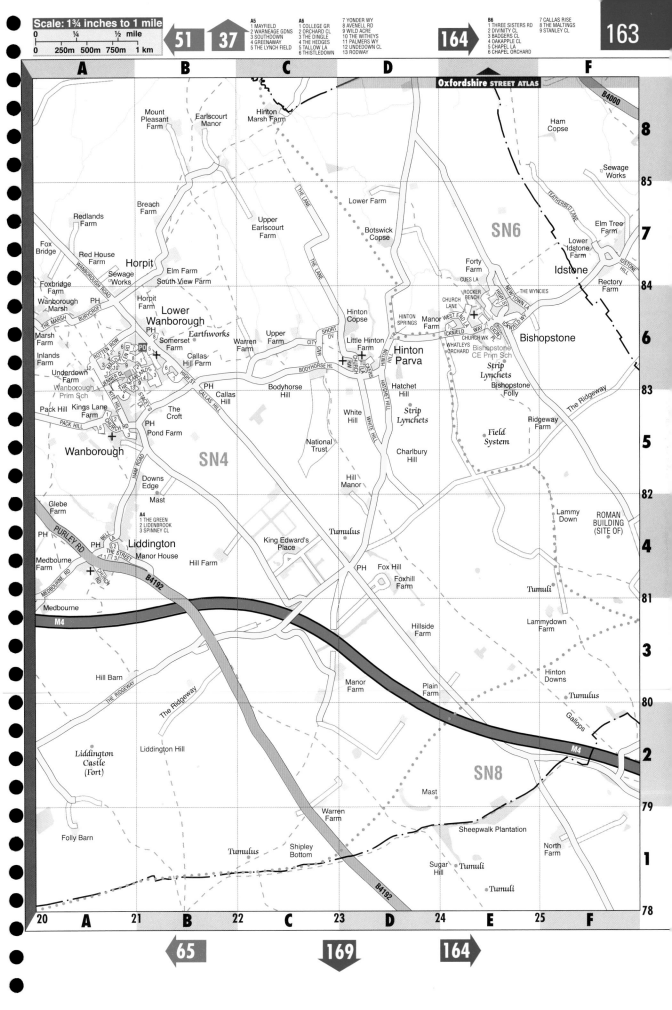

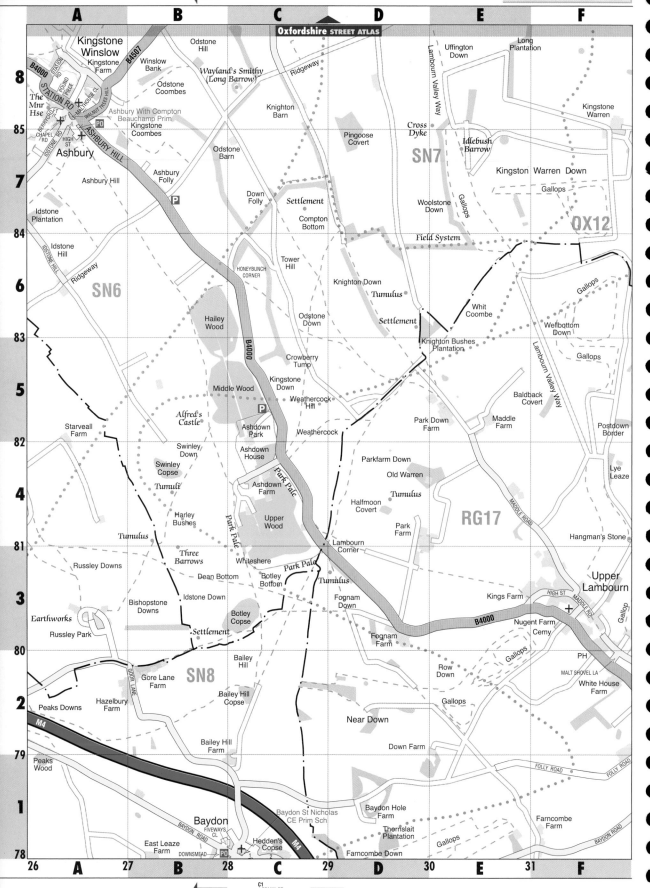

Scale: 1¾ inches to 1 mile

Oxfordshire STREET ATLAS

C1
1 ERMIN ST
2 FINCHES LA

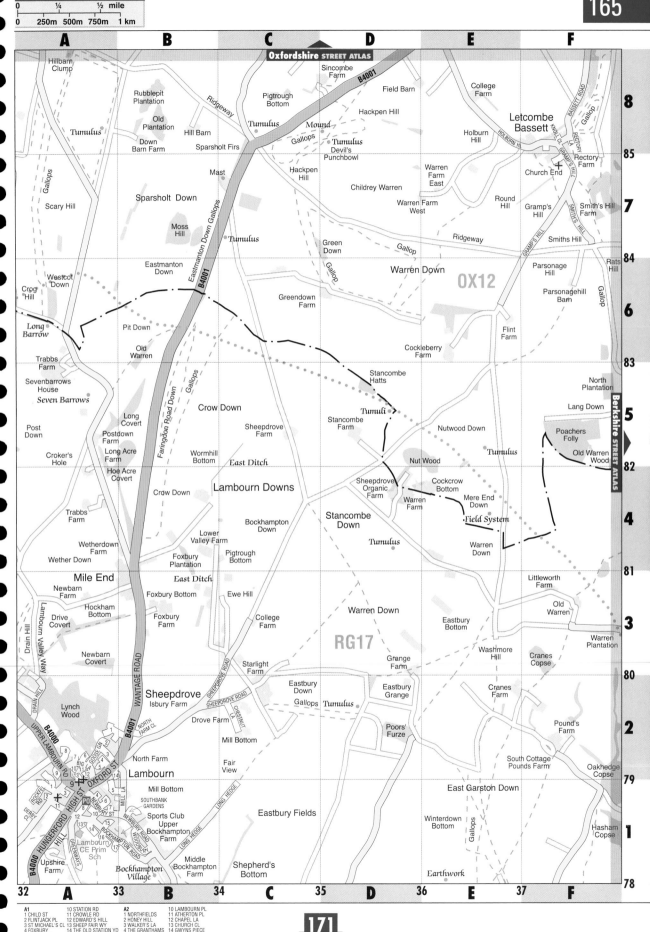

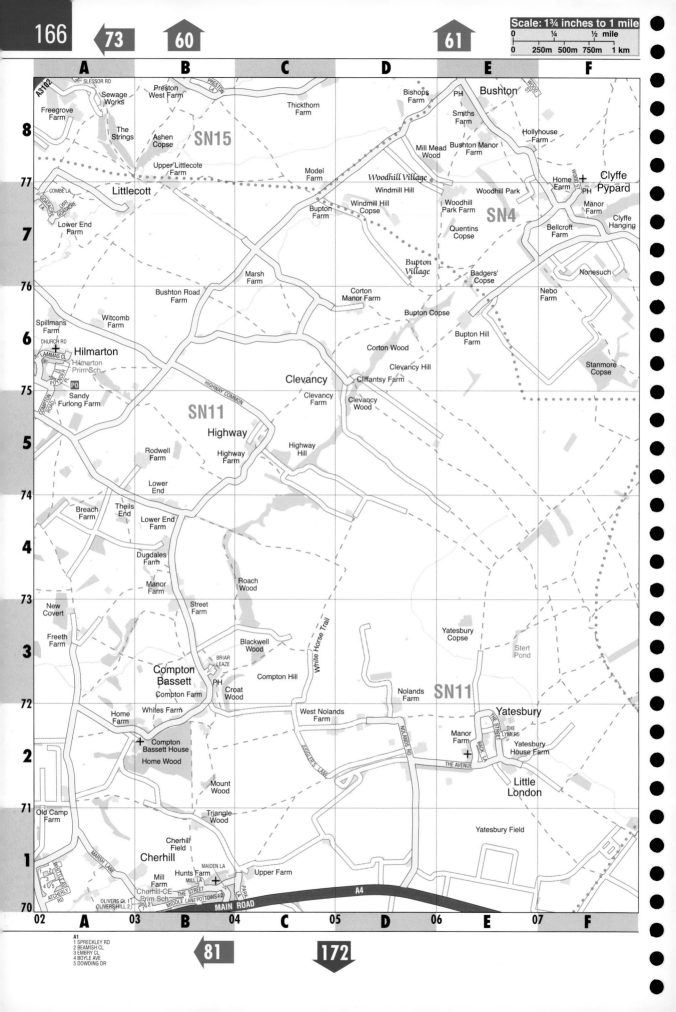

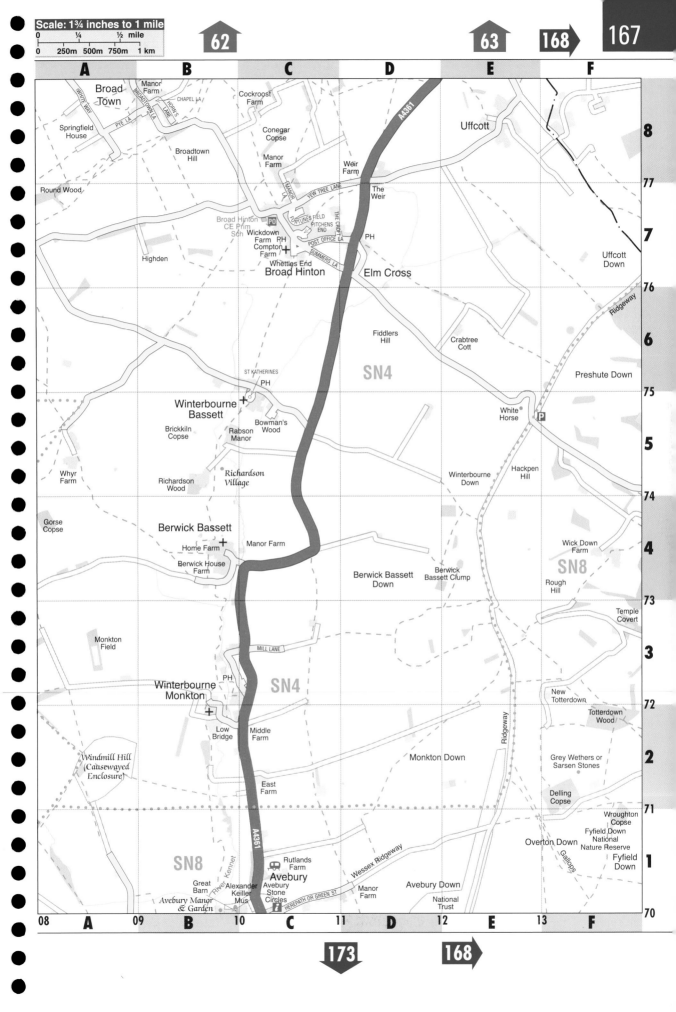

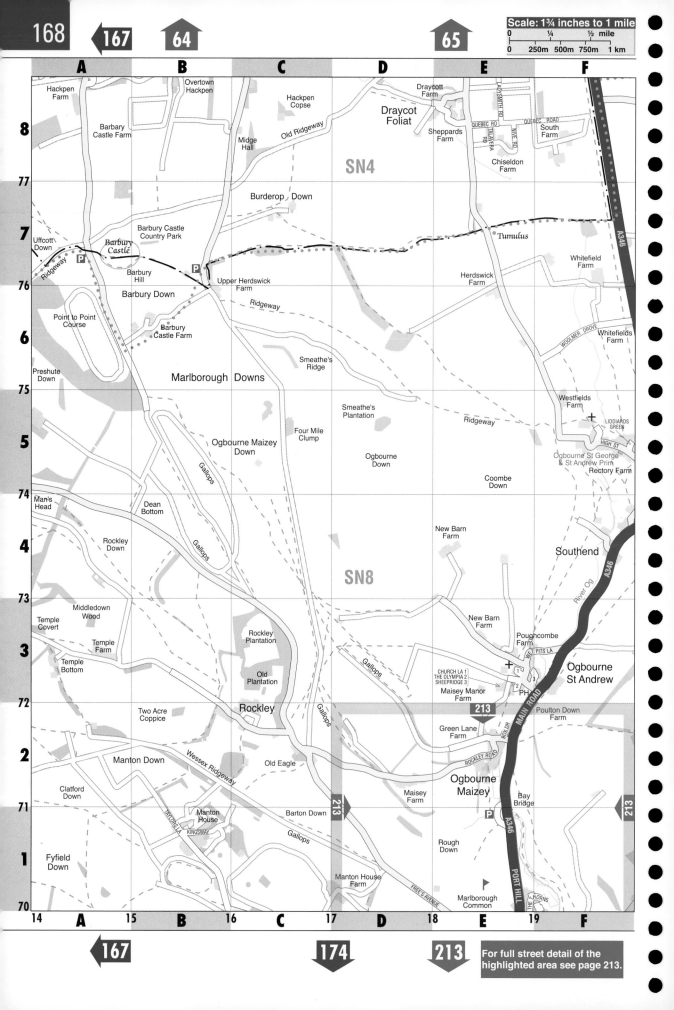

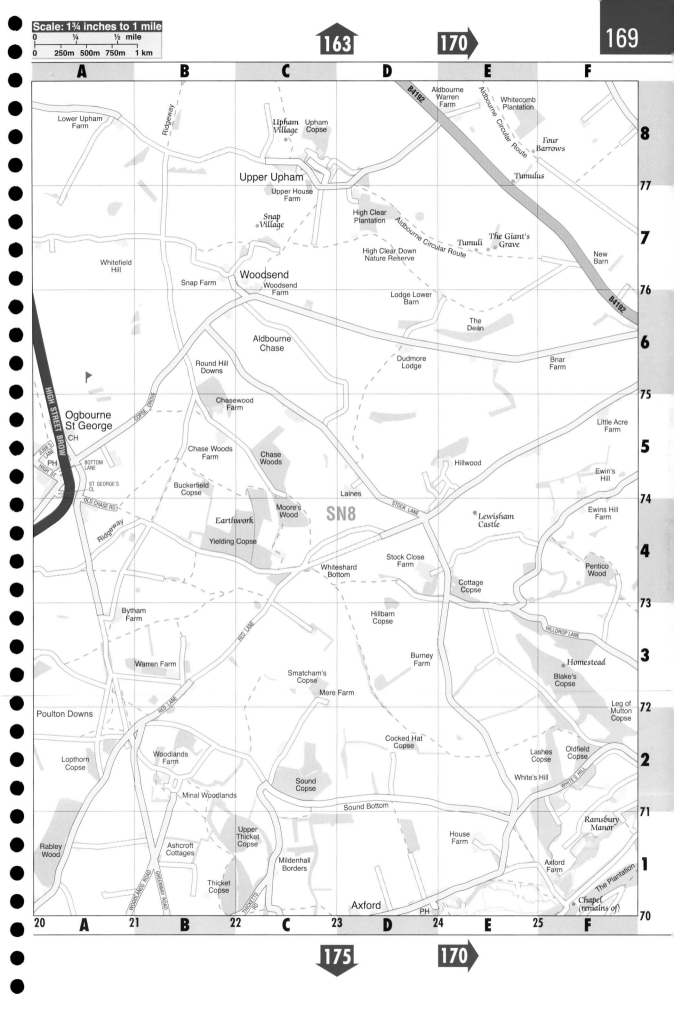

A   B   C   D   E   F

8
77
7
76
6
75
5
74
4
73
3
72
2
71
1
70

Lower Upham Farm

Ridgeway

Upham Village

Upham Copse

B4192

Aldbourne Warren Farm

Aldbourne Circular Route

Whitecomb Plantation

Four Barrows

Upper Upham

Upper House Farm

Snap Village

High Clear Plantation

Tumulus

Tumulus

The Giant's Grave

B4192

New Barn

Whitefield Hill

Snap Farm

Woodsend

Woodsend Farm

High Clear Down Nature Reserve

Aldbourne Circular Route

Lodge Lower Barn

The Dean

Aldbourne Chase

Dudmore Lodge

Briar Farm

Round Hill Downs

COPSE DROVE

Chasewood Farm

HIGH STREET BROW

Ogbourne St George

CH

JUBB'S LANE

PH

HIGH ST

BOTTOM LANE

ST GEORGE'S CL

Chase Woods Farm

Buckerfield Copse

Chase Woods

Hillwood

Little Acre Farm

Laines

STOCK LANE

Ewin's Hill

OLD CHASE RD

Ridgeway

Earthwork

Moore's Wood

SN8

Lewisham Castle

Ewins Hill Farm

Yielding Copse

Whiteshard Bottom

Stock Close Farm

Cottage Copse

Pentico Wood

Bytham Farm

RED LANE

Hillbarn Copse

HILLDROP LANE

Warren Farm

RED LANE

Smatcham's Copse

Mere Farm

Burney Farm

Homestead

Blake's Copse

Leg of Mutton Copse

Poulton Downs

Cocked Hat Copse

Lashes Copse

Oldfield Copse

Lopthorn Copse

Woodlands Farm

Sound Copse

White's Hill

WHITE'S HILL

Minal Woodlands

Sound Bottom

Ramsbury Manor

WOODLANDS ROAD

GREENWAY ROAD

Ashcroft Cottages

Upper Thicket Copse

House Farm

Axford Farm

Rabley Wood

Thicket Copse

THICKETS RD

Mildenhall Borders

Axford

PH

Chapel (remains of)

The Plantation

20   21   22   23   24   25

A   B   C   D   E   F

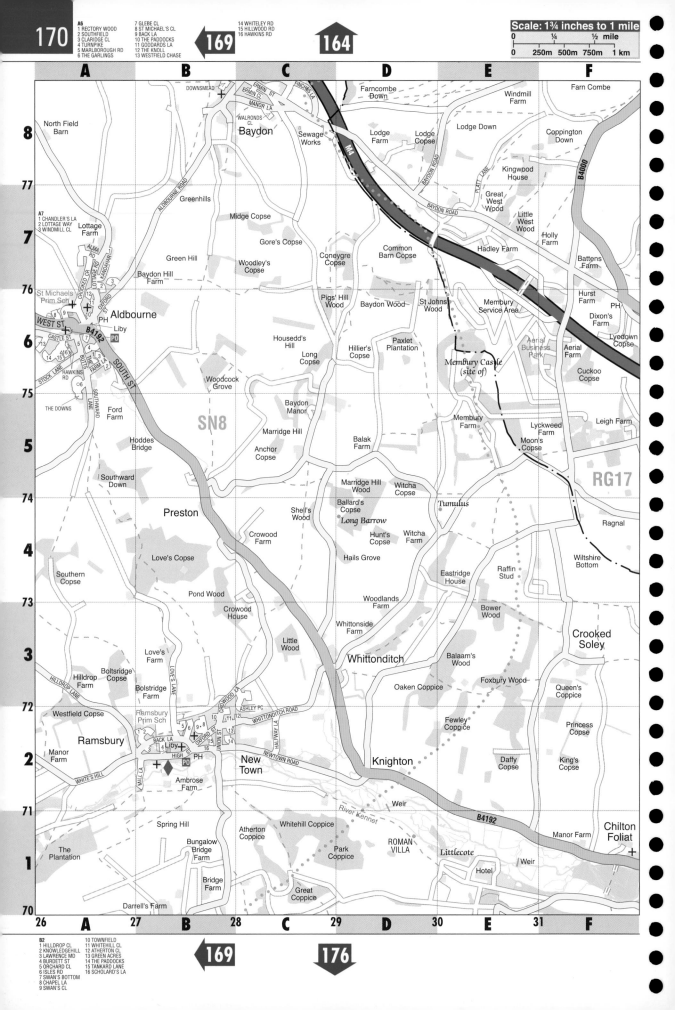

A6
1 RECTORY WOOD
2 SOUTHFIELD
3 CLARIDGE CL
4 TURNPIKE
5 MARLBOROUGH RD
6 THE GARLINGS

7 GLEBE CL
8 ST MICHAEL'S CL
9 BACK LA
10 THE PADDOCKS
11 GODDARDS LA
12 THE KNOLL
13 WESTFIELD CHASE

14 WHITELEY RD
15 HILLWOOD RD
16 HAWKINS RD

169   164

Scale: 1¾ inches to 1 mile

0   ¼   ½   mile

0   250m   500m   750m   1 km

A   B   C   D   E   F

DOWNSMEAD
ERMIN ST
ERMIN CL
MANOR LA
WALRONDS CL
FINCHES LA
Farncombe Down
Windmill Farm
Farn Combe

8 North Field Barn
Baydon
Sewage Works
Lodge Farm
Lodge Copse
Lodge Down
Coppington Down

77 Greenhills
Midge Copse
M4
BAYDON ROAD
PLATT LANE
B4000

A7
1 CHANDLER'S LA
2 LOTTAGE WAY
3 WINDMILL CL

7 Lottage Farm
Green Hill
Gore's Copse
Woodley's Copse
Coneygre Copse
Common Barn Copse
Hadley Farm
Great West Wood
Kingwood House
Little West Wood
Holly Farm
Battens Farm

ALMA RD
KANDAHAR
CROOKED CR
LOTTAGE RD
OXFORD RD

76 Baydon Hill Farm
St Michaels Prim Sch
PH Aldbourne
Liby PO
Pigs' Hill Wood
Baydon Wood
St Johns Wood
Membury Service Area
Hurst Farm
Dixon's Farm
PH
Lyedown Copse

WEST ST
CASTLE ST
B4192
THE BUTTS
SOUTH ST
Housedd's Hill
Long Copse
Hillier's Copse
Paxlet Plantation
Aerial Business Park
Aerial Farm
Cuckoo Copse

6 HAWKINS RD
THE DOWNS
STOCK LANE
SOUTHEND LANE
Woodcock Grove
Membury Castle (site of)

75 Ford Farm
Hoddes Bridge
Baydon Manor
Marridge Hill
Membury Farm
Lyckweed Farm
Moon's Copse
Leigh Farm

SN8
Southward Down
Anchor Copse
Balak Farm
RG17

5

74 Marridge Hill Wood
Witcha Copse
Tumulus
Preston
Shell's Wood
Ballard's Copse
Long Barrow
Hunt's Copse
Witcha Farm
Ragnal

4 Southern Copse
Love's Copse
Crowood Farm
Hails Grove
Eastridge House
Raffin Stud
Wiltshire Bottom

73 Pond Wood
Crowood House
Woodlands Farm
Bower Wood
Crooked Soley

3 Love's Farm
Little Wood
Whittonside Farm
Whittonditch
Balaam's Wood
Foxbury Wood
Queen's Copse

HILLDROP LANE
Hilldrop Farm
Boltsridge Copse
Bolstridge Farm
LOVE'S LANE
CROWOOD LA
ASHLEY PC
WHITTONDITCH ROAD
Oaken Coppice
Fewley Coppice
Princess Copse

72 Westfield Copse
Ramsbury Prim Sch
BACK LA
UNION ST
King's Copse

2 Manor Farm
Ramsbury
Liby
HIGH ST PO PH
New Town
NEWTOWN ROAD
Knighton
Daffy Copse

WHITE'S HILL
MILL LA
Ambrose Farm
HALFWAY LA

71 Spring Hill
Bungalow Bridge Farm
Atherton Coppice
Whitehill Coppice
River Kennet
Weir
B4192
Manor Farm
Chilton Foliat

1 The Plantation
Bridge Farm
Park Coppice
ROMAN VILLA
Littlecote
Hotel
Weir

70 Darrell's Farm
Great Coppice

26   A   27   B   28   C   29   D   30   E   31   F

B2
1 HILLDROP CL
2 KNOWLEDGEHILL
3 LAWRENCE MD
4 BURDETT ST
5 ORCHARD CL
6 ISLES RD
7 SWAN'S BOTTOM
8 CHAPEL LA
9 SWAN'S CL

10 TOWNFIELD
11 WHITEHILL CL
12 ATHERTON CL
13 GREEN ACRES
14 THE PADDOCKS
15 TANKARD LANE
16 SCHOLARD'S LA

169   176

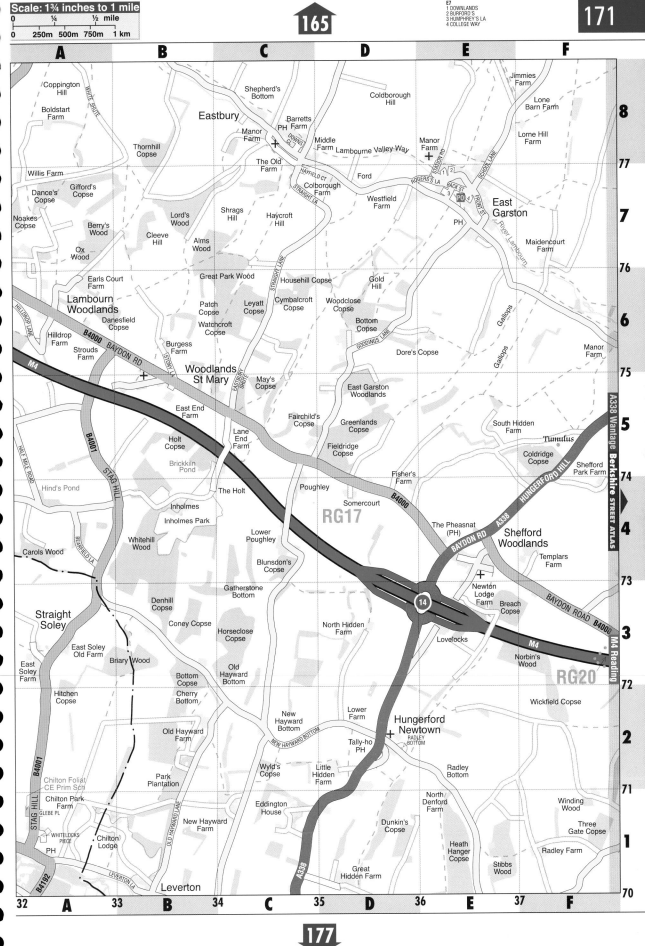

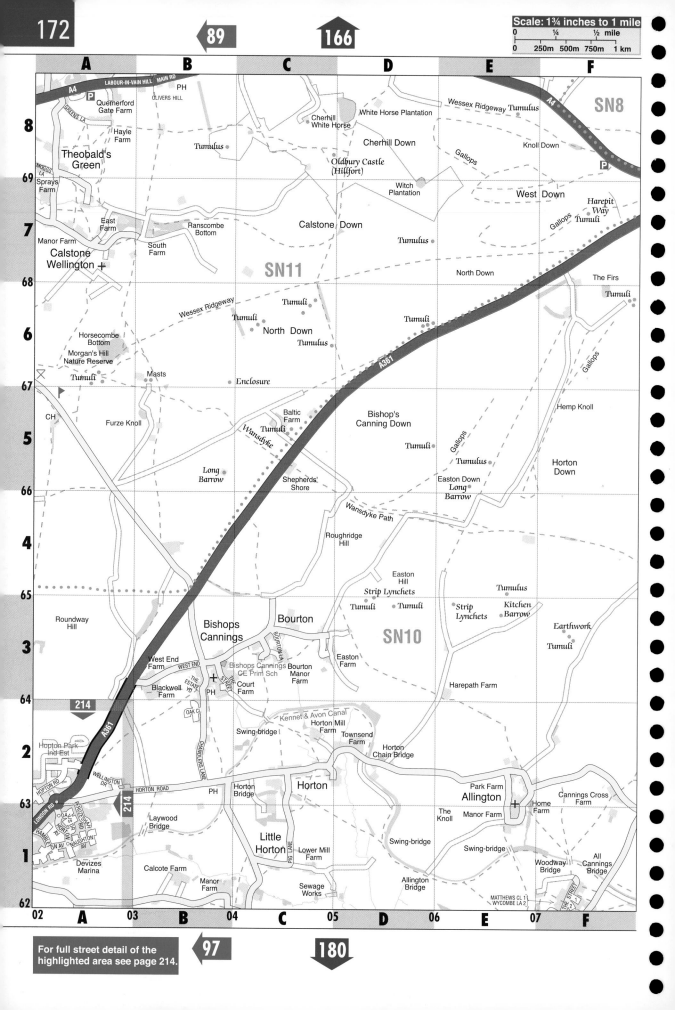

Scale: 1¾ inches to 1 mile

0   ¼   ½ mile
0 250m 500m 750m 1 km

SN8

LABOUR-IN-VAIN HILL MAIN RD
A4
P
Quemerford
Gate Farm
OLIVERS HILL
PH

Hayle
Farm

Theobald's
Green

GREENS LA

MOGGS LA

Sprays
Farm

East
Farm

Manor Farm

Calstone
Wellington

South
Farm

Ranscombe
Bottom

Tumulus

Cherhill
White Horse

White Horse Plantation

Cherhill Down

Wessex Ridgeway Tumulus

Knoll Down

West Down

Oldbury Castle
(Hillfort)

Witch
Plantation

A4

P

Harepit
Way
Tumuli

Calstone Down

SN11

Wessex Ridgeway

Tumuli

Tumuli

North Down

Tumulus

North Down

Tumulus

Gallops

The Firs

Tumuli

Horsecombe
Bottom

Morgan's Hill
Nature Reserve

Tumuli

Masts

Enclosure

Tumuli

North Down

Tumulus

Tumuli

A361

Bishop's
Canning Down

Tumuli

Gallops

Hemp Knoll

Gallops

CH

Furze Knoll

Wansdyke

Baltic
Farm

Tumuli

Tumulus

Gallops

Tumulus

Horton
Down

Long
Barrow

Shepherds'
Shore

Wansdyke Path

Easton Down
Long
Barrow

Roughridge
Hill

Roundway
Hill

Bishops
Cannings

West End
Farm

WEST END

WEST END

Blackwell
Farm

THE ESTATE YD

OAK CL

BOURTON LA

Bishops Cannings
CE Prim Sch

PH

THE STREET

Court
Farm

Bourton

Bourton
Manor
Farm

Easton
Farm

Easton
Hill

Strip Lynchets

Tumuli

Tumuli

Tumulus

Strip
Lynchets

Tumulus

Kitchen
Barrow

Earthwork

Tumuli

SN10

Harepath Farm

214

A361

Hopton Park
Ind Est

WELLINGTON DR

HOPTON RD

214

CHANDLERS LANE

Kennet & Avon Canal

Swing-bridge

Horton Mill
Farm

Townsend
Farm

Horton
Chain Bridge

Park Farm

Allington

Cannings Cross
Farm

LONDON RD

FERGUSON DR

HORTON ROAD

PH

Horton
Bridge

Horton

The
Knoll

Manor Farm

Home
Farm

Devizes
Marina

HAMBL
ON AV
NAUGHTON AV

Laywood
Bridge

Calcote Farm

Little
Horton

PIG LANE

Lower Mill
Farm

Sewage
Works

Swing-bridge

Allington
Bridge

Swing-bridge

Woodway
Bridge

All
Cannings
Bridge

THE STREET

Manor
Farm

MATTHEWS CL 1
WYCOMBE LA 2

For full street detail of the
highlighted area see page 214.

97

180

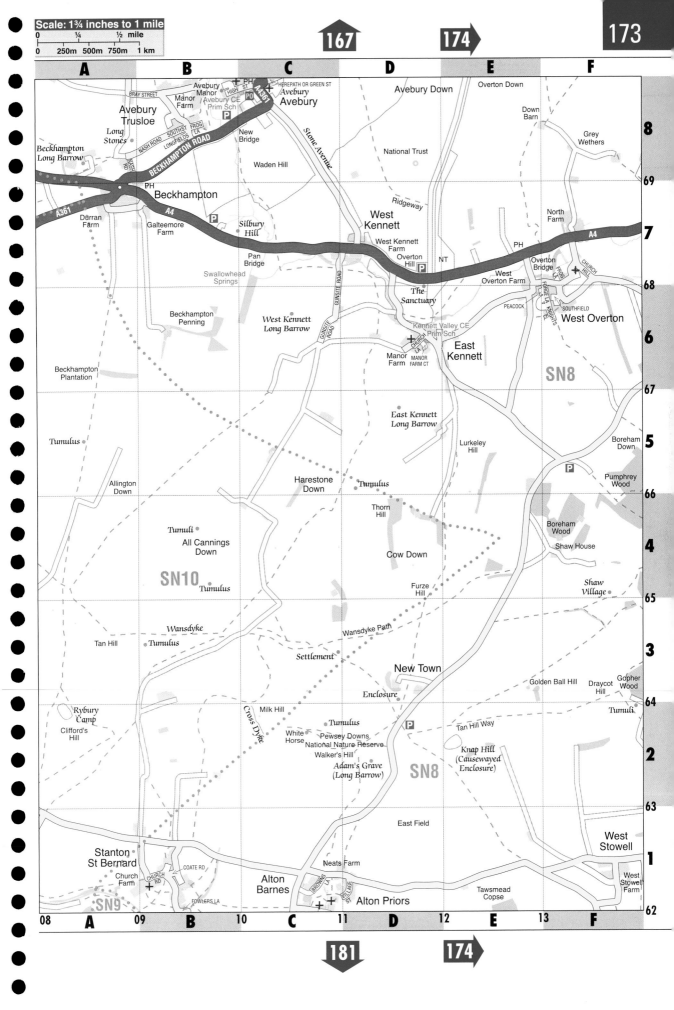

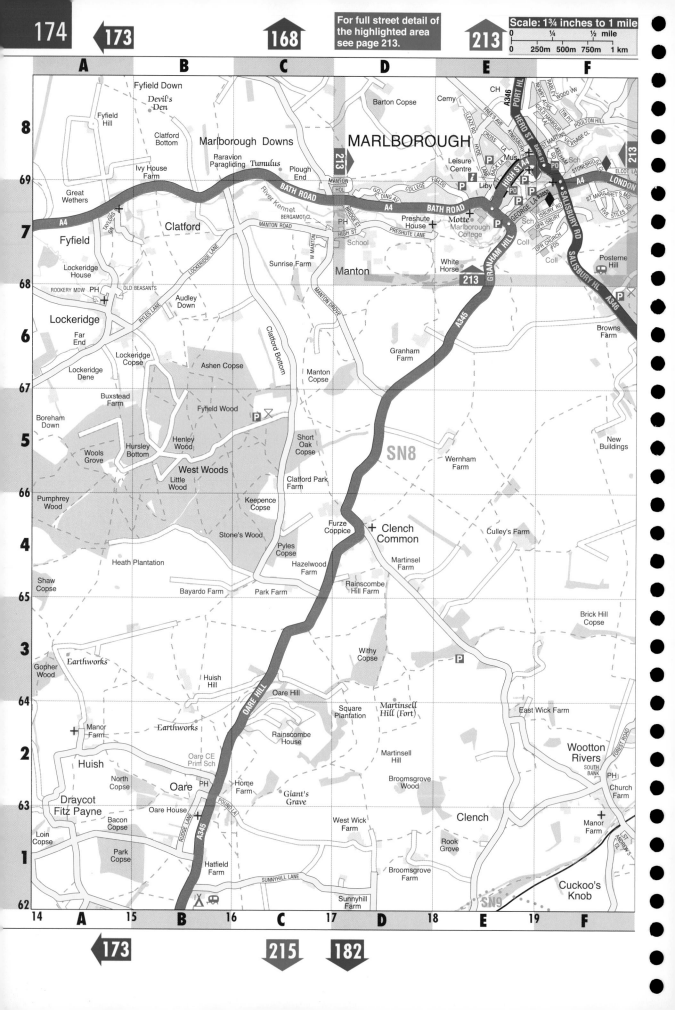

174

◀ 173

▲ 168

For full street detail of
the highlighted area
see page 213.

213 ▲

Scale: 1¾ inches to 1 mile
0   ¼   ½ mile
0   250m 500m 750m 1 km

A   B   C   D   E   F

8

Fyfield Down

Devil's
Den

Fyfield
Hill

Clatford
Bottom

Marlborough Downs

Barton Copse

Cemy

CH

MARLBOROUGH

69

Paravion
Paragliding   Tumulus

Plough
End

213 ▲

MANTON
HOL

Leisure
Centre

Ivy House
Farm

BATH ROAD

River Kennet

A4

Liby

i

Ivy House
Farm

7

Great
Wethers

A4

Clatford

BERGAMOT CL

MANTON ROAD

PH

BATH ROAD

Preshute
House

Motte

Marlborough
College

Posterne
Hill

Fyfield

PRESHUTE LANE

HIGH ST

School

Manton

White
Horse

213 ▲

Coll

Coll

68

Lockeridge
House

RYLES LANE

OLD BEASANTS

ROOKERY MDW PH

Audley
Down

W MANTON

MANTON DROVE

6

Lockeridge

Far
End

Lockeridge
Copse

Ashen Copse

Clatford Bottom

Manton
Copse

Granham
Farm

A345

Browns
Farm

Lockeridge
Dene

67

Buxstead
Farm

Fyfield Wood

P

5

Boreham
Down

Wools
Grove

Hursley
Bottom

Henley
Wood

West Woods

Little
Wood

Short
Oak
Copse

Clatford Park
Farm

SN8

Wernham
Farm

New
Buildings

66

Pumphrey
Wood

Keepence
Copse

Stone's Wood

Pyles
Copse

Furze
Coppice

Clench
Common

Culley's Farm

4

Heath Plantation

Hazelwood
Farm

Martinsel
Farm

65

Shaw
Copse

Bayardo Farm

Park Farm

Rainscombe
Hill Farm

Brick Hill
Copse

3

Gopher
Wood

Earthworks

Huish
Hill

OARE HILL

Oare Hill

Withy
Copse

P

East Wick Farm

64

Manor
Farm

Earthworks

Square
Plantation

Martinsell
Hill (Fort)

2

Huish

North
Copse

Oare

RUDGE LANE

A345

PH

Home
Farm

POUND LA

Rainscombe
House

Giant's
Grave

Oare CE
Prim Sch

Martinsell
Hill

Broomsgrove
Wood

Wootton
Rivers

SOUTH
BANK

PH

Church
Farm

63

Draycot
Fitz Payne

Bacon
Copse

Oare House

West Wick
Farm

Clench

Manor
Farm

ST ANDREW'S

Loin
Copse

1

Park
Copse

Hatfield
Farm

SUNNYHILL LANE

Rook
Grove

Broomsgrove
Farm

Cuckoo's
Knob

62

Sunnyhill
Farm

SN9

14   A   15   B   16   C   17   D   18   E   19   F

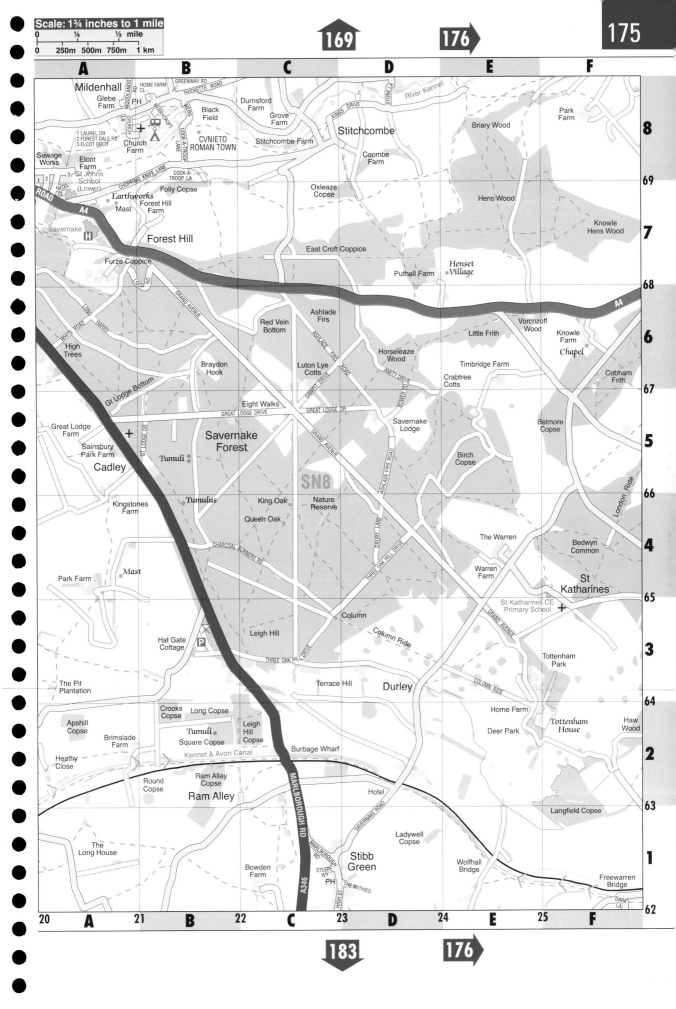

Scale: 1¾ inches to 1 mile

0 ¼ ½ mile
0 250m 500m 750m 1 km

8

The Plantation

Burnt Wood
Scrope Farm
Little Copse
Rudge
Bottom Coppice
Lawn Coppice
Brickkiln Copse

69

Scrope's Wood
Rudge Manor Farm
Rudge Farm House
Littlecote Park Farm
Cake Wood

7

Froxfield
Highclose Farm

BATH ROAD

68

Harrow Farm
A4 BATH ROAD
Green Farm
MANOR PK
Sewage Works
PH
Lock
RG17

6

Noke Wood
Almshouse Copse
Lock
Firth Copse
Oak Hill
North Standen House

67

Withy Copse
Round Copse
Bushelleys Copse
Trindledown Copse
Jugg's Wood
Long Walk
Lady's Wood

5

Upper Horsehall Hill Farm
Lower Farm
Chisbury
CHURCH ST
Fore Bridge
Stype Wood
Catmore Copse

LONDON RIDE
Chisbury Lane Farm
Oldhouse Wood
Strouds Farm
CHISBURY LANE
Chisbury Manor Farm
SCHOOL LA
Lock
Little Bedwyn

66

CHISBURY LA
St Martin's Chapel
Stype Grange
Cowleaze Coppice

Tumuli
Faggotty Copse
Park Copse
Chisbury Camp
SN8
HIGH ST
PH
Barn Copse
Furze Copse
Bagshot

4

Bewley Farm
Chisbury Wood
Great Bedwyn CE Prim Sch
WANSDYKE RD
Little Bonning's Copse
Wentworth's Copse
Hillcroft Copse
Westcott Copse

Brimley Copse
KESTON ROAD
Parlow Bottom
Bonning's Copse
ANNETT SEA
Eastcourt Farm
SIX ACRE LA

65

Horse Copse
BROWN'S LANE
Lock
Strockeridge Copse
Burridge Heath
Gully Copse
Polesdon House
Baverstock's Copse
A338

Stokke Manor
FOREST HILL
PH
FARM LANE
WILLIS CL
Sewage Works
Burridgeheath Plantation

3

Stock Common
Shawgrove Copse
Great Bedwyn
PO
Bedwyn
GALLEY LANE
Bedwyn Dyke
Foxbury Wood
Foxwood Farm
Shalbourne Heath Plantation

BACK LA
FROG LA

64

Lock
CHURCH STREET
BROOK STREET
Round Copse
Birch Copse
Long Copse

Bedwyn Stone Museum
Sewage Works

2

Haw Wood
Mill Bridge
Ivy's Copse
Folly Farm
Newtown
Shalbourne CE Prim Sch

Bloxham Lodge
Bloxham Copse
Brail Farm
Castle Copse
Shalbourne

KENNET & AVON CANAL
CROFTON ROAD

63

Lock
West Farm
Baverstock Farm
PO
Ropewind Farm

Lock
Harding Copse
KINGSTON RD
COX'S LANE

1

Crofton Farm
Weir
Wilton Brail
Bedwyn Brail
Harding Farm
CARVERS HILL
Westcourt Farm
BURR LA
RIVAR RD
THE LYNCH

Crofton
LC
Crofton Beam Engines
Wilton Water
Dodsdown Farm
Wilton Common
A338

62

Lock
Tumulus
Wilton Down
Marlmere Farm

26 A 27 B 28 C 29 D 30 E 31 F

B3
1 NAPIERS
2 COPYHOLD
3 CASTLE RD
4 FAIRFIELD
5 COSTER VIEW
6 GRANARY RD
7 MANOR RD

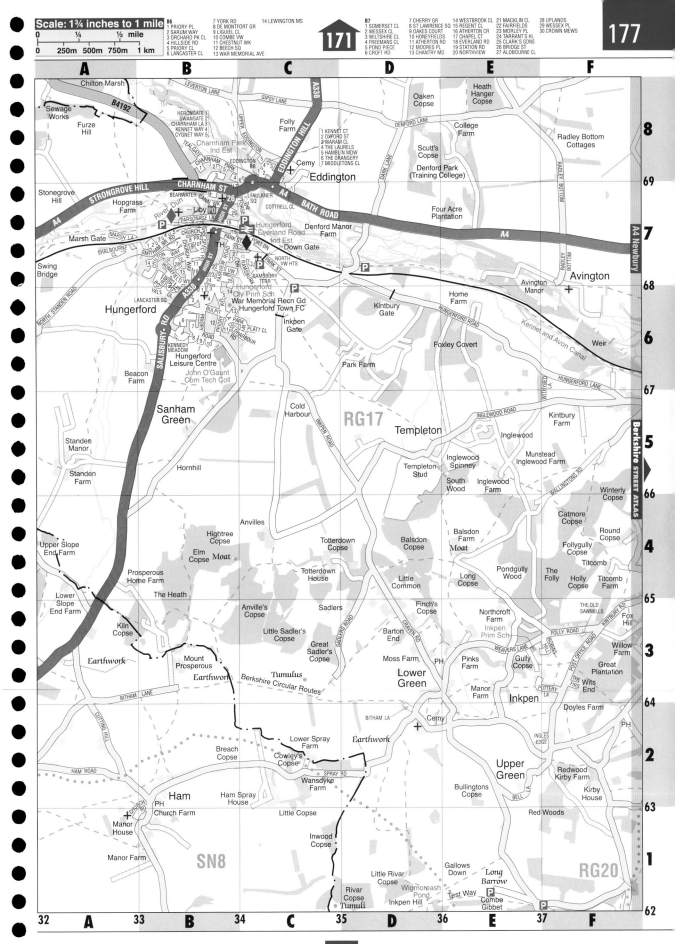

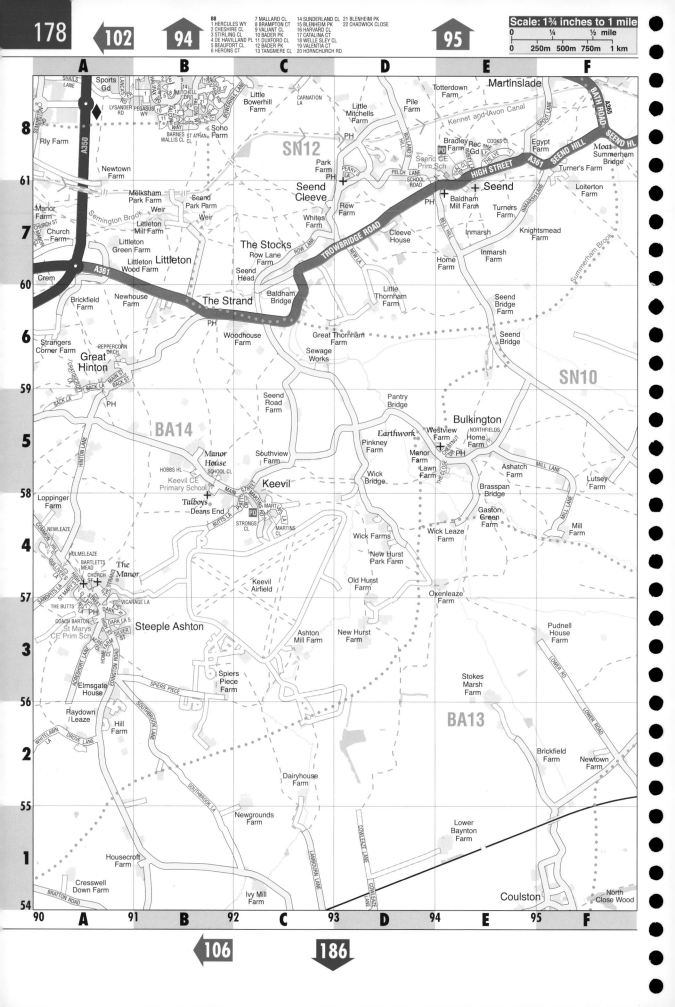

102
94
95

B8
1 HERCULES WY
2 CHESHIRE CL
3 STIRLING CL
4 DE HAVILLAND PL
5 BEAUFORT CL
6 HERONS CT
7 MALLARD CL
8 BRAMPTON CT
9 VALIANT CL
10 BADER PK
11 DUXFORD CL
12 BADER PK
13 TANGMERE CL
14 SUNDERLAND CL
15 BLENHEIM PK
16 HARVARD CL
17 CATALINA CT
18 WELLE SLEY CL
19 VALENTIA CT
20 HORNCHURCH RD
21 BLENHEIM PK
22 CHADWICK CLOSE

Scale: 1¾ inches to 1 mile

0   ¼   ½ mile
0   250m   500m   750m   1 km

Martinslade

Kennet and Avon Canal

Totterdown Farm

SN12

Little Bowerhill Farm

CARNATION LA

Pile Farm

Little Mitchells Farm

Bradley Farm

Rec Gd

Seend CE Prim Sch

Egypt Farm

Moat

Summerham Bridge

Turner's Farm

Park Farm

PH

Seend Cleeve

Rew Farm

HIGH STREET

SEEND HILL

SEEND HL

BATH ROAD

A365

Seend

Loiterton Farm

Whites Farm

Baldham Mill Farm

Turners Farm

Semington Brook

Melksham Park Farm

Weir

Seend Park Farm

Weir

Littleton Mill Farm

The Stocks

Row Lane Farm

TROWBRIDGE ROAD

Cleeve House

Inmarsh

Knightsmead Farm

Summerham Brook

Manor Farm

Church Farm

Crem

A361

Littleton Green Farm

Littleton Wood Farm

Littleton

Seend Head

The Strand

Baldham Bridge

Little Thornham Farm

Home Farm

Inmarsh Farm

Seend Bridge Farm

Brickfield Farm

Newhouse Farm

PH

Woodhouse Farm

Great Thornham Farm

Seend Bridge

Strangers Corner Farm

PEPPERCORN ORCH

Sewage Works

SN10

Great Hinton

BACK LA

BACK ST

MAIN ST

BACK LA

PH

Seend Road Farm

Pantry Bridge

Bulkington

NORTHFIELDS

Westview Farm

Home Farm

BA14

HINTON LANE

Manor House

SCHOOL CL

HOBBS HL

Keevil CE Primary School

Southview Farm

Earthwork

Pinkney Farm

Manor Farm

THE CLOSE

DR PH

Lawn Farm

Ashatch Farm

MILL LANE

Lutsey Farm

Loppinger Farm

NEWLEAZE

Keevil

MAIN STREET

MARTINS RD

STRONGS CL

PO

MART'S LA

MARTINS CL

Wick Bridge

Brasspan Bridge

Gaston Green Farm

Mill Farm

Talboys

Deans End

BUTTS LA

Wick Leaze Farm

Wick Farms

HOLMELEAZE

COMMON HILL

BULVER'S CL

BARTLETTS MEAD

The Manor

CHURCH ST

Keevil Airfield

New Hurst Park Farm

Old Hurst Farm

Oxenleaze Farm

ST MARY'S

SANDBITS LA

VICARAGE LA

DARK LA

Steeple Ashton

Ashton Mill Farm

New Hurst Farm

Pudnell House Farm

LOWER RD

THE BUTTS

COACH BARTON

St Marys CE Prim Sch

ACRE LA

HOME FARM

SILVER ST

EDINGTON ROAD

DARK LA S

PH

Spiers Piece Farm

Stokes Marsh Farm

Elmsgate House

SPIERS PIECE

SOUTHBROOK LANE

BA13

Raydown Leaze

Hill Farm

Brickfield Farm

Newtown Farm

WHITELAWN LA

DROVE LANE

SOUTHBROOK LA

Dairyhouse Farm

Lower Baynton Farm

Housecroft Farm

Newgrounds Farm

LAMBOURN LANE

COWLEAZE LANE

Cresswell Down Farm

BRATTON ROAD

Ivy Mill Farm

COWLEAZE

Coulston

North Close Wood

106
186

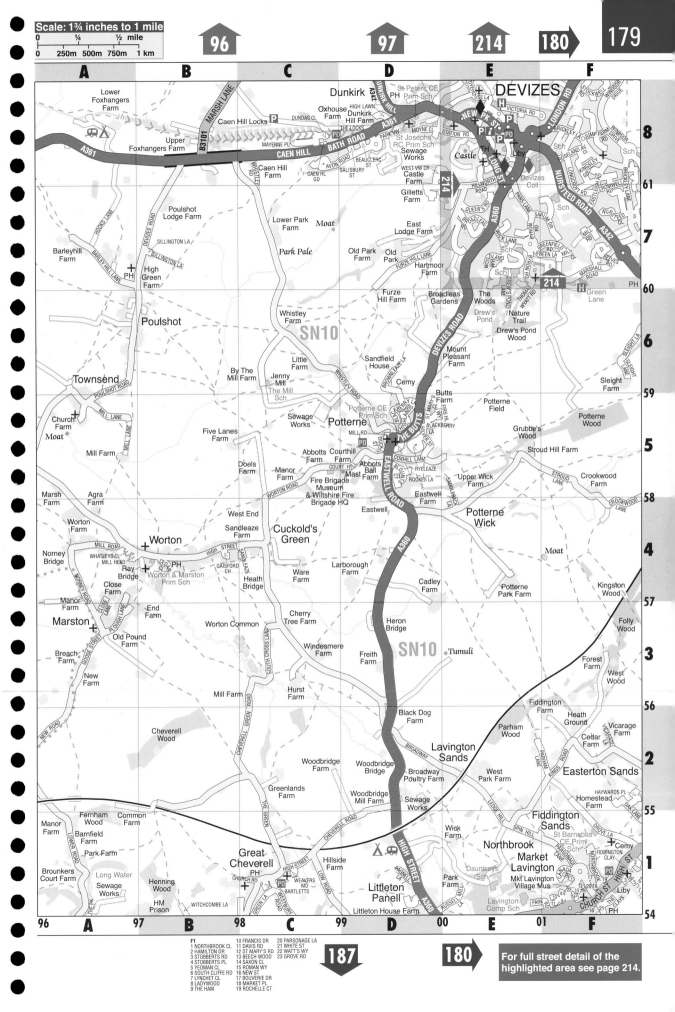

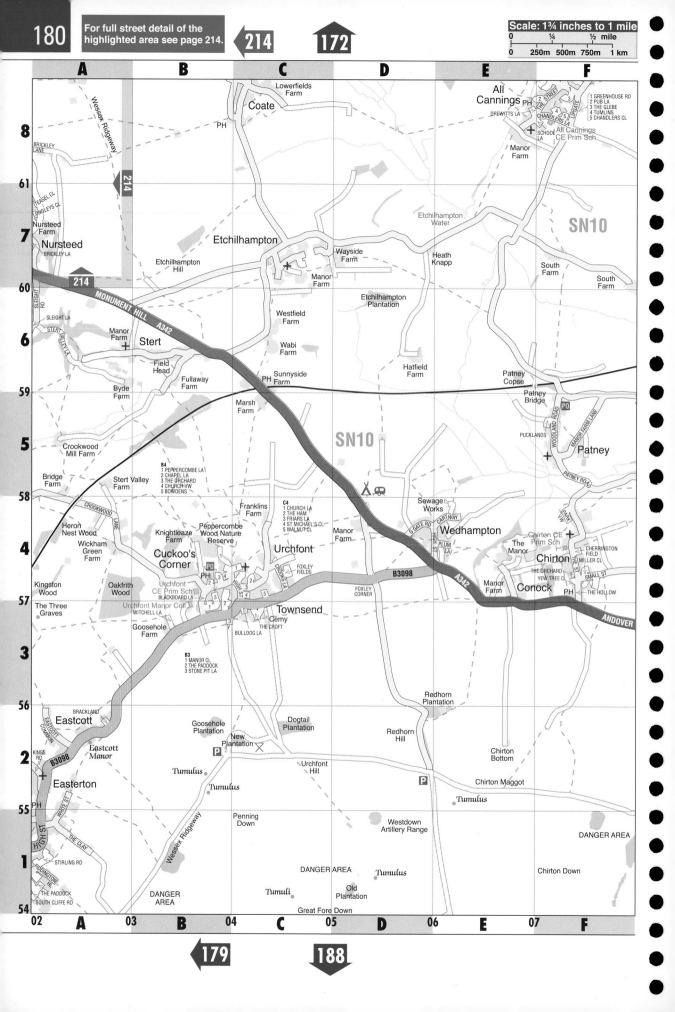

180

For full street detail of the highlighted area see page 214.

214

172

Scale: 1¾ inches to 1 mile

0   ¼   ½   mile
0   250m 500m 750m   1 km

A   B   C   D   E   F

8

61

7

60

6

59

5

58

4

57

3

56

2

55

1

54

Wessex Ridgeway

214

214

BRICKLEY LANE

TEASEL CL
LONGLEYS CL
Nursteed Farm

Nursteed

BRICKLEY LA

SLEIGHT RD
SLEIGHT LA
STERT VALLEY LA

MONUMENT HILL
A342

Manor Farm
Stert

Field Head

Byde Farm

Fullaway Farm

Crookwood Mill Farm

Bridge Farm

CROOKWOOD LANE

Heron Nest Wood

Wickham Green Farm

Kingston Wood

The Three Graves

Stert Valley Farm

Knightleaze Farm

Cuckoo's Corner

Oakfrith Wood

Goosehole Farm

B4
1 PEPPERCOMBE LA
2 CHAPEL LA
3 THE ORCHARD
4 CHURCH VW
5 BOWDENS

Peppercombe Wood Nature Reserve

Franklins Farm

C4
1 CHURCH LA
2 THE HAM
3 FRIARS LA
4 ST MICHAEL'S CL
5 WALNUT CL

Urchfont

PO
PH

Urchfont CE Prim Sch
BLACKBOARD LA
HIGH ST
CROWS LA

Urchfont Manor Coll
WITCHELL LA

Townsend

Cemy
THE CROFT
BULLDOG LA

B3
1 MANOR CL
2 THE PADDOCK
3 STONE PIT LA

Lowerfields Farm

Coate

PH

Etchilhampton

Etchilhampton Hill

Wayside Farm

Manor Farm

Westfield Farm

Wabi Farm

Sunnyside Farm

PH

Marsh Farm

SN10

Etchilhampton Water

Heath Knapp

Etchilhampton Plantation

Hatfield Farm

Manor Farm

Foxley Fields

FOXLEY CORNER

B3098

Sewage Works

G GATE RD
CART WAY
HIGH ST
PLUM LA

Wedhampton

A342

Manor Farm

All Cannings
PH

DREWITTS LA

Manor Farm

THE STREET
CHANDLERS LA
LIPGATE
SCHOOL LA

All Cannings CE Prim Sch

1 GREENHOUSE RD
2 PUB LA
3 THE GLEBE
4 TUMLINS
5 CHANDLERS CL

SN10

South Farm

South Farm

Patney Copse

Patney Bridge

PUCKLANDS

WOODLAND ROAD
MANOR FARM LANE
PO

Patney

PATNEY ROAD

Chirton CE Prim Sch

The Manor

CHERRINGTON FIELD
MILLER CL

Chirton

THE ORCHARD
YEW TREE CL

Conock

SMALL ST

PH

THE HOLLOW

ANDOVER

Eastcott

BRACKLAND

EASTCOTT COMMON

Eastcott Manor

KINGS RD
B3098

Easterton

PH

WHITE ST
THE CLAY

HIGH ST

STIRLING RD

FIDDINGTON HL

THE PADDOCK
SOUTH CLIFFE RD

DANGER AREA

Goosehole Plantation

New Plantation
P

Tumulus

Tumulus

Wessex Ridgeway

Penning Down

DANGER AREA

Tumuli

Dogtail Plantation

Urchfont Hill

Great Fore Down

Redhorn Plantation

Redhorn Hill

P

Chirton Maggot

Tumulus

Westdown Artillery Range

Tumulus

Old Plantation

Chirton Bottom

Chirton Down

DANGER AREA

02   A   03   B   04   C   05   D   06   E   07   F

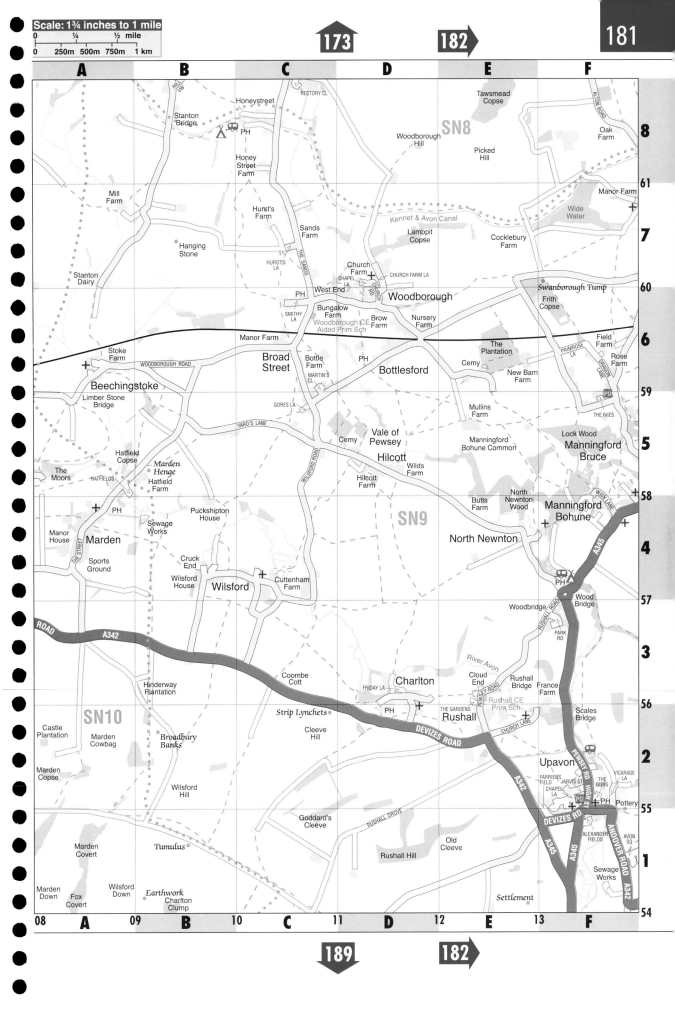

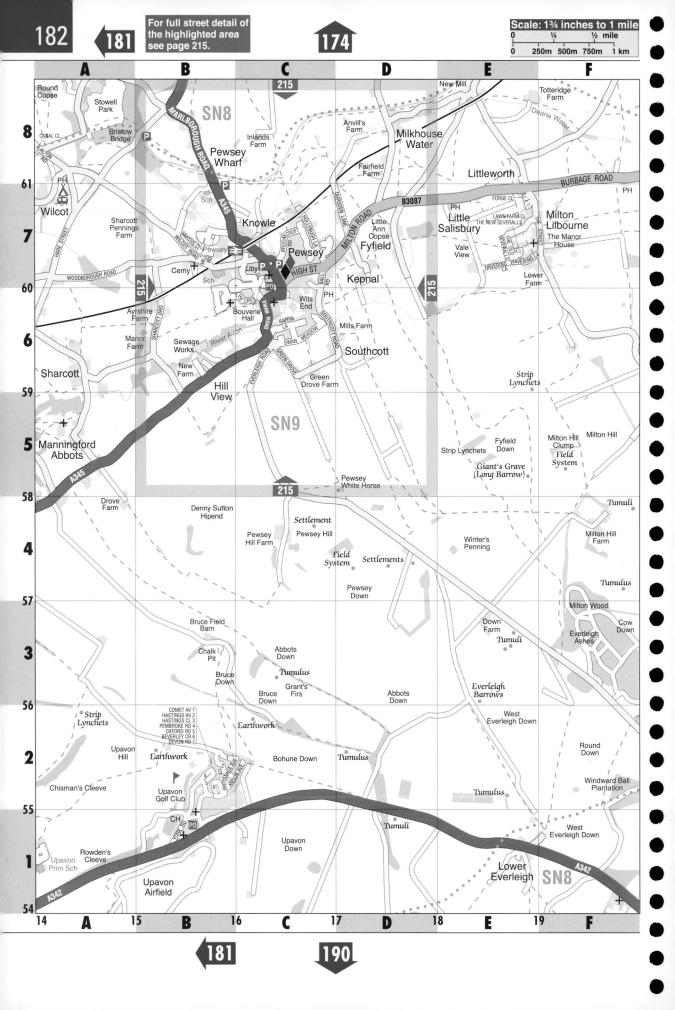

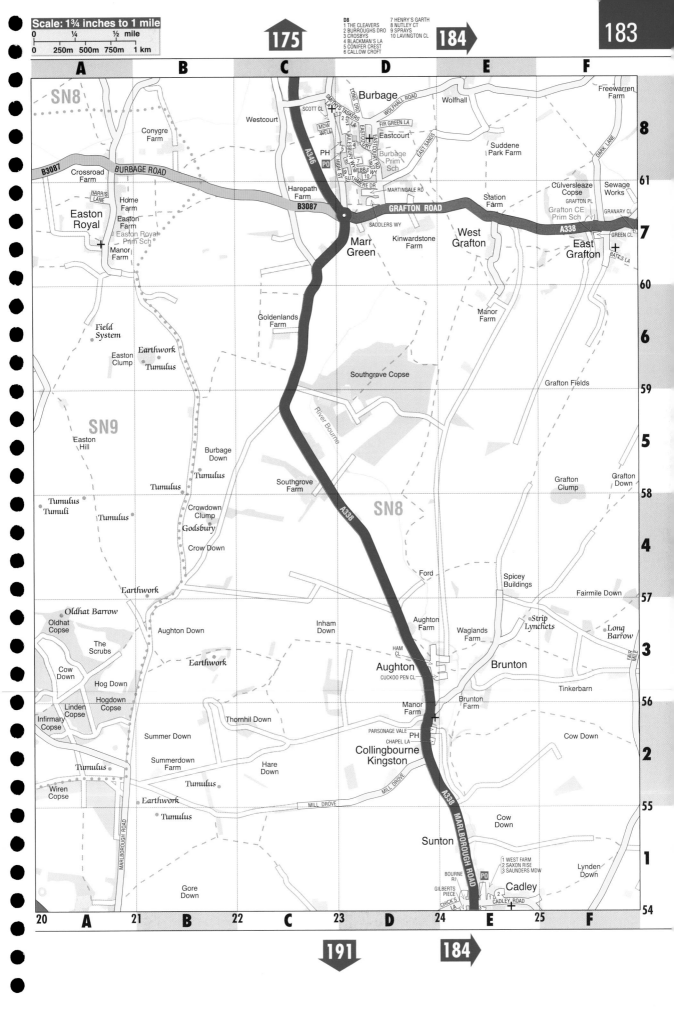

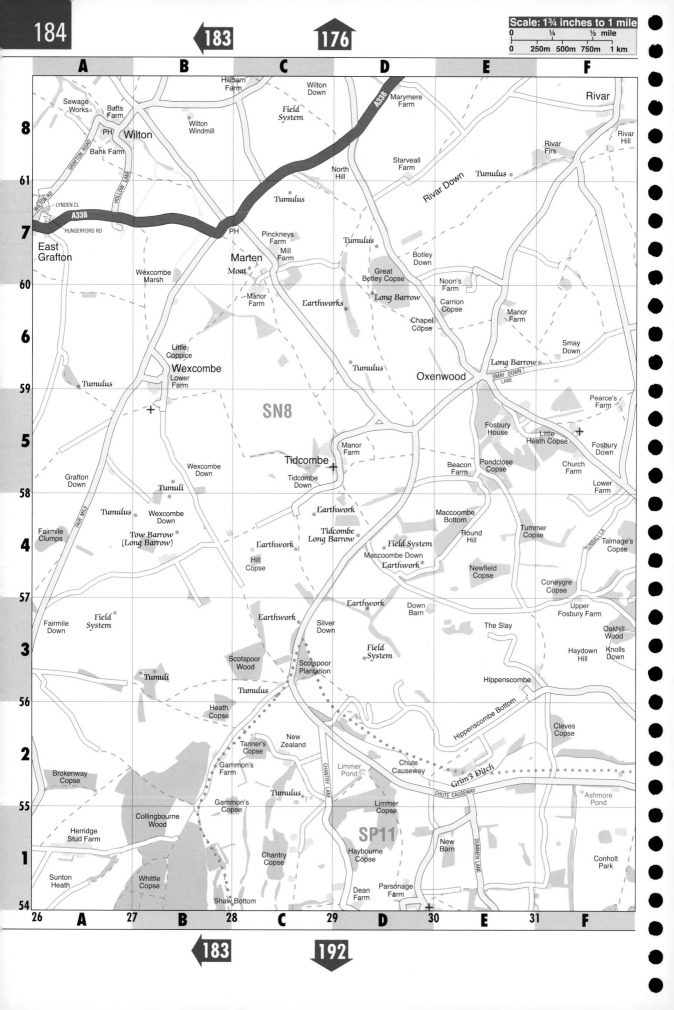

Scale: 1¾ inches to 1 mile

0   ¼   ½   mile
0   250m   500m   750m   1 km

A   B   C   D   E   F

Rivar

Sewage Works
Batts Farm
PH
Wilton
Bank Farm
Hillbarn Farm
Wilton Windmill
Wilton Down
Field System
Marymere Farm
Rivar Firs
Rivar Hill

8

GRAFTON ROAD
HOLLOW LANE
61

WILTON RD
LYNDEN CL
A338
HUNGERFORD RD
North Hill
Starveall Farm
Rivar Down
Tumulus
Rivar Down

7
PH
East Grafton
Wexcombe Marsh
Marten
Moat
Pinckneys Farm
Mill Farm
Tumulus
Great Botley Copse
Botley Down
Noon's Farm
Manor Farm

60
Manor Farm
Earthworks
Long Barrow
Carrion Copse
Chapel Copse
Smay Down

6
Little Coppice
Wexcombe
Lower Farm
Tumulus
Long Barrow
Oxenwood
SMAY DOWN LANE

59
Tumulus
SN8
Fosbury House
Pearce's Farm
Little Heath Copse
Fosbury Down
Church Farm

5
Grafton Down
Wexcombe Down
Tidcombe
Manor Farm
Tidcombe Down
Beacon Farm
Pondclose Copse
Lower Farm

58
Tumuli
Wexcombe Down
Earthwork
Tidcombe Long Barrow
Maccoombe Bottom
Round Hill
Tummer Copse
Talmage's Copse

4
Fairmile Clumps
FAIR MILE
Tumulus
Tow Barrow (Long Barrow)
Earthwork
Hill Copse
Field System
Maccoombe Down
Earthwork
Newfield Copse
Coneygre Copse
TURRILL LA

57
Fairmile Down
Field System
Earthwork
Earthwork
Down Barn
The Slay
Upper Fosbury Farm
Oakhill Wood
Knolls Down

3
Tumuli
Silver Down
Field System
Haydown Hill
Scotspoor Wood
Scotspoor Plantation
Hippenscombe

56
Heath Copse
Tumulus
Hippenscombe Bottom
Cleves Copse

2
Tanner's Copse
New Zealand
Gammon's Farm
CHANTRY LANE
Limmer Pond
Chute Causeway
Grim's Ditch
Ashmore Pond

55
Brokenway Copse
Gammon's Copse
Tumulus
Limmer Copse
Chute Causeway
SP11
DUMMER LANE

1
Herridge Stud Farm
Collingbourne Wood
Chantry Copse
Haybourne Copse
New Barn
Conholt Park

54
Sunton Heath
Whittle Copse
Shaw Bottom
Dean Farm
Parsonage Farm

26   A   27   B   28   C   29   D   30   E   31   F

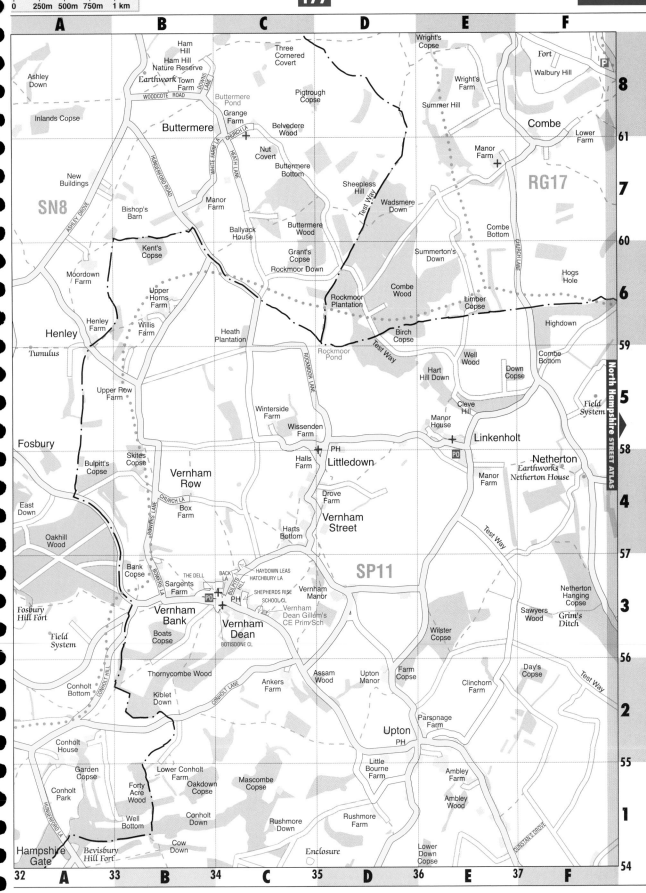

	A	B	C	D	E	F

8 Ashley Down, Inlands Copse, Ham Hill, Ham Hill Nature Reserve, Earthwork, Town Farm, Woodcote Road, Three Cornered Covert, Pigtrough Copse, Wright's Copse, Fort, Walbury Hill, P

61 New Buildings, Buttermere, Grange Farm, Buttermere Pond, Belvedere Wood, Nut Covert, Wright's Farm, Summer Hill, Combe, Manor Farm, Lower Farm, RG17

7 SN8, Ashley Drove, Bishop's Barn, Manor Farm, White Farm La, Church La, Heath Lane, Buttermere Bottom, Sheepless Hill, Test Way, Wadsmere Down, Combe Bottom, Church Lane

60 Moordown Farm, Hungerford Road, Kent's Copse, Ballyack House, Buttermere Wood, Grant's Copse, Rockmoor Down, Summerton's Down, Combe Wood, Hogs Hole, Highdown

6 Henley, Henley Farm, Upper Horns Farm, Willis Farm, Heath Plantation, Rockmoor Plantation, Rockmoor Pond, Test Way, Birch Copse, Limber Copse, Combe Bottom, Down Copse, Well Wood

59 Tumulus, Upper Row Farm, Rockmoor Lane, Hart Hill Down, Field System

5 Fosbury, Skites Copse, Winterside Farm, Wissenden Farm, Halls Farm, Littledown, PH, Manor House, Cleve Hill, Linkenholt, PO, Netherton, Earthworks, Netherton House

58 Bulpitt's Copse, Vernham Row, Church La, Box Farm, Harts Bottom, Drove Farm, Vernham Street, Manor Farm

4 East Down, Oakhill Wood, Bowers Lane, Test Way, Netherton Hanging Copse

57 Bank Copse, The Dell, Back La, Haydown Leas, Hatchbury La, Sargents Farm, PO, Bulpitts Hill, PH, Shepherds Rise, School Cl, Vernham Manor, SP11, Sawyers Wood, Grim's Ditch

3 Fosbury Hill Fort, Field System, Vernham Bank, Vernham Dean, Boats Copse, Botisdone Cl, Vernham Dean Gillum's CE Prim Sch, Wilster Copse, Netherton Hanging Copse

56 Thornycombe Wood, Conholt Bottom, Conholt Lane, Ankers Farm, Assam Wood, Upton Manor, Farm Copse, Clinchorn Farm, Day's Copse, Test Way

2 Kiblet Down, Parsonage Farm, Upton, PH, Conholt House, Lower Conholt Farm, Oakdown Copse, Mascombe Copse, Little Bourne Farm, Ambley Farm, Dunstan's Drove

55 Garden Copse, Conholt Park, Forty Acre Wood, Conholt Down, Ambley Wood

1 Conholt Down, Well Bottom, Rushmore Down, Rushmore Farm, Lower Down Copse

54 Hampshire Gate, Bevisbury Hill Fort, Cow Down, Enclosure, Hungerford La

32	A	33	B	34	C	35	D	36	E	37	F

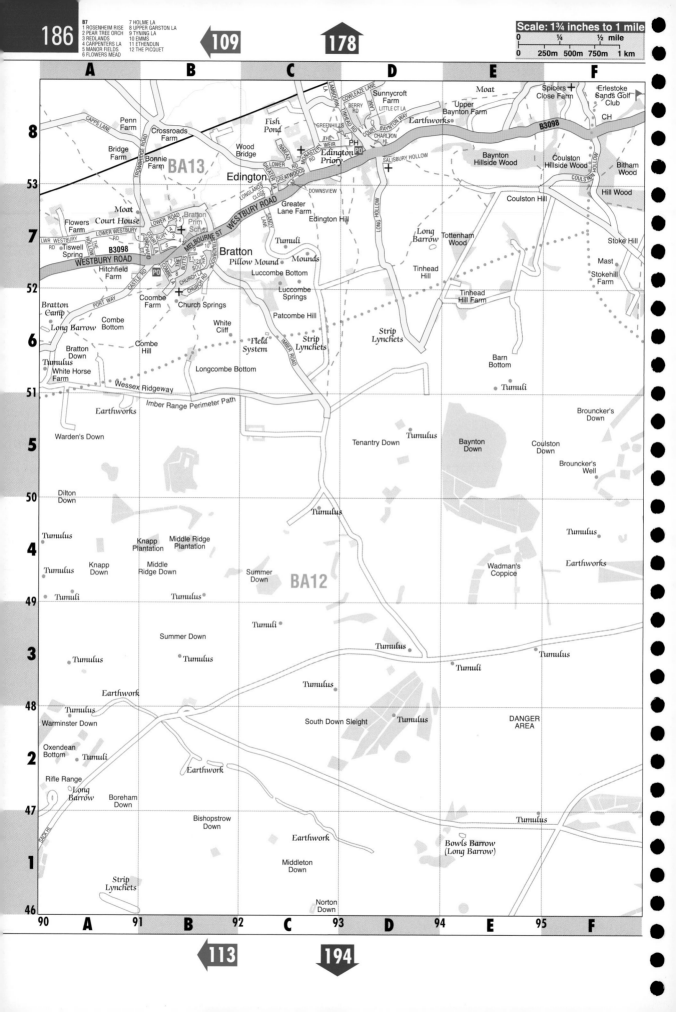

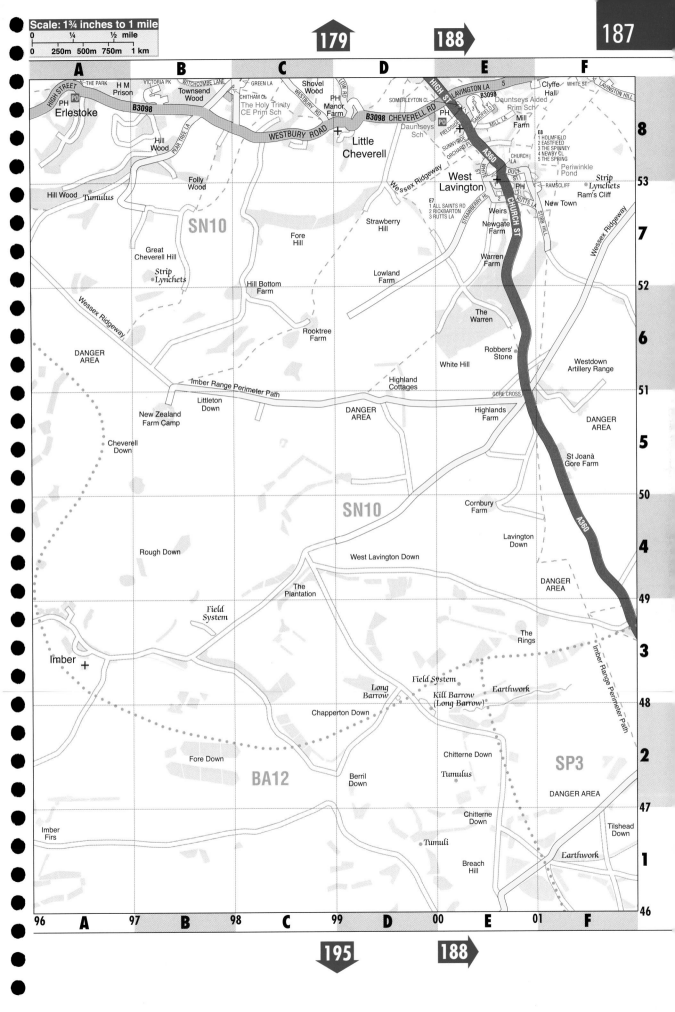

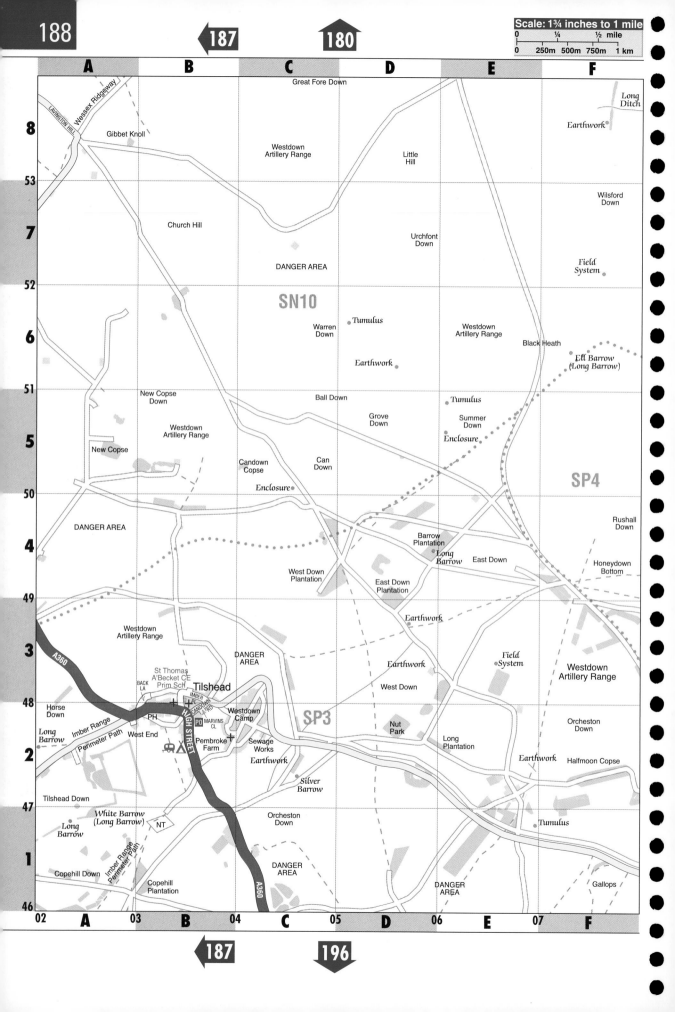

Scale: 1¾ inches to 1 mile
0   ¼   ½ mile
0   250m 500m 750m 1 km

A   B   C   D   E   F

Long Ditch

8

Wessex Ridgeway
LAVINGTON HILL

Earthwork

Gibbet Knoll

53

Great Fore Down

Westdown
Artillery Range

Little
Hill

Wilsford
Down

7

Church Hill

Urchfont
Down

Field
System

52

DANGER AREA

SN10

6

Warren
Down

Tumulus

Westdown
Artillery Range

Black Heath

Earthwork

Ell Barrow
(Long Barrow)

51

New Copse
Down

Ball Down

Grove
Down

Tumulus

Westdown
Artillery Range

Summer
Down

5

New Copse

Candown
Copse

Can
Down

Enclosure

SP4

Enclosure

50

Rushall
Down

DANGER AREA

Barrow
Plantation

Long
Barrow

East Down

Honeydown
Bottom

4

West Down
Plantation

East Down
Plantation

49

Westdown
Artillery Range

Earthwork

Field
System

Westdown
Artillery Range

3

A360

DANGER
AREA

Earthwork

St Thomas
A'Becket CE
Prim Sch

BACK
LA

Tilshead

IMBER
PL

West Down

CANDOWN
RD

48

Horse
Down

PH

HIGH STREET

PO

MARVINS
CL

Westdown
Camp

SP3

Nut
Park

Orcheston
Down

Long
Barrow

Imber Range

Perimeter Path

West End

Pembroke
Farm

Sewage
Works

Long
Plantation

Earthwork

2

Long
Barrow

Earthwork

Halfmoon Copse

47

Tilshead Down

Silver
Barrow

White Barrow
(Long Barrow)

NT

Orcheston
Down

Tumulus

Long
Barrow

1

Copehill Down

Imber Range
Perimeter Path

Copehill
Plantation

DANGER
AREA

A360

DANGER
AREA

Gallops

46

02   A   03   B   04   C   05   D   06   E   07   F

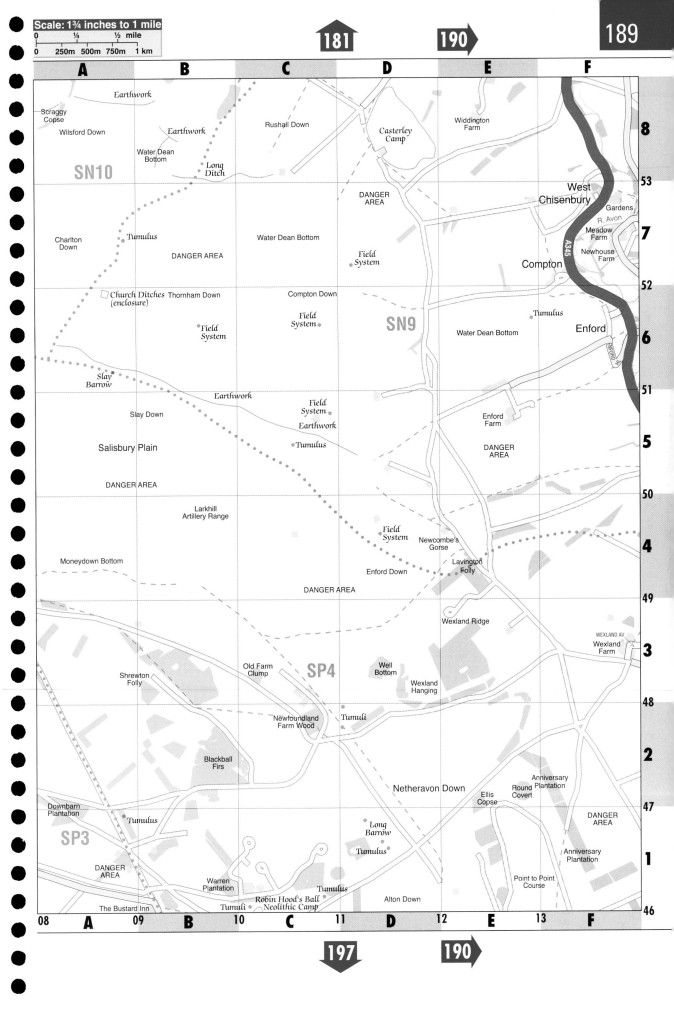

A   B   C   D   E   F

Earthwork

Scraggy
Copse

Wilsford Down   Earthwork   Rushall Down   Casterley   Widdington
Camp   Farm

Water Dean
Bottom   West
Chisenbury

SN10   Long   8
Ditch   Gardens

53   R. Avon

DANGER   Meadow
AREA   Farm   7

Charlton   Tumulus   Water Dean Bottom   Newhouse
Down   Field   Farm

System   Compton   52

DANGER AREA

Church Ditches   Thornham Down   Compton Down   Tumulus   6
(enclosure)

Field   SN9   Enford
System

Field   Water Dean Bottom
System

Slay   51
Barrow   Earthwork   Field
System

Slay Down   Earthwork   Enford
Farm   5

Salisbury Plain   Tumulus   DANGER
AREA

DANGER AREA   50

Larkhill   Field   Newcombe's
Artillery Range   System   Gorse   4

Moneydown Bottom   Lavington
Folly

Enford Down   49

Wexland Ridge

WEXLAND AV
Wexland   3
Farm

Old Farm   Well
Clump   SP4   Bottom

Shrewton   Wexland   48
Folly   Hanging

Newfoundland   Tumuli   2
Farm Wood

Blackball
Firs   Anniversary
Plantation

Netheravon Down   Round
Ellis   Covert
Copse   47

Downbarn   DANGER
Plantation   Tumulus   AREA

SP3   Long   1
Barrow

DANGER   Tumulus   Anniversary
AREA   Plantation

Warren   Point to Point
Plantation   Tumulus   Course

The Bustard Inn   Robin Hood's Ball   Alton Down   46
Tumuli   Neolithic Camp

08   A   09   B   10   C   11   D   12   E   13   F

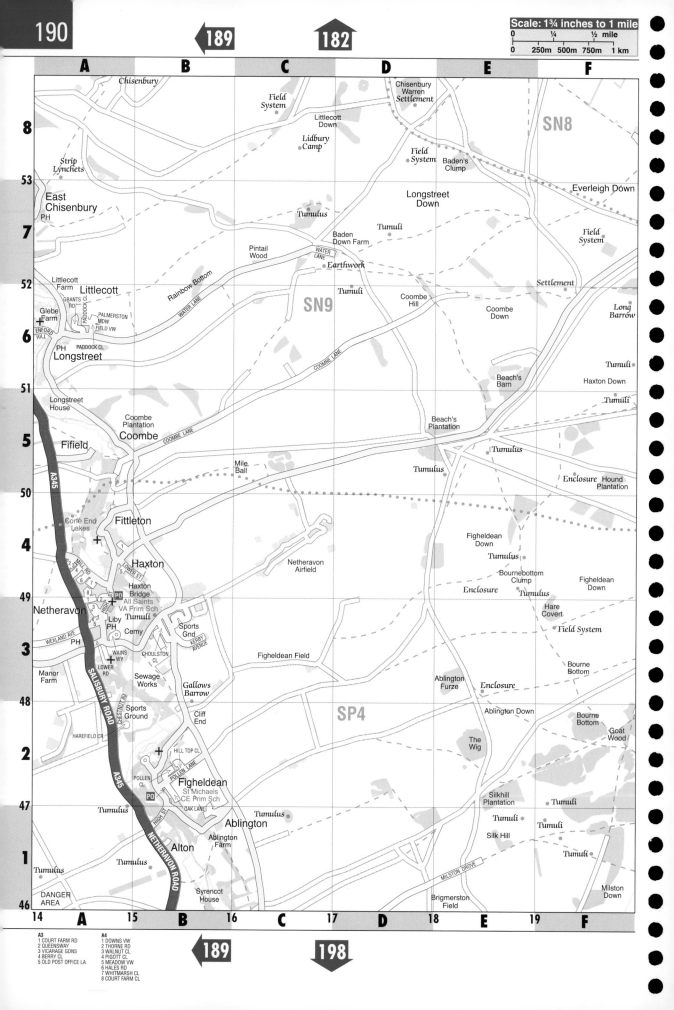

Scale: 1¾ inches to 1 mile
0   ¼   ½ mile
0 250m 500m 750m 1 km

A B C D E F

8

Chisenbury

Field
System

Littlecott
Down

Chisenbury
Warren
Settlement

SN8

Lidbury
Camp

53

Strip
Lynchets

Field
System

Baden's
Clump

Everleigh Down

East
Chisenbury
PH

7

Tumulus

Longstreet
Down

Tumuli

Field
System

52

Littlecott
Farm

Littlecott

Rainbow Bottom

Pintail
Wood

Baden
Down Farm

WATER
LANE

Earthwork

SN9

Tumuli

Coombe
Hill

Settlement

Coombe
Down

Long
Barrow

Glebe
Farm

GRANTS
RD

PADDOCK CL

PALMERSTON
MDW
FIELD VW

WATER
LANE

6

ENFORD
HILL

PH

PADDOCK CL

Longstreet

COOMBE LANE

Tumuli

Beach's
Barn

Haxton Down

Tumuli

51

Longstreet
House

Coombe
Plantation

COOMBE LANE

Beach's
Plantation

Tumulus

5

Fifield

Coombe

COOMBE LANE

Mile
Ball

Tumulus

Tumulus

Enclosure Hound
Plantation

50

Corfe End
Lakes

Fittleton

Netheravon
Airfield

Figheldean
Down

Tumulus

A345

4

Haxton

Tumulus

Bournebottom
Clump

Figheldean
Down

MILL RD

Haxton
Bridge
All Saints
VA Prim Sch

Enclosure

Tumulus

Hare
Covert

49

Netheravon

HIGH ST

PO

Liby
PH

Tumuli

Sports
Gnd

KERBY
AVENUE

Field System

LOWER ST

Cemy

3

WEXLAND AVE

PH

WAINS
WY

LOWER
RD

CHOULSTON
CL

Sewage
Works

Figheldean Field

Bourne
Bottom

CHESTNUT AV

Manor
Farm

HAREFIELD CR

Gallows
Barrow

SP4

Ablington
Furze

Enclosure

Bourne
Bottom

Goat
Wood

48

Sports
Ground

Cliff
End

Ablington Down

SALISBURY ROAD

HILL TOP CL

The
Wig

2

POLLEN LANE

POLLEN
CL

Figheldean

Silkhill
Plantation

Tumuli

A345

PO

St Michaels
CE Prim Sch

HIGH ST

OAK LANE

Tumulus

Silk Hill

Tumuli

Tumuli

47

Tumulus

Ablington

Tumuli

NETHERAVON ROAD

Ablington
Farm

Milston
Down

1

Alton

Tumuli

Tumulus

MILSTON DROVE

Tumuli

46

DANGER
AREA

Syrencot
House

Brigmerston
Field

14 A 15 B 16 C 17 D 18 E 19 F

A3
1 COURT FARM RD
2 QUEENSWAY
3 VICARAGE GDNS
4 BERRY CL
5 OLD POST OFFICE LA

A4
1 DOWNS VW
2 THORNE RD
3 WALNUT CL
4 PIGOTT CL
5 MEADOW VW
6 HALES RD
7 WHITMARSH CL
8 COURT FARM CL

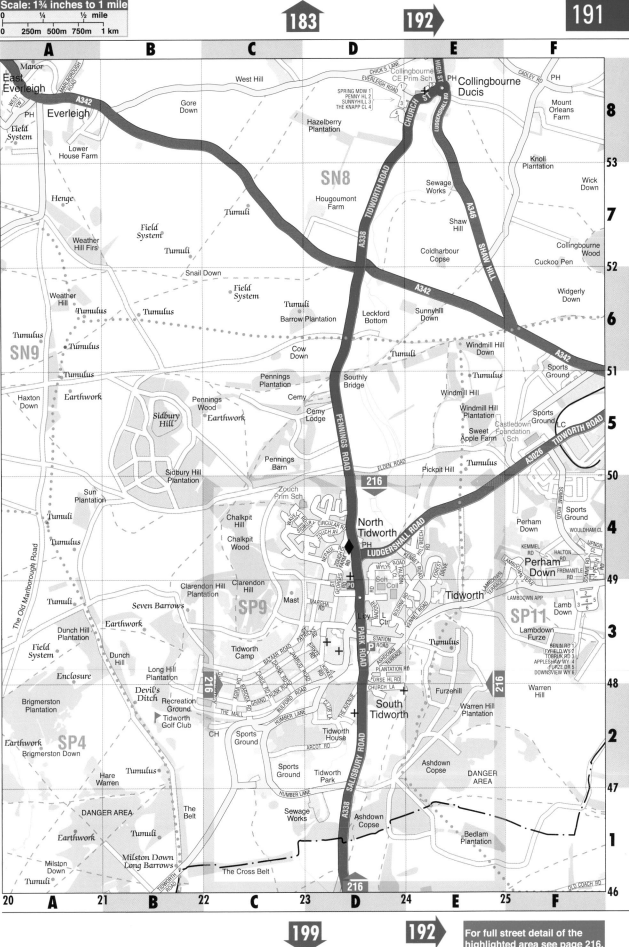

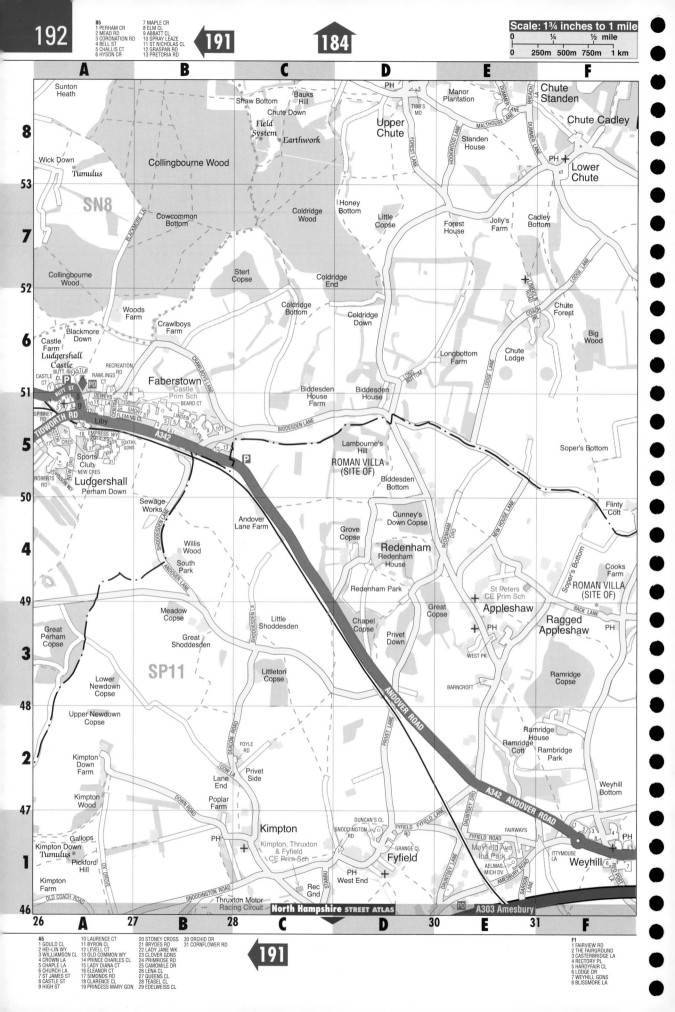

Scale: 1¾ inches to 1 mile

North Hampshire STREET ATLAS

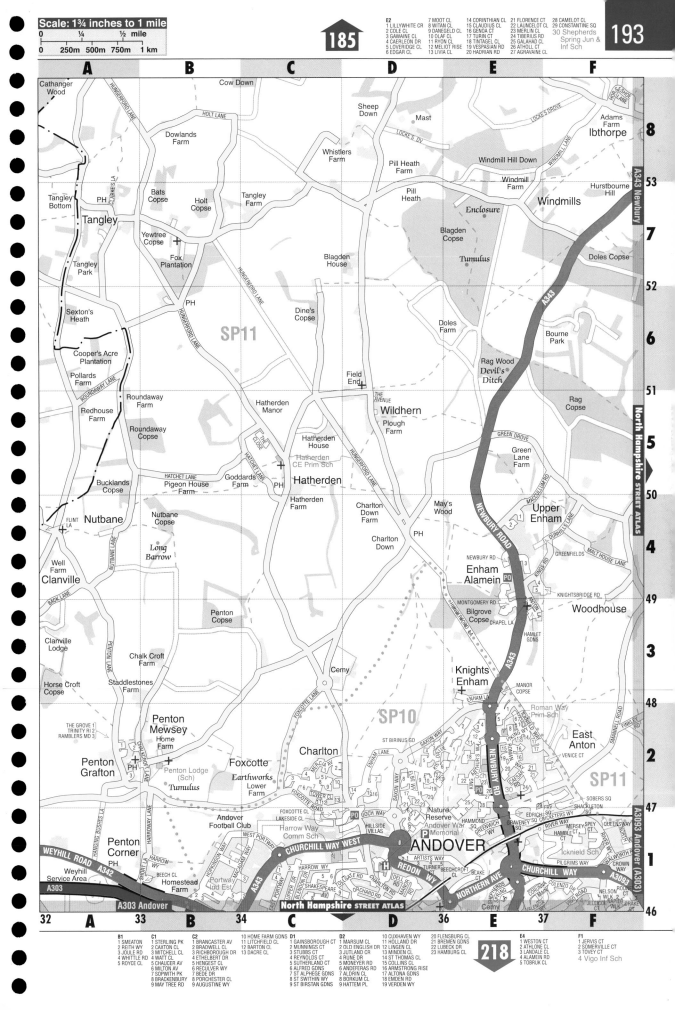

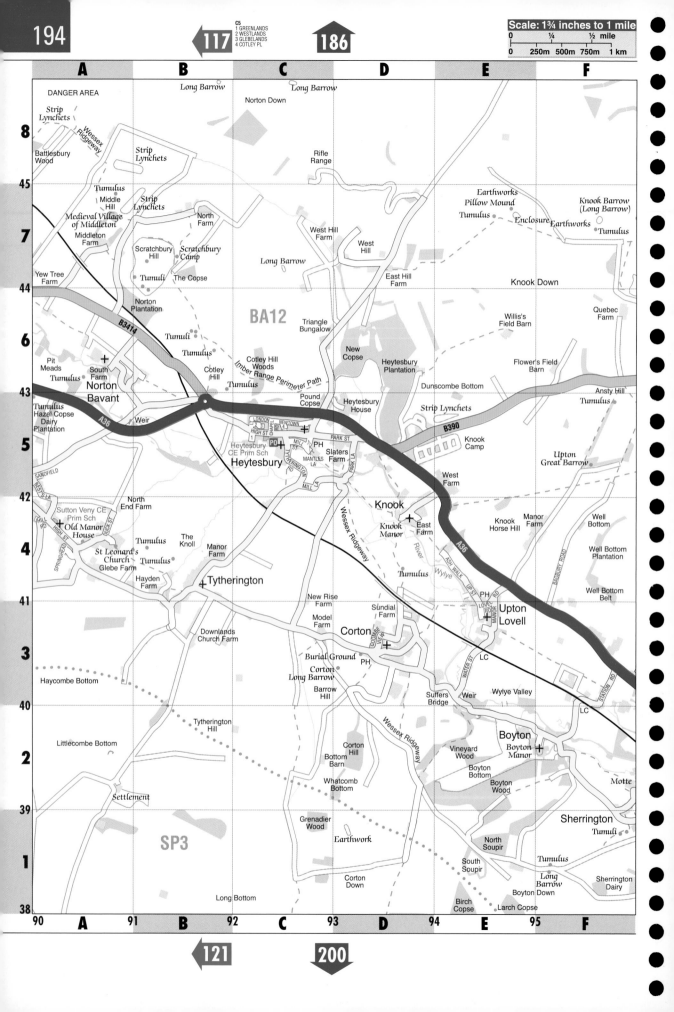

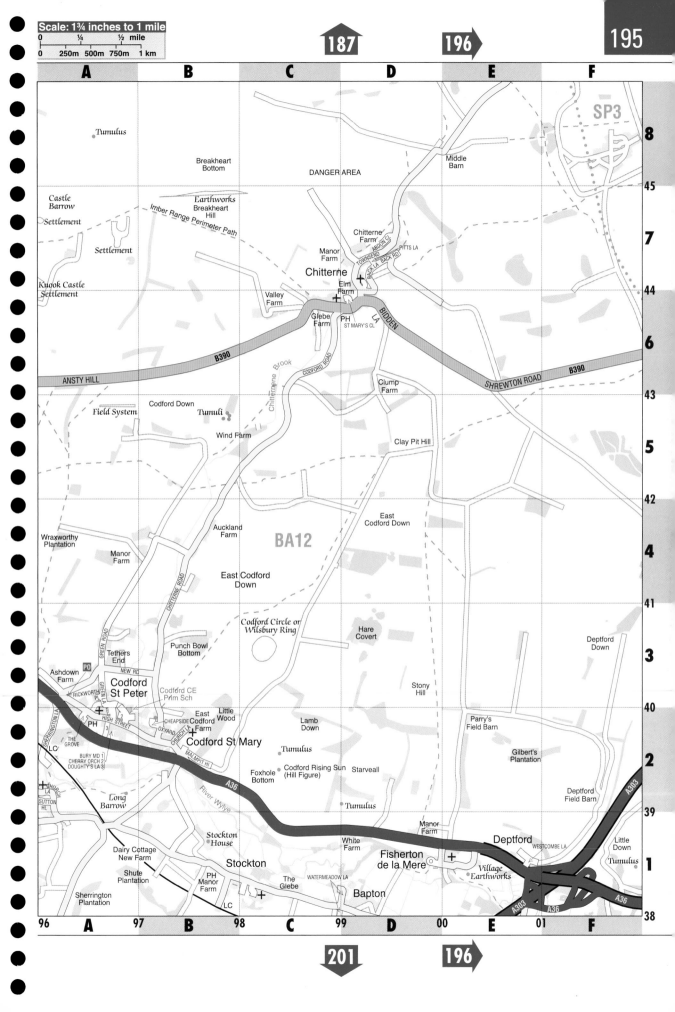

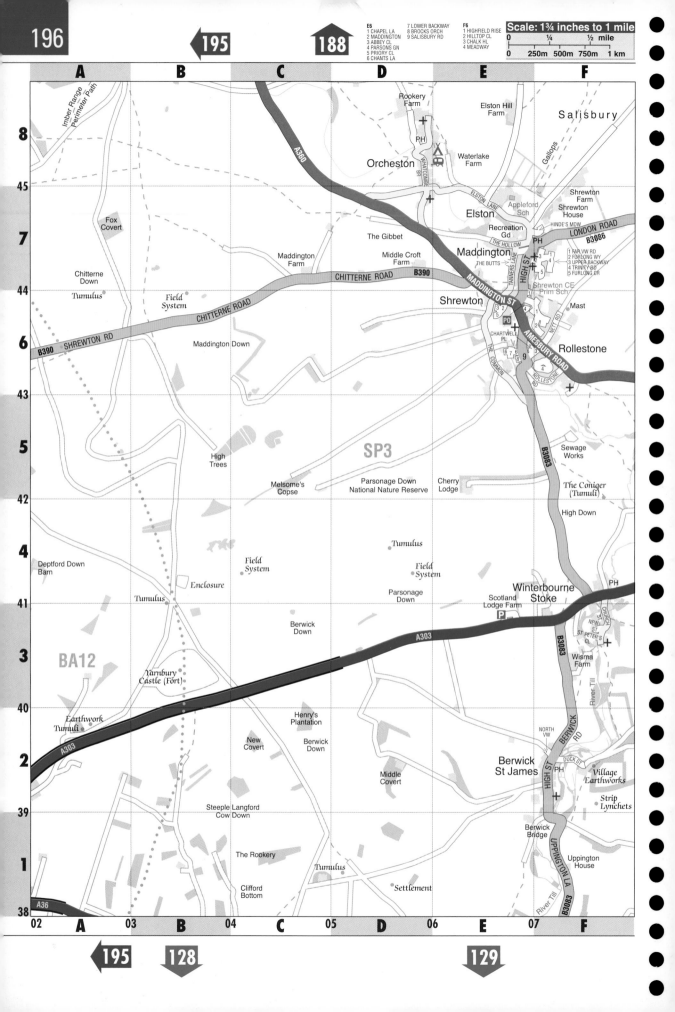

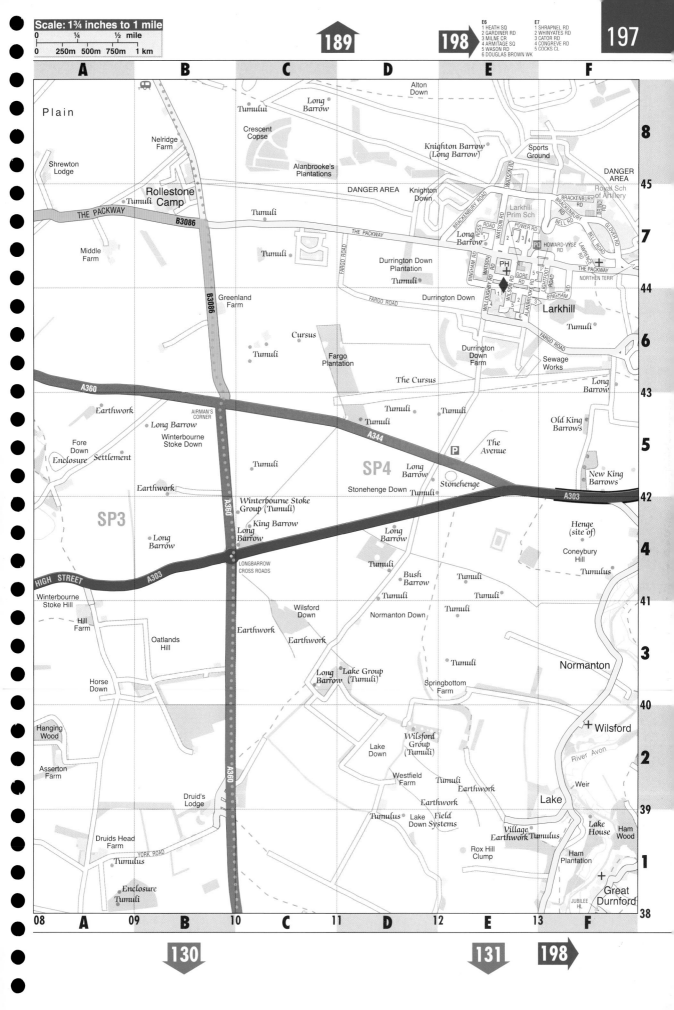

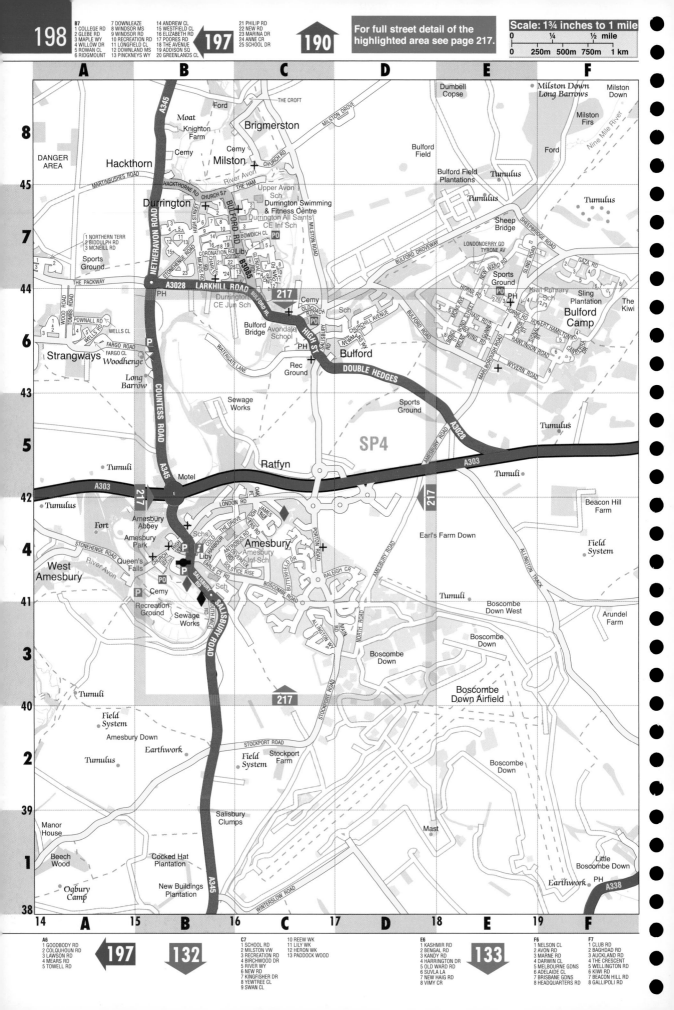

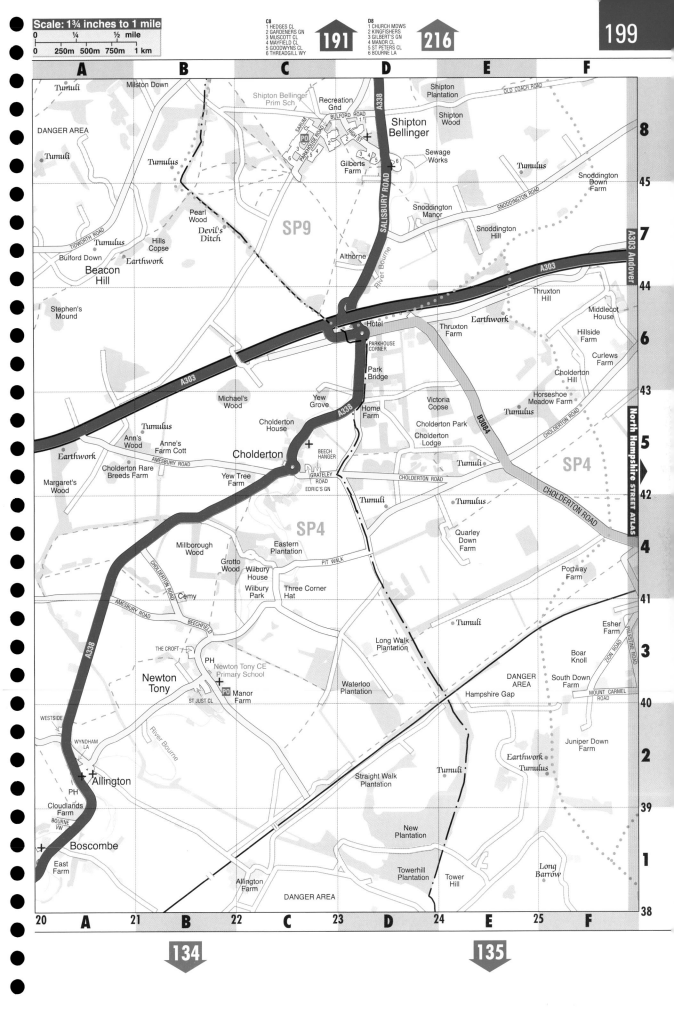

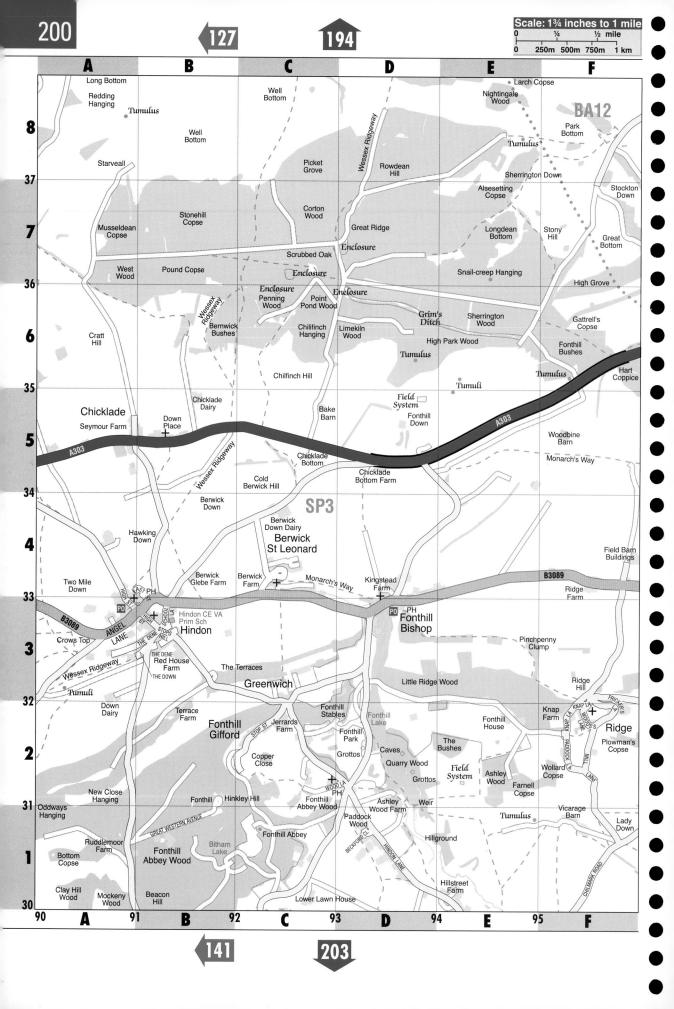

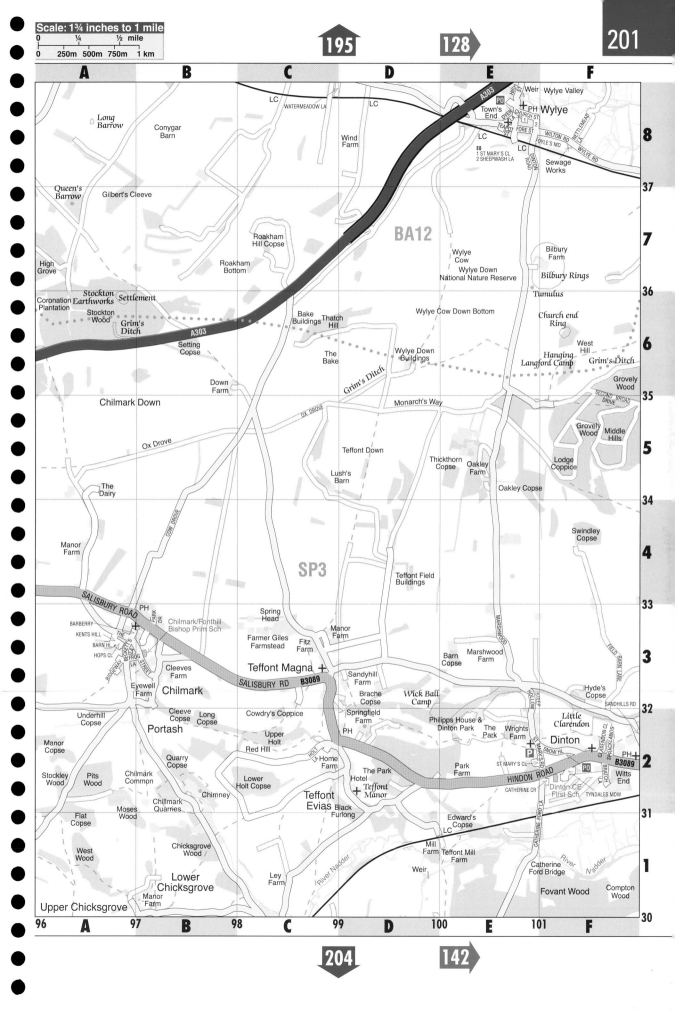

140

141

Scale: 1¾ inches to 1 mile

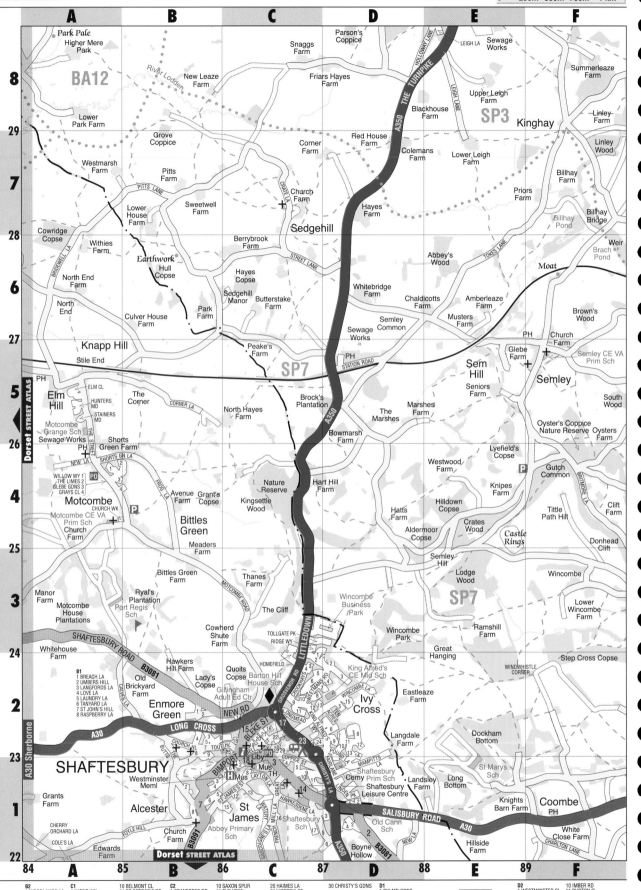

206

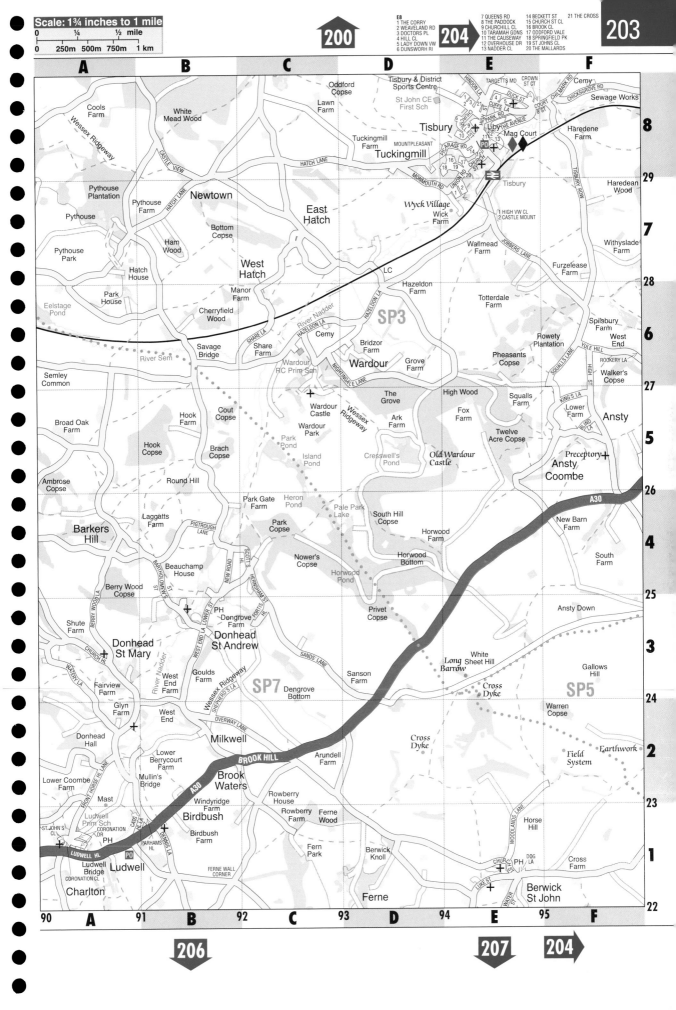

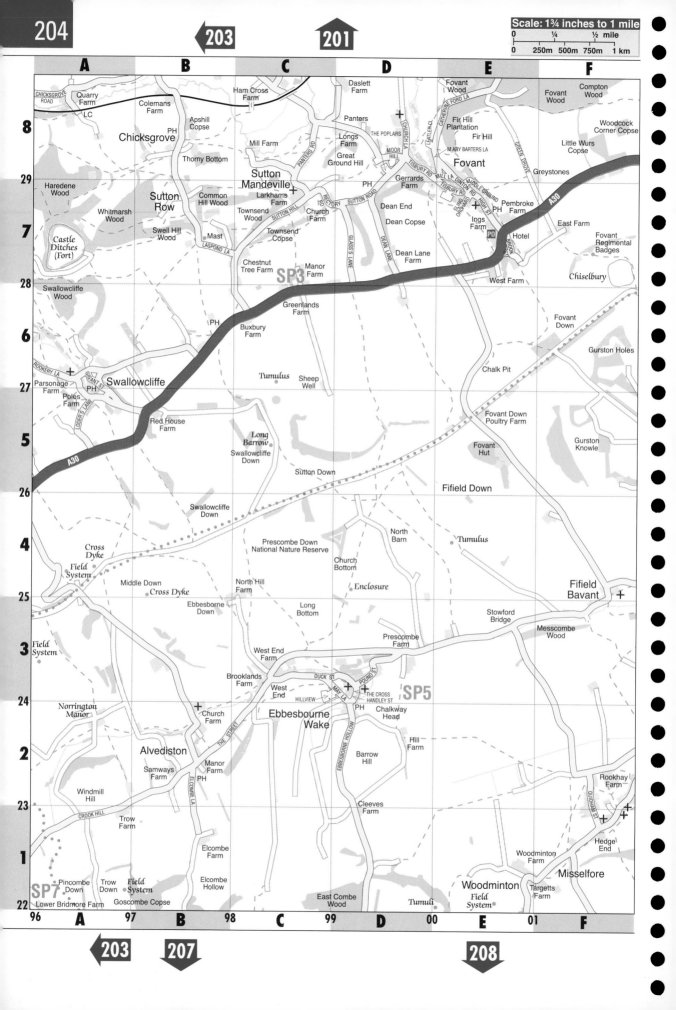

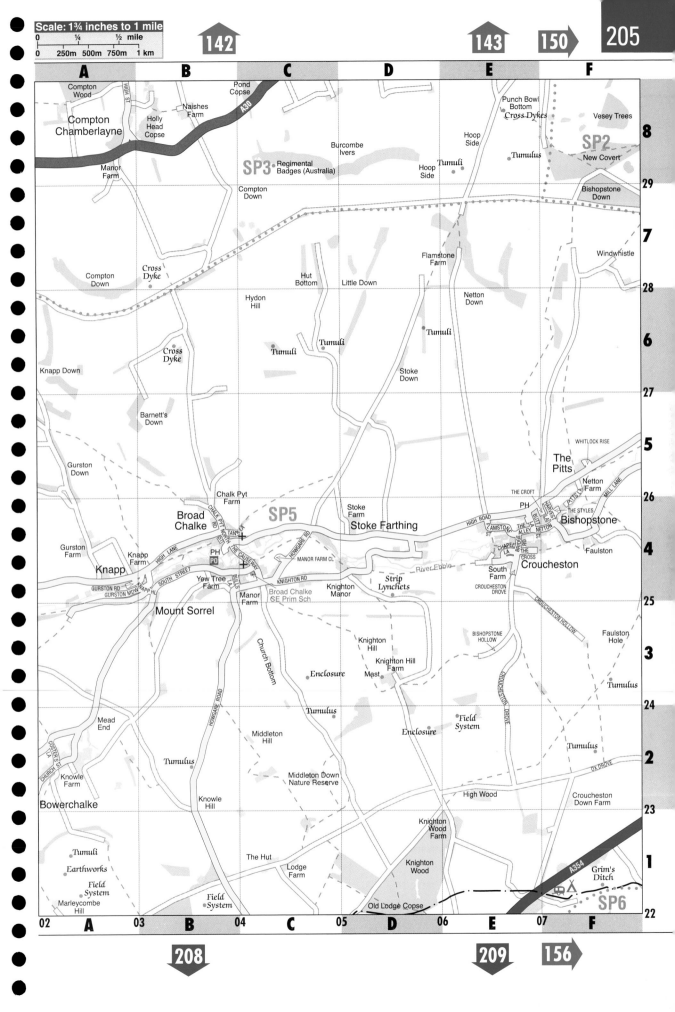

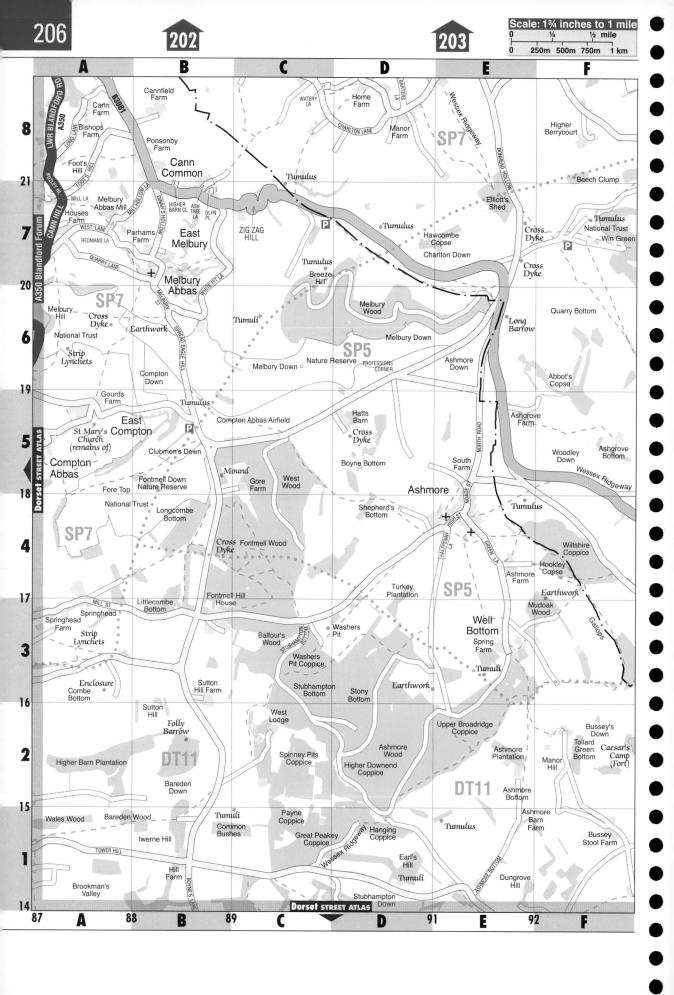

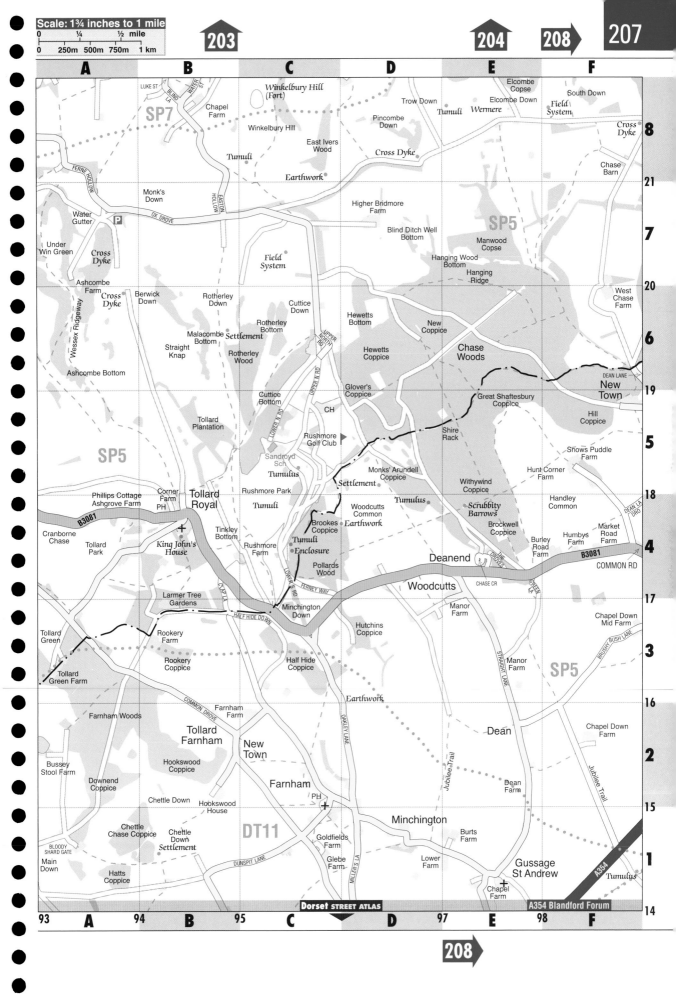

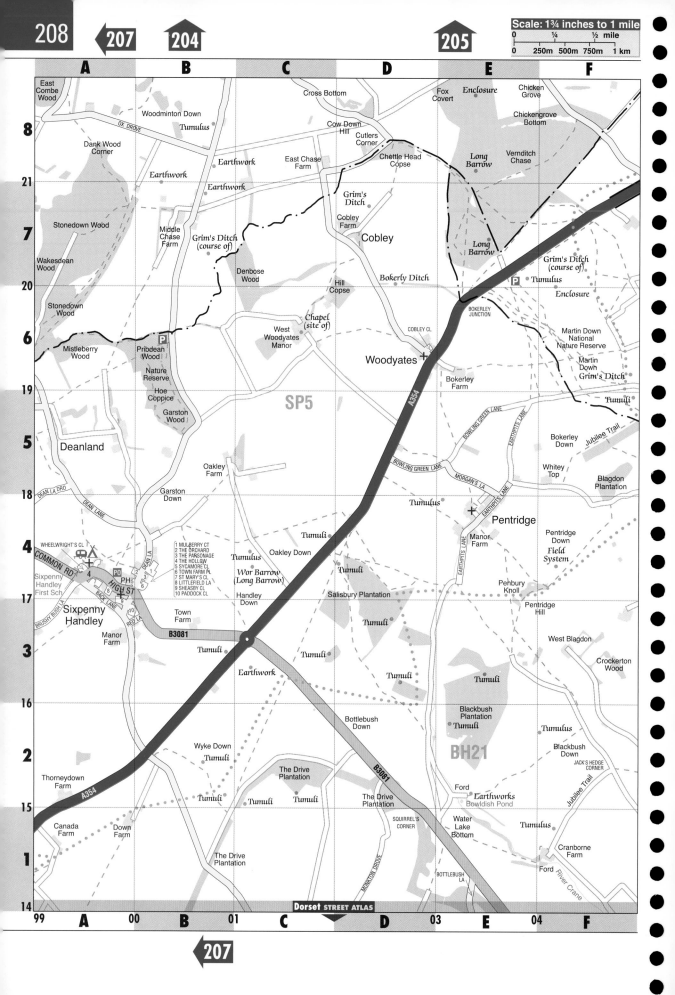

Scale: 1¾ inches to 1 mile

0   ¼   ½   mile
0 250m 500m 750m 1 km

A B C D E F

East Combe Wood

Woodminton Down

OX DROVE

Tumulus

Cross Bottom

Cow Down Hill

Fox Covert

Enclosure

Chicken Grove

Chickengrove Bottom

8

Dank Wood Corner

Earthwork

East Chase Farm

Cutlers Corner

Chettle Head Copse

Long Barrow

Vernditch Chase

21

Earthwork

Earthwork

Grim's Ditch

Long Barrow

7

Stonedown Wood

Middle Chase Farm

Grim's Ditch (course of)

Cobley Farm

Cobley

Grim's Ditch (course of)

Wakesdean Wood

Denbose Wood

Hill Copse

Bokerly Ditch

P

Tumulus

Enclosure

20

Stonedown Wood

Chapel (site of)

COBLEY CL

BOKERLEY JUNCTION

6

Mistleberry Wood

Pribdean Wood

P

West Woodyates Manor

Woodyates

Bokerley Farm

Martin Down National Nature Reserve

Nature Reserve

A354

Martin Down

Grim's Ditch

Hoe Coppice

SP5

Tumuli

19

Garston Wood

BOWLING GREEN LANE

Bokerley Down

Jubilee Trail

5

Deanland

Oakley Farm

Garston Down

BOWLING GREEN LANE

MORGAN'S LA

EARTHPITS LANE

Whitey Top

Blagdon Plantation

18

DEAN LA DRO

DEAN LANE

Tumulus

Pentridge

Pentridge Down

Field System

4

WHEELWRIGHT'S CL

1 MULBERRY CT
2 THE ORCHARD
3 THE PARSONAGE
4 THE HOLLOW
5 SYCAMORE CL
6 TOWN FARM PL
7 ST MARY'S CL
8 LITTLEFIELD LA
9 SHEASBY CL
10 PADDOCK CL

Tumulus

Oakley Down

Tumuli

Manor Farm

EARTHPITS LANE

Penbury Knoll

Pentridge Hill

COMMON RD

Sixpenny Handley First Sch

PO

PH

DEAN LA

HIGH ST

Wor Barrow (Long Barrow)

Tumuli

Salisbury Plantation

West Blagdon

Crockerton Wood

3

Sixpenny Handley

BACK LANE

RED LA

Town Farm

Handley Down

B3081

Tumuli

Earthwork

Tumuli

Tumuli

Tumuli

Blackbush Plantation

Tumuli

Tumulus

Blackbush Down

16

Manor Farm

Bottlebush Down

BH21

2

BRUSHY BUSH LA

Thorneydown Farm

A354

Wyke Down

Tumuli

The Drive Plantation

B3081

JACK'S HEDGE CORNER

15

Canada Farm

Down Farm

Tumuli

Tumuli

Tumuli

The Drive Plantation

Ford

Earthworks
Bowldish Pond

Squirrel's Corner

Water Lake Bottom

Tumulus

Cranborne Farm

1

The Drive Plantation

MONKTON DROVE

BOTTLEBUSH LA

Ford

Jubilee Trail

River Crane

14

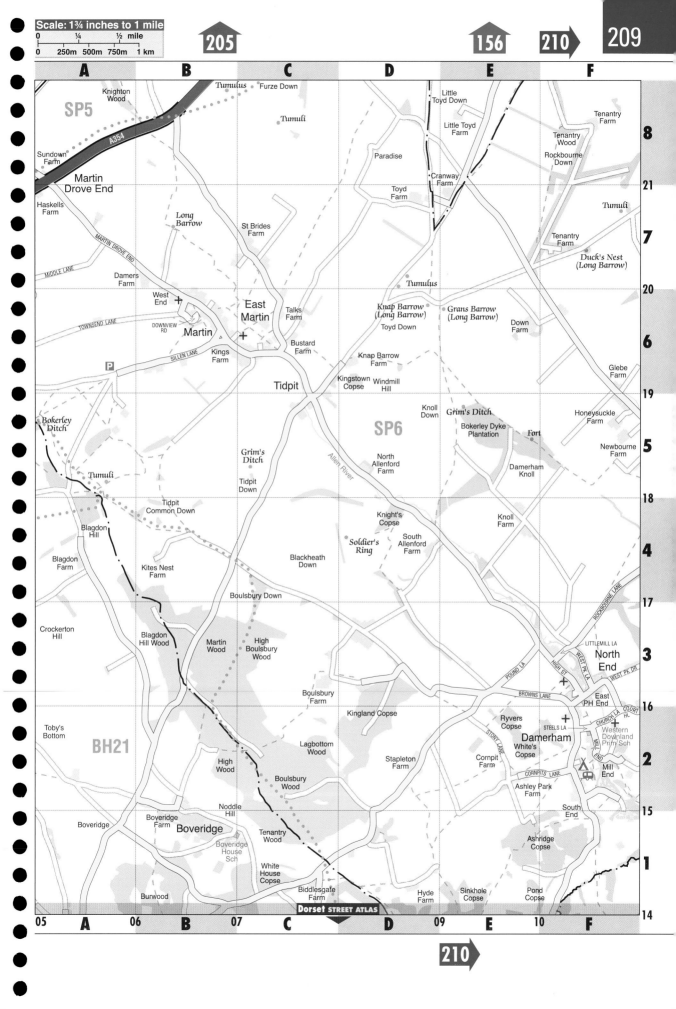

A   B   C   D   E   F

SP5

Knighton Wood

Tumulus   Furze Down

Tumuli

Little Toyd Down

Little Toyd Farm

Tenantry Farm

Tenantry Wood

Rockbourne Down

8

Sundown Farm

Martin Drove End

Paradise

Cranway Farm

21

Haskells Farm

Long Barrow

St Brides Farm

Toyd Farm

Tumuli

7

MARTIN DROVE END

MIDDLE LANE

Damers Farm

Tumulus

Tenantry Farm

Duck's Nest (Long Barrow)

TOWNSEND LANE

West End

East Martin

Talks Farm

Knap Barrow (Long Barrow)

Grans Barrow (Long Barrow)

Down Farm

20

DOWNVIEW RD

Martin

Toyd Down

6

P

SILLEN LANE

Kings Farm

Bustard Farm

Knap Barrow Farm

Glebe Farm

Tidpit

Kingstown Copse

Windmill Hill

19

Bokerley Ditch

SP6

Knoll Down

Grim's Ditch

Honeysuckle Farm

Bokerley Dyke Plantation

Fort

5

Tumuli

Grim's Ditch

Tidpit Down

North Allenford Farm

Damerham Knoll

Newbourne Farm

18

Tidpit Common Down

Knight's Copse

Knoll Farm

Blagdon Hill

Soldier's Ring

South Allenford Farm

4

Blagdon Farm

Kites Nest Farm

Blackheath Down

17

Boulsbury Down

Crockerton Hill

Blagdon Hill Wood

Martin Wood

High Boulsbury Wood

LITTLEMILL LA

North End

WEST PK LA

3

POUND LA

HIGH ST

WEST PK DR

Boulsbury Farm

BROWNS LANE

East PH End

16

Toby's Bottom

BH21

High Wood

Kingland Copse

Ryvers Copse

STEELS LA

CHURCH LA

COURT HL

Western Downland Prim Sch

STONY LANE

Lagbottom Wood

Damerham

White's Copse

2

Boveridge Farm

Noddle Hill

Boulsbury Wood

Stapleton Farm

Cornpit Farm

CORNPITS LANE

Mill End

Boveridge

Boveridge

Tenantry Wood

Ashley Park Farm

South End

15

Burwood

White House Copse

Biddlesgate Farm

Hyde Farm

Sinkhole Copse

Pond Copse

Ashridge Copse

1

Boveridge House Sch

Dorset STREET ATLAS

14

05   A   06   B   07   C   08   D   09   E   10   F

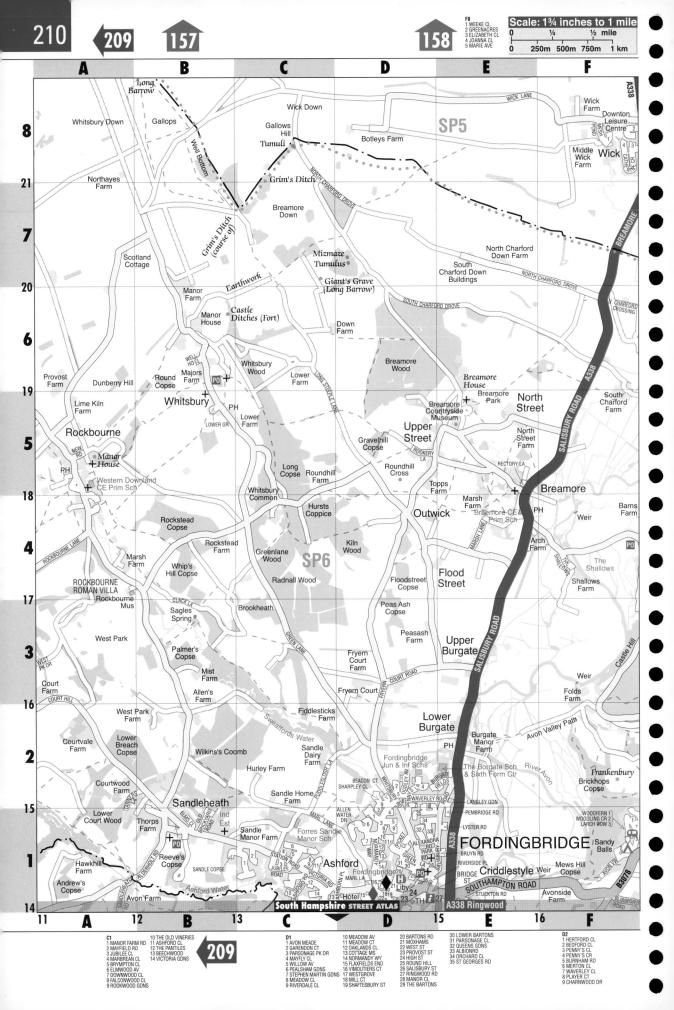

210
209 157 158

Scale: 1¾ inches to 1 mile
0   ¼   ½ mile
0   250m 500m 750m 1 km

F8
1 WEEKE CL
2 GREENACRES
3 ELIZABETH CL
4 JOANNA CL
5 MARIE AVE

A B C D E F

8
21
7
20
6
19
5
18
4
17
3
16
2
15
1
14

Long Barrow
Gallops
Whitsbury Down
Northayes Farm
Scotland Cottage
Grim's Ditch
(course of)
Earthwork
Manor Farm
Manor House
Castle Ditches (Fort)
Round Copse
Majors Farm
Whitsbury
Rockbourne
Manor House
Dunberry Hill
Lime Kiln Farm
Provost Farm
Whitsbury Wood
Lower Farm
Lower Farm
Whitsbury Common
Rockstead Copse
Rockstead Farm
Whip's Hill Copse
Greenlane Wood
SP6
Radnall Wood
Long Copse
Roundhill Farm
Hursts Coppice
Kiln Wood
Wick Down
Gallows Hill
Tumuli
Grim's Ditch
Breamore Down
Mizmaze
Tumulus
Giant's Grave
(Long Barrow)
Down Farm
Gravelhill Copse
Roundhill Cross
Topps Farm
Marsh Farm
Botleys Farm
SP5
Wick Lane
Wick Farm
Downton Leisure Centre
Wick
Middle Wick Farm
North Charford Down Farm
NORTH CHARFORD DROVE
South Charford Down Buildings
SOUTH CHARFORD DROVE
Breamore Wood
Breamore House
Breamore Park
Breamore Countryside Museum
Upper Street
North Street
North Street Farm
RECTORY LA
Breamore
Outwick
Breamore CE Prim Sch
MARSH LANE
SALISBURY ROAD
A338
BREAMORE
South Charford Farm
Barns Farm
Weir
Arch Farm
The Shallows
Shallows Farm
Flood Street
Floodstreet Copse
Peas Ash Copse
Peasash Farm
Upper Burgate
Weir
Folds Farm
Castle Hill
Rockbourne Lane
Marsh Farm
ROCKBOURNE ROMAN VILLA
Rockbourne Mus
Sagles Spring
CLACK LA
Brookheath
GREEN LANE
Fryern Court Farm
Fryern Court
FRYERN COURT ROAD
Lower Burgate
Burgate Manor Farm
Avon Valley Path
West Park
WEST PK DR
Court Farm
COURT HILL
West Park Farm
Palmer's Copse
Mist Farm
Allen's Farm
Fiddlesticks Farm
Sweatfords Water
Sandle Dairy Farm
River Avon
Frankenbury Brickhops Copse
Courtvale Farm
Lower Breach Copse
Wilkins's Coomb
Hurley Farm
Sandle Home Farm
FORDINGBRIDGE
Sandy Balls
Courtwood Farm
Sandleheath
Ind Est
Thorps Farm
Reeve's Copse
Sandle Manor Farm
Forres Sandle Manor Sch
Ashford
Fordingbridge Jun & Inf Schs
The Burgate Sch & Sixth Form Ctr
Criddlestyle
Mews Hill Copse
Avonside Farm
Lower Court Wood
Hawkhill Farm
Andrew's Copse
Avon Farm
Ashford Water
SOUTHAMPTON ROAD
A338 Ringwood
South Hampshire STREET ATLAS

11 A 12 B 13 C 14 D 15 E 16 F
209

C1
1 MANOR FARM RD
2 MAYFIELD RD
3 JUBILEE CL
4 MARBREAN CL
5 BRYMPTON CL
6 ELMWOOD AV
7 DOWNWOOD CL
8 FALCONWOOD CL
9 ROOKWOOD GDNS
10 THE OLD VINERIES
11 ASHFORD CL
12 THE PANTILES
13 BEECHWOOD
14 VICTORIA GDNS

D1
1 AVON MEADE
2 GARENDON CT
3 PARSONAGE PK DR
4 MAYFLY CL
5 WILLOW AV
6 PEALSHAM GDNS
7 STEPHEN MARTIN GDNS
8 MEADOW CL
9 RIVERDALE AV
10 MEADOW AV
11 MEADOW CT
12 OAKLANDS CL
13 COTTAGE MS
14 NORMANDY WY
15 FLAXFIELDS END
16 VIMOUTIERS CT
17 WESTGROVE
18 MILL CT
19 SHAFTESBURY ST
20 BARTONS RD
21 MOXHAMS
22 WEST ST
23 PROVOST ST
24 HIGH ST
25 ROUND HILL
26 SALISBURY ST
27 RINGWOOD RD
28 MANOR CL
29 THE BARTONS
30 LOWER BARTONS
31 PARSONAGE CL
32 QUEENS GDNS
33 ALBIONRD
34 ORCHARD CL
35 ST GEORGES RD
D2
1 HERTFORD CL
2 BEDFORD CL
3 PENNY'S CL
4 PENNY'S CR
5 BURNHAM RD
6 MERTON CL
7 WAVERLEY CL
8 PLAYER CT
9 CHARNWOOD DR

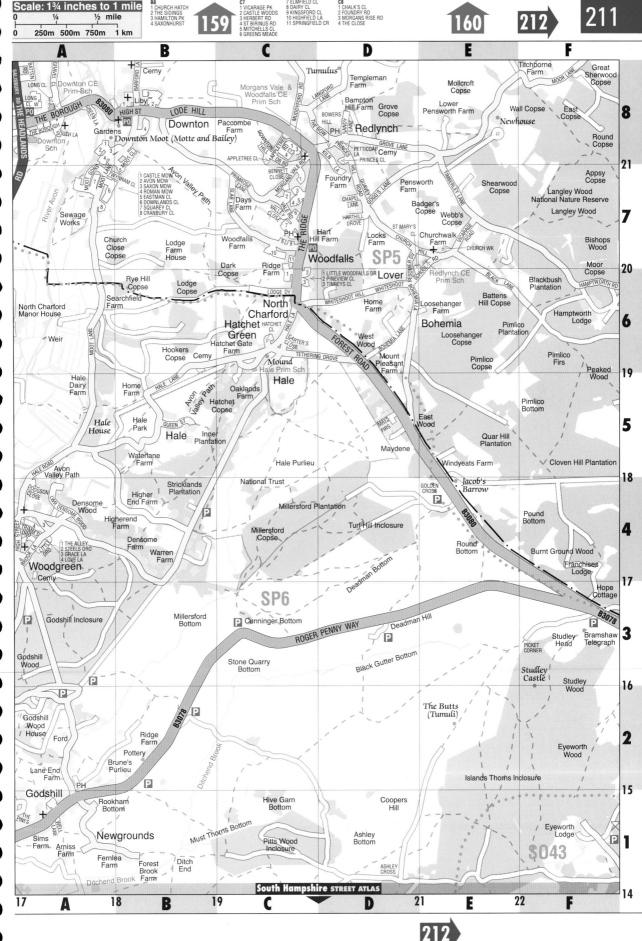

B8
1 CHURCH HATCH
2 THE SIDINGS
3 HAMILTON PK
4 SAXONHURST

C7
1 VICARAGE PK
2 CASTLE WOODS
3 HERBERT RD
4 ST BIRINUS RD
5 MITCHELLS CL
6 GREENS MEADE

7 ELMFIELD CL
8 DAIRY CL
9 KINGSFORD CL
10 HIGHFIELD LA
11 SPRINGFIELD CR

C8
1 CHALK'S CL
2 PINEVIEW CL
3 MORGANS RISE RD
4 THE CLOSE

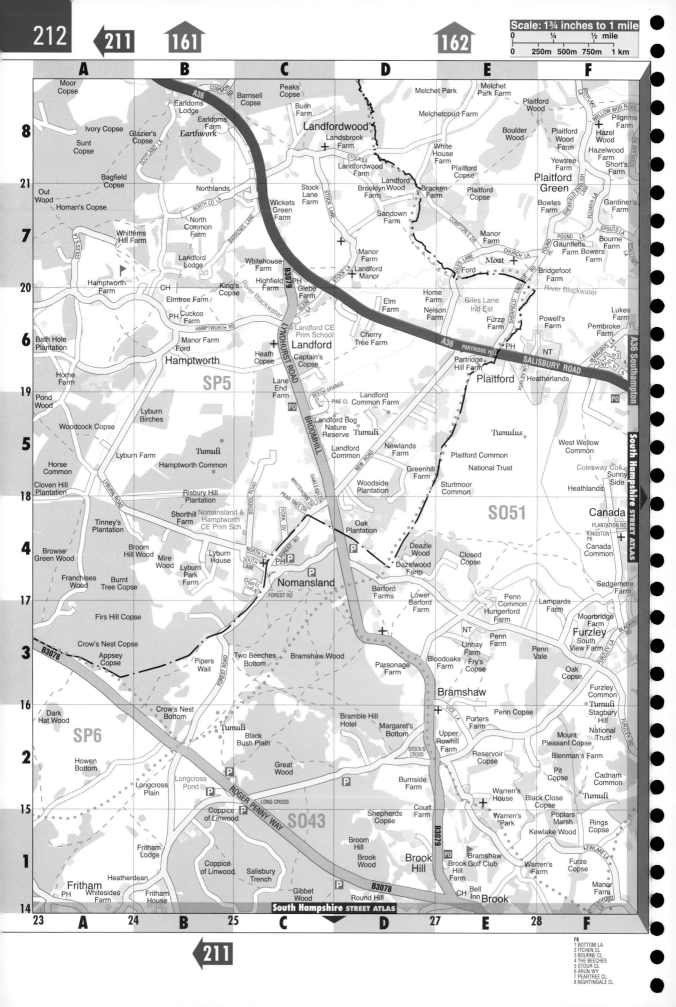

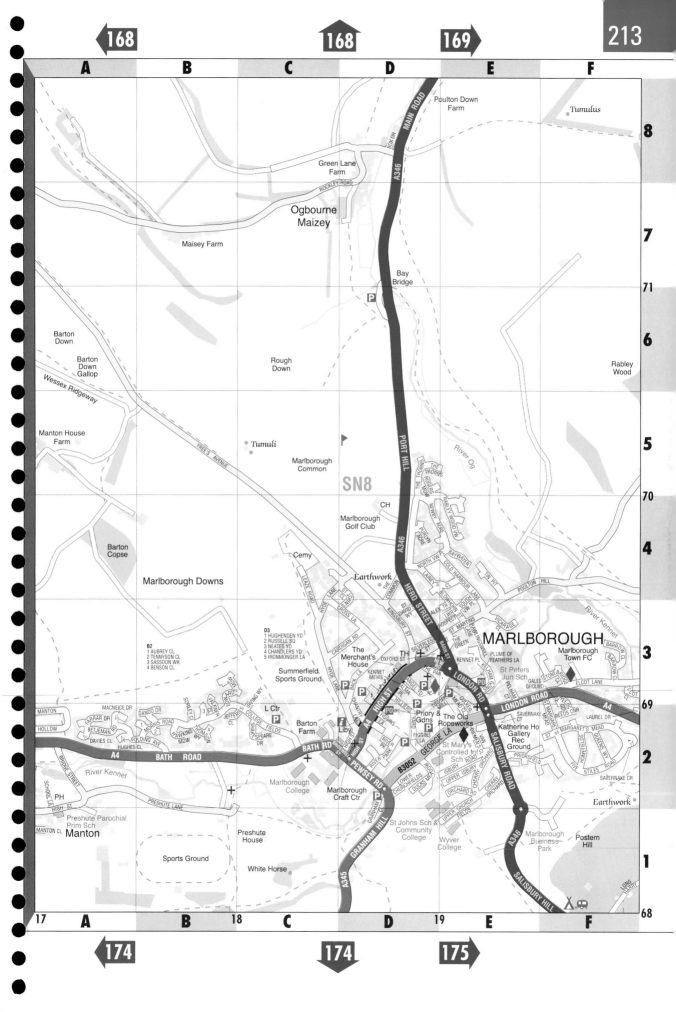

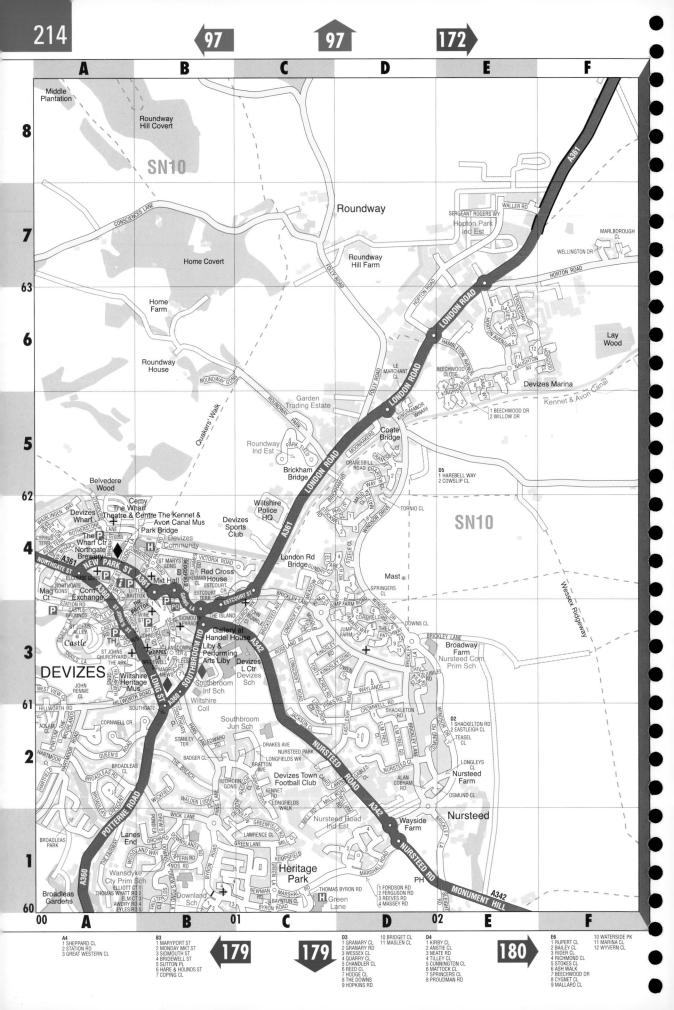

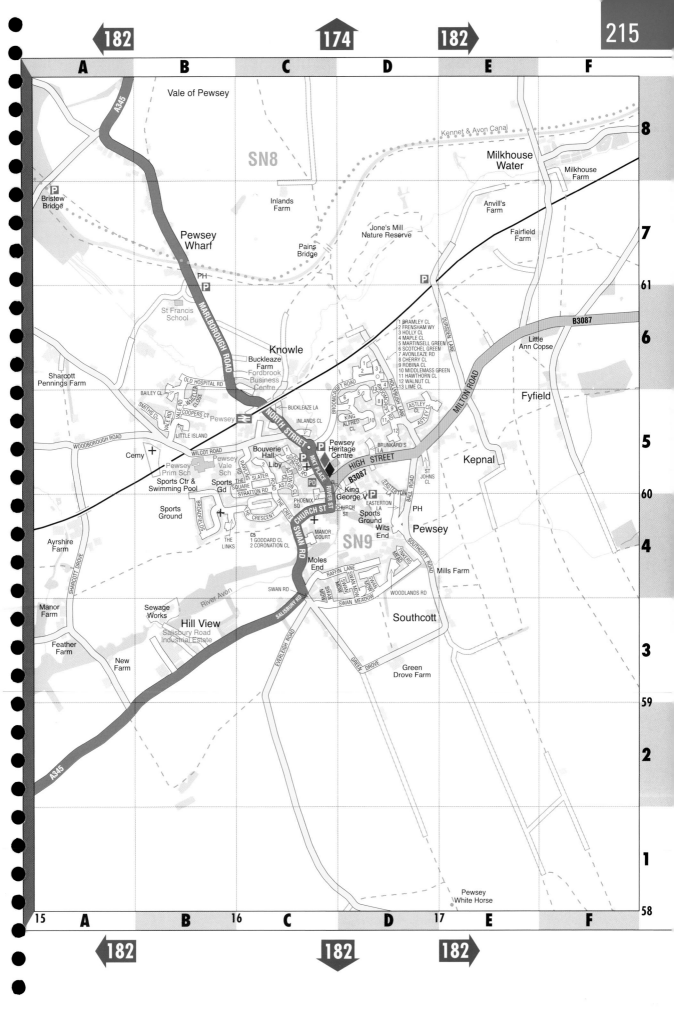

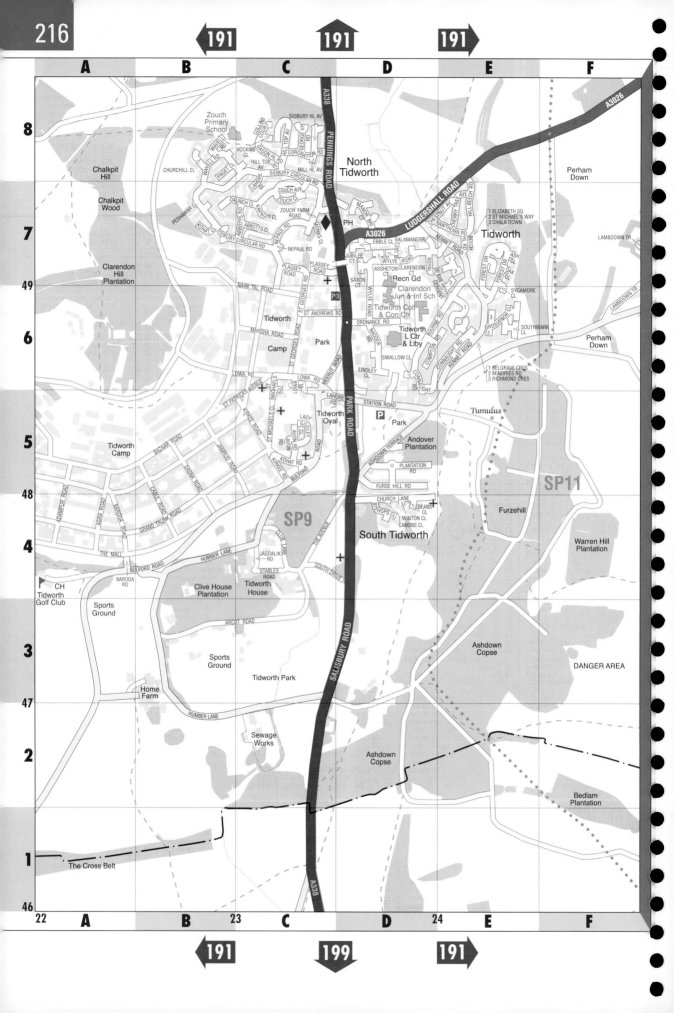

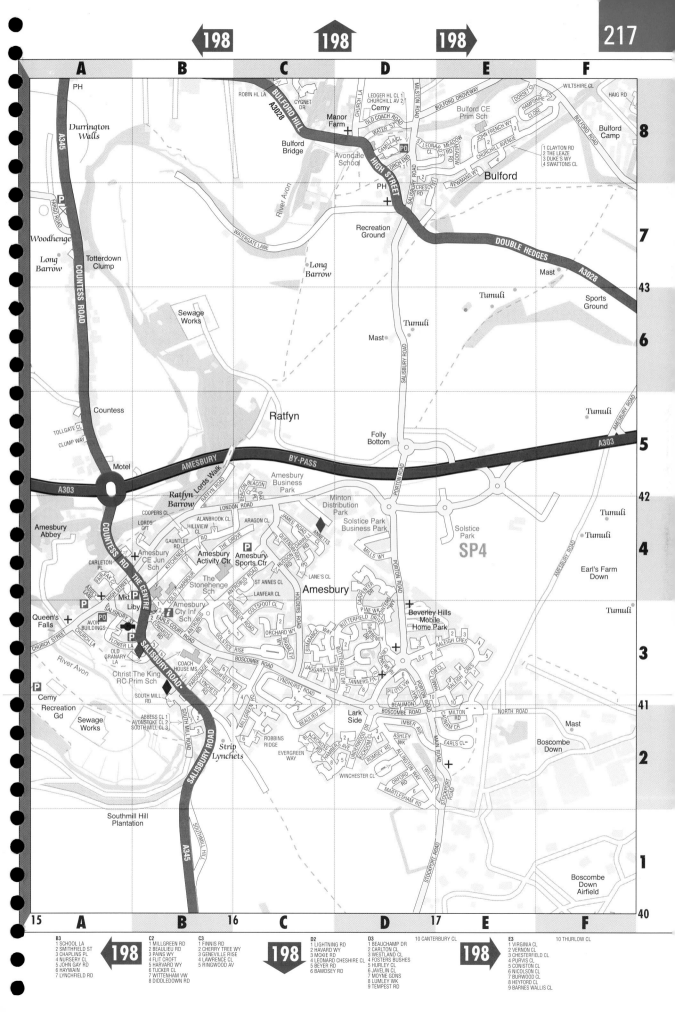

Frome

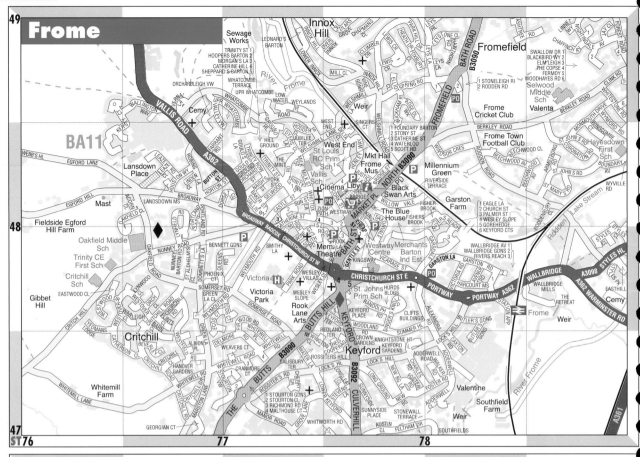

Andover

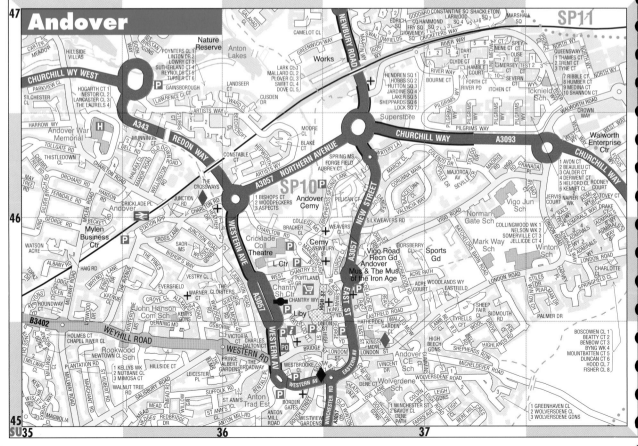

Index

Place name May be abbreviated on the map
Location number Present when a number indicates the place's position in a crowded area of mapping
Locality, town or village Shown when more than one place has the same name
Postcode district District for the indexed place
Page and grid square Page number and grid reference for the standard mapping

Church Rd 6 Beckenham BR2..........53 C6

Public and commercial buildings are highlighted in magenta **Places of interest** are highlighted in blue with a star★

Abbreviations used in the index

Acad	**Academy**	Comm	**Common**	Gd	**Ground**	L	**Leisure**	Prom	**Promenade**
App	**Approach**	Cott	**Cottage**	Gdn	**Garden**	La	**Lane**	Rd	**Road**
Arc	**Arcade**	Cres	**Crescent**	Gn	**Green**	Liby	**Library**	Recn	**Recreation**
Ave	**Avenue**	Cswy	**Causeway**	Gr	**Grove**	Mdw	**Meadow**	Ret	**Retail**
Bglw	**Bungalow**	Ct	**Court**	H	**Hall**	Meml	**Memorial**	Sh	**Shopping**
Bldg	**Building**	Ctr	**Centre**	Ho	**House**	Mkt	**Market**	Sq	**Square**
Bsns, Bus	**Business**	Ctry	**Country**	Hospl	**Hospital**	Mus	**Museum**	St	**Street**
Bvd	**Boulevard**	Cty	**County**	HQ	**Headquarters**	Orch	**Orchard**	Sta	**Station**
Cath	**Cathedral**	Dr	**Drive**	Hts	**Heights**	Pal	**Palace**	Terr	**Terrace**
Cir	**Circus**	Dro	**Drove**	Ind	**Industrial**	Par	**Parade**	TH	**Town Hall**
Cl	**Close**	Ed	**Education**	Inst	**Institute**	Pas	**Passage**	Univ	**University**
Cnr	**Corner**	Emb	**Embankment**	Int	**International**	Pk	**Park**	Wk, Wlk	**Walk**
Coll	**College**	Est	**Estate**	Intc	**Interchange**	Pl	**Place**	Wr	**Water**
Com	**Community**	Ex	**Exhibition**	Junc	**Junction**	Prec	**Precinct**	Yd	**Yard**

Index of localities, towns and villages

A

Ablington 190 B1
Acton Turville 52 F6
Alcester 202 B1
Alcombe 82 F8
Aldbourne 170 A6
Alderbury 153 C3
Alderton 39 F2
All Cannings 180 E8
Allington
Amesbury 199 A2
Chippenham 69 E3
Devizes 172 E2
Allington Bar 69 F2
Alton 190 B1
Alton Barnes 173 C1
Alton Priors 173 D1
Alvediston 204 B2
Amesbury 217 C4
Ansty 203 F5
Ansty Coombe 203 F5
Appleshaw 192 E3
Ashbury 164 A7
Ashford 210 C1
Ashley
Box 83 A6
Tetbury 3 A2
Ashmore 206 D5
Ashton Common 102 F1
Ashton Keynes 6 F1
Atworth 92 F8
Aughton 183 D3
Avebury 173 C8
Avebury Trusloe 173 B8
Avington 177 F7
Avon 71 F6
Avoncliff 99 F4
Axford 169 D1

B

Badbury 65 F5
Badbury Wick 65 D8
Badminton 38 F2
Bagshot 176 F4
Ballard's Ash 47 D5
Bapton 195 D1
Barford St Martin 143 A3
Barkers Hill 203 A4
Barrow 136 C5
Barrow Street 139 F2
Batheaston 82 B4
Bathford 82 B2
Baverstock 142 B4
Baydon 170 C8
Beanacre 94 A8
Beckhampton 173 B7
Beechingstoke 181 A6
Bemerton 145 C2
Bemerton Heath 145 C4
Berkley 111 A7
Berkley Down 110 C5
Berryfield 93 F1
Berwick Bassett 167 B4
Berwick St James 196 E2
Berwick St John 203 E1
Berwick St Leonard 200 C4
Bewley Common 86 E5
Biddestone 76 F8
Birdbush 203 B1
Bishopdown 146 C4
Bishops Cannings 172 B3
Bishopstone
Salisbury 205 F4
Swindon 163 E6
Bishopstrow 117 E4
Bittles Green 202 B4
Blackland 89 F6
Bleet 102 F2
Blue Vein 83 D3
Blunsdon St Andrew 34 E8
Bodenham 152 F1
Bohemia 211 E6
Boreham 117 C5
Boscombe 199 A1
Bottlesford 181 D6
Bourton
Bishops Cannings 172 C3
Gillingham 137 E2
Boveridge 209 B1
Bowden Hill 87 B4
Bowerchalke 205 A2
Bowerhill 94 D1
Bowldown 70 E8
Box 83 D6
Box Hill 83 F7
Boyton 194 E2
Bradenstoke 59 C3
Bradford Leigh 91 F1
Bradford-on-Avon 100 E6
Bramshaw 212 E3
Bratton 186 B7
Breamore 210 F5
Bremhill 80 E7
Brigmerston 198 C8
Brinkworth 45 E5
Britford 152 E5
Brixton Deverill 120 E2
Broad Blunsdon 21 C2
Broadbush 21 D1
Broad Chalke 205 B4
Broad Hinton 167 C7
Broad's Green 88 F3
Broad Street 181 C6
Broad Town 167 A8
Brokenborough 27 D7
Brokerswood 107 F5
Bromham 96 A7
Brook 212 E1
Brook Hill 212 D1
Brook Waters 203 B2
Broomfield 55 A1
Broughton Gifford 93 C4
Brunton 183 E3
Bugley 116 C6
Bulbridge 144 B1
Bulford 217 E8
Bulford Camp 198 F6
Bulkington 178 E5
Bullenhill 106 E8
Bullock's Horn 15 E1
Burbage 183 D8
Burcombe 143 E2
Burton
Acton Turville 53 B4
Mere 139 D5
Buscot Wick 12 D8
Bushton 166 E8
Buttermere 185 B8

C

Cadley 175 A5
Calcutt 20 A7
Callow Hill 46 D6
Calne 81 B2
Calne Marsh 81 C4
Calstone Wellington 172 A7
Canada 212 F4
Cann Common 206 B8
Castle Combe 68 A7
Castle Eaton 10 B4
Catcomb 73 D6
Cerney Wick 7 F5
Chalford 113 A8
Chapel Barton 115 D6
Chapel Knapp 85 D5
Chapel Plaister 84 A5
Chapmanslade 111 C4
Charlcutt 72 F4
Charlton
Andover 193 C2
Malmesbury 29 A6
Pewsey 181 D3
Shaftesbury 203 A1
Charlton-All-Saints 159 A4
Charlton Heath 29 D6
Charlton Musgrove 136 B4
Charnage 139 E4
Chedglow 14 C7
Chelworth 4 C1
Chelworth Lower Green 19 A5
Chelworth Upper Green 19 A6
Cheney Manor 34 F1
Cherhill 166 B1
Chicklade 200 A5
Chicksgrove 204 B8
Chilmark 201 B3
Chilton Foliat 170 F1
Chippenham 78 E7
Chirton 180 F4
Chisbury 176 B5
Chiseldon 65 D3
Chitterne 195 C7
Chittoe 87 E2
Cholderton 199 C5
Christian Malford 58 B2
Churchfields 145 D1
Chute Cadley 192 F8
Chute Standen 192 F8
Clanville
Andover 193 A4
Stanton St Quintin 56 E4
Clatford 174 B7
Claverton 90 B5
Clearwood 111 F8
Clench 174 E1
Clench Common 174 D4
Clevancy 166 C6
Cleverton 44 D8
Cloatley 15 E2
Cloatley End 16 B1
Clyffe Pypard 166 F8
Coate
Devizes 180 C8
Swindon 51 C2
Cobley 208 D7
Codford St Mary 195 B2
Codford St Peter 195 A3
Cold Harbour
Trowbridge 102 F2
Warminster 116 F8
Colerne 75 B3
Collingbourne Ducis 191 E8
Collingbourne
Kingston 183 D2
Combe 185 F8
Common Platt 33 F2
Compton 189 F7
Compton Abbas 206 A5
Compton Bassett 166 B3
Compton
Chamberlayne 205 A8
Conkwell 90 C1
Conock 180 E4
Coombe
Durrington 190 B5
Shaftesbury 202 F1
Coombe Bissett 150 F1
Coped Hall 47 F4
Corsham 85 A8
Corsley 111 D2
Corsley Heath 115 B8
Corston 42 F5
Corton 194 D3
Cotmarsh 62 B4
Cotswold Community 6 D4
Coulston 178 E1
Covingham 51 D7
Cowesfield Green 161 F4
Cricklade 19 E7
Criddlestyle 210 E1
Crockerton 116 E1
Crockerton Green 116 F2
Crofton 176 A1
Crooked Soley 170 F3
Cross Keys 77 A3
Croucheston 205 F4
Crudwell 14 E6
Cuckold's Green 179 C4
Cuckoo's Corner 180 B4
Cuckoo's Knob 174 F1
Culkerton 3 A5
Culverslade 66 A2

D

Damerham 209 F2
Dauntsey 45 B1
Dauntsey Lock 59 B5
Dean 207 E2
Deanend 207 E4
Deanland 208 A5
Deptford 195 E1
Derry Fields 17 F8
Derry Hill 79 F2
Dertfords 115 B7
Devizes 214 A3
Didmarton 24 C3
Dilton Marsh 112 B8
Dinton 201 F2
Ditchampton 144 C4
Ditteridge 83 B8
Dogridge 32 F3
Donhead St Andrew 203 B3
Donhead St Mary 203 A3
Dorcan 51 D5
Down Ampney 8 D7
Downton 211 B8
Draycot Cerne 56 F1

Draycot Fitz Payne 174 A2
Draycot Foliat 168 D8
Drynham 105 E5
Dunfield 10 A8
Dunge 106 E1
Dunkirk 179 D1
Durley 175 D3
Durrington 198 B7
Dursley 105 E1

E

East Anton 193 F2
Eastbury 171 C8
East Chisenbury 190 A7
East Compton 206 A5
Eastcott 180 A2
Eastcourt 15 D6
East End 74 A8
Easterton 180 A2
Easterton Sands 179 F2
East Everleigh 191 A8
East Garston 171 E7
East Gomeldon 133 E4
East Grafton 183 F7
East Grimstead 154 E4
East Hatch 203 C7
East Kennett 173 E6
East Knoyle 141 C6
Eastleaze 49 B6
East Martin 209 C6
East Melbury 206 B7
Easton 77 D2
Easton Grey 26 C3
Easton Royal 183 A7
Easton Town 25 D1
Eastrip 75 D4
East Town 106 E4
East Tytherton 72 B2
East Winterslow 149 C8
East Woodlands 114 B5
Ebbesbourne Wake 204 C2
Eddington 177 C8
Eden Vale 108 E3
Edington 186 C8
Elcombe 63 E5
Eldene 51 C5
Elliots Green 114 D8
Elm Cross 167 D7
Elm Hill 202 A5
Elston 196 E7
Enford 189 F6
Englands 78 F5
Enham Alamein 193 E4
Enmore Green 202 B2
Erlestoke 187 A8
Etchilhampton 180 C7
Even Swindon 49 E6
Everleigh 191 A8
Ewen 5 C8

F

Faberstown 192 B6
Fairford 1 E7
Fairwood 108 B4
Farleigh Hungerford . . . 103 F2
Farleigh Wick 90 F5
Farley 154 D8
Farnham 207 C2
Ferne 203 D1
Fiddington Sands 179 F1
Fifield 190 A5
Fifield Bavant 204 E4
Figheldean 190 B2
Filands 28 A6
Firsdown 148 C8
Fisherton de la Mere . . . 195 D1
Fittleton 190 A4
Flaxlands 47 D6
Flood Street 210 E4
Fonthill Bishop 200 D3
Fonthill Gifford 200 B2
Ford
  Chippenham 68 A2
  Salisbury 146 D7
Fordingbridge 210 E1
Forest Hill 175 B7
Forewoods Common . . . 101 C7
Fosbury 185 A5
Foscote 54 E3
Fovant 204 E8
Foxcotte 193 E2
Foxham 72 D7
Foxley 41 F8
Fresh Brook 49 A4
Freshford 99 B5
Fritham 212 A4
Frogmore 109 A4
Frome 110 A5
Fromefield 110 A6
Froxfield 176 D7
Fugglestone St Peter . . . 144 F4
Furzley 212 F3
Fyfield
  Andover 192 D1
  Pewsey 215 E5

G

Gare Hill 118 A5
Garsdon 29 B4
Gasper 137 C7
Gastard 85 D6
Giddeahall 68 D2

Goatacre 73 F7
Godshill 211 A1
Gomeldon 133 D4
Gorse Hill 35 D1
Grange Park 48 F5
Great Ashley 91 A1
Great Bedwyn 176 B3
Great Chalfield 92 E3
Great Cheverell 179 C1
Great Durnford 197 F1
Greatfield 47 F8
Great Hinton 178 A6
Great Somerford 44 B2
Great Wishford 129 F3
Green Hill 32 D1
Greenmeadow 35 B4
Greenwich 200 C3
Grittenham 46 C2
Grittleton 54 D5
Gussage St Andrew 207 E1

H

Hackthorn 198 A8
Hailstone Hill 8 A1
Halcombe 27 E3
Hale 211 C5
Halfway 113 A4
Half Way Firs 76 C1
Ham 177 B2
Ham Green 101 C8
Hampshire Gate 185 A1
Hampton 22 D5
Hampton Hill 22 E5
Hamptworth 212 B6
Hanging Langford 128 C7
Hankerton 15 C2
Hannington 22 B7
Hannington Wick 11 A4
Hardway 122 A4
Haresfield 23 B8
Harnham 151 E6
Hatchet Green 211 C6
Hatherden 193 C5
Hawkeridge 108 E8
Haxton 190 B4
Haydon Wick 34 E5
Hayes Knoll 19 E2
Heddington 89 B1
Heddington Wick 88 E2
Henley
  Box 83 C4
  Shalbourne 185 A6
Heritage Park 214 F2
Heytesbury 194 C5
Heywood 109 A8
Higher Pertwood 127 E4
Highway 166 B5
Highworth 23 B5
Hilcott 181 D5
Hill Corner 110 E7
Hill Deverill 120 F5
Hill View 215 B3
Hilmarton 166 A6
Hilperton 102 A3
Hilperton Marsh 101 F5
Hindon 200 B3
Hinton
  Charterhouse 98 E1
Hinton Parva 163 D6
Hisomley 112 C7
Hodson 65 A5
Hoggington 104 D4
Holloway 141 A1
Holt 92 E1
Holwell 139 B5
Homington 151 D1
Hook 47 F6
Hook Street 48 B6
Horningsham 119 A7
Horpit 163 B7
Horton 172 C2
Hudswell 84 C8
Huish 174 A2
Hullavington 41 E1
Hungerford 177 A6
Hungerford
  Newtown 171 D2
Huntenhull Green 111 C3
Hurdcott 146 F8
Hyde 35 D7

I

Ibthorpe 193 B5
Idmiston 133 F8
Idstone 163 F7
Imber 187 A3
Inglesham 2 B1
Inkpen 177 E3
Ireland 105 B2
Ivy Cross 202 D2

K

Keevil 178 C5
Kellaways 71 E4
Kemble 4 E7
Kemble Wick 4 E4
Kempsford 10 E6
Kepnal 215 E5
Kilmington 123 E5
Kilmington Common . . . 123 D4
Kimpton 192 C1
Kinghay 202 F3

Kingsdown
  Bathford 82 F3
  Stratton St Margaret . . . 35 F5
Kingshill 50 B5
Kingston Deverill 126 B6
Kingstone Winslow 164 A8
Kington Langley 70 E7
Kington St Michael 70 A8
Knapp 205 A4
Knapp Hill 202 A5
Knighton 170 D2
Knights Enham 193 E3
Knockdown 24 F5
Knook 194 D4
Knowle 215 C6

L

Lacock 86 D5
Lake 197 F2
Lambourn 165 B2
Lambourn Woodlands . . 171 A6
Landford 212 C6
Landfordwood 212 D8
Lane End 115 A8
Langley Burrell 71 A3
Larkhill 197 F6
Latton 8 C4
Laverstock 146 E2
Lavington Sands 179 E2
Lawn 50 F3
Lea 28 F1
Leafield 84 E7
Lechlade-on-Thames 2 D4
Leigh 18 C5
Leigh Delamere 55 C3
Letcombe Bassett 165 F8
Leverton 171 B1
Liddington 163 B4
Liden 51 D3
Limpers Hill 139 D4
Limpley Stoke 99 A6
Linkenholt 185 C1
Little Ashley 91 A2
Little Badminton 38 E5
Little Bedwyn 176 D5
Little Chalfield 92 C3
Little Cheverell 187 D8
Littlecott
  Calne 166 A7
  Durrington 190 A6
Littledown 185 D4
Little Durnford 131 D1
Little Faringdon 2 F8
Little Horton 172 C1
Little Langford 129 A6
Little London 166 E2
Little Marsh 102 F4
Little Salisbury 182 E2
Little Somerford 44 B5
Littleton 178 B7
Littleton Drew 53 E5
Littleton Panell 179 D1
Littleworth 182 E8
Lockeridge 174 A6
Longbridge Deverill 120 F6
Long Cross 138 B5
Long Dean 68 C4
Longfield 105 E8
Longhedge 115 D5
Long Newnton 13 C5
Longstreet 190 A6
Lopcombe Corner 135 D3
Lover 211 D6
Lower Blunsdon 21 B3
Lower Burgate 210 D2
Lower Chicksgrove 201 B1
Lower Chute 192 F8
Lower Everleigh 182 E1
Lower Green 177 D3
Lower Moor 17 A4
Lower Rudge 107 D4
Lower Seagry 57 F7
Lower Stanton St
  Quintin 56 D6
Lower Stratton 36 B2
Lower Studley 105 E6
Lower Wanborough 163 B6
Lower Woodford 131 C3
Lower Wraxall 91 E5
Lower Zeals 138 D5
Luckington 39 E4
Ludgershall 192 A5
Ludwell 203 A1
Lydiard Green 48 B8
Lydiard Millicent 33 D1
Lydiard Plain 32 B1
Lydiard Tregoze 48 E6
Lye Green 100 A4
Lye's Green 111 B1
Lyneham 60 B2

M

Maddington 196 E7
Maiden Bradley 118 D2
Malmesbury 28 B3
Manningford Abbots . . . 182 A5
Manningford Bohune . . . 181 F4
Manningford Bruce 181 F5
Manton 213 A1
Marden 181 A4
Market Lavington 179 E1
Marlborough 213 B2
Marr Green 183 D7
Marshfield 74 A8

Marston 179 A3
Marston Hill 1 C4
Marston Meysey 9 D7
Marten 184 C7
Martin 209 B6
Martin Drove End 209 A8
Martinslade 178 E8
Melksham Abbas 206 B7
Melksham 94 A5
Melksham Forest 94 B6
Mere 139 B5
Meysey Hampton 1 A5
Middlehill 83 A6
Middlewick 76 D3
Middle Winterslow 149 B7
Middle Woodford 131 B4
Midford 98 C5
Milbourne 28 D4
Mildenhall 175 A8
Mile Elm 89 A7
Mile End 165 A3
Milford 152 E8
Milkhouse Water 215 E8
Milkwell 203 B2
Milston 198 B8
Milton 141 B3
Milton Lilbourne 182 F7
Minchington 207 D1
Minety 17 B2
Minety Common 31 C8
Misselfore 204 F1
Monk's Park 85 A6
Monkton Combe 98 E8
Monkton Deverill 126 D7
Monkton Farleigh 90 F7
Moor Green 84 D6
Moredon 34 E3
Motcombe 202 A4
Mountain Bower 66 F4
Mount Sorrel 205 B3
Murcott 14 F4

N

Neston 84 E6
Netheravon 190 A3
Netherhampton 151 A8
Netherton 185 F4
Nettleton 53 C1
Nettleton Green 53 B1
Nettleton Shrub 67 C7
Netton 131 E6
Newbury 119 C8
Newgrounds 211 B1
Newton 161 B2
Newton Grove 27 E4
Newton Tony 199 B3
Newtown
  Shalbourne 176 E2
  West Tisbury 203 B7
New Town
  Alton 173 D3
  Farnham 207 C2
  Ramsbury 170 C2
  Sixpenny Handley 207 F6
  Swindon 50 D6
Nine Elms 49 A8
Nomansland 212 C4
Norleaze 108 F8
Normanton 197 F3
Norrington Common 93 C6
North Bradley 105 D4
North Brewham 122 A6
Northbrook 179 E1
North Charford 211 C6
Northend 82 A5
North End 6 E2
North Newnton 181 E4
North Street 210 E5
North Tidworth 216 D8
North Wraxall 67 B3
North Wroughton 64 B8
Norton 41 D5
Norton Bavant 194 A6
Norton Ferris 124 C6
Notton 86 B8
Nunton 152 D1
Nursteed 214 E1
Nutbane 193 A4
Nythe 51 C7

O

Oaksey 15 F7
Oare 174 B2
Odstock 152 A1
Ogbourne Maizey 213 C2
Ogbourne St Andrew . . . 168 F3
Ogbourne St George . . . 169 A5
Okus 50 A4
Oldbury on the Hill 24 B5
Old Town 50 D3
Orcheston 196 D8
Outmarsh 102 F7
Outwick 210 D4
Overtown 64 D4
Oxenwood 184 E6

P

Park Corner 99 A4
Park North 51 A5
Park South 51 A4
Patney 180 F5
Paxcroft 102 C3

Pear Ash 137 C4
Peckingell 71 B2
Penhill 35 C5
Penknap 112 E8
Penleigh 108 D2
Penselwood 137 B4
Penton Corner 193 A1
Penton Grafton 193 A2
Penton Mewsey 193 B2
Pentridge 208 E4
Perham Down 191 F4
Perry Green 29 B7
Petersfinger 152 E7
Petty France 38 B8
Pewsey 215 D4
Pewsey Wharf 215 B7
Pickwick 76 E2
Pinckney Green 90 E5
Pinehurst 35 D3
Pitton 148 C3
Plaitford 212 E6
Plaitford Green 212 F8
Poole Keynes 5 C4
Portash 201 B2
Porton 133 D6
Potterne 179 D5
Potterne Wick 179 C4
Poulshot 179 B6
Preston
  Aldbourne 170 B4
  Lyneham 60 D1
Priory Vale 34 C8
Purlpit 93 A8
Purton 33 B4
Purton Common 33 A5
Purton Stoke 19 C1

Q

Queen Oak 138 A3
Queen Street 31 B3
Quemerford 89 D8
Quidhampton 145 A2

R

Ragged Appleshaw 192 F3
Ram Alley 175 B2
Ramsbury 170 A2
Ratford 80 E5
Ratfyn 217 C5
Redenham 192 D4
Redlands 22 F3
Redlynch 211 D8
Redstocks 95 A2
Restrop 33 A2
Reybridge 86 D7
Ridge 200 F2
Rivar 184 F8
Rockbourne 210 A5
Rockley 168 C2
Rodbourne
  Malmesbury 43 A3
  Swindon 35 A1
Rodbourne Bottom 43 A2
Rodbourne Cheney 35 B2
Rode Hill 103 F1
Rodmarton 3 C8
Rollestone 196 F6
Rollestone Camp 197 B7
Rood Ashton 106 D4
Rook Street 139 A4
Roughmoor 34 B1
Roundway 214 D7
Rowde 96 D2
Rudge 107 D5
Rudloe 76 B1
Rushall 181 E2

S

St Andrew Ridge 35 A8
St Edith's 96 D5
St James 202 C1
St Katharines 175 F4
Salisbury 152 C7
Salterton 131 D4
Sambourne 116 F5
Sandleheath 210 B2
Sandy Lane 88 B4
Sanham Green 177 B5
Sawyers Hill 17 A2
Sedgehill 202 C7
Seend 178 E7
Seend Cleeve 178 C7
Sells Green 95 E1
Semington 102 E5
Semley 202 F5
Serrington 129 C7
Sevenhampton 23 B2
Sevington 55 A2
Shaftesbury 202 A1
Shalbourne 176 F2
Sharcott 182 A6
Sharpstone 99 A4
Shaw
  Melksham 93 D7
  Swindon 49 B7
Sheepdrove 165 B2
Shefford Woodlands . . . 171 E4
Sherrington 194 F1
Sherston 25 B1
Sherston Parva or
  Pinkney 25 E2

Shipton Bellinger 199 D8
Shipton Moyne. 26 E8
Shockerwick. 82 E5
Shorncote 6 A6
Shrewton 196 E6
Sixpenny Handley 208 A3
Slaughterford 76 A8
Sodom 59 C7
Somerford Keynes 5 F3
Sopworth 24 D1
South Brewham 122 A4
Southbrook 139 B4
South Cerney 7 A6
Southcott. 215 D3
Southend 168 F4
South Marston 36 F5
South Newton 130 B2
South Tidworth 216 D4
Southwick 104 F3
South Wraxall 91 D6
Spirthill 73 B4
Standerwick 107 B2
Stanley 80 A6
Stanton Fitzwarren. 22 B1
Stanton St Bernard. . . . 173 A1
Stanton St Quintin 56 B4
Stapleford 129 E7
Startley 43 D1
Staverton 101 C6
Steeple Ashton 178 B3
Steeple Langford 128 D8
Stert 180 B6
Stibb Green. 175 D1
Stitchcombe 175 D8
Stockley 89 C4
Stockton 195 B1
Stoford 130 A3
Stoke Farthing 205 D4
Stonebridge 110 C7
Stormore 112 A8
Stourton 123 F1
Straight Soley 171 A3
Strangways 198 A6
Stratford sub Castle . . . 145 F5
Stratford Tony 150 C2
Stratton St Margaret 36 A3
Studley 80 B3
Studley Green 104 F7
Sturford 115 E6
Sunton 183 E1
Sutton Benger 57 C2
Sutton Mandeville 204 C8
Sutton Row 204 B7

Sutton Veny 117 F1
Swallett Gate 59 A6
Swallowcliffe 204 A6
Swanborough. 22 C4
Swindon. 50 E4

T

Tangley 193 A7
Tanis 96 F2
Teffont Evias 201 C2
Teffont Magna 201 C3
Tellisford 103 E4
Temple 115 C6
Templeton 177 D5
The Causeway 139 C4
The Common
  Brinkworth. 46 B7
  Melksham 93 B5
  Winterslow 149 C6
The Fox 33 F3
The Gibb 53 F3
The Green 141 A3
The Ham 108 E5
The Linleys 85 B6
Theobald's Green 172 A8
The Pitts 205 F5
The Ridge 85 B5
The Shoe 66 F1
The Spa 94 C2
The Stocks 178 C7
The Strand 178 B6
Thickwood 75 D6
Thingley 77 F1
Thornend 58 C1
Thornhill 61 F1
Tidcombe 184 C5
Tiddleywink 68 F4
Tidpit 209 C6
Tidworth 216 E7
Tilshead 188 B3
Tisbury 203 D8
Tockenham 60 E3
Tockenham Wick 60 D7
Tollard Farnham 207 B2
Tollard Royal 207 B4
Toothill 49 C4
Townsend
  Poulshot. 179 A6
  Urchfont 180 C3
Trowbridge. 101 E3
Trowle Common 100 F2

Tuckingmill. 203 D8
Tucking Mill 98 D8
Turleigh 99 F6
Tytherington. 194 B4
Tytherton Lucas 71 D1

U

Uffcott 167 E8
Ugford 144 A3
Underhill 140 F2
Upavon 181 F2
Upper Burgate 210 E3
Upper Castle Combe . . . 68 B8
Upper Chicksgrove 201 A1
Upper Chute 192 D8
Upper Enham 193 F4
Upper Green 177 E2
Upper Inglesham 12 B5
Upper Lambourn 164 F3
Upper Minety 16 D3
Upper Pickwick 76 C3
Upper Seagry 57 D6
Upper Stratton 35 E4
Upper Street 210 D5
Upper Studley 105 A5
Upper Town 58 D4
Upper Up 6 E6
Upper Upham 169 C8
Upper Woodford 131 C7
Upper Wraxall 66 E2
Upton
  Mere 141 A5
  Vernhams Dean 185 D2
Upton Lovell 194 E3
Upton Scudamore 112 E5
Urchfont 180 C4

V

Vastern. 60 F8
Vernham Bank 185 B3
Vernham Dean 185 C3
Vernham Row 185 B4
Vernham Street 185 D4

W

Wadswick 84 B4
Walcot East. 50 F6

Walcot West 50 E5
Wanborough. 163 A5
Wardour. 203 D6
Warleigh 90 D5
Warminster. 116 E7
Warminster Common . . . 116 E5
Waterhay 18 C7
Wedhampton 180 E4
Well Bottom 206 E3
West Amesbury 198 A4
West Ashton 106 B3
Westbrook. 95 E8
Westbury 109 B2
Westbury Leigh 108 E1
West Chisenbury 189 F7
West Crudwell 14 D7
West Dean. 155 F3
West Grafton 183 E7
West Grimstead 154 C2
West Hatch 203 C7
West Hill 85 B1
West Kennett 173 D7
West Kington 66 F7
West Kington Wick 67 B6
West Knoyle 140 E6
West Lavington 187 E8
Westlea 49 D5
Westonbirt 25 D8
West Overton 173 F6
Westrop 77 C1
West Stowell 173 F1
Westwells 84 C6
West Winterslow 148 F5
Westwood
  Bradford-on-Avon 99 F2
  Salisbury 145 B5
West Yatton 68 D3
Wexcombe 184 B6
Weyhill 192 F1
Whaddon
  Alderbury 153 E1
  Hilperton 102 C7
Whitbourne Moor. 115 C7
Whitbourne Springs. . . . 115 E5
White Cross 137 E5
White Hill 139 C2
Whiteparish 161 D4
Whitepits 126 A7
Whitley 85 C1
Whitsbury 210 B5
Whittonditch 170 D3
Wick 210 F8
Widbrook. 100 E4

Widham 33 C5
Wilcot 182 A7
Wildhern 193 D5
Willesley 25 C6
Wilsford
  Amesbury 197 F2
  Pewsey 181 B4
Wilton
  Burbage. 184 A8
  Salisbury 144 C3
Windmills 193 F7
Wingfield 104 C6
Winsley 99 E7
Winterbourne Bassett . . 167 B5
Winterbourne Dauntsey 133 B2
Winterbourne Earls . . . 133 A1
Winterbourne Gunner . . 133 D3
Winterbourne Monkton 167 B3
Winterbourne Stoke. . . 196 F4
Wolverton 138 B4
Woodborough 181 D6
Woodcock 117 C6
Woodcutts 207 D4
Woodfalls 211 D7
Woodgreen 211 A4
Woodhouse 193 F3
Woodlands St Mary . . . 171 B6
Woodminton 204 E1
Woodsend 169 C7
Woodshaw 48 A2
Woodyates 208 D6
Woolley 100 E7
Woolley Green 100 F8
Woolverton 103 C1
Wootton Bassett 47 C2
Wootton Rivers 174 F2
Worton 179 B4
Wroughton 64 A5
Wylye 201 F8

Y

Yarnbrook 105 F3
Yatesbury 166 E2
Yatton Keynell 68 E6

Z

Zeals 137 F4

A

Abberd La SN11 ....81 D3
Abberd Way SN11 ....81 C3
Abbess Cl SP4 ....217 B2
Abbey Cl
  Chippenham SN15 ....79 B5
  3 Shrewton SP3 ....196 E6
Abbey House Gdns★
  SN16 ....28 A3
Abbey La
  Amesbury SP4 ....217 A4
  Hinton Charterhouse BA2 ....99 A3
Abbey Meads Prim Sch
  SN25 ....35 A7
Abbey Prim Sch SP3 ....202 B1
Abbey Rw SN16 ....28 A3
Abbey Stadium SN25 ....35 A8
Abbey View Rd SN25 ....34 E3
Abbey Wlk **6** SP7 ....202 C1
Abbeyfield Sch SN15 ....79 B6
Abbot Rd SP1 ....146 C4
Abbots Wlk GL7 ....2 D4
Abbotsbury Way SN25 ....35 A8
Abbotts Cl SP9 ....216 C7
Abbotts Gdn SN16 ....28 A3
Abbotts Rd SP9 ....216 C7
Abdon Cl BA12 ....195 D7
Abingdon Ct La SN6 ....19 E8
Abington Way SN2 ....35 D5
Abney Moor SN3 ....51 E2
Abotts Cl BA13 ....108 F3
Above Hedges SP5 ....148 C3
Acacia Cl SN14 ....70 A1
Acacia Cres BA14 ....105 A8
Acacia Dr BA11 ....110 C7
Acacia Gr SN2 ....35 C2
Academy Dr SN13 ....76 E2
Acorn Cl SN3 ....51 C5
Acorn Meadow BA14 ....105 A5
Acre Cl BA14 ....178 A3
Acres Rd SN10 ....214 C3
Acreshort La BA14 ....178 A3
Activity Zone Leisure Ctr
  SN16 ....27 F3
Acton Turville Rd GL9 ....52 A4
Adam's Grave (Long
  Barrow)★ SN8 ....173 D2
Adampur Rd SP9 ....216 A4
Adcroft Dr BA14 ....101 D1
Adcroft St BA14 ....101 C1
Adderwell BA11 ....110 A3
Adderwell Cl BA11 ....110 A3
Adderwell Rd BA11 ....110 A3
Addington Cl SN10 ....214 C2
Addison Cres SN2 ....35 F3
Addison Rd SN12 ....93 F6
Addison Sq **19** SP4 ....198 B7
Adelaide Cl **6** SP4 ....198 F6
Adlam Cl SN10 ....214 A2
Adwalton Cl SN5 ....49 B4
Aelmas Mich Dro
  SP11 ....192 E1
Aerial Bsns Pk RG17 ....170 E6
Affleck Cl SN5 ....49 C5
Agra Rd SP9 ....216 A4
Agravaine Cl **27** SP10 ....193 E2
Ailesbury Cl SN15 ....79 A4
Ailesbury Way SN8 ....183 D8
Ainsworth Rd SN3 ....51 A4
Aintree **7** RG17 ....165 A1
Aintree Ave BA14 ....105 E4
Aintree Dr SN14 ....77 F6
Airman's Cnr SP3 ....197 B5
Aisne Rd SN4 ....65 D1
Akenfield Cl SN25 ....34 F5
Akers Ct SN26 ....21 C2
Akers Way SN2 ....34 E2
Alamein Rd **4** SP11 ....193 E4
Alan Cobham Rd
  SN10 ....214 D2
Alan Powell La BA13 ....112 B8
Alanbrooke Cres SN2 ....35 A2
Alanbrooke Rd SP4 ....197 E6
Alba Cl **11** SN5 ....48 F8
Albany Cl BA14 ....101 F2
Albany Rd SP1 ....146 B1
Albert Rd BA14 ....101 F3
Albert St SN1 ....50 D4
Albion Bglws SP2 ....145 A3
Albion Dr BA14 ....105 B8
Albion Rd **33** SP6 ....210 D1
Albion St SN1 ....50 A5
Alcock Crest BA12 ....116 F6
Aldborough Cl **2** SN5 ....49 C6
Aldbourne Cl
  Blunsdon St Andrew SN2 ....35 C6
  27 Hungerford RG17 ....177 B7
Aldbourne Four Barrows★
  SN8 ....169 E8
Aldbourne Rd SN8 ....170 B7
Aldeburgh Pl BA14 ....104 F6
Alder Cl Swindon SN2 ....34 D4
  Trowbridge BA14 ....105 B5
Alder Way SN12 ....94 A4
Alder Wlk **5** BA11 ....110 B7
Alderbury & W Grimstead
  Sch SP5 ....153 E3
Alderholt Rd SP6 ....210 B1
Alderney Cl **6** SN4 ....48 A2
Alders The SP2 ....145 A3

Alderton Rd
  Grittleton SN14 ....54 D5
  Luckington SN14 ....53 D6
Alderton Way BA14 ....105 D5
Aldrin Cl **7** SP10 ....193 D2
Aldworth Dr **3** SP1 ....146 C5
Alexander Fields SN9 ....181 F1
Alexander Keiller Mus★
  SN8 ....167 B1
Alexander Rd SN16 ....27 F4
Alexander Terr SN13 ....77 A1
Alexandra Cl SP2 ....145 C3
Alexandra Rd
  Fordingbridge SP6 ....210 D1
  Frome BA11 ....110 A4
  1 Swindon SN1 ....50 C7
Alexandra Terr SN8 ....213 D3
Alfred Gdns **6** SP10 ....193 D2
Alfred St Swindon SN1 ....50 C7
  Westbury BA13 ....109 A4
Alfred's Castle★ RG17 ....164 B5
Alfred's Twr★ BA10 ....122 F3
All Cannings CE Prim Sch
  SN10 ....180 D8
All Saints CE Prim Sch
  Farley SP5 ....154 E8
  Whiteparish SP5 ....161 D3
All Saints Cres **2** BA13 ....109 A3
All Saints Rd **1** SN10 ....187 E7
All Saints VA Prim Sch
  SP4 ....190 A3
Allen Rd Corsham SN13 ....84 C3
  Trowbridge BA14 ....105 B7
Allen Wr Dr SP6 ....210 D2
Allenby Rd SP4 ....133 C2
Allengrove La SN14 ....39 C3
Alley The
  Bishopstone SP5 ....205 E4
  Woodgreen SP6 ....211 A4
Allington Rd SN2 ....35 B5
Allington Tk SP4 ....198 E4
Allington Way
  Amesbury SP4 ....217 D2
  2 Chippenham SN14 ....70 A1
Alma Pl SN8 ....213 D3
Alma Rd SN8 ....170 A7
Alma St BA14 ....105 E8
Alma Terr SN11 ....81 B3
Almond Gr BA14 ....105 B5
Alnwick SP5 ....49 B4
Aloeric Prim Sch SN12 ....94 A3
Alpine Cl **8** SN5 ....49 A7
Alton Barnes White Horse★
  SN8 ....173 C2
Alton Cl SN2 ....35 C5
Alton Rd SN8 ....181 F8
Altona Gdns **17** SP10 ....193 D2
Alum Cl BA14 ....105 E7
Alvescot Rd SN3 ....50 D5
Alveston Cl SN5 ....49 C6
Amber Ct SN1 ....50 D7
Amberley Cl Calne SN11 ....81 A4
  Swindon SN25 ....35 C4
Ambrose House Con &
  Management Ctr SN1 ....50 B6
Ambrose Rd SN1 ....50 C2
American Mus In Britain★
  BA2 ....90 A5
Amersham Rd SN3 ....51 B3
Amesbury Bsns Pk
  SP4 ....217 C5
Amesbury By-Pass
  SP4 ....217 B5
Amesbury CE Jun Sch
  SP4 ....217 B4
Amesbury Cl **4** SN2 ....35 C4
Amesbury Cty Inf Sch
  SP4 ....217 B3
Amesbury Rd
  Amesbury SP4 ....217 F4
  Amport SP11 ....192 E1
  Newton Tony SP4 ....199 A3
  Shrewton SP3 ....196 E4
Amesbury Sports Ctr
  SP4 ....217 C4
Amity Dr SN8 ....175 D6
Amouracre BA14 ....105 F8
Ancaster Cl BA14 ....101 A1
Anchor Rd SN11 ....81 C2
Ancona Cl **12** SN5 ....49 A7
Andeferas Rd **6** SP10 ....193 D2
Anderson Cl SN3 ....51 D3
Anderson Rd SP1 ....146 C4
Andover La SP11 ....192 B4
Andover Rd
  Amport SP11 ....192 E2
  Chirton SN10 ....180 D3
  Fyfield SP11 ....192 D3
  Upavon SN9 ....181 F1
Andover St **4** SN1 ....50 A5
Andrew Cl **14** SP4 ....198 B7
Andrews Cl SN14 ....78 B7
Andrews Way SP2 ....151 F5
Angel La Hindon SP3 ....200 A3
  Mere BA12 ....139 A5
  27 Shaftesbury SP7 ....202 C2
Angel Yd SN8 ....213 D3
Angelica Cl **6** SN2 ....34 D4
Angler Rd
  Salisbury SP2 ....145 C5
  Swindon SN5 ....49 B7
Anglesey Cl **5** SN5 ....49 C6
Anglesey Mead SN15 ....79 A4
Angrove Cotts SN16 ....43 D4
Angus Cl SN1 ....49 B7
Anise Cl **4** SN2 ....34 C4
Anne Cres **24** SP4 ....198 B7
Annett's La RG17 ....176 F4

Annetts Cl SP4 ....217 C4
Anson Ave SN9 ....182 B2
Anson Gr SN12 ....94 C1
Anson Pl SN14 ....56 C7
Anstey Pl SN15 ....79 A4
Ansty Hill BA12 ....195 A6
Ansty Wlk SN2 ....35 B6
Anthony Cl SN16 ....25 C1
Anthony Rd SN4 ....64 A7
Anton La SP1 ....193 E4
Antrobus Rd SP4 ....217 B3
Apollo Cl SN25 ....34 B7
Apollo Rd SN15 ....59 E3
Apostle Way SP1 ....146 C5
Appleford SP3 ....196 E7
Appleshaw Way
  Perham Down SP11 ....191 F3
  Salisbury SP1 ....146 D5
Appletree Cl SP5 ....211 C8
Appletree Rd SP5 ....211 C8
Applewood Cl SN14 ....78 B8
Applewood Ct SN5 ....49 D5
Apsley Cl BA14 ....102 B2
Aragon Cl SP4 ....217 C4
Aragon Ct SN3 ....51 A4
Arc Theatre The BA14 ....105 A6
Arcade The **8** SN1 ....50 B6
Archer Cl SN2 ....35 F5
Archers Ct SP2 ....146 A2
Archers The SN6 ....22 F5
Arches La SN16 ....27 F2
Arcot Rd SP9 ....216 B3
Arden Cl SN12 ....94 C5
Argosy Rd SN15 ....60 B1
Argyle Dr SN14 ....70 C3
Argyle St SN2 ....35 D1
Ark The SN10 ....214 A3
Arkwright Rd SN25 ....34 B7
Arley Cl SN25 ....35 A5
Arlington Cl SN3 ....51 B7
Armitage Sq **4** SP4 ....197 E6
Armoury Yd **16** SP7 ....202 C2
Armstrong Rd BA11 ....110 B5
Armstrong Rise **16**
  SP10 ....193 D2
Armstrong St **2** SN1 ....50 C7
Arn Hill Down & Nature
  Reserve★ BA12 ....117 B8
Arn View
  Cold Harbour BA12 ....112 F1
  2 Warminster BA12 ....117 A8
Arnfield Moor SN3 ....51 E2
Arnhem Cross SN15 ....60 B2
Arnold Rd BA14 ....104 E3
Arran Cl **5** SN4 ....48 A2
Arran Way SN6 ....22 F7
Arras Cl SN14 ....70 A1
Arthur Bennett Ct SN1 ....50 A5
Artis Ave SN4 ....64 B7
Arun Rd SN25 ....34 F3
Arun Way **6** SO51 ....212 F6
Arundel Cl
  Chippenham SN14 ....78 A7
  Swindon SN3 ....50 F3
Arundell Cl BA13 ....109 B4
Ascham Rd SN5 ....49 A5
Ascot Cl SN14 ....78 A5
Ascott Cl SN25 ....34 F7
Ash Cl Lyneham SN15 ....60 B2
  4 Shaftesbury SP7 ....202 D2
  Swindon SN5 ....34 A2
  Tidworth SP9 ....216 E7
Ash Cres SP1 ....146 C5
Ash Dr BA14 ....105 C3
Ash Gdns SN3 ....36 E4
Ash Gr **1** Melksham SN12 ....94 A2
  Swindon SN2 ....35 C2
Ash Rd SN14 ....75 A5
Ash Tree La SP7 ....206 B7
Ash Wlk
  Upton Lovell BA12 ....194 E4
  Warminster BA12 ....117 A7
Ashburn Pl **5** SP6 ....210 D1
Ashburnham Cl **7** SN5 ....49 A4
Ashbury Ave SN3 ....51 B7
Ashbury Hill SN6 ....164 A7
Ashbury with Compton
  Beauchamp Prim Sch
  SN6 ....164 A8
Ashcroft Cotts SN8 ....169 B1
Ashdown Dr SN12 ....94 D6
Ashdown Pk★ RG17 ....164 C5
Ashdown Terr SP9 ....216 D5
Ashdown Way SN2 ....34 C4
Ashe Cl SN15 ....70 D1
Ashe Cres SN15 ....70 D1
Ashen Copse Rd SN4 ....62 F7
Ashes La Freshford BA2 ....99 A4
  Kington Langley SN15 ....70 E7
Ashfield Rd
  Chippenham SN15 ....70 D1
  Salisbury SP2 ....145 E1
Ashford Cl **11** SP6 ....210 C1
Ashford Rd
  Fordingbridge SP6 ....210 C1
  Swindon SN1 ....50 B4
Ashford Trad Est SP2 ....145 E1
Ashgrove BA12 ....139 B4
Ashie Cl SN5 ....34 B2
Ashkirk Cl SN3 ....50 E6
Ashlade Firs Rd SN8 ....175 C6
Ashlands SP4 ....146 D6
Ashleigh Cl SP2 ....130 B2
Ashleigh Gr BA14 ....105 C7
Ashley Cl
  Atworth/Whitley SN12 ....85 D1

Ashley Cl continued
  Bradford-on-Avon BA15 ....100 B8
  Swindon SN3 ....50 F6
Ashley Coombe BA12 ....117 A4
Ashley Dro SN8 ....185 A7
Ashley La BA15 ....99 F7
Ashley Piece SN8 ....170 C2
Ashley Pl BA12 ....116 F4
Ashley Rd Bath BA1 ....82 C2
  Bradford-on-Avon BA15 ....91 B1
  Salisbury SP2 ....145 F2
Ashley Wlk SP4 ....217 D2
Ashleycross SP6 ....211 D1
Ashmead BA14 ....105 D6
Ashmead Ct BA14 ....105 D7
Ashmore Bottom
  DT11 ....206 E1
Ashmore Cl
  Swindon SN3 ....51 C6
  Whiteparish SP5 ....161 D4
Ashmore La
  West Dean SP5 ....155 E2
  Whiteparish SP5 ....161 D6
Ashton Cl SN15 ....60 B2
Ashton Keynes CE Prim Sch
  SN6 ....17 E8
Ashton Rd
  Ashton Keynes SN16 ....17 E7
  Siddington GL7 ....6 D8
  Trowbridge BA14 ....102 A2
Ashton Rise BA14 ....102 A2
Ashton St BA14 ....105 E8
Ashtree Rd BA11 ....110 A7
Ashwell Cl SN3 ....50 F5
Ashwood Rd SN13 ....76 A1
Ashworth Rd SN5 ....49 E6
Askerton Cl **5** SN5 ....48 F8
Askew Cl **3** SN5 ....48 F5
Aspen Cl Colerne SN14 ....74 F6
  Frome BA11 ....110 B7
  Wootton Bassett SN4 ....47 E3
Assheton Ct SP9 ....216 D7
Assisi Rd SP1 ....146 A4
Astley Cl SN5 ....215 D5
Aston Cl SN9 ....215 C5
Aston Mead SP1 ....146 C3
Astor Cres SP11 ....192 A5
Atbara Cl SN25 ....35 A3
Atcherly Rd SN5 ....166 A1
Athelstan Mus★ SN16 ....28 A3
Athelstan Rd SN16 ....27 F4
Athena Ave SN2 ....35 E1
Athenaeum Ctr **2** BA14 ....117 A7
Atherton Cl **12** SN8 ....170 B2
Atherton Cres **18** RG17 ....177 B7
Atherton Pl **11** RG17 ....165 A2
Atherton Rd **11** RG17 ....177 B7
Athlone Cl **2** SP11 ....193 E4
Atholl Ct **26** SP10 ....193 C2
Attlee Cres SN2 ....35 E3
Attwood Rd SP1 ....146 A3
Atwell-Wilson Motor Mus★
  SN11 ....89 D7
Atworth Cl SN2 ....35 B6
Atworth La SN13 ....84 E4
Atworth Prim Sch SN12 ....92 E8
Atyec Cl BA13 ....112 B8
Atyeo Cl BA13 ....112 B8
Aubrey Rise **6** SN16 ....28 A5
Auckland Rd **3** SP4 ....198 F7
Auden Cl SN25 ....34 F5
Audley Cl **2** SN5 ....48 F4
Audley Gate BA13 ....108 E2
Audley Rd SN14 ....78 C8
Augusta Cl SN25 ....34 C7
Augustine Way **9** SP10 ....193 C2
Austen Cres SN3 ....51 D4
Australian Ave SP2 ....145 D2
Avebury CE Prim Sch
  SN8 ....173 B8
Avebury Cl Calne SN11 ....81 A3
  Westbury BA13 ....108 F1
Avebury Manor & Gdns★
  SN8 ....167 B1
Avebury Mus★ SN8 ....167 B1
Avebury Rd
  Chippenham SN14 ....78 A6
  Swindon SN2 ....35 B5
Avebury Stone Circles★
  SN8 ....167 C1
Avenell Rd **8** SN4 ....163 A6
Avening St SN2 ....35 C1
Avens Cl SN2 ....34 D4
Avenue La Fleche
  SN15 ....78 D6
Avenue Rd Frome BA11 ....110 A4
  Swindon SN1 ....50 C4
  Trowbridge BA14 ....105 B8
Avenue Sch BA12 ....117 B7
Avenue The★
  Amesbury SP4 ....197 E5
  Cherhill SN11 ....166 E2
  Claverton BA2 ....90 A4
  Durnford SP4 ....131 D1
  18 Durrington/Bulford
  SP4 ....198 B7
  Porton SP4 ....133 D6
  Salisbury SP1 ....146 C1
  South Tedworth SP9 ....216 C4
  Stanton Fitzwarren SN6 ....22 B1
  Tangley SP11 ....193 D5
  Tisbury SP3 ....203 E8
  Warminster BA12 ....117 A7
  Westbury BA13 ....109 A3
  Wilton SP2 ....144 F5
  Woodford SP2 ....145 A8
Avil's La SN14 ....56 F6

Avocet Cl SN3 ....51 E6
Avon App SP2 ....146 A1
Avon Bldgs SP4 ....217 A3
Avon Cl
  Bradford-on-Avon BA15 ....100 E5
  Calne SN11 ....81 A5
Avon Ct BA1 ....82 A4
Avon Dr SP5 ....153 E2
Avon Mead SN15 ....78 F8
Avon Meadow **1** SP6 ....210 D1
Avon Meadow SN5 ....211 A8
Avon Meadows SP4 ....131 C5
Avon Mid Sch SP2 ....145 D4
Avon Mills SN16 ....28 B2
Avon Pl Sh Ctr SP12 ....94 A4
Avon Rd Devizes SN10 ....179 C8
  2 Durrington/Bulford
  SP4 ....198 F6
  Malmesbury SN16 ....27 F4
  Melksham SN12 ....94 A6
  Tidworth SP9 ....216 C5
  Warminster BA12 ....117 A5
Avon Reach SN15 ....78 D7
Avon Rise SN14 ....39 C4
Avon Sq SN9 ....181 F1
Avon Terr
  Devizes SN10 ....214 A4
  Salisbury SP2 ....145 F2
Avon Valley Nature Reserve★
  SP1 ....145 F3
Avon View SP6 ....210 F1
Avon Way SP4 ....101 D3
Avoncliff Sta BA15 ....99 E5
Avondale Sch SP4 ....217 D8
Avondown Rd SP4 ....198 C7
Avonfield BA14 ....101 F8
Avonfield Ave BA15 ....100 E5
Avonleaze Rd SN9 ....215 D5
Avonmead SN25 ....34 F4
Avonside Enterprise Pk
  SN12 ....94 A5
Avonstoke Cl SP4 ....217 B2
Avonvale Rd BA14 ....101 D2
Avonweir La SN15 ....57 F3
Avro Way SN12 ....94 C1
Awdry Ave SN12 ....94 C6
Awdry Cl
  Chippenham SN14 ....77 F7
  Heddington SN11 ....89 A2
Awdry Rd SN10 ....214 B1
Axbridge Cl SN3 ....51 A5
Axe & Cleaver La
  BA14 ....105 C4
Axis Bsns Ctr SN5 ....49 D7
Aylesbury St SN1 ....50 C7
Ayleswade Rd SP2 ....152 A6
Aymer Pl SN3 ....51 C5
Ayr Cl SN14 ....77 F5
Ayrshire Cl
  Salisbury SP2 ....145 B5
  Swindon SN5 ....49 B7
Azalea Cl SN11 ....81 C1
Azalea Dr
  Trowbridge BA14 ....105 A4
  Warminster BA12 ....116 E7
Azelin Ct SN3 ....36 B3

B

Babington Pk **9** SN5 ....48 F5
Back La
  9 Aldbourne SN8 ....170 A6
  Blunsdon St Andrew SN26 ....21 B3
  Calne Without SN15 ....88 B4
  Cherhill SN11 ....166 E2
  Chitterne BA12 ....195 D7
  Great Bedwyn SN8 ....176 B3
  Great Hinton BA14 ....178 A6
  Maiden Bradley with Yarnfield
  BA12 ....118 F2
  Marlborough SN8 ....213 D3
  Penton Grafton SP11 ....193 A3
  Ramsbury SN8 ....170 B2
  Sixpenny Handley SP5 ....208 A4
  Tilshead SP3 ....188 B3
  Vernhams Dean SP11 ....185 C3
Back Rd Calne SN11 ....81 B2
  Chitterne BA12 ....195 D7
Back St
  Ashton Keynes SN6 ....6 F1
  East Garston RG17 ....171 E7
  Great Hinton BA14 ....178 A6
  Trowbridge BA14 ....101 C1
Bader Pk **10** SN12 ....178 B8
Badger Cl
  Devizes SN10 ....214 B2
  2 Wootton Bassett SN4 ....47 F2
Badgers Brook SN4 ....64 A5
Badgers Cl **3** SN4 ....163 B6
Badminton House★
  GL9 ....38 C3
Badminton Pk★ GL9 ....38 F3
Bagbury La SN5 ....33 B1
Bagbury Rd BA12 ....194 F4
Baghdad Rd **2** SP4 ....198 F7
Bailey Cl SN9 ....215 B5
Bailey's Mead SN4 ....48 A2
Baileys Barn BA15 ....100 D5
Baileys Farm Gdns SN3 ....51 A6
Baileys Way SN4 ....64 B7
Bailiffe Piece SN6 ....8 D1
Bainbridge Cl **2** SN5 ....49 A5
Bainton Cl BA15 ....100 D7
Baird Cl SN5 ....49 B8
Bakehouse Cl SN15 ....78 E6
Bakers Cnr SN13 ....84 C4
Bakers Ct SN3 ....36 B2

Bakers Field SN15 . . . . . .60 A3
Bakers Rd SN4 . . . . . . .64 B5
Balden Cl SN4 . . . . . . .63 F6
Bale Cl **6** SN5 . . . . . .48 F5
Ball Rd SN9 . . . . .215 D4
Ballands Castle★ BA9 .137 A2
Balmoor Cl BA12 . . . . .139 B3
Balmoral Cl
  Chippenham SN14 . . . . . .77 F7
  Swindon SN3 . . . . .51 A3
Balmoral Rd
  Salisbury SP1 . . . . . .146 B4
  Trowbridge BA14 . . . .105 B5
Bampton Gr SN3 . . . . .50 E6
Banbury Cl SN3 . . . . . .50 F3
Bancroft BA15 . . . . . .100 D7
Bancroft Cl SN5 . . . . . .48 F6
Bank St SN12 . . . . . . .94 A4
Bank The SN14 . . . . . .75 C3
Bankfoot Cl **3** SN5 . . . .49 B7
Banks The SN15 . . . . . .59 E4
Bankside SN1 . . . . . . .49 F4
Bankwaters Rd SN13 . . .84 B8
Bannerdown Cl BA1 . . .82 B4
Bannerdown Dr BA1 . . .82 A4
Bannerdown Rd BA1 . . .82 C5
Banwell Ave SN3 . . . . .51 A5
Barbara's Rd SN13 . . . .84 D8
Barbel Cl SN11 . . . . . .81 B5
Barber's La SP5 . . . . .151 C1
Barberry SP3 . . . . . . .201 A3
Barbury Castle★ SN4 .168 A7
Barbury Castle Ctry Pk★
  SN4 . . . . .168 B7
Barbury Cl SN25 . . . . . .34 F3
Barcelona Cres SN4 . . .64 A7
Barcete Cl SN3 . . . . . .34 D7
Bardsey Cl **5** SN4 . . . .47 F2
Barford La SP5 . . . . . .159 C1
Barford St Martin CE Fst Sch
  SP3 . . . . .143 A3
Bargates SN13 . . . . . .83 D6
Barken Rd
  4 Chippenham SN14 . . .70 A1
  Chippenham SN14 . . . . . .78 A8
Barkstead Cl **3** SN5 . . .49 B4
Barley Cl
  Malmesbury SN16 . . . . . .28 A2
  Warminster BA12 . . . .117 C5
Barley Hill La SN10 . . .179 A7
Barlow Cl SN25 . . . . . .35 A8
Barn Cl
  Chippenham SN14 . . . . . .78 A8
  Corsham SN13 . . . . . . .76 E1
Barn End SN14 . . . . . .74 A8
Barn Glebe BA14 . . . .101 E1
Barn Hill SP3 . . . . . .201 A3
Barn Moor Cl SN3 . . . .51 E3
Barn Owl Rd SN14 . . . .70 B2
Barn Piece Box SN13 . .83 D6
  Bradford-on-Avon BA15 . . .100 D4
Barn St SN8 . . . . . . .213 D3
Barnack Cl BA14 . . . .101 A1
Barnard Cl SN3 . . . . . .51 B7
Barnard St **1** SP1 . . . .152 B8
Barnards Hill Dr SP2 . .145 C4
Barncroft SN13 . . . . .192 E3
Barnes Cl BA14 . . . . .105 A7
Barnes Gn SN15 . . . . .45 F6
Barnes Pl BA12 . . . . .139 A5
Barnes Rd SN14 . . . . .70 B2
Barnes Wallis Cl
  9 Amesbury SP4 . . . . .217 E3
  Melksham Without BA14 . .178 B8
Barnetts Hill SN13 . . . .83 F7
Barnfield Cl SN2 . . . . .49 F7
Barnfield Rd SN2 . . . . .49 E7
Barnfield Way BA1 . . . .82 B4
Barnstaple Cl SN3 . . . .51 B5
Barnum Ct SN2 . . . . . .50 A7
Baroda Rd SP9 . . . . . .216 B5
Baron Cl Lyneham SN15 . .59 C4
  4 Swindon SN3 . . . . . .36 B3
Barons Mead SN14 . . . .78 A8
Barra Cl SN6 . . . . . . .22 E6
Barracks SN14 . . . . . .74 F4
Barrett La SN15 . . . . . .57 D2
Barrett Way SN4 . . . . .64 B6
Barrington Cl SN3 . . . .51 D3
Barrington Rd SP1 . . . .146 C3
Barrow Cl SN8 . . . . . .213 F3
Barrow Gn SN15 . . . . .70 E2
Barrow La BA9 . . . . . .136 B5
Barrow St La
  Mere BA12 . . . . .139 F3
  West Knoyle BA12 . . . .140 A4
Barrow Water La BA9 .136 A5
Barrowby Gate SN4 . . . .36 A4
Barrows La SP5 . . . . .212 B7
Barry Glen Cl SN2 . . . .35 E1
Barry Pl SN11 . . . . . . .79 F2
Barters La SP7 . . . . .206 D8
Bartlett Cl **11** BA11 . . .110 C6
Bartlett Rd SP1 . . . . .146 B4
Bartletts SN10 . . . . . .179 C1
Bartletts Mead BA14 . .178 A4
Bartletts The BA12 . . .139 B4
Barton Cl **12** SP10 . . .193 C2
Barton Farm Ctry Pk★
  BA15 . . . . .100 A5
Barton Hill **22** SP7 . . .202 C2
Barton Hill House Sch
  SP7 . . . . .202 C2
Barton La SN14 . . . . . .74 A1
Barton Lodge BA14 . . .105 A6
Barton Orch BA15 . . . .100 C6
Barton Rd SN25 . . . . . .34 E3

Barton Way SN16 . . . . .42 E4
Bartons Rd **20** SP6 . . .210 D1
Bartons The **29** SP6 . .210 D1
Basepoint Bsns Ctr
  SN5 . . . . .49 C8
Basil Cl SN2 . . . . .34 D4
Basil Hill Rd SN13 . . . .84 C7
Basingstoke Cl **6** SN5 . .49 A4
Baskerville Rd SN3 . . . .51 E7
Bassett Rd OX12 . . . . .165 E8
Bassetts Pasture
  BA15 . . . . .100 D4
Bassetts The SN13 . . . .83 D6
Batch The BA2 . . . . . . .98 E1
Bath Acad of Art SN13 . .77 A2
Bath Rd Atworth SN12 . .84 D2
  Atworth/Whitley SN12 . . .93 A8
  Box SN13 . . . . .83 A6
  Bradford-on-Avon BA15 . . .91 C1
  Chippenham Without
    SN14 . . . . .77 F5
  Colerne SN14 . . . . . . .74 F3
  Corsham SN13 . . . . . . .77 A8
  Cricklade SN6 . . . . . . .19 D8
  Devizes SN10 . . . . . .179 C8
  Frome BA11 . . . . . . .110 A6
  Hungerford RG17 . . . .176 F7
  Marlborough SN8 . . . .213 B2
  Melksham SN12 . . . . . .94 A5
  Melksham Without SN12 . .93 E7
  Preshute SN8 . . . . . .174 C7
  Seend SN12 . . . . .95 C1
  Swindon SN1 . . . . . . .50 C4
  Upton Scudamore BA12 . .112 D2
  Warminster BA12 . . . .112 E1
  Westonbirt with Lasborough
    GL8 . . . . .25 D8
  Wootton Bassett SN4 . . .47 C1
Bath Rd Ind Est SN14 . .78 B6
Bathampton St SN1 . . . .50 A6
Bathford CE VC Sch
  BA1 . . . . .82 C2
Bathford Hill BA1 . . . . .82 B2
Bathurst Rd SN1 . . . . .50 D6
Batt's La SN8 . . . . . . .183 F7
Batten Rd SP5 . . . . . .211 A8
Battens The **3** SN10 . . .70 A1
Battlesbury Barracks
  BA12 . . . . .117 E6
Battlesbury Hill Fort★
  BA12 . . . . .117 F8
Battlesbury Rd BA12 . .117 E7
Battlewell SN5 . . . . . . .33 A3
Baverstock La SP3 . . . .142 B5
Bawdsey Rd **6** SP4 . . .217 D2
Baxter Cl SN25 . . . . . .35 A7
Bay Cl SN11 . . . . .89 C8
Bay Tree Ct SN2 . . . . . .35 C2
Baydon Cl Swindon SN25 . .34 F3
  Trowbridge BA14 . . . .105 C5
Baydon Gr SN11 . . . . . .81 B4
Baydon Rd
  Aldbourne SN8 . . . . . .164 B1
  Great Shefford RG17 . . .171 A4
  Lambourn RG17 . . . . .171 A6
Baydon St Nicholas CE Prim
  Sch SN8 . . . . .164 C1
Baydons La SN15 . . . . .78 E6
Bayleaf Ave SN2 . . . . .34 D4
Bayliffes Cl SN15 . . . . .79 A7
Baynton Way BA13 . . .186 D8
Bayntun Cl
  Bromham SN15 . . . . . .96 A7
  Devizes SN10 . . . . . .214 C1
Baywater SN8 . . . . . .213 E4
Bazaar Rd SP9 . . . . . .216 B5
Beacon Cl
  Amesbury SP4 . . . . . .217 C4
  8 Swindon SN1 . . . . . .49 F4
Beacon Ct SP6 . . . . . .210 D2
Beacon Hill Rd **7** SP4 . .198 F7
Beacon View BA12 . . . .116 D6
Beaconsfield Way
  BA11 . . . . .110 B7
Beale Cl SN14 . . . . . . .78 B7
Beale Ct SN14 . . . . . . .78 A7
Beale's Barton BA14 . .101 F8
Beales Cl SN1 . . . . . . .50 B7
Beales Farm Rd **15**
  RG17 . . . . .165 A1
Beamish Cl **2** SN11 . . .166 A1
Beanacre Old Manor★
  SN12 . . . . .94 A8
Beanacre Rd
  Melksham SN12 . . . . . .94 A7
  Melksham Without SN12 . .86 A1
Beanlands The SN4 . . .163 A6
Bear Cl BA15 . . . . . . .100 B7
Beard Ct SP11 . . . . . .192 B5
Bearfield Bldgs BA15 . .100 C8
Bearfield La RG17 . . . .171 A4
Bearwater RG17 . . . . .177 B7
Beatrice Rd SP1 . . . . .146 A4
Beatrice St SN2 . . . . . .50 C8
Beatrice Way BA14 . . .105 E8
Beatty Ct SN3 . . . . . . .50 D4
Beauchamp Dr **1** SP4 . .217 D3
Beauclerc St SN10 . . . .179 D8
Beaufort Cl **6** SN12 . . .178 B8
Beaufort Gn SN3 . . . . .51 B5
Beaufort Rd SN4 . . . . .64 C4
Beaufoy Cl **9** SP7 . . . .202 D2
Beaulieu Cl SN5 . . . . .49 C4
Beaulieu Rd **2** SP4 . . .217 C2
Beaumaris Rd SN5 . . . .49 B5
Beaumont Rd SN3 . . . .50 E6
Beaumont Way SP4 . . .217 D2
Beaven Cl **2** SN15 . . . .78 F4

Beavens Ct BA12 . . . . .117 B7
Beck Cl SN25 . . . . . . .35 A3
Becket Way SP1 . . . . .146 D1
Beckett Pl BA13 . . . . .108 F1
Beckett St **14** SP3 . . . .203 E8
Beckett's La SP3 . . . . .201 A3
Beckford Cl
  Tisbury SP3 . . . . . . .200 D1
  Warminster BA12 . . . .117 B6
Bedford Rd
  Salisbury SP2 . . . . . .145 E2
  6 Swindon SN3 . . . . . .50 F6
Bedwin St SP1 . . . . . .146 B1
Bedwyn Cl SN2 . . . . . .35 C1
Bedwyn Dyke★ SN8 . .176 C3
Bedwyn Stone Mus★
  SN8 . . . . .176 B2
Beech Ave
  Melksham SN12 . . . . . .94 A3
  Swindon SN2 . . . . . . .35 A2
  Warminster BA12 . . . .116 F6
Beech Cl Andover SP11 .193 B1
  Porton SP4 . . . . .133 D6
Beech Ct BA11 . . . . . .110 B7
Beech Dr SN5 . . . . . . .34 A2
Beech Gr Highworth SN6 . .22 F5
  Trowbridge BA14 . . . .105 B6
Beech Grange SP5 . . . .212 C5
Beech Hanger SP4 . . . .199 C5
Beech Hill Rd SP9 . . . .216 E7
Beech Lea
  Broad Blunsdon SN26 . . . .21 C1
  Meysey Hampton GL7 . . . . .1 A4
Beech Rd Colerne SN14 . .75 A5
  Corsham SN13 . . . . . . .83 E7
Beech Sq **12** RG17 . . . .177 B6
Beech Wlk SN4 . . . . . .131 C1
Beech Wood **13** SN10 . .179 F1
Beechcroft Cl SP10 . . .193 D1
Beechcroft Inf Sch
  SN25 . . . . .35 E4
Beechcroft Rd
  Salisbury SP1 . . . . . .146 D1
  Swindon SN2 . . . . . . .35 E4
Beeches Cl SN25 . . . . .148 C3
Beeches La SN15 . . . . .59 A5
Beeches The
  Bradford-on-Avon BA15 .101 A5
  Coombe Bissett SP5 . . .156 F7
  Lydiard Millicent SN5 . . .33 B1
  Melksham Without SN12 . .93 C7
  5 Salisbury SP1 . . . .152 C8
  15 Shaftesbury SP7 . .202 C2
  Trowbridge BA14 . . . .101 F2
  Warminster BA12 . . . .116 F6
  4 West Wellow SO51 . .212 F6
Beechfield SN5 . . . . . .199 B3
Beechfield Dr SN10 . . .214 E5
Beechfield Rd SN13 . . . .76 E1
Beechgrove BA12 . . . .117 B8
Beechwood **13** SP6 . . .210 C1
Beechwood Ave BA11 . .110 A5
Beechwood Cl
  Frome BA11 . . . . . . .110 A5
  Roundway SN10 . . . . .214 E6
Beechwood Rd SN14 . . .78 B8
Beehive Cl **1** SN5 . . . .49 A8
Begle Cl SN5 . . . . . . .34 B7
Belcombe Ct★ BA15 . .100 B6
Belcombe Rd BA15 . . .100 B6
Belfast Mead SN15 . . . .60 C2
Belfry Dr SN14 . . . . . .41 E4
Belgrave Cres SP9 . . . .216 E6
Belgrave St SN1 . . . . . .50 C5
Bell Cl BA12 . . . . . . .116 F5
Bell Gdns SN3 . . . . . . .36 E4
Bell Hill Seend SN12 . . .178 E7
  Warminster BA12 . . . .116 F5
Bell La Inkpen RG17 . . .177 C2
  Lechlade GL7 . . . . . . .2 C3
  Liddington SN4 . . . . . .163 A4
  Sutton Benger SN15 . . . .57 D2
Bell Piece SN15 . . . . . .57 D2
Bell Rd SP4 . . . . .197 F7
Bell St
  4 Ludgershall SP11 . . .192 B5
  Shaftesbury SP7 . . . . .202 C2
Bellamy La SP1 . . . . . .152 B8
Belle Vue Rd
  Salisbury SP1 . . . . . .146 A1
  Swindon SN1 . . . . . . .50 D4
Bellefield Cres BA14 . . .101 D1
Bellinger Cl SN15 . . . . .70 C3
Bellingham La SN6 . . . .23 A2
Bellot Dr
  3 Corsham SN13 . . . .76 E1
  Corsham SN13 . . . . . . .84 E8
Bellott Dr SN13 . . . . . .84 E8
Bells La BA12 . . . . . . .137 F7
Bellver SN5 . . . . .49 B5
Belmont Cl
  10 Shaftesbury SP7 . . .202 C1
  Swindon SN3 . . . . . . .36 A4
Belmont Cres SN1 . . . .50 A4
Belmont Sch SP2 . . . . .146 B1
Belsay SN5 . . . . .49 C4
Belthane Pl SN12 . . . . .93 C8
Belvedere Rd SN3 . . . .51 A3
Bembridge Cl SN3 . . . .51 B4

Bemerton St Johns CE Fst
  Sch SP2 . . . . .145 C2
Ben La SP5 . . . . .154 F7
Bences La SN13 . . . . . .77 A2
Bendy Bow SN16 . . . . .15 F7
Benin Rd SP11 . . . . . .191 F3
Bennett Cl SP5 . . . . . .211 C7
Bennett Hill Cl **3** SN4 . .47 F2
Bentham Cl SN5 . . . . . .49 D6
Bentham La SN5 . . . . . .33 A8
Bentley Cl SN3 . . . . . .51 A6
Bentley Gr SN11 . . . . .81 C2
Bentley Way SP5 . . . . .149 D5
Benwell Cl SN5 . . . . . .49 C6
Beranburh Field SN4 . . .64 C2
Berenger Cl SN1 . . . . .50 D3
Beresford Cl **1** SN3 . . .51 C4
Bergamot Cl SN8 . . . .174 C7
Bergman Cl SN25 . . . . .35 B6
Berhills La SN10 . . . . .95 C5
Bericot La SN4 . . . . . .65 E6
Berkeley Cl
  Melksham SN12 . . . . . .94 A2
  South Cerney GL7 . . . . . .6 F6
Berkeley Lawns SN3 . . .50 F3
Berkeley Rd
  Trowbridge BA14 . . . .105 A8
  Wroughton SN4 . . . . . .64 B7
Berkely Cl **2** SN14 . . . .78 A7
Berkley CE Fst Sch
  BA11 . . . . .111 A7
Berkley Cross BA11 . . .110 F6
Berkley La BA11 . . . . .110 D8
Berkley Rd BA11 . . . . .110 A5
Berkley St BA11 . . . . .107 B1
Berkshire Dr SN5 . . . . .49 A4
Berkshire Rd SP2 . . . .151 E7
Bermerton Heath & Barnards
  Folly Nature Reserve★
  SP2 . . . . .145 C4
Berrington Rd SN3 . . . .51 A3
Berry Cl **4** SP4 . . . . .190 A3
Berry Rd BA13 . . . . . .186 D8
Berry Wood La SP7 . . .203 A3
Berrycroft
  Ashbury SN6 . . . . . . .164 A7
  Mildenhall SN8 . . . . . .175 B8
Berryfield Cl SN12 . . . .93 F1
Berryfield La SN12 . . . .93 F1
Berryfield Pk SN12 . . . .93 F1
Berryfield Rd BA15 . . .100 D8
Bertha's Field GL9 . . . .24 B4
Berton Cl SN26 . . . . . .21 C2
Berwick La SP3 . . . . . .207 D5
Berwick Rd
  Berwick St James SP3 . .196 F2
  Stapleford SP3 . . . . . .129 E7
Besomer Dro SP5 . . . .211 D6
Bess Rd SN5 . . . . .48 F4
Bessemer Cl SN2 . . . . .35 A1
Bessemer Rd E SN2 . . .35 A1
Bessemer Rd W SN2 . . .34 F1
Best's La SP4 . . . . . . .194 A5
Bethel Rd SN13 . . . . . .76 E1
Betjeman Ave SN4 . . . .47 E3
Betjeman Rd SN8 . . . .213 A2
Betony Cl SN25 . . . . . .34 E5
Bettertons Cl GL7 . . . . .1 F7
Bevan Cl SN2 . . . . . . .35 F3
Beverley Cl SN12 . . . . .94 C1
Beverley Cres SN9 . . . .182 B2
Beverley Hills Mobile Home
  Pk SP4 . . . . .217 D3
Beverley Way SN4 . . . .77 F5
Beversbrook La SN11 . . .81 B5
Beverstone Gr SN3 . . . .50 F8
Bevil SN5 . . . . .49 A3
Bevisbury Hill Fort★
  SP11 . . . . .185 A1
Bevisland SN3 . . . . . . .51 C3
Bewley Ct★ SN15 . . . . .86 F6
Bewley La SN15 . . . . . .86 F5
Bewley Rd **1** BA14 . . .105 C5
Beyer Rd **5** SP4 . . . . .217 D2
Bibury Rd SN3 . . . . . .50 E5
Bicton Rd SN5 . . . . . .34 F6
Biddel Springs SN6 . . .23 B6
Bidden La BA12 . . . . .195 D6
Biddesden La SN14 . . . .68 E3
Biddestone Manor★
  SN14 . . . . .76 F7
Biddulph Rd SP4 . . . . .198 A7
Bideford Cl SN3 . . . . . .51 A5
Big La RG17 . . . . .165 A2
Bilborough Dr **2** SN3 . .50 F5
Bilbury Rings★ BA12 . .201 E7
Bill Turpin Ct SN3 . . . . .51 B4
Bimport SP7 . . . . .202 B1
Bincknoll Castle★ SN4 . .62 F3
Bindon Cl SN5 . . . . . . .49 A5
Bingham Rd
  Durrington SP4 . . . . . .197 E7
  Salisbury SP1 . . . . . .146 C4
Binknoll La SN4 . . . . . .47 F1
Birch Gdns BA14 . . . . .102 B2
Birch Glade SN6 . . . . . .8 C4
Birch Gr Bower Hill SN12 . .94 C1
  Chippenham SN15 . . . . .70 E1
Birch St SN1 . . . . .49 F5
Birch Wlk **4** BA11 . . . .110 B7
Birchenleaze BA14 . . . .105 D3
Birches The SN3 . . . . . .51 B2
Birchill La BA11 . . . . .110 A1
Birchwood Cl BA12 . . .115 C3
Birchwood Dr **4** SP4 . .198 C7
Birchwood Rd SN3 . . . .36 B2

Birdbrook Rd SN2 . . . . .35 E5
Birdcombe Rd **1** SN5 . .49 C5
Birds Marsh View SN15 . .70 E2
Bishop Rd SN11 . . . . . .81 B4
Bishop Wordsworths Sch
  SP1 . . . . .152 A8
Bishop's Palace★ SP1 .152 A7
Bishop's Wlk SP1 . . . .152 A8
Bishopdale Cl **2** SN5 . .34 A1
Bishopdown Rd SP1 . . .146 B3
Bishops Cannings CE Pri Sch
  SN10 . . . . .172 B3
Bishops Cl
  Chippenham SN15 . . . . .78 F4
  Mere BA12 . . . . .139 A6
  Tidworth SP9 . . . . . . .216 D4
Bishops Dr SP2 . . . . . .151 E4
Bishops Mead SP1 . . . .146 E4
Bishopsfield **6** SN6 . . .19 D8
Bishopstone CE Prim Sch
  SN6 . . . . .163 E6
Bishopstone Hollow
  SP5 . . . . .205 E3
Bishopstrow Rd BA12 . .117 E4
Bisley SN16 . . . . .29 A6
Bisley Cl SN3 . . . . . . .51 A5
Biss Cl BA12 . . . . . . .112 F4
Biss Meadow BA14 . . .105 A8
Bitham Brook Prim Sch
  BA13 . . . . .109 B4
Bitham La Ham RG17 . .177 A3
  Westbury BA13 . . . . . .109 A3
Bitham Mill BA13 . . . .109 B3
Bitham Pk BA13 . . . . .109 B4
Bittern Rd SN3 . . . . . .51 E6
Black Bridge Rd SN15 . .78 F8
Black Dog Hill
  Calne Without SN11 . . . .80 D2
  Chapmanslade BA13 . . .111 E4
Black Horse La
  Westbury BA13 . . . . . .108 D1
  Winterbourne SP4 . . . .146 F8
Black La
  Pitton & Farley SP5 . . . .148 C5
  Redlynch SP5 . . . . . .211 E6
Blackbarn Rd SN4 . . . .134 B5
Blackberry Cl SN14 . . . .70 A2
Blackberry La
  Potterne SN10 . . . . . .179 D5
  Winsley BA15 . . . . . . .90 C1
Blackbird Way BA11 . . .110 B6
Blackboard La SN10 . . .180 B4
Blackcross SN15 . . . . . .78 F6
Blackcross Rd SP4 . . . .217 C2
Blackdown Cl **10** BA12 .117 A8
Blackford La SN6 . . . . .10 C4
Blackfriars Way SP1 . . .152 B8
Blackhill Rd SN5 . . . . .212 F3
Blacklands Crossroads
  SN11 . . . . .89 C6
Blackman Gdns SN1 . . .50 D3
Blackman's La **4** SN8 . .183 D8
Blackmoor Copse Nature
  Reserve★ SP5 . . . . .155 A7
Blackmore Cl **1** SN3 . .51 E7
Blackmore La SN8 . . . .192 A7
Blackmore Rd
  Melksham SN12 . . . . . .94 C4
  3 Shaftesbury SP7 . . .202 D2
Blackstone Ave SN3 . . .51 C4
Blackthorn Cl SN4 . . . .47 E4
Blackthorn Mews SN5 . .78 F5
Blackthorn Way BA14 . .101 D4
Blackworth SN6 . . . . . .22 F8
Blagdon Wlk BA11 . . . .110 C7
Blagrove Ind Est SN1 . .49 A2
Blair Rd BA14 . . . . . . .105 B7
Blake Cres SN3 . . . . . .36 C3
Blake Ct SN14 . . . . . .101 D4
Blakehill Farm Nature
  Reserve★ SN6 . . . . . .19 A3
Blakeney Ave SN3 . . . .51 B7
Blakesley Cl **3** SN3 . . .50 F4
Blakey Rd SP1 . . . . . .152 C8
Blandford Alley SN6 . . .23 A5
Blandford Ct SN3 . . . . .51 B6
Blandford Rd SP5 . . . .150 F1
Blaygrove Ind Est SN1 . .49 A2
Bleak St BA9 . . . . . . .137 C3
Blease Cl BA14 . . . . . .101 D4
Bleke St SP7 . . . . . . .202 C2
Blendon Dr SP10 . . . . .193 C1
Blenheim Gdns SN14 . . .56 C6
Blenheim Pk
  15 Bowerhill SN12 . . .178 B8
  21 Bowerhill SN12 . . .178 B8
Blenheim Rd SN4 . . . . .64 A7
Blenhiem Cl BA12 . . . .116 F7
Bletchley Cl **5** SN3 . . .51 C4
Blick's Hill SN16 . . . . .28 B4
Blicks Cl SN14 . . . . . .41 F1
Blicks Hill SN16 . . . . .28 B3
Blind La Ansty SP3 . . . .203 F5
  Berwick St John SP7 . . .207 B8
  Southwick BA14 . . . . .104 F2
Blissford Rd SP6 . . . . .210 F1
Blissmore La **8** SP11 . .192 F1
Bloody Shard Gate
  DT11 . . . . .207 A1
Bloomsbury Cl **2** SN5 . .49 B4
Blounts Ct SN10 . . . . .179 D5
Blowhorn St SN8 . . . . .213 D4
Blue Boar Row SP1 . . .146 A1
Bluebell Dr SN14 . . . . .70 B3
Bluebell Gr SN11 . . . . .81 B5

Blunsdon Abbey SN25 . .34 F8
Blunsdon Rd SN25 . . . . . .34 F4
Blunsdon Sta SN5 . . . . . .33 F8
Blyth Way SP1 . . . . .146 D4
BMI Ridgeway Hospl
SN4 . . . . .64 C6
Boar St BA12 . . . . .139 A5
Boatman Cl SN25 . . . . . .34 A7
Bobbin La BA15 . . . . .99 F4
Bobbin Pk BA15 . . . . .99 F3
Bockhampton Rd
RG17 . . . . .165 A1
Bockhampton Village★
RG17 . . . . .165 B1
Bodiam Dr SN5 . . . . .49 D4
Bodiam Dr N 4 SN5 . . . .49 D5
Bodiam Dr S 3 SN5 . . . .49 D4
Bodman Cl SN15 . . . . . . .78 F4
Bodmin Cl SN3 . . . . .51 A6
Bodyhorse Hill SN4 . . .163 C6
Bohemia La SP5 . . . . . .211 D6
Bokerley Ditch★ SP6 . .209 A5
Bokerley Junc SP5 . . . .208 E6
Boldrewood SN3 . . . . . . .51 D3
Bolehyde Manor★
SN14 . . . . .69 E4
Boleyn Cl SN5 . . . . .49 A6
Bolingbroke Cl SN5 . . . . .47 F6
Bolingbroke Rd SN2 . . . .34 F2
Bolland's Hill SN12 . . . .178 D8
Bonaker Cl SP4 . . . . . . .133 D6
Bond St
Durrington/Bulford SP4 . .198 E6
Trowbridge BA14 . . . . . . .105 C7
Bond St Bldgs BA14 . . .105 C7
Boness Rd SN4 . . . . .64 A7
Bonham La BA12 . . . . . .137 E7
Bonner Cl 10 SN5 . . . . . .48 F5
Bonners Cl SN16 . . . . . . .28 A5
Bonnewe Rise SP4 . . . .217 D3
Boothmead SN14 . . . . . . .78 B8
Borage Cl SN2 . . . . .34 D5
Border Cl SN25 . . . . .34 C5
Bore Hill BA12 . . . . .116 F4
Boreham Cl BA12 . . . . .117 C6
Boreham Field BA12 . . .117 D6
Boreham Rd BA12 . . . . .117 E5
Borgate Sch & Sixth Form Ctr
The SP6 . . . . .210 E2
Borkum Cl 8 SP10 . . . .193 D2
Borough Fields SN4 . . . .47 D2
Borough Parade Sh Ctr
SN15 . . . . .78 D7
Borough The SP5 . . . . .211 A8
Boscombe Down Airfield
SP4 . . . . .198 E3
Boscombe Rd
Amesbury SP4 . . . . .217 C3
Swindon SN25 . . . . .34 E4
Bosham Cl 6 SN5 . . . . . . .49 B4
Boswell Rd BA15 . . . . . . .99 F3
Bosworth Rd SN5 . . . . . . .49 A5
Botany SN6 . . . . .22 E5
Bothwell Rd SN3 . . . . . . .50 F7
Botisdone Cl SP11 . . . .185 C3
Botley Copse SN5 . . . . . .34 A2
Bottlebush La BH21 . . .208 E1
Bottom La
Ogbourne St George
SN8 . . . . .169 A5
1 West Wellow SO51 . . . .212 F6
Bouchers Way SP2 . . . .152 A5
Boulton Cl BA13 . . . . . .108 E1
Boundary Ave BA11 . . .110 B5
Boundary Cl
Lyneham SN15 . . . . .59 C3
Swindon SN2 . . . . .35 F6
Boundary Rd
Chippenham SN15 . . . . . . .78 F8
Salisbury SP1 . . . . .146 E2
Boundary Wlk BA14 . . .105 C4
Bourbon Cl BA12 . . . . . .117 B5
Bourne Ave SP1 . . . . . .146 C2
Bourne Cl Porton SP4 . .133 D6
1 Salisbury SP1 . . . . . . .152 D8
Warminster BA12 . . . . . . .117 A5
3 West Wellow SO51 . . . .212 F6
Bourne Gdns SP4 . . . . .133 D6
Bourne Hill SP1 . . . . . .146 B1
Bourne La 6 SP9 . . . . . .199 D8
Bourne Lake Pk SN6 . . . .18 E6
Bourne Pk★ SP11 . . . . .193 F6
Bourne Rd Swindon SN2 . .34 F2
Tidworth SP9 . . . . .216 D6
Bourne Ret Pk SP1 . . . .152 D7
Bourne Rise SN8 . . . . . .183 E1
Bourne Vale RG17 . . . . .177 B7
Bourne Valley Cl SP4 . .133 E5
Bourne View SP4 . . . . . .199 A1
Bourne Way SP1 . . . . . .152 D7
Bourton Ave SN3 . . . . . . .36 B2
Bourton La SN10 . . . . . .172 C3
Bouverie Ave
Salisbury SP2 . . . . .152 A6
Swindon SN3 . . . . .50 D3
Bouverie Ave S SP2 . . .151 F5
Bouverie Cl SP2 . . . . . .151 F6
Bouverie Dr 17 SN10 . . .179 F1
Bouverie Pk SN14 . . . . . .56 B5
Boveridge House Sch
BH21 . . . . .209 B1
Bow Ct SN1 . . . . .50 C4
Bow Wow GL7 . . . . .7 A7
Bowd's La SN15 . . . . .60 A6
Bowden Cres SN12 . . . . .94 C6
Bowden Pk★ SN15 . . . . .87 B5
Bowdich Cl SP4 . . . . . . .198 C7
Bower Gdns SP1 . . . . . .152 C8
Bower Hill Rd SP1 . . . .146 C2
Bower Rd SN8 . . . . .175 D5
Bowerhill La SN12 . . . . .94 E1
Bowerhill Prim Sch
SN12 . . . . .94 C1
Bowers Hill SP5 . . . . . .211 D8
Bowers La SP11 . . . . . . .185 B4
Bowes Lyon Ct SP2 . . . .145 D3
Bowldown Rd GL8 . . . . . .25 F8
Bowles Rd SN25 . . . . .35 A5
Bowleymead SN3 . . . . . .51 D5
Bowling Gn La
Pentridge SP5 . . . . .208 D5
Swindon SN1 . . . . .50 C3
Bowls Barrow (Long
Barrow)★ BA12 . . . . . .186 E1
Bowman Cl 5 SN3 . . . . . .36 B3
Bowman Ct SN4 . . . . .47 C1
Bowmans Ct SN12 . . . . . .94 C6
Bowood Cl SN11 . . . . . . .79 F3
Bowood House & Gdns★
SN11 . . . . .88 C8
Bowood Rd SN1 . . . . .50 B4
Box CE Prim Sch SN13 . .83 C6
Box Dr SN8 . . . . .213 D8
Box Highlands Prim Sch
SN13 . . . . .84 B8
Box Hill Box SN13 . . . . . . .76 A1
Corsham SN13 . . . . .83 F7
Box Rd BA1 . . . . .82 C3
Box View SN14 . . . . .75 B2
Boxbush Rd GL7 . . . . .7 A7
Boxfields Rd SN13 . . . . . .83 F7
Boydell Cl SN5 . . . . .49 B8
Boyle Ave 4 SN11 . . . . .166 A1
Boyne's La DT11 . . . . . .206 B1
Boyton Manor★ BA12 . .194 E2
Bozley Hill SP7 . . . . . . .206 A8
Brabant Way 4 BA13 . . .108 E1
Bracken Cl SP5 . . . . . . .153 D3
Brackenbury 8 SP10 . . .193 C1
Brackenbury Rd SP4 . . .197 E7
Brackland SN10 . . . . . . .180 A2
Bradbury Cl SN15 . . . . . .79 A5
Bradene Cl 3 SN4 . . . . . .47 E2
Bradenham Rd SN5 . . . . .49 A5
Bradenstoke Abbey★
SN15 . . . . .59 B3
Bradfield Cl BA12 . . . . .117 D5
Bradford Rd
Atworth SN12 . . . . .92 E7
Bathford BA1 . . . . .82 B2
Box SN13 . . . . .83 F3
Broughton Gifford SN12 . . .93 F4
Corsham SN13 . . . . .76 C1
Holt BA14 . . . . .101 D8
Melksham SN12 . . . . .94 A5
Rode BA11 . . . . .103 F1
Swindon SN1 . . . . .50 C4
Trowbridge BA14 . . . . . . .101 B1
Winsley BA15 . . . . .99 D6
Bradford-on-Avon Com
Hospl BA15 . . . . .100 D8
Bradford-on-Avon Mus★
BA15 . . . . .100 D6
Bradford-on-Avon Sta
BA15 . . . . .100 C6
Bradford-on-Avon
Swimming Pool
BA15 . . . . .100 C6
Bradley Cl Holt BA14 . . .101 F8
Warminster BA12 . . . . . . .116 E4
Bradley La Holt BA14 . . . .92 F1
Maiden Bradley with Yarnfield
BA12 . . . . .118 C3
Bradley Mound★
BA12 . . . . .118 F2
Bradley Pk★ BA12 . . . . .118 F1
Bradley Rd
Southwick BA14 . . . . .105 B2
Swindon SN2 . . . . .35 D4
Trowbridge BA14 . . . . . . .105 C5
Warminster BA12 . . . . . . .116 E4
Bradon Forest Sch SN5 . .33 B3
Bradwell Cl 2 SP10 . . . .193 C2
Bradwell Moor SN3 . . . . .51 D2
Braemar Cl SN3 . . . . .50 F3
Braemar Rise SP1 . . . . .146 B4
Braemor Rd SN11 . . . . . .81 A4
Braemore CE Prim Sch
SP6 . . . . .210 E4
Braithwaite Way 3
BA11 . . . . .110 C6
Brake Mead SN15 . . . . . .78 F7
Brakspear Dr SN13 . . . . .76 E1
Bramble Cl SN2 . . . . .35 E1
Bramble Dr
Chippenham SN15 . . . . . . .79 A4
Westbury BA13 . . . . .108 F5
Bramble Rd SN2 . . . . .35 E1
Brambles The
Hinton Charterhouse BA2 . .98 E1
Salisbury SP1 . . . . .146 C2
Trowbridge BA14 . . . . . . .101 D2
Bramdean Cl 6 SN25 . . . .34 F6
Bramley Cl
Pewsey SN9 . . . . .215 D6
4 Warminster BA12 . . . . .116 F7
Bramley Dr BA11 . . . . . .110 C6
Bramley Hill BA12 . . . . .138 F5
Bramley La BA14 . . . . . .105 D7
Bramley Way SP4 . . . . .217 C3
Bramleys The SP5 . . . . .161 D3
Brampton Ct 8 SN12 . . .178 B8
Bramptons The SN5 . . . .49 B7
Bramshaw Telegraph★
SP6 . . . . .211 F3
Bramwell Cl SN2 . . . . . . .35 E6
Brancaster Ave 1 SP10 193 C2
Branch Rd BA2 . . . . .98 F2
Branders 4 SN6 . . . . .19 D8
Brandon Cl SN5 . . . . .49 A5
Branksome Rd SN25 . . . .34 E3
Branscombe Dr SN4 . . . .47 E1
Bransdown Hill
Easton Grey SN16 . . . . . . .26 A3
Sherston SN16 . . . . .25 F2
Brassknocker Hill BA2 . .90 A1
Bratch La SP3 . . . . .201 F2
Bratton Ave SN10 . . . . .214 C2
Bratton Camp★ BA13 . .186 A6
Bratton Cl SN2 . . . . .35 B5
Bratton Prim Sch
BA13 . . . . .186 B7
Bratton Rd
West Ashton BA14 . . . . . .106 B4
Westbury BA13 . . . . .109 C4
Bray St SN8 . . . . .173 A8
Braybrooke Cl 2 SN5 . . .48 F8
Braydon Ct SN2 . . . . .35 C5
Braydon La SN6 . . . . .18 F4
Breach Cl SP8 . . . . .137 E2
Breach La Chute SP11 . .192 E8
1 Shaftesbury SP7 . . . . . .202 B1
Southwick BA14 . . . . .105 A3
Wootton Bassett SN4 . . . . .61 B5
Breach The SN10 . . . . .214 B2
Bread St BA12 . . . . .116 F5
Bream Cl Calne SN11 . . . .81 A5
Melksham SN12 . . . . .94 D6
Breamore Countryside Mus★
SP6 . . . . .210 E5
Breamore House★
SP6 . . . . .210 E6
Breamore Rd SP5 . . . . .210 F7
Brecon Cl
Melksham SN12 . . . . .94 D4
Swindon SN3 . . . . .50 E2
Bremen Gdns 21 SP10 . .193 D2
Bremeridge Cl BA13 . . .109 B3
Bremeridge Rd BA13 . . .109 B3
Bremhill Cl SN2 . . . . .35 C4
Bremhill View SN11 . . . . .81 A4
Bremilham Rd SN16 . . . .27 F4
Bremilham Rise SN16 . . .27 E3
Brendon Wlk SN3 . . . . . .51 B6
Breton Rd BA13 . . . . . . .108 F2
Brettingham Gate SN3 . .64 F8
Brewer Mead SN15 . . . . .78 F4
Brewers La SN11 . . . . . . .81 C1
Brewery St SN6 . . . . .23 A5
Brewery Wlk BA14 . . . .101 D1
Briar Cl Frome BA11 . . .110 B7
Westbury BA13 . . . . .108 F4
Briar Fields SN1 . . . . . . .50 E7
Briar Leaze SN11 . . . . .166 B3
Briars Cl SN4 . . . . .47 E3
Briarswood Ct SN3 . . . . .51 D3
Briary Rd GL7 . . . . .2 C6
Brick Hill SN15 . . . . .95 D6
Brick La Salisbury SP2 . .145 C2
Trowbridge BA14 . . . . . . .101 D3
Brickham Rd 1 SN10 . . .214 D5
Brickley La SN10 . . . . . .214 D2
Bricksteed Ave SN10 . . .214 C3
Brickworth La SP5 . . . .160 E4
Brickyard La SP8 . . . . . .137 E1
Bridewell La SP7 . . . . . .202 A6
Bridewell Sq SN10 . . . .214 B3
Bridewell St SN8 . . . . . .213 C2
Bridge Ave BA14 . . . . . .105 A8
Bridge Ct BA13 . . . . . . .108 E4
Bridge End Rd SN3 . . . . .35 F1
Bridge Rd SP5 . . . . .205 E4
Bridge St Bourton SP8 . .137 E2
Bradford-on-Avon BA15 . .100 D6
Fordingbridge SP6 . . . . . .210 D1
26 Hungerford RG17 . . . . .177 B7
Marlborough SN8 . . . . . . .213 A2
Salisbury SP2 . . . . .152 A8
Swindon SN1 . . . . .50 B6
3 Trowbridge BA14 . . . . .105 D7
Bridge The SN15 . . . . . . .78 D7
Bridgeman Cl SN3 . . . . . .36 B2
Bridgemead Cl SN5 . . . . .49 D7
Bridgemead Ret Pk
SN5 . . . . .49 E5
Bridgewater Cl SN2 . . . .50 A7
Bridlewood Prim Sch
SN25 . . . . .34 F7
Bridport Rd SN3 . . . . . . .51 B4
Brier Ct SP2 . . . . .145 C4
Briery Cl SN3 . . . . .36 A4
Bright Cl 3 SN15 . . . . . .78 F5
Bright St SN2 . . . . .50 D8
Brighton Way SN14 . . . . .77 F6
Brimble Hill SN4 . . . . . . .64 D5
Brimble Hill Specl Sch
SN3 . . . . .51 B5
Brimhill Rise BA13 . . . .111 D4
Brind Cl SN3 . . . . .51 E6
Brind Rd SP4 . . . . .197 F7
Brindley Cl SN2 . . . . .34 E1
Brington Rd SN3 . . . . . . .51 B8
Brinkworth Cl SN14 . . . .77 F7
Brinkworth Earl Danby's CE
Prim Sch SN15 . . . . . . .45 E5
Brinkworth House Bsns &
Events Ctr SN15 . . . . . .45 C6
Brinkworth Rd SN15 . . . .45 C3
Brinscombe La 6 SP7 . .202 D1
Brionne Way 13 SP7 . . .202 D2
Brisbane Gdns 7 SP4 . .198 F6
Bristol Rd
Chippenham SN14 . . . . . . .78 C8
Chippenham Without
SN14 . . . . .69 E2
Luckington SN14 . . . . .39 D3
Bristol St
3 Malmesbury SN16 . . . . .28 A3
Swindon SN1 . . . . .50 A6
Britannia Ave SN9 . . . . .182 B2
Britannia Cres SN15 . . . .60 B2
Britannia Pl SN1 . . . . . . .50 D4
Britannia Trade Pk SN3 .35 F3
Britford CE Prim Sch
SP5 . . . . .152 D5
Britford La SP2 . . . . . . .152 B6
Britford La W 1 SP2 . . .152 A6
British Row BA14 . . . . .101 C1
Britmore La SP7 . . . . . .202 F4
Brittain Cl SN14 . . . . . . .77 F7
Britten Rd SN25 . . . . . . .34 E7
Brittox The SN10 . . . . . .214 B3
Brixham Ave SN3 . . . . . . .50 E5
Broad Chalke CE Prim Sch
SP5 . . . . .205 C4
Broad Hinton (Hackpen)
White Horse★ SN4 . . .167 E5
Broad Hinton CE Prim Sch
SN4 . . . . .167 C7
Broad St Swindon SN1 . . .50 C7
Trowbridge BA14 . . . . . . .101 C1
Broad Stones BA15 . . . . .90 E7
Broad Town CE Prim Sch
SN4 . . . . .62 B1
Broad Town White Horse★
SN4 . . . . .62 D1
Broadacres SN4 . . . . .62 B2
Broadbury Banks★
SN9 . . . . .181 B2
Broadcloth E La BA14 .105 E7
Broadcloth La BA14 . . .105 E7
Broadfield Rd SP4 . . . .133 D3
Broadfields SN9 . . . . . . .215 B4
Broadlands Cl SP1 . . . .146 B4
Broadleas Cl SN10 . . . .214 A2
Broadleas Cres SN10 . .214 A2
Broadleas Gdns★
SN10 . . . . .214 A1
Broadleas Pk SN10 . . . .214 A1
Broadleas Rd SN10 . . . .214 A2
Broadleaze
Down Ampney GL7 . . . . .8 E8
Seagry SN15 . . . . .57 D6
Broadley Pk BA14 . . . . .105 D3
Broadmead
Corsham SN13 . . . . .85 B7
Trowbridge BA14 . . . . . . .101 A1
Broadmead La BA12 . . .116 E1
Broadmead Wlk SN3 . . . .51 B7
Broadmoor Rd SN3 . . . . .36 D7
Broadstone SN13 . . . . . .85 B7
Broadtown La
Broad Town SN4 . . . . .62 B3
Wootton Bassett SN4 . . . . .61 F5
Broadway
Market Lavington SN10 . .179 D2
Warminster BA12 . . . . . . .116 E5
Broadway Cl GL7 . . . . . . .10 D7
Broadway E BA13 . . . . .108 D6
Broadway La GL7 . . . . .7 A5
Broadway N BA13 . . . . .108 C7
Broadway The SN25 . . . .35 A3
Broadwood Ave SN13 . . .84 B8
Broadwood Cl 1 BA12 . .117 A8
Brockley Rise SN2 . . . . .36 A5
Brocks Orch 8 SP3 . . . .196 E6
Broken Cross
Calne SN11 . . . . .81 B3
Laverstock SP4 . . . . .146 F6
Brokerswood Ctry Pk★
BA13 . . . . .107 F6
Brokerswood Rd
BA14 . . . . .105 A1
Bromley Cl 2 SN3 . . . . . .50 E6
Bronte Cl 2 SN3 . . . . . . .51 D4
Brook Cl 16 SP3 . . . . . .203 E8
Brook Dr SN13 . . . . .85 B7
Brook Dro BA13 . . . . . .108 C4
Brook Field Prim Sch
Sn5 . . . . .49 A8
Brook Hill
Donhead St Andrew SP7 . .203 B2
Sherston SN16 . . . . .40 C8
Brook La
Westbury BA13 . . . . .108 D4
Woodgreen SP6 . . . . .211 A4
Brook Rd BA14 . . . . .101 B1
Brook St
Chippenham SN14 . . . . . . .78 B8
Fovant SP3 . . . . .204 E7
Great Bedwyn SN8 . . . . . .176 C3
Warminster BA12 . . . . . . .116 E5
Brook Way SN11 . . . . . . .81 C3
Brookdene SN25 . . . . . . .34 E4
Brooke Cres SN2 . . . . . . .34 C5
Brookfield SN6 . . . . .22 F7
Brookfield Rise SN12 . . .85 D1
Brookfields SO51 . . . . .212 F6
Brooklands SN15 . . . . . .45 E5
Brooklands Ave SN2 . . . .34 F1
Brookleaze SN13 . . . . . .84 E5
Brooklime Cl 1 SN2 . . . .34 D4
Brookmead BA14 . . . . .105 A3
Brooks Cl SN2 . . . . .35 E5
Brooksby Way SN3 . . . . .51 B8
Brookside
Crudwell SN16 . . . . .14 E6
Hullavington SN14 . . . . . . .41 F2
Brookside Cl BA1 . . . . . .82 A5
Brookwell Cl SN14 . . . . .70 C2
Broomcroft Rd SN9 . . .215 C5
Broome Manor La SN3 . .50 F2
Broomfield SN15 . . . . . . .70 D2
Broomground BA15 . . . .99 E7
Broomhill SP5 . . . . .212 C5
Brotherton Cl SN15 . . . . .78 F5
Broughton Grange 6
SN3 . . . . .50 F4
Broughton Rd 2 BA14 .105 C5
Brouncker's Well★
BA12 . . . . .186 F5
Brow The SN25 . . . . .34 E4
Brown St
3 Salisbury SP1 . . . . . . .146 B1
Salisbury SP1 . . . . .152 B8
Trowbridge BA14 . . . . . . .105 D7
Brown's Folly★ BA1 . . . .82 C1
Brown's La SN8 . . . . . . .176 B3
Browning Cl 1 SN3 . . . . .36 B3
Brownings The SN13 . . . .83 D5
Brownleaze La SN10 . . .179 D6
Browns La Alton SN8 . . .173 C1
Damerham SP6 . . . . .209 E3
Broxburn Rd BA12 . . . .116 D6
Bruce St SN2 . . . . .49 F7
Bruddel Gr SN3 . . . . .50 E2
Bruges Cl SN15 . . . . .78 F7
Brunel Cl SN13 . . . . .76 F1
Brunel Ct SN15 . . . . .78 B6
Brunel Ctr The SN1 . . . . .50 B6
Brunel Rd SP2 . . . . .145 D1
Brunel Way Box SN13 . . .83 D6
Frome BA11 . . . . .110 C7
Brunkard's La SN9 . . . .215 D5
Brunswick St SN1 . . . . . .50 C4
Brushy Bush La SP5 . . .207 F3
Bruton Wlk SN3 . . . . .51 A4
Bruyn Rd SP6 . . . . .210 E1
Bryans Cl Rd SN11 . . . . .81 B3
Bryanston Way SN3 . . . . .51 C6
Bryant Rd SN25 . . . . . . .34 C5
Brydes Rd 21 SP11 . . . .192 A5
Brympton Cl 5 SP6 . . . .210 C1
Brynards Hill SN4 . . . . . .47 E1
Bryony Way SN2 . . . . . . .34 D4
Bryworth La GL7 . . . . .2 A6
Buckhurst Cres SN3 . . . .51 A6
Buckingham Rd
Chippenham SN15 . . . . . . .79 A5
Swindon SN3 . . . . .51 A3
Buckland Cl SN3 . . . . . . .51 A6
Buckleaze Cl BA14 . . . .105 D5
Buckleaze La SN9 . . . . .215 C5
Bucklebury Cl SN3 . . . . .36 A1
Buckthorn Dr SN2 . . . . . .34 D4
Budbury Circ BA15 . . . .100 C7
Budbury Cl BA15 . . . . . .100 C7
Budbury Pl BA15 . . . . . .100 C7
Budbury Ridge BA15 . . .100 C7
Budbury Tyning BA15 . .100 C7
Bude Rd SN5 . . . . .49 F6
Budge La BA11 . . . . . . .114 A8
Buettell Way SN16 . . . . . .27 F5
Buie Cl SN5 . . . . .34 B2
Bulbridge Rd SP2 . . . . .144 B1
Bulford CE Prim Sch
SP4 . . . . .217 E8
Bulford Droveway
SP4 . . . . .198 D7
Bulford Hill SP4 . . . . . .217 C8
Bulford Rd Bulford SP4 .217 F8
Durrington/Bulford SP4 . .198 B7
Shipton Bellinger SP9 . . .199 C8
South Tedworth SP9 . . . . .216 A4
Bull La BA12 . . . . .116 F2
Bull Pit BA15 . . . . .100 D6
Bulldog La SN10 . . . . . .180 C3
Buller St SN2 . . . . .35 D1
Bullfinch Cl SN3 . . . . . . .51 D6
Bullock's Horn La
Charlton SN16 . . . . .29 D7
Hankerton SN16 . . . . .15 D1
Bulls La Box SN13 . . . . . .83 D6
Broad Chalke SP5 . . . . . .205 B4
Bulpit La RG17 . . . . . . .177 B6
Bulpits Hill SP11 . . . . . .185 C3
Bumper's Batch BA2 . . . .98 A8
Bumpers Fram Ind Est
SN14 . . . . .70 A1
Bumpers Way SN14 . . . . .70 A1
Bunce Rd SN3 . . . . .36 A2
Bungalows The SN2 . . . .35 C2
Bunnies La SN10 . . . . . .96 D2
Bunns La BA11 . . . . . . .114 A2
Bunny La SP5 . . . . .162 C4
Buntings The SN3 . . . . . .51 D7
Bupton Village★
SN11 . . . . .166 D7
Burbage Prim Sch
SN8 . . . . .183 D8
Burbage Rd
Easton SN9 . . . . .183 A8
Milton Lilbourne SN9 . . . .182 F7
Swindon SN2 . . . . .35 C6
Burbage Wharf★ SN8 . .175 C2
Burcombe La SP2 . . . . .144 B2
Burcot Cl SN25 . . . . .34 C7
Burden Cl SN3 . . . . .36 C1
Burderop Cl
1 Trowbridge BA14 . . . . .105 D5
Wroughton SN4 . . . . .64 B8
Burderop Pk★ SN4 . . . . .64 F5
Burdett St 4 SN8 . . . . . .170 B2
Burford Ave
Salisbury SP2 . . . . .152 B6
Swindon SN3 . . . . .50 E5
Burford La SP2 . . . . . . .152 B6

Burford Rd SP2 . . . . .152 B6
Burford St GL7 . . . . .2 C4
Burford's 2 RG17 . . . . . . .171 E7
Burgate Fields SP6 . . . . .210 D2
Burgess Cl SN3 . . . . .36 A1
Burgess Gn SP1 . . . . . . .146 C4
Burghley Cl SN3 . . . . .51 A6
Burlands Rd SN15 . . . . . . .78 E6
Burleaze SN15 . . . . .78 C5
Burn Rd SN13 . . . . .76 E1
Burnet Cl
  Melksham SN12 . . . . . . .94 B2
  Swindon SN2 . . . . .34 D5
Burnet Way SP1 . . . . . . .146 D4
Burnett Rd BA14 . . . . . . .105 D6
Burnham Rd
  5 Fordingbridge SP6 . . . .210 D2
  Swindon SN3 . . . . .51 B6
Burnhams Cl 1 SP10 . . . .193 E2
Burnivale SN16 . . . . .28 A3
Burns Way SN2 . . . . .35 E4
Burnston Cl SN12 . . . . . . .94 D5
Burr La SN8 . . . . .176 F1
Burroughs Dro 2 SN8 . .183 D8
Burton Cl 11 SP7 . . . . . .202 D2
Burton Farm Cl SN14 . . . .53 B3
Burton Hill SN16 . . . . .28 B2
Burton Hill Sch SN16 . . . .28 A1
Burton Rd GL9 . . . . .52 F6
Burtons La SN13 . . . . .83 C5
Burwood Cl 7 SP4 . . . . .217 E3
Bury Camp (Hill Fort) ★
  SN14 . . . . .67 B1
Bury Fields SN5 . . . . .33 D1
Bury Hill (Settlement) ★
  SN6 . . . . .18 B1
Bury La BA13 . . . . .186 B7
Bury Mead BA12 . . . . . . .195 A2
Burycroft SN4 . . . . .163 A6
Burytown La SN26 . . . . . . .21 C2
Buscot Cl SN25 . . . . .34 F7
Buscot Old Parsonage ★
  SN7 . . . . .2 E1
Bush Barrow ★ SP4 . . . .197 D4
Bush Farm Bison Ctr ★
  BA12 . . . . .140 B3
Bustlers Hill SN16 . . . . . . .40 D8
Bute Cl SN6 . . . . .22 F7
Butleigh Rd SN25 . . . . . . .34 C7
Butler Cl SP2 . . . . .152 B6
Butler's Field GL7 . . . . . . .2 C5
Butler's Gdns BA11 . . . . .110 A4
Butlers Cl SN16 . . . . .25 C1
Butt Cl SP11 . . . . .192 A6
Butt La SP5 . . . . .205 E4
Butt St SP11 . . . . .192 A5
Butt's La SP15 . . . . .90 F7
Butter Furlong Rd
  SP5 . . . . .154 C3
Buttercup Cl SN14 . . . . . . .70 B3
Butterfield Dr 2 SP4 . . . .217 D3
Butterfly World ★ SN1 . . .48 F1
Buttermere SN3 . . . . .51 E3
Butterworth St SN1 . . . . . .50 A5
Buttons Yd BA12 . . . . . . .117 B7
Butts (Tumuli) The ★
  SP6 . . . . .211 E2
Butts Cl SN14 . . . . .76 E7
Butts Hill SP3 . . . . .129 E7
Butts La
  Kilmington BA12 . . . . . .123 E6
  Steeple Ashton BA14 . . .178 A3
Butts Mead 3 SP7 . . . . .202 D1
Butts Rd Chiseldown SN4 .65 D5
  Salisbury SP1 . . . . .146 A2
Butts Terr SP2 . . . . .146 A2
Butts The
  Aldbourne SN8 . . . . . . .170 A6
  Biddestone SN14 . . . . . . .76 D7
  Bratton BA13 . . . . .186 B7
  Chippenham SN15 . . . . . .78 E6
  Crudwell SN16 . . . . .14 E6
  Lydiard Millicent SN5 . . . .48 C8
  Potterne SN10 . . . . .179 D5
  Shaftesbury SP7 . . . . . .202 B2
  Shrewton SP3 . . . . .196 E7
  Steeple Ashton BA14 . . .178 A3
  Westbury BA13 . . . . . . .109 A2
By Brook Valley CE Prim Sch
  SN14 . . . . .68 F5
Bydemill Gdns SN6 . . . . . .22 E5
Byfield Way SN3 . . . . .51 B8
Byre Cl SN6 . . . . .19 D7
Byrd Cl 13 SN5 . . . . .48 F5
Byron Ave SN4 . . . . .47 F2
Byron Cl 11 SP11 . . . . . .192 A5
Byron Ct SN3 . . . . .36 E5
Byron Rd SN10 . . . . .214 B1
Byron St 3 SN1 . . . . .50 C5
Bythebrook SN14 . . . . . . .70 B1
Bythesea Rd BA14 . . . . . .105 C8
Byways Cl 4 SP1 . . . . . .152 C8

C

Cabot Dr SN5 . . . . .48 F6
Cabul Rd SP9 . . . . .216 B5
Cadby Cl BA14 . . . . .105 F8
Caddy La BA12 . . . . .138 F5
Cadley Cl SN2 . . . . .35 D2
Cadley Clay Shooting Gd
  SN8 . . . . .175 A5
Cadley Rd SN8 . . . . .183 E1
Cadnam Cres SP4 . . . . . .217 E2
Caen Hill SN10 . . . . .179 C8
Caen Hill Gdns SN10 . . . .179 C8

Caen Hill Locks ★
  SN10 . . . . .179 C8
Caen View SN1 . . . . .49 E4
Caerleon Dr 4 SP10 . . . .193 C2
Caesar Rd SP10 . . . . . . .193 C2
Cagney Dr SN25 . . . . .35 A5
Caird Lawns SN10 . . . . . .214 C2
Cairndow Way SN2 . . . . . .35 E5
Calcutt St SN6 . . . . .19 E8
Calder Cl SN25 . . . . .34 F5
Callaghan Cl 2 SN3 . . . . .36 B2
Callas Hill SN4 . . . . .163 B5
Callas Rise 7 SN4 . . . . .163 B6
Callenders SN5 . . . . .49 E5
Callow Croft 6 SN8 . . . .183 D8
Callows Cross SN15 . . . . .46 C6
Calne Heritage Ctr ★
  SN11 . . . . .81 B2
Calne Rd SN15 . . . . .60 A1
Calstock Rd SN25 . . . . . . .34 B6
Calvert Rd SN3 . . . . .50 E6
Calves La SP7 . . . . .202 A2
Camargue Rd BA13 . . . . .108 E1
Cambrai Rd SN4 . . . . .65 D1
Cambria Bridge Rd
  SN1 . . . . .50 A5
Cambria Pl SN1 . . . . .50 A5
Cambridge Cl SN3 . . . . . . .50 F4
Cambridge Rd SP1 . . . . .146 B3
Camden Cl SN5 . . . . .49 A5
Camellia Dr BA12 . . . . . .116 E7
Camelot Cl 28 SP10 . . . .193 E2
Cameron Cl SN3 . . . . .36 A1
Camilla Cl SP4 . . . . .217 D8
Camomile Dr 25 SP11 . . .192 A5
Campbell Rd SP1 . . . . . .146 B2
Campden Rd SN3 . . . . . . .50 E5
Campion Cl Calne SN11 . . .81 A5
  Westbury BA13 . . . . . . .109 A5
Campion Dr
  Melksham SN12 . . . . . . .94 C2
  Trowbridge BA14 . . . . . .105 D6
Campion Gate SN5 . . . . . .48 F5
Camton Rd SN5 . . . . .48 F7
Canada Rd SO51 . . . . . . .212 F5
Canada Rise SN10 . . . . . .179 F1
Canadian Ave SP2 . . . . . .145 D2
Canal Cl Calne SN11 . . . . .81 A2
  Wilcot SN8 . . . . .182 A8
Canal La SP5 . . . . .153 E2
Canal Rd
  Chippenham SN15 . . . . . .78 F5
  Trowbridge BA14 . . . . . .101 D3
Canal Rd Ind Est
  BA14 . . . . .101 D3
Canal Way SN10 . . . . . . .214 E6
Canal Wlk
  Hungerford RG17 . . . . . .177 B7
  Swindon SN1 . . . . .50 B6
Canalside SP5 . . . . .153 E2
Canberra Dr SP4 . . . . . . .198 F6
Candown Rd SP3 . . . . . . .188 B2
Canford Cl SN3 . . . . .51 C6
Cann Hill SP7 . . . . .206 A7
Canney Cl SN4 . . . . .65 D4
Cannimore Cl BA12 . . . . .116 E5
Cannimore Rd BA12 . . . . .116 D5
Cannon Sq SN12 . . . . .94 A4
Cannon St SN1 . . . . .50 C5
Cannwood La BA10 . . . . .122 D8
Canons Cl
  Tidworth SP9 . . . . .216 D4
  Warminster BA12 . . . . . .117 C5
Canons Ct SN12 . . . . .94 A4
Cantax Hill SN15 . . . . .86 C6
Cantelo Ct SN25 . . . . .34 F7
Canterbury Cl
  10 Amesbury SP4 . . . . . .217 D3
  Swindon SN3 . . . . .50 F3
Canterbury St SN14 . . . . . .78 C8
Cantors Way SN16 . . . . . . .17 C2
Capesthorne Dr SN25 . . . .34 E6
Capitol Cl SN3 . . . . .36 D1
Capps La BA13 . . . . .109 E7
Caprice Cl 1 SN5 . . . . . . .49 A7
Capulet Rd SP1 . . . . .145 F4
Caradon Wlk SN25 . . . . . .34 C7
Caraway Dr SN2 . . . . .34 C4
Carders Cnr 7 BA14 . . . .105 D7
Cardigan Cl SN3 . . . . .50 E4
Cardigan Rd SN8 . . . . . . .213 C3
Cardwell Cl 1 SN3 . . . . . .51 B7
Carey Cl SN3 . . . . .49 A5
Carfax Cl 1 SN1 . . . . .50 C6
Carfax St SN1 . . . . .50 C6
Carisbrook Rd SN12 . . . . .94 B2
Carisbrook Terr SN4 . . . . .65 C3
Carisbrooke Cres
  BA14 . . . . .101 E5
Carleton Pl SP4 . . . . .217 A4
Carlisle Ave SN3 . . . . .50 D3
Carlton Cl 2 SP4 . . . . . .217 D3
Carlton Gate SN3 . . . . . . .50 F1
Carlton Row BA14 . . . . . .105 C6
Carman Cl SN3 . . . . .36 B3
Carmel Wlk SN3 . . . . .50 F5
Carmelite Way SP1 . . . . .152 B7
Carnarvon Cl SN14 . . . . . .78 A7
Carnation La SN12 . . . . . .178 C8
Carp Rd SN11 . . . . .81 A5
Carpenter Cl 5 SN5 . . . . .78 F5
Carpenter Dr SP4 . . . . . .217 D4
Carpenter's Cl SN11 . . . . .80 F4
Carpenters Cl SN16 . . . . . .25 D1
Carpenters La
  4 Bratton BA13 . . . . . . .186 B7

Carpenters La continued
  Swindon SN2 . . . . .50 D8
Carr St SN1 . . . . .50 B6
Carrick Cl SN15 . . . . .79 A8
Carrion Pond Dro
  SP2 . . . . .151 D7
Carroll Cl SN3 . . . . .51 D4
Carronbridge Rd SN5 . . . .49 B6
Carshalton Rd SN3 . . . . . .51 B3
Carstairs Ave SN3 . . . . . . .51 A3
Carter Cl SN25 . . . . .35 C6
Carter's Cl SP6 . . . . .211 C6
Cartway SN10 . . . . .180 E4
Cartwright Dr SN5 . . . . . . .49 B8
Carvers Hill SN8 . . . . . . .176 E1
Cary Glen SN15 . . . . .79 A4
Casley La BA11 . . . . .107 C7
Caspian Gdns BA13 . . . . .108 F1
Cassini Dr SN25 . . . . .34 B7
Casson Rd SN3 . . . . .36 A2
Castell Cl BA14 . . . . .106 B8
Casterbridge La 3
  SP11 . . . . .192 F1
Casterley Camp ★
  SN9 . . . . .189 D8
Castilian Mews SN5 . . . . .49 A7
Castle Barrow ★ BA12 . .195 A4
Castle Combe Motor Racing
  Circuit ★ SN14 . . . . .68 C6
Castle Combe Motte &
  Baileys ★ SN14 . . . . . . .67 F8
Castle Ct SP11 . . . . .192 A6
Castle Ditches Hill Fort ★
  SP3 . . . . .204 A7
Castle Dore SN5 . . . . .49 A5
Castle Grounds SN10 . . . .214 A3
Castle Hill (Fort) ★
  SN26 . . . . .21 D3
Castle Hill Cl 9 SP7 . . . .202 B2
Castle Hill Cres BA14 . . . .139 A6
Castle Hill La BA12 . . . . .139 A5
Castle Keep
  Salisbury SP1 . . . . .145 E4
  4 Wilton SP2 . . . . .144 D3
Castle La Alderbury SP5 . .153 E1
  Wilton SP2 . . . . .144 D3
Castle Meadow SP5 . . . . .211 A8
Castle Pl Sh Ctr BA14 . . .105 D8
Castle Prim Sch SP11 . . . .192 B5
Castle Rd Bratton BA13 . .186 A6
  Devizes SN10 . . . . .214 A3
  3 Great Bedwyn SN8 . . .176 B3
  Salisbury SP1 . . . . .146 A3
Castle St
  Aldbourne SN8 . . . . . . .170 A6
  Calne SN11 . . . . .81 B2
  8 Ludgershall SP11 . . . .192 A5
  Mere BA12 . . . . .138 F5
  Salisbury SP2 . . . . .146 A2
  Trowbridge BA14 . . . . . .105 D8
Castle View
  West Tisbury SP3 . . . . . .203 B8
  Westbury BA13 . . . . . . .109 B3
Castle View Cl SN4 . . . . . .65 E4
Castle View Rd
  Chiseldown SN4 . . . . . . .65 D5
  Swindon SN3 . . . . .36 C1
Castle Wlk SN11 . . . . .81 A2
Castle Woods 2 SP5 . . . .211 C7
Castledown Foundation Sch
  SP11 . . . . .191 F5
Castlefield Cl 3 SN5 . . . . .49 C6
Castlefields SN11 . . . . .81 A3
Castlehaven Cl SN15 . . . . .79 A5
Castleton Rd SN5 . . . . .49 A7
Castley Rd BA14 . . . . . . .102 A2
Catalina Ct 17 SN12 . . . .178 B8
Cathedral Cl SP1 . . . . . . .152 B8
Catherine Cres
  Dinton SP3 . . . . .201 E2
  Downton SP5 . . . . .210 F8
Catherine Ct SP1 . . . . . . .152 A8
Catherine Ford La
  Dinton SP3 . . . . .201 E1
  Fovant SP3 . . . . .204 E8
Catherine St
  Salisbury SP1 . . . . .152 B8
  5 Swindon SN1 . . . . . . .50 B6
Catherine Way BA1 . . . . . .82 A5
Catherine Wayte Cl
  SN25 . . . . .34 F4
Catherine Wayte Prim Sch
  SN25 . . . . .34 F5
Catmint Cl SN2 . . . . .34 D4
Cator Rd 3 SP4 . . . . . . .197 E2
Cats Hill La SP7 . . . . . . .203 A1
Catterick Cl 7 SN14 . . . . .77 F6
Caulfield Rd SN2 . . . . .50 D8
Causeway Cl SN15 . . . . . .78 E7
Causeway The
  Brinkworth SN15 . . . . . . .45 D6
  Broad Chalke SP5 . . . . .205 B4
  Chippenham SN15 . . . . . .78 E7
  The Common SP5 . . . . .149 C7
  11 Tisbury SP3 . . . . . . .203 E8
Cavendish Dr BA14 . . . . .104 F6
Cavendish Sq SN3 . . . . . . .51 A4
Caversham Cl SN3 . . . . . . .50 F5
Cavie Cl SN5 . . . . .49 A8
Caxton Cl
  2 Andover SP10 . . . . . .193 C1
  2 Swindon SN3 . . . . . . .50 F4
Caxton Rd BA11 . . . . . . .110 A3
Cayenne Pk SN2 . . . . .34 C4
Cecil Ave SN2 . . . . .152 A5
Cecil Rd SN3 . . . . .51 A6
Cecil Terr SP2 . . . . .145 D1

Cedar Cl Melksham SN12 . .94 A3
  Salisbury SP2 . . . . .145 B4
  Worton SN10 . . . . .179 B4
Cedar Gr
  Chippenham SN15 . . . . . .70 E1
  Trowbridge BA14 . . . . . .105 B6
Cedars Cl SN2 . . . . .35 A2
Celandine Way SN14 . . . . .70 B2
Cemetery La BA15 . . . . . .100 F7
Central St SP11 . . . . .192 A5
Central Trad Est 50 D3
Centre The SP4 . . . . .217 A4
Centurion Cl
  Chippenham SN15 . . . . . .79 A5
  1 Salisbury SP2 . . . . . .145 D2
Centurion Way SN3 . . . . . .51 C8
Cerney Wick La GL7 . . . . . .7 D5
Chaddenwick Hill
  BA12 . . . . .140 B7
Chadwick Cl 22 SN12 . . .178 B8
Chaffeymoor Hill SP8 . . . .137 B1
Chaffinch Ave BA11 . . . . .110 B6
Chaffinch Dr 2 BA14 . . . .105 B8
Chafyn Gr Sch SP1 . . . . . .146 C2
Chain Dro
  South Newton SP3 . . . . .130 B6
  Stapleford SP3 . . . . . . .129 F7
Chain Hill SP3 . . . . .129 F7
Chain La BA12 . . . . .117 C6
Chalcot La
  Chapmanslade BA13 . . . .111 F5
  Upton Scudamore BA13 .112 A6
Chalet Specl Sch The
  . . . . .51 D3
Chalfield Cres SN12 . . . . . .94 C5
Chalfont Cl BA14 . . . . . . .105 A8
Chalford Ave SN3 . . . . . . .51 B7
Chalgrove Field SN5 . . . . .49 A3
Chalk Down SP9 . . . . . . .216 E7
Chalk Hill 8 SP3 . . . . . . .196 F6
Chalk Pyt Rd SP5 . . . . . .205 B4
Chalk's Cl 1 SP5 . . . . . .211 C8
Chalkcroft La SP11 . . . . .193 A2
Challis Ct 5 SP11 . . . . . .192 B5
Chalvedon Gn SN3 . . . . . .51 A5
Chamberlain Rd
  Chippenham Without
  SN14 . . . . .77 F7
  Swindon SN3 . . . . .36 A2
Chambers Ave SP4 . . . . . .217 C2
Chambon Cl SN16 . . . . . . .17 A2
Champneys Rd 6 BA11 . .110 A4
Chancel Way GL7 . . . . .2 C4
Chancellor Cl SN5 . . . . . . .48 F6
Chancery Cl 1 SP2 . . . . .145 E2
Chancery La BA12 . . . . . .117 C6
Chandler Cl SN3 . . . . .50 D5
Chandler Way 3 SN15 . . . .78 F4
Chandler's La 1 SN8 . . . .170 A7
Chandlers Cl SN10 . . . . . .180 F8
Chandlers La
  All Cannings SN10 . . . . .180 F8
  Bishops Cannings SN10 .172 B2
Chandos Cl SN5 . . . . .49 A6
Chantry Gdns BA14 . . . . .104 F3
Chantry La Chute SP11 . . .184 C2
  Marlborough SN8 . . . . . .213 D2
  Westbury BA13 . . . . . . .109 A3
Chantry Mead 13 RG17 . .177 B7
Chantry Mews BA12 . . . . .117 A7
Chantry Rd Swindon SN2 . .34 F2
  Wilton SP2 . . . . .144 C1
Chantry The ★ BA12 . . . .139 A5
Chants La 6 SP3 . . . . . . .196 E6
Chapel Cl GL7 . . . . .10 D6
Chapel Cnr SN14 . . . . .41 F1
Chapel Ct 17 RG17 . . . . .177 B7
Chapel Hill
  Broad Blunsdon SN26 . . . .21 B2
  Grimstead SP5 . . . . . . .154 B2
  Lacock SN15 . . . . .86 C6
Chapel La
  Acton Turville GL9 . . . . . .53 A6
  Andover SP11 . . . . .193 E3
  Bishopstone SP5 . . . . . .205 E4
  Box SN13 . . . . .83 D5
  Broad Town SN4 . . . . . .167 B8
  Chippenham SN15 . . . . . .78 E7
  Collingbourne Kingston
  SN8 . . . . .183 D2
  Corsham SN13 . . . . .84 E4
  Downton SP5 . . . . .159 B5
  Hankerton SN16 . . . . . . .15 C2
  12 Lambourn RG17 . . . .165 A2
  5 Ludgershall SP11 . . . .192 A5
  Melksham Without SN12 . .86 A1
  Minety SN16 . . . . .17 A2
  Nomansland SP5 . . . . . .212 C4
  Pen Selwood BA9 . . . . . .137 C3
  8 Ramsbury SN8 . . . . . .170 B2
  Redlynch SP5 . . . . .211 D7
  1 Shrewton SP3 . . . . . .196 E6
  South Marston SN3 . . . . .36 E5
  Stapleford SP3 . . . . . . .129 E7
  Upavon SN9 . . . . .181 F2
  5 Wanborough SN4 . . . .163 B6
  Wingfield BA14 . . . . . . .104 C6
  Woodborough SN9 . . . . .181 D7
  Zennor SN4 . . . . .75 A5
Chapel Mews SN15 . . . . . .78 E7
Chapel Orch 6 SN4 . . . . .163 B6
Chapel Path SN14 . . . . . . .75 B3
Chapel Pl 1 SP2 . . . . . . .146 A1
Chapel Rd
  Ashbury SN6 . . . . .164 A7
  Heytesbury BA12 . . . . . .194 C5
  Kempsford GL7 . . . . .10 D7

Bur – Che 225

Chapel Rise SN12 . . . . . . .92 E8
Chapel St
  Horningsham BA12 . . . . .119 A7
  Swindon SN2 . . . . .50 D8
  Warminster BA12 . . . . . .116 F5
Chapel Wlk GL9 . . . . .24 B3
Chaplins Pl 3 SP4 . . . . . .217 B3
Chapmanslade CE Prim Sch
  BA13 . . . . .111 C4
Charcoal Burners Rd
  SN8 . . . . .175 B4
Charcroft Hill BA10 . . . . .122 A5
Charfield Cl SN3 . . . . .51 A4
Charlbury Cl SN25 . . . . . . .34 E3
Charles Garrett Cl 39
  SP7 . . . . .202 C2
Charles McPherson Gdns
  SN3 . . . . .51 C5
Charles Rd SP4 . . . . .198 B7
Charles St
  Corsham SN13 . . . . .76 F2
  2 Salisbury SP2 . . . . . .145 F1
Charlham La GL7 . . . . .8 D7
Charlieu Ave SN11 . . . . . . .89 C8
Charlock Path SN25 . . . . . .34 E5
Charlotte Ct BA14 . . . . . .101 D1
Charlotte Mews SN3 . . . . .50 D4
Charlotte Sq SN4 . . . . . . .101 D1
Charlotte St BA14 . . . . . .101 D1
Charlton Cl SN2 . . . . .35 D5
Charlton Hill BA13 . . . . . .186 D6
Charlton La SP7 . . . . .202 F1
Charlton Pk ★ SN16 . . . . .28 E7
Charlton Rd SN16 . . . . . . .28 E5
Charlwood Rd SN13 . . . . . .84 F8
Charminster Cl SN3 . . . . . .51 C6
Charnham La RG17 . . . . .177 B8
Charnham Pk RG17 . . . . .177 B8
Charnham Pk Ind Est
  RG17 . . . . .177 B8
Charnwood Dr 9 SP6 . . . .210 D2
Charnwood Rd
  Salisbury SP2 . . . . .145 B1
  Trowbridge BA14 . . . . . .101 A1
Charter Cl 3 SN10 . . . . . .214 D5
Charter Prim Sch SN15 . . .78 F6
Charter Rd SN15 . . . . .78 D7
Charterhouse Dr 4
  BA11 . . . . .110 C7
Chartley Gn 1 SN5 . . . . . .49 A5
Chartwell Pl SP3 . . . . . . .196 E6
Chartwell Rd SN25 . . . . . . .34 F7
Chase Cres SP5 . . . . .207 C4
Chase Wood SN5 . . . . .34 A2
Chatham Cl SP1 . . . . .145 F4
Chatham Ct BA12 . . . . . . .117 B7
Chatsworth Rd SN25 . . . . .34 F5
Chaucer Ave 5 SP10 . . . .193 C1
Chaucer Cl SN4 . . . . .47 E3
Chaveywell Ct SN11 . . . . . .81 B2
Cheapside BA12 . . . . .195 A2
Cheddar Cl BA11 . . . . . . .110 C7
Cheddar Rd SN25 . . . . . . .34 E3
Chedworth Gate SN3 . . . . .50 F1
Cheese Mkt 6 SP1 . . . . .146 A1
Cheese Wharf ★ SN7 . . . . .2 F1
Chelmsford Rd SN5 . . . . . .49 C7
Cheltenham Dr SN14 . . . . .78 A5
Cheltenham St SN1 . . . . . .50 B7
Chelwood Cl SN14 . . . . . . .78 B6
Chelworth House SN16 . . . .4 B1
Chelworth Rd SN6 . . . . . . .19 B6
Chemical Rd BA13 . . . . . .108 C6
Cheney Manor Ind Est
  SN2 . . . . .34 E1
Cheney Manor Rd SN2 . . . .34 F2
Chepston Pl BA14 . . . . . .100 F1
Chepstow Cl
  4 Chippenham SN14 . . . .78 A5
  Swindon SN5 . . . . .49 C3
Cheraton Cl SN3 . . . . .51 B7
Cherbury Wlk SN3 . . . . . . .51 A6
Cherhill CE Prim Sch
  SN11 . . . . .166 B1
Cherhill Cl SN25 . . . . .34 E3
Cherhill White Horse ★
  SN11 . . . . .172 C8
Cherrington Field
  SN10 . . . . .180 F4
Cherry Cl Pewsey SN9 . . .215 D5
  Salisbury SP2 . . . . .145 D1
Cherry Gdns SN4 . . . . . . .102 A3
Cherry Gdns Ct BA14 . . . .105 D7
Cherry Gr 7 RG17 . . . . . .177 B7
Cherry Orch
  Codford St Peter BA12 . .195 A2
  Highworth SN6 . . . . .23 A5
  Marlborough SN8 . . . . . .213 E2
Cherry Orch E SN2 . . . . . .35 E2
Cherry Orch La
  Cann SP7 . . . . .202 A2
  Luckington SN14 . . . . . . .39 C5
  Salisbury SP2 . . . . .145 D1
Cherry Orch N SN2 . . . . . .35 E2
Cherry Orch W SN2 . . . . . .35 D2
Cherry Rd SN14 . . . . .75 A5
Cherry Tree Ave SP9 . . . .216 E6
Cherry Tree Ct SN11 . . . . .81 B4
Cherry Tree Gr SN2 . . . . . .35 C2
Cherry Tree Rd SN6 . . . . . .19 D8
Cherry Tree Way 2
  SP4 . . . . .217 C3
Chervil Cl 3 SN2 . . . . . . .34 C4
Chesford Cl SN3 . . . . .51 A3

Cheshire Cl
2 Bower Hill SN12 178 B8
Salisbury SP2 145 C4
Chester St SN1 50 B6
Chester Way SN14 78 A5
Chesterfield Cl
3 Amesbury SP4 217 E3
4 Swindon SN5 49 C6
Chesters The SN5 49 C6
Chestnut Ave
Netheravon SP4 190 A2
Swindon SN2 35 C3
Tidworth SP9 216 D7
Chestnut Cl
Down Ampney GL7 8 D7
Frome BA11 110 B7
Rowde SN10 96 D2
Salisbury SP1 146 D3
Chestnut Dr SN10 178 E5
Chestnut Gr
Trowbridge BA14 105 B5
Westwood BA15 99 F4
Chestnut Grange SN13 76 D1
Chestnut La RG17 165 C2
Chestnut Mews SN12 94 A3
Chestnut Rd
Chippenham SN14 78 B8
Sutton Benger SN15 57 D2
Chestnut Springs SN5 33 D1
Chestnut Wlk 11 RG17 177 B6
Chetcombe Rd BA12 139 B6
Chevalier Cl 13 SN5 48 F8
Cheverell Ave SP1 146 C3
Cheverell Cl BA14 105 D5
Cheverell Gn Rd SN10 179 C2
Cheverell Rd
Cheverell Parva SN10 179 C1
West Lavington SN10 187 D8
Cheviot Cl Swindon SN5 49 A6
Trowbridge BA14 105 E7
Chevral Cl SN14 70 B2
Cheyney Wlk BA13 109 B4
Chichester Cl SP2 152 B6
Chichester Pk BA13 109 A4
Chick's La SN8 183 E1
Chickerell Rd SN3 51 A6
Chicksgrove Rd SP3 203 F8
Chicory Cl SN2 34 C3
Child St 1 RG17 165 A1
Chilmark Rd
Tisbury SP3 200 F1
Trowbridge BA14 101 A1
Chilmark/Fonthill Bishop Pri Sch SP3 201 B3
Chiltern Cl
Melksham SN12 94 C4
9 Warminster BA12 117 A8
Chilton Foliat CE Prim Sch RG17 171 A2
Chilton Gdns SN25 34 F3
Chilton Way RG17 177 B7
Chilvester Hill SN11 80 E2
Chilworth Cl SN25 34 E6
Chine Rd SP4 131 C7
Chippenham Com Hospl SN15 78 C6
Chippenham La SN14 77 B7
Chippenham Mus & Heritage Ctr★ SN15 78 E7
Chippenham Rd
Lyneham & Bradenstoke SN15 59 E3
Marshfield SN14 74 A8
Chippenham Sta SN15 78 E8
Chipper La SP1 146 A1
Chirton CE Prim Sch SN10 180 F4
Chirton Pl 6 BA14 105 D6
Chisbury Camp★ SN8 176 C4
Chisbury La SN8 176 C5
Chiselbury Gr SP2 152 A6
Chiseldon Ct SN4 65 D4
Chiseldon Prim Sch SN4 65 E4
Chitham Cl SN10 187 C8
Chitterne Rd
Codford BA12 195 B3
Shrewton SP3 196 B6
Chittoe Heath SN15 88 A2
Chivers Rd
Chippenham SN15 78 E5
Devizes SN10 214 D3
Chives Way SN2 34 D4
Chobham Cl SN2 36 A5
Cholderton Rare Breeds Farm★ SP4 199 A5
Cholderton Rd
Amport SP4 199 D5
Quarley SP4 199 F5
Chopping Knife La SN8 175 A7
Choristers Sq 1 SP1 152 A8
Choulston Cl SP4 190 B3
Christ the King RC Prim Sch SP4 217 B3
Christchurch CE Prim Sch BA15 100 E8
Christchurch Rd BA15 100 D8
Christchurch Terr BA12 116 F5
Christian Malford CE Prim Sch SN15 58 A2
Christie Cl SN3 51 D4
Christie Miller Rd SP2 145 E2
Christie Miller Sports Ctr SN12 94 B1
Christin Ct BA14 105 A8
Christopher Cl 2 SP2 151 F5
Christopher Dr SN15 79 A4
Christy's Gdns 30 SP7 202 C2
Christy's La 23 SP7 202 C2
Chubb Cl SN16 28 A5
Chudleigh SN5 49 B4
Chur St SP4 198 E6
Church Acre
Bradford-on-Avon BA15 100 C7
Seagry SN15 57 F6
Church Bottom SP4 131 A5
Church Cl Bath BA1 82 B2
Bourton SP8 137 D1
13 Lambourn RG17 165 A2
Church Farm La
South Marston SN3 36 E4
Woodborough SN9 181 D7
Church Farm Mews SN15 60 A2
Church Fields BA14 105 A5
Church Furlong SP3 129 E7
Church Hatch 1 SP5 211 B8
Church Hill
Bromham SN15 95 F7
Donhead St Mary SP7 203 A3
Limpley Stoke BA2 99 B5
Nettleton SN14 53 B3
Redlynch SP5 211 D7
Shaftesbury SP7 202 B2
West Overton SN8 173 F7
Wroughton SN4 63 F5
Church Hill Rise SN15 96 A7
Church La
Amesbury SP4 217 A3
Bishopstone SP5 150 A1
Bishopstone SN6 163 E6
Box SN13 83 C5
Bratton BA13 186 B7
Britford SP5 152 E5
Brokenborough SN16 27 D7
Buttermere SN8 185 C7
Codford St Peter BA12 195 B2
5 Cricklade SN6 19 D8
Damerham SP6 209 F2
Dauntsey SN15 44 E1
Downton SP5 159 A5
Durrington/Bulford SP4 217 D8
East Kennet SN8 173 D6
Fovant SP3 204 D8
Great Somerton SN15 44 E1
Hankerton SN16 15 C2
Hawkesbury GL9 38 E5
Kington Langley SN15 70 E6
Limpley Stoke BA2 99 A5
6 Ludgershall SP11 192 A5
Lyneham SN15 60 A2
Marshfield SN14 74 A8
Melchet Park & Plaitford SO51 212 E7
Melksham SN12 94 C6
Mildenhall SN8 175 A8
Norton SN16 41 D5
Ogbourne St Andrew SN8 168 E3
Pitton & Farley SP5 148 C4
Rushall SN9 181 E2
Salisbury SP2 145 C2
2 Shaftesbury SP7 202 C1
Sherfield English SO51 162 F3
Sherrington BA12 194 F2
Sopworth SN14 24 D1
South Cerney GL7 6 F7
Stanton St Quintin SN14 56 B5
Tidworth SP9 216 D4
Trowbridge BA14 105 A5
Vernhams Dean SP11 185 B4
West Lavington SN10 187 E8
Westbury BA13 108 E1
Wingfield BA14 104 C6
Church Mdws 1 SP9 199 D8
Church Piece SN15 57 D2
Church Pk SN15 59 C3
Church Pl
Lydiard Millicent SN5 33 C1
Swindon SN1 50 A6
Church Rails SP3 141 B1
Church Rd
Biddestone SN14 76 E7
Bratton BA13 186 B6
Calne Without SN11 80 A2
Cheverell Magna SN10 179 B1
Christian Malford SN15 58 A2
Derry Hill/Studley SN11 79 F2
Froxfield SN8 176 D7
Ham SN8 177 A1
Heddington SN13 89 B1
Hilmarton SN11 73 F3
Idmiston SP4 133 F8
Kemble GL7 4 F7
Kilmington BA12 123 E5
Kington Langley SN15 70 E6
Liddington SN4 163 A4
Luckington SN14 39 E4
Milston SP4 198 C8
Norleaze BA13 108 F8
Pitton & Farley SP5 154 E7
St Paul Malmesbury Without SN16 43 A3
Salisbury SP1 146 E3
Sherston GL8 25 B5
Silton SP8 138 A1
Stanton St Bernard SN8 173 B1
Swindon SN1 50 D4
Wanborough SN4 163 A5
Woodborough SN9 181 D7
Church Rise SN13 84 E5
Church Row SN4 163 D6
Church St
Amesbury SP4 217 A3
Atworth SN12 92 D8
Bath BA1 82 B2
Berwick St John SP7 203 E1
Bower Chalke SP5 205 A2
Bradford-on-Avon BA15 100 C6
Calne SN11 81 B2
Chiseldown SN4 65 D4
Collingbourne Ducis SN8 191 E8
Corsham SN13 77 A2
Durrington/Bulford SP4 198 B7
Great Bedwyn SN8 176 B2
Grimstead SP5 154 C2
Horningsham BA12 119 B7
Hungerford RG17 177 B7
Keevil BA14 178 A4
Lacock SN15 86 D6
Little Bedwyn SN8 176 D5
Longbridge Deverill BA12 120 F7
Maiden Bradley with Yarnfield BA12 118 E2
Market Lavington SN10 179 F1
Melksham SN12 94 A4
Mere BA12 139 A5
Pewsey SN9 215 D4
Purton SN5 33 C4
Semington BA14 102 F6
Sherston SN16 25 C1
Southwick BA14 104 F3
Swindon SN3 36 B3
Tisbury SP3 203 E8
Trowbridge BA14 101 D1
Warminster BA12 116 F7
West Lavington SN10 187 E7
Westbury BA13 109 A3
Winterbourne Stoke SP3 196 F3
Wootton Bassett SN4 47 C2
Wylye BA12 201 E8
Church St Cl 15 SP3 203 E8
Church Tk SP8 137 D1
Church View
Castle Eaton SN6 10 B4
Chippenham SN14 70 C2
Church Way
Hungerford RG17 177 B7
7 Swindon SN3 36 B3
Church Wlk
Ashton Keynes SN6 6 E1
Bishopstone SN6 163 E6
Devizes SN10 214 C3
Melksham SN12 94 A4
Motcombe SP7 202 A4
Redlynch SP5 211 E7
Swindon SN2 35 E3
Church Wlk N SN25 34 F3
Church Wlk S SN2 34 F3
Churches BA15 100 C7
Churchfield SN25 34 F4
Churchfields BA15 91 E6
Churchfields Ind Est SP2 145 E1
Churchfields Rd SP2 145 E1
Churchfields Sch SN3 50 F5
Churchill Ave
Broad Blunsdon SN26 21 C2
Durrington/Bulford SP4 217 D8
Melksham SN12 94 D5
Churchill Cl Calne SN11 81 C1
North Tidworth SP9 216 B8
9 Tisbury SP3 203 E8
3 Wootton Bassett SN4 47 F3
Churchill Ct SP2 144 D3
Churchill Est SP3 203 E8
Churchill Way SN13 76 F3
Churchill Way E SP1 146 B1
Churchill Way N SP1 146 A2
Churchill Way S SP1 152 B7
Churchill Way W
Charlton SP10 193 C1
Salisbury SP2 146 A1
Churchlands BA14 105 D2
Churchward Ave SN2 35 A1
Churchward Dr BA11 110 C7
Churchway SN26 21 C2
Churn Cl GL7 6 F7
Chute Cswy SP11 184 E2
Circle The SN2 35 C2
Cirencester Rd
Fairford GL7 1 F6
Latton GL7 7 E8
Cirencester Way SN2 50 D8
City Cnr SN4 163 C6
City The SN12 94 A5
Clack La SP6 210 B3
Clanfield Rd SN3 51 B5
Clap La SP5 207 B4
Clardon La SN5 33 C6
Clare Wlk SN5 49 B4
Clarence Cl 18 SP11 192 A5
Clarence Rd
Chippenham SN14 77 F7
Trowbridge BA14 105 F8
Clarence St SN1 50 C6
Clarendon Ave BA14 105 E8
Clarendon Cl SP3 201 F2
Clarendon Ct SP9 216 D7
Clarendon Dr SN4 47 E1
Clarendon Jun & Inf Sch SP9 216 D6
Clarendon La 1 SN1 50 A5
Clarendon Pal★ SP5 147 C1
Clarendon Rd
Alderbury SP5 153 D3
Clarendon Park SP5 152 F6
Clarendon Rd *continued*
Grimstead SP5 154 A4
Salisbury SP1 146 C1
Trowbridge BA14 105 E8
Clarendon Sch The BA14 105 C6
Claridge Cl 3 SN8 170 A6
Clark Ave SN11 81 C5
Clark's Gdns 25 RG17 177 B7
Clark's Pl 3 BA14 105 E8
Clarke Dr SN5 49 B8
Clarke's La SP11 193 A7
Clarkes Leaze SN14 68 F6
Clary Rd SN2 34 D5
Classics The 16 RG17 165 A1
Clattinger Farm Nature Reserve★ SN16 16 E7
Claudius Cl 15 SP10 193 E2
Claverton Pumping Sta★ BA1 90 C5
Clay Cl BA13 112 C8
Clay St
Little Somerford SN15 44 C6
Longbridge Deverill BA12 116 E1
Whiteparish SP5 161 C3
Clay The SN10 180 A1
Clayfurlong Gr GL7 4 F8
Clayhill Copse SN5 34 A2
Clays Cl SN2 35 E3
Clays The SN10 179 F1
Clayton Rd SP4 217 E8
Clearbury Ring★ SP5 158 C5
Clearwood BA13 111 F8
Clearwood View BA13 111 D4
Cleasby Cl SN5 49 D6
Cleavers The 1 SN8 183 D8
Cleaves Ave SN14 75 A3
Cleeve Lawns SN3 50 F3
Cleeve The
Corsham SN13 85 A8
West Knoyle BA12 140 A6
Cleevedale Rd SN13 85 A8
Cleeves Cl SN5 49 A6
Cleeves The SP3 143 B3
Clement's La BA12 139 B4
Clementine Rd SN25 34 B7
Clevedon Cl SN3 51 A6
Cleveland Gdns BA14 101 E2
Cleveland Way BA13 108 E2
Cleverton Ct SN2 35 C5
Cleves Cl SN5 49 A6
Cley Hill (Hill Fort)★ BA12 116 A6
Cley View 6 BA12 116 E6
Cleyhill Gdns BA13 111 D5
Cliff Rd SN16 40 C8
Cliffe Dr BA2 99 A6
Cliffords SN6 19 C8
Clift Ave SN15 70 E1
Clift Cl SN13 84 A8
Clifton Cl SN14 78 B8
Clifton Rd SP2 145 F2
Clifton St SN1 50 B5
Clifts Bldgs BA11 110 A4
Clink Farm Ct 6 BA11 110 C6
Clink Rd BA11 110 E6
Clinton Cl SN5 48 F4
Clipsham Rise BA14 101 A1
Clivey BA13 107 E1
Cloatley Manor★ SN16 15 D2
Cloatley Mdws Nature Reserve★ SN16 15 E2
Cloatley Rd SN16 15 C2
Cloche Way SN2 35 E3
Cloford Cl BA14 101 A1
Cloister Gdn★ SN16 28 A3
Close End 8 RG17 165 A1
Close La Marston SN10 179 A3
Rowde SN10 96 D2
Close The
Bulkington SN10 178 E5
Chippenham SN14 77 E8
Corsham SN13 85 C6
Kington St Michael SN14 70 A8
Laverstock SP4 146 D8
Lechlade GL7 2 C5
Lydiard Millicent SN5 48 D8
Melksham SN12 94 B3
4 Redlynch SP5 211 C8
Salisbury SP1 152 A8
Tangley SP11 193 C5
Warminster BA12 117 A7
Cloth Yd 1 BA14 105 E7
Clothier Leaze 2 BA14 105 D7
Cloudberry Rd SN25 34 E5
Clough La SP5 149 B7
Clouts Wood SN5 34 A2
Clouts Wood Nature Reserve★ SN4 63 F4
Clover Cl SN12 94 C3
Clover Dean SN14 78 A6
Clover Gdns 28 SP11 192 A5
Clover Pk SN2 34 D4
Cloverlands SN25 34 D4
Club La SP9 216 C4
Club Rd 1 SP4 198 F7
Clump Way SP4 217 A5
Clydesdale Cl
5 Swindon SN5 49 A7
Trowbridge BA14 105 C5
Clydesdale Rd SN13 83 D5
Coach Barton BA14 178 A3
Coach Hill SP11 192 E6
Coach Ho Mews SP4 217 B3
Coach Rd
Bradford-on-Avon BA15 100 C6
Westbury BA13 109 B5
Coalpit Rd BA1 82 A4
Coalway La BA11 110 C7
Coate Rd SN8 173 B1
Coate Wr Ctry Pk★ SN3 51 A1
Coate Wr Nature Reserve★ SN3 51 B1
Cob Pl BA13 108 F1
Cobbett Cl SN25 35 A7
Cobbett Pl BA12 116 F6
Cobbett Rise BA12 117 E4
Cobden Rd SN2 50 A8
Cobley Cl SP5 208 D6
Cock Hill BA14 101 A1
Cock Rd
Horningsham BA12 118 F8
Rowde SN10 95 F2
Cock-a-Troop La SN8 175 B8
Cocklebury La SN15 70 F1
Cocklebury Rd SN15 78 E8
Cocks Cl 5 SP4 197 E7
Codford CE Prim Sch BA12 195 B3
Codford Circ or Wilsbury Ring★ BA12 195 C3
Codford Rd BA12 195 C6
Codford Rising Sun (Hill Figure)★ BA12 195 C2
Coker's La BA12 123 F7
Colbert Pk SN25 34 F6
Colborne Cl SN15 79 B5
Colbourne St SN1 50 D7
Colchester Cl SN5 49 D4
Cold Harbour SP4 217 B3
Cold Harbour La SN8 213 E4
Coldharbour La SP2 145 F2
Coldharbour Rd RG17 177 B6
Cole Cl 2 Andover SP10 193 E2
Swindon SN3 51 D6
Cole's La SP7 202 A1
Colebrook Jun & Inf Sch SN3 51 C8
Colebrook Rd SN3 36 B1
Coleridge Cl
Warminster BA12 116 D6
Wootton Bassett SN4 47 E3
Coleridge Rd SN25 34 F6
Colerne Airfield SN14 74 E3
Colerne CE Prim Sch SN14 75 B3
Colerne Pk★ SN14 75 F6
Coles's La SP5 212 A7
Colesway Coll SO51 212 F5
College Cl SN15 78 F8
College Fields SN8 213 C2
College Gdns BA14 105 D3
College Gr 1 SN4 163 A6
College Rd
1 Durrington/Bulford SP4 198 B7
Purton SN5 33 C4
Trowbridge BA14 105 B6
College St
Salisbury SP1 146 B1
Swindon SN1 50 C6
College Way 4 RG17 171 E7
Collen Cl 1 SN14 78 A7
Collett Ave SN2 35 A1
Collett Pl SN6 8 C3
Collett Way BA11 110 C7
Collingbourne CE Prim Sch SN8 191 E8
Collingbourne Cl 2 BA14 105 D5
Collingsmead SN3 51 C5
Collingwood Wlk 4 SP10 193 F1
Collins Cl 15 SP10 193 D2
Collins Ct SP9 216 C8
Collins La SN5 33 E5
Colman Pk SN25 35 A6
Coln Cres SN25 35 A4
Colquhoun Rd 2 SP4 198 A6
Colston Cl SN3 51 A4
Colston Rd SN10 214 A3
Coltsfoot Cl SP4 217 C3
Column Ride SN8 175 E3
Combe La
Bratton BA13 186 B7
Hilmarton SN11 73 F6
Combe View
10 Hungerford RG17 177 B6
Yatton Keynell SN14 68 F5
Comet Ave SN9 182 B2
Comet Cl SN15 60 B2
Comfrey Cl Swindon SN2 34 D4
Trowbridge BA14 105 E6
Commerce Bsns Ctr BA13 108 E7
Commercial Rd
Devizes SN10 214 A4
Swindon SN1 50 B5
Common Dro DT11 207 B3
Common Hill
Cricklade SN6 19 B7
Great Hinton BA14 102 F2
Steeple Ashton BA14 106 F8
Common Platt SN5 34 A2
Common Rd
St Paul Malmesbury Without SN16 27 D1
Sixpenny Handley SP5 207 F4
Whiteparish SP5 161 E1
Common Slip SN15 78 E7
Common The
Bromham SN15 95 E6
Holt BA14 92 F1
Kington Langley SN15 70 E6

Common The *continued*
Marlborough SN8 . . . . . . .213 D4
Minety SN16 . . . . .17 C1
Shrewton SP3 . . . . .196 E6
The Common SP5 . . . . . . .149 D6
Commonweal Rd SN1 . . .50 B3
Commonweal Sch The
SN1 . . . . .50 B3
Commonwood La SN16 . .40 D5
Compton Abbas Airfield
SP5 . . . . .206 C5
Compton Cl
4 Swindon SN3 . . . . .51 C4
Trowbridge BA14 . . . . . .101 E4
Compton Gdns BA11 . . .110 C7
Compton Pk★ SP3 . . . . .142 C1
Compton Rd
Hilmarton SN11 . . . . .73 F3
Tidworth SP9 . . . . .216 D6
Compton's Dr SO51 . . . .212 E7
Conan Doyle Wlk SN3 . .51 D4
Concord Wlk SN3 . . . . . .51 A5
Conference Cl **1** BA12 . .116 F7
Congreve Rd **4** SP4 . . . .197 E7
Conholt Hill SP11 . . . . .185 A2
Conholt La SP11 . . . . . .185 B2
Conholt Pk★ SP11 . . . . .184 F1
Conifer Crest **5** SN8 . .183 D8
Conifers The SN16 . . . . .17 A2
Coniger the (Tumuli)★
SP3 . . . . .196 F5
Conigre BA14 . . . . .101 C1
Conigre Cl SN12 . . . . . . .94 A3
Conigre Hill BA15 . . . . .100 C7
Conigre Mead Nature
Reserve★ SN12 . . . . .94 A4
Conisborough SN5 . . . . . .49 C5
Coniston Cl **5** SP4 . . . . .217 E3
Coniston Rd
Chippenham SN14 . . . . . .77 F6
Trowbridge BA14 . . . . . .101 E2
Connaught Rd SP9 . . . . .216 D6
Conrad Cl SN3 . . . . .51 D4
Consciences La SN10 . . .214 A7
Constable Rd SN2 . . . . . .35 E2
Constable Way SP2 . . . .151 E7
Constantine Sq 29 SP10 193 E2
Convent The★ BA10 . . . .123 B2
Conway Cres SN12 . . . . .94 B2
Conway Rd
Chippenham SN14 . . . . . .78 A7
Swindon SN3 . . . . .51 C3
Conyers Cl **5** SN5 . . . . . .48 F4
Cookham Rd SN25 . . . . .34 C7
Cooks Cl
Hullavington SN14 . . . . . .56 D6
Salisbury SP2 . . . . .145 B5
Seend SN12 . . . . .178 E8
Cooks La SO51 . . . . .162 F7
Coombe Barn La
BA12 . . . . .124 D5
Coombe Bissett CE Prim Sch
SP5 . . . . .150 F1
Coombe Cl SN4 . . . . .64 C5
Coombe La
Atworth SN12 . . . . .92 C7
Enford SN9 . . . . .190 C6
Coombe Rd
Salisbury SP2 . . . . .151 F5
Swindon SN25 . . . . .34 F3
Coombe St BA9 . . . . . . .137 D3
Coombe View BA12 . . . .194 D3
Cooper Fields SN25 . . . . .35 A5
Coopers Cl
Amesbury SP4 . . . . .217 B4
2 Malmesbury SN16 . . . .28 A5
Coopers Ct SN9 . . . . . . .215 B5
Cop Croft SN11 . . . . .81 B3
Copheap La BA12 . . . . . .117 B7
Copheap Rise BA12 . . . .117 B8
Copper Beeches SN6 . . . .22 F5
Coppice Cl Swindon SN2 .34 D3
Warminster BA12 . . . . . .117 A7
Coppice Hill BA15 . . . . .100 D7
Coppice La SN16 . . . . . . .15 D6
Coppice St SP7 . . . . . . .202 C1
Copse Ave SN1 . . . . .50 E8
Copse Dro SN8 . . . . .169 B5
Copse The
Alderbury SP5 . . . . .153 D2
Frome BA11 . . . . .110 B6
Copyhold **2** SN8 . . . . . .176 B3
Corbin Rd BA14 . . . . . . .101 F1
Corby Ave SN3 . . . . .50 E3
Corfe Cl SN25 . . . . .35 A4
Corfe Cres SN1 . . . . .81 A4
Corfe Rd Melksham SN12 .94 B3
Swindon SN5 . . . . .49 B4
Coriander Way SN2 . . . . .34 D5
Corinthian Cl **14** SP10 .193 E2
Corn Gastons SN16 . . . . .27 E3
Corner Gd BA12 . . . . . . .117 E5
Corner La SP7 . . . . .202 B5
Cornfield Rd SN10 . . . . .214 D3
Cornflower Cl SN11 . . . . .81 C5
Cornflower Cl SN25 . . . . .34 D5
Cornflower Way
51 Ludgershall SP11 . . . .192 A5
Melksham SN12 . . . . .94 B3
Cornmarket BA12 . . . . . .117 B7
Cornmarsh Way SN3 . . . .51 E7
Cornpits La SP6 . . . . . . .209 E2
Cornwall Ave SN2 . . . . . .35 A1
Cornwall Cres SN12 . . . . .94 C4
Cornwall Rd SP1 . . . . . .146 A3
Cornwell Cres SN10 . . . .214 A2

Coronation Cl
Christian Malford SN15 . . .58 A1
Donhead St Mary SP7 . . .203 A1
2 Pewsey SN9 . . . . .215 C5
Sutton Benger SN15 . . . . .57 F1
Coronation Dr SP7 . . . . .203 A1
Coronation Rd
Atworth/Whitley SN12 . . .92 E8
Durrington/Bulford SP4 . .198 B7
Frome BA11 . . . . .110 B5
3 Ludgershall SP11 . . . .192 B5
Melksham SN12 . . . . .94 B3
Salisbury SP2 . . . . .145 D3
Tidworth SP9 . . . . .216 C8
Wroughton SN4 . . . . .64 A6
Coronation Sq SP2 . . . .144 F3
Coronation St
Fairford GL7 . . . . .1 F7
4 Trowbridge BA14 . . . .105 D7
Corporation St SN2 . . . . .50 C7
Corral Cl SN5 . . . . .34 A1
Corry The **1** SP3 . . . . . .203 E8
Corsham Ct★ SN13 . . . . .77 A2
Corsham Media Pk
SN13 . . . . .84 C6
Corsham Pk★ SN13 . . . . .77 B2
Corsham Prim Sch
SN13 . . . . .77 B1
Corsham Rd
Atworth/Whitley SN12 . . .85 D1
Lacock SN13 . . . . .85 F8
Swindon SN2 . . . . .35 C5
Corsham Regis Prim Sch
SN13 . . . . .76 F2
Corsham Sch The SN13 .76 F1
Corsham Sports Club
SN13 . . . . .77 A1
Corsley CE Prim Sch
BA12 . . . . .111 D2
Corton (Long Barrow)★
SN5 . . . . .194 D3
Corton Cres SN5 . . . . . . .49 B6
Cory Way BA13 . . . . . . .108 E7
Coster View **5** SN8 . . . .176 B3
Coster's La SP5 . . . . . . .205 A2
Cote La BA12 . . . . .123 E4
Cotley Pl **4** BA12 . . . . . .194 C5
Cotswold Cl Calne SN11 .81 D2
Melksham SN12 . . . . .94 C4
8 Warminster BA12 . . . .117 A8
Cotswold Wr Pk★ SN6 . . .6 F4
Cotswold Wr Pk Gateway
Ctr★ GL7 . . . . .7 E6
Cottage Mews **18** SP6 .210 D1
Cottars Cl **3** SN3 . . . . . .36 B3
Cottington Cl SN5 . . . . . .49 A4
Cottle Mead SN14 . . . . . .84 E8
Cottles La BA15 . . . . .99 F6
Cotton House Gdns
BA12 . . . . .117 B7
Cottrell Cl RG17 . . . . . .177 C7
Couch La SN10 . . . . .214 A4
Coulston Hollow BA13 .186 F8
Coulston Rd SN13 . . . . . .77 A3
Council Houses The
SN15 . . . . .44 A4
Countess Rd SP4 . . . . . .217 A4
County Bsns Pk SN1 . . . .50 F8
County Rd SN1 . . . . .50 D7
County Way BA14 . . . . . .101 E1
Court Farm Cl **8** SP4 . . .190 A4
Court Farm Rd **1** SP4 . .190 A3
Court Gdns Bath BA1 . . .82 A3
Stanton St Quintin SN14 . .56 B4
Court Hill
Damerham SP6 . . . . .209 F2
Potterne SN10 . . . . .179 C5
Court La Bathford BA1 . .82 B1
Bratton BA13 . . . . .186 B7
Corsley BA12 . . . . .111 B1
Edington BA13 . . . . .186 D8
Court St Sherston SN16 .25 C1
Tisbury SP3 . . . . .203 E8
Trowbridge BA14 . . . . . .105 D8
Court St Cl SP3 . . . . . . .203 E8
Courtenay Rd SN3 . . . . . .51 A6
Courts Gdns The★
BA14 . . . . .101 E8
Courtsknap Ct **7** SN1 . . .50 A5
Courtwood Cl **3** SP1 . . .152 C5
Coventry Cl SN4 . . . . . . .64 B7
Covingham Dr SN3 . . . . .51 C8
Covingham Pk Jun & Inf Sch
SN3 . . . . .51 C7
Covingham Sq SN3 . . . . .51 C7
Cow Dro SP3 . . . . .201 B4
Cow La Kimpton SP11 . .192 B2
Laverstock SP1 . . . . . . .146 C1
Cow St SN5 . . . . .19 B1
Cowbridge Cres SN16 . . .28 C1
Cowdrey Cl SN5 . . . . . . .49 B4
Cowleaze Cres SN4 . . . . .63 F6
Cowleaze La BA13 . . . . .186 D8
Cowleaze Wlk SN2 . . . . .35 F4
Cowley Way SN15 . . . . . .57 D1
Cowley Wlk SN3 . . . . . . .51 B6
Cowslip Gr SN11 . . . . . . .81 B5
Cowslip Way SN14 . . . . .70 B3
Cox's Hill
Ashton Keynes SN6 . . . . . .6 E2
Calne SN11 . . . . .81 B2
Cox's La SN8 . . . . .176 F1
Coxhill La SN10 . . . . . . .179 D5
Coxstalls SN4 . . . . .47 D5
Crab La BA12 . . . . .138 A2
Crab Mill La SN16 . . . . . .28 E1
Crabtree Copse SN5 . . . .34 A2
Crampton Rd SN3 . . . . . .51 A7

Cranborne Chase SN2 . .34 C4
Cranborne Dr **1** SP7 . . .202 C2
Cranbury Cl SP5 . . . . . . .211 A7
Crandon Lea BA14 . . . . . .92 F1
Crane Furlong SN6 . . . . .23 A7
Crane St SP1 . . . . .152 A8
Cranebridge Rd SP2 . . . .152 A8
Cranesbill Cl SN10 . . . . .214 D5
Cranesbill Rd SN10 . . . .214 D5
Cranmore Ave SN3 . . . . .51 A3
Cranmore Cl BA14 . . . . .101 A1
Cranwell Cl **6** SN14 . . . .78 A6
Cratchcroft La BA14 . . .178 A6
Crate La SP7 . . . . .202 C7
Craven Rd RG17 . . . . . . .177 D3
Crawford Cl SN5 . . . . . . .49 A4
Crawlboys La SP11 . . . . .192 B6
Crawley Ave SN3 . . . . . . .36 B1
Crawley Cres BA14 . . . .105 A8
Craybourne Rd SN12 . . . .94 C5
Crays The SN12 . . . . .94 C5
Crench Comm Airfield
SN8 . . . . .174 E4
Crescent Rd
Durrington/Bulford SP4 . .217 D7
Melksham SN12 . . . . .94 C6
Crescent The
Bromham SN15 . . . . .96 C7
Calne SN11 . . . . .89 F8
Chiseldown SN4 . . . . .65 C3
4 Durrington/Bulford
SP4 . . . . .198 F7
Pewsey SN9 . . . . .215 B4
Swindon SN5 . . . . .33 F2
Westbury BA13 . . . . .109 A3
Wilton SP2 . . . . .144 B2
Cresswell Rd BA14 . . . . .102 B2
Cresswell La SN15 . . . . . .44 B4
Crestmount Dr SP2 . . . .145 C3
Creswells SN13 . . . . .84 F8
Cricketts La SN15 . . . . . .78 F5
Cricklade Leisure Ctr
SN6 . . . . .19 C8
Cricklade Mus★ SN6 . . .19 E8
Cricklade Rd
Highworth SN6 . . . . .22 F5
Purton SN5 . . . . .19 C2
Swindon SN25 . . . . .35 D1
Cricklade St SN1 . . . . . . .50 D5
Crieff Cl SN3 . . . . .51 B6
Crispin Cl **6** SN3 . . . . . .36 B3
Crockerton CE Prim Sch
BA12 . . . . .116 D2
Crockford Rd SP5 . . . . . .154 B2
Croft Cl SN6 . . . . .8 C4
Croft Hts SP5 . . . . .161 D3
Croft La SN6 . . . . .8 C4
Croft Rd
6 Hungerford RG17 . . . .177 B7
Swindon SN1 . . . . .50 C1
Croft Sports Hall SN1 . . .50 D3
Croft The
Bishopstone SP5 . . . . . .205 E5
Broad Hinton SN4 . . . . . .167 D7
Milston SP4 . . . . .198 C8
Newton Tony SP4 . . . . . .199 B3
Trowbridge BA14 . . . . . .105 C6
Urchfont SN10 . . . . .180 C3
Crofton Beam Engines★
SN8 . . . . .176 A1
Crofton Rd SN8 . . . . . . .176 A1
Crombey St SN1 . . . . .50 B5
Cromer Ct SN3 . . . . .51 D3
Cromhall La SN14 . . . . . .69 A7
Crompton Rd SN25 . . . . .35 D6
Cromwell Cl SN5 . . . . . . .49 B3
Cromwell Rd SN10 . . . . .214 D2
Crook Hill SP5 . . . . .204 A1
Crooked Cnr SN8 . . . . . .170 A6
Crookhays SP7 . . . . .202 C2
Crooks La SN10 . . . . . . .180 C5
Crookwood La SN10 . . . .179 F4
Crosby Wlk SN3 . . . . .51 A3
Crosbys **8** SN3 . . . . . . .183 D8
Croscombe Gdns
BA11 . . . . .110 D6
Cross Hayes La SN16 . . . .28 A3
Cross Keys Chequer **5**
SP1 . . . . .146 B1
Cross Keys Rd SN13 . . . .77 A3
Cross La SN8 . . . . .213 D3
Cross St Swindon SN1 . . .50 C5
Trowbridge BA14 . . . . . .101 D1
Cross The
Bishopstone SP5 . . . . . .205 E4
Ebbesborne Wake SP5 . .204 D3
21 Tisbury SP3 . . . . .203 E8
Cross Tree Cres GL7 . . . .10 C7
Crossing La SN15 . . . . . . .71 B3
Crossways SN4 . . . . .46 D6
Crossways Ave SN25 . . . .35 C3
Crosswood Rd SN3 . . . . .51 A3
Croucheston Dro SP5 . . .205 E3
Croucheston Hollow
SP5 . . . . .205 E4
Crowdys Hill Specl Sch
SN2 . . . . .35 D2
Crowe Hill BA2 . . . . .99 B6
Crowe La BA2 . . . . .99 B5
Crowle Rd **11** RG17 . . . .165 A1
Crown Cl
Chippenham SN15 . . . . . .79 A5
Salisbury SP2 . . . . .145 D3
Crown La **4** SP11 . . . . . .192 A5
Crown Mews **30** RG17 . .177 C7
Crown Way SP10 . . . . . .193 F1
Crowood La SN8 . . . . . . .170 B2

Crudwell CE Prim Sch
SN16 . . . . .14 F6
Crudwell La
Crudwell SN16 . . . . .14 B6
Long Newnton GL8 . . . . .13 D6
Crudwell Way SN25 . . . . .35 C6
Crusades The **6** SP1 . . .146 C5
Cruse Cl SN4 . . . . .77 F8
Cuckoo La BA11 . . . . . . .110 A8
Cuckoo Pen Cl SN8 . . . .183 D3
Cuckoo's Mead SN3 . . . . .51 E6
Cues La SN6 . . . . .163 E7
Cuffs La SP3 . . . . .203 E8
Cullerne Rd SN3 . . . . . . .36 C1
Cullerns The SN6 . . . . . .23 A6
Culver Rd BA15 . . . . . . .100 E5
Culver St **7** SP1 . . . . . .152 B8
Culvermead Cl SN8 . . . .213 E3
Culverwell Rd BA14 . . . . .78 A7
Cumberland Rd SN3 . . . .50 E6
Cunetio Rd SN8 . . . . . . .213 C8
Cunnage La BA12 . . . . . .139 F1
Cunningham Rd SN2 . . . .35 A2
Curlcroft Rd SN13 . . . . . .84 D7
Curlew Dr SN14 . . . . .70 A2
Curnicks The SN4 . . . . . .65 C4
Cursus The★
Amesbury SP4 . . . . .197 D6
Lechlade GL7 . . . . .2 C5
Curtis Orch SN12 . . . . . . .93 B4
Curtis St SN1 . . . . .50 B5
Curzon Cl SN11 . . . . .81 A3
Curzon St SN11 . . . . .81 A3
Cusance Way BA14 . . . .102 A1
Cuthwine Pl GL7 . . . . .2 C5
Cutting Hill RG17 . . . . . .177 A4
Cuttle La SN14 . . . . .76 E8
Cutts Cl SN15 . . . . .46 A7
Cuxhaven Way **10** SP10 .193 D2
Cygnet Dr SP4 . . . . .217 C8
Cygnet Way BA14 . . . . . .101 D5
Cygney Way RG17 . . . . .177 B8
Cyppa Ct SN15 . . . . .78 E6
Cypress Gr SN2 . . . . .35 A3
Cypress Way **7** BA11 . . .110 C7
Cypress Wlk SN14 . . . . . .74 F6
Cyprus Terr SN10 . . . . . .214 A4

D

Dacre Cl **13** SP10 . . . . . .193 C2
Dacre Rd SN3 . . . . .51 A6
Dairy Cl **8** SP5 . . . . .211 C2
Dairy Mdw La SP1 . . . . .152 D7
Dairy Rd
Barford St Martin SP3 . .143 A4
Chiseldon SN4 . . . . .64 F4
Daisy Cl Melksham SN12 .94 C3
Swindon SN2 . . . . .34 C3
Dales Cl SN25 . . . . .35 A7
Dales Rd BA13 . . . . .108 E2
Dalewood Rise SP1 . . . .146 E2
Dallas Ave SN3 . . . . .51 B7
Dallas Rd SN14 . . . . .78 C8
Dalton Cl SN3 . . . . .50 F7
Dalwood Cl SN3 . . . . .51 B3
Damask Way BA12 . . . . .117 A5
Dammas Bsns Ctr SN1 . . .50 D4
Dammas La SN3 . . . . .50 D4
Damy Gn SN13 . . . . .84 E5
Dando Dr SN8 . . . . .213 B2
Dane Cl BA15 . . . . .99 E7
Dane Rise BA15 . . . . .99 E7
Danegeld Cl **9** SP10 . . . .193 E2
Danes Cl SN15 . . . . .78 F5
Danestone Cl SN5 . . . . . .48 F7
Daniel Cl **9** SN1 . . . . . . .49 F4
Daniel's Well★ SN16 . . . .28 A3
Daniell Crest BA12 . . . . .116 F6
Danvers Mead SN15 . . . . .79 A4
Danvers Rd SN13 . . . . . . .76 E1
Danvers Way BA13 . . . . .109 B4
Darby Cl SN2 . . . . .34 E1
Darcey Cl SN5 . . . . .48 F6
Darcy Cl SN15 . . . . .78 F8
Darius Way SN25 . . . . . . .35 A6
Dark La Berkley BA11 . . .110 E8
Castle Combe SN14 . . . . .68 B7
Grafton SN8 . . . . .175 F1
Kintbury RG17 . . . . .177 D8
Limpley Stoke BA2 . . . . . .99 B5
Malmesbury SN16 . . . . . .27 F3
Mere BA12 . . . . .139 A5
Dark La N BA14 . . . . . . .178 A3
Dark La S BA14 . . . . . . .178 A3
Darnley Cl SN3 . . . . .50 F6
Darrell Rd SP4 . . . . .217 C4
Dart Ave SN25 . . . . .35 A3
Dartmoor Cl **7** SN1 . . . . .49 F4
Dartmoor Rd **2** BA13 . . .108 E1
Darwin Cl
4 Durrington/Bulford
SP4 . . . . .198 F6
Swindon SN3 . . . . .51 B7
Dasna Rd SP9 . . . . .216 B5
Daunch Cl SP9 . . . . .216 B7
Dauntsey Dro SP11 . . . . .192 E1
Dauntsey La SP11 . . . . . .192 E1
Dauntsey Pk★ SN15 . . . .44 F2
Dauntsey Rd SN15 . . . . . .44 C2
Dauntseys Aided Prim Sch
SN10 . . . . .187 E8
Dauntseys Sch
Market Lavington SN10 . .179 E1
West Lavington SN10 . . .187 D8

Dave Watkins Ct SN2 . . .35 F3
Davenham Cl SN3 . . . . . .51 A3
Davenwood SN2 . . . . .35 F4
David Stoddart Gdns
SN2 . . . . .35 B1
David's Gdn SP5 . . . . . . .148 C3
Davies Cl SN13 . . . . .213 A2
Davies Dr SN10 . . . . .214 E6
Davis Pl SN1 . . . . .50 B6
Davis Rd **11** SN10 . . . . . .179 F1
Dawbeney Dr SP4 . . . . . .217 D3
Dawlish Rd SN3 . . . . .51 B5
Dawneys The SN16 . . . . .14 E6
Day Ho La SN3 . . . . .51 C2
Day's Cl SN3 . . . . .36 A1
Day's La SN15 . . . . .56 D2
Days Ct SN16 . . . . .14 E6
De Havilland Pl **4** SN12 178 B8
De Montfort Gr **8** RG17 .177 B6
De Vaux Pl SP1 . . . . .152 A7
Deacon Rd SP11 . . . . . . .192 B2
Deacon St SN1 . . . . .50 B5
Dean Cl Frome BA11 . . . .110 C6
Melksham SN12 . . . . .94 C6
Dean La Fovant SP3 . . . .204 D7
Sixpenny Handley SP5 . .207 F6
Whiteparish SP5 . . . . . . .161 D4
Dean La Dro SP5 . . . . . .207 F5
Dean Rd SP5 . . . . .155 B3
Dean St SN1 . . . . .49 F5
Dean Sta SP5 . . . . .155 F3
Deans Cl SP9 . . . . .216 D4
Deansfield SN6 . . . . .19 D7
Deansway SN12 . . . . .70 D2
Deben Cres SN25 . . . . . . .34 F5
Deburgh St SN2 . . . . .49 F6
Deep La BA12 . . . . .111 D2
Deer Pk★ SN8 . . . . .175 E2
Deerhurst Way **1** SN5 . . .49 D4
Delamere Dr SN3 . . . . . . .36 A4
Delamere Rd BA14 . . . . .101 D2
Dell The SP11 . . . . .185 B3
Delta Bsns Pk SN5 . . . . . .49 D6
Delta Office Pk SN5 . . . . .49 D5
Denbeck Wood SN5 . . . . .49 B6
Denbigh Cl SN3 . . . . .50 E3
Dene The Hindon SP3 . . .200 B3
Warminster BA12 . . . . . .117 E6
Deneb Dr SN25 . . . . .34 B7
Denes Ave BA12 . . . . . . .139 A6
Denford La RG17 . . . . . . .177 D8
Denholme Rd SN3 . . . . . .51 A3
Denison Rise SP1 . . . . . .146 C3
Dennis La SP7 . . . . .203 B1
Derby Cl
Chippenham SN15 . . . . . .78 F5
Lambourn RG17 . . . . . . .165 A1
Derby St SN3 . . . . .50 E6
Derriads Gn SN14 . . . . . .78 A7
Derriads La **3** SN14 . . . . .77 F6
Derry Hill CE Prim Sch
SN11 . . . . .80 A2
Derry Pk SN16 . . . . .17 C2
Derry The SN6 . . . . .17 F8
Derwent Dr SN2 . . . . .35 F4
Desborough SN5 . . . . . . .49 A3
Deva Cl SN3 . . . . .51 D8
Devenish Nature Reserve★
SP4 . . . . .131 D2
Deverell Cl BA15 . . . . . .100 E4
Devereux Cl **8** SN5 . . . . .48 F5
Devereux Rd SP4 . . . . . .217 B3
Deverill Rd
Sutton Veny BA12 . . . . .117 E1
Warminster BA12 . . . . . .116 F4
Devils Bed & Bolster The★
BA11 . . . . .107 A8
Devizes Castle★ SN10 .214 A3
Devizes Com Hospl
SN10 . . . . .214 B4
Devizes Leisure Ctr
SN10 . . . . .214 B3
Devizes Rd Box SN13 . . .83 E4
Bromham SN15 . . . . .88 B4
Calne Without SN11 . . . . .87 F7
Charlton SN9 . . . . .181 D2
Derry Hill/Studley SN11 . .79 F1
Hilperton BA14 . . . . .102 C3
Potterne SN10 . . . . .179 D6
Poulshot SN10 . . . . .179 B7
Rowde SN10 . . . . .96 F2
Salisbury SP2 . . . . .145 E2
Swindon SN1 . . . . .50 D4
Trowbridge BA14 . . . . . .102 B3
Wroughton SN4 . . . . .64 B6
Devizes Sch SN10 . . . . .214 C3
Devizes Sports Club
SN10 . . . . .214 C4
Devizes White Horse★
SN10 . . . . .97 F5
Devon Cl **5** SN14 . . . . . .77 F6
Devon Dr BA13 . . . . .109 A5
Devon Rd Swindon SN2 . .35 B1
Upavon Down SN9 . . . . .182 B2
Devonshire Pl SN12 . . . . .94 C5
Devonshire Rd SP1 . . . . .146 A3
Dew Cl SN13 . . . . .85 A8
Dew's Rd SP2 . . . . .145 F1
Dewell Mews SN1 . . . . . .50 D3
Dewey Cl SN4 . . . . .65 D4
Deweys La SP11 . . . . . . .192 A5
Dexter Cl SN5 . . . . .49 B7
Dial Cl SN12 . . . . .178 E8
Dianmer Cl SN4 . . . . .47 F5
Dickens Ave SN13 . . . . . .76 F2

Dickens Cl SN3 ....51 D3
Dickenson Rd SN25 ....34 C5
Dicketts Rd SN13 ......85 A7
Dickson Rd SN15 ....60 A1
Dickson Way **2** SN15 ...78 F5
Diddledown Rd **8** SP4 .217 C2
Dilton Ct BA13 ....112 B6
Dilton Marsh CE Prim Sch
  BA13 ....112 B8
Dilton Marsh Sta
  BA13 ....108 C1
Dinah's Hollow SP7 ....206 B7
Dingle The **8** SN3 ......163 A6
Dinmore Rd SN25 ....34 F6
Dinton CE Fst Sch
  SP3 ....201 F2
Dinton Rd Fovant SP3 ..204 E8
  Wylye BA12 ....201 E8
Dione Cres SN25 ....34 B7
Discover Salisbury (Medieval
  Hall)★ SP1 ....152 A8
Distillery Mdws Nature
  Reserve★ SN16 ....31 B7
Divinity Cl **2** SN4 ......163 B6
Dixon St SN1 ....50 B5
Dixon Way SN11 ....81 B4
Dobbin Cl SN3 ....51 E7
Dobson Cl SN25 ....35 A8
Dockle Way SN2 ....35 F4
Doctors Hill SN3 ....83 B5
Doctors Pl **8** SP3 ......203 E8
Dodford La SN15 ....58 D6
Dodgson Cl SP6 ....211 A4
Dog Kennel La BA13 ...109 A1
Dog La SP7 ....203 E1
Dog Trap La SN16 .....16 E1
Doggetts La BA13 .....109 A4
Dogridge SN5 ....33 A3
Dolphin Ind Est SP1 ...152 D7
Dolphin St SP1 ....152 B8
Don Cl SN25 ....35 A4
Donaldson Rd SP1 .....146 A2
Doncaster Cl SN14 ....77 F5
Doncombe Hill SN14 ..74 E7
Doncombe La SN14 ....75 A6
Donhead Hollow SP7 ..206 E8
Donnington Gr SN3 ....50 F4
Dorcan Bsns Village
  SN3 ....51 E6
Dorcan Ind Est SN3 ...51 E5
Dorcan Tech Coll SN3 .51 E6
Dorcan Way SN3 ....51 A8
Dorchester Rd SN3 ....50 F3
Dores Ct SN2 ....35 E3
Dores Rd SN2 ....35 D3
Doris Archer Ct SN2 ...35 B2
Dormers The SN6 ......23 A6
Dorney Cl BA13 ....108 F1
Dorney Rd SN25 ....34 C8
Dorset Cl SP4 ....217 E8
Dorset Cres SN12 ......94 C3
Dorset Dr BA13 ....109 A5
Dorset Gn SN2 ....34 F2
Dorset Rd SP1 ....146 B3
Double Hedges SP4 ....217 E7
Doubledays SN6 ....19 D8
Doughty's La BA12 ....195 A2
Douglas Brown's Wlk **6**
  SP4 ....197 E6
Douglas Haig Rd SP1 ..146 A3
Douglas Rd **5** SN3 .....50 F6
Doulting Ct BA1 ....110 D7
Dovecote Cl **8** BA14 ...105 B8
Dovecote Dr SN13 .....76 F2
Dover St
  Chippenham SN14 .....78 C7
  Swindon SN1 ....50 C5
Dovers La BA1 ....82 C2
Dovers Pk BA1 ....82 C2
Doves La SP5 ....161 C3
Dovetrees SN3 ....51 D7
Doveys Terr SN15 .....70 E7
Dowding Ave SN3 ......84 B8
Dowding Dr **5** SN11 ....166 A1
Dowding Way SN12 .....94 C1
Dowling St SN1 ....50 C5
Down Ampney House★
  GL7 ....8 D6
Down Ampney Rd GL7 ..8 B6
Down Barn Cl SP4 .....133 B4
Down Barn Rd SP4 ....132 F6
Down Rd Kimpton SP11 .192 B2
  Marshfield SN14 ....66 C2
Down The Hindon SP3 ..200 B3
  Trowbridge BA14 ....101 D2
Down View SN14 ....78 A7
Down View Rd SP1 ....146 E2
Downavon BA15 ....100 D5
Downham Mead SN15 ..78 F8
Downhayes Rd BA14 ...101 D2
Downing St SN14 ......78 C8
Downland Rd
  Calne SN11 ....81 A2
  Swindon SN2 ....34 D4
Downland Sch SN10 ...214 B1
Downland Way **12** SP4 .198 B7
Downlands **1** RG17 ....171 E7
Downlands Cl SP5 .....211 A7
Downlands The BA12 ..114 A7
Downleaze **7** SP4 ......198 B7
Downs Cl
  Bradford-on-Avon BA15 .100 B7
  Devizes SN10 ....214 D3
  Lambourn RG17 ....171 C8
Downs La SN8 ....185 B8

Downs Rd SN4 ....65 E4
Downs The SN8 ....170 A5
Downs View
  Bradford-on-Avon BA15 .100 B7
  Highworth SN6 ....23 A6
  1 Netheravon SP4 ....190 A4
  Warminster BA12 ....117 C6
  Wootton Bassett SN4 ..47 D1
Downs View Rd **8** SN3 .50 F2
Downside Cl BA12 .....139 A6
Downside Pk BA14 ....101 E2
Downslands Rd SN10 ..214 B1
Downsmead SN8 ....164 B1
Downsview BA13 ....186 C7
Downsview Rd BA13 ...109 A4
Downsview Way SP11 ..191 F3
Downsway SP1 ....146 B4
Downton Bus Ctr SP5 .159 A1
Downton CE Prim Sch
  SP5 ....211 A8
Downton Hill SP5 .....211 C8
Downton L Ctr SP5 ...210 F8
Downton Meml Gdns★
  SP5 ....211 A8
Downton Rd
  Salisbury SP2 ....152 B5
  Swindon SN2 ....35 B5
Downton Sch SP5 .....211 A8
Downview Rd SP6 .....209 B6
Downwood Cl **7** SP6 ..210 C1
Doyle Ave SN10 ....214 C2
Dr Behr Ct SN2 ....35 B2
Dragon La SN9 ....181 F6
Drain Hill RG17 ....165 A2
Drake Cl SP1 ....146 C5
Drake Cres SN14 ......77 F6
Drake Ct SP10 ....193 F1
Drake's Way SN1 ......50 E6
Drakes Ave SN10 .....214 C2
Drakes Mdw Bsns Pk
  SN3 ....50 F7
Drakes Way Bsns Ctr
  SN3 ....51 A7
Draycot Cl SN4 ....65 C3
Draycott Cl SN3 ....51 A5
Drew St SN2 ....49 E7
Drew's Pond La SN10 .214 B1
Drewitts La SN10 .....180 E8
Drifton Hill SN14 ......66 E7
Drive The
  Melchet Park & Plaitford
  SO51 ....162 C1
  Swindon SN3 ....51 B7
Drove Cl SP5 ....150 F2
Drove La
  Coombe Bissett SP5 ...150 F3
  Market Lavington SN10 .179 F1
  Steeple Ashton BA14 ..178 A2
Drove Prim Sch SN1 ..50 D6
Drove Rd SN1 ....50 D5
Drove The
  Amesbury SP4 ....217 B4
  Hawkeridge BA13 ......108 D7
Droves The SP5 ....207 E4
Druley Hill BA10 ......123 B7
Drury Cl SN5 ....47 F5
Drury La SN8 ....175 D4
Dry Hill BA12 ....116 E2
Dryden Cl SP2 ....152 B5
Dryden St SN1 ....50 B5
Drynham La BA14 .....105 D5
Drynham Pk BA14 .....105 D6
Drynham Rd BA14 .....105 D5
Duchess Way SN2 .....35 D5
Duck Cl
  Barford St Martin SP3 .143 B3
  Laverstock SP1 ....152 E8
  Salisbury SP1 ....146 D2
Duck Pool La BA11 ....107 B6
Duck St
  Berwick St James SP3 .196 F2
  Ebbesborne Wake SP5 .204 C3
  Potterne SN10 ....179 D5
  Steeple Langford SP3 .128 D7
  Sutton Veny BA12 .....194 A4
  Tisbury SP3 ....203 E8
  West Lavington SN10 ..187 D8
Duck's Nest (Long Barrow)★
  SP6 ....209 F7
Ducks Meadow SN8 ...213 D6
Dudley Ave SP6 ....210 D2
Dudley Rd SN3 ....50 D6
Dudmore Rd SN3 .....50 D6
Duke St BA14 ....101 D1
Duke's La BA12 ....118 A1
Duke's Way SP4 ......217 E8
Dukes Cl SN2 ....35 E5
Dulverton Ave SN3 ...51 A5
Dumbarton Terr **2** SN1 .50 C5
Dummer La SP11 ......184 E1
Dummer Way SN15 ....79 A5
Dunbar Rd SN4 ....64 A7
Dunbeath Ct SN2 .....35 E1
Dunbeath Rd SN2 ....35 E1
Duncan St SN1 ....81 B5
Duncan's Cl SP11 .....192 D1
Dunch La SN12 ....93 F7
Dundas Aqueduct★
  BA2 ....90 B2
Dundas Cl SN10 ......179 C8
Dunford Cl BA14 ......105 D6
Dunhills La SP11 ......193 F4
Dunkirk Hill
  Devizes SN10 ....179 D8
  Rowde SN10 ....97 A1
Dunley Cl SN25 ....34 D7
Dunley Way SP1 ......146 C5
Dunn Cl SN25 ....34 F7
Ebor Gdns SN11 ......89 C8
Dunn's La SP8 ....138 A1

Dunnet Cl SN11 ......81 B4
Dunnington Rd SN4 ..61 D8
Dunns La 68 B8
Dunraven Cl SN3 .....50 F4
Dunsdon Cl SN1 ......49 F4
Dunstable Cnr SP5 ...148 E7
Dunstan's Dro SP11 ..185 E1
Dunster Cl SN3 ....50 F8
Dunvant Rd SN25 ....34 C7
Dunwich Dr SN5 ......49 D4
Dunworth Rise **6** SP3 .203 E8
Durham St SN1 ....50 C5
Durlett Rd SN10 ......95 F2
Durley Pk SN13 ....84 D6
Durnford Rd SN2 .....35 C3
Durrington All Saints CE Inf
  Sch SP4 ....198 C7
Durrington CE Jun Sch
  SP4 ....198 B6
Durrington Swimming &
  Fitness Ctr SP4 ......198 C7
Durrington Walls★
  SP4 ....217 A8
Durrington Wlk SN2 ..35 C5
Dursden La SN9 ......215 E6
Dursley Rd
  Heywood BA13 ....108 F8
  North Bradley BA13 ...105 E1
Dutts BA13 ....108 B1
Duxford Cl **11** SN12 ...178 B8
Dyehouse La SN10 ....214 A4
Dyer La BA12 ....201 E8
Dyer's Cl SN15 ....79 A6
Dyke Mews SN4 ......65 D4
Dymocks La BA12 .....121 F8
Dymott Sq BA14 ......102 A3

E

Eagle Cl SN3 ....51 E7
Eagle Field SP2 ......145 D4
Earl Cl SN5 ....48 F7
Earl's Rise SP4 ......133 A1
Earls Cl SP4 ....217 E2
Earls Cnr SN16 ......15 E8
Earls Ct Rd SP4 .....217 B3
Earthpits La SP5 .....208 E4
East Dunley Cotts SN14 .40 E1
East End BA12 ....117 B6
East End Ave BA12 ..117 B6
East End La SN15 ...44 D5
East Gomeldon Rd
  SP4 ....133 E4
East Kennett (Long
  Barrow)★ SN8 ....173 D5
East La SN12 ....93 B3
East Portway SP10 ..193 C1
East Sands SN8 .....183 D8
East St Bourton SP8 .137 C1
  Hindon SP3 ....200 A4
  Lacock SN15 ....86 D6
  Salisbury SP2 ....145 C1
  10 Swindon SN1 ......50 B6
  Warminster BA12 ......117 B6
East Town Rd BA14 ..106 D3
East Woodlands Rd
  BA11 ....114 A7
East Yewstock Cres
  SN15 ....70 C1
Eastbourne Gdns
  BA14 ....101 E1
Eastbourne Rd BA14 ..101 E1
Eastbury Shute RG17 ..171 C5
Eastbury Way SN25 ..34 E7
Eastcott Cmn SN10 ..180 A2
Eastcott Hill **5** SN1 ..50 C5
Eastcott Rd SN1 .....50 C5
Eastcourt SN8 ....183 D8
Eastcourt Rd SN8 ....183 D8
Eastern Ave
  Chippenham SN15 .....78 F8
  Swindon SN3 ....50 E6
Easterton La SN9 ....215 D4
Eastfield
  Ashton Keynes SN6 ...6 F1
  2 Littleton Panell SN10 .187 E8
Easthill BA11 ....110 B4
Eastleaze Rd SN5 ...49 C6
Eastleigh Cl **4** BA11 ..110 A7
Eastleigh Rd SN10 ...214 D2
Eastman Cl SP5 ......211 B7
Eastmere SN3 ....51 E3
Easton Comm Hill
  SP5 ....149 E6
Easton Hollow SP5 ..207 B7
Easton La SN14 ......77 F3
Easton Royal Prim Sch
  SN9 ....183 A4
Easton Sq SN16 .....25 D1
Easton Town SN16 ..25 C1
Eastrip La SN14 .....75 C3
Eastrop SN6 ....23 B5
Eastrop Inf Sch SN6 ..23 A5
Eastview Rd BA14 ...105 A7
Eastville Rd SN25 ...35 C3
Eastwell Rd SN10 ...179 D5
Eastwood SO51 .....162 E1
Eaton Cl **1** SN3 ....51 A4
Eaton Wood SN5 ....34 A2
Ebbesborne Hollow
  SP5 ....204 D2
Ebble Cl SP9 ....216 D7
Ebble Cres BA12 ....117 A5
Ebor Cl SN25 ....34 F7
Ebor Paddock SN11 ..89 C8
Eccleston Cl SN3 ....51 B3
Echo Lodge Mdws Nature
  Reserve★ SN15 .....46 E7
Ecklington SN3 ......51 C5
Edale Moor SN3 .....51 E3
Eddington Hill RG17 .177 C8
Edelweiss Cl **23** SP11 .192 A5
Eden Gr SN12 ....85 D1
Eden Pk Cl BA1 ......82 A4
Eden Pk Dr BA1 .....82 A4
Eden Vale Rd BA13 ..108 F3
Edencroft SN6 ....23 B8
Edgam Pl SP2 ....144 F3
Edgar Cl **6** SP10 ...193 E2
Edgar Row Cl **1** SN4 .64 A6
Edgecorner La SN14 .53 A3
Edgehill SN5 ....49 B3
Edgeware Rd SN1 ...50 C6
Edgeworth Cl **4** SN5 .49 B7
Edinburgh Rd SN11 ..81 F1
Edinburgh St SN2 ...35 D1
Edinburgh Way SN13 .84 E7
Edington Cl SN5 .....49 B5
Edington Priory★
  BA13 ....186 C8
Edington Rd BA14 ...178 A3
Edison Bsns Pk SN3 ..51 C5
Edison Rd
  Salisbury SP2 ....151 E8
  Swindon SN3 ....51 C5
Edmund St SN1 ......50 C5
Edric's Gn SP4 ......199 C5
Edrich Rd SP10 .....193 E1
Edridge Cl SN15 ....78 F8
Edridge Pl **1** SN13 ..76 C1
Edward Rd SN10 ....214 B2
Edward Richardson & Phyllis
  Amey Nature Reserve★
  GL6 ....2 C6
Edward St BA13 .....109 A3
Edwards Hill **12** RG17 .165 A1
Edwards Meadow
  SN8 ....213 B3
Edwards Rd SP4 ....217 B3
Egerton Cl SN3 .....51 B7
Eider Ave SN15 .....60 A1
Elbe Way SP10 .....193 D2
Elborough Rd SN2 ..34 D3
Elcombe Ave **8** SN4 .64 A6
Elcombe Cl BA14 ....105 C5
Elcombe Gdns SN10 .214 A4
Elcombe La SP5 .....204 B2
Elcot Cl SN8 ....213 F3
Elcot La SN8 ....213 F3
Elcot Orch SN8 .....175 A8
Elden Dr SP9 ....191 D5
Eldene Dr SN3 ......51 C4
Eldene Prim Sch SN3 ..51 C5
Elder Cl SN2 ....34 C3
Eleanor Ct **16** SP11 ..192 A5
Elgar Cl SN25 ......34 E7
Elgin Dr SN2 ....35 E1
Eliot Cl SN3 ....51 D3
Elizabeth Cl
  8 Downton SP5 ....210 F8
  Melksham Without SN12 .93 F1
Elizabeth Dr SN10 ..214 C4
Elizabeth Gdns GL7 ..1 A5
Elizabeth Pl SN15 ..79 A4
Elizabeth Rd
  16 Durrington/Bulford
  SP4 ....198 B7
  Wilton SP2 ....144 B5
Elizabeth Sq SP9 ...216 E7
Elley Gn SN13 ......84 E6
Ellingdon Rd SN4 ..63 F7
Elliott Cl SN10 .....214 B1
Elliott Gn SP4 ......133 C4
Elliott Pl BA14 .....101 A1
Elm Cl Bower Hill SN12 .94 C1
  Calne SN11 ....89 C8
  8 Ludgershall SP11 ..192 B5
  Lyneham SN15 ....60 B2
  Motcombe SP7 ....202 A5
  Pitton & Farley SP5 ..148 C4
  Rowde SN10 ....96 D1
  Salisbury SP1 ....146 D3
  Staverton BA14 ....101 D6
  Trowbridge BA14 .....105 C3
  Wootton Bassett SN4 .47 E4
Elm Ct SN10 ....214 B1
Elm Gr Corsham SN13 .76 E1
  Salisbury SP1 ....146 C1
  Swindon SN5 ....49 A8
Elm Gr Pl SP1 ......146 B1
Elm Gr Rd SP1 .....146 B1
Elm Hayes SN13 ....85 A7
Elm Hill BA12 ......113 C1
Elm Leigh BA11 ....110 C6
Elm Pk SN15 ....47 D1
Elm Rd Colerne SN14 .75 A5
  Swindon SN2 ....35 A2
Elm Tree Cl SN10 ..214 D2
Elm Tree Gdns SN10 .214 D2
Elm View GL7 ......5 F4
Elmdale Cl BA14 ...105 A7
Elmdale Rd BA14 ...105 A7
Elmer Cl SN16 .....28 A5
Elmfield BA15 ......100 C7
Elmfield Cl **7** SP5 ..211 C7
Elmina Rd SN1 .....50 C7
Elmore SN3 ....51 C5
Elms Cl SN5 ....210 B1
Elms Cross Dr BA15 .100 C5
Elms The
  Bradford-on-Avon BA15 .100 B7
  Highworth SN6 ....22 F5

Elms The continued
  Holt BA14 ....92 F1
  Swindon SN5 ....48 F8
Elmswood **8** SN2 ...35 E5
Elmwood SN15 .....70 E2
Elmwood Ave **6** SP6 .210 C1
Elsham Way SN25 ...35 A5
Elston La SP3 ......196 E7
Elstree Way
  Haydon Wick SN25 ...34 F6
  Swindon SN25 ....35 A7
Ely Cl SN5 ....49 C4
Embankment SN1 ...50 D3
Embry Cl **8** SN11 ..166 A1
Emden Rd **18** SP10 .193 D2
Emerson Cl SN25 ...35 A6
Emery Gate SN15 ..78 E7
Emery La SN15 .....78 E7
Emlyn Sq SN1 ....50 B6
Emmanuel Cl SN25 .35 A4
Emmaus Sch BA14 ..101 D5
Emmett Hill Mdws Nature
  Reserve★ SN16 .....16 G1
Emms La **10** BA13 ..186 B7
Empire Rd SP2 .....145 C2
Empress Way SP11 ..192 A5
Emwell St BA12 ....117 A7
Endless St SP1 .....146 A1
Enford Ave SN2 ....35 C6
Enford Hill SN9 ....189 F6
Engineer Rd BA13 ..108 C6
Englefield SN4 ....47 E1
Enham La SP10 ....193 E3
Eningen View SN11 ..81 B1
Ensor Cl SN25 .....35 A8
Epping Cl BA12 ....117 A8
Epping Dr SN12 ....94 C6
Epsom Cl SN14 ....77 F6
Epsom Rd BA14 ....105 E4
Erin Ct **2** SN1 .....50 A5
Eriskay Gdns BA13 ..108 F2
Erleigh Dr SN15 ....78 C7
Erlestoke Way SN25 .35 C5
Ermin Cl SN8 ......170 C8
Ermin St **1** Baydon SN8 .170 C8
  Blunsdon St Andrew SN26 ..20 F2
  Swindon SN2 ....35 F4
Ernestson Cres SN13 .76 F1
Ernle Rd SN11 .....81 C4
Erskine Barracks SP2 .144 F4
Escott Cl **4** SN15 ..78 F4
Eshton Wlk SN3 ...51 A3
Esmead SN15 ......78 F8
Espringham Pl SN2 ..35 E4
Essex Pl **7** RG17 ..165 A2
Essex Sq SP2 ......151 D6
Essex Wlk SN3 ....50 F6
Estate Yd The SN8 ..172 B3
Estcourt Cres SN10 .214 B4
Estcourt Rd SP1 ...146 B1
Estcourt St SN10 ..214 B3
Estcourt Terr SN10 .214 B5
Eston Medieval Village of★
  SN14 ....69 D8
Ethelbert Dr **4** SP10 .193 C2
Ethelred Pl SN13 ..76 E1
Ethendun **11** BA13 ..186 B7
Euclid St SN1 ......50 C6
Euro Way SN1 .....48 F3
Europa & Brittania Pk
  SN3 ....51 A8
Evans Cl SN15 .....70 C1
Eveleigh Rd SN4 ...47 E2
Evelyn St SN1 .....50 D3
Even Swindon Inf Sch
  SN2 ....49 F7
Even Swindon Jun Sch
  SN2 ....49 F7
Eveque Ct SP2 .....144 F3
Evergreen Way SP4 .217 C2
Evergreens Cl SN3 ..36 C1
Everland Rd **18** RG17 .177 B7
Everland Rd Ind Est
  RG17 ....177 C7
Everleigh Barrows★
  SN9 ....182 E3
Everleigh Cl BA14 ..105 D5
Everleigh Rd
  Collingbourne Ducis
  SN8 ....191 D8
  Pewsey SN9 ....215 C3
  Swindon SN3 ....35 C5
Eworth Cl SN5 .....48 F5
Exbury Cl **2** SN25 ..35 A6
Exe Cl SN25 ....35 A4
Exeter Cl SN14 ....77 F5
Exeter House Specl Sch
  SP1 ....146 B3
Exeter St Salisbury SP1 .152 B7
  Swindon SN1 ....50 A6
Exmoor Cl **1** SN2 ..34 C4
Exmoor Rd **6** BA13 .108 C1
Exmouth St SN1 ...50 A5
Eyles Rd SN10 .....214 B1
Eyres Dr SP5 ......153 C2
Eyres Way SP1 ....152 B8

F

Factory Hill SP8 ...137 F3
Factory La BA12 ...116 F6
Fair Mile
  Collingbourne Kingston
  SN8 ....183 F3
  Grafton SN8 ....184 A4
Fair View Rd SP2 ..144 E4

Fairdown Ave BA13 ....109 B3
Fairfax CI
　Amesbury SP4 ....217 A4
　Swindon SN3 ....50 F7
Fairfield 1 Cricklade SN6 ..19 D8
　4 Great Bedwyn SN8 ...176 B3
　Rode BA11 ....103 F1
　Wootton Bassett SN4 ...47 E3
Fairfield CI
　Frome BA11 ....110 A7
　Marshfield SN14 ......74 A8
Fairfield Meadows
　BA14 ....104 F3
Fairfield Rd
　Salisbury SP1 ....146 A4
　Warminster BA12 .....117 B7
Fairfields 22 RG17 .....177 B7
Fairfoot CI SN14 ....78 A7
Fairford Airfield GL7 ....1 E1
Fairford Cres SN25 ....35 C3
Fairground The 2 SP11 .192 F1
Fairhaven BA13 ....108 D1
Fairholme Way SN2 ....35 F4
Fairlane SP7 ....202 C1
Fairlawn SN3 ....51 D3
Fairleigh Rise SN15 ....70 F7
Fairview Colerne SN14 ..75 C6
　Swindon SN1 ....50 B5
Fairview Rd
　1 Andover SP11 .....192 F1
　Hungerford RG17 .....177 B7
　Salisbury SP1 ....146 C1
Fairway Calne SN11 ....89 C8
　Melksham SN12 ....94 C5
Fairway The SN10 .....214 A1
Fairways Amport SP11 ..192 E1
　Dilton Marsh BA13 ....108 D1
Fairwood CI BA14 .....102 A2
Fairwood Rd
　Dilton Marsh BA13 ....108 C3
　North Bradley BA13 ...107 F5
Falcon Rd SN11 ....81 D3
Falcon Way SN12 .....94 D1
Falconer Mews SN25 ..35 B6
Falconscroft SN3 ......51 C8
Falconsway SP2 ......152 A5
Falconwood CI 8 SP6 .210 C1
Falkirk Rd SN4 ....64 A7
Falkner CI SN8 ....213 B3
Fallow Field CI SN14 ...70 B2
Falmouth Gr SN3 ......50 E4
Fanshaw Way BA12 ...117 A5
Fanstones Rd SN3 ....51 C4
Fantley La SP8 ....138 B1
Far View Rd SP3 ......196 F7
Faraday Pk SN3 ....51 E5
Faraday Rd
　Salisbury SP2 ....145 E1
　Swindon SN3 ....51 E5
Fareham CI SN3 ....51 B5
Farfield La SN6 ....19 E4
Fargo CI SP4 ....198 A6
Fargo Rd SP4 ....217 A7
Faringdon Rd 2 SN1 ...50 B6
Farleigh Ave
　Melksham SN12 ....94 B3
　Trowbridge BA14 .....105 A7
Farleigh Castle ★ BA2 .103 E8
Farleigh CI
　1 Chippenham SN14 ..77 F6
　Westbury BA13 ....108 F4
Farleigh Coll BA2 ....103 D6
Farleigh Cres SN3 .....50 E3
Farleigh Pk ★ BA2 ....103 D5
Farleigh Rd BA2 ......103 A5
Farleigh Rise BA1 .....82 D1
Farley CI BA11 ....110 C6
Farley Rd SP1 ....152 C7
Farm La Aldbourne SN8 .170 A6
　Great Bedwyn SN8 ...176 B3
　Salisbury SP2 ....145 E1
Farman CI SN3 ....51 C4
Farmer CI SN15 ....70 E1
Farmer Cres SN25 ....35 C6
Farmer Giles Farmstead ★
　SP3 ....201 C3
Farmhouse CI SN15 ...78 F4
Farmhouse Dr SN15 ...78 A4
Farnborough Rd SN3 ..51 B3
Farne Way SN4 ....48 A2
Farnsby St SN1 ....50 B6
Farrar Dr SN8 ....213 A2
Farrells Field SN14 ....68 F4
Farrfield SN2 ....35 E4
Farriers CI SN1 ....50 E8
Farriers Field SN9 ....181 F2
Farthing Row BA11 ...103 E1
Faulkner Sq RG17 .....177 C7
Faverole Way BA14 ...102 A2
Fayre Gdns GL7 ....1 F6
Feather Wood SN5 ....49 D5
Featherbed La SN6 ...163 F7
Fell Rd BA13 ....108 E2
Feltham Dr BA11 .....110 A3
Feltham La BA11 .....110 A2
Fenland CI
　8 Swindon SN5 ......48 F8
　5 Swindon SN5 ......49 A8
Fennel CI SN2 ....34 D4
Fennel Rd BA12 ......139 B6
Fenton Ave SN25 .....34 E7
Ferguson Rd SN10 ...214 D1
Fermoy BA11 ....110 B6
Ferndale Jun & Inf Sch
　SN2 ....50 B8
Ferndale Rd SN2 ......49 F8
Ferne Hollow SP5 ....207 A8
Ferne Wall Cnr SP7 ..203 B1

Ferney Way SP5 ......207 C4
Fernham Rd SN25 .....34 E3
Ferozeshah Rd SN10 .214 E6
Ferrers Dr SN5 ....48 F4
Ferris Gr SN12 ....94 C4
Ferris Mead BA12 ....117 A6
Festival Ave SP2 .....145 C3
Feversham Rd SP1 ...146 B3
Fiddington Clay SN10 .179 F1
Fiddington Hill SN10 ..180 A1
Fiddle The SN6 ....19 C7
Field Barn La SP3 ....201 F3
Field CI South Cerney GL7 ..7 A7
　Westbury BA13 ......109 A4
Field La BA9 ....137 B3
Field Rise SN1 ....50 A3
Field View
　Chippenham SN15 ....78 D7
　Enford SN9 ....190 A6
Field Way BA14 ......104 F6
Fieldfare SN3 ....51 D7
Fieldins BA15 ....99 E7
Fields The Mere BA12 .139 B6
　Swindon SN3 ....36 A1
Fieldside SN10 ....187 E8
Figgins La SN8 ......213 D2
Finchley Rd SP2 ......145 E2
Finkley Rd SP11 .....193 F2
Finnis Rd 1 SP4 .....217 C3
Fir Gn La SN8 ....183 D8
Fir Gr SN11 ....89 D8
Fir Rd SN14 ....74 F6
Firbank Cres BA12 ...117 C8
Fire Brigade Mus ★
　SN10 ....179 C5
Firecrest View 3 SN3 ..51 E6
Firs CI SP5 ....148 C2
Firs Hill Way SN10 ..179 C5
Firs Rd Alderbury SP5 .153 E2
　Firsdown SP5 ....148 B7
Firs The
　Chippenham SN14 ....78 A6
　Inkpen RG17 ....177 F3
　Limpley Stoke BA2 ...99 A5
First Broad Dr
　Barford St Martin SP3 .129 A1
　Wilton SN2 ....144 A7
First La SN12 ....85 C1
Firth CI SN25 ....35 A3
Fish Row SP1 ....152 A8
Fishers Brook BA11 ..110 A5
Fisherton Island SP2 .145 F1
Fisherton Manor Mid Sch
　SP2 ....145 E2
Fisherton St SP2 .....145 F1
Fison Wlk SP1 ....146 D4
Fitwell Rd SN25 ......34 C7
Fitzmaurice CI
　Bradford-on-Avon BA15 .100 A4
　Calne Without SN11 ..79 F2
　Swindon SN3 ....51 D7
Fitzmaurice Pl BA15 .100 D5
Fitzmaurice Prim Sch
　BA15 ....100 D5
Fitzroy Rd SN1 ....50 C2
Fitzwarren CI SN15 ...79 A4
Five Ash La BA12 ....117 C2
Five Rivers Leisure Ctr
　SP1 ....145 F3
Five Stiles Rd SN8 ...213 F2
Five Thorn La SN15 ..57 D6
Fiveways CI SN8 .....164 B1
Flamstone St SP5 ....205 E4
Flashett The SP5 ....149 D6
Flaxfields End 18 SP6 .210 D1
Flayburn Rd RN25 ....34 E7
Fleece Cotts 2 BA14 .105 E7
Fleet CI SN15 ....78 D8
Fleet St SN1 ....50 B6
Fleetwood CI SN13 ...84 E6
Fleetwood Rise SN12 .93 A8
Fleming CI SP11 .....192 A5
Fleming Way SN1 .....50 C5
Flensburg CI 20 SP10 .193 D2
Flers Ct BA12 ....117 A6
Fleur De Lys Dr BA14 .105 A4
Flint Hill SN5 ....49 C4
Flint La SP11 ....193 A4
Flintjack Pl 2 RG17 ...165 A1
Flisteridge Rd SN16 ..16 C3
Flit Croft 4 SP4 .....217 C2
Flood The SP4 ......149 B2
Florence Ct 21 SP10 ..193 E2
Florence St SN2 ......50 C8
Flower La
　Amesbury SP4 ....217 A3
　Melchet Park & Plaitford
　SO51 ....212 F7
Flowers Mead 6 BA13 .186 B7
Flowers Yd SN13 .....78 E7
Foghamshire SN15 ...78 D7
Folkestone CI SN14 ..78 A6
Folkestone Rd
　Salisbury SP2 ....151 F6
　Swindon SN1 ....50 B4
Folly Barrow ★ DT11 .206 B2
Folly CI Highworth SN6 .23 A7
　Salisbury SP2 ....151 F5
Folly Cres SN6 ....23 A7

Folly Dr SN6 ....23 A7
Folly La Alderbury SP5 .153 C3
　Melksham Without SN12 .93 B8
Folly La E SN15 ....86 C5
Folly La W SN15 ......86 B5
Folly Rd Inkpen RG17 ..177 F3
　Lambourn SN8 ....164 F1
　Roundway SN10 ......214 C7
Folly The SN15 ....44 A2
Folly View SP2 ......145 C5
Folly Way SN6 ....23 A7
Follyfield
　Bradford-on-Avon BA15 .100 D4
　Hankerton SN16 ......15 B2
Fonthill Wlk SN3 ......50 E5
Foot's Hill Cann SP7 .206 A7
　Salisbury SP2 ....145 A3
Ford St SN1 ....50 A5
Fordbrook Bsns Ctr
　SN9 ....215 C6
Fordingbridge Hospl
　SP6 ....210 D1
Fordingbridge Jun & Inf Sch
　SP6 ....210 D1
Fordson Rd SN10 ....214 D1
Fore St Ashton Keynes SN6 .6 F1
　Trowbridge BA14 ....101 D1
　Warminster BA12 ....116 F5
　Westbury BA13 ......109 A4
　Wylye BA12 ....201 E8
Foreminster Ct BA12 .116 F5
Forest & Sandridge CE Prim
　Sch SN12 ....94 F5
Forest Dale Rd SN8 ..175 A8
Forest Dr SP9 ....216 E7
Forest Hill SN8 ......176 B3
Forest La
　Chippenham SN15 ....78 E3
　Chute SP11 ....192 D8
　Melksham Without SN12 .86 F2
Forest Rd
　Bramshaw SP5 ......212 B3
　7 Frome BA11 ....110 B7
　Horningsham BA12 ..118 D8
　Melksham SN12 ......94 B5
　Redlynch SP6 ....211 D6
　Wootton Rivers SN8 .174 F2
Forest Rd Cnr BA12 ..118 E7
Forest Wlk BA13 .....111 C4
Forester CI 5 SN3 ....51 D4
Foresters Pk Rd SN12 .94 C4
Forge CI
　Milton Lilbourne SN9 .182 E7
　South Newton SP2 ..130 B1
Forge Fields SN5 .....48 D8
Forge La
　West Overton SN8 ...173 F7
　Zennor BA12 ....137 F3
Forge The
　Hungerford RG17 ....177 C7
　Lower Stanton St Quinton
　SN14 ....56 D6
Forman St SN1 ....81 C3
Forres Sandle Manor Sch
　SP6 ....210 C1
Forrester Gn SN14 ...75 B3
Forsey CI 4 SN3 .....51 E7
Fortis Hill SP7 ....203 C3
Fortune Way SN15 ...78 F5
Fortunes Field SN4 ..167 C7
Forty Acres Rd SN10 .214 C3
Forty The SN6 ....19 D7
Forum CI SN3 ....51 C8
Fosbury Hill Fort ★
　SN8 ....185 A3
Foss Way SN14 ......74 E5
Fosse CI SN2 ....49 F6
Fosse Cotts SN16 ....27 A6
Fosse La BA1 ....82 A4
Fosseway CI SN14 ...75 B3
Foster Rd BA11 ......110 A3
Fosters Bushes 4 SP4 .217 D3
Fotherby Cres SP1 ..146 C4
Foundry La SN15 .....70 E1
Foundry Rd
　3 Malmesbury SN16 ..28 A4
　2 Redlynch SP5 ....211 C8
Fountain Mead 3 SP7 .202 C2
Four Acre CI SN6 .....18 A8
Fourmile Hill SP4 ....132 B3
Fovant CI SN5 ....34 A1
Fovant Regimental Badges ★
　SP3 ....204 F7
Fowey SN5 ....49 A3
Fowler's Hill SP1 ....152 C8
Fowler's Rd SP1 .....152 B8
Fowlers La SN8 ......173 B1
Fox Brook SN4 ....47 F2
Fox CI SN14 ....70 B1
Fox Croft Wlk SN15 ..78 F8
Fox Talbot Mus ★ SN15 .86 D5
Fox Wood SN5 ....49 D5
Foxbridge SN3 ....51 D7
Foxbury 4 RG17 .....165 A1
Foxcote Gdns 2 BA11 .110 C7
Foxcott SN6 ....8 C4
Foxcotte CI SP10 ....193 C1
Foxcotte La SP11 ....193 C2
Foxcotte Rd SP10 ...193 C2
Foxdown Cl SN12 ....94 C3
Foxglove Cl SN25 ....34 D5
Foxglove Dr BA14 ...101 A4
Foxglove Rd SN25 ...34 D5
Foxglove Way SN11 ..81 B5
Foxgrove SN14 ....70 A2
Foxhill CI SN25 ....34 F3
Foxleaze SN6 ....8 D1

Foxley CI SN2 ....35 E4
Foxley Cnr SN16 .....180 D4
Foxley Fields SN10 ..180 C4
Foxley Rd Norton SN16 ..41 E8
　St Paul Malmesbury Without
　SN16 ....27 D2
Foxtail Gdns SP11 ...192 A5
Foyle Hill SP7 ....202 B1
Foyle Rd SP11 ....192 C2
Foyle's Mead BA12 ..201 E8
Frampton CI SN5 .....49 B6
Frampton Ct BA14 ...105 A6
Francis Rd 10 SN10 ..179 F1
Francis St SN10 ......101 C1
Francis Way SP2 .....152 A5
Francomes SN25 .....34 A4
Francomes Field 17
　RG17 ....165 A1
Frank Warman Ct 8 SN3 .36 B3
Frankenbury ★ SP6 ..210 F2
Frankland St SN1 .....48 E3
Frankton Gdns 2 SN3 .36 B2
Fraser CI SN3 ....51 B7
Frederick Taylor Ct
　BA12 ....116 F4
Fredericks Ave SN14 ..77 F7
Fredericks Way SN14 .53 B3
Free's Ave SN8 ......213 B5
Freegrove Dr SN15 ...73 F8
Freegrove Rd SN15 ..73 F8
Freemans CI 4 RG17 .177 B7
Freesia CI 2 BA12 ...116 E7
Freestone Way SN13 ..76 D1
Fremantle Rd SP11 ..191 F4
French Mill La SP7 ...202 C1
French Mill Rise 16 SP7 .202 C1
Frensham Way SN15 .105 D6
Fresden Village ★ SN6 ..23 A7
Freshbrook Prim Sch
　SN5 ....49 A3
Freshbrook Way SN5 ..49 B4
Freshford CE Prim Sch
　BA2 ....99 B5
Freshford La BA2 .....99 A4
Freshford Sta BA2 ....99 C5
Friar's Orch 4 SP1 ...152 B8
Friars CI BA13 ....112 C8
Friars The BA12 ......94 C6
Friary CI BA15 ....99 E4
Friary La SP1 ....152 B7
Friary The SP1 ......152 B8
Fricker's La SP3 .....200 F3
Friday La SN9 ....181 D3
Friday St SN15 ....58 C3
Fridays Ham La SN6 ...7 B3
Friesian CI SN5 ....49 A7
Friesland CI SN5 .....49 A7
Friggle St BA11 .....110 D1
Frilford Dr SN3 ....36 A1
Frith Copse SN5 .....34 A2
Fritillary Mews SN1 ..50 D6
Frobisher Dr SN3 .....50 F6
Frog La Avebury SN8 .173 B8
　Chilmark SP3 ....201 A3
　Great Bedwyn SN8 ..176 C3
　Great Somerford SN15 .44 B3
　Hullavington SN14 ...41 F1
　Longbridge Deverill
　BA12 ....121 A6
　Motcombe SP7 ......202 B4
　West Overton SN8 ...173 F7
Frogmore Rd BA13 ...108 F5
Frogwell SN14 ....77 F8
Frogwell Pk SN14 ....78 A8
Frogwell Prim Sch
　SN14 ....78 A7
Frome Com Coll BA11 .110 A7
Frome Leisure Ctr
　BA11 ....110 A7
Frome Rd
　Bradford-on-Avon BA15 .100 C5
　Maiden Bradley with Yarnfield
　BA12 ....118 D5
　Southwick BA14 .....104 F3
　Swindon SN25 ....34 F4
　Trowbridge BA14 ....105 C2
　Westwood BA15 .....100 C3
　Wingfield BA14 .....104 C6
Frome Sta BA11 .....110 B4
Frome View BA12 ...118 E3
Front Horse Hill La
　SP7 ....203 A1
Front La SN26 ....21 A4
Front St RG17 ....171 E7
Fruitfields CI SN10 ..214 B1
Fry CI 2 SN1 ....49 F4
Fry Sq SP10 ....193 F1
Fryern Ct Rd SP6 ....210 D3
Fugglestone SP2 ....144 F3
Fulford Rd BA14 .....101 C2
Fuller Ave SN13 ......84 E8
Fuller CI SN2 ....35 F5
Fuller's CI SN12 ......94 B5
Fullers Ave SN6 ......19 D8
Fullerton Wlk 6 SN1 ..49 F4
Fulmar CI SN12 ......94 D1
Fulney CI BA14 ......101 F2
Furlong BA12 ....117 B6
Furlong CI Rowde SN10 ..96 E1
　Swindon SN25 ....34 E5
Furlong Cres SP3 ...196 F7
Furlong Gdns BA14 ..101 E1
Furlong Way SP3 ...196 F7
Furnax La BA12 .....112 F1
Furse Hill Rd SP9 ...216 D5
Furze CI SN5 ....34 A2
Furze Dr SP11 ....191 F3
Furze Hill La SN10 ..179 D7

Furzehill SN13 ....84 F8
Furzley La SO51 .....212 F3
Furzley Rd SO51 ....212 F2
Fussells Lodge (Long
　Barrow) ★ SP5 .....147 D5
Fyfield Ave SN2 ....35 C5
Fyfield CI 2 SP1 .....146 D5
Fyfield Down National Nature
　Reserve ★ SN8 .....167 C3
Fyfield La SP11 .....192 D1
Fyfield Rd SP11 .....192 E1
Fyfield Way SP11 ...191 F3
Fynamore Com Prim Sch
　SN11 ....81 A4
Fyne CI 3 SN5 ....34 B2

G

Gable CI SN2 ....35 B6
Gables CI SN10 .....214 D2
Gabriel CI 4 BA11 ..110 C6
Gains La SN10 ....214 B4
Gainsborough Ave SN4 .47 F3
Gainsborough CI SP2 .145 C3
Gainsborough Ct 1
　SP10 ....193 D1
Gainsborough Rise
　BA14 ....105 A6
Gainsborough Way
　SN5 ....49 A3
Gairlock CI SN5 ....34 B2
Gaisford Chase SN10 .179 B4
Galahad CI 25 SP10 ..193 E2
Gales CI SN8 ....78 F8
Gales Gd SN8 ....213 E3
Gallery at Handel House ★
　SN10 ....214 B3
Galley La SN8 ....176 C3
Gallipoli Rd 8 SP4 ..198 F5
Galloway CI 13 SN5 ..49 A7
Galloway Dr SN2 .....34 C5
Gallows Barrow ★ SP4 .190 B3
Gallows Leap SN11 ...81 A5
Galsworthy CI SN3 ...51 D4
Galton Way SN2 .....49 F8
Gambia St SN1 ......50 D6
Gamekeepers CI SN25 .34 F7
Gantlettdene SN3 ....51 E6
Ganton Way SN2 .....35 C1
Garden The SN2 .....35 E5
Garden Trading Est
　SN10 ....214 C5
Gardeners Gn 2 SP9 .199 C8
Gardens The
　Rushall SN9 ....181 E3
　Heddington SN11 ....89 B1
　Swindon SN25 ....35 A3
　Upavon SN9 ....181 F2
Gardiner Rd 2 SP4 ..197 E6
Gardners Dr SN14 ....55 E8
Garendon Ct 2 SP6 .210 D1
Garfield CI SN3 ......51 C3
Garlings The 6 SN8 .170 A6
Garrard Way SN3 ....51 A8
Garraways 6 SN4 ....47 F2
Garsdon Mill SN15 ...28 F5
Garsington Dr SN25 ..34 C7
Garston BA11 ....110 A4
Garston CI 3 BA11 ..110 A4
Garston Rd BA11 ....110 A4
Garstons The BA1 ...82 D2
Garth CI SN14 ....70 B1
Gartons Rd SN5 ......48 F7
Gas La Cricklade SN6 ..19 D8
　Salisbury SP2 ....145 F1
Gascelyn CI SN14 ....78 A3
Gascoigne's La SP7 .202 C1
Gason Hill Rd SP9 ..216 C8
Gasper St BA12 .....137 C6
Gassons Rd GL7 ......2 C5
Gassons Way GL7 .....2 C4
Gaston La SN16 ......40 C8
Gaston's Rd SN14 ....78 C8
Gastons Rd SN16 ....27 A7
Gaters La SP4 ....133 A2
Gauntlet Rd SP4 ....217 B4
Gaveller Rd SN25 ....34 C7
Gawaine CI 3 SP10 ..193 E2
Gawthorne Dr SP2 ..151 F6
Gay's Pl SN2 ....35 F4
Gaynor CI SN25 ....35 A6
Gayton Way SN3 .....51 B8
Gaza Rd SP4 ....198 F4
Geneville Rise 3 SP4 .217 C3
Genoa Ct 16 SP10 ...193 E2
Gentle St BA12 .....119 C7
George CI SN11 ......81 C3
George Gay Gdns 7 SN3 .50 F4
George La SN8 ......213 D2
George St (South) 6
　SP2 ....145 F1
George St
　Salisbury SP2 ....145 F1
　Swindon SN1 ....50 A6
　Trowbridge BA14 ...101 D1
　Warminster BA12 ....117 A7
George St Pl BA12 ..117 A7
George VI Rd SP9 ...216 C8
George Ward Sch The
　SN12 ....93 F6
Gerard Wlk SN5 ......49 A6
Germain's La SN14 ...76 A8
Geys Hill BA12 ......115 A7

Giant's Cave (Long Barrow)★ SN14 39 C2
Giant's Chair The (Tumulus)★ SP5 158 E2
Gibbs Cl 2 Salisbury SP1 146 C5
Swindon SN3 51 E7
Westbury BA13 109 B4
Gibbs La SN14 55 F8
Gibbs Leaze BA14 102 A1
Gibson Cl SN12 94 C1
Gifford Rd SN3 36 B3
Giffords The BA14 102 A4
Gigant St Salisbury SP1 152 B8
Swallowcliffe SP3 204 A6
Gilbert Way SP1 146 C4
Gilbert's Gn 3 SP9 199 D8
Gilberts Piece SN8 183 E1
Giles Ave 1 SN6 19 D7
Giles La SO51 212 E7
Giles La Ind Est SP5 212 E6
Gilling Way SN3 51 D6
Gillingham Adult Ed Ctr SP7 202 B1
Gilman Cl SN25 35 A8
Giotto Cl SN25 34 B7
Gipsy La
Chippenham SN15 78 D6
Frome BA11 110 B7
Holt BA14 92 F2
Hungerford RG17 177 C8
Swindon SN2 50 E8
Warminster BA12 117 B5
Gladstone Rd
Chippenham SN15 78 D7
Trowbridge BA14 105 B7
Gladstone St SN1 50 C7
Gladys Plumley Gdns SN2 50 C8
Glass's La SP3 204 D7
Glebe Cl
7 Aldbourne SN8 170 A6
Pitton & Farley SP5 148 C4
Glebe Field BA12 117 A6
Glebe Gdns SP7 202 A4
Glebe La Kemble GL7 4 F7
Landford SP5 212 C6
Glebe Pl RG17 171 A1
Glebe Rd
2 Durrington/Bulford SP4 198 B7
Trowbridge BA14 105 A7
Wootton Bassett SN4 47 D1
Glebe The
All Cannings SN10 180 F8
Calne SN11 81 C3
Freshford BA2 99 B4
Hinton Charterhouse BA2 98 D2
Glebe Way SN13 76 E1
Glebelands 3 BA12 194 C5
Glendale Cres SP1 152 D8
Glendale Rd SP4 198 C7
Gleneagles Cl SN15 78 F7
Glenfield Cl SP5 149 D6
Glenmore Rd
Haydon Wick SN25 34 C5
Salisbury SP1 146 C3
Glenside SN12 94 C6
Glenville Cl SN4 61 E8
Glenwood Cl SN1 50 C2
Glevum Cl SN5 33 C5
Glevum Rd SN3 36 C1
Globe St SN1 50 C4
Gloucester Cl 3 SN14 78 A6
Gloucester Rd
Calne Without SN11 81 F1
8 Malmesbury SN16 28 A3
Trowbridge BA14 105 B7
Gloucester Sq SN12 94 C4
Gloucester St SN1 50 B7
Gloucester Wlk BA13 109 A4
Glover Rd SP4 197 F7
Glyn Pl SP7 206 B7
Glyndebourne Cl SP2 145 C3
Goatacre La SN11 73 F7
Goddard Ave SN1 50 B4
Goddard Cl 1 SN9 215 C5
Goddard Pk Prim Sch SN3 51 A4
Goddard Rd SN9 215 C5
Goddards La 11 SN8 170 A6
Godley Rd SP2 152 A6
Godolphin Cl SN5 49 A3
Godolphin Prep Sch SP1 146 C1
Godolphin Sch The SP1 152 C8
Godwin Ct SN1 50 C4
Godwin Rd SN3 36 B3
Godwins Cl SN12 84 E1
Gogg's La SP5 211 D7
Gold Hill 8 SP7 202 C1
Gold View SN1 49 F4
Goldcrest Wlk SN3 51 E7
Golden Cross SP6 211 E4
Golding Ave SN8 213 A2
Goldney Ave SN14 78 C7
Goldsborough Cl SN5 49 B6
Gomeldon Medieval Village of★ SP4 133 C4
Gomeldon Prim Sch SP4 133 C4
Gomeldon Rd SP4 133 D5
Gooch Cl BA11 110 D6
Gooch St SN1 50 C7
Goodbody Rd 1 SP4 198 A6
Goodes Hill SN13 85 D3
Goodings La RG17 171 D6
Goodwin Cl BA12 117 E8
Goodwood Cl BA14 105 E4
Goodwood Way 3 SN14 77 F5
Goodwyns Cl 5 SP9 199 C8
Goor La SN8 164 B2
Goose Gn RG17 165 A2
Goose St Marston SN10 179 A3
Southwick BA14 105 A2
Gooselands
Crudwell SN16 14 D5
Westbury BA13 108 F2
Gordon Gdns 4 SN1 50 C6
Gordon Rd 5 SN1 50 C6
Gore Cl SN25 34 F6
Gore Cross SN10 187 E5
Gore La BA13 111 B4
Gore Rd SP4 197 E7
Gores La SN9 181 C5
Gorringe Rd SP2 145 D1
Gorse Hill Inf Sch SN2 35 D1
Gorse Hill Jun Sch SN2 35 D1
Gosditch
Ashton Keynes SN6 17 E8
Latton SN6 8 C4
Goughs Way SN4 47 E2
Gould Cl 1 SP11 192 A5
Goulding Cl 3 SN3 36 B2
Gower Cl Swindon SN2 35 F2
1 Swindon SN5 48 F5
Gower Rd 14 SP7 202 D2
Grace Cl SP2 145 B5
Grace La SP6 211 A4
Graemar La SO51 162 E1
Grafton CE Prim Sch SN8 183 F7
Grafton Pl SN8 183 F7
Grafton Rd
Burbage SN8 183 D7
Swindon SN2 35 C5
Graham St SN1 50 D7
Grailey Cl SN3 51 C4
Gramp's Hill OX12 165 F7
Gramshaw Rd 2 SP2 145 D2
Granary Cl
East Grafton SN8 183 F7
4 Swindon SN5 48 F8
Granary Rd 6 SN8 176 B3
Grand Ave SN8 175 E3
Grand Trunk Rd SP9 216 B4
Grandison Cl SN5 49 A6
Grange Cl
Atworth/Whitley SN12 85 D1
Fyfield SP11 192 D1
Highworth SN6 23 A5
Grange Com Inf Sch SN3 36 B3
Grange Dr SN3 36 B1
Grange Gdns SP1 146 C2
Grange Jun Sch SN3 36 B2
Grange La
St Paul Malmesbury Without SN16 43 B5
Warminster BA12 117 E5
Grange Pk Way SN5 48 F5
Grange Rd BA11 110 A7
Grange View BA15 100 E7
Granger Cl SN15 78 F4
Granham Cl SN8 213 D1
Granham Hill SN8 213 D1
Grans Barrow (Long Barrow)★ SP6 209 E6
Grantham Cl SN5 49 B3
Granthams The 4 RG17 165 A2
Grantley Cl SN3 51 A3
Grants Rd SN9 190 A6
Granville Gdns 28 SP7 202 C2
Granville Rd SN12 94 A6
Granville St SN1 50 C6
Grasmere
Bower Hill SN12 94 D1
Swindon SN3 51 E3
Trowbridge BA14 101 E2
Grasmere Cl 1 SP2 151 F6
Graspan Rd 12 SP11 192 B5
Grateley Rd SP4 199 C5
Gravel Cl SP5 211 A8
Gravel The BA14 92 E1
Graveney Sq SP10 193 E1
Grays Cl SP7 202 A4
Grays Leaze BA14 105 C2
Graythwaite Cl 3 SN25 34 F6
Great Barn★ SN8 167 B1
Great Bedwyn CE Prim Sch SN8 176 B4
Great Chalfield Manor★ BA14 92 D3
Great Croft SP5 148 C7
Great Dro SP4 132 F1
Great Ground 15 SP7 202 D2
Great Hill BA9 137 B3
Great La SP7 202 C1
Great Lodge Dr SN8 175 B5
Great Parks BA14 92 F1
Great Roc Rd BA13 108 E3
Great Western Ave SP3 200 B1
Great Western Hospl The SN3 51 D1
Great Western Way SN5 48 F3
Great Wethers★ SN8 174 A7
Great Wishford CE Fst Sch SP2 130 A4
Greater La BA13 186 C8
Greatwoods BA13 186 C8
Green Acres 13 SN8 170 B2
Green Beeches SN12 93 D8
Green Cl
East Grafton SN8 183 F7
Holt BA14 101 F8
Whiteparish SP5 161 D4
Green Dro Fovant SP3 204 E8
Grimstead SP5 154 B4
Pewsey SN9 215 D3
Smannell SP11 193 E5
Green Farm Rise SN8 176 D7
Green Gate Rd SN10 180 D4
Green La Ashmore SP5 206 E4
Cheverell Magna SN10 179 C1
Codford BA12 195 A3
Colerne SN14 75 A3
Deanend SP5 207 E4
Devizes SN10 214 B1
Downton SP5 211 A8
Fordingbridge SP6 210 D1
Hinton Charterhouse BA2 98 E1
Laverstock SP4 146 D8
Rockbourne SP6 210 C3
Salisbury SP1 146 D6
Sherston SN16 25 C1
Southwick BA14 104 D2
Steeple Ashton BA14 102 C1
Trowbridge BA14 105 E8
Westbury BA13 108 F2
Winsley BA15 99 E6
Green La Hospl SN10 214 B1
Green La Wood Nature Reserve★ BA14 106 C8
Green Mdw Ave SN25 34 F4
Green Pk La BA11 107 A6
Green Rd Codford BA12 195 A3
Corsham SN13 85 B4
Swindon SN2 35 E3
Green Ride BA12 123 E5
Green St SN8 167 C1
Green Terr BA14 101 C2
Green The
Alderbury SP5 153 C3
Biddestone SN14 76 E8
Brokenborough SN16 27 D7
Calne SN11 81 B2
Cheverell Magna SN10 179 C2
Dauntsey SN15 59 A8
Fairford GL7 1 F7
Highworth SN6 22 F5
1 Liddington SN4 163 A4
Lyneham & Bradenstoke SN15 60 A4
Marlborough SN8 213 E3
Oaksey SN16 15 F7
Pitton & Farley SP5 148 C3
Salisbury SP1 146 D2
Upper Woodford SP4 131 D7
Whiteparish SP5 161 D4
Green Valley Ave SN25 34 F4
Greenacres
Dilton Marsh BA13 112 A8
2 Downton SP5 210 F8
Greenacres Way SN11 80 F4
Green's Ct 3 SP1 152 B8
Green's La SN4 64 B5
Greenaway 4 SN4 163 A5
Greenbridge Ind Est SN3 51 A7
Greenbridge Rd SN3 51 A7
Greenbridge Ret Pk SN3 51 A8
Greencroft St SP1 146 B1
Greencroft The 6 SP1 146 B1
Greendown Com Sch SN5 48 F5
Greenfield Rd SN10 214 C1
Greenfields
Grimstead SP5 154 C2
Smannell SP11 193 F4
South Marston SN3 36 E5
Greenham Wlk SN3 51 B6
Greenhill
Sutton Veny BA12 117 F1
Westwells SN13 84 D7
Greenhill Gdns
Sutton Veny BA12 117 F1
Trowbridge BA14 102 A4
Greenhill Rd SN2 34 E2
Greenhills BA13 186 C8
Greenhouse Rd SN10 180 F8
Greenland Cl SN12 92 E8
Greenland View BA15 100 D6
Greenlands 1 BA12 194 C5
Greenlands Cl 20 SP4 198 B7
Greenlands Rd SN2 35 E3
Greenlane Cl SP4 146 D6
Greenmeadow Prim Sch SN25 35 A4
Greens Cl SN14 41 F1
Greens La SN11 172 A8
Greens Meade 6 SP5 211 C7
Greensand Cl SN25 34 F7
Greentrees Prim Sch SP1 146 C5
Greenway SN4 60 F2
Greenway Ave SN15 70 D1
Greenway Cl SN3 51 B7
Greenway Ct SN15 70 D2
Greenway Dr SN15 73 F8
Greenway Gdns
Chippenham SN15 70 D1
Trowbridge BA14 101 E3
Greenway La SN15 70 D2
Greenway Pk SN15 70 D1
Greenway Rd SN8 169 B1
Greenways RG17 165 A1
Greenwich Cl SN25 35 A5
Greenwood Ave SP1 146 D1
Greenwood Rd SN12 94 A3
Gregory Cl SN15 57 C1
Grenadier Cl 2 BA12 116 F7
Gresham Cl SN3 50 F6
Grey Wethers or Sarsen Stones★ SN8 167 F2
Grey's Cnr BA9 136 A5
Greyfriars Cl SP1 152 B7
Greyhound La 1 SP2 144 D3
Greystones SN15 96 B8
Greywethers Ave SN3 50 E3
Grierson Cl SN11 81 B3
Griffin Alley 6 SN16 28 A3
Griffins Ct 3 SP2 146 A1
Griffiths Cl SN3 36 B1
Grimstead Beeches★ SP5 160 D7
Grimstead Rd SP5 153 F1
Grindal Dr SN5 48 F5
Grittleton House Sch SN14 54 E4
Grocyn Cl SN14 75 B3
Grosmont Dr SN5 49 B5
Grosvenor close SP9 216 E6
Grosvenor Rd
Shaftesbury SP7 202 C2
Swindon SN1 50 A4
Ground Cnr BA14 101 D8
Groundwell SN25 35 C6
Groundwell Ind Est SN25 35 D6
Groundwell Rd SN1 50 D5
Grove Hill SN6 23 A7
Grove La
Kington St Michael SN14 69 F8
Redlynch SP5 211 D8
Yatton Keynell SN14 69 A6
Grove Leaze BA15 100 B6
Grove Orch SN6 22 F7
Grove Prim Sch BA14 105 B5
Grove Rd Corsham SN13 77 A1
23 Market Lavington SN10 179 F1
Sherston SN16 40 C8
Grove The
Codford St Peter BA12 195 A2
Crudwell SN16 4 C1
Penton Mewsey SP11 193 A2
Warminster BA12 117 A7
Grovelands Ave SN1 50 C3
Grovelands Way BA12 116 E7
Groveley Rd SP3 143 B3
Grovely Castle★ SP3 128 F4
Grovely Cl SN5 34 A1
Grovely Rd SP3 129 E2
Grovely View SP2 144 B1
Groves St SN2 49 F6
Groves The SN25 35 B3
Grundys SN3 51 D3
Gryphon Cl BA13 108 E3
Guilder La SP1 152 B8
Guildford Ave SN3 50 F3
Guildhall Sq 3 SP1 152 A8
Gullet The SN13 83 F7
Gulliver's La BA14 178 A4
Gundry Cl
Chippenham SN15 78 F5
Devizes SN10 214 C4
Gunner St SP4 198 E6
Gunsite Rd SN8 173 C6
Gunville Hill SP5 149 E6
Gunville Rd SP5 149 D6
Guppy St SN2 49 F7
Gurston Meadow SP5 205 A4
Gurston Rd SP5 205 A4
Gutherie CE Inf Sch SN11 81 C4
Guthrie Cl SN11 81 C4
Guyers La SN13 76 D2
Gwyns Piece 14 RG17 165 A2

H

Ha'penny Bridge★ GL7 2 C3
Habrel's Cl SN15 78 F6
Hackett Cl SN2 35 E4
Hackleton Rise SN3 51 B8
Hackney Way BA13 108 E3
Hackpen Cl SN4 64 B7
Hackthorne Rd SP4 198 B7
Haddon Cl 14 SN5 48 F5
Haddons Cl SN16 27 E2
Haden Rd 6 BA14 105 D7
Hadleigh Cl SN5 49 C6
Hadleigh Rise SN2 36 A5
Hadrian Rd 20 SP10 193 E2
Hadrians Cl
Salisbury SP2 145 C1
Swindon SN3 51 C8
Haig Cl SN2 35 E4
Haig Rd SP4 217 F8
Haimes La 20 SP7 202 C2
Hale House★ SP6 211 A5
Hale La SP6 211 B5
Hale Prim Sch SP6 211 C6
Hale Rd SP6 211 A5
Hales Castle★ BA11 114 D5
Hales Rd 6 SP4 190 A4
Half Hide Down SP5 207 B3
Half Mile Rd RG17 171 A5
Halfpenny La SP5 206 E4
Halfpenny Row BA11 103 E1
Halfway Cl BA14 101 F2
Halfway Firs SN13 76 C1
Halfway La SN8 170 C2
Halifax Cl SN4 64 A7
Halifax Rd SN12 94 C1
Hall Cl SN4 64 A6
Hallam Moor SN3 51 E2
Hallsfield SN6 8 D1
Hallum Cl SP1 146 D4
Halton Rd SP11 191 F4
Halve The BA14 101 D1
Ham Cl SN8 183 D3
Ham Hill Nature Reserve★ SN8 185 B8
Ham La Biddestone SN14 76 C8
Kempsford GL7 10 E6
South Cerney GL7 6 F6
Ham Rd Ham RG17 177 A2
Liddington SN4 163 A5
Ham The
Durrington/Bulford SP4 198 C7
Kington St Michael SN14 70 A8
9 Market Lavington SN10 179 F1
Westbury BA13 108 E5
Hambidge La GL7 2 C5
Hamble Ct SP10 193 F1
Hamble Rd SN25 34 F4
Hambleton Ave SN10 214 E6
Hamblin Meadow RG17 177 C8
Hamilton Cl
Amesbury SP4 217 E3
Swindon SN3 50 F7
Hamilton Dr
Chippenham SN14 77 F5
2 Market Lavington SN10 179 F1
Hamilton Pk 3 SP5 211 B8
Hamilton Rd SP1 146 A2
Hamlet Ct SN15 70 D1
Hamlet Gdns SP11 193 E3
Hamlet The SN15 70 E1
Hammer St BA10 122 C7
Hammond Way BA14 101 D4
Hammonds SN6 19 E8
Hampshire Cl
Durrington/Bulford SP4 217 E8
7 Swindon SN5 49 A7
Hampshire Gdns BA13 109 A4
Hampshire Pl SN12 94 B5
Hampsley Rd SN13 89 C1
Hampstead Way SN25 34 F7
Hampton Cl SN12 94 C1
Hampton Ct SP2 144 F2
Hampton Dr SN5 48 F5
Hamptworth Rd SP5 211 F6
Hamshill Ditches★ SP3 143 B7
Hamworthy Rd SN3 51 C6
Hanbury Rd SN3 51 A4
Hancock Cl SN15 79 A5
Handel St SN2 50 C8
Handley St SP5 204 D3
Hanging Bushes La SP11 193 A1
Hanging Langford Camp★ BA12 201 F6
Hanging Stone★ SN9 181 B7
Hangman's Stone★ RG17 164 F4
Hankerton Priory SN16 15 B4
Hankerton Rd SN16 16 C2
Hanks Cl SN16 28 A5
Hannington Cl SN2 35 B6
Hanover Cl BA14 101 E4
Hanover Ct SN3 51 D7
Harbour Cl SN25 34 F3
Harcourt Mews 5 BA11 110 A4
Harcourt Rd SN2 50 A8
Harcourt Terr SP2 151 F8
Hardenhuish Ave SN15 70 C1
Hardenhuish La SN14 70 B1
Hardenhuish Pk★ SN14 70 C1
Hardenhuish Sch SN14 70 C2
Hardens Cl SN15 79 A5
Hardens Mead SN15 79 A6
Hardhams Rise SN13 84 F8
Hardie Cl SN3 36 A1
Harding St 6 SN1 50 B6
Hardwick Cl SN25 35 A5
Hardyfair Cl 5 SP11 192 F1
Hare Cl SN2 35 F5
Hare Knapp BA15 100 B6
Hare St Bremhill SN15 72 C5
Pewsey SN9 182 A7
Hare Warren Cl SP2 144 C1
Harebell Cl SN25 34 D5
Harefield Cres SP4 190 A2
Harepit Way★ SN11 172 F7
Hares Patch SN14 70 B2
Haresdown Hill GL7 3 F7
Harford Cl 4 SN15 78 F5
Harford St 4 BA14 105 E8
Hargreaves Rd
Swindon SN25 35 D6
Trowbridge BA14 105 E7
Harlech Cl SN5 49 B4
Harlestone Rd SN3 51 B8
Harmony Pl 8 BA14 105 D7
Harnham CE Jun Sch SP2 151 F6
Harnham Inf Sch SP2 151 F6
Harnham Rd SP2 151 F7
Harnham Trad Est SP2 151 D7
Harnish Way SN14 70 B2
Harnwood Rd SP2 151 E6
Harper Rd SP2 145 D2
Harper's La SN16 27 F3
Harptree Cl SN5 49 A8
Harriers The SN3 51 C7

Harrington Dr 4 SP4 198 E6
Harrington Wlk SN3 51 A7
Harris Cl 5 RG17 165 A2
Harris La SN9 183 A7
Harris Rd
Ashton Keynes SN6 7 A1
Calne SN11 81 C5
Swindon SN2 35 A2
Harrow Cl SN3 36 A1
Harrow Gr SN15 60 B2
Harrow Way SP11 193 B1
Harrow Way Com Prim Sch SP10 193 C1
Harroway La SP11 193 B1
Hartfield SN10 214 A2
Hartham La SN13 76 E5
Harthill Dro SP5 211 D7
Hartington Rd
Salisbury SP2 145 E2
Swindon SN25 34 C7
Hartland Cl SN3 51 A5
Hartley Way SP1 146 D5
Hartmoor Cl SN10 214 A2
Hartmoor Rd SN10 214 A2
Harts La SN14 76 E8
Hartsthorn Cl SN2 34 D3
Harvard Cl
16 Bower Hill SN12 178 B8
1 Salisbury SP2 151 F5
Harvest La SP5 205 F4
Harvester Cl 7 SN5 48 F8
Harvey Gr SN2 34 F2
Hastings Ave SN9 182 B2
Hastings Cl SN9 182 B2
Hastings Dr SN15 60 B2
Hastings Rd SN13 85 A8
Hatch La SP3 203 C8
Hatch Rd SN3 36 B4
Hatchbury La SP11 185 C3
Hatcher's Cres SN26 21 B2
Hatches La SP1 152 D7
Hatchet Cl SP6 211 C6
Hatchet Hill SN4 163 D6
Hatchet La SP11 193 B5
Hatfield Cl SN25 34 E6
Hatfields SN10 181 A5
Hathaway Cl SP1 145 F4
Hathaway Rd SN2 35 E5
Hathaway Ret Pk SN15 78 E8
Hatherden CE Prim Sch SP11 193 C5
Hatherell Rd SN15 78 F4
Hatherhall Cl SN3 36 C2
Hatherleigh Ct SN3 51 B6
Hatherley Rd SN3 51 B7
Hathersage Moor SN3 51 E2
Hattem Pl 23 SP10 193 D2
Hatton Gr SN3 50 F6
Hatton Way SN13 76 E1
Havard Way 2 SP4 217 D2
Havelock Sq SN1 50 B6
Havelock St
Swindon SN1 50 B5
Trowbridge BA14 105 C7
Haven Cl SN3 51 B8
Havering La SN9 182 E7
Havisham Dr SN25 34 D6
Hawcroft BA14 92 E1
Hawfinch Cl SN3 51 E5
Hawk's Worth Cl 6 BA11 110 C7
Hawker Rd SN3 51 C4
Hawkeridge Pk BA13 108 E5
Hawkeridge Rd BA14 105 E2
Hawkesdene 17 SP7 202 C1
Hawkesdene La SP7 202 C1
Hawkins Cl SN15 78 F5
Hawkins Meadow SN8 213 B2
Hawkins Rd 16 SN8 170 A6
Hawkins St SN2 50 A7
Hawksridge 4 SP2 152 A5
Hawkstreet SN15 96 B6
Hawkswood SN3 51 D8
Hawksworth Trad Est SN2 50 A8
Hawksworth Way SN2 50 A7
Hawthorn Ave SN2 35 C2
Hawthorn Cl
Pewsey SN9 215 D5
1 Salisbury SP2 145 F1
2 Shaftesbury SP7 202 D2
Hawthorn Gr BA14 105 C5
Hawthorn Rd
Chippenham SN15 70 E1
Frome BA11 110 A6
Tidworth SP9 216 D7
Hay La SN5 48 F6
Hay St SN14 74 A8
Haydock Cl 4 SN14 77 F5
Haydon Ct SN25 34 E5
Haydon Ct Dr SN25 34 E5
Haydon End La SN25 34 D6
Haydon St SN1 50 C7
Haydon View Rd SN25 35 C3
Haydon Wick Prim Sch SN25 34 E4
Haydonleigh Dr SN25 34 E4
Haydonleigh Prim Sch SN25 34 E5
Haydown Leas SP11 185 C3
Haye's La GL9 38 E2
Hayes Cl BA14 101 E3
Hayes Knoll Sta SN5 19 F2
Hayesdown Fst Sch BA11 110 B5
Hayfield SN14 74 A8
Hayfield Ct RG17 171 C7
Haygrove Cl BA12 116 D6
Hayle Rd SN5 49 F6
Haynes Cl SN3 51 C4
Haynes Rd BA13 109 A3
Haywain 6 SP4 217 B3
Haywain Cl SN25 35 C6
Hayward Cl
Chippenham SN15 78 F5
Swindon SN25 35 A6
Hayward Pl BA13 108 F5
Haywards Pl SN10 179 F2
Hazel Cl
Marlborough SN8 175 A7
Salisbury SP2 145 B3
Hazel Copse 2 SN14 77 F6
Hazel End SN4 47 E1
Hazel Gr Calne SN11 81 B1
Swindon SN2 35 C3
Trowbridge BA14 105 B5
Hazel Way SN14 75 A5
Hazelbury Cres SN3 51 C7
Hazelbury Hill SN13 83 D6
Hazelbury Manor Gdns* SN13 83 F5
Hazeldon La SP3 203 D6
Hazelwood Rd SN12 94 A3
Hazlemere Cl SN3 51 B4
Hazzard's Hill BA12 139 B5
Headington Hts SN11 89 B1
Headlands Gr SN2 35 E3
Headlands Sch SN2 35 D3
Headquarters Rd
8 Durrington/Bulford SP4 198 F6
Westbury BA13 108 C6
Heale Gdn* SP4 131 D5
Heath Cl BA12 115 B8
Heath La
Buttermere SN8 185 C7
Great Somerford SN15 43 D2
Heath Rd SP2 145 D4
Heath Sq 1 SP4 197 E6
Heath View Dr SP2 145 C3
Heath Way SN3 51 B8
Heathcote Rd SN12 94 C5
Heather Ave SN12 94 C4
Heather Cl BA13 108 F4
Heather Shaw BA14 105 E8
Heather Way SN11 81 C1
Heathfield SN15 70 E2
Heathfields Way 2 SP7 202 C2
Heathlands The BA12 116 F5
Heathway BA12 115 C8
Heaton Cl SN25 35 A6
Heaven's Gate* BA12 115 C1
Hebden Rd BA15 99 F3
Heddington CE Prim Sch SN11 89 B1
Heddington Cl
Swindon SN2 35 B5
Trowbridge BA14 105 C5
Hedge Row SN15 79 A4
Hedgeditch La GL8 26 D7
Hedges Cl
1 Shipton Bellinger SP9 199 C8
Swindon SN3 36 B3
Hedges The 4 SN4 163 A6
Hedgesparrow La SN13 83 F8
Hei-lin Way 2 SP11 192 A5
Heights The SN1 50 A4
Helena Rd SN25 34 C8
Helena Terr 7 SP1 146 B1
Helmdon Rd BA14 101 A1
Helmsdale SN25 34 F4
Helmsdale Wlk SN3 51 A4
Helps Well Rd BA14 102 B2
Helston Rd SN3 51 A5
Henderson Cl BA14 105 B7
Hendon Pl SN12 94 E1
Henfords Marsh BA12 117 B4
Hengest Cl 5 SP10 193 C2
Henley Dr SN6 23 A7
Henley La SN13 83 C4
Henley Rd 2 SN3 51 A4
Henman Cl
Devizes SN10 214 B4
Swindon SN25 35 A5
Henn La SN15 57 C6
Henry St 9 Swindon SN1 50 B6
1 Swindon SN1 50 B6
Henry's Garth 7 SN8 183 D8
Henset Village* SN8 175 E7
Hepworth Rd 5 SN25 34 F6
Herbert Rd
3 Redlynch SP5 211 C7
Salisbury SP2 145 C3
Hercules Way 1 SN12 178 B8
Herd St SN8 213 D4
Hereford Cl SN14 78 A5
Hereford Lawns SN3 50 F3
Herepath SN8 167 C1
Herman Miller Ind Est SN14 78 B5
Hermitage La SN2 35 E3
Hernsham St SP7 203 C4
Heron Cl SN11 81 D3
Heron Way SN14 77 F6
Heron Wlk 12 SP4 198 C7
Heronbridge Cl 2 SN5 49 C5
Herongate RG17 177 B8
Herons Ct 6 SN12 178 B8
Heronscroft SN3 51 D7
Heronslade BA12 117 D5
Heronswood SP2 152 A5
Herschell Cl SN25 34 B7
Hertford Cl
1 Fordingbridge SP6 210 D2
4 Swindon SN3 50 F6
Hesketh Cres SN1 50 D3
Hewitt Cl Swindon SN3 51 C4
Trowbridge BA14 105 E7
Hewlett Cl SN15 79 A5
Hexham Cl
4 Chippenham SN14 77 F6
Swindon SN5 49 B5
Heyford Cl 8 SP4 217 E3
Heytesbury CE Prim Sch BA12 194 C5
Heytsbury Gdns 4 SN5 48 F4
Heywood Cl SN2 35 B5
Heywood Prep Sch SN13 77 A2
Hicks Cl SN4 64 A6
Hidcot Ct SN25 34 E7
High Bannerdown BA1 82 B4
High Clear Down Nature Reserve* SN8 169 D7
High La SP5 205 B4
High Lawn SN10 179 D8
High Mead SN4 47 F2
High Rd
Ashton Keynes SN6 6 F1
Bishopstone SP5 205 E4
Britford SP5 152 D4
High St Alderbury SP5 153 C3
Amesbury SP4 217 A3
Ansty SP3 203 F6
Ashbury SN6 164 A7
Ashmore SP5 206 E4
Avebury SN8 173 B8
Badminton GL9 38 E2
Bath BA1 82 D2
Berwick St James SP3 196 F2
Bishopstone SN6 163 E6
Box SN13 83 C5
Broad Blunsdon SN26 21 B1
Bromham SN15 96 A7
Bulford SP4 217 D8
Burbage SN8 175 C1
Calne SN11 81 B3
Chapmanslade BA13 111 B4
Cheverell Magna SN10 179 C1
Chippenham SN15 78 D7
Chiseldown SN4 65 D4
Codford BA12 195 A2
Colerne SN14 75 B3
Collingbourne Ducis SN8 191 E8
Compton Chamberlayne SP3 205 A8
Corsham SN13 77 A1
Cricklade SN6 19 E8
Damerham SP6 209 F3
Downton SP5 211 B8
Durrington/Bulford SP4 198 B7
Erlestoke SN10 187 A8
Figheldean SP4 190 B1
24 Fordingbridge SP6 210 D1
Fovant SP3 204 E7
Great Bedwyn SN8 176 B3
Heytesbury BA12 194 C5
Highworth SN6 23 A5
Hindon SP3 200 A4
Hinton Charterhouse BA2 98 E1
Hungerford RG17 177 B7
Idmiston SP4 133 D5
Kempsford GL7 10 C7
Lacock SN15 86 D5
Lambourn RG17 164 F3
Lechlade GL7 2 C4
Limpley Stoke BA2 99 B5
Little Bedwyn SN8 176 D4
Littleton Panell SN10 187 D8
9 Ludgershall SP11 192 A5
Maiden Bradley with Yarnfield BA12 118 E3
Malmesbury SN16 28 A3
Market Lavington SN10 179 F1
Marlborough SN8 213 A1
Melksham SN12 94 A4
Meysey Hampton GL7 1 A5
Netheravon SP4 190 A3
Ogbourne St George SN8 168 F5
Pewsey SN9 215 D5
Pitton & Farley SP5 148 C3
Porton SP4 133 D6
Purton SN5 33 B4
Ramsbury SN8 170 B2
Rode BA11 103 F1
Rowde SN10 96 D2
Salisbury SP1 152 A8
Seend SN12 178 E8
Semington BA14 102 F6
18 Shaftesbury SP7 202 C1
Sherston SN16 40 C8
Shipton Bellinger SP9 199 D8
Shrewton SP3 196 E7
Sixpenny Handley SP5 208 A4
South Cerney GL7 6 F6
Steeple Ashton BA14 178 A3
Stourton with Gasper BA12 123 F1
Sutton Benger SN15 57 C2
Sutton Veny BA12 117 F1
Swindon SN25 34 E4
Swindon SN3 50 D4
Tilshead SP3 188 B2
Tisbury SP3 203 E8
Upavon SN9 181 F2
Urchfont SN10 180 C4
Wanborough SN4 163 B6
Warminster BA12 117 A7
West Lavington SN10 179 D1
Westbury BA13 109 A3
Winterbourne Stoke SP3 197 A4
Woodgreen SP6 211 A4
Wootton Bassett SN4 47 D1
High St *continued*
Worton SN10 179 B4
Wroughton SN4 64 A5
Wylye BA12 201 E8
Zeale SP8 137 F3
High St Brow SN8 169 A6
High View Cl SP3 203 E7
Highbury Ave SP2 145 E2
Highbury Cl 2 SP2 145 E2
Highbury Pk BA12 117 C6
Highbury Prim Sch SP2 145 E2
Highclere Ave SN3 50 F4
Highdown Way SN25 35 A7
Higher Barn Cl SP7 206 B7
Higher Blandford Rd 2 SP7 202 D1
Higher Mere Pk* BA12 202 A8
Highfield SN15 96 C7
Highfield Cl BA14 102 F5
Highfield Cres SP5 149 B6
Highfield La 10 SP5 211 C7
Highfield Rd
Amesbury SP4 217 B3
Bradford-on-Avon BA15 100 D7
Salisbury SP2 145 E2
Highfield Rise 1 SP3 196 F6
Highfold SN4 47 F1
Highgate Cottage SN4 46 F5
Highgrove Cl SN11 81 D2
Highland Cl 8 SN5 49 A7
Highland View SP2 130 A2
Highlands SN10 179 D5
Highlands Cl SN13 84 A8
Highlands Rd SP2 152 A6
Highlands Way SP5 161 D4
Highmoor Copse SN5 34 A1
Highnam Cl SN3 36 A1
Highridge Cl SN5 33 A3
Highway Comm SN11 166 B6
Highway The SP5 158 F5
Highwood Cl 4 SN2 34 D4
Highworth Ind Est SN6 23 A7
Highworth Rd
Highworth SN6 22 D1
Shrivenham SN6 23 E1
South Marston SN3 36 E6
Highworth Recn Ctr SN6 22 F5
Highworth Warneford Sch SN6 23 A5
Hill Beech Rd SP9 216 E7
Hill Cl 4 SP3 203 E8
Hill Cnr Rd SN15 70 E2
Hill Deverill Manor* BA12 120 F5
Hill Deverill Medieval Village of* BA12 120 F5
Hill Hayes La SN14 41 E1
Hill Rd
Norton Bavant BA12 194 A4
Salisbury SP1 146 E2
Hill Rise SN15 70 E2
Hill Side SP3 129 E8
Hill St BA14 101 C1
Hill The
Limpley Stoke BA2 99 C5
Little Somerford SN15 44 B6
Hill Top Ave SP9 216 C8
Hill Top Cl SP4 190 B2
Hill View SN8 181 B8
Hill View Rd
6 Salisbury SP1 152 B8
Swindon SN3 36 C1
Hillary Cl SN25 35 C4
Hillbourne Cl BA12 117 B7
Hillcote Hospl SP1 146 C1
Hillcrest Colerne SN14 75 C6
Malmesbury SN16 28 B2
Hillcroft SN11 81 C2
Hilldrop Cl 1 SN8 170 B2
Hilldrop La
Lambourn RG17 171 A6
Ramsbury SN8 169 F3
Hilliers Yd SN8 213 D3
Hillingdon Rd SN3 51 B4
Hillmead Dr SN5 34 B1
Hillmead Ent Pk SN5 49 B8
Hillocks The SN4 60 B5
Hillside Leigh SN6 18 C5
Nettleton SN14 53 A4
Hillside Ave SN1 50 A4
Hillside Cl
Heddington SN11 89 B1
Mere BA12 138 E5
West Tytherley SP5 155 F2
Hillside Ct SN1 50 A4
Hillside Dr SP4 133 D3
Hillside Pk BA13 109 B3
Hillside Rd
4 Hungerford RG17 177 B6
South Newton SP2 130 B2
Hillside Villas SP10 193 D1
Hillside Way SN26 21 A1
Hilltop Cl 2 SP3 196 F6
Hilltop Way SP1 146 A5
Hillview SP5 204 C3
Hillview Cl SP4 217 B4
Hillwell SN16 15 B2
Hillwood Cl BA12 116 F5
Hillwood La BA12 116 F5
Hillwood Rd 15 SN8 170 A6
Hillworth Gdns SN10 214 A3
Hillworth Rd SN10 214 A2
Hillyard Cl 3 SN5 48 F4
Hilmarton Ave 1 SN2 35 C5
Hilmarton Prim Sch SN11 166 A6
Hilperton CE Prim Sch BA14 102 A3
Hilperton Dr BA14 102 A2
Hilperton Rd BA14 101 E1
Hinde's Meadow SP3 196 F7
Hindon La SP3 200 D1
Hindon Rd
Chilmark SP3 201 B3
East Knoyle SP3 141 C2
Kingston Deverill BA12 126 D7
Hinkson Cl SN25 34 F8
Hinton Hill
Bishopstone SN4 163 D6
Hinton Charterhouse BA2 98 A1
Hinton Ho* BA2 98 E1
Hinton La BA14 178 A5
Hinton Priory* BA2 98 F3
Hinton Springs SN6 163 D6
Hinton St SN2 50 D8
Hitchings Skilling SN14 75 B3
Hither Cl SN14 78 A8
Hither Spring SN13 84 F8
Hither Way SN15 86 D5
Hoadley Gn SP1 146 D4
Hobbes Cl SN16 27 F4
Hobbs Hill BA14 178 B5
Hobbs Wlk SN13 77 A1
Hobhouse Cl BA15 100 E4
Hobley Dr SN3 36 A3
Hocketts Cl SN15 60 A3
Hodds Hill SN5 34 B2
Hodge La SN16 27 F4
Hodges Barn Gdns* GL8 26 F8
Hodson Rd SN4 65 C4
Hoggington La BA14 104 D4
Hoggs La SN5 33 A4
Holbein Cl 6 SN5 49 A5
Holbein Ct SN5 49 A5
Holbein Field 12 SN5 49 A4
Holbein Mews 5 SN5 49 A5
Holbein Pl SN5 49 A5
Holbein Sq 10 SN5 49 A4
Holbein Wlk 11 SN5 49 A4
Holborn Hill OX12 165 E8
Holbrook La BA14 105 D6
Holbrook Prim Sch BA14 105 D6
Holbrook Vale SN12 93 F1
Holbrook Way SN1 50 B6
Holcombe La BA2 82 A1
Holdcroft Cl SN26 21 C2
Holden Cres SN25 35 A6
Holden Garson Rd SN25 35 B6
Holders Rd SP4 217 C4
Holford Cres GL7 10 E6
Holinshead Pl 4 SN5 49 A5
Holinshed Mews 3 SN5 49 A5
Holland Cl SN15 79 A4
Holland Dr 11 SP10 193 D2
Holliday Cl SN25 35 A6
Hollies La BA1 82 A6
Hollins Moor SN3 51 D2
Hollis Gdns SN14 39 E4
Hollis Way BA14 104 F3
Hollow La SN8 184 A7
Hollow St SN15 43 F2
Hollow The
Bratton BA13 186 A7
Chirton SN10 180 F4
Corsley BA12 111 B1
Dilton Marsh BA13 112 C8
Shrewton SP3 196 E7
Sixpenny Handley SP5 208 A4
Steeple Langford SP3 128 C5
Hollow Way SN15 59 D3
Holloway SN16 28 A3
Holloway Hill SN14 66 E8
Holloway La SP3 141 B1
Hollows Cl SP2 151 F6
Hollows The SP2 144 B4
Holly Cl Calne SN11 81 C1
Pewsey SN9 215 D6
Swindon SN2 35 A2
Holly Ct BA11 110 B7
Holly Dr SN14 74 F6
Hollybush Cl
Acton Turville GL9 53 A6
Chippenham Without SN14 70 A2
Winsley BA15 99 E7
Hollybush La SN9 215 D6
Hollybush Rd BA12 117 A8
Holmbury Cl BA11 110 C6
Holme La 7 BA13 186 B7
Holmeleaze BA14 178 A4
Holmes Cl SN15 78 F4
Holmfield 1 SN10 187 E8
Holmleigh SN25 34 E4
Holmoak Ct SN3 50 D4
Holt La Tangley SP11 193 B8
Teffont SP3 201 C2
Holt Rd
Bradford-on-Avon BA15 100 E6
Witham Friary BA11 123 C8
Holt VC Prim Sch BA14 92 F1
Holy Family Cath Prim Sch SN3 51 B6
Holy Rd Church* SN3 50 E4
Holy Rood Cath Inf Sch SN1 50 C5

Holy Rood Cath Jun Sch
SN3 ....**50** D5
Holy Trinity CE Prim Sch
Calne SN11 ....**81** C1
Cheverell Magna SN10 ...**187** B8
Holyrood Cl BA14 .....**105** B5
Home Cl Chiseldown SN4 ..**65** C4
Trowbridge BA14 ......**105** D7
Home Farm Cl
Heddington SN11 ......**89** B1
Mildenhall SN8 ....**175** B8
Steeple Ashton BA14 ..**178** A3
Home Farm Gdns 10
SP10 ....**193** C2
Home Farm Rd SP2 ....**144** C1
Home Fields SN14 .....**68** F5
Home Gd Cricklade SN6 ..**19** C8
Wootton Bassett SN4 ...**48** A2
Home Mill Bldgs
BA14 ....**105** D8
Homefarm SN6 ....**22** F6
Homefield Mere BA12 ..**138** F5
Motcombe SP7 ....**202** C2
Wootton Bassett SN4 ....**47** E2
Homefield Way RG17 ..**177** B7
Homefields
Longbridge Deverill
BA12 ....**120** F6
Marlborough SN8 ......**213** F2
Homelands The 1
BA12 ....**116** E5
Homes Mead SN13 .....**76** D1
Homington Rd
Britford SP5 ....**151** D3
Coombe Bissett SP5 ....**157** B8
Honey Garston SN11 ...**81** C3
Honey Hill 2 RG17 ....**165** A2
Honey Knob Hill SN14 ..**55** F1
Honey La Norton SN16 ..**41** E6
Westbury BA13 ....**112** D8
Honeybone Wlk SN3 ...**51** E7
Honeybrook Cl SN14 ...**78** B8
Honeybunch Cnr SN6 ..**164** C6
Honeyfields 10 RG17 ...**177** B7
Honeylight View 3 SN25 ..**35** A6
Honeymans Cl BA14 ...**105** F8
Honeymead SN11 ......**81** C3
Honeysuckle Cl
Calne Without SN11 .....**80** F4
Chippenham Without
SN14 ....**70** B3
Swindon SN25 ....**34** D5
4 Trowbridge BA14 ...**105** E7
Honiton Rd SN3 ....**51** B5
Hook Cl SN5 ....**34** A1
Hook St Hook SN4 ......**47** F6
Swindon SN5 ....**48** F4
Hooks Hill SN5 ....**33** C4
Hooks La SN10 ....**179** A4
Hookwood La SP11 ....**192** E8
Hoopers Pl SN1 ....**50** D4
Hop Gdns The SP5 ....**161** C3
Hopgood Cl SN10 ......**214** F6
Hopkinson Way SP10 ..**193** B1
Hops Cl SP3 ....**201** A3
Hopton Cl SN5 ....**49** B3
Hopton Pk Ind Est
SN10 ....**214** E7
Hopton Rd SN10 ....**214** D6
Horace St SN2 ....**49** F7
Horcott Rd Fairford GL7 ..**1** F6
Roughmoor SN5 ....**34** B2
Horder Mews SN3 .....**50** D4
Horham Cres SN3 ......**51** A4
Horn's La SN4 ....**167** B8
Hornbeam Cl 1 BA11 ..**110** C6
Hornbeam Cres SN12 ...**94** A3
Hornbeam Ct SN2 ......**35** B2
Hornbury Cl SN16 .....**17** A2
Hornbury Hill SN16 ....**17** A2
Hornchurch Rd 20 SN12 ..**178** B8
Horne Rd SP4 ....**198** E6
Horningsham Prim Sch
BA12 ....**119** B7
Hornsey Gdns SN2 .....**36** A5
Horse Barrow★ SP4 ..**133** D3
Horse Fair La SN6 .....**19** E8
Horse Rd BA14 ....**101** F4
Horse Shoe La SP3 ....**142** C3
Horsebrook Pk SN11 ...**81** B2
Horsebrook The SN11 ..**81** C2
Horsefair La SN15 .....**59** C3
Horsell Cl 2 SN4 ......**47** E2
Horseponds 8 SP7 ....**202** B2
Horsepool SN15 ....**96** B8
Horseshoe Cres SN5 ...**34** A1
Horseshoe La SP11 ....**193** F8
Horton Ave SN10 ......**214** E6
Horton Cl BA15 ....**100** E4
Horton Rd
Bishops Cannings SN10 ..**172** A2
Devizes SN10 ....**214** F7
Swindon SN2 ....**35** E6
Hospital Rd BA13 ......**109** A2
Hossil La SN6 ....**22** B1
Houldsworth Ave
BA12 ....**117** D8
Howard Cl SN3 ....**51** D6
Howard-Vyse Rd SP4 ..**197** F7
Howgare Rd SP5 ......**205** B2
Hread Parkway Sch
SN2 ....**34** E3
Hubble View SN5 ......**34** B6
Hubert Hamilton Rd
SP4 ....**198** E6

Huddleston Cl SN2 .....**50** D8
Hudson Rd
Amesbury SP4 ....**217** C4
Malmesbury SN16 .....**27** F4
Salisbury SP1 ....**145** F3
Hudson Way SN5 ......**35** A5
Hudswell La SN13 .....**84** C8
Hughes Cl SN8 ....**213** A2
Hughes St SN2 ....**49** F7
Hugo Dr SN25 ....**35** A6
Hulbert Cl SN13 ....**76** E1
Hullavington Airfield
SN14 ....**56** A7
Hullavington CE Prim Sch
SN14 ....**41** F1
Hulse Rd SP1 ....**146** A2
Humber La SP9 ....**216** B4
Humber Rd SN12 .....**94** D5
Humphrey's La 3 RG17 ..**171** E7
Hungerford Ave SN14 ..**78** A5
Hungerford Ave SP4 ..**105** A7
Hungerford City Prim Sch
RG17 ....**177** B7
Hungerford Hill
Great Shefford RG17 ..**171** F4
Lambourn RG17 ......**165** A1
Hungerford La
Andover SP10 ....**193** E3
Chute SP11 ....**185** A1
Kintbury RG17 ....**177** F6
Tangley SP11 ....**193** A8
Hungerford Leisure Ctr
RG17 ....**177** B6
Hungerford Rd
Buttermere SN8 ......**185** B7
Calne SN11 ....**81** B4
Chippenham SN15 .....**70** D1
Grafton SN8 ....**184** A7
Hungerford RG17 .....**177** D6
Hungerford Sta RG17 ..**177** C7
Hunsdon Rd SN3 ....**51** A6
Hunt Cl The BA14 .....**102** F5
Hunt St SN1 ....**50** C5
Huntenhull La BA13 ...**111** D4
Hunter's Gr SN2 ....**35** B1
Hunters Chase BA13 ...**108** F2
Hunters Mead SP7 ....**202** A5
Hunters Meadow SN4 ..**68** F5
Huntingdon Pl BA15 ...**100** C7
Huntingdon Rise
BA15 ....**100** C7
Huntingdon St BA15 ...**100** C8
Huntingdon Way SN14 ..**78** A6
Huntley Cl SN3 ....**50** F7
Hunts Hill SN26 ....**21** B2
Hunts Mead SN15 .....**96** A7
Hunts Mill Rd SN4 .....**61** A8
Hunts Rise SN3 ....**36** C7
Huntsland SN4 ....**47** F2
Hurdcott La SP4 ......**146** F8
Hurley Cl 5 SP4 ......**217** D3
Hurricane Rd SN12 ....**94** C1
Hurst Cres SN2 ....**35** C3
Hurst's La SN9 ....**181** C7
Huxley Ct GL7 ....**7** A7
Hyam Cotts SN16 .....**27** C4
Hyde La
Marlborough SN8 .....**213** C3
Purton SN5 ....**33** C4
Hyde Rd Swindon SN25 ..**35** D6
Trowbridge BA14 .....**101** C2
Hyde The SN5 ....**33** D4
Hylder Cl SN2 ....**34** D4
Hyson Cres 6 SP11 ...**192** B5
Hysopp Cl SN2 ....**34** C4
Hythe Rd SN1 ....**50** B5

Icknield Sch SP10 .....**193** F1
Icknield Way
Andover SP10 ....**193** E3
Bishopstone SN6 .....**163** E6
Icomb Cl SN5 ....**49** C4
Idlebush Barrow★
SN4 ....**164** E7
Idmiston CE Prim Sch
SP4 ....**133** C6
Idmiston Rd SP4 ......**133** E6
Idovers Dr SN5 ....**49** C4
Idstone Hill SN6 ......**163** F7
Idstone Rd SN6 ......**164** A7
Iffley Rd SN2 ....**49** F8
Iford Fields BA15 ......**99** E3
Iford Hill BA15 ....**99** E2
Iford La BA15 ....**99** D3
Iford Manor★ BA15 ...**99** E3
Iles La SN14 ....**73** F7
Ilkeston Rd SN25 ......**34** C7
Ilynton Ave SP5 ......**148** C2
Imber Ave
Amesbury SP4 ....**217** D2
Warminster BA12 .....**117** C7
Imber Pl SP3 ....**188** B3
Imber Rd Bratton BA12 ..**186** C6
10 Shaftesbury SP7 ...**202** D2
Warminster BA12 .....**117** D8
Imber Wlk SN2 ....**35** B6
Imberwood Cl BA12 ...**117** C7
Imby Cl BA12 ....**117** F1
India Ave SP2 ....**145** E2
Indigo Gdns BA13 ....**108** F3
Indigo La BA13 ....**108** F3
Ingles Edge RG17 .....**177** E2
Inglesham Cl 3 BA14 ..**105** D5
Inglesham Rd SN25 ....**34** D8
Inglesham Village★ SN6 ..**2** B1
Inglewood Rd RG17 ...**177** E5

Ingram Pl BA13 ....**108** F4
Ingram Rd SN12 ....**94** D5
Ingram St SN16 ....**28** A3
Inkpen Prim Sch
RG17 ....**177** E3
Inkpen Rd RG17 ....**177** C5
Inlands Cl SN9 ....**215** C5
Inmarsh La SN12 .....**178** E7
Inmead BA13 ....**186** C8
Innox Mill Cl BA14 ....**101** B1
Innox Rd BA14 ....**101** B1
Intercity Trad Est SN12 ..**94** A5
Inverary Rd SN4 ....**64** A7
Ipswich St SN2 ....**50** C8
Ironstone Cl SN25 .....**34** E7
Irston Way 4 SN5 ......**49** B4
Irving Way SN3 ....**213** C2
Isbury Rd SN8 ....**213** E2
Isis Cl Calne SN11 .....**81** A4
Swindon SN25 ....**35** A3
Island The SN10 ......**214** B3
Islandsmead SN3 .....**51** C6
Islay Cres SN6 ....**22** F6
Isles Rd 6 SN8 ....**170** B2
Islington BA14 ....**101** D1
Islington St SN1 ....**50** C6
Itchen Cl 2 SO51 .....**212** F6
Ivies The SN9 ....**181** F5
Ivy Fields SN13 ......**77** A2
Ivy La
Broad Blunsdon SN26 ...**21** B2
Chippenham SN15 .....**78** D7
South Wraxall BA15 ...**91** E5
Ivy La Sch SN15 ......**78** D8
Ivy Mead BA12 ....**139** B5
Ivy Rd SN15 ....**78** D7
Ivy Rd Ind Est SN15 ..**78** D7
Ivy St SN12 ....**152** B8
Ivy Terr BA15 ....**100** D7
Ixworth Cl 10 SN5 ....**49** A7

Jack Paul Cl BA12 .....**139** A6
Jack Thorne Cl SN5 ...**34** A2
Jack's Hedge Cnr
BH21 ....**208** F2
Jackaments Barn GL7 ..**4** B6
Jacksom's La SN15 ....**70** D5
Jackson Cl SN10 ......**214** C2
Jacobs Wlk SN3 ......**51** D4
Jagdalik Rd SP9 ......**216** C4
Jaggard View SP4 ....**217** C3
Jaggards La SN13 .....**84** D5
James Cl SN15 ....**79** A4
James Rd SN4 ....**217** C4
James St Salisbury SP2 ..**145** F1
Trowbridge BA14 ....**101** D2
James Watt Cl SN2 ...**50** A7
James's Hill BA10 ....**122** A7
Jamrud Rd SP9 ....**216** B5
Jarvis St SN9 ....**181** F2
Jasmine Cl Calne SN11 ..**81** B1
Chippenham SN14 ....**70** A1
Swindon SN2 ....**34** D4
Jasmine Way BA14 ...**105** E2
Javelin Cl 4 SP4 .....**217** D3
Jay Cl BA11 ....**110** B6
Jeanneau Cl 24 SP7 ..**202** C2
Jefferies Ave SN2 .....**35** D2
Jefferies Cl SN8 ......**213** B2
Jellicoe Ct SP10 ......**193** F1
Jenkins St BA14 ......**101** C1
Jenner Cl SN4 ....**163** A6
Jennings St SN2 ......**49** F6
Jerram Gall The★
SP1 ....**152** B8
Jersey Pk SN5 ....**49** B8
Jervis Ct 1 SP10 .....**193** F1
Jewel Cl 2 SN5 ......**48** F5
Jewell Cl SP1 ....**146** D4
Joanna Cl 4 SP5 .....**210** F4
Jobbers La SP3 ....**203** E7
Jockey La SN15 ......**96** A7
John Alder Cl SN4 ....**65** C3
John Aubrey Cl SN14 ...**68** F6
John Bentley Sch
Calne SN11 ....**81** B1
Calne SN11 ....**89** B8
John Betjeman Cl 1
SN16 ....**28** A5
John French Way SP4 ..**217** E8
John Gay Rd 5 SP4 ...**217** B3
John Herring Cres SN3 ..**36** A1
John Ivie Ctr Pru SP1 ..**152** B7
John O'Gaunt Com Tech Coll
RG17 ....**177** B6
John of Gaunt Rd GL7 ..**10** D6
John of Gaunt Sch The
BA14 ....**105** B8
John Rennie Cl
Bradford-on-Avon BA15 ..**100** E4
Devizes SN10 ....**214** A2
John Rumble Cl SN10 ..**214** C5
John St SN1 ....**50** B6
Johnson Way SP11 ...**192** A5
Joiner La SN1 ....**50** D4
Jole Cl SN2 ....**35** E5
Joles La BA11 ....**110** F1
Jolliffe St 8 SN1 .....**50** A5
Jone's Mill Nature Reserve★
SN9 ....**215** D7
Jones Hill BA15 ......**100** C5
Jordan Cl SN15 ......**78** F5
Joseph St 5 SN1 .....**50** A5
Joule Rd 3 SP10 ....**193** B1

Joyce Cl SN25 ....**35** A6
Jubb's La SN8 ....**169** A5
Jubilee Cl
Bermerton Heath SP2 ..**145** C3
3 Sandleheath SP6 ...**210** C1
Westbury BA13 ......**109** A3
Jubilee Ct
North Tidworth SP9 ...**216** D7
3 Salisbury SP2 .....**145** F2
Jubilee Gdns GL7 .....**6** F7
Jubilee Hill SP4 ......**197** F1
Jubilee Rd
Devizes SN10 ....**214** D3
Sandleheath SP6 .....**210** C1
Swindon SN2 ....**34** D3
Juggler's La SN11 ....**166** C2
Juliana Cl 2 SN5 .....**49** A7
Juniper Cl SN3 ....**51** B8
Juniper Dr SP1 ....**146** A5
Juniper Rd SP5 ......**148** C2
Juno Way SN1 ....**49** F4
Junction Rd
Alderbury SP5 ....**153** E3
Bradford-on-Avon BA15 ..**100** D6
Juniper Cl SN3 ....**51** B8
Jutland Cres 3 SP10 ..**193** D2

Kandahar SN8 ....**170** A7
Kandy Rd 3 SP4 .....**198** E6
Karachi Cl SP9 ....**216** C7
Karslake Cl 6 SN3 ....**51** C4
Kashmir Rd 1 SP4 ...**198** E6
Katherine House Gall★
SN8 ....**213** E2
Katherine's Wlk GL7 ...**2** D4
Katifer La SN16 ....**28** A3
Keates Cl SN4 ....**101** C1
Keats Cl SN4 ....**47** F3
Keats Cres SN2 ....**35** F4
Keble Cl Lechlade GL7 ..**2** C7
Swindon SN3 ....**51** C7
Keels SN11 ....**8** C1
Keevil Airfield BA14 ..**178** C4
Keevil Ave SN11 ......**81** A3
Keevil CE Prim Sch
BA14 ....**178** B5
Kelham Cl 3 SN3 .....**50** F4
Kelham Gdns SN8 ....**213** E3
Kellsborough Rd SN4 ...**63** F7
Kelly Gdns SN11 .....**34** F6
Kelmscot Rd SN25 ....**35** C3
Kelsey Rd SP1 ....**146** B1
Kelso Ct 3 SN14 .....**78** A5
Kelston Rd SN8 ......**176** C4
Kelvin Rd SN3 ....**51** A7
Kemble Bsns Pk GL7 ...**4** A3
Kemble Dr SN2 ....**50** A7
Kemble Sta GL7 ......**4** F8
Kembles Cl SN16 .....**28** C2
Kembrey Bsns Pk SN2 ..**35** E2
Kembrey St SN2 ......**35** D2
Kemerton Wlk SN3 ...**51** A3
Kemmel Rd SP11 .....**191** F4
Kemp Cl SN10 ....**214** C3
Kemp's La BA11 ......**110** F7
Kempsfield SN10 .....**214** C1
Kempton Pk Ct 10 SN14 ..**77** F6
Ken Savage Cl SN3 ...**51** A6
Kendal SN5 ....**49** B4
Kendrick Cl BA13 ....**109** A3
Kendrick Ind Est SN2 ...**49** E8
Kenilworth Gdns SN12 ..**94** B3
Kenilworth Lawns SN3 ..**50** F3
Kennedy Ave SN12 ...**85** D1
Kennedy Dr SN3 .....**51** D4
Kennedy Meadow
RG17 ....**177** B6
Kennel Dr GL9 ....**38** E2
Kennet & Avon Canal Mus
The★ SN10 ....**214** B4
Kennet Ave SN25 ....**35** B3
Kennet Cl
Melksham SN12 ....**94** A6
Warminster BA12 .....**117** A5
Kennet Ct RG17 ......**177** C8
Kennet Gdns BA15 ...**100** D5
Kennet Mews SN8 ...**213** D3
Kennet Pl SN8 ....**213** E3
Kennet Rd
Devizes SN10 ....**214** C2
South Tedworth SP9 ..**216** D6
Wroughton SN4 ......**64** A7
Kennet Way
Hungerford RG17 .....**177** B8
Trowbridge BA14 .....**101** D3
Kennett Valley CE Prim Sch
SN8 ....**173** D8
Kensington Cl SN10 ..**214** D2
Kensington Fields
BA14 ....**104** F7
Kensington Rd 1 SP2 ..**145** F2
Kensington Way SN14 ...**77** F7
Kent Cl SN14 ....**78** A6
Kent End SN6 ....**7** A1
Kent Rd Salisbury SP2 ..**151** E6
Swindon SN1 ....**50** B4
Kenton Cl SN3 ....**51** B6
Kenton Dr BA14 .....**101** C1
Kents Hill SP3 ....**201** A3
Kenwin Cl SN3 ....**36** B2
Kenwood Cl BA14 ....**105** F8
Kerby Ave SP4 ....**190** B3
Kerrs Way SP4 ....**64** A6

Kerry Cl
Derry Hill/Studley SN11 ..**79** F2
Swindon SN5 ....**49** A7
Kershaw Rd SN3 .....**51** C4
Kestrel Dr SN3 ....**51** E6
Keswick Rd SN3 ......**51** B3
Kettle La BA14 ......**106** A2
Ketton Cl BA14 ......**101** A1
Kew Dr 4 BA14 .....**105** A7
Kewlake La SO51 ....**212** F1
Keynes Ctry Pk★ GL7 ..**6** B5
Keynston Rd SN3 .....**50** F5
Keynsham Wlk SN3 ...**51** B4
Kibblewhite Cl SN5 ...**33** B3
Kickdom Cl SP4 ......**217** D2
Kidston Way SN13 ....**84** A8
Kiel Dr SP10 ....**193** D2
Kilben Cl SN5 ....**48** F7
Kilda Rd SN6 ....**22** E7
Kill Barrow (Long Barrow)★
BA12 ....**187** D3
Kiln Cl Alderbury SP5 ..**153** F1
Devizes SN10 ....**214** D3
Kiln La Redlynch SP5 ..**211** D8
Swindon SN2 ....**34** F1
Kilns The SN11 ....**81** C4
Kilsby Dr SN3 ....**51** B8
Kilsyth Cl SN5 ....**49** B5
Kilverts Cl SN14 .....**78** A6
Kimberley Rd SN3 ....**51** A4
Kimbolton Cl 6 SN5 ..**49** A4
Kimmeridge Cl SN3 ..**51** C6
Kimpton Thruxton & Fyfield
CE Prim Sch SP11 ...**192** C1
King Alfred Cl SN9 ...**215** D5
King Alfred St SN15 ...**78** C8
King Alfred Way BA15 ...**99** D7
King Alfred's CE Mid Sch
SP7 ....**202** D2
King Alfred's Way
SP7 ....**202** C2
King Alfreds Cl BA12 ...**126** B7
King Arthur's Way
SP10 ....**193** E2
King Barrow★
Bishopstrow BA12 ....**117** F5
Winterbourne Stoke
SP4 ....**197** C4
King Charles Rd SN5 ...**49** B4
King Henry Dr
Chippenham SN15 ....**79** A4
Swindon SN5 ....**48** F4
King John St SN1 ....**50** D4
King John's House★
SP5 ....**207** B4
King La BA12 ....**116** E5
King Oak★ SN8 ......**175** C4
King St Melksham SN12 ..**94** A3
3 Swindon SN1 .....**50** B6
Warminster BA12 .....**116** E5
Wilton SP2 ....**144** D4
King William St SN1 ...**50** C4
King William St CE Prim Sch
SN1 ....**50** C4
King's House★ SP1 ...**152** A7
King's La SP3 ....**203** F5
King's Rd 5 SP1 .....**146** A2
King's Wall SN16 .....**28** A3
Kingdom Ave BA13 ..**108** C5
Kingdown Com Sch
BA12 ....**117** D6
Kingfisher Cl SP2 ....**152** A5
Kingfisher Dr
Bower Hill SN12 .....**94** D1
Devizes SN10 ....**214** E5
7 Durrington/Bulford
SP4 ....**198** C7
Swindon SN3 ....**51** D7
Westbury BA13 ......**109** A4
Kingfishers 2 SP9 ...**199** D8
Kingham Cl SN14 ....**78** C7
Kings Ave
Chippenham Without
SN14 ....**77** F6
Corsham SN13 ....**76** F2
Highworth SN6 ....**23** A5
Kings Ct 5 BA12 .....**116** E5
Kings Dr SN8 ....**175** C8
Kings Gate SP2 ......**144** E4
Kings Gdns BA14 ....**101** E5
Kings Hill 18 SP7 ....**202** C2
Kings Lodge Prim Sch
SN15 ....**79** A5
Kings Meadow SN16 ...**14** D5
Kings Orch BA12 .....**116** E5
Kings Paddock SP5 ...**149** A5
Kings Rd
Easterton SN10 ......**180** A2
Enham Alamein SP11 ..**193** E4
Market Lavington SN10 ..**179** F2
Kings Rise BA12 .....**116** E5
Kingsbere La 5 SP7 ..**202** D2
Kingsbourne Cl SP4 ...**133** B1
Kingsbury Cl SN12 ...**94** B3
Kingsbury Sq 3 SP2 ..**144** D3
Kingsbury St
Calne SN11 ....**81** B2
Marlborough SN8 ....**213** D3
Kingscote Cl 1 SN5 ...**48** F8
Kingsdown Gr BA1 ...**82** F2
Kingsdown Ind Est SN2 ..**36** A6
Kingsdown La SN25 ...**35** D8
Kingsdown Rd
Stratton St Margaret SN2 ..**36** A6
Swindon SN2 ....**35** F5
3 Trowbridge BA14 ..**105** C5
Kingsdown Sch SN2 ...**35** F5
Kingsettle Hill BA10 ..**122** C2

Kingsfield BA15 . . . . .100 D7
Kingsfield Grange Rd
  BA15 . . . . .100 E7
Kingsford Cl 9 SP5 . . . . .211 C7
Kingshill Rd SN1 . . . . . . .50 A4
Kingsland Rd SP2 . . . . . .145 F2
Kingsley Ave SN4 . . . . . . .47 E3
Kingsley Gdns SN10 . . . .214 C3
Kingsley Pl BA14 . . . . . .100 F1
Kingsley Rd
  Chippenham SN14 . . . . .78 B6
  Devizes SN10 . . . . .214 C3
Kingsley Way SN2 . . . . . .35 D5
Kingsman La 13 SP7 . . . .202 C1
Kingsmanor Wharf
  SN10 . . . . .214 D5
Kingsmead Lechlade GL7 . .2 C5
  Stoford SP2 . . . . .130 A3
Kingsmead House
  SN15 . . . . .44 A5
Kingsmead Mill★ SN15 .43 F6
Kingsthorpe Gr SN3 . . . . .51 C8
Kingston SN16 . . . . .43 F8
Kingston Ave SN3 . . . . . .100 E5
Kingston La BA12 . . . . . .118 F2
Kingston Pk SO51 . . . . . .212 F4
Kingston Rd
  Bradford-on-Avon BA15 . .100 D6
  Shalbourne SN8 . . . . .176 F1
  Swindon SN3 . . . . .51 A4
Kingsway Preshute SN8 . .168 B1
  Wilton SP2 . . . . .144 E5
Kingsway Cl 1 SN3 . . . . .50 F4
Kingswood
  Trowbridge BA14 . . . . . . .104 F6
  Wroughton SN4 . . . . .64 A5
Kingswood Ave SN3 . . . . .51 A5
Kington La SN14 . . . . .56 B4
Kington St Michael CE Prim
  Sch SN14 . . . . .70 A8
Kingway View SN16 . . . . .42 E4
Kintbury Rd RG17 . . . . . .177 F3
Kipling Gdns SN2 . . . . . . .35 A4
Kirby Cl SN3 . . . . .50 F4
Kirby Rd SN13 . . . . .76 E1
Kirkee Rd SP9 . . . . .216 C5
Kirkstall Cl SN5 . . . . .49 C4
Kirktonhill Rd SN5 . . . . . .49 D6
Kishorn Cl 5 SN5 . . . . . . .34 B2
Kitchen Barrow★
  SN10 . . . . .172 E3
Kitchener Rd SP4 . . . . . . .217 B4
Kitchener St SN2 . . . . . . .50 C8
Kite Hill SN4 . . . . .163 A5
Kite's Nest La SP8 . . . . . .137 E2
Kitefield 2 SN6 . . . . .19 D8
Kivel Ct SP2 . . . . .146 A4
Kiwi Prim Sch SP4 . . . . .198 E6
Kiwi Rd 6 SP4 . . . . .198 F7
Kiwi The★ SP4 . . . . .198 F6
Knap Barrow (Long
  Barrow)★ SP6 . . . . .209 D6
Knap Hill (Causewayed
  Enclosure)★ SN8 . . . . .173 E2
Knap La SP3 . . . . .200 F2
Knap The BA14 . . . . .102 A3
Knapp Cl SN2 . . . . .35 A2
Knapp Hill SP5 . . . . .205 A4
Knapp The Calne SN11 . . .81 C3
  Great Bedwyn SN8 . . . . . .176 B3
  7 Shaftesbury SP7 . . . . .202 B2
Knapps The BA14 . . . . . .102 F5
Knighton Barrow (Long
  Barrow)★ SP4 . . . . . . .197 E8
Knighton Rd SP5 . . . . . . .205 C4
Knights Cl
  1 Chippenham SN15 . . . . .78 F4
  West Overton SN8 . . . . . .173 F6
Knights Enham Prim Sch
  SP10 . . . . .193 E2
Knightsbridge Rd
  SP11 . . . . .193 F4
Knockdown Rd SN16 . . . . .25 C1
Knoll Cl OX12 . . . . .165 F8
Knoll The
  12 Aldbourne SN8 . . . . . .170 A6
  Kempsford GL7 . . . . .10 D7
  Westbury BA13 . . . . .109 B4
Knolton Wlk SN3 . . . . . . .51 A4
Knook Barrow (Long
  Barrow)★ BA12 . . . . . .194 F7
Knook Castle★ BA12 . . .195 A7
Knook Manor★ BA12 . . .194 D4
Knowlands SN6 . . . . .23 A7
Knowle The SN13 . . . . . . .84 F8
Knowledge Hill 2 SN8 . .170 B2
Knowsley Rd SN3 . . . . . . .51 A4
Kohat Cl SP9 . . . . .216 B7
Komat Rd SP9 . . . . .216 C5
Kyneton Way SN14 . . . . . .70 A8

L

La Retraite Swan SP1 .146 B2
Labour-in-Vain Hill
  SN11 . . . . .172 A8
Laburnum Dr SN4 . . . . . . .47 E3
Laburnum Cl 3 BA11 . . .110 B7
Laburnum Dr SN12 . . . . . .94 A3
Laburnum Gr BA14 . . . . .105 B6
Laburnum Rd SN2 . . . . . . .35 C3
Lacemakers Rd SN16 . . . .28 A5
Lackham Cir SN14 . . . . . . .78 B6
Lackham Ctry Pk★
  SN15 . . . . .78 F1
Lackham Mus SN15 . . . . .78 F1

Lacock Abbey★ SN15 . .86 D5
Lacock CE Prim Sch
  SN15 . . . . .86 D5
Lacock Gdns BA14 . . . .102 B2
Lacock Pottery★ SN15 .86 D6
Lacock Rd
  Corsham SN13 . . . . .85 D8
  Swindon SN2 . . . . .35 C4
Ladbrook La SN13 . . . . . .77 C1
Ladds La SN15 . . . . .78 E7
Lady Coventry Rd SN15 .78 F7
Lady Diana Ct 15 SP11 . .192 A5
Lady Down View 5 SP3 203 E8
Lady Godley Cl SP9 . . . .216 C5
Lady Jane Wlk 22 SP11 .192 A5
Lady La SN25 . . . . .21 B1
Lady Margaret Hungerford
  Almshouse★ SN13 . . . . .77 A1
Lady Mead SN6 . . . . .19 D8
Ladydown SN11 . . . . .81 B4
Ladyfield Rd SN14 . . . . . .78 B7
Ladysmith SP4 . . . . .133 D3
Ladysmith Rd
  Chiseldon SN4 . . . . .65 D1
  Salisbury SP2 . . . . .145 D3
Ladywood 8 SN10 . . . . . .179 F1
Laggar The SN13 . . . . . . .77 A2
Lagos St 3 SN1 . . . . .50 C7
Lagpond La SP3 . . . . .204 B7
Lahore Cl SP9 . . . . .216 C7
Lahore Rd SP9 . . . . .216 C5
Laines Head SN14 . . . . . .70 C2
Lainesmead Prim Sch
  SN3 . . . . .50 E5
Lainey's Cl SN8 . . . . .213 D4
Lake Group (Tumuli)★
  SP4 . . . . .197 D3
Lake House★ SP4 . . . . . .197 F1
Lake View SN11 . . . . .89 D8
Lakeside Fairford GL7 . . . .1 F6
  South Cerney GL7 . . . . .7 B7
  Swindon SN3 . . . . .50 E3
Lakeside Cl SP10 . . . . . .193 C1
Lamb Ale Gn BA14 . . . . .105 D6
Lambdown App SP11 . . .191 F3
Lambdown Terr
  North Tidworth SP11 . . . .216 F6
  Perham Down SP11 . . . . . .191 F4
Lambert Cl SN5 . . . . .49 B3
Lamberts SN14 . . . . .78 A8
Lambourn Ave SN3 . . . . . .50 E3
Lambourn CE Prim Sch
  RG17 . . . . .165 A1
Lambourn La BA13 . . . . .186 C8
Lambourn Pl 10 RG17 . . .165 A2
Lambourne Cres SN12 . . .94 B4
Lambrok Cl BA14 . . . . . .104 F6
Lambrok Rd BA14 . . . . . .104 F6
Lammas Cl SN11 . . . . . . .166 A6
Lamora Cl 12 SN5 . . . . . .48 F8
Lampeter Rd SN25 . . . . . .34 C6
Lamplighters Wlk
  BA14 . . . . .105 C2
Lanac Rd SN3 . . . . .36 A1
Lancaster Cl 6 RG17 . . .177 B6
Lancaster Mews SN3 . . . .36 C6
Lancaster Pl SN3 . . . . . . .36 C6
Lancaster Rd
  Bower Hill SN12 . . . . .94 B4
  Kempsford GL7 . . . . .10 E6
  Wroughton SN4 . . . . .64 A6
Lancaster Sq
  Hungerford RG17 . . . . . . .177 B6
  Lyneham SN15 . . . . .60 A2
Landale Cl 3 SP11 . . . . .193 E4
Landford CE Prim Sch
  SP5 . . . . .212 C6
Landor Rd SN25 . . . . .34 F8
Lane The SN4 . . . . .163 C7
Lane-side 9 SP7 . . . . . . .202 C2
Lane's Cl SP4 . . . . .217 C4
Lanes End SN13 . . . . .85 D5
Lanes End Hill BA12 . . .115 A8
Lanfear Cl 4 SP4 . . . . . .217 C4
Langdale Dr SN5 . . . . . . .49 B3
Langet GL7 . . . . .6 E6
Langford Gr SN3 . . . . .50 E6
Langford La SP5 . . . . . . .160 A3
Langford Rd
  Great Wishford SP2 . . . . .129 F4
  Trowbridge BA14 . . . . . . .101 C2
Langfords La 3 SP7 . . . .202 B1
Langham Pl BA11 . . . . . .103 F1
Langholm Ave BA12 . . . .116 D6
Langholm Cl BA12 . . . . .116 D6
Langley Fitzurse CE Prim Sch
  SN15 . . . . .70 E6
Langley Gdn SP6 . . . . . .210 E2
Langley Pk SN15 . . . . . . .70 E1
Langley Rd
  Chippenham SN15 . . . . . . .70 E1
  Swindon SN5 . . . . .34 B1
  Trowbridge BA14 . . . . . . .105 C5
Langley Wood National
  Nature Reserve★
  SP5 . . . . .211 F7
Langport Cl 1 SN5 . . . . .49 B4
Langstone Way SN5 . . . . .49 C6
Lanham's Cl BA13 . . . . . .109 A2
Lanhill (Long Barrow)★
  SN14 . . . . .69 B2
Lanhill View SN14 . . . . . .70 B2
Lanhydrock Cl 9 SN5 . . .49 A4
Lansbury Dr SN2 . . . . . . .35 F4
Lansdown Cl
  Melksham SN12 . . . . .94 D6
  Trowbridge BA14 . . . . . . .105 B7
Lansdown Gr SN15 . . . . . .70 D1

Lansdown Rd SN1 . . . . . .50 B4
Lansdowne Cl SN11 . . . . .81 A4
Lansdowne Cres SN11 . . .79 F2
Lansdowne Terr SN10 . .214 A3
Lapwing Cl 1 SN3 . . . . . .51 E6
Lapwing Cres SN14 . . . . .70 B2
Larch Cl SN12 . . . . .94 A3
Larch Gr BA14 . . . . .105 B6
Larch Rd SN14 . . . . .74 F6
Lark Row SP6 . . . . .210 F1
Larchfield Cl BA11 . . . . .110 B7
Larchmore Cl SN25 . . . . .35 A3
Lark Cl SP9 . . . . .216 D7
Lark Down BA14 . . . . . . .101 E1
Larkham Rise SN15 . . . . .78 F6
Larkhill Prim Sch SP4 . .197 E7
Larkhill Rd SP4 . . . . .198 B7
Larkrise Sch BA14 . . . . .101 E1
Larksfield SN3 . . . . .51 C8
Larkspur BA14 . . . . .101 C1
Larmer Tree Gdns★
  SP5 . . . . .207 B3
Late Broads BA15 . . . . . .99 D7
Latimer Gdns SN14 . . . . .41 E1
Latton Cl SN2 . . . . .35 B6
Laughton Way SN25 . . . . .35 A6
Launcelot Cl 22 SP10 . . .193 E2
Laundry La 5 SP7 . . . . . .202 B1
Laura Pl SN13 . . . . .83 F7
Laurel Cl BA11 . . . . .110 B7
Laurel Dr Colerne SN14 . .74 F6
  Marlborough SN8 . . . . . . .213 F2
Laurel Gr BA14 . . . . .105 C6
Laurels The
  Hungerford RG17 . . . . . . .177 C8
  Melksham Without SN12 . . .86 A1
  Westwood BA15 . . . . .99 F3
Laurence Ct 10 SP11 . . .192 A5
Lavender Cl
  4 Trowbridge BA14 . . . . .105 C2
Lavender Ct BA11 . . . . . .110 B7
Lavender Dr SN11 . . . . . . .81 B1
Laverstock Pk SP1 . . . . .146 D1
Laverstock Pk W SP1 . .146 D2
Laverstock Rd SP1 . . . . .146 C1
Laverton Cl 1 BA13 . . . .109 A3
Laverton Gn BA13 . . . . .108 F1
Laverton Rd BA13 . . . . . .108 F1
Lavington Cl 10 SN8 . . . .183 D8
Lavington Comp Sch
  SN10 . . . . .179 E1
Lavington Hill SN10 . . . .187 F8
Lavington La SN10 . . . . .187 E8
Lawn Farm Cl SN9 . . . . .182 E7
Lawn Prim Sch SN3 . . . . .50 F2
Lawns The SN4 . . . . .47 D2
Lawrence Cl
  4 Amesbury SP4 . . . . . . .217 C3
  Devizes SN10 . . . . .214 C1
  Swindon SN3 . . . . .51 C4
Lawrence Mead 3 SN8 .170 B2
Lawrence Rd SP4 . . . . . .197 F7
Lawson Rd 3 SP4 . . . . . .198 A6
Lawton Cl SN3 . . . . .51 A3
Layton La SP7 . . . . .202 C1
Le Marchant Cl 2 SN10 214 D5
Lea & Garsdon CE Prim Sch
  SN16 . . . . .28 F2
Lea Cl SN25 . . . . .35 A7
Lea House SN16 . . . . .28 D1
Leaden Hall Sch SP1 . . .152 A7
Leafield Ind Est SN13 . . .84 E6
Leafield Pl BA14 . . . . . . .100 F1
Leafield Rd SN13 . . . . . . .84 E6
Leafield Way SN13 . . . . . .84 E6
Leafy La SN13 . . . . .76 A1
Leamington Gr SN3 . . . . .50 F2
Leap Gate
  Hilperton BA14 . . . . .102 A1
  Trowbridge BA14 . . . . . . .106 A8
Leatler Cl SP3 . . . . .204 D8
Leaze Rd
  Marlborough SN8 . . . . . . .213 C4
  Melksham SN12 . . . . .94 C6
Leaze The
  Ashton Keynes SN6 . . . . . . .6 F1
  Durrington/Bulford SP4 . .217 E8
  South Cerney GL7 . . . . .6 F6
Lechlade Rd Buscot SN7 . .2 C2
  Highworth SN6 . . . . .23 A7
  Inglesham SN6 . . . . .12 A6
Ledge Rd SN10 . . . . .179 E2
Ledger Hill Cl SP4 . . . . .217 D8
Lee Cres SN15 . . . . .57 C7
Lees Ct SP2 . . . . .145 F2
Legate Cl SN15 . . . . .79 B5
Leicester St SN1 . . . . .50 D6
Leigh Cl BA13 . . . . .108 E1
Leigh La SP3 . . . . .202 E8
Leigh Pk Rd BA15 . . . . . .100 D8
Leigh Rd
  Bradford-on-Avon BA15 . . .91 E1
  Holt BA14 . . . . .92 C1
  Swindon SN2 . . . . .35 C4
  Westbury BA13 . . . . .108 F1
Leighton Ave SN3 . . . . . .50 F4
Leighton Gn BA13 . . . . . .109 A2
Leighton La BA13 . . . . . .109 A1
Leighton Pk N 4 BA13 .108 F1
Leighton Pk Rd 5 BA13 108 F1
Leighton Pk W 2 BA13 .108 F1
Leland Cl 5 SN16 . . . . . . .28 A5
Lena Ct 26 SP11 . . . . . . .192 A5
Lennards The GL7 . . . . . . .7 A7
Lennox Dr SN3 . . . . .50 E6
Lenta Bsns Ctr SN1 . . . . .50 B6
Lenton Cl SN14 . . . . .77 F7

Leonard Cheshire Cl 4
  SP4 . . . . .217 D2
Lesley Anne Skeete Ct
  SN3 . . . . .51 B4
Leslie Cl SN5 . . . . .49 A4
Leslie Rise BA15 . . . . . . .99 F3
Lethbridge Prim Sch
  SN1 . . . . .50 C3
Lethbridge Rd SN1 . . . . . .50 C3
Letterage Rd SN5 . . . . . . .34 A2
Levell Ct 12 SP11 . . . . . .192 A5
Leven SN5 . . . . .49 A7
Leversedge Rd 2 BA11 . .110 A7
Leverton Gate SN3 . . . . . .51 F1
Leverton La SP11 . . . . . .171 B1
Lewington Mews 14
  RG17 . . . . .177 B6
Lewis Cl SN25 . . . . .34 F6
Lewisham Castle★
  SN8 . . . . .169 E4
Lewisham Cl SN25 . . . . . .34 F3
Ley The SN13 . . . . .83 D5
Leylands Rd SN13 . . . . . .76 B1
Leys Hill BA11 . . . . .110 A6
Leys La BA11 . . . . .110 A6
Leystone Cl BA11 . . . . . .110 A6
Lichen Cl 3 SN2 . . . . .34 D4
Lickhill Rd SN11 . . . . .81 A4
Lidbury Camp★ SN9 . . .190 C8
Liddiards Gn SN8 . . . . . .168 F5
Liddington Castle (Fort)★
  SN4 . . . . .163 A2
Liddington St SN2 . . . . . .35 C3
Liddington Way BA14 . . .105 D5
Liden Dr SN3 . . . . .51 D4
Liden Prim Sch SN3 . . . . .51 D3
Lidenbrook 2 SN4 . . . . . .163 A4
Light Cl SN13 . . . . .77 A2
Light's La SP5 . . . . .153 C2
Lightfoot Rd SP4 . . . . . .197 F7
Lightning Rd 1 SP4 . . . .217 D2
Liguiel Cl 9 RG17 . . . . . .177 B6
Lilac Ct SN2 . . . . .35 B2
Lilac Gr BA14 . . . . .105 B5
Lilac Way SN11 . . . . .81 B1
Lilian Lock Gdns SN2 . . .35 C5
Lillywhite Cres 1 SP10 .193 E2
Lily Wlk 11 SP4 . . . . . . .198 C7
Lime Ave Badminton GL9 . .38 C1
  Melksham SN12 . . . . .94 A3
Lime Cl Colerne SN14 . . . .75 A5
  Frome BA11 . . . . .110 B7
Lime Kiln
  SN15 . . . . .60 C2
  Pewsey SN9 . . . . .215 D6
Lime Kiln Way SP2 . . . . .152 A5
Lime Tree Cl SN11 . . . . . .81 A3
Lime Trees SN5 . . . . .58 A2
Limekiln Rd SP11 . . . . . .192 E6
Limes Ave SN2 . . . . .35 B3
Limes Pl SN6 . . . . .8 C4
Limes Rd GL7 . . . . .4 F7
Limes The
  Badminton GL9 . . . . .38 E2
  Motcombe SP7 . . . . .202 A4
  Porton SP4 . . . . .133 E6
  South Ceney SN6 . . . . .7 A6
Limpley Stoke Rd BA15 . .99 D6
Lincoln Gn SN12 . . . . .94 C7
Lincoln Gr SN12 . . . . .94 C1
Lincoln St SN1 . . . . .50 C6
Linden Ave SN2 . . . . .35 C3
Linden Cl Calne SN11 . . . .81 B2
  Colerne SN14 . . . . .74 F6
  Ludgershall SP11 . . . . . . .192 B5
  Salisbury SP1 . . . . .146 D1
Linden Cres BA15 . . . . . .100 A3
Linden Gr 2 SN12 . . . . . .94 A2
Linden Lea GL7 . . . . .8 E8
Linden Pk SP7 . . . . .202 D1
Linden Pl BA14 . . . . .101 B1
Linden Way SN5 . . . . .34 C2
Lindford Rd SP1 . . . . . . .146 D5
Lindisfarne 1 SN4 . . . . . .48 A2
Lindlar Cl 13 SP7 . . . . . .202 C2
Lindley Cl SP9 . . . . .216 D6
Lineacre Cl SN5 . . . . .48 F4
Lingen Cl 12 SP10 . . . . .193 D2
Lingfield Cl 6 SN14 . . . .77 F5
Link Ave SN5 . . . . .49 B5
Link La BA15 . . . . .83 A1
Link Leisure Ctr SN5 . . . .49 B5
Link Rd BA13 . . . . .108 E7
Link Way SP1 . . . . .146 C3
Links The Corsham SN13 . .84 B7
  Pewsey SN9 . . . . .215 B4
Linley Cl SN1 . . . . .50 C2
Linley Rd SN26 . . . . .21 C2
Linnet Way BA11 . . . . . .110 B6
Linnetsdene
  6 Salisbury SP2 . . . . . . .152 A5
  Swindon SN3 . . . . .51 C8
Linslade SN2 . . . . .50 A7
Linslade St SN2 . . . . .49 F6
Linsvale Cl BA11 . . . . . . .110 C5
Linsvale Dr BA11 . . . . . .110 C5
Lipgate SN10 . . . . .180 F8
Liskeard Way SN5 . . . . . .49 B4
Lisle Cl SN5 . . . . .49 A5
Lismore Rd SN6 . . . . .22 E6
Lister Gr BA15 . . . . .99 F3
Lister Rd SN4 . . . . .64 B7
Litchfield Cl 11 SP10 . . .193 C2
Little Ave SN2 . . . . .35 A1

Little Badminton La
  SN16 . . . . .28 F2
Little Brittox SN10 . . . . .214 A3
Little Challows SN14 . . . .76 D7
Little Clarendon★
  SP3 . . . . .201 F2
Little Comm BA14 . . . . .105 D3
Little Content La 17
  SP7 . . . . .202 C2
Little Ct La BA13 . . . . . .186 D8
Little Down SN14 . . . . . . .78 B7
Little Dro SP6 . . . . .211 A4
Little Englands SN15 . . .78 E6
Little Hill BA12 . . . . .116 E2
Little Ingleburn SN16 . . .28 A2
Little Island SN9 . . . . . . .215 B5
Little London
  Heytesbury BA12 . . . . . . .194 C5
  Swindon SN1 . . . . .50 D4
Little Mead SN8 . . . . . . .176 F1
Little Parks BA14 . . . . . . .92 F1
Little Pk Cl SN15 . . . . . . .59 F1
Little Rose La SN26 . . . . .20 F5
Little Sands SN14 . . . . . . .68 F5
Little Woodbury★
  SP5 . . . . .152 B4
Little Woodfalls Dr
  SP5 . . . . .211 C6
Littlecote Cl 3 SN5 . . . .49 D5
Littlecote Rd
  Chippenham SN14 . . . . . . .78 A6
  Froxfield SN8 . . . . .176 D7
Littlecote Roman Villa★
  RG17 . . . . .170 D1
Littledown SP7 . . . . .202 C2
Littlefield La SN7 . . . . . .208 A4
Littlejohn Ave SN12 . . . . .94 C6
Littlemead SN13 . . . . .83 B5
Littlemill La SP6 . . . . . . .209 F3
Littleton Drew La GL9 . . .53 A6
Littleworth La SN12 . . . . .85 C2
Livery Rd
  West Dean SP5 . . . . .155 B7
  Winterslow SP5 . . . . .149 B4
Livia Cl 18 SP10 . . . . . . .193 E2
Lock's Hill BA11 . . . . . . .110 A3
Lock's La SP2 . . . . .145 A3
Locke's Dro SP11 . . . . . .193 E8
Lockeridge Cl BA14 . . . .105 D5
Lockeridge La SN8 . . . . .174 B2
Locking Cl SN12 . . . . . . .178 B8
Locks Cross SN13 . . . . . .84 E5
Locks La SN5 . . . . .33 B5
Locks The SN10 . . . . .179 D8
Locksgreen Cres 1 SN2 .34 E3
Lockside 1 SN5 . . . . .78 F5
Lockswell Cl SN15 . . . . . .79 A4
Loddon Way BA15 . . . . . .100 E5
Lode Hill SP5 . . . . .211 B8
Loder's La SP3 . . . . .204 A5
Lodersfield GL7 . . . . .2 C4
Lodge Cl SN11 . . . . .81 A3
Lodge Ct BA14 . . . . .105 F8
Lodge Dr 6 SP11 . . . . . .192 F1
Lodge Dro SP5 . . . . .211 C6
Lodge Hill BA11 . . . . . . .110 F5
Lodge La SP11 . . . . .192 E6
Lodge Rd
  Chippenham SN15 . . . . . . .79 A5
  Horningsham BA12 . . . . . .119 A8
Lodowicks SN11 . . . . .80 D7
Logan Cl 1 SN3 . . . . .50 E6
Lomond Cl SN5 . . . . .34 B2
London La SN3 . . . . .17 C1
London Rd
  Amesbury SP4 . . . . .217 B4
  Bishops Cannings SN10 . .214 E6
  Box SN13 . . . . .83 D7
  Calne SN11 . . . . .81 B2
  Chippenham SN15 . . . . . . .78 F6
  Marlborough SN8 . . . . . . .213 E2
  Salisbury SP1 . . . . .146 C3
  Shrewton SP3 . . . . .196 F7
London Rd E BA1 . . . . . . .82 A3
London Ride SN8 . . . . . . .176 A5
London St SN1 . . . . .50 B6
Londonderry Gdns
  SP4 . . . . .198 E2
Long Acre SN5 . . . . .33 B4
Long Barrow Rd SN11 . . .81 A3
Long Bottom SP11 . . . . .192 D6
Long Cl
  Chippenham SN15 . . . . . . .78 F6
  Downton SP5 . . . . .211 A8
Long Cl Ave SN13 . . . . . .76 B1
Long Cl W SP5 . . . . .211 A8
Long Cross
  Bramshaw SO43 . . . . .212 C2
  Shaftesbury SP7 . . . . .202 B2
Long Dro Burbage SN8 . .183 D8
  Grimstead SP5 . . . . .154 B4
Long Harry SN8 . . . . .213 F1
Long Hedge RG17 . . . . . .165 B4
Long Hill BA12 . . . . .138 F5
Long Hollow BA13 . . . . . .186 D7
Long La Bourton SP8 . . . .137 B1
  Cann SP7 . . . . .206 A8
Long Leaze La SN12 . . . .94 C3
Long Ridings SN14 . . . . . .70 C2
Long River Rd SN13 . . . .109 D2
Long Row SN6 . . . . .10 B4
Long St SN10 . . . . .214 B3
Long Steeple La SP6 . . . .210 C6
Long Stones★ SN8 . . . . .173 A8

Longbarrow Cross Roads
SP4 ....197 C4
Longcombe Dr BA12 ....115 E3
Longcroft Ave SN10 ...214 C3
Longcroft Cres SN10 ...214 C3
Longcroft Rd SN10 .....214 C3
Longfellow Cl SN25 ....35 A8
Longfellow Cres SN4 ...47 F3
Longfield Cl 11 SP4 ..198 B7
Longfield Rd BA14 .....105 D7
Longfields SN8 ....173 B8
Longfields Wlk SN10 ..214 C2
Longford Castle★
SP5 ....153 A2
Longford Pk★ SP5 .....152 E2
Longford Rd SN10 ......94 A2
Longhill Dr 11 SP2 ....152 B5
Longland SP2 ....145 E1
Longlands BA13 ....186 C7
Longleat Gdns SN2 .....35 C4
Longleat House★
BA12 ....114 F3
Longleat Safari Pk★
BA12 ....115 B4
Longleaze SN4 ....47 E3
Longleaze Prim Sch
SN4 ....47 E3
Longleys Cl SN10 ......214 E2
Longmead SP7 ....202 C2
Longmeadow Prim Sch
BA14 ....105 E7
Longsplatt SN13 ......83 D3
Longstock Ct SN5 ......49 B6
Longstone Rd 11 SN14 ..70 A1
Longthorpe Cl SN5 .....49 D4
Longworth Dr SN25 .....34 B7
Lonsdale SN26 ....21 C2
Lonsdale Gdns SN12 ...94 A2
Loop Rd SN8 ....175 A7
Lopcombe Cnr SP4 .....135 D3
Lopes Way BA13 ....108 F4
Lord's La SN15 ....78 E7
Lord's Mead SN14 ......78 A8
Lords Croft SP4 ....217 B4
Lordsmead Rd BA12 ...139 B4
Lorne St SN1 ....50 A5
Lottage Rd SN8 ....170 A7
Lottage Way 2 SN8 ..170 A7
Lotts The SN6 ....17 F8
Loughborough Cl 11 SN5 48 F4
Louviers Way SN1 ......50 C2
Lovage Way BA12 .....139 B6
Love La Box SN13 .....83 F7
Salisbury SP1 ....152 B8
4 Shaftesbury SP7 ...202 B1
Woodgreen SP6 ....211 A4
Loveage Cl 5 SN2 .....34 D4
Love's La SN8 ....170 B3
Lovel Rd BA12 ....194 E3
Lovell Cl SN3 ....51 D7
Lover's La SN16 ....28 A4
Loveridge Cl
5 Andover SP10 .....193 E2
Swindon SN2 ....35 E6
Loves La BA14 ....104 C7
Lovett Gn SP1 ....146 C4
Low La SN11 ....81 D2
Low Rd SN10 ....179 C1
Lowa Cl SP9 ....216 C6
Lowa Rd SP9 ....216 B6
Lowbourne Inf Sch
SN12 ....94 B5
Lowbourne Jun Sch
SN12 ....94 B4
Lowden SN15 ....78 C7
Lowden Ave SN14 ......78 C8
Lowden Hill SN15 ......78 C7
Lower Alma St SN14 ...105 E8
Lower Backway 7 SP3 ..196 E6
Lower Bartons 30 SP6 ..210 D1
Lower Blandford Rd
Cann SP7 ....206 A8
5 Shaftesbury SP7 ..202 D1
Lower Churchfields
SN8 ....213 D2
Lower Ct BA14 ....101 D1
Lower Densome Wood
SP6 ....211 A4
Lower Folly SP2 ....144 B1
Lower Goatacre SN11 ..166 A7
Lower Gr SP6 ....210 B5
Lower Ho SN5 ....15 B8
Lower Kingsdown Rd
SN13 ....83 A4
Lower Marsh Rd BA12 ..117 A5
Lower N Rd SP5 ....207 C1
Lower Prospect SN8 ...213 E3
Lower Rd Bratton BA13 ..186 B7
Britford SP5 ....152 C5
Coombe Bissett SP5 ...151 C1
Downton SP5 ....159 B4
Edington BA13 ....186 C8
Erlestoke BA13 ....178 F2
Netheravon SP4 ....190 A3
Odstock SP5 ....152 A4
Salisbury SP2 ....144 F2
Lower S Rd SP5 ....207 C4
Lower St
Donhead St Andrew SP7 .203 B3
Netheravon SP4 ....190 A4
Rode BA11 ....103 E1
Salisbury SP2 ....151 E7
Lower Stoke
Limpley Stoke BA2 .....99 A6

Lower Stoke continued
Monkton Combe BA2 .....90 A1
Lower Westbury Rd
BA13 ....109 E5
Lower Wharf SN10 .....214 A4
Lower Woodrow SN12 ..86 F1
Lowes Cl 2 SN5 ....34 B2
Lowmead BA14 ....101 E1
Loxley Cl SN12 ....94 B6
Loxley Wlk SN3 ....51 B3
Loyalty St SN14 ....78 C7
Lubeck Dr 22 SP10 ....193 D2
Lucerne Cl
10 Swindon SN5 ....48 F8
Wootton Bassett SN4 ..47 D4
Lucewood La SP5 ......154 C7
Luckett Way SN11 ......81 C4
Luckington Com Sch
SN14 ....39 E5
Luckington Ct★ SN14 ..39 F5
Lucknam Pk★ SN14 ....75 B6
Luddesdown Rd SN5 ....49 C4
Ludgershall Castle★
SP11 ....192 A6
Ludgershall Rd
Collingbourne Ducis SN8 .191 E8
4 Swindon SN1 ....49 F4
Tidworth SP9 ....216 D7
Ludgershall Sports Club
SP11 ....192 A5
Ludlow Cl
Chippenham SN15 ......79 A5
10 Frome BA11 ....110 C6
Swindon SN3 ....50 F4
Warminster BA12 ......116 F4
Westbury BA13 ....108 F4
Ludmead Rd SN13 ......85 A8
Ludwell Hill SP7 ....203 A1
Ludwell Prim Sch
SP7 ....203 A1
Lugbury (Long Barrow)★
SN14 ....53 E2
Lukas Cl SN25 ....34 F7
Luke St SP7 ....203 E1
Lulworth Rd SN25 ......34 F7
Lumley Cl 2 Swindon SN5 49 A4
Westwood SP2 ....145 B5
Lumley Wlk 8 SP4 .....217 D3
Luxfield Rd BA12 ....116 E7
Lyall Cl SN25 ....34 F8
Lyburn Rd SP5 ....212 A5
Lyddon Way SN25 ......34 F4
Lydford Cl 4 SN5 ......49 A8
Lydiard Fields Bsns Pk
SN5 ....48 E3
Lydiard Millicent CE Prim
Sch SN5 ....48 B8
Lydiard Pk★ SN5 ......48 E6
Lydiard Rd SN14 ....78 A6
Lydiard Way BA14 .....105 D5
Lye The SN12 ....178 E8
Lyes Gr BA13 ....112 B8
Lymers The SN11 ......166 E2
Lynch Cl BA12 ....139 B5
Lynch Field The 5 SN4 .163 A5
Lynch La 6 RG17 ......165 A2
Lynch The SN8 ....176 F1
Lynchets Rd SP4 ......217 B3
Lynchfield Rd 7 SP4 ..217 B3
Lynden Cl SN8 ....184 A7
Lyndhurst Cres SN3 ....51 A6
Lyndhurst Rd
Amesbury SP4 ....217 C3
Landford SP5 ....212 C6
Lyneham Cl SN2 ....35 B6
Lyneham Jun & Infants Sch
SN15 ....60 B2
Lyneham Way BA14 ...105 F8
Lynmouth Rd SN5 ......49 F6
Lynt Farm Cotts SN6 ...12 B6
Lynt Rd SN6 ....12 A5
Lynton Rd SN14 ....34 E1
Lynwood Gr SN2 ....34 D3
Lynwood Rd BA14 .....101 A1
Lyons Wlk 11 SP7 .....202 C1
Lypiatt SN13 ....84 F6
Lypiatt Mead SN13 .....85 A8
Lypiatt Prim Sch SN13 ..84 F6
Lypiatt Rd SN13 ....85 A7
Lysander Rd
Bower Hill SN12 ....94 B1
Laverstock SP4 ....146 C4
Melksham Without SN12 .178 B8
Lysley Cl SN15 ....79 A5
Lyster Rd SP6 ....210 C1
Lytchett Way SN3 ......51 C6
Lytham Cl SN15 ....78 F7

M

MacAdam Way SP10 ...193 B1
MacCullum Rd SP11 ....193 B1
MacKenzie Cl 11 SN3 ..51 D4
Mackintosh Davidson Wood
Nature Reserve★
BA12 ....140 D3
MacKlin Cl 21 RG17 ....177 B7
MacKlin Rd SP2 ....145 E2
MacNeice Dr SN3 ......213 A2
Maddington 2 SP3 .....196 E6
Maddington St SP3 .....196 F2
Maddle Rd RG17 ....164 E4
Maddock's Hill 4 BA12 .116 E5
Maddocks Rd BA14 .....101 D4

Magdalen La BA14 .....104 B7
Magdalen Rd SN4 ......163 A6
Magdalene La 7 SP7 ..202 C1
Magic Rdbt SN1 ....50 E6
Magister Rd SN12 ......94 D1
Magnolia Cl 11 BA11 ...110 C7
Magnolia Ct SN2 ....35 B2
Magnolia Rise
Calne SN11 ....81 B1
Trowbridge BA14 ....105 E7
Magnon Rd BA15 ....100 B7
Magpie La SN3 ....51 E6
Magpie Mews SN6 .....214 B3
Maidavale SN25 ....34 D6
Maiden La SN11 ....166 B1
Maidencroft Cotts GL7 ..10 E6
Maidstone Rd SN1 ......50 B4
Main Rd Amesbury SP4 ..217 D2
Cherhill SN11 ....166 B1
Christian Malford SN15 ..58 E5
Ogbourne St Andrew
SN8 ....213 D8
St Paul Malmesbury Without
SN16 ....42 E4
Sutton Benger SN15 ....57 F2
Main St
Great Hinton BA14 .....178 A6
Westbury BA13 ....108 C6
Main St E BA13 ....108 C6
Maitland Cl SN15 ....79 A4
Maitland Rd SN3 ....51 A7
Majestic Cl 4 SN5 .....49 A7
Maldwyn Cl 9 SN5 .....48 F8
Mall The
South Tedworth SP9 ....216 A4
Swindon SN1 ....50 B3
Mallard Ave SN15 ......60 B1
Mallard Cl
7 Bower Hill SN12 ....178 B8
Calne SN11 ....81 D2
Salisbury SP2 ....151 E1
Swindon SN3 ....51 E6
Westbury BA13 ....109 B4
Mallards The 20 SP3 ...203 E8
Mallow Cl 3 Swindon SN2 34 D4
5 Trowbridge BA14 ...105 D6
Malmesbury Abbey★
SN16 ....28 A3
Malmesbury CE Prim Sch
SN16 ....28 A4
Malmesbury Com Hospl
SN16 ....28 B1
Malmesbury House★
SP1 ....152 A8
Malmesbury Ind Est
SN16 ....28 A4
Malmesbury Rd
Chippenham SN15 ......70 C1
Leigh SN5 ....17 E3
Malmesbury Sch SN16 ..27 E3
Malmesbury Swimming Pool
SN16 ....27 E4
Malmpit Hill BA12 .....195 B2
Malt House La SP11 ....193 F4
Malt Shovel La RG17 ...164 F1
Malthouse Cl
Ashbury SN6 ....164 A8
Broad Blunsdon SN26 ..21 C2
Malthouse La
Chute SP11 ....192 E8
4 Salisbury SP2 .....146 A1
Maltings The
Malmesbury SN16 ......28 A3
Salisbury SP2 ....146 A1
8 Wanborough SN4 ...163 B6
Warminster BA12 ......116 F6
Wootton Bassett SN4 ..47 D1
Yatton Keynell SN14 ...68 F6
Malvern Cl
Melksham SN12 ....94 D4
7 Warminster BA12 ...117 A4
Malvern Rd SN2 ....35 C1
Malvern Way SP4 ......133 D6
Mampitts La SP7 ......202 D1
Manchester Rd SN1 ....50 C7
Mand Wood BA14 ......101 F8
Manley Cl BA14 ....101 C1
Manning Cl 8 SP1 .....146 C5
Mannington La SN5 .....49 D5
Mannington Pk SN2 ....49 F7
Mannington Ret Pk
SN1 ....49 E4
Manor Bridge Ct SP9 ...216 D7
Manor Cl
Broad Blunsdon SN26 ..21 C2
28 Fordingbridge SP6 ..210 D1
Semington BA14 ....102 F5
Sherston SN16 ....25 C1
4 Shipton Bellinger SP9 .199 D8
Trowbridge BA14 ......105 A6
Wroughton SN4 ....64 B5
Manor Copse SP11 .....193 E3
Manor Cotts SN14 ......24 D1
Manor Cres SN2 ....34 F2
Manor Ct SN9 ....215 C4
Manor Dr BA1 ....82 B2
Manor Farm Cl SP5 ....205 C4
Manor Farm Ct SN8 ...173 D6
Manor Farm Dr SN15 ...57 C2
Manor Farm La
Great Wishford SP2 ....129 F4
Patney SN10 ....180 F5
Manor Farm Rd
Salisbury SP1 ....146 C1
1 Sandleheath SP6 ...210 C1
Manor Fields 5 BA13 ..186 B7
Manor Gdns
Swindon SN2 ....34 F1

Manor Gdns continued
Warminster BA12 ......117 A7
Manor Ho SP4 ....48 E6
Manor House The★
SN9 ....182 F7
Manor La Baydon SN8 ..170 C8
Broad Hinton SN4 .....167 C7
Manor Orch SN6 ....19 E8
Manor Pk
Froxfield SN8 ....176 D6
Great Somerford SN15 ..44 A2
South Marston SN3 ....36 E4
Manor Rd
Chippenham SN14 .....78 A8
Corsham SN13 ....76 F2
7 Great Bedwyn SN8 ..176 B3
Mere BA12 ....138 F7
Salisbury SP1 ....146 C1
Swindon SN1 ....49 F5
Trowbridge BA14 ......105 A6
Upton Lovell BA12 .....194 E3
Manor The★
Keevil BA14 ....178 A4
Longbridge Deverill
BA12 ....120 F5
Manor View SN16 ......28 F2
Mansion House Mews
SN13 ....77 A1
Mantles La BA12 ....194 C5
Manton Cl
Marlborough SN8 ......213 A1
Trowbridge BA14 ......105 C6
Manton Dro SN8 ....174 C6
Manton Hollow SN8 ...213 A2
Manton Rd SN8 ....174 C7
Manton St SN2 ....49 F7
Maple Cl Calne SN11 ...81 B1
Melksham SN12 ....94 D5
Pewsey SN9 ....215 D6
5 Shaftesbury SP7 ...202 C2
Maple Cres
7 Ludgershall SP11 ...192 B5
Wilton SP2 ....144 F3
Maple Ct 8 BA11 ......110 A7
Maple Dr Firsdown SP5 .148 C7
Wootton Bassett SN4 ..47 E4
Maple Gr Swindon SN2 ..35 C2
Trowbridge BA14 ......105 C6
Maple Way
Chippenham SN15 ......70 D2
3 Durrington/Bulford
SP4 ....198 B7
Maplecroft 3 SP2 .....152 A5
Mapperton Hill SP8 ....138 E1
Maranatha Christian Sch
SN6 ....22 E1
Marbrean Cl 4 SP6 ....210 C1
March Cl SN25 ....35 A6
Marchment Cl SN1 .....50 F6
Marden Henge★ SN9 ..181 B5
Marden Way SN11 ......81 A2
Marden Wlk 2 BA14 ...105 D6
Margaret Leckie Ct 5
SN3 ....50 F6
Margaret Stancomb Infants'
Sch BA14 ....101 C1
Margha Rd SP9 ....216 C1
Marie Ave 5 SP5 ......210 D6
Marigold Cl
Melksham SN12 ....94 C3
Swindon SN2 ....34 D4
Marina Dr BA14 ....101 D4
Marina Rd
23 Durrington/Bulford
SP4 ....198 B7
Salisbury SP1 ....152 C7
Marine Cl SN4 ....64 B7
Mariner Rd SN25 ....34 B7
Maristow St BA13 .....109 A3
Marjoram Cl SN2 ....34 D5
Markan Rd SP4 ....133 F7
Markenfield 2 SN5 .....49 D4
Market Hill SN11 ....81 B3
Market Lavington Mus★
SN10 ....179 F1
Market Pl Box SN13 ...83 D6
Chippenham SN15 ......78 E7
Colerne SN14 ....75 B3
Lechlade GL7 ....2 C4
18 Market Lavington SN10 179 F1
Marshfield SN14 ....74 A8
Pewsey SN9 ....215 C5
Warminster BA12 ......117 A7
2 Westbury BA13 ....109 A4
Market Pl The SN10 ....214 A4
Market Sq The SN3 ....50 D4
Market St
Bradford-on-Avon BA15 ..100 D7
4 Malmesbury SN16 ...28 A3
Swindon SN1 ....50 B6
Trowbridge BA14 ......105 D8
Markham Cl SN3 ....50 F7
Markham Rd SN4 ......64 A5
Marl La SP6 ....210 D1
Marlborough Bsns Pk
SN8 ....213 E1
Marlborough Cl SN10 ..214 F7
Marlborough Coll
SN8 ....213 C2
Marlborough Craft Ctr★
SN8 ....213 C2
Marlborough Ct SN14 ..78 C7
Marlborough Leisure Ctr
SN8 ....213 C2
Marlborough Rd
5 Aldbourne SN8 .....170 A6
Bulford SP4 ....198 E6

Marlborough Rd continued
Burbage SN8 ....175 C1
Chiseldon SN3 ....51 C2
Collingbourne Ducis SN8 .183 E1
Everleigh SN8 ....183 A1
Liddington SN4 ....51 E1
Pewsey SN9 ....215 B6
Salisbury SP1 ....146 A2
Swindon SN3 ....50 D3
Wootton Bassett SN4 ..61 E7
Wroughton SN4 ....64 B6
Marlborough St 6 SN1 ..50 A5
Marlborough White Horse★
SN8 ....213 C1
Marlowe Ave SN3 ......50 F7
Marlowe Way SN4 .....47 F3
Marne Rd 3 SP4 ......198 F6
Marney Rd SN5 ....49 A5
Marsh Farm La SN1 ....50 E7
Marsh La
Breamore SP6 ....210 E4
Cherhill SN11 ....166 A1
Coombe Bissett SP5 ...150 F2
Hungerford RG17 ......177 A7
Nettleton SN14 ....53 C4
Pen Selwood BA9 .....137 A4
Rowde SN10 ....96 D2
Salisbury SP2 ....145 F2
Marsh Rd Berkley BA11 ..107 C1
Rode BA11 ....103 F1
Trowbridge BA14 ......101 E5
Marsh St BA12 ....117 A5
Marsh The SN4 ....51 D3
Marshall Rd
Roundway SN10 ....214 D1
Swindon SN5 ....49 B8
Marshall St SN14 ......78 C7
Marshfield Rd SN15 ....78 C8
Marshfield VC CE Prim Sch
SN14 ....74 B8
Marshfield Way SN3 ....36 A2
Marshgate SN1 ....50 F8
Marshmead BA14 ......101 F4
Marshmead CF SN5 ...152 F6
Marshwood SP3 ....201 E3
Marsland Rd SN2 ......35 D2
Marston Ave SN2 ......35 D4
Marston Rd BA14 ......105 B4
Marsum Cl 11 SP10 ....193 D2
Martha's La SP3 ....140 F4
Marti Cl SN2 ....94 C4
Martigny Rd SN12 .....94 B3
Martin Cl SP9 ....216 E6
Martin Crest BA12 .....116 E5
Martin Dro End SP6 ...209 A7
Martin Way SN11 ......81 D3
Martin's Cl SN9 ....181 C6
Martin's St 4 SP7 .....202 C1
Martinbushes Rd SP4 ..198 A7
Martinfield SN3 ....51 D7
Martingale Rd SN8 ....183 D7
Martingate SN13 ......77 A1
Martins Cl
Chippenham SN15 ......79 A8
2 Salisbury SP2 .....152 A5
Steeple Ashton BA14 ..178 C4
Martins Croft SN14 ....75 B3
Martins La BA14 ......178 C4
Martins Rd BA14 ....178 C5
Martins Rise SP5 ......161 C4
Martinsell Gn SN9 .....215 D5
Martinsell Hill (Fort)★
SN8 ....174 F2
Martlesham Rd SP4 ...217 D2
Martlet Cl SN12 ....94 D1
Martor Ind Est SN14 ...66 A2
Marvins Cl SP3 ....188 E2
Mary Barters La SP3 ...204 E8
Maryland Cl SP2 ....145 B5
Masefield SN4 ....47 F3
Masefield Ave SN2 .....35 C4
Masefield Rd BA12 ....116 E6
Maskeleyne Way SN4 ..63 F6
Mason Rd SN25 ....35 B6
Masons La BA15 ......100 D7
Masons The SN5 ....33 A3
Masons Way SN13 .....76 D1
Massey Cl SN15 ....78 E5
Massey Rd 4 SN10 ...214 D1
Massinger Wlk SN3 ....50 F6
Matford Hill SN15 ......79 A8
Matilda Way SN10 .....214 D4
Matley Moor SN3 ......51 E2
Matravers Cl BA13 .....108 F3
Matravers Sch BA13 ...108 F4
Matrons Cotts SP5 .....153 F1
Matthews Cl SN10 .....172 F1
Maud Cl SN10 ....214 D4
Maud Heath Ct SN15 ..78 E8
Maud Heath Prim Sch
SN15 ....72 A2
Maud Heath's Cswy
Chippenham SN15 ......70 E1
Langley Burrell Without
SN15 ....71 B3
Maud Heath's Mon★
SN11 ....80 C8
Maud Heath's Stone★
SN11 ....80 C8
Maulton Cl BA14 ......101 D8
Maunders Dr BA14 ....101 D4
Maundrell Cl SN10 .....96 D2
Maundrell Rd SN11 ....81 C5
Maunsell Way SN4 .....63 F7
Maur Cl SN15 ....78 C8
Maurys La SO51 ....212 F6
Maxcroft La BA14 .....101 E5
Maxey Cl SN5 ....49 B8

Maxwell St SN1 ....50 A6
May Cl SN2 ....35 C1
May La SP5 ....204 D3
May Tree Rd 9 SP10 ...193 C1
May's La SN4 ....65 D4
Mayenne Pl SN10 .....179 C8
Mayfair Rd SP1 ......146 D1
Mayfield 1 SN4 ....163 A5
Mayfield Ave Ind. Pk
SP11 ....192 E1
Mayfield Cl
4 Shipton Bellinger SP9 .199 C8
Swindon SN3 ....51 B7
Mayfield Rd 2 SP6 ......210 C1
Mayfly Cl 4 SP6 ....210 D1
Mayfly Rd SN25 ....34 A7
Mayo Cl SN13 ....76 E2
Mays Firs SP6 ....211 D5
Maytree Cl 6 BA11 .....110 B7
McArthur Glen Designer
Outlet Village SN2 .....50 A6
McKie Rd 3 SP4 ....217 D2
McNeill Rd SP4 ....198 A7
Mead Pk SN12 ....84 F1
Mead Prim Sch The
BA14 ....102 B1
Mead The
Ashton Keynes SN6 ....17 F8
Warminster BA12 ....117 A7
Westbury BA13 ....109 A5
Winsley BA15 ....99 E7
Mead Way SN5 ....34 B2
Meade Rd 2 SP11 .....192 B5
Meadens La SP5 ....151 A1
Meadland SN13 ....76 E1
Meadow Ave 10 SP6 ...210 D1
Meadow Cl
Chippenham SN14 ....78 A7
8 Fordingbridge SP6 ....210 D1
Yatton Keynell SN14 ......68 F6
Meadow Ct
11 Fordingbridge SP6 ....210 D1
Whiteparish SP5 ....161 E4
Meadow Dr SN10 ......214 C3
Meadow La
Little Somerford SN15 .....44 A5
Westbury BA13 ....109 A4
Meadow Pk BA1 ....82 B3
Meadow Rd (South) 5
SP2 ....145 F1
Meadow Rd
Durrington/Bulford SP4 ..217 E8
Melksham SN12 ....94 C7
3 Salisbury SP2 ....145 F1
Swindon SN2 ....49 E7
Meadow Springs SN5 ...48 E8
Meadow View
5 Fittleton SP4 ....190 A4
Kempsford GL7 ....10 C7
Meadow Way
Chiseldon SN4 ....65 E7
South Cerney GL7 ....6 F7
Meadow Well SN8 .....183 C8
Meadowcroft SN2 ....35 F3
Meadowfield BA15 ....100 B6
Meadows The
Bourton SP8 ....137 F2
Lydiard Tregoze SN5 ......47 F5
Salisbury SP1 ....152 D8
Meadowsweet Cl 2
SN25 ....34 E5
Meadowsweet Dr SN11 .80 F3
Meads Rd SP4 ....198 B7
Meads The SN14 ....53 B3
Meadway
4 Shrewton SP3 ....196 F6
Wingfield BA14 ....105 A8
Meares Dr SN5 ....49 B8
Mears Rd 4 SP4 ....198 A6
Medbourne SN4 ....163 A3
Medbourne Rd SN4 .....163 A4
Medgbury Pl SN1 ....50 D6
Medgbury Rd SN1 ......50 C6
Medieval Hall★ SP1 ...152 C8
Medina Way SN2 ....35 F4
Medlar Ct SN2 ....35 B2
Medway SN25 ....34 F4
Medway Rd SN25 ....34 F4
Meerut Rd SP9 ....216 C6
Melbourne Cl SN3 ......50 F3
Melbourne Gdns 5 SP4 198 F6
Melbourne St BA13 ....186 B7
Melbury Abbas Mill★
SP7 ....206 A7
Melbury Down★ SP5 ..206 C6
Melbury St SP7 ....206 B6
Melbury Way 12 SP7 ...202 D2
Melchet Cl SO51 ......162 D1
Melford Wlk SN3 ....51 C7
Melfort Cl SN5 ....34 B2
Meliot Rise 12 SP10 ....193 E2
Melksham Blue Pool
SN12 ....94 A4
Melksham Cl SN2 ......35 B6
Melksham Com Hospl
SN12 ....94 B3
Melksham La SN12 .....93 C4
Melksham Rd
Chippenham SN15 ....78 B5
Holt SN12 ....93 A2
Lacock SN15 ....86 D5
Melksham Sta SN12 ....94 A6
Mellow Gd SN25 ....34 E5
Melrose Ave BA12 .....116 E6
Melrose Cl
1 Swindon SN5 ....49 C6
4 Warminster BA12 .....116 E6
Melsome Rd SN15 ......59 F1
Melton Rd BA14 ......101 C2
Melville Cl 3 SN3 ......50 F6
Melvin Cl SP1 ....146 D1
Mendip Cl
3 Frome BA11 ....110 A7
Melksham SN12 ....94 C4
Swindon SN25 ....35 C3
6 Warminster BA12 .....117 A8
Mendip Dr BA11 ......110 A7
Menham Cl SN2 ....35 D2
Merchants House The★
SN8 ....213 D3
Mercia Ave SP10 .....193 C2
Mere Ave SN14 ....41 F1
Mere Castle★ BA12 ...138 F6
Mere Mus★ BA12 .....139 A5
Mere Sch BA12 ....139 B5
Meriden Wlk SN3 ......51 B4
Meridian Wlk BA14 ....105 A8
Meriton Ave SN13 ......77 A1
Merlin Cl 23 SP10 ......193 E2
Merlin Theatre BA11 ..110 A7
Merlin Way
Bower Hill SN12 ....94 B1
Stratton St Margaret SN3 ..51 D8
Swindon SN3 ....36 D1
Merrifield Rd SP4 .....146 C6
Merrivale Gr SN3 ......50 E5
Mersey Ct SP10 ....193 F1
Merton Ave SN2 ....35 D4
Merton Cl 6 SP6 ......210 D2
Merton St 2 SN1 ....50 C6
Mervyn Webb Pl SN2 ...50 D8
Mesh Pond SP5 ....210 F8
Methuen Ave SN12 .....94 B6
Methuen Cl BA15 .....100 E4
Methuen Dr 1 SP1 .....152 C8
Methuen Pk 5 SN14 .....77 F5
Methuen Way SN13 .....76 F2
Mews The
Highworth SN6 ....23 A6
Lydiard Millicent SN5 .....48 D8
Warminster BA12 ....117 A7
Meyrick Ave SP2 ......152 A5
Meysey Cl GL7 ....1 A5
Michael Pym's Rd SN16 .28 A5
Middle Field Cl SN10 ..214 C3
Middle Gd Cricklade SN6 .19 C8
Fovant SP3 ....204 E7
Wootton Bassett SN4 .....48 A2
Middle La
Atworth/Whitley SN12 ....85 D1
Cherhill SN11 ....166 B1
Martin SP6 ....209 A7
Trowbridge BA14 ....101 F2
Middle St SP2 ....151 F7
Middle Stoke BA2 ......99 A6
Middleleaze Dr SN5 ....48 F8
Middlemass Gn SN9 ...215 D5
Middleton SP5 ....149 B7
Middleton Cl
Swindon SN3 ....50 F6
5 Warminster BA12 .....116 E6
Middleton Medieval Village
of★ BA12 ....194 A7
Middleton Rd
Salisbury SP2 ....145 F2
The Common SP5 ....149 B7
Middletons Cl RG17 ....177 C8
Middlewick La SN13 ....76 D3
Midford Hill BA2 ....98 C4
Midford La BA2 ....98 E7
Midford Rd BA2 ....98 B7
Midhurst Ave SN3 ......51 B5
Midlands Ind Est The
BA14 ....92 E1
Midlands The BA14 .....92 E1
Midwinter Cl SN5 ......34 B2
Midwinter Gdns SN3 ...36 A2
Milbourne La SN16 .....28 C4
Milbourne Pk SN16 .....28 C4
Mildenhall Way SN2 ....35 B6
Mildmay Cl 12 SN5 .....48 F5
Mile Dr SN15 ....44 E1
Miles's La SP5 ....161 E5
Milestone Way SN15 ....70 C2
Milford Hill SP1 ....152 B8
Milford Hollow 6 SP1 ..152 C8
Milford Ind Est SP1 ...152 C8
Milford Manor Gdns
SP1 ....152 D8
Milford Mill Rd SP1 ...152 D8
Milford Pk SP1 ....152 D8
Milford St
Salisbury SP1 ....152 B8
Swindon SN1 ....50 C6
Milford Way SN15 ......78 F4
Mill Cl Devizes SN10 ...214 C1
Longbridge Deverill
BA12 ....120 F6
South Cerney GL7 ....7 A7
Winterbourne SP4 ....133 B4
Wroughton SN4 ....64 B6
Mill Ct 18 SP6 ....210 D1
Mill Dro SN8 ....183 C1
Mill End SP6 ....209 F2
Mill Head SN10 ....179 A4
Mill Hill Ave SP9 .....216 C8
Mill Hollow La SP7 ....206 A7
Mill La Bishopstone SP5 .150 A1
Bourton SP8 ....137 E2
Box SN13 ....83 C7
Bradford-on-Avon BA15 ..100 D6
Broughton Gifford SN12 ...93 C3
Bulkington SN10 ....178 E5
Cherhill SN11 ....166 B1
Chilmark SP3 ....200 F2
Fairford GL7 ....1 F7
Mill La *continued*
Fovant SP3 ....204 D8
Heytesbury BA12 ....194 C5
Lambourn RG17 ....165 B1
Lechlade GL7 ....2 F4
Little Somerford SN15 .....43 F5
Malmesbury SN16 ....28 A3
Melbury Abbas SP7 .....206 A7
Mere BA12 ....139 B5
Monkton Combe BA2 ......98 E8
Poulshot SN10 ....179 A5
Ramsbury SN8 ....170 B2
St Paul Malmesbury Without
SN16 ....42 E5
Salisbury SP1 ....145 E5
Selwood BA11 ....114 F8
Shalbourne SN8 ....176 F2
Stanton Fitzwarren SN6 ...22 A2
Swindon SN1 ....50 A3
The Common SP5 ....149 E6
West Lavington SN10 ....187 E8
Westbury BA13 ....112 D8
Winterbourne Monkton
SN4 ....167 C3
Winterslow SP5 ....149 D7
Zeale SP8 ....137 F2
Mill Rd Devizes SN10 ..214 C1
Netheravon SP4 ....190 A4
Potterne SN10 ....179 D5
Salisbury SP2 ....145 F1
Worton SN10 ....179 A4
Mill Rise SP8 ....137 E2
Mill Sch The SN10 ....179 C6
Mill St Calne SN11 .....81 B2
Fontmell Magna SP7 .....206 A3
Heytesbury BA12 ....194 C5
Trowbridge BA14 ....105 D8
Mill Stream App SP2 ..146 A1
Millard Cl SN25 ....35 B6
Millard Cl 2 SN15 ......78 F4
Millbourn Cl BA15 .....99 D7
Millbrook 2 SP1 ......146 B2
Millbrook La SP3 .....141 C1
Millbuck Cl SN2 ....35 E1
Millennium Visitor Ctr★
GL7 ....6 B4
Millennium Way SP2 ..152 B5
Miller Cl Chirton SN10 ..180 F4
Salisbury SP1 ....145 E5
Swindon SN5 ....48 F8
Miller's La DT11 ......207 D1
Millfield 5 RG17 ......165 A1
Millgreen Rd 1 SP4 ...217 C2
Millhand Villas BA14 ..105 E7
Millington Dr 3 BA14 ..105 A7
Mills Rd SN12 ....94 C4
Mills Way SP4 ....217 D4
Milne Cres 3 SP4 .....197 E6
Milne Rd SP4 ....198 E6
Milston Ave SN2 ....35 C5
Milston Down (Long
Barrows)★ SP4 ......198 E8
Milston Dro SP4 ....190 E1
Milston Rd Bulford SP4 .198 C7
Durrington/Bulford SP4 ..217 D8
Milston View 2 SP4 ...198 C7
Milton Ave
6 Andover SP10 ....193 C1
Melksham SN12 ....94 B4
Milton Pl GL7 ....1 F6
Milton Rd
Amesbury SP4 ....217 E2
Pewsey SN9 ....215 E5
Salisbury SP2 ....152 B6
Swindon SN1 ....50 B6
Milton St GL7 ....1 F6
Milton's Way SN4 ......47 C1
Milverton Ct SN3 ......51 A5
Minden Cl 13 SP10 ....193 D2
Minety CE Prim Sch
SN16 ....17 B2
Minety La SN16 ....16 A7
Minety Rd SN2 ....35 B5
Minnow Cl SN25 ....34 A7
Minories Rd SP9 ......216 E6
Minster CE Prim Sch
BA12 ....116 F7
Minster Cl SN25 ....34 F7
Minster St
7 Salisbury SP1 ....146 A1
Wilton SP2 ....144 D3
Minster View BA12 ....116 F7
Minster Way SN14 .....78 A5
Mint Cl SN2 ....34 D4
Minton Distribution Pk
SP4 ....217 C4
Minty's Top SN15 ......96 A7
Mir Cres SN25 ....34 B7
Mitchell Cl 3 SP10 ....193 C1
Mitchell Dr SN12 .....178 B8
Mitchell Rd SP2 ......151 D8
Mitchells Cl 5 SP5 ....211 C7
Mizmaze★ SP6 ....210 D7
Moat Rd BA13 ....108 D6
Moberly Rd SP1 ......146 B3
Moffat Rise SN16 ....28 A5
Moggs La SN11 ....172 A8
Mompesson Ho★ SP2 .152 A8
Monastery Rd BA13 ...186 C8
Monet Cl SN25 ....34 F6
Moneyer Rd 5 SP10 ...193 D2
Monk's La SN13 ....85 B6
Monkley La BA14 .....104 C1
Monks Cl SP9 ....216 C7
Monks Pk SN16 ....28 D4
Monks Pk Gdns SN13 ..85 B5
Monks Way SN15 ......79 A4
Monkton Cl SN3 ....51 B4
Monkton Dro BH21 ...208 D1
Monkton Farleigh & S
Wraxall CE VC Prim Sch
BA15 ....90 E7
Monkton Hill SN15 .....78 D7
Monkton House★ SN12 .93 C1
Monkton Pk SN15 ......78 F7
Monkton Pk Prim Sch
SN15 ....78 E7
Monmouth Cl 4 SN3 ....50 F4
Monmouth Dr BA11 ...110 B5
Monmouth Rd SP3 ....203 D8
Mons Ave SP4 ....198 E6
Mons La SN15 ....86 D8
Montagu St SN2 ....49 F7
Montague Cl SN15 .....79 A7
Montague Ct BA14 ....102 A1
Montague Pl SN12 .....94 C5
Montague Rd SP2 .....151 D7
Monteagle Cl SN5 ......49 A4
Montgomery Ave SN2 ..35 B2
Montgomery Gdns
SP2 ....145 E2
Montgomery Rd SP11 .193 E3
Montrose Cl SN2 ....34 E2
Monument Hill SN10 ..214 E1
Monxton Cl 3 SP1 .....146 D5
Moody's Hill SP5 .....155 E2
Moon Cl SN14 ....75 B3
Moonrakers SN10 .....214 D5
Moor Barton SN13 .....84 D6
Moor Hill SP3 ....204 D8
Moor La
Charlton Heath SN16 .....29 D6
Whiteparish SP5 ....161 A1
Moor Pk SN13 ....84 C6
Moore Cl SN4 ....64 C8
Moore's Pl 12 RG17 ....177 B7
Moores Yd BA14 ......104 C6
Moorgate GL7 ....2 B4
Moorhen Cl
Swindon SN3 ....51 E5
Trowbridge BA14 ....101 D4
Moorings The SN1 .....50 A5
Moorlands SN15 ....70 E2
Moorlands The SN10 ..214 A2
Moormead Rd SN4 .....64 B6
Moors Cl SN15 ....70 C5
Moot (Motte & Bailey) The★
SP5 ....211 B8
Moot Cl 7 Andover SP10 193 E2
Downton SP5 ....211 B7
Moot Gdns SP5 ....211 A7
Moot La SP5 ....211 A7
Mopes La SN5 ....33 C7
Moray Rd SN2 ....35 E1
Moredon Inf Sch SN2 ..34 D2
Moredon Jun Sch SN2 ..34 E2
Moredon Pk SN2 ....34 D3
Moredon Rd SN25 ......34 F3
Moresby Cl SN5 ....49 C6
Morgan Wlk BA13 .....108 E2
Morgan's La
Pentridge SP5 ....208 E5
Winterbourne SP4 ....133 A2
Morgans Rise Rd 3
SP5 ....211 C8
Morgans Vale & Woodfalls
CE Prim Sc SP5 ......211 C8
Morgans Vale Rd SP5 .211 C7
Morie Cl SN5 ....34 B1
Morley Field BA12 ....117 C7
Morley Pl 23 RG17 ....177 B7
Morley St SN1 ....50 C5
Morris La Bath BA1 .....82 B3
Devizes SN10 ....214 B3
Morris Rd SN8 ....213 B2
Morris St SN2 ....49 E6
Morrison St SN2 ....49 F7
Morse Cl SN15 ....78 E4
Morse St SN1 ....50 B5
Morstone Rd SN4 ......61 D8
Mortimer Cl 5 SN5 ....49 B7
Mortimer St BA14 ....105 C7
Moss Mead SN14 ......77 F8
Motcombe CE VA Prim Sch
SP7 ....202 A4
Motcombe Grange Sch
SP7 ....202 A5
Motcombe Rd SP7 ....202 B3
Moulton Dr BA15 .....100 D4
Mount Carmel Rd
SP11 ....199 F3
Mount Hts SP5 ....135 E3
Mount La
Barford St Martin SP3 ....143 B4
Warminster BA12 ....117 A5
Mount Pleasant
Atworth SN12 ....85 A1
Atworth/Whitley SN12 ....93 A8
Bradford-on-Avon BA15 ..100 D7
Chippenham SN14 ....70 A1
Lechlade GL7 ....2 C4
South Newton SP2 ......130 A4
Mount The BA14 ......101 D2
Mountain Wood BA1 ...82 B2
Mountford Manor Prim Sch
SN3 ....50 F6
Mountings The SN4 ....64 B8
Mountpleasant SP3 ...203 D8
Mountsfield BA11 .....110 A2
Moxhams 21 SP6 ......210 D1
Moyle Pk BA14 ....102 A1
Moyne Cl SN10 ....179 D8
Moyne Gdns 7 SP4 ....217 D3
Mud La SN5 ....32 F2
Muddyford Rd SP5 ....211 C8
Muirfield SN25 ....34 D7
Mulberry Cl SN14 .....70 B1
Mulberry Ct
Frome BA11 ....110 B7
Sixpenny Handley SP5 ...208 B4
Mulberry Gr SN2 ....35 A2
Mulcaster Ave SN5 ....48 F5
Mulling Cl SN14 ....75 A3
Mundy Ave SN3 ....51 C4
Munks Cl 3 SP2 ....151 E7
Munnings Ct 2 SP10 ..193 D1
Munro Cl SN3 ....50 E6
Murdock Rd SN3 ....51 E6
Murray Rd BA14 ......101 D2
Murray Wlk SN12 ......94 B5
Murrayfield SN15 ......70 E1
Muscott Cl 3 SP9 .....199 C8
Muscovey Cl SN15 .....60 A2
Mustons La 26 SP7 ....202 C2
Mycroft Rd SN25 ....34 C6
Myrrfield Rd 7 SP1 ...146 D5
Myrtle Ave BA12 .....116 F6
Myrtle Gdns SN2 ....35 C2
Mythern Meadow
BA15 ....100 E5

N

Nadder Cl 13 SP3 .....203 E8
Nadder La SP2 ....144 F2
Nadder Rd SP9 ....216 D6
Nadder Terr SP2 ......144 C2
Naini Tal Rd SP9 .....216 C6
Nantwich SN5 ....49 A3
Napier Cl SN2 ....50 A7
Napier Cres SP1 ......146 D1
Napier Wlk SP10 ......193 F1
Napiers 1 SN8 ....176 B3
Narrow Wine St BA14 .105 D8
Nash Cl SN25 ....35 A8
Nash Rd SN8 ....173 A8
National Monuments Records
Ctr★ SN2 ....50 A7
Naughton Ave SN10 ...214 E6
Naunton Rd SN3 ....51 A6
Navigator Cl BA14 ....101 E4
Neal Cl 1 SP1 ....146 C5
Neale's Barrow★ SP2 .150 A6
Neeld Cl SN14 ....68 F6
Neeld Cres SN14 ....78 B8
Neigh Bridge Ctry Pk★
GL7 ....5 F2
Nell Hill SN6 ....22 A7
Nelson Cl 1 SP4 ......198 F6
Nelson Rd SP2 ....146 A2
Nelson St SN1 ....49 F5
Nelson Wlk SP10 .....193 F1
Nepaul Rd SP9 ....216 C7
Ness Cl 1 SN5 ....34 B2
Nestings The BA14 ....105 A5
Neston Cres SN13 ......84 E6
Neston Pk★ SN13 ......84 E3
Neston Prim Sch SN13 .84 E5
Netheravon Cl SP1 ....146 B3
Netheravon Rd
Durrington SP4 ....198 B7
Figheldean SP4 ....190 B1
Salisbury SP1 ....146 B2
Nethercote Hill SN15 ..86 D6
Netherhampton Rd
Netherhampton SP2 .....150 F8
Quidhampton SP2 ....144 F1
Nethermore SN13 ......84 D6
Netherstreet SN15 .....96 D6
Netherton Cl SN3 ......51 B4
Netherton House★
SP11 ....185 F4
Nett Rd SP3 ....196 F6
Nettlebed Nursery 14
SP7 ....202 C2
Nettlecombe 6 SP7 ...202 D2
Nettlemead La BA12 ..201 F8
Nettleton Rd SN14 .....53 B3
Netton St SP5 ....205 E4
Neville Cl SP1 ....146 C4
Neville Terr SN15 .....57 D1
Nevis Cl SN5 ....34 B2
New Bottom Rd SP4 ...145 E7
New Bridge Cl 4 SN1 ..50 C7
New Bridge Rd SP1 ...152 A7
New Bridge Sq 5 SN1 ..50 C7
New Broughton Rd
SN12 ....94 A5
New Canal SP1 ....152 A8
New Cl Bourton SP8 ....137 E2
West Knoyle BA12 ......140 E7
New Cl Cty Prim Sch
BA12 ....117 B6
New Coll SN3 ....50 F5
New Coll Wlk SN3 .....50 F5
New Cres SP11 ....192 A5
New Cut BA12 ....139 A6
New Dro SP11 ....192 A5
New Haig Rd 7 SP4 ...198 E6
New Hall Hospl SP5 ..158 F8
New Harnham Rd SP2 .152 A6
New Hayward Bottom
RG17 ....171 C2
New House La SP11 ...192 E4
New King Barrows★
SP4 ....197 F5
New La Cann SP7 ......202 D1
Seend SN12 ....178 D7
New Lawns SN12 ......94 B4
New Pk Rd SN10 ......214 B4

New Pk St SN10 ......214 A4
New Rd Bath BA1 ....82 C2
 Bradford-on-Avon BA15 ..100 E7
 Bromham SN15 ....96 A5
 Calne SN11 ....81 B2
 Calne Without SN11 .....79 F3
 Chippenham SN15 ....78 D7
 Chiseldon SN4 ....65 D3
 Codford BA12 ....195 A3
 Donhead St Andrew SP7 .203 B4
 22 Durrington/Bulford
 SP4 ....198 B7
 East Knoyle SP3 ......141 B3
 Erlestoke BA13 ....179 A2
 Kilmington BA12 ......123 D6
 Landford SP5 ....212 D5
 Limpley Stoke BA2 .....99 B5
 Maiden Bradley with Yarnfield
 BA11 ....123 D8
 Marlborough SN8 ......213 D3
 Melksham Without SN12 ..94 E7
 Purton SN5 ....33 C5
 Rockbourne SP6 ....210 A5
 2 Shaftesbury SP7 ...202 B2
 1 Trowbridge BA14 ...105 D7
 Wootton Bassett SN4 ...47 D1
 Zeale SP8 ....138 A3
New Severalls The
 SN9 ....182 E7
New St
 16 Market Lavington SN10 179 F1
 Salisbury SN1 ....152 A8
 Winterbourne Stoke SP3 .196 F3
New Terr BA14 ....101 C7
New Town La SN8 ......163 E6
New Ward Rd SP4 .....198 A2
New Zealand Ave SP4 ...145 D2
Newall Tuck Rd SN15 ...78 F7
Newark Cl SN5 ....49 B3
Newbourne Gdns SN14 ..56 D6
Newburgh Pl SN6 ....22 F6
Newburn Cres SN1 .....49 F5
Newbury Ave SN11 .....80 F4
Newbury Dr
 Chippenham SN14 ......77 F5
 Swindon SN5 ....49 B3
Newbury Rd
 Andover SP10 ....193 E2
 Lambourn RG17 ....165 B1
Newbury St RG17 .....165 A1
Newby Acre SN8 ......213 D4
Newby Cl **4** SN10 ...187 E8
Newcastle St SN1 ......50 D6
Newcombe Dr SN2 ......50 A7
Newcombe Trad Est
 SN2 ....50 B7
Newcroft Cl SN11 .....81 B4
Newcroft Rd SN11 .....81 B4
Newhall St SN1 ....50 B5
Newhurst Pk BA14 .....102 A2
Newland Rd SN25 ......35 A3
Newlands Cl SN15 .....70 E7
Newlands Rd SN13 .....77 A1
Newleaze
 Steeple Ashton BA14 ...178 A4
 Trowbridge BA14 ......101 F4
Newleaze Pk SN12 .....93 B4
Newman Rd SN10 ......214 C1
Newmans Way SP4 ....217 E7
Newmarket Ave BA14 ..105 E4
Newmarket Cl **9** SN14 ..77 F6
Newmeadow Copse
 SN5 ....34 A1
Newopual Way BA12 ...116 F8
Newport BA12 ....117 A7
Newport St SN1 ....50 D3
Newstead Cl **1** SN25 ...34 F6
Newth's La SN5 ....19 D2
Newton Abbot Cl **6**
 SN14 ....77 F6
Newton Barrow★ SP2 .130 E3
Newton Cl SP5 ....161 C3
Newton La SP5 ....161 B3
Newton St SN15 ......145 D1
Newton Tony CE Prim Sch
 SP4 ....199 B3
Newton Way SN2 ....35 C4
Newtown
 Bradford-on-Avon BA15 .100 C6
 Heytesbury BA12 ......194 C5
 Hullavington SN14 .....41 F1
 Trowbridge BA14 ......105 C8
 Westbury BA13 ....109 C3
Newtown Com Prim Sch
 BA14 ....105 C8
Newtown Rd SN8 ......170 C2
Nicolson Cl **6** SP4 ...217 E3
Niebull Cl SN16 ....28 A5
Nightingale Ave BA11 .110 B6
Nightingale Cl **8** SO51 .212 F6
Nightingale Dr BA13 ..109 B4
Nightingale La
 South Marston SN3 .....36 F4
 Tisbury SP3 ....203 C6
Nightingale Rd BA14 ..105 A8
Nightingale Wlk SP2 ..145 E2
Nightwood Copse **3**
 SN5 ....34 A1
Nindum Rd SN3 ....36 C1
Nine Acre Dr SN13 .....76 D1
Nive Rd SN4 ....168 E8
Noade St SP5 ....206 E4
Noble St SN16 ....40 C8
Nolan Cl SN25 ....34 F8
Nolands Rd SN11 ......166 D2

Nomansland & Hamptworth
 CE Prim Sch SP5 .....212 B4
Norcliffe Rd SN3 ....51 B4
Nore Marsh Rd SN4 ....47 E1
Noredown Way SN4 ....47 E1
Noremarsh Jun Sch
 SN4 ....47 E1
Norfolk Cl **1** SN3 ....50 F6
Norfolk Rd SP2 ....151 E7
Norley La SN11 ....80 C3
Norman Cl SN15 ....79 A4
Norman Rd SN2 ....35 C1
Normandy Way **14** SP6 ..210 D1
Norney Rd BA13 ......179 A4
Norridge View **4** BA12 .116 E7
Norrington Manor★
 SP5 ....204 A2
Norris Cl SN4 ....65 C3
Norris Rd BA14 ....102 B3
North Bank Rise SN4 ...47 F2
North Bradley CE Prim Sch
 BA14 ....105 D2
North Charford Crossing
 SP6 ....210 F6
North Charford Dro
 SP6 ....210 C8
North Comm La SP5 ...212 B7
North Cote SN11 ....81 A4
North End SN11 ....81 A4
North End Gdns SN16 ..25 C1
North Farm Cl RG17 ..165 B2
North La SP5 ....212 C4
North Leaze Cl SN2 ...34 F4
North Mdw National Nature
 Reserve★ SN6 ....8 C1
North Mdw Rd SN6 .....8 C1
North Rd
 Amesbury SP4 ....217 E2
 Ashmore SP5 ....206 E5
 Mere BA12 ....139 A6
North Row BA12 ....117 A7
North St
 Broad Chalke SP5 .....205 B4
 Calne SN11 ....81 B4
 Mere BA12 ....139 A5
 Pewsey SN9 ....215 C5
 Salisbury SP2 ....145 F1
 Swindon SN1 ....50 C5
 Wilton SP2 ....144 D3
North Standen Rd
 RG17 ....177 A6
North Star Ave SN2 ....50 B8
North Star Ind Est SN2 .50 B7
North View
 Berwick St James SP3 .196 F2
 Highworth SN6 ....22 F5
North View Hts RG17 ..177 C7
North View Pl SN8 ....213 D4
North Wall SN6 ....19 D8
North Way Calne SN11 ..81 A4
 Trowbridge BA14 ......105 A4
North Wlk SP1 ....152 A8
Northampton St SN1 ...50 D6
Northbourne Rd SN25 ..35 A7
Northbrook SN10 .....179 F1
Northbrook Cl **1** SN10 .179 F1
Northbrook Rd SN2 ....93 F7
Northcote Cres **7** BA11 .110 A7
Northcroft Rd **1** SN13 ..76 B1
Northen Cl GL7 ....10 C6
Northen Terr
 Durrington SP4 ....197 F7
 Larkhill SP4 ....198 A7
Northern Rd SN2 ......35 A1
Northfield BA15 ....99 F7
Northfield La SN14 ....66 A2
Northfield Way SN3 ....51 B7
Northfields
 Bulkington SN10 .....178 E5
 Calne SN11 ....81 A4
 1 Lambourn RG17 ...165 A2
Northgate Gdns SN10 .214 A4
Northgate St SN10 ...214 A4
Northlands Ind Est
 BA12 ....117 B7
Northleaze SN13 ....76 D1
Northleigh BA15 ....91 E1
Northmoor La GL7 .....6 F8
Northside SP4 ....146 B8
Northview **20** RG17 ..177 B7
Northview Prim Sch
 SN6 ....23 A7
Northway SP4 ....134 B7
Northwood SN15 ......70 E2
Norton Dr SP4 ....146 D6
Norton Gr SN3 ....50 D5
Norton Rd BA12 ......117 F1
Norwood Castle (site of)★
 SN16 ....4 F2
Norwood Cl **3** SN3 ...51 D4
Notton House Sch
 SN15 ....86 B8
Noyes Cl
 Chippenham SN14 ......77 F8
 Haydon Wick SN2 ......34 C5
Nuffield Cl SN5 ....49 B8
Nunns Pk SN5 ....161 D4
Nunton Dro SP5 ......152 D1
Nurseries The
 Christian Malford SN15 .58 A4
 Swindon SN1 ....50 A5
Nursery Cl
 1 Amesbury SP4 .....217 B3
 Atworth/Whitley SN12 ..92 E8
 Trowbridge BA14 .....102 A3

Nursery Cl continued
 Wroughton SN4 ....64 A5
Nursery Gdns
 Corsham SN13 ....85 A8
 Mere BA12 ....139 A5
Nursery Rd
 Colerne SN14 ....75 A3
 Salisbury SP2 ....145 E1
Nursery The SN16 .....27 F6
Nursteed Cl SN10 ....214 D2
Nursteed Com Prim Sch
 SN10 ....214 E3
Nursteed Pk SN10 ....214 D1
Nursteed Rd SN10 ....214 C2
Nursteed Rd Ind Est
 SN10 ....214 C1
Nutbane La SP11 .....193 A4
Nuthatch Cl **4** SN3 ...51 E6
Nutley Ct **8** SN8 ....183 D8
Nutmeg Cl **7** SN2 ....34 D4
Nyland Rd SN3 ....51 C7
Nyland Sch SN3 ....51 B7
Nythe Cty Prim Sch
 SN3 ....51 B8
Nythe Rd SN3 ....36 B1

O

O'Donnell Cl SN15 .....70 E1
Oak Ash Gn SP2 ......144 C2
Oak Cl
 Bishops Cannings SN10 .172 B2
 Pitton & Farley SP5 ...154 E7
 South Newton SP2 .....130 B2
 Tidworth SP9 ....216 F7
Oak Dr Alderbury SP5 ..153 D2
 Highworth SN6 ....22 F5
 Trowbridge BA14 .....105 C3
Oak Gdns SN3 ....36 A4
Oak Hill SN8 ....176 E6
Oak La Easterton SN10 .179 F2
 Figheldean SP4 ......190 B2
 Mere BA12 ....139 B4
Oak Lodge SN14 ....78 C8
Oak Pl SP4 ....217 C4
Oak Rd
 Chippenham Without
 SN14 ....77 C6
 Colerne SN14 ....74 F5
 Down Ampney GL7 ......8 E6
Oak St GL7 ....2 C4
Oak Tree Ave SN2 .....35 D3
Oak Tree Bsns Pk SN3 ..36 C7
Oak Tree Cl BA14 ....101 B1
Oak Tree Prim Sch
 SN3 ....51 A4
Oak Way GL7 ....6 F6
Oakapple Cl **3** SN4 ..163 B6
Oakbournes The **5** SP1 146 C5
Oakes Ct **9** RG17 ...177 B7
Oakes La GL9 ....52 B5
Oakford La SN14 ......74 B2
Oakford Wlk SN3 ......51 A6
Oakham Cl SN5 ....49 C5
Oakhurst Way SN25 ...34 C7
Oakie Cl SN25 ....35 A5
Oaklands SN15 ....70 D2
Oaklands Cl **12** SP6 ..210 D1
Oaklea La SP5 ....153 E2
Oakleaze SN16 ....17 B2
Oakleigh Dr SP5 .....212 C5
Oakley Flats GL7 ....10 D6
Oakley La DT11 ......207 D2
Oaks The
 Chippenham SN15 .....70 D2
 Kemble GL7 ....4 F7
 Warminster BA12 ....117 A8
Oaksey Rd Minety SN16 .16 C4
 Swindon SN2 ....35 C4
Oakwood Dr SN12 .....94 B4
Oakwood Gr SP5 .....153 D3
Oakwood Rd SN5 ......49 C7
Oamaru Way SN10 ...214 D3
Oare Hill SN8 ....174 C2
Oare Prim Sch SN8 ..174 B2
Oasis Leisure Ctr SN2 ..50 B7
Oasthouse Cl **3** SN5 ..49 A8
Oate Hill SN15 ....78 F6
Oatfields BA14 ....101 D4
Oathill La SP5 ....3 B8
Oathills SN13 ....84 F8
Oatmeal Row **5** SP1 ..152 A8
Obelisk Terr **6** BA12 ..116 F7
Oberon Way SN25 .....35 A5
Ocotal Way SN1 ....50 D8
Odcroft Cl SN15 ....79 A7
Oddford Vale **17** SP3 ..203 E8
Odstock Prim Sch
 SP5 ....152 B1
Odstock Rd
 Britford SP2 ....152 B4
 Swindon SN2 ....35 C6
Ogbourne SN14 ....75 B3
Ogbourne St George & St
 Andrew Prim Sch SN8 .168 F5
Ogbury Camp★ SP4 ..198 A1
Ogilvie Sq SN11 ....81 C3
Okebourne Pk SN3 ....51 C3
Okeford Cl SN3 ....51 C7
Okus Gr SN2 ....35 D4
Okus Rd SN1 ....49 F3
Okus Trad Est SN3 .....50 A4
Olaf Cl **10** SP10 ....193 E2
Old Alexander Rd SN16 .27 F4
Old Bakery Cl SN16 ....28 C7
Old Barn GL8 ....3 C5
Old Batch The BA15 ..100 B8

Old Beasants SN8 ....174 A6
Old Blandford Rd SP2 .151 F6
Old Boundary Rd **5**
 SP7 ....202 C1
Old Brickyard Rd SP6 .210 B1
Old Broughton Rd
 SN12 ....94 A5
Old Cann Sch SP7 ....202 D1
Old Castle Rd SP1 ...146 A5
Old Chapel Cl SP5 ...153 D3
Old Chase Rd SN8 ...169 A4
Old Coach Rd
 Durrington/Bulford SP4 .217 D8
 North Wraxall SN14 ...67 D2
 Shipton Bellinger SP11 .191 F1
Old Comm Way **13** SP11 192 A5
Old Ct SN4 ....47 D1
Old Dairy Cl SP2 .....145 C3
Old Dairy Ct SN12 .....94 C5
Old Dairy The SP5 ....152 D1
Old Derry Hill SN15 ....79 D2
Old Dilton Rd BA13 ...112 E7
Old Down Rd GL9 ......52 C8
Old English Dr **2** SN10 .193 D2
Old Forge Cl SN15 ....45 E6
Old Granary La SP4 ..217 D7
Old Hardenhuish La
 SN14 ....70 B1
Old Hayward La RG17 .171 B1
Old Hollow BA12 .....139 B6
Old Hospl Rd SN6 ....215 B6
Old King Barrows★
 SP4 ....197 F5
Old Malmesbury Rd
 SN4 ....47 E4
Old Malthouse La BA14 .147 B7
Old Manor Hospl SP2 .145 E1
Old Manor House★
 BA12 ....194 A4
Old Mdws Wlk SP2 ...151 E2
Old Midford Rd BA2 ...98 A7
Old Mill La SN3 ....50 D3
Old Orch The SN16 ....28 A6
Old Post Office La **5**
 SP4 ....190 A3
Old Pound Ct SP8 ....137 D1
Old Rd Alderbury SP5 .153 C4
 Chippenham SN15 .....78 D8
 Derry Hill/Studley SN11 .80 B2
Old Rly Cl **1** SN8 ....28 A4
Old Ropeworks The★
 SN8 ....213 E2
Old Sarum★ SP1 .....145 F6
Old Sarum Barracks
 SP4 ....146 C8
Old Sarum Bsns Pk
 SP4 ....146 C8
Old Sarum Pk SP4 ...146 D8
Old Sawmills The
 RG17 ....177 F3
Old Sch Cl SN15 ......96 C7
Old Sch Ct SN3 ....51 B6
Old Sch Yd SN13 ......85 A8
Old Severalls The SN9 .182 E7
Old Shaft Rd SN13 ....84 C7
Old Shaftesbury Dro
 SP2 ....150 A6
Old Shaftesbury Dro
 SP2 ....151 A6
Old Shaw La SN5 ......48 F8
Old Sodom La SN15 ...59 B8
Old St SP2 ....152 A6
Old Sta Yd The **14** RG17 .165 A1
Old Track BA2 ....98 F7
Old Vicarage La GL7 ...4 F7
Old Vineries The **10**
 SP6 ....210 C1
Old Ward Rd **5** SP4 ..198 E6
Old Wardour Castle★
 SP3 ....203 D1
Oldbury Castle (Hill Fort)★
 SN11 ....172 C6
Oldbury Prior SN11 ....81 C1
Oldbury Way SN11 ....81 A3
Oldenburgh Rd **3** BA13 108 E1
Oldfield Pk BA13 .....108 E3
Oldfield Rd
 Salisbury SP1 ....146 C5
 Westbury BA13 ......108 E4
Oldford Hill BA11 ....110 A8
Oldhat Barrow★ SN9 .183 A3
Oldlands Wlk SN3 .....51 A3
Olive Gr SN2 ....35 D4
Olivemead La SN15 ...45 C1
Oliver Ave SN13 ....76 F2
Oliver Cl SN5 ....49 B5
Oliver Tomkins Jun & Inf Sch
 SN5 ....49 B5
Oliver's Castle (Fort)★
 SN10 ....97 C6
Oliver's La **5** SN16 ...28 A3
Olivers Cl SN11 ......166 B3
Olivers Hill SN11 ....166 B1
Olivier Cl SP2 ....145 C5
Olivier Rd Swindon SN25 .35 B6
 Wilton SP2 ....144 B3
Olympia The SN8 ....168 E3
Olympiad L Ctr SN15 ..78 E8
Omdurman St SN2 .....35 B1
Orange Cl SN6 ....23 A6
Orangery The RG17 ..177 C6
Orbital Sh Pk SN10 ...34 E6
Orchard Cl Calne SN11 ..81 C2
 Devizes SN10 ....214 B1
 34 Fordingbridge SP6 ..210 D1
 Lechlade GL7 ....2 B1
 5 Ramsbury SN8 ....170 B2
 2 Wanborough SN4 ..163 A6

Orchard Cl continued
 Warminster BA12 ....117 B8
 West Ashton BA14 ...106 B4
 Westbury BA13 ......112 C8
 Westwood BA15 ....99 F3
Orchard Cres SN14 ....78 B7
Orchard Ct
 Bratton BA13 ....186 A7
St Paul Malmesbury Without
 SN16 ....28 A7
Orchard Dr BA14 ....104 E2
Orchard End SP4 ....217 D8
Orchard Gdns
 Melksham SN12 ....94 A3
 Purton SN5 ....33 A3
Orchard Gr
 Bromham SN15 ....96 D7
 Swindon SN2 ....35 D3
Orchard Mead **3** SN4 ..48 A2
Orchard Pk Cl **3** RG17 .177 B6
Orchard Pl SN10 .....187 E8
Orchard Rd
 Chippenham SN14 .....78 B7
 Corsham SN13 ....77 A2
 Marlborough SN8 ....213 E2
 Redlynch SP5 ....211 C8
 Salisbury SP2 ....145 D2
 Trowbridge BA14 ....105 D7
 Westbury BA13 ......109 A3
Orchard The
 Chirton SN10 ....180 F4
 Kington St Michael SN14 ..70 A8
 Limpley Stoke BA2 ....99 C5
 Semington BA14 .....102 F6
 Sixpenny Handley SP5 .208 B4
 Upton Scudamore BA12 .112 F4
Orchard Way
 Amesbury SP4 ....217 C3
 Longbridge Deverill
 BA12 ....116 E1
 Trowbridge BA14 ....105 C3
Orchid Cl SN25 ....35 C3
Orchid Dr **30** SP11 ..192 A5
Ordnance Rd SP9 ....216 D6
Orford Rd SP4 ....217 D2
Orkney Cl SN5 ....49 B7
Orlando Cl **4** SN5 ....48 F5
Orpington Way BA14 .102 B5
Orrin Cl SN5 ....34 B1
Orwell Cl
 Malmesbury SN16 .....28 A5
 Swindon SN25 ....35 A5
Osborne Rd BA14 ....101 E3
Osborne St SN2 ....50 B8
Oslings La BA1 ....82 B2
Osmund Cl SN10 .....214 D3
Osmund Rd SN10 ....214 D2
Osprey Cl
 Bower Hill SN12 ......94 D1
 Swindon SN3 ....51 E6
Osterley Rd SN5 ......34 E6
Otter Way SN4 ....47 F2
Overbrook SN3 ....51 C3
Overhouse Dr **12** SP3 .203 E8
Overton Gdns SN3 ....36 B2
Overtown Hill SN4 ....64 C5
Overway La SP7 .....203 B2
Owen Cl SN10 ....214 D3
Owl Cl SN3 ....51 E6
Owlets The SN3 ....51 E6
Owlswood **9** SP2 ...152 A5
Ox Dro
 Berwick St John SP5 ..207 B7
 Bishopstone SP5 .....205 F2
 Bower Chalke SP5 ...208 A8
 Kimpton SP11 ....192 A1
 Teffont SP3 ....201 C5
Ox Row **4** SP1 ......152 A8
Oxencroft **8** SP7 ...202 C2
Oxford Brooks Univ
 SN2 ....50 A8
Oxford Rd Calne SN11 ..81 B3
 Swindon SN3 ....36 A1
 Upavon Down SN9 ....182 B2
Oxford St
 Aldbourne SN8 ......170 A6
 Hungerford RG17 ....177 C8
 Lambourn RG17 .....165 A1
 Malmesbury SN16 .....28 A3
 Marlborough SN8 ....213 D3
 Ramsbury SN8 ......170 B2
 Swindon SN1 ....50 B6
Oxon Pl SN6 ....163 E6
Oxyard BA12 ....195 B2

P

Pack Hill SN4 ....51 F2
Pack Horse La BA2 ....98 A7
Packhorse Bridge★
 SN15 ....86 E5
Packhorse La SN5 .....33 E8
Packington Cl SN5 ....49 B7
Packway The
 Durrington SP4 ......197 D7
 Shrewton SP3 ....197 A7
Paddington Dr SN5 ....49 E5
Paddock Cl
 Great Somerford SN15 ..44 A2
 4 Shaftesbury SP7 ..202 D1
 Sixpenny Handley SP5 .208 A3
 Swindon SN25 ....34 E5
 Winterbourne SP4 ...133 D2
Paddock End SN14 ....70 A7
Paddock La
 Chilmark SP3 ....200 F2
 Corsham SN13 ....84 D8

Paddock The
Highworth SN6 . . . . .23 A5
Market Lavington SN10 . . .180 A1
8 Tisbury SP3 . . . . .203 E8
Paddock Way SP1 . . . . .146 E2
Paddock Wood 13 SP4 .198 B7
Paddocks The
10 Aldbourne SN8 . . . . . .170 A6
Chippenham SN15 . . . . . .78 E6
Mere BA12 . . . . .139 A5
14 Ramsbury SN8 . . . . . . .170 B2
5 Swindon SN3 . . . . .36 A2
Padfield Gdns SN12 . . .93 F1
Padstow Rd SN5 . . . . . . .49 F5
Page Cl Calne SN11 . . . .81 C3
Chippenham SN14 . . . . . .78 A7
Paget Cl SP9 . . . . .216 B8
Pagnell La SN10 . . . . . .179 D1
Pagoda Pk SN5 . . . . . . .49 D7
Pains Way 3 SP4 . . . . .217 C2
Painters Mead BA14 . .102 A2
Pakenham Rd SN3 . . . . .51 B4
Palairet Cl BA15 . . . . . .100 D4
Palestine Rd SP11 . . . .199 F3
Palm Rd SN14 . . . . .75 A5
Palmer Dr BA15 . . . . . .100 D8
Palmer Rd
Salisbury SP2 . . . . .145 E2
Trowbridge BA14 . . . . . .101 D2
Palmer St SN14 . . . . . . .78 C7
Palmers Way 11 SN4 .163 A6
Palmerston Meadow
SN9 . . . . .190 A6
Pampas Ct 1 BA12 . . .116 E6
Pans La SN10 . . . . .214 B2
Panters Rd SP3 . . . . . .204 C8
Pantiles The 12 SP6 . .210 C1
Parade The
Marlborough SN8 . . . . . .213 D3
Swindon SN1 . . . . .50 C6
Paradise La BA12 . . . .116 E1
Parham Wlk 7 SN5 . . . .48 F5
Parham La SN10 . . . . . .179 E2
Parhams Ct SN4 . . . . . . .47 E1
Parhams Hill SP7 . . . .203 B1
Park Ave
Chippenham SN14 . . . . . .78 B8
Corsham SN13 . . . . .84 A8
Highworth SN6 . . . . .23 A5
Park Cl Calne SN11 . . . .81 C2
Malmesbury SN16 . . . . . .27 F4
Salisbury SP1 . . . . .146 A4
Trowbridge BA14 . . . . . .105 D3
Park Dr SP3 . . . . .201 B3
Park End SN6 . . . . .17 F8
Park Field SN10 . . . . . .214 C5
Park Fields SN15 . . . . .78 C8
Park La
Castle Combe SN14 . . . . .68 A7
Cherhill SN11 . . . . .166 C1
Chippenham SN15 . . . . . .78 D8
Corsham SN13 . . . . .76 D1
Great Somerford SN15 . .44 A2
Heytesbury BA12 . . . . .194 D5
Heywood BA13 . . . . .109 C7
Lea & Cleverton SN16 . .29 D3
Lydiard Millicent SN5 . .48 D7
Malmesbury SN16 . . . . . .27 E5
North Wraxall SN14 . . . .68 A2
Odstock SP5 . . . . .152 D4
Salisbury SP1 . . . . .146 A3
Sutton Benger SN15 . . . .57 D2
Swindon SN1 . . . . .50 A6
West Dean SP5 . . . . . . .149 F1
Park Mead SN16 . . . . . .27 F4
Park Pl SN6 . . . . .6 F1
Park Rd
Fordingbridge SP6 . . . .210 D1
Malmesbury SN16 . . . . . .27 E4
Market Lavington SN10 .179 E1
Rushall SN9 . . . . .181 F3
Salisbury SP1 . . . . .146 D2
Tidworth SP9 . . . . .216 D5
Tisbury SP3 . . . . .203 E8
Trowbridge BA14 . . . . . .105 D8
Westbury BA13 . . . . . . .112 B8
Park Springs SN5 . . . . .49 C5
Park St Charlton SN16 .29 A6
Heytesbury BA12 . . . . .194 C5
Hungerford RG17 . . . . .177 B7
Salisbury SP1 . . . . .146 B2
Swindon SN3 . . . . .36 C2
Trowbridge BA14 . . . . . .105 C7
Park Terr SN15 . . . . . . .78 C8
Park The
Erlestoke SN10 . . . . . . .179 A1
8 Lambourn RG17 . . . .165 A2
Park View
Chirton SN10 . . . . .180 F4
Devizes SN10 . . . . .179 D8
Park View Dr
Lydiard Millicent SN5 . .48 D8
1 Westbury BA13 . . . .108 F1
Park Way RG17 . . . . . . .177 B6
Parkers La SN15 . . . . . .70 D6
Parkhouse Cnr SP4 . . .199 D6
Parkhouse Rd SP9 . . .199 C8
Parkland Way SP4 . . .133 D6
Parklands
Malmesbury SN16 . . . . . .27 E4
Trowbridge BA14 . . . . . .101 D2
Parklands Cl SN16 . . . .27 E4
Parklands Rd SN3 . . . .50 D5
Parklands The SN14 . .55 E8
Parkside
Chippenham SN15 . . . . . .78 D8
Swindon SN3 . . . . .36 A3
Parkstone Wlk SN3 . . .51 B3

Parkwater Rd SP5 . . . .161 E1
Parliament Row SN16 .28 A2
Parliament St SN14 . . .78 B7
Parr Cl SN5 . . . . .49 A6
Parsley Cl SN2 . . . . . . .34 D5
Parsonage Cl
81 Fordingbridge SP6 . .210 D1
Salisbury SP1 . . . . .145 E5
Parsonage Down National
Nature Reserve★
SP3 . . . . .196 D5
Parsonage Gn SP2 . . .151 E6
Parsonage Hill SP5 . .154 D7
Parsonage La
Charlton Musgrove BA9 .136 C2
Hungerford RG17 . . . . .177 B7
9 Lambourn RG17 . . . .165 A1
20 Market Lavington SN10 179 F1
Parsonage Pk Dr 3
SP6 . . . . .210 D1
Parsonage Pl 9 RG17 .165 A1
Parsonage Rd
Amesbury SP4 . . . . .217 B3
Swindon SN3 . . . . .36 A3
Trowbridge BA14 . . . . . .102 A1
Parsonage The SP5 . .208 B4
Parsonage Vale SN8 .183 D2
Parsonage Way SN15 .70 F1
Parsons Cl SP4 . . . . . .133 D5
Parsons Gn 4 SP3 . . .196 E6
Parsons La BA12 . . . . .116 E2
Parsons Pool 19 SP7 .202 C2
Parsons Way SN4 . . . . .47 E1
Partridge Cl
Chippenham SN14 . . . . .70 B2
Corsham SN13 . . . . .76 E1
Swindon SN3 . . . . .51 E6
Partridge Hill SP5 . . .212 E6
Partridge Way SP4 . .146 C3
Passmore Cl SN3 . . . .51 E7
Pasture Ct SN2 . . . . . . .49 E7
Pastures The BA15 . . .99 E3
Pat-yat GL7 . . . . .4 B5
Patchway SN14 . . . . . . .78 B8
Patchway The SN10 . .214 D3
Pathfinder Way
Bowerhill SN12 . . . . .94 C2
Swindon SN25 . . . . .34 B7
Patney Rd SN10 . . . . . .180 F5
Paul St SN13 . . . . .76 F1
Paul's Dene Cres SP1 .146 A5
Paul's Dene Rd SP1 . .146 A5
Paulet Cl 3 SN5 . . . . .49 A4
Pauls Croft SN6 . . . . . .19 D7
Pavely Cl SN5 . . . . .78 C6
Pavely Gdns BA14 . . .102 A1
Paven Cl SN5 . . . . .33 A4
Pavenhill SN5 . . . . .33 A4
Paxcroft Prim Sch
BA14 . . . . .101 A1
Paxcroft Way BA14 . .105 F8
Paxmans Rd BA13 . . .108 E5
Payne Cl SN15 . . . . . .78 E4
Payne's Hill 2 SP1 . .152 B8
Peacock SN8 . . . . .173 E6
Peak The SN5 . . . . .33 B3
Peaks Down SN5 . . . . .34 B2
Pealsham Gdns 6 SP6 .210 D1
Pear Ash La BA9 . . . .137 C4
Pear Tree Dr SP4 . . .212 C5
Pear Tree La SN10 . . .187 B8
Pear Tree Orch 2 BA13 186 B7
Pearce Cl SN2 . . . . .35 E6
Pearce Way SP1 . . . . .146 D5
Pearl Rd SN5 . . . . .49 A7
Peartree Cl
Atworth/Whitley SN12 . .85 C1
Purton SN5 . . . . .33 C5
7 West Wellow SO51 . .212 F6
Peatmoor Com Prim Sch
SN5 . . . . .34 A2
Peatmoor Way SN5 . . .34 A1
Peel Cir SN13 . . . . .84 D8
Peel Cl SN12 . . . . .94 A3
Pegasus Way SN12 . . .94 C1
Pelch La SN12 . . . . . .178 D8
Pelham Ct SN8 . . . . . .213 E3
Pembridge Rd SP6 . .210 E1
Pembroke Cl 1 BA14 .105 D6
Pembroke Ctr SN2 . . .34 E1
Pembroke Gdns SN25 .34 E3
Pembroke Gn SN16 . . .28 F1
Pembroke Pk Fst Sch
SP2 . . . . .145 C3
Pembroke Rd
Chippenham SN15 . . . . .79 A4
Melksham SN12 . . . . . . .94 B4
Salisbury SP2 . . . . .145 C2
Upavon Down SN9 . . . .182 B2
Pembroke St SN1 . . . . .50 B4
Pen Cl SN25 . . . . .35 A4
Pen Hill BA10 . . . . . . .122 F1
Pen Mill Hill BA9 . . .137 E3
Pendennis Rd SN5 . . .49 A3
Penfold Gdns SN1 . . .50 C4
Penhill Dr SN2 . . . . . . .35 C4
Penhill Prim Sch SN2 .35 C5
Penleigh Cl SN13 . . . .84 F8
Penleigh Rd BA13 . . .108 D2
Penn Hill Rd SN11 . . .81 C3
Penneys Piece 2 BA11 .110 C6
Pennine Cl SN12 . . . . .94 D4
Pennine Way SN25 . . .34 F7
Penning Rd SP2 . . . . .145 B4
Pennings Dro SP5 . . .157 A8
Pennings Rd
North Tidworth SP9 . . .191 D5
Tidworth SP9 . . . . .216 C8

Penny Hill SN8 . . . . . . .191 E8
Penny La
Chippenham SN15 . . . . . .78 A2
Swindon SN3 . . . . .50 F7
Penny Royal Cl SN11 .80 F3
Penny's Cl 3 SP6 . . . .210 D2
Penny's Cres 4 SP6 .210 D2
Penny's La
Pitton & Farley SP5 . . .154 E7
2 Wilton SP2 . . . . . . .144 D3
Pennycress Cl SN25 . .34 E4
Pennycress Dr SN12 . .94 C3
Pennyfarthing St SP1 .146 B1
Pennys La SP6 . . . . . .210 D2
Penrose Wlk SN3 . . . . .51 A5
Penruddock Cl SP2 . .145 C5
Pensford Way BA14 . .110 D6
Penton La SP11 . . . . .193 A3
Penton Lodge Sch
SP11 . . . . .193 B2
Pentridge Cl SN3 . . . .51 C7
Pentylands Cl SN6 . . .22 F7
Penzance Dr SN5 . . . .49 F5
Pepper Pl BA12 . . . . . .117 D7
Pepperacre La BA14 .101 E1
Pepperbox Hill SN5 . .34 B2
Pepperbox Rise SN5 .153 E2
Pepperbox The★ SP5 .160 C6
Peppercombe Wood Nature
Reserve★ SN10 . . . . .180 B4
Peppercorn Orch
BA14 . . . . .178 A6
Percheron Cl 11 SN5 .49 A7
Percheron Pl BA13 . .108 D2
Percy St SN2 . . . . .49 F7
Peregrine Cl SN2 . . . . .34 C3
Perham Cres 1 SP11 .192 B5
Periwinkle Cl SN2 . . . .34 C3
Perrinsfield GL7 . . . . . . .2 D1
Perriwinkle Cl BA12 . .116 D6
Perry's La Seend SN12 .178 D8
Wroughton SN4 . . . . .64 A6
Perth Rd SP11 . . . . . . .191 F4
Peshawar St SP9 . . . .216 B7
Peter Furkins Ct SN1 .50 A5
Peters Finger Rd SP5 .152 E7
Petersfield Rd SN3 . . .51 B4
Peto Gdn The★ BA15 .99 E2
Petter Cl SN4 . . . . .64 B7
Petticoat La
Redlynch SP5 . . . . .211 D8
Westbury BA13 . . . . . .112 C8
Pettridge La BA12 . . .139 A5
Petty La SN11 . . . . .79 F3
Pevensey Way SN5 . . .49 C5
Pew Hill SN15 . . . . . . .70 E2
Pewsey Downs National
Nature Reserve★
SN8 . . . . .173 C2
Pewsey Prim Sch SN9 .215 B5
Pewsey Rd
Marlborough SN8 . . . . . .213 D2
Rushall SN9 . . . . .181 E2
Pewsey Sports Ctr &
Swimming Pool SN9 . .215 B5
Pewsey Sta SN9 . . . . .215 B5
Pewsey Vale Sch SN9 .215 B5
Pewsey White Horse★
SN9 . . . . .215 E1
Pewsham Lock SN15 . .78 E5
Pewsham Rd SN2 . . . .35 D5
Pewsham Way SN15 . .78 E4
Pheasant Bsns Pk SN14 .78 B5
Pheasant Cl
8 Chippenham Without
SN14 . . . . .77 F6
Swindon SN3 . . . . .51 E5
Pheasantry The GL7 . . .8 E7
Philip Cl SN12 . . . . . . .94 C6
Philip Ct SP2 . . . . .145 D3
Philip Rd
21 Durrington/Bulford
SP4 . . . . .198 B7
Wilton SP2 . . . . .144 B5
Philipps House & Dinton Pk★
SP3 . . . . .201 B4
Phillip Cl SN10 . . . . . .214 C4
Phillips Cl SN14 . . . . .77 F7
Phillips La
Salisbury SP4 . . . . .145 E6
Swindon SN1 . . . . .50 D4
Phillips Way BA14 . . .105 E2
Phipps Cl BA13 . . . . . .108 F4
Phoebe Way SN25 . . . .34 B7
Phoenix Rise BA13 . .108 E3
Phoenix Sq SN9 . . . .215 C4
Picket Cl SN6 . . . . . . .210 D1
Picket Cnr SP6 . . . . .211 F3
Picket Post Gate
BA12 . . . . .116 A4
Picketleaze SN14 . . . .78 A7
Pickford Way SN25 . .35 B6
Pickwick SN13 . . . . . . .76 F2
Pickwick Cl SN2 . . . . .35 E5
Pickwick Rd SN13 . . .76 F2
Picquet The 12 BA13 .186 B7
Picton Rd SN5 . . . . . . .49 A7
Pictor Cl SN13 . . . . . . .76 D1
Pig La
Bishops Cannings SN10 172 C1
Hullavington SN16 . . . .41 A3
Pigeon House La SN3 .36 A3
Pigott Cl 4 SP4 . . . . .190 A4
Pigtrough La SP7 . . . .203 B4
Pike Cnr SN16 . . . . . . .17 C7
Pike House La SN6 . . .19 C8
Pikefield Cres SN16 . .29 A6
Pilgrim Cl SN5 . . . . . . .49 A7

Pilgrims Mead SP1 . . .146 C5
Pill Hill SP5 . . . . .161 C4
Pilots View SP4 . . . . .217 D3
Pilton Cl SN5 . . . . .49 A8
Pimperleaze Rd BA12 .139 F1
Pinckneys Way 13 SP4 .198 B7
Pine Cl Corsham SN13 .76 A1
Landford SP5 . . . . .212 C5
Melksham SN12 . . . . . .94 A3
Pine Ct 2 BA11 . . . . .110 B7
Pine Wlk
Amesbury SP4 . . . . .217 D3
Trowbridge BA14 . . . . . .105 C3
Pinehurst Inf Sch SN2 .35 B2
Pinehurst Jun Sch SN2 .35 B2
Pinehurst Rd SN2 . . . .35 C2
Pinehurst Sports Ctr
SN2 . . . . .35 B3
Pines Rd SN10 . . . . . .214 C2
Pines The SP6 . . . . . .211 A1
Pinetree Rise SN2 . . .35 B3
Pinetum Cl SN10 . . . .214 A2
Pineview Cl SP5 . . . . .211 C6
Pinewood Way
Colerne SN14 . . . . .74 F7
Salisbury SP2 . . . . .145 B4
Pinewoods Cl SP2 . . .145 B4
Pinfield La SN15 . . . . .78 F4
Pinhills SN11 . . . . .81 A2
Pink La SN16 . . . . .29 E5
Pinkney Pk★ SN16 . . .25 F1
Pinnegar Way SN3 . . .51 E6
Pinnocks Pl SN2 . . . .35 F4
Pintail Ct SN5 . . . . . . .60 B1
Pintail Way BA13 . . .109 B4
Pioneer Cl 3 SN5 . . . .49 A7
Pipehouse La BA2 . . .98 F4
Pipers Cl SN4 . . . . . . .61 D8
Pipers Way SN1 . . . . .50 C1
Pipitdene SN3 . . . . . . .51 D7
Piplar Gd BA15 . . . . . .100 D4
Pippin The SN11 . . . . .81 B3
Pippins The 3 BA12 . .116 F7
Pipsmore Rd
5 Chippenham SN14 . .70 A1
Chippenham SN14 . . . . .78 A8
Pit Wlk SP4 . . . . .199 C4
Pitchens End SN4 . . .167 C2
Pitchens The SN4 . . . .64 B5
Pitman Ave BA14 . . .105 B7
Pitman Ct BA14 . . . . .105 B6
Pitton CE Prim Sch
SP5 . . . . .148 B3
Pitton Rd SP5 . . . . . .154 D8
Pitts Croft SN13 . . . . .84 E5
Pitts La
Bishopstone SP5 . . . . .205 F4
Chitterne BA12 . . . . . .195 D7
Sedgehill & Semley SP7 .202 B7
Pittsfield SN6 . . . . .19 D7
Pix Mead Gdns 1 SP7 .202 D1
Place Rd SN12 . . . . . . .94 A4
Plane Tree Cl SN12 . .85 C1
Planks The SN3 . . . . .50 D4
Plantation Rd
Chippenham SN14 . . . . .78 C8
Tidworth SP9 . . . . .216 D5
Wellow SO51 . . . . .212 F4
Plantation The SP5 . .149 A5
Plants Gn BA12 . . . . .117 B6
Plassey Rd SP9 . . . . .216 C7
Platford St SN11 . . . . .81 B2
Platt Cl RG17 . . . . . . .177 C6
Platt La RG17 . . . . . . .170 E7
Plattes Cl SN5 . . . . . . .49 B8
Play Cl SN5 . . . . .33 C4
Player Ct 8 SP6 . . . .210 D2
Playhouse Salisbury★
SP2 . . . . .146 A1
Pleydell Rd SN1 . . . . .50 C2
Pleydells 3 SN6 . . . . .19 D8
Plough La
Kington Langley SN15 . .70 C5
Marston SN10 . . . . . . .179 A3
Plum La SN10 . . . . . . .180 E4
Plume of Feathers La
SN8 . . . . .213 E3
Plummer Cl SN4 . . . . .64 A6
Plumpton Cl SN14 . . .77 F6
Plymouth St SN1 . . . . .50 D6
Poachers Way SN25 . .34 F7
Pockeredge Dr SN13 .84 C7
Pockeridge Rd SN13 .84 E7
Pointers Way SP4 . . .217 D3
Polaris Way SN2 . . . . .50 B7
Polden Rd 1 SP1 . . .152 C7
Polebarn Rd BA14 . .105 D8
Pollen Cl SP4 . . . . . . .190 B2
Pollen La SP4 . . . . . . .190 B2
Poltondale SN3 . . . . . .51 D7
Pomeroy La BA14 . . .104 B6
Pond La SN5 . . . . .19 B1
Pond St SN25 . . . . . . .34 F5
Ponting St SN1 . . . . . .50 C7
Ponting's Cl SN26 . . .21 C2
Pool Gastons Rd SN16 .27 F3
Pool Gn SN13 . . . . . . .84 E6
Poole Keynes House
GL7 . . . . .5 B4
Poole Rd SN25 . . . . . .34 A5
Poores Rd 17 SP4 . . .198 B7
Pope Cl SN25 . . . . . . .34 F5
Popham Ct SN15 . . . .78 E6
Poplar Ave SN2 . . . . . .35 C4
Poplar Tree La BA14 .104 B3
Poplar Way
Colerne SN14 . . . . .75 A5
Salisbury SP1 . . . . .146 C5

Poplars The
Chippenham SN14 . . . . .70 A1
Fovant SP3 . . . . .204 D8
Trowbridge BA14 . . . . . .105 A5
Popplechurch Dr 5 SN3 .51 E7
Poppy Cl SN11 . . . . . . .80 F4
Porchester Cl 8 SP10 .193 C2
Port Down RG17 . . . . .177 C7
Port Hill SN8 . . . . . . .213 D5
Port Regis Sch SP7 . . .202 A3
Port Way BA13 . . . . . .186 A6
Portal Ave SN13 . . . . .84 B8
Portal Cl SN15 . . . . . . .70 C1
Portal Pl SN15 . . . . . . .60 A1
Portal Rd SN2 . . . . . .35 A2
Porte Marsh Ind Est
SN11 . . . . .81 C5
Porte Marsh Rd SN11 .81 C5
Portfield Rd SP5 . . . .150 A4
Portland Ave
Britford SP2 . . . . .151 F5
Swindon SN1 . . . . .50 A4
Portland Way SN11 . .81 C2
Portman Rd SN12 . . . .94 A6
Portmore Cl SN5 . . . . .34 C2
Portnell's La BA12 . . .137 F4
Porton Rd SP4 . . . . . .217 D3
Portsmouth St SN1 . .50 D6
Portway
Chippenham SN14 . . . . .78 B6
Frome BA11 . . . . .110 A4
Laverstock SP4 . . . . . .146 E2
Warminster BA12 . . . .117 A7
Winterbourne SP4 . . .133 A3
Portway Ind Est SP10 .193 B1
Portway La BA12 . . . .117 A8
Portway The SP1 . . . .145 F4
Portwell 3 SN6 . . . . . .19 C7
Post Office La
Broad Hinton SN4 . . . .167 C7
Corsham SN13 . . . . . . .77 A1
Post Office Rd RG17 .177 F3
Poston Way BA15 . . .99 D7
Pot La BA11 . . . . .110 F8
Potley La SN13 . . . . .84 E7
Potterdown Rd 3 SN2 .35 C5
Potterne CE Prim Sch
SN10 . . . . .179 D5
Potterne Rd SN10 . . .214 A1
Potters Way SP1 . . . .152 C5
Pottery La RG17 . . . .177 E3
Pottle St BA12 . . . . . .119 A6
Pottows Field SN11 . .166 B1
Poulsen Cl BA12 . . . .117 A5
Poulshot Rd SN10 . . .179 A5
Poulton BA15 . . . . . . .100 D5
Poulton Hill SN8 . . . .213 D4
Poulton La BA15 . . . .100 E5
Poulton St SN2 . . . . . .50 C8
Pound Cl Lyneham SN15 .60 A3
Semington BA14 . . . . .102 F6
Pound Farm Cl BA14 .101 E4
Pound Hill
Melchet Park & Plaitford
SO51 . . . . .212 F7
St Paul Malmesbury Without
SN16 . . . . .43 A3
Pound La
Bradford-on-Avon BA15 .100 C5
Damerham SP6 . . . . . .209 E3
Melchet Park & Plaitford
SO51 . . . . .212 F7
Semington BA14 . . . . .102 E6
Shaftesbury SP7 . . . . .202 C2
Swindon SN2 . . . . .35 B2
Wilcot SN8 . . . . .174 B2
Pound Mead SN13 . . .84 F8
Pound Piece
Ashbury SN6 . . . . .164 A8
5 Hungerford RG17 . .177 B7
Pound Pill SN13 . . . . .77 A1
Pound Rd SN6 . . . . . . .22 F7
Pound Row BA12 . . . .116 F6
Pound St
Ebbesborne Wake SP5 .204 D3
Warminster BA12 . . . .116 F6
Pound The
Bromham SN15 . . . . . .96 B7
Mere BA12 . . . . .139 B5
Powell Rise SN16 . . .28 B5
Powells Way GL8 . . . .13 B4
Power Rd SP4 . . . . . .197 C2
Pownall Rd SP4 . . . .198 A6
Poynder Pl SN11 . . . .166 A6
Poynder Rd SN13 . . .76 E1
Poynings Way SN5 . .48 F4
Prescombe Down National
Nature Reserve★
SP5 . . . . .204 C4
Preshute La SN8 . . . .213 B2
Preshute Parochial Prim Sch
SN8 . . . . .213 B1
Prestbury Dr BA12 . .117 C3
Prestly Wood 3 SN13 .76 B1
Preston La SN15 . . . . .60 B1
Pretoria Rd 13 SP11 .192 B5
Priddy Cl BA11 . . . . .110 C7
Priestley Gr SN11 . . .81 C2
Priestley Prim Sch
SN11 . . . . .81 C2
Priestly Wood Rd 6
SN13 . . . . .76 B1
Primrose Cl Calne SN11 .81 B5
Swindon SN2 . . . . .34 D5
Primrose Dr SN12 . . .94 C4

Primrose Hill
Tockenham SN4 . . . . .60 D6
Wilton SP2 . . . . .144 D4
Primrose La
Manningford SN9 . . . . . .181 F6
Redlynch SP5 . . . . .211 D8
Primrose Rd
24 Ludgershall SP11 . . . . .192 A5
Salisbury SP2 . . . . .145 C4
Primrose Way SN14 . . . .70 B2
Primrose Wlk 1 BA12 . .116 E7
Prince Charles Cl 14
SP11 . . . . .192 A5
Prince Charles Dr
SN11 . . . . .81 C3
Princecroft La 3 BA12 .116 E6
Princecroft Prim Sch
BA12 . . . . .116 E6
Princes Cl SP5 . . . . . . .211 D8
Princes Hill SP5 . . . . . .211 D8
Princes St 4 SN1 . . . . . .50 C5
Princess Anne Rd 9
BA11 . . . . .110 A7
Princess Gdns
Trowbridge BA14 . . . . . .101 E4
Warminster BA12 . . . . . .117 D6
Princess Margaret Hospl
SN3 . . . . .51 D1
Princess Mary Gdns 19
SP11 . . . . .192 A5
Prior Pk Prep Sch SN6 . . .19 E7
Prior's Hill SN4 . . . . . . .64 B5
Priorsfield SN8 . . . . . . .213 E2
Priory Ave RG17 . . . . . .177 B6
Priory Cl Alderbury SP5 .153 F2
Bradford-on-Avon BA15 . .100 C7
5 Hungerford RG17 . . . .177 B6
5 Shrewton SP3 . . . . . .196 E6
Wilton SP2 . . . . .144 C2
Priory Gn SN6 . . . . .23 A6
Priory New Rd SN13 . . . .76 F2
Priory Pk BA15 . . . . . . .100 D7
Priory Pl 1 RG17 . . . . . .177 B6
Priory Rd
Hungerford RG17 . . . . . .177 B6
Swindon SN3 . . . . .51 A4
Priory Sq 5 SP2 . . . . . .146 A1
Priory St SN13 . . . . . . .76 F2
Pritchard Cl SN2 . . . . . . .35 F5
Private Rd BA11 . . . . . .123 C8
Privet La SP11 . . . . . . .192 D2
Pro Logis Pk SN3 . . . . . . .36 C6
Proby Pl BA14 . . . . . . .102 A1
Professions Cnr SP5 . . . .206 D6
Prospect Box SN13 . . . . .83 B4
Corsham SN13 . . . . .85 A7
Prospect Hill SN1 . . . . . .50 C5
Prospect Pl
Bathford BA1 . . . . .82 D2
Mere BA12 . . . . .138 F5
Swindon SN1 . . . . .50 C4
Trowbridge BA14 . . . . . .101 D1
Prospect Rd RG17 . . . . .177 B7
Prospect Sq 3 BA13 . . .109 B3
Proud Cl SN5 . . . . .33 B3
Providence La SN13 . . . .76 F1
Providence Terr SN15 . . .78 D7
Provis Mead SN15 . . . . . .79 A4
Provost St 28 SP6 . . . . .210 D1
Pub La SN10 . . . . .180 F8
Puck Well Nature Reserve★
BA12 . . . . .140 C4
Pucklands SN10 . . . . . .180 E5
Puddleslosh La SP6 . . . .210 C2
Pullman Dr SP2 . . . . . .145 B3
Pulsar Rd SN25 . . . . . . .34 B2
Pump La Bathford BA1 . . .82 B1
Long Newnton GL8 . . . . . .13 C4
Purbeck Cl SN3 . . . . . . .51 C7
Purbeck Pl SN11 . . . . . . .81 C2
Purleigh Rd SN13 . . . . . .76 E1
Purley Ave SN3 . . . . . . .51 B3
Purley Rd SN4 . . . . .51 F1
Purley Way SO51 . . . . . .212 E6
Purlpit SN12 . . . . .85 A1
Purlyn Acre SN8 . . . . . .213 D4
Purton Rd SN2 . . . . .34 C3
Purton Mus★ SN5 . . . . . .33 C4
Purton Rd SN2 . . . . .34 C3
Purvis Cl 4 SP4 . . . . . .217 E3
Pyatts Cnr BA14 . . . . . .178 C4
Pye La SN4 . . . . .167 A8

Q

Quadrangle The SN15 . . .78 C6
Quakers Wlk SN11 . . . . . .73 F7
Quantock Cl
Melksham Without SN12 . . .94 D4
5 Warminster BA12 . . . .117 A8
Quarr Barton SN11 . . . . .81 B5
Quarries The SN1 . . . . . .50 C3
Quarry Cl BA2 . . . . .99 D6
Quarry Cres SN6 . . . . . . .22 F6
Quarry Fields Ind Est
BA12 . . . . .138 E5
Quarry Hill SN13 . . . . . .83 E5
Melbury Abbas SP7 . . . . .206 A7
Quarry La Colerne SN14 . .75 B3
Quarry Mews SN1 . . . . . .50 C3
Quarry Rd SN1 . . . . .50 C4
Quarrybrook Cl SN3 . . . .36 E5
Quarrydale Cl SN11 . . . . .81 B2

Quartermaster Rd
BA13 . . . . .108 D6
Quarterway La BA14 . . . .101 E1
Quavey Rd SP5 . . . . . . .211 D7
Quebec Rd SN4 . . . . . . .168 E8
Queen Alexandra Rd
SP2 . . . . .145 D3
Queen Elizabeth Dr
SN2 . . . . .34 C4
Queen Manor Rd
Clarendon Park SP5 . . . .147 B1
Laverstock SP5 . . . . . . .152 E8
Queen Mary Rd SP2 . . .145 D3
Queen Oak★ SN8 . . . . .175 C4
Queen St Hale SP6 . . . .211 B5
Salisbury SP1 . . . . .146 A1
Swindon SN1 . . . . .50 B6
Wilton SP2 . . . . .144 D4
Queen's Barrow★
SP2 . . . . .201 A7
Queen's Dr SN3 . . . . . . .50 E6
Queen's Rd
Devizes SN10 . . . . .214 A2
Westbury BA13 . . . . . . .108 E3
Wootton Bassett SN4 . . . .47 A2
Queenborough SN5 . . . . .49 C4
Queens Ave
Corsham SN13 . . . . .76 F3
Highworth SN6 . . . . .23 A6
Queens Chase BA12 . . . .117 A8
Queens Cl
27 Ludgershall SP11 . . . .192 A5
Sutton Benger SN15 . . . . .57 D2
Queens Club Gdns
BA14 . . . . .105 A8
Queens Cres SN14 . . . . .78 A6
Queens Cres Sch SN14 . . .78 A6
Queens Dr SN3 . . . . . . .51 B2
Queens Gdns
32 Fordingbridge SP6 . . .210 D1
Trowbridge BA14 . . . . . .101 E4
Queens Gr BA9 . . . . . . .137 C3
Queens Rd
Hannington SN6 . . . . . . .21 F8
Mere BA12 . . . . .139 B6
Salisbury SP1 . . . . .146 B2
7 Tisbury SP3 . . . . . . .203 E8
Trowbridge BA14 . . . . . .101 C2
Queens Sq SN15 . . . . . .78 F6
Queens Way SN8 . . . . . .213 F2
Queensberry Rd
Amesbury SP4 . . . . .217 C4
Salisbury SP1 . . . . .146 A3
Queensfield SN2 . . . . . . .35 D5
Queensway
Andover SP10 . . . . .193 F1
Melksham SN12 . . . . . . .94 C4
2 Netheravon SP4 . . . . .190 A3
Warminster BA12 . . . . . .117 D6
Queintin Rd SN1 . . . . . . .50 D3
Quemerford Calne SN11 . .81 C1
Calne Without SN11 . . . . .89 D8
Quidham St SP5 . . . . . .204 F2
Quilling Cl BA14 . . . . . .105 E7

R

Rabley Wood View
SN8 . . . . .213 E4
Radcliffe Rd SP2 . . . . . .152 A6
Radcot Cl SN5 . . . . .34 A1
Radley Bottom
Hungerford Newtown
RG17 . . . . .171 D2
Kintbury RG17 . . . . .177 F7
Radley Cl SN3 . . . . .51 C7
Radnor Cl SN10 . . . . . .214 C2
Radnor Pk SN16 . . . . . . .42 E4
Radnor Pl 3 SN12 . . . . .94 A2
Radnor Rd SP1 . . . . . . .146 A3
Radnor St SN1 . . . . .50 A5
Radstock Ave SN3 . . . . . .51 B6
Radway Rd SN3 . . . . . . .35 F3
Raffin La SN9 . . . . .215 C4
Raggett St SN1 . . . . . . .50 C5
Raglan Cl SN3 . . . . .50 E2
Ragleth Gr BA14 . . . . . .101 E2
Railway Village Mus★
SN1 . . . . .50 B6
Rainer Cl SN3 . . . . .36 B3
Raleigh Ave SN3 . . . . . . .50 F6
Raleigh Cres SP4 . . . . . .217 E3
Rambler Cl BA14 . . . . . .105 A8
Ramblers Mead SP11 . . .193 A2
Rambridge Cres SP2 . . .145 B5
Ramleaze Dr
Salisbury SP2 . . . . .145 C5
Swindon SN5 . . . . .49 A7
Rampart Rd SP1 . . . . . .146 B1
Ramsbury Ave SN2 . . . . .35 B6
Ramsbury Dr RG17 . . . .177 C7
Ramsbury Manor★
SN8 . . . . .169 F1
Ramsbury Prim Sch
SN8 . . . . .170 B2
Ramsbury Terr RG17 . . .177 C7
Ramsbury Wlk BA14 . . . .105 D6
Ramscliff SN10 . . . . . . .187 F7
Ramscombe La BA1 . . . . .82 A6
Ramsden Rd SN1 . . . . . . .48 F3
Ramsthorn Cl SN2 . . . . . .34 D4
Randall Cres SN5 . . . . . . .49 A7
Randall Ct SN13 . . . . . . .76 D1
Randall's Croft Rd
SP2 . . . . .144 B2
Randolph Cl SN3 . . . . . . .50 F5
Rank The BA14 . . . . . . .105 C3

Rannoch Cl 4 SN5 . . . . . .34 B2
Ransome Cl SN5 . . . . . . .49 B8
Raspberry La 8 SP7 . . .202 B1
Ratcliff's Gdn 15 SP7 . .202 C1
Ratcoombe Rd SN4 . . . . .34 A2
Ratfyn Barrow★ SP4 . . .217 E5
SP4 . . . . .217 D5
Ratfyn Rd SP4 . . . . . . .217 D5
Raven Cl SP9 . . . . .216 D6
Ravenglass Rd SN5 . . . . .49 C6
Ravenhurst SN16 . . . . . . .14 E6
Ravens Wlk SN4 . . . . . . .48 A2
Ravenscroft
7 Salisbury SP2 . . . . . .152 A5
Swindon SN3 . . . . .51 C8
Ravenscroft Gdns
BA14 . . . . .101 F1
*Ravensroost Wood & Mdws
Nature Reserve*★
SN16 . . . . .31 A5
Rawlence Rd
Salisbury SP2 . . . . .145 B3
Wilton SP2 . . . . .144 C2
Rawlings Cl SN3 . . . . . . .36 E4
Rawlings Ct 3 SN11 . . . .192 A5
Rawlingswell La SN8 . . .213 E3
Rawlins Rd SN9 . . . . . . .215 C5
Rawlinson Rd SP4 . . . . .198 E6
Rawston Cl SN3 . . . . . . .51 C6
Ray Cl Chippenham SN15 . .78 F5
Swindon SN25 . . . . .35 A4
Raybrook Cres SN2 . . . . .49 E6
Rayfield Gr SN2 . . . . . . .50 B8
Read St SN1 . . . . .50 A5
Reading St 4 SN1 . . . . . .50 B6
Recreation Rd
10 Durrington/Bulford
SP4 . . . . .198 B7
Ludgershall SN1 . . . . . . .192 A6
Rectory Cl Alton SN8 . . .181 C8
Stanton St Quintin SN14 . . .56 B4
11 Warminster BA12 . . .117 A8
Rectory Hill SP5 . . . . . .155 F3
Rectory La
Alderbury SP5 . . . . .153 E2
Breamore SP5 . . . . .210 E5
Charlton Musgrove BA9 . .136 B1
Cricklade SN6 . . . . .19 E8
Letcombe Bassett OX12 . .165 F8
Rectory Pl 4 SP11 . . . . .192 A5
Rectory Rd
Alderbury SP5 . . . . .153 E2
Salisbury SP2 . . . . .151 F8
Sutton Mandeville SP3 . . .204 C1
Rectory Wood SN4 . . . . .170 A6
Reculver Way 6 SP10 . .193 C2
Red Cross House★
SN10 . . . . .214 B4
Red Gables Cl SN5 . . . . . .33 A3
Red La Mildenhall SN8 . .169 B2
Sixpenny Handley SP5 . . .208 A3
Red Lion La SN6 . . . . . . .19 E8
Red Pit BA13 . . . . .112 A8
Red Post La SP11 . . . . . .192 F1
Red Way The BA12 . . . .115 F3
Redbridge Cl 1 SN1 . . . .49 C6
Redcap Gdns SN5 . . . . . .49 A7
Redcliffe St SN2 . . . . . . .49 F6
Redenham Dro SP11 . . .192 E4
Redford Cl SP1 . . . . . . .146 B3
Redgrave Cl BA14 . . . . .105 D6
Redhill Cl SN11 . . . . .79 F2
Redhills SN4 . . . . .62 B1
Redhorn Gdns SN10 . . .214 B2
Redhouse Way SN25 . . . .34 D7
Redland SN14 . . . . .78 B8
Redland La BA13 . . . . . .108 F2
Redland Prim Sch
SN14 . . . . .78 B8
Redlands 3 BA13 . . . . .186 B7
Redlands Cl SN16 . . . . . .23 A4
Redlynch CE Prim Sch
SP5 . . . . .211 E6
Redlynch Cl SN2 . . . . . . .35 C5
Redman Rd SN11 . . . . . . .81 C6
Redmans La SP7 . . . . . .206 A7
Redposts Dr SN1 . . . . . . .49 E4
Redruth Cl SN3 . . . . .51 B5
Redstocks La SN12 . . . . .95 A2
Redwing Ave SN14 . . . . .70 B2
Redwood Way SN4 . . . . .75 A5
Reed Wlk 10 SP4 . . . . .198 C7
Reeds SN6 . . . . .19 C8
Reeds Cnr SN8 . . . . . . .213 E2
Reeds Farm Rd SN16 . . . .28 A4
Reeds Gd SN8 . . . . .213 F3
Reeves Cl 2 SN3 . . . . . .51 C4
Reeves Rd SN10 . . . . . .214 D1
Regent Cir SN1 . . . . . . .50 C5
Regent Cl
16 Hungerford RG17 . . .177 B7
Swindon SN1 . . . . .50 C6
Regent St 6 SN1 . . . . . . .50 C5
Regents Pl
Bradford-on-Avon BA15 . .100 D5
Studley Green BA14 . . . .104 F6
Reid's Piece SN5 . . . . . . .33 B3
Reith Way 2 SP10 . . . . .193 B1
Rendall's Barn GL7 . . . . .4 C5
Rendells Ct SN10 . . . . . .214 B3
Renoir Cl SN25 . . . . .35 A8
Restrop Rd SN5 . . . . . . .33 A4
Restrop View SN5 . . . . . .33 A4
Retingham Way SN2 . . . .36 A5
Reto Gr BA15 . . . . .99 F3
Retreat The
Frome BA11 . . . . .110 A4
Highworth SN6 . . . . .22 F6
Revell Cl SN2 . . . . .35 E4

Reynolds Ct 4 SP10 . . . .193 D1
Reynolds Way SN25 . . . .35 A8
Rhine Cl SN1 . . . . .49 F4
Rhuddlan SN5 . . . . .49 B4
Ricardo Rd SN15 . . . . . . .78 D8
Richard Jefferies Mus★
SN3 . . . . .51 B2
Richard Webb Mews
SN1 . . . . .50 B3
Richards Cl SN4 . . . . . . .47 D1
Richards Way SP2 . . . . .151 E7
Richborough Dr 3
SP10 . . . . .193 C2
Richmond Cl 2 BA14 . . .105 A7
Richmond Cres SP9 . . . .216 E6
Richmond Ct SN6 . . . . . . .6 F1
Richmond Rd
Calne Without SN11 . . . . .81 A4
2 Salisbury SP2 . . . . . .145 C2
Rickbarton 2 SN10 . . . .187 E7
Rickfield BA15 . . . . .100 B6
Rickworth Pl BA12 . . . . .195 A3
Ridge Gn SN5 . . . . .49 B7
Ridge Nether Moor
SN3 . . . . .51 D2
Ridge The
Broad Blunsdon SN26 . . . .21 B2
Redlynch SP5 . . . . .211 C7
Ridgemead SN1 . . . . . . .81 B4
Ridgeway SP3 . . . . .201 A3
Ridgeway Cl SN2 . . . . . . .34 F2
Ridgeway Ct BA12 . . . . .117 B6
Ridgeway La SN15 . . . . . .44 E1
Ridgeway Rd
Salisbury SP1 . . . . .146 B2
Swindon SN2 . . . . .35 E5
Ridgeway Sch The SN4 . . .64 B7
Ridgeway The
Chiseldon SN4 . . . . .65 D2
Crudwell SN16 . . . . .14 E6
Liddington SN4 . . . . . . .163 A2
Warminster BA12 . . . . . .117 B6
Ridgmount 6 SP4 . . . . .198 B7
Ridings Mead SN14 . . . . .70 C2
Ridings The SN14 . . . . . .70 A8
Rigsby's La SN6 . . . . . . .19 E7
Ringsbury Camp★ SN5 . . .32 E2
Ringsbury Cl SN5 . . . . . . .32 F3
Ringwood Ave 5 SP4 . . .217 C3
Ringwood Cl SN3 . . . . . .51 B6
Ringwood Rd 27 SP6 . . .210 D1
Rinsdale Cl SN3 . . . . . . .34 B1
Ripley Rd SN1 . . . . .50 C4
Ripon Cl SN14 . . . . .78 A5
Ripon Way SN3 . . . . .51 A3
Ripple Field SN5 . . . . . . .49 B4
Rise The SN11 . . . . .89 C8
Risingham Mead SN5 . . . .49 C5
Rivar Rd SN8 . . . . .176 F1
Rivenhall Rd SN5 . . . . . . .49 C5
River Par SN8 . . . . .78 D7
River Pk SN8 . . . . .213 D2
River Ray Ind Est SN2 . . .49 E7
River St
Chippenham SN15 . . . . . .78 E2
Pewsey SN9 . . . . .215 C5
River Way
5 Durrington/Bulford
SP4 . . . . .198 C7
South Cerney GL7 . . . . . . .6 F7
Trowbridge BA14 . . . . . .101 C1
Riverbourne Rd
Laverstock SP1 . . . . . . .146 D1
Salisbury SP1 . . . . .152 D8
Riverdale Cl
9 Fordingbridge SP6 . . .210 D1
Swindon SN5 . . . . .50 C2
Riverdale Wlk SN1 . . . . . .50 C2
Rivergate SN5 . . . . .49 C8
Rivermead SP4 . . . . . . .133 F8
Rivermead Dr SN5 . . . . . .49 C7
Rivermead Ind Est SN5 . . .49 C7
Rivers Reach 6 BA11 . . .110 A4
Rivers Way SN6 . . . . . . .22 F6
Riverside Calne SN11 . . . .89 D8
Wilton SP2 . . . . .144 D4
Riverside Cl
Salisbury SP1 . . . . .146 D2
South Newton SP2 . . . . .130 A4
Riverside Dr
Chippenham SN15 . . . . . .79 A8
Melksham SN12 . . . . . . .94 A6
Riverside Pk SN15 . . . . . .44 A2
Riverside Pl SP6 . . . . . .210 E1
Riverside Rd SP1 . . . . . .146 D2
Riverside Terr SP3 . . . . .129 E7
Roach's La GL9 . . . . .38 C1
Road Hill Box SN13 . . . .83 F8
Colerne SN14 . . . . .74 D1
Robbers' Stone★
SN10 . . . . .187 E6
Robbins Ridge SP4 . . . . .217 C2
Robert Franklin Way
GL7 . . . . .7 A7
Robert Le King Prim Sch
SN1 . . . . .50 A5
Roberts Cl SN4 . . . . .64 B5
Roberts of Kandahar Rd
BA12 . . . . .113 F1
Roberts Rd
North Tidworth SP11 . . . .192 A5
Salisbury SP2 . . . . .145 D3
Robin Cl BA12 . . . . .117 C6
Robin Hill La SP4 . . . . .217 C2
Robin Hood's Ball★
SP4 . . . . .189 C1

Robin Hood's Bower★
BA12 . . . . .117 B1
Robinia Cl SN9 . . . . . . .215 D5
Robins Cl
Chippenham SN14 . . . . . .70 B2
Wootton Bassett SN4 . . . .48 A2
Robins Hill RG17 . . . . . .177 F3
Robinsgreen SN3 . . . . . . .51 D7
Robinson Cl SN3 . . . . . . .51 D6
Rochdale Ave SN11 . . . . .81 B4
Roche Cl SN3 . . . . .51 D4
Roche Ct★ SP5 . . . . . . .135 E1
Rochelle Ct 19 SN10 . . .179 F1
Rocher Cl BA13 . . . . . . .108 F3
Rochester Cl 5 SN5 . . . . .49 A4
Rochford Cl BA12 . . . . . . .49 A5
Rock La BA12 . . . . .117 D6
Rock Rd BA14 . . . . .105 B7
Rockbourne La SP6 . . . .209 F3
Rockbourne Mus★
SP6 . . . . .210 A3
Rockbourne Roman Villa★
SP6 . . . . .210 A4
Rockdown Ct SN2 . . . . . .35 D4
Rocker Bench SN6 . . . . .163 E6
Rockfel Rd RG17 . . . . . .165 A1
Rockfield SN14 . . . . .75 B3
Rockley Rd SN8 . . . . . . .213 C7
Rockmoor La SP11 . . . . .185 C5
Rodbourne Cheney Prim Sch
SN25 . . . . .35 A3
Rodbourne House
SN16 . . . . .43 B4
Rodbourne Rd
St Paul Malmesbury Without
SN16 . . . . .42 F4
Swindon SN2 . . . . .49 F7
Rodden Manor★
BA11 . . . . .110 D4
Rodden Rd BA11 . . . . . .110 A5
Roddenbury Cl BA11 . . . .110 B5
Roddenbury View
BA12 . . . . .115 A8
Rode Bridge★ BA11 . . . .103 E1
Rode Hill BA11 . . . . . . .103 F1
Rode Tropical Bird Gdns★
BA11 . . . . .103 D2
Rodney Ct SP10 . . . . . . .193 F1
Rodsleigh BA14 . . . . . . .104 F6
Rodway 13 SN4 . . . . . . .163 A6
Rodwell Cl 3 SN3 . . . . . .51 A4
Rodwell Pk BA14 . . . . . .101 E2
Roebuck Cl SN4 . . . . . . .47 F2
Roger Penny Way
SP6 . . . . .211 C3
Rogers Cl
Quidhampton SP2 . . . . . .145 A3
Swindon SN3 . . . . .51 A7
Rogers Meadow SN8 . . .213 C5
Rogers's La RG17 . . . . .171 D7
Rolleston St 1 SN1 . . . . .50 C5
Rollestone Rd SP3 . . . . .196 E6
Rollestone St 1 SP1 . . . .146 B1
Roman Cres SN1 . . . . . . .50 B3
Roman Meadow SP5 . . .211 A8
Roman Rd SP2 . . . . .145 D2
Roman Way
Andover SP10 . . . . .193 C2
Chippenham SN15 . . . . . .79 B5
Highworth SN6 . . . . .22 F5
Lechlade GL7 . . . . .2 C4
15 Market Lavington SN10 179 F1
Roman Way Prim Sch
SP10 . . . . .193 E2
Romer Rd SP2 . . . . .152 A6
Romney Way SN5 . . . . . .49 A4
Romsey Rd
Amesbury SP4 . . . . .217 D2
Whiteparish SP5 . . . . . .162 B3
Romsey St SN2 . . . . .49 F7
Ron Golding Cl SN16 . . . .28 A5
Rook St BA12 . . . . .139 A4
Rookery Cottages SP5 . .155 F4
Rookery La Ansty SP3 . . .203 F6
Breamore SP6 . . . . .210 D5
Swallowcliffe SP3 . . . . . .204 A6
Rookery Meadow SN8 . .174 A6
Rookery Pk SN11 . . . . . . .89 C7
Rookes La SN10 . . . . . . .179 D5
Rooks La BA11 . . . . .110 D6
Rooks Nest Cl SN15 . . . . .78 F4
Rookwood Gdns 9 SP6 .210 C1
Rope Wlk SN12 . . . . .94 B3
Rope Yd SN4 . . . . .47 D1
Rosary The SN4 . . . . . . .47 E2
Rose St SN2 . . . . .49 F7
Rosebery St SN1 . . . . . . .50 D7
Rosebrock Gdns SN12 . . .94 C3
Rosedale Gdns BA14 . . . .101 A1
Rosedale Rd SN3 . . . . . . .51 B4
Rosefield Way BA13 . . . .108 F4
Rosehill Cl SN15 . . . . . . .59 D3
Roseland Ave SN10 . . . .214 C3
Rosemary Cl Calne SN11 . .80 F4
Laverstock SP1 . . . . . . .146 D1
Swindon SN2 . . . . .34 D5
Rosemary La
Freshford BA2 . . . . .99 B4
2 Salisbury SP1 . . . . . .152 A8
Rosenheim Rise 1
BA13 . . . . .186 B7
Rosetta Cl SN25 . . . . . . .34 B7
Rosewood Ct SN3 . . . . . .51 D3
Ross Gdns SN2 . . . . .36 A4
Ross Rd SP4 . . . . .197 E2
Rossett Gdns BA14 . . . . .105 A8
Rothe Rise BA13 . . . . . .108 F1
Rother Cl SN25 . . . . .34 F5

Rotherstone SN10 ......214 A4
Rotten Row SN4 ......163 A6
Rougemont St SP1 ...146 B1
Rough St SN13 ....84 F5
Roughmoor Way SN5 ...34 A1
Round Barrow Cl SN14 .75 B3
Round Hill
25 Fordingbridge SP6 ...210 D1
West Kington SN14 ....67 A7
Round House SN11 .....81 D1
Roundaway La SP11 ...193 A5
Roundhills Mead SN6 ..23 B6
Roundpond SN12 ......93 F6
Roundponds SN12 .....93 F6
Roundstone Prep Sch
BA14 ....105 E8
Roundstone St BA14 ..101 D1
Roundway Cl SN11 .....89 B1
Roundway Down SN5 ...49 B3
Roundway Gdns SN10 .214 B6
Roundway Ind Est
SN10 ....214 C5
Roundway Pk SN10 ....214 C5
Roundwood View SN8 .58 A3
Rovers Farm & Visitor Ctr★
SN6 ....37 B6
Roves La SN6 ....23 B1
Row La SN12 ....178 C7
Row The SP5 ....211 C8
Rowan Cl Colerne SN14 .75 A5
5 Durrington/Bulford
SP4 ....198 B7
Salisbury SP2 ....145 B4
Rowan Ct Frome BA11 .110 B7
Melksham SN12 ....94 A3
Rowan Dr SN4 ....47 E1
Rowan Rd SN2 ....35 A3
Rowans The SN16 ......27 F4
Rowbarrow SP2 ....152 B5
Rowbarrow Cl SP2 ....152 B5
Rowde CE Prim Sch
SN10 ....96 E2
Rowde Ct Rd SN10 ....96 D1
Rowdeford Sch SN10 ..96 D3
Rowden Hill SN15 .....78 C6
Rowden La
Bradford-on-Avon BA15 .100 D4
Chippenham SN15 .....78 C5
Rowden Rd SN15 ......78 C6
Rowe Mead SN15 ......78 E5
Rowe's Hill BA12 .....119 C8
Rowland Hill Cl SN3 ..51 E4
Rowlands Cl BA1 ......82 B2
Rowley Medieval Village of★
BA15 ....99 F1
Rowley Pl SN12 ....94 B4
Rowton Heath Way
SN5 ....49 A4
Royal Cescent The
SP9 ....216 D7
Royal Cl SN15 ....78 D6
Royal Cres SP9 ......216 D7
Royal Field Cl SN14 ..55 E8
Royal Oak Cl SN15 ....78 F6
Royce Cl 5 SP10 .....193 B1
Royston Rd SN3 ....51 A4
Rubens Cl SN25 ....34 F8
Ruckley Gdns SN3 .....36 B2
Rudge Hill BA11 ......107 D5
Rudge La
Beckington BA11 ......107 B6
Wilcot SN8 ....174 B1
Rudge Rd BA11 ....107 B2
Rumble Dene SN15 ....78 E5
Rune Dr 4 SP10 .....193 D2
Rushall CE Prim Sch
SN9 ....181 E3
Rushall Cl SN2 ....35 B5
Rushall Dro SN9 .....181 D1
Rushall Rd SN9 ......181 F3
Rushcroft Cl SN16 ....28 F1
Rushey La BA15 ....91 F3
Rushmead La SN14 ...66 A3
Rushmere Path SN25 .34 E5
Rushmore Pk★ SP5 ..207 C5
Rushton Rd SN3 ....51 A3
Rushy Platt Ind Est
SN5 ....49 E4
Rushy Platt Nature Reserve★
SN1 ....49 F4
Ruskin Ave
Melksham SN12 ....94 B4
Swindon SN2 ....35 F3
Ruskin Dr
Warminster BA12 .....116 D6
Wootton Bassett SN4 ...47 F3
Ruskin Jun Sch SN2 ..35 F4
Russell Mill La SN10 .179 D1
Russell Rd SP2 ....145 E2
Russell St SP2 ....144 D3
Russell Wlk SN3 ......50 E6
Russet Ct BA12 ......116 F7
Russley Cl SN3 ....53 F1
Russley Pk★ SN8 ....164 A3
Rusty La SN12 ....178 E8
Rutland Cl SN12 ......94 C3
Rutland Cres BA14 ...105 C6
Rutland Rd 1 SN3 ....50 F5
Rutts La 3 SN10 .....187 E2
Ruxley Cl SN4 ....47 D1
Ryan Ave SN14 ....78 A4
Ryan Cl SN5 ....34 B2
Rybury Camp (Hill Fort)★
SN10 ....173 A2
Rycote Cl SN5 ....49 A6
Rydal Cl SN25 ....34 F5
Rye Cl SN5 ....49 A7
Ryeland Way BA14 ...105 E7

Ryeleaze SN10 ....179 D5
Rylands Way SN4 .....47 E2
Ryles La SN8 ....174 B6
Ryon Cl 11 SP10 .....193 E2

S

Sack Hill BA12 ....113 F1
Sackville St SN3 ......50 F7
Saddleback Cl SN11 ..81 C2
Saddleback La SN10 .179 E5
Saddleback Rd SN5 ...49 A7
Saddlers Mead SP2 ..144 C3
Saddlers Way SN8 ...183 D7
Sadler Wlk SN3 ....50 F5
Sadlers Mead SP2 ....78 E8
Sadlers Rd RG17 .....177 C3
Saffron Cl 2 Swindon SN2 .34 E3
Wootton Bassett SN4 ...47 E4
Saffron Meadows SN11 .80 F3
Sage Cl SN2 ....34 D5
St Albans Cl
Salisbury SP1 ....146 D5
Swindon SN2 ....49 E7
St Aldhelm Rd BA14 .100 E5
St Aldhelms Rd SN16 .27 F4
St Alphege Gdns 7
SP10 ....193 D1
St Ambrose Cl SN3 ...51 D6
St Andrew CE Prim Sch
SN26 ....21 C1
St Andrew's Cl
Wilton SP2 ....144 B2
Wooton Rivers SN8 ..174 F1
St Andrew's Rd
Melksham SN12 ....94 C5
Salisbury SP2 ....145 C2
South Newton SP2 ...130 A3
St Andrews SP1 ......146 D2
St Andrews CE Prim Sch
SP1 ....146 E3
St Andrews Cl SN4 ...64 B7
St Andrews Gn SN3 ..51 E7
St Andrews Rd
Tidworth SP9 ....216 C6
Warminster BA12 ....116 D6
St Ann Pl SP1 ....152 B8
St Ann St SP1 ....152 B8
St Annes Cl SN4 .....217 C4
St Arild's Rd GL9 .....24 B4
St Athan Cl SN14 ....178 B8
St Augustine's Rd 5
BA14 ....105 B8
St Augustines Cath Coll
BA14 ....105 B8
St Austell Way SN5 ...49 F6
St Barnabas CE Prim Sch
SN10 ....179 F1
St Bartholomew's St
SP7 ....203 B4
St Bartholomews CE Prim
Sch SN4 ....47 E2
St Bedes Cl 5 SP1 ..146 D5
St Birinus Gdns SP10 .193 D2
St Birinus Rd 4 SP5 .211 C7
St Birstan Gdns 9
SP10 ....193 D1
St Brendans Cl SP1 ..146 C5
St Catherines Cl SN11 .81 C4
St Catherines RC Prim Sch
SN2 ....35 F5
St Christophers Cl 4
SP1 ....146 D5
St Clair Rd SP2 ......152 B6
St Clements Ct SN3 ..51 A4
St Clements Way SN1 .146 C5
St David's Way SN8 ..213 D3
St Davids Cl SP1 .....146 D5
St Dennis Rd 7 SN16 .28 A3
St Dunstan CE Prim Sch
SN11 ....81 C4
St Dunstan Cl SN11 ..81 B5
St Edith's Cl SP2 ....144 C1
St Edith's Marsh SN16 .96 D5
St Edmund RC Prim Sch
SP1 ....81 C5
St Edmund's Church St 2
SP1 ....146 B1
St Edmunds CE Girls Sch
SP1 ....146 E3
St Edwards 12 SP7 ..202 C2
St Edwards Meadow
SN4 ....133 B2
St Edwards Sch S051 .162 B2
St Francis CE VA Prim Sch
SN25 ....34 C5
St Francis Rd SP1 ...146 A4
St Francis Sch SN9 ..215 B6
St George's Cl
Ogbourne St George
SN8 ....169 A5
Warminster BA12 ....117 E5
St George's Rd
Salisbury SP1 ....151 D7
Semington BA14 .....102 E5
11 Shaftesbury SP7 ..202 C1
St Georges CE Prim Sch
BA14 ....102 E6
St Georges CE Sch
SP8 ....137 E1
St Georges Hospl
BA14 ....102 E5
St Georges Pl BA14 .102 E6
St Georges RC Prim Sch
BA12 ....117 D5

St Georges Rd
35 Fordingbridge SP6 ...210 D1
Tidworth SP9 ....216 C6
St Giles Cl SN16 ......29 A2
St Gregory's Ave SP2 .145 D2
St Helens View SN1 ..49 F4
St Ives Ct SN3 ....51 B7
St James SN15 ....59 A7
St James Cl SN2 ......35 D5
St James Gdns SN4 .214 B4
St James St 7 SP11 .192 A5
St James's Cl SP1 ...146 D5
St James's St SP7 ...202 B1
St John CE Fst Sch
SP3 ....203 D8
St John Rd SN4 ....64 A6
St Johns Cl
Donhead St Mary SP7 ...203 A1
Marlborough SN8 ....213 D4
2 Salisbury SP1 .....152 D8
St John's Cres BA14 .104 F6
St John's Ct SP2 .....144 C3
St John's Hill 7 SP7 .202 B1
St John's Priory Pk GL7 ..2 C3
St John's Rd
Frome BA11 ....110 B5
Warminster BA12 ....117 C5
St John's St
Devizes SN10 ....214 A3
Lechlade GL7 ....2 C4
Malmesbury SN16 ....28 B2
Salisbury SP1 ....152 B8
St Johns Alley SN1 ..214 A3
St Johns Cath Prim Sch
BA14 ....105 B8
St Johns CE Prim Sch
BA12 ....117 C6
St Johns Churchyard
SN10 ....214 A3
St Johns Cl
Pewsey SN9 ....215 D5
19 Tisbury SP3 ....203 E8
St Johns Sch & Com Coll
SN8 ....213 D1
St Johns Sch (Lower)
SN8 ....175 A8
St Joseph's Cath Sch
SN3 ....50 E7
St Josephs Cath Sch
SP1 ....146 E3
St Josephs Cl SP1 ...146 C4
St Josephs RC Comp Lower
Sch SN3 ....50 E7
St Josephs RC Prim Sch
Dunkirk SN10 ....179 D8
Malmesbury SN16 ....28 B3
St Judes Cl SN14 ....146 D4
St Just Cl SP4 ....199 B3
St Katharines CE Prim Sch
SN8 ....175 A4
St Katherine Gn 2 SN3 .51 E7
St Katherines SN4 ...167 C6
St Laurence CE Prim Sch
GL7 ....2 D3
St Laurence Rd BA15 .100 E5
St Laurence Sch BA15 .100 C7
St Lawrence Cl SP1 ..145 C4
St Lawrence Cres 6
SP7 ....202 C2
St Lawrence Rd GL7 ...2 C4
St Lawrence Sq 8
RG17 ....177 B7
St Leonard's Cl SP4 .217 B4
St Leonards Cl SN16 ..16 D3
St Lukes Cl 8 SP1 ...146 D5
St Lukes Dr SN15 ....78 C6
St Lukes Sch 7 SN15 .78 C6
St Margaret's Cl 2 SP1 .152 C8
St Margaret's Gdns
SN12 ....94 C5
St Margaret's Gn 1 SN3 .36 B2
St Margaret's Hill
BA15 ....100 D6
St Margaret's Mead
SN8 ....213 D4
St Margaret's Pl BA15 .100 D6
St Margaret's Rd SN1 .50 D3
St Margaret's St BA15 .100 D6
St Margaret's Villas
BA15 ....100 D6
St Margarets Cl SN11 ..81 A4
St Margarets Gdns
SN15 ....78 C6
St Margarets Hospl
SN3 ....36 B4
St Margarets Ret Pk
SN4 ....36 D2
St Mark's Ave SP1 ..146 B3
St Mark's Rd SP1 ...146 B2
St Marks CE Jun Sch
SP1 ....146 B3
St Martin's Chapel★
SN8 ....176 C4
St Martin's Church St 5
SP1 ....152 B8
St Martin's Cl SP3 ..143 A4
St Martins SN8 ......213 E3
St Martins Church St
SP1 ....152 C8
St Martins Cl SP3 ...143 A4
St Mary St SN15 ......78 E7
St Mary's BA14 ......178 A3

St Mary's Church (remains
of)★ SP7 ....206 A5
St Mary's Cl
Chitterne BA12 ....195 D6
Dinton SP3 ....201 E2
Kempsford GL7 ....10 E6
Lyneham SN15 ....59 C3
Potterne SN10 ....179 D5
Redlynch SP5 ....211 D7
Sixpenny Handley SP5 ..208 A4
Trowbridge BA14 ....101 E4
Wilton SP2 ....144 C1
Wylye BA12 ....201 E8
St Mary's Controlled Inf Sch
SP1 ....213 E2
St Mary's Gdns BA14 .101 E4
St Mary's La 2 SN3 ..28 A3
St Mary's Pl SN15 ....78 D8
St Mary's Rd
Dinton SP3 ....201 E2
Frome BA11 ....110 B5
12 Market Lavington SN10 .179 F1
Salisbury SP1 ....151 F7
St Mary's St 1 SN3 ..28 A3
St Marys Cath Prim Sch
SN3 ....35 A1
St Marys CE Prim Sch
Broughton Gifford SN12 ..93 B3
Purton SN5 ....33 C4
Steeple Ashton BA14 .178 A3
St Marys Field GL7 ....1 A1
St Marys Gdns SN10 .214 B4
St Marys Gr SN2 .....35 A3
St Marys La
Dilton Marsh BA13 ..108 B1
Westbury BA13 ......112 C8
St Marys RC Prim Sch
SN15 ....78 C6
St Marys Sch
Calne SN11 ....81 B3
Coombe SP7 ....202 E1
St Matthews Cl
Rowde SN10 ....96 D2
6 Salisbury SP1 .....146 D5
St Mellion Cl SN15 ...78 F7
St Michael's Ave SN6 .22 E6
St Michael's Cl
8 Aldbourne SN8 ....170 A6
Brinkworth SN15 ......45 E6
3 Lambourn RG17 ...165 A1
Trowbridge BA14 ....102 A3
Wilton SP2 ....144 B1
St Michael's Rd
Melksham SN12 ....94 A3
Salisbury SP2 ....145 C4
St Michael's Way SN2 .216 E7
St Michaels CE Controlled
Prim Sch SN12 ....94 B4
St Michaels CE Prim Sch
SP4 ....190 B2
St Michaels Cl
Lyneham & Bradenstoke
SN15 ....59 F4
Tidworth SP9 ....216 C5
St Michaels Prim Sch
SN8 ....170 A6
St Nicholas CE VC Prim Sch
SN15 ....96 A7
St Nicholas Cl
Calne SN11 ....81 C4
11 Ludgershall SP11 ..192 B5
Trowbridge BA14 ....105 D3
Wilton SP2 ....144 B1
Winsley BA15 ....99 D7
St Nicholas Sch SN14 .70 C2
St Nicholas' Rd SP1 .152 A7
St Osmund's Cl SP1 .146 A5
St Osmunds RC Prim Sch
SP1 ....152 A7
St Patricks Ave SP9 .216 B5
St Patricks RC Prim Sch
SN13 ....77 A1
St Paul St SN15 ......78 D8
St Paul's Dr SN3 ......51 E6
St Paul's Rd SP2 ....145 F1
St Paul's St SN2 ......35 C1
St Pauls Prim Sch
SN15 ....70 D2
St Peter's Church★
SP3 ....127 D4
St Peter's Cl
Wilton SP2 ....144 B2
Winterbourne Stoke SP3 .196 F3
St Peter's Pump★
BA12 ....123 C3
St Peters CE Prim Sch
Appleshaw SP11 .....192 E4
Chippenham SN14 ....78 A8
Dunkirk SN10 ....179 D8
St Peters Cl
Chippenham SN15 ....78 C6
5 Shipton Bellinger SP9 .199 D8
St Peters Jun Sch
SN8 ....213 E3
St Peters Rd SP1 ....146 C5
St Philip's Rd SN2 ...35 E3
St Rumbold's Rd 9 SP7 .202 C1
St Sampsons CE Jun Sch
SN6 ....19 D8
St Sampsons Inf Sch
SN6 ....19 D8
St Stephen's Pl BA14 .105 D8
St Swithin Way 8 SP10 .193 D1
St Teresa's Dr SN15 ..78 C7
St Teresas Cl 7 SP1 ..146 C5
St Thomas a' Becket CE Prim
Sch SP3 ....188 B3
St Thomas Cl 14 SP10 .193 D2

Rot – San 239

St Thomas' Rd BA14 .101 D1
St Thomas's Sq SP1 .146 A1
St Thomas's Way SP1 .146 C5
St Ursula's Cl 9 SP1 .146 D5
Saintes Cl 1 SP1 ....146 D5
Salamander Ct SP9 .216 D7
Salcombe Gr SN3 .....50 E5
Salisbury & S Wiltshire Mus
& Stonehenge Gall★
SP1 ....152 A7
Salisbury Arts Ctr★
SP1 ....146 B1
Salisbury Bsns Pk
SP1 ....152 D7
Salisbury Cath★ SP1 .152 A8
Salisbury Cath Sch
SP1 ....152 A7
Salisbury Cl 1 SN14 ..78 A6
Salisbury Coll SP1 ..152 B8
Salisbury District Hospl
SP5 ....152 B3
Salisbury Hill SN8 ..213 E1
Salisbury Hollow
BA13 ....186 D8
Salisbury Mus & Stonehenge
Gallery★ SP1 ....152 A7
Salisbury Racecourse
SP2 ....150 E5
Salisbury Rd
Amesbury SP4 ....217 B3
Breamore SP6 ....210 F5
Chilmark SP3 ....201 A4
Downton SP5 ....211 A8
Fordingbridge SP6 ...210 E1
Hungerford RG17 ....177 B6
Marlborough SN8 ....213 B2
Netheravon SP4 .....190 A3
Pewsey SN9 ....215 C3
Plaitford/Landford SO51 .212 E6
14 Shaftesbury SP7 ..202 C1
Shipton Bellinger SP9 ..199 D7
9 Shrewton SP3 .....196 E6
South Tedworth SP9 .216 C3
Steeple Langford SP3 ..128 C8
Wilton SP2 ....144 E3
Salisbury Rd Ind Est
SN9 ....215 B3
Salisbury Sch of English
SP1 ....152 B8
Salisbury St
Amesbury SP4 ....217 A3
Devizes SN10 ....179 D8
26 Fordingbridge SP6 ..210 D1
Mere BA12 ....139 A5
3 Shaftesbury SP7 ..202 C1
Swindon SN1 ....50 D7
Salisbury Sta SP2 ...145 F1
Salisbury Swimming Baths
SP1 ....146 B2
Sally In the Wood BA1 ..90 C6
Sally Kings La 5 SP7 .202 B2
Salmons Leap SN11 ..81 A5
Salt La Salisbury SP1 .146 B1
Winterbourne SP4 ...133 C3
Salt Spring Dr SN4 ...47 C1
Salt Way Prim Sch SN5 .49 A7
Saltash Rd SN5 ....49 F5
Salter Cl BA14 ....105 E7
Saltersford La SN14 ..78 A5
Saltram Cl SN3 ....51 C6
Salzgitter Dr SN25 ...35 A8
Sambourne CE Prim Sch
BA12 ....116 F6
Sambourne Chase
BA12 ....117 A7
Sambourne Gdns
BA12 ....117 A6
Sambourne Rd
Minety SN5 ....17 D2
Warminster BA12 ....117 A6
Sambre Rd SN4 ....65 D1
Sams La SN26 ....21 C1
Sanctuary The★ SN8 .173 D6
Sand Hole La
6 Westbury BA13 ....108 F1
Westbury BA13 ......112 E8
Sand St BA12 ....121 A6
Sandacre Rd
1 Swindon SN5 ....34 A1
3 Swindon SN5 ....48 F8
Sandalwood Rd 1
BA13 ....108 E1
Sand's La SN10 ....96 D2
Sanden Cl RG17 .....177 B7
Sanders Rd BA14 ....101 C2
Sandes Cl SN15 ....78 C7
Sandfield
Littleton Panell SN10 .187 E8
Sutton Veny BA12 ...194 A5
Sandford Pk BA14 ...104 F7
Sandgate SN3 ....36 B1
Sandhills Rd SP3 ....142 A4
Sandle Copse SP6 ...210 B1
Sandlea Cl SN14 ......68 F5
Sandleaze SN10 .....179 C4
Sandleheath Rd SP6 .210 A1
Sandown Ave SN3 ....50 E3
Sandown Ctr BA14 ..105 E4
Sandown Dr SN14 ....77 F6
Sandown Pl 7 SP2 ...145 F1
Sandpiper Bridge SN3 .51 E2
Sandpiper Gdns SN14 .70 A2
Sandpit Hill SP3 ....141 A2
Sandpit Rd SN11 .....81 D4

Sandpits La
Sherston SN16 . . . . .25 C1
Steeple Ashton BA14 . . . .106 E6
Sandridge Comm SN12 .94 D5
Sandridge Hill SN12 . . . .95 A6
Sandridge La SN15 . . . . . .95 C7
Sandridge Pk★ SN12 . . .95 B6
Sandridge Rd SN12 . . . . .94 B5
Sandringham Rd
Swindon SN3 . . . . .50 F3
Trowbridge BA14 . . . . . . .105 B5
Sandringhams The
SP5 . . . . .153 E1
Sandroyd Sch SP5 . . . . .207 C5
Sands Cl SN10 . . . . .96 D1
Sands The SN9 . . . . .181 C7
Sands' La SP7 . . . . .203 C3
Sandstone Rd SN25 . . . .34 F7
Sandwood Cl SN5 . . . . . .34 B2
Sandy La
Edington BA13 . . . . .186 C7
Redlynch SP5 . . . . .211 D8
Swindon SN1 . . . . .50 B4
Sandy Lea Ave 5 SN13 . .76 B1
Sandy Leaze BA15 . . . . .100 C6
Sandy Ridge SN11 . . . . . .81 C1
Sanford St 3 SN1 . . . . . .50 C6
Sangster Ave SN12 . . . . .94 B4
Sarsen Cl SN1 . . . . .49 F4
Sarson La SP11 . . . . .192 E1
Sarum Ave SN12 . . . . . . .94 B2
Sarum Cl Salisbury SP2 .145 E3
Shipton Bellinger SP9 . . .199 C8
Sarum Dr SN10 . . . . .214 C2
Sarum Gdns BA13 . . . . .109 A4
Sarum Rd SN14 . . . . .78 A6
Sarum St Pauls CE Prim Sch
SP2 . . . . .145 F2
Sarum Way Calne SN11 . .81 A3
2 Hungerford RG17 . . . .177 B6
Sassoon Cl BA12 . . . . . .116 D6
Saunders Gr SN13 . . . . . .76 D1
Saunders Meadow
SN8 . . . . .183 E1
Savernake Ave SN12 . . . .94 C6
Savernake Cl 4 BA12 . . .117 A8
Savernake Cres SN8 . . . .213 F2
Savernake Ct SN8 . . . . . .213 E2
Savernake Hospl SN8 . . .175 A7
Savernake Rd
Burbage SN8 . . . . .175 D1
Corsham SN13 . . . . .84 D8
Savernake St SN1 . . . . . . .50 B5
Savill Cres SN3 . . . . .63 F7
Sawpit Dr SN8 . . . . .175 C5
Sawpit Hill BA14 . . . . . .140 B4
Sawyer Cl SN25 . . . . .35 B6
Sawyers Cl SN16 . . . . . . .17 A2
Sawyers Cres SN13 . . . . .76 D1
Sawyers Hill SN16 . . . . . .17 A2
Saxby Rd SN15 . . . . .70 E1
Saxifrage Bank SN12 . . . .94 C3
Saxon Cricklade SN6 . . . .19 D7
14 Market Lavington SN10 179 F1
Sherston SN16 . . . . .25 C1
Westbury BA13 . . . . .109 A4
Saxon Ct
North Tidworth SP9 . . . . .216 D7
Swindon SN3 . . . . .50 D4
Saxon Dr BA14 . . . . .101 E4
Saxon Leas SP5 . . . . . . .149 C6
Saxon Meadow SN8 . . . .211 A8
Saxon Mill SN4 . . . . .65 D5
Saxon Rd SP2 . . . . .151 F6
Saxon Rise SN8 . . . . . . .183 E1
Saxon Spur 10 SP7 . . . . .202 C2
Saxon St SN14 . . . . .78 B8
Saxon Way
Andover SP10 . . . . .193 C2
Winsley BA15 . . . . .99 F7
Saxonhurst 4 SP11 . . . .211 B8
Saxons Acre BA12 . . . . .116 D6
Saxton Wlk SN5 . . . . .49 B8
Scallows La SO51 . . . . . .212 F7
Scamell's Rd SP2 . . . . . .146 A2
Scarborough Rd SN2 . . . .49 F8
Scarlet Cl SN25 . . . . .34 F7
Scholard's La 16 SN8 . . .170 E2
School Cl
Chiseldown SN4 . . . . .65 E4
Keevil BA14 . . . . .178 B5
St Paul Malmesbury Without
SN16 . . . . .28 A1
Vernhams Dean SP11 . . .185 C3
School Dr 28 SP4 . . . . . .198 B7
School Hill
Alderbury SP5 . . . . .153 C2
Brinkworth SN15 . . . . .45 E5
School La
All Cannings SN10 . . . . . .180 F8
1 Amesbury SP4 . . . . . .217 B3
Badminton GL9 . . . . .38 E2
Bromham SN15 . . . . .96 A7
Castle Combe SN14 . . . . .68 A7
Castle Eaton SN6 . . . . . . .10 B4
East Garston RG17 . . . . .171 E8
Grittleton SN14 . . . . .54 E5
Hindon SP3 . . . . .200 B3
Lea SN16 . . . . .29 A2
Little Bedwyn SN8 . . . . . .176 C5
Marlborough SN8 . . . . . . .213 A2
Meysey Hampton GL7 . . . . .1 A4
South Cerney GL7 . . . . . . .6 F7
Staverton BA14 . . . . .101 D5
Westbury BA13 . . . . .108 E1

School La continued
Wroughton SN4 . . . . .64 A6
School Rd Calne SN11 . . .81 A4
1 Durrington/Bulford
SP4 . . . . .198 C7
Kemble GL7 . . . . .4 F7
Nomansland SP5 . . . . . . .212 C4
Redlynch SP5 . . . . .211 E6
Seend SN12 . . . . .178 D8
School Wlk SN14 . . . . . . .78 A7
Scotby Ave SN3 . . . . .50 E2
Scotchel Gn SN9 . . . . . .215 D5
Scotland Hill SN15 . . . . .57 A5
Scotland La
Beckington BA11 . . . . . . .107 C4
Landford SP5 . . . . .212 B8
Scotland Rd SN12 . . . . . .94 A6
Scotney Cres 2 SN25 . . .34 C4
Scots La SP1 . . . . .146 A1
Scott Cl SN8 . . . . .183 C8
Scott's Hill SP7 . . . . .203 C4
Scotts Cl SN11 . . . . .89 B2
Scratchbury Camp★
BA12 . . . . .194 B7
Scrubbity Barrows★
SP5 . . . . .207 E4
Seaford Cl SN5 . . . . .49 A6
Seagrim Rd SP2 . . . . . . .144 C2
Seagry CE Prim Sch
SN15 . . . . .57 D6
Seagry Ct SN25 . . . . .35 B5
Seagry Hill SN15 . . . . . . .57 D3
Seagry Rd
Hullavington SN14 . . . . . .56 F5
Sutton Benger SN15 . . . . .57 D2
Seaton Cl SN25 . . . . .34 F5
Second Broad Dr SP3 . . .128 C2
Sedgebrook SN3 . . . . .51 D2
Sedgefield Gdns SN10 . .214 B4
Sedgefield Way SN14 . . . .77 F6
Seend CE Prim Sch
SN12 . . . . .178 D8
Seend Hill SN12 . . . . . . .178 F8
Sefton Way SN25 . . . . . . .34 C7
Selby Cres SN5 . . . . .49 B4
Seldon Cl 4 SN3 . . . . . . .50 E6
Selions Cl SN14 . . . . .70 B2
Selwood Anglican/Methodist
Mid Sch BA11 . . . . . . .110 B6
Selwood Cres 1 BA11 . . .110 A7
Semington Rd
Berryfield SN12 . . . . .94 A1
Melksham Without BA14 . .178 A8
Semley Ceva Prim Sch
SP7 . . . . .202 F5
Senior Dr SP2 . . . . .152 A5
Sergeant Rogers Way
SN10 . . . . .214 E7
Seth Ward Dr SP1 . . . . . .146 D4
Seven Barrows★
Lambourn RG17 . . . . . . .165 A5
South Tedworth SP9 . . . .191 B3
Seven Fields Nature
Reserve★ SN25 . . . . . . .35 B5
Seven Fields Prim Sch
SN2 . . . . .35 B4
Sevenfields SN6 . . . . .23 A7
Severn Ave SN25 . . . . . . .35 A4
Severn Cl SN11 . . . . .81 A5
Severn Rd SN12 . . . . .94 A6
Seymour Ct BA14 . . . . . .101 C1
Seymour Rd
Chippenham SN15 . . . . . .78 F4
Swindon SN3 . . . . .50 F6
Trowbridge BA14 . . . . . . .101 C4
Seymours Ct★ BA11 . . .107 A6
Shackleton Cl SN12 . . . . .94 D1
Shackleton Rd SN10 . . . .214 C2
Shackleton Sq SP10 . . . .193 F2
Shady Bower SP1 . . . . . .152 C8
Shady Bower Cl SP1 . . . .152 C8
Shaftesbury Ave SN3 . . . .51 B4
Shaftesbury Ct BA14 . . . .105 A6
Shaftesbury Dro SP2 . . .151 E5
Shaftesbury Leisure Ctr
SP7 . . . . .202 C1
Shaftesbury Mus★
SP7 . . . . .202 C1
Shaftesbury Prim Sch
SP7 . . . . .202 D1
Shaftesbury Rd
Barford St Martin SP3 . . .143 B3
Mere BA12 . . . . .139 B4
Motcombe SP7 . . . . .202 A3
Wilton SP2 . . . . .144 B3
Shaftesbury Sch SP7 . . .202 C1
Shaftesbury St 19 SP6 . .210 D1
Shails La
Melksham Without
SN12 . . . . .178 A8
Trowbridge BA14 . . . . . . .101 C1
Shakespeare Ave
SP10 . . . . .193 C1
Shakespeare Dr SN8 . . . .213 C2
Shakespeare Path SN3 . . .35 F3
Shakespeare Rd
Salisbury SP1 . . . . .145 F4
Wootton Bassett SN4 . . . .47 F3
Shalbourne CE Prim Sch
SN8 . . . . .176 F2
Shalbourne Cl
Hungerford RG17 . . . . . . .177 A7
Swindon SN2 . . . . .35 B5
Shalford La BA9 . . . . . . .136 A3
Shallow Wagon La
BA13 . . . . .108 F6
Shallowbrooks La SN14 . .39 F8

Shallows The SP6 . . . . . .210 F4
Shambles The BA15 . . . .100 D7
Shanklin Rd SN2 . . . . . . .34 E4
Shaplands 4 SN3 . . . . . . .36 A2
Shapwick Cl SN3 . . . . . . .51 C7
Sharcott Dro SN9 . . . . . .215 A4
Share La SP3 . . . . .203 C6
Sharp Cl SN5 . . . . .49 B7
Sharpley Cl SP6 . . . . . . .210 D2
Sharratt Ave 4 SP1 . . . .146 C5
Shaw La BA10 . . . . .122 A4
Shaw CE Prim Sch
SN12 . . . . .93 D8
Shaw Hill
Collingbourne Ducis SN8 .191 E7
Melksham Without SN12 . .93 D7
Shaw Rd SN5 . . . . .49 B7
Shaw Ridge Leisure Pk★
SN5 . . . . .49 B6
Shaw Ridge Prim Sch
SN5 . . . . .49 B7
Shaw Village★ SN8 . . . .173 F4
Shawgrove SN8 . . . . .176 B3
Shear Cross BA12 . . . . . .116 E1
Shearman St BA14 . . . . .105 D7
Shearwater Way SN13 . . .84 D7
Shearwood Rd SN5 . . . . .34 A1
Sheasby Cl SP5 . . . . .208 A3
Sheen Cl Salisbury SP2 . .145 B5
4 Swindon SN5 . . . . .49 A4
Sheep Fair Way 13
RG17 . . . . .165 A1
Sheep St Devizes SN10 . .214 B3
Highworth SN6 . . . . .23 A6
Sheepbridge Rd SP4 . . . .198 E7
Sheepcote Barton 3
BA14 . . . . .105 E7
Sheepdrove Rd RG17 . . .165 B2
Sheepridge SN8 . . . . .168 C3
Sheepscroft SN14 . . . . . .70 B2
Sheepwash La BA12 . . . .201 E8
Sheerwold Cl SN3 . . . . . . .36 B3
Sheffield La SN13 . . . . . . .76 D1
Shelburne Rd SN11 . . . . .81 C1
Shelburne Way SN11 . . . .79 F2
Sheld Dr SN15 . . . . .60 A1
Sheldon Manor & Gdns★
SN14 . . . . .69 D1
Sheldon Rd SN14 . . . . . . .78 B7
Sheldon Sch SN14 . . . . . .70 B1
Shelfinch SN5 . . . . .49 D4
Shelley Ave 2 SN4 . . . . . .47 F3
Shelley Gdns SN12 . . . . .94 B4
Shelley Dr SP1 . . . . .145 F4
Shelley St SN1 . . . . .50 B5
Shelley Way BA12 . . . . . .116 D6
Shelly's Wlk GL7 . . . . .2 D4
Shenton Cl SN3 . . . . .36 B3
Shepherd Spring Jun & Inf
Sch 30 SP10 . . . . .193 E4
Shepherd's La
Donhead St Andrew SP7 .203 B2
Selwood BA11 . . . . .114 D6
Shepherds SN13 . . . . .84 D6
Shepherds Breach 1
. . . . .47 E2
Shepherds Cl
Coombe Bissett SP5 . . . .151 A1
Odstock SP5 . . . . .152 A1
Shepherds Mead
BA13 . . . . .112 A8
Shepherds Rise SP11 . . .185 C3
Sheppard Cl SN15 . . . . . .78 F5
Sheppard St SN1 . . . . . . .50 B7
Sheppards Rise SN15 . . .46 B7
Shepperton Way SN25 . . .34 F6
Sherborne Pl SN3 . . . . . . .51 B7
Sherborne Rd BA14 . . . . .100 F1
Sherborne St GL7 . . . . .2 C4
Sherfield SN4 . . . . .133 A2
Sherfield English La
SO51 . . . . .212 F7
Sherfield English Rd
SP5 . . . . .212 E6
Sherfields SN4 . . . . .47 E1
Sherford Rd SN25 . . . . . .34 E4
Sheridan Dr SN4 . . . . .47 F3
Sheringham Ct SN3 . . . . .51 D3
Sherington Mead SN15 . .79 B4
Sherrington La BA12 . . . .195 A2
Sherrington Mead
SN15 . . . . .79 B4
Sherston Ave SN2 . . . . . . .35 C5
Sherston Rd
Brokenborough SN16 . . . .27 E4
Luckington SN14 . . . . .39 E5
Sherwood Ave SN12 . . . . .94 C6
Sherwood Cl 3 BA12 . . .117 A8
Sherwood Rd SN3 . . . . . . .51 B4
Shetland Cl
Swindon SN5 . . . . .49 B7
Westbury BA13 . . . . .108 D2
Shetland Gdns SN5 . . . . .49 A7
Shipley Dr SN25 . . . . .34 F6
Shipton Bellinger Prim Sch
SP9 . . . . .199 C8
Shipton Gr SN3 . . . . .50 E5
Shiptons La SN15 . . . . . . .43 F2
Shire Cl SN5 . . . . .49 A7
Shire Ct 3 SN1 . . . . .50 A5
Shire Hill SN14 . . . . .66 A7
Shire Way BA13 . . . . .108 E2
Shires Sh Ctr The
BA14 . . . . .105 C8
Shirley Cl SN3 . . . . .50 F7
Shockerwick La BA1 . . . . .82 D4
Shoddesden La SP11 . . . .192 B4
Shoemaker La SN15 . . . . .45 F6

Shop La Badminton GL9 . . .38 E2
Wingfield BA14 . . . . .104 C6
Shore Pl BA14 . . . . .100 F1
Shoreland Cl BA13 . . . . .108 F3
Short Dro SN4 . . . . .163 C6
Short La Andover SP11 . . .193 B1
Barford St Martin SP3 . . .143 A4
Short River Rd BA13 . . . .109 D2
Short St
Ludgershall SP11 . . . . . . .192 A5
Melksham SN12 . . . . .94 C6
Shortlands SP2 . . . . .144 B3
Shorts Gn La SP7 . . . . . .202 A4
Shoscombe Gdns 3
BA11 . . . . .110 C7
Showfield SN4 . . . . .47 D3
Shrapnel Rd 1 SP4 . . . . .197 E2
Shrewsbury Rd SN3 . . . . .50 F6
Shrewton CE Prim Sch
SP3 . . . . .196 E7
Shrewton Cl BA14 . . . . . .105 D6
Shrewton Rd BA12 . . . . . .195 E6
Shrewton Wlk SN25 . . . . .35 C5
Shrivenham Rd
Highworth SN6 . . . . .23 B4
Swindon SN1 . . . . .50 E7
Swindon SN3 . . . . .36 E2
Shropshire Cl
Salisbury SP2 . . . . .145 C5
1 Swindon SN5 . . . . .49 B7
Shurnhold SN12 . . . . .93 F5
Shute End Rd SP5 . . . . . .153 B4
Shutts La SP5 . . . . .151 A1
Sidbury Circular Rd
SP9 . . . . .216 B7
Sidbury Hill Ave SP9 . . . .216 C8
Sidings The 2 SP5 . . . . .211 B8
Sidmouth Par SN10 . . . . .214 B3
Sidney Cl Swindon SN5 . . .48 F4
3 Swindon SN3 . . . . .50 E6
Sidney St SP2 . . . . .145 F1
Sidney Wood Ct SN14 . . . .78 C7
Signal St SN4 . . . . .198 E6
Signal Way SN1 . . . . .50 D3
Silbury Cl
Chippenham SN14 . . . . . .78 A6
Westbury BA13 . . . . .108 F4
Silbury Hill★ SN8 . . . . .173 C7
Silbury Mews SN25 . . . . .34 E3
Silbury Rd SN11 . . . . .81 A3
Silchester Way SN5 . . . . .49 C6
Sillen La SP6 . . . . .209 B6
Sillington La SN10 . . . . . .179 B7
Silman Cl SN13 . . . . .76 C1
Silton Rd SP8 . . . . .137 F2
Silver Barrow★ SP3 . . . .188 D2
Silver Birch Rd BA14 . . . .105 B5
Silver Cl SN16 . . . . .17 B2
Silver La BA11 . . . . .114 C6
Silver Meadows BA14 . . .105 A5
Silver St Alderbury SP5 . .153 B2
Bradford-on-Avon BA15 . .100 D6
Calne SN11 . . . . .81 B1
Calne Without SN11 . . . . .89 B8
Colerne SN14 . . . . .75 B3
Corsham SN13 . . . . .85 C6
Kington Langley SN15 . . . .70 F7
Malmesbury SN16 . . . . . . .28 A3
Minety SN16 . . . . .17 B2
Potterne SN10 . . . . .179 D5
Salisbury SP1 . . . . .152 A8
Sherston SN16 . . . . .40 C8
South Cerney GL7 . . . . . . .6 F7
Steeple Ashton SN14 . . . .178 A3
Trowbridge BA14 . . . . . . .105 D8
Warminster BA12 . . . . . . .117 A7
Westbury BA13 . . . . .112 C8
Wilton SP2 . . . . .144 D3
Silver St La
Bromham SN15 . . . . .87 D1
Trowbridge BA14 . . . . . . .105 B5
Silver Wood SP5 . . . . . . .153 C3
Silverless St SN8 . . . . . . .213 D5
Silverton Rd SN3 . . . . . . .51 B6
Silverwood Dr SP1 . . . . . .146 E2
Simmance Way SP4 . . . .217 C3
Simnel Cl SN5 . . . . .48 F5
Simonds Rd 17 SP11 . . .192 A5
Six Acre La
Shalbourne RG17 . . . . . . .176 F3
West Knoyle BA12 . . . . . .140 A4
Sixpenny Handley Fst Sch
SP5 . . . . .208 A4
Skew Bridge Cl SN4 . . . . .47 C1
Skew Bridge Rd SP2 . . . .145 D2
Skew Rd SP2 . . . . .145 B2
Skinner's Cl SN6 . . . . .22 B7
Skye Cl SN6 . . . . .22 F7
Slab La SP5 . . . . .211 C7
Slade Dr SN3 . . . . .36 B1
Slades The SN11 . . . . .81 C3
Sladesbrook BA15 . . . . . .100 E8
Slag La BA13 . . . . .108 F5
Slate Way SP5 . . . . .148 B3
Slater Rd SN9 . . . . .215 C5
Slaughterford Rd SN14 . . .68 C1
Sleight La SN10 . . . . .179 F6
Sleight Rd SN10 . . . . .214 E1
Slessor Rd
Lyneham SN15 . . . . .60 D1
Lyneham & Bradenstoke
SN15 . . . . .166 A8
Sling Orch SP3 . . . . .204 E7
Sling Rd SP4 . . . . .198 E7
Slipper La SN4 . . . . .65 D4
Slipway The BA14 . . . . . .101 D4
Slodbrook La SP8 . . . . . .138 C1
Slowgrove Cl BA14 . . . . .105 E7

Small St SN10 . . . . .180 F4
Smallbrook Gdns
BA14 . . . . .101 D5
Smallbrook La BA12 . . . .117 D5
Smallbrook Mdws Nature
Reserve★ BA12 . . . . . .117 C5
Smallbrook Rd BA12 . . . .117 D5
Smannell Rd SP11 . . . . . .193 F2
Smay Down La SN8 . . . . .184 E6
Smeaton Rd
1 Andover SP10 . . . . . . .193 B1
Salisbury SP2 . . . . .145 E1
Smitan Brook SN3 . . . . . . .51 D6
Smith St SN14 . . . . .67 A6
Smitham Bridge Rd
RG17 . . . . .177 B7
Smith's Hill OX12 . . . . . .165 F7
Smithfield St 2 SP4 . . . .217 B3
Smiths Cl SN9 . . . . .215 B5
Smiths Yd SN13 . . . . .177 A2
Smithy La SN9 . . . . .181 C6
Smithys La SN8 . . . . .183 C8
Smithywell Cl BA14 . . . . .105 F8
Snail-Creep Hanging★
SP3 . . . . .200 E7
Snails' La SN10 . . . . .214 A3
Snap Village★ SN8 . . . . .169 C7
Snappersnipes BA13 . . . .109 A3
Snapps Cl SN4 . . . . .64 B5
Snarlton La SN12 . . . . . . .94 D5
Snoddington Rd
Fyfield SP11 . . . . .192 D1
Shipton Bellinger SP9 . . .199 E7
Snow Hill Dinton SP3 . . .201 F2
Hilmarton SN11 . . . . .73 F5
Snowberry La SN12 . . . . .94 C3
Snowdon Pl SN2 . . . . .35 E4
Snowdrop Cl SN25 . . . . . .34 D5
Snowshill Cl SN25 . . . . . .34 F5
Snowswick La SN7 . . . . . .12 E7
Snuff St SN10 . . . . .214 A4
Sobers Sq SP11 . . . . .193 C2
Sock's La BA10 . . . . .122 A7
Sodom La SN15 . . . . .59 C7
Soldier's Ring★ SP6 . . . .209 D4
Solstice Pk Bsns Park
SP4 . . . . .217 D4
Solstice Rise SP4 . . . . . .217 B3
Somerdale Cl 6 SN5 . . . .49 C6
Somerford Cl SN2 . . . . . . .35 C4
Somerford Lakes Reserve★
GL7 . . . . .9 D2
Somerfords Walter Powell CE
VA Prim Sch SN15 . . . . .44 B2
Somerleyton Cl SN10 . . .187 D8
Somerset Cl 1 RG17 . . . .177 B7
Somerset Cres SN12 . . . .94 B3
Somerset Dr BA13 . . . . . .109 A5
Somerset Rd
Salisbury SP1 . . . . .146 B3
Swindon SN2 . . . . .34 F1
Somerset Way BA14 . . . .102 F6
Somerton Gdns BA11 . . .110 C9
Somerville Ct 2 SP10 . . .193 F1
Somerville Rd SN3 . . . . . .50 F6
Somme Rd SP11 . . . . . . .191 F4
Sopwith Pk 7 SP10 . . . . .193 C1
Sopworth Rd SN14 . . . . . .39 E5
Sorley Cl SN8 . . . . .213 B3
Sorrel Cl Melksham SN12 . .94 C3
Trowbridge BA14 . . . . . . .105 D5
Wootton Bassett SN4 . . . .47 E4
Sorrel Dr SN14 . . . . .70 B3
Sound Copse SN5 . . . . . . .34 B2
South Alley 6 BA12 . . . . .116 E5
South Bank SN8 . . . . .174 F2
South Charford Dro
SP6 . . . . .210 D6
South Cliffe Rd 6 SN10 .179 F1
South Cross La SN10 . . . .179 C3
South Dr SP9 . . . . .216 C4
South Hills Sch SP2 . . . .150 D8
South La Downton SP5 . . .211 A8
Nomansland SP5 . . . . . . .212 C4
South Marston CE Prim Sch
SN3 . . . . .36 C4
South Marston Park
SN3 . . . . .36 C7
South Mdw La SN5 . . . . . .19 F3
South Mill Cl SN4 . . . . . .217 B2
South Mill Rd SP4 . . . . . .217 B2
South Pk★ SP11 . . . . . . .192 B4
South Pl Calne SN11 . . . . .81 B2
Corsham SN13 . . . . .77 A1
South St
Aldbourne SN8 . . . . .170 A6
Avebury SN8 . . . . .173 B8
Broad Chalke SP5 . . . . . .205 B4
Corsham SN13 . . . . .77 A1
Great Wishford SP2 . . . . .130 A3
8 Salisbury SP2 . . . . . . .145 F1
Swindon SN1 . . . . .50 A4
Warminster BA12 . . . . . . .116 E5
Wilton SP2 . . . . .144 C1
South Ugford Medieval
Village of★ SP2 . . . . . .144 A2
South View RG17 . . . . . . .177 B7
South View Ave SN3 . . . . .50 E5
South View Pl SN8 . . . . . .213 C6
South Way
Alderbury SP5 . . . . .153 E2
Trowbridge BA14 . . . . . . .105 D7
South Western Rd
SP2 . . . . .145 F1
South Wilts Gram Sch
SP1 . . . . .146 A3
Southampton Rd
Alderbury SP5 . . . . .153 D3

Southampton Rd *continued*
Fordingbridge SP6 . . . .**210** E1
Salisbury SP1 . . . .**152** C7
Southampton St SN1 . . . .**50** D6
Southay BA13 . . . .**186** B7
Southbank Gdns RG17 . . .**165** B1
Southbank Glen SN4 . . . . .**47** F2
Southbourne Way
SP4 . . . .**133** D6
Southbrook BA12 . . . .**139** C4
Southbrook Gdns
BA12 . . . .**139** B4
Southbrook La BA13 . . . .**178** B1
Southbrook Rd SN12 . . . .**93** F6
Southbrook St SN2 . . . . . .**35** B5
Southbroom Inf Sch
SN10 . . . .**214** C2
Southbroom Jun Sch
SN10 . . . .**214** C2
Southbroom Rd SN10 . . . .**214** B3
Southcott Rd SN9 . . . . . .**215** D4
Southcroft Dr BA13 . . . . .**111** D4
Southcroft Rd 2 SN13 . . .**76** B1
Southdown 3 SN4 . . . . . .**163** A5
Southernwood Dr SN2 . . .**34** C4
Southerwicks SN13 . . . . . .**84** F8
Southey Cl SN25 . . . .**34** F8
Southfield
2 Aldbourne SN8 . . . .**170** A6
Southwick BA14 . . . .**104** F2
West Overton SN8 . . . . . .**173** F6
Southfield Jun Sch
SN6 . . . .**23** A5
Southfields BA11 . . . .**110** A3
Southgate SN10 . . . .**214** B2
Southgate Cl SN10 . . . . . .**214** B2
Southleigh BA15 . . . .**100** C5
Southleigh View BA12 . . .**117** C5
Southmead SN14 . . . .**78** B6
Southmill Hill SP4 . . . . . .**217** D1
Southside
Laverstock SP4 . . . .**146** D8
Shipton Moyne GL8 . . . . . .**26** E7
Southview Rd BA14 . . . .**105** D6
Southville Rd BA15 . . . . .**100** C5
Southward La SN8 . . . . . .**170** A6
Southwark Cl SP9 . . . . . .**216** E6
Southway SP4 . . . .**134** B2
Southway Rd BA15 . . . . . .**100** D4
Southwell Cl 2 SN14 . . . .**78** D4
Southwick Ave SN2 . . . . .**35** B5
Southwick CE Prim Sch
BA14 . . . .**104** F3
Southwick Ctry Pk ★
BA14 . . . .**104** F5
Southwick Rd BA14 . . . . .**105** C2
Southwold SN25 . . . .**34** B6
Southwood Rd BA14 . . . .**105** F8
Sovereign Ct SP2 . . . . . .**145** F1
Soyuz Cres SN25 . . . .**34** E7
Spa Cl SN6 . . . .**23** B6
Spa Ct SN12 . . . .**94** B3
Spa Rd SN12 . . . .**94** B3
Spackman La SN13 . . . . . .**84** E8
Spanbourn Ave SN14 . . . .**78** D7
Sparcells Dr SN5 . . . .**34** B2
Speedwell Cl
Melksham SN12 . . . .**94** C2
1 Swindon SN25 . . . .**34** E5
3 Trowbridge BA14 . . . . .**105** D6
Spencer Cl
Melksham SN12 . . . .**94** A6
Swindon SN5 . . . .**48** F7
Spencers Orch
Bradford-on-Avon BA15 . .**100** D5
Wroughton SN4 . . . .**64** B6
Spenser Cl SN3 . . . .**51** A7
Speresholt SN5 . . . .**49** D4
Spey Ct SP10 . . . .**193** F1
Spiders Island SP5 . . . . .**153** F2
Spiers Piece BA14 . . . . . .**178** B3
Spin Hill SN10 . . . .**179** E1
Spindle Tree Ct SN2 . . . .**35** B2
Spine Rd (East) GL7 . . . . . .**7** C4
Spine Rd W GL7 . . . .**6** A2
Springfield Rd BA12 . . . .**139** B5
Spinners Croft 5 BA14 . .**105** D6
Spinners Way BA12 . . . . .**139** B6
Spinney Cl
Chippenham SN14 . . . .**78** A6
3 Liddington SN4 . . . .**163** A4
Spinney Rd SP11 . . . .**192** A5
Spinney The
Lechlade GL7 . . . .**2** C4
3 Littleton Panell SN10 . .**187** E8
Trowbridge BA14 . . . .**105** F8
Spital La SN6 . . . .**19** E7
Spitfire Rd SN14 . . . .**146** D8
Spitfire Way SN3 . . . .**36** C2
Spode Cl SN25 . . . .**34** D7
Spout La SO51 . . . .**178** F8
Spouts La SO51 . . . .**212** F1
Spracklands SP3 . . . .**201** F2
Sprats Barn Cres SN4 . . .**47** D3
Spratsgate La GL7 . . . .**6** B4
Spray Leaze 10 SP11 . . . .**192** B5
Spray Rd RG17 . . . .**177** C2
Sprays 9 SN8 . . . .**183** D8
Spread Eagle Hill SP7 . .**206** B6
Spreckley Rd 1 SN11 . . . .**166** A1
Spring Cl SN1 . . . .**50** C6
Spring Gdns Lechlade GL7 . . .**2** C4
Swindon SN1 . . . .**50** C6
Spring La SN13 . . . .**84** C7
Spring Meadow SN8 . . . .**191** D8
Spring Meadows
BA14 . . . .**105** A5
Spring Rd BA11 . . . .**110** A6

Spring The 5 SN10 . . . .**187** E8
Spring Tining SN13 . . . . .**76** F1
Springers Cl SN10 . . . . . .**214** D4
Springfield BA15 . . . .**100** A5
Springfield Bldgs
SN15 . . . .**78** D3
Springfield Cl
Corsham SN13 . . . .**84** A8
7 Shaftesbury SP7 . . . . . .**202** C2
Trowbridge BA14 . . . .**101** E1
Springfield Cres
11 Redlynch SP5 . . . .**211** C7
Wootton Bassett SN4 . . . .**47** D2
Springfield Dr SN11 . . . . .**81** A3
Springfield Gdns SN12 . .**85** C1
Springfield Pk
18 Tisbury SP3 . . . .**203** E8
Trowbridge BA14 . . . .**101** E1
Springfield Rd
Rowde SN10 . . . .**96** D1
Swindon SN1 . . . .**50** C4
Westbury BA13 . . . .**108** F2
Springfield Sports Ctr
SN13 . . . .**76** F1
Springfields Sch SN11 . . .**81** A3
Springhead BA12 . . . .**194** A4
Springhill Cl 3 SN5 . . . . .**49** C5
Spur Way SN2 . . . .**35** C4
Squalls La SP3 . . . .**203** F6
Square The Calne SN11 . . .**81** B3
Mere BA12 . . . .**139** A5
Pewsey SN9 . . . .**215** C5
Swindon SN3 . . . .**50** D4
Squarey Cl SP5 . . . .**211** A7
Squires Copse SN5 . . . . . .**34** A1
Squires Hill Cl
4 Wootton Bassett SN4 . . .**47** F2
7 Wootton Bassett SN4 . . .**48** A2
Squirrel Cres 1 SN4 . . . .**47** F2
Squirrel's Cnr BH21 . . . .**208** D1
Stables Rd SP9 . . . .**216** C4
Stacey's La SN4 . . . .**163** B6
Stafford St SN1 . . . .**50** B5
Stag Hill RG17 . . . .**171** A1
Stainers Mead SP7 . . . . .**202** A5
Stallard St BA14 . . . .**105** C8
Stalls The BA12 . . . .**114** F5
Stamford Cl SN5 . . . .**49** B5
Stanbridge Pk 9 SN5 . . . .**49** A7
Stanbury Rd SP11 . . . . . .**192** C1
Stancomb Ave BA14 . . . .**101** E1
Stancombe Pk 1 SN5 . . . .**49** D5
Standen Way SN25 . . . . . .**35** A7
Standings Cl 6 SN5 . . . . .**49** A8
Stanford Rd SN25 . . . .**34** C7
Stanier Cl BA11 . . . .**110** D6
Stanier Rd SN11 . . . .**81** C6
Stanier St SN1 . . . .**50** B5
Stanley Cl 9 SN4 . . . .**163** B6
Stanley Honey Ct 7 SN3 . .**50** F6
Stanley La SN15 . . . .**79** D6
Stanley Little Rd SP2 . . .**145** B3
Stanley St SN1 . . . .**50** C5
Stanley Terr SN10 . . . . . .**214** B2
Stanmore St SN1 . . . .**50** A5
Stansfield Cl 5 SN5 . . . . .**49** D4
Stanton Cl BA14 . . . .**105** D5
Stanton La SN11 . . . .**56** A1
Stanton Ctry Pk ★ SN6 . . .**36** B8
Stanton Pk Farm ★ SN6 . . .**36** B8
Stanton Pk Nature Reserve ★
SN6 . . . .**36** B8
Stanton St Quintin Prim Sch
SN14 . . . .**56** B4
Stanway Cl 5 SN3 . . . .**51** A4
Stapleford Castle Ring &
Bailey ★ SP3 . . . .**129** D8
Stapleford Cl SN15 . . . . . .**78** E4
Stapleford Way SN2 . . . . .**35** B6
Staples Hill BA2 . . . .**99** C3
Stapleton Cl SN6 . . . .**22** F5
Star La SN14 . . . .**74** D8
Star The BA14 . . . .**101** E7
Stardust Cres SN25 . . . . . .**34** B7
Staring Cl 6 SN5 . . . .**48** F8
Station App
4 Frome BA11 . . . .**110** A4
Melksham SN12 . . . .**94** A6
Minety SN16 . . . .**17** C2
Swindon SN1 . . . .**50** D3
Westbury BA13 . . . .**108** D4
Station Hill SN15 . . . .**78** D8
Station Ind Est SN1 . . . . .**50** B6
Station Rd
Ashbury SN6 . . . .**164** A8
Badminton GL9 . . . .**38** F1
Calne SN11 . . . .**81** B2
Chiseldown SN4 . . . .**65** D4
Christian Malford SN15 . . .**58** A2
Codford BA12 . . . .**194** F3
Corsham SN13 . . . .**77** A1
Devizes SN10 . . . .**214** A3
East Garston RG17 . . . . . .**171** C4
Great Wishford SP2 . . . . .**129** F3
Highworth SN6 . . . .**22** F6
Holt BA14 . . . .**92** E1
19 Hungerford RG17 . . . .**177** B7
Kemble GL7 . . . .**4** F7
10 Lambourn RG17 . . . . .**165** A1
Lechlade GL7 . . . .**2** D5
Limpley Stoke BA2 . . . .**99** C5
Minety SN16 . . . .**17** C1
Purton SN5 . . . .**33** C5
Sandleheath SP6 . . . .**210** C1
Sedgehill & Semley SP7 . .**202** D5
South Cerney GL7 . . . .**7** C1
Swindon SN1 . . . .**50** D4
Tidworth SP9 . . . .**216** D5
Warminster BA12 . . . . . .**117** B7

Station Rd *continued*
Westbury BA13 . . . .**108** E5
Wootton Bassett SN4 . . . .**47** D1
Station Terr 4 SP2 . . . . .**145** F1
Station Way BA14 . . . . . .**105** C8
Staverton CE Prim Sch
BA14 . . . .**101** C6
Staverton Way 2 SN2 . . . .**35** C6
Stavordale Priory ★
BA9 . . . .**136** D5
Steadings The
Salisbury SP4 . . . .**146** D6
Wootton Bassett SN4 . . . . .**47** F1
Steam Mus of the Great
Western Rly ★ SN2 . . . . . .**50** A6
Stedham Wlk SN3 . . . .**51** B4
Steel's La BA9 . . . .**137** A3
Steele Cl SN10 . . . .**214** D4
Steels Dro SP6 . . . .**211** A4
Steels La SP6 . . . .**209** F2
Steep Hollow SP3 . . . . . .**201** E3
Steep St BA12 . . . .**139** A6
Steepe Way SN8 . . . .**175** C1
Steeple Langford CE Fst Sch
SP8 . . . .**128** C8
Stephen Martin Gdns 7
SP6 . . . .**210** D1
Stephens Cl 1 SP2 . . . . . .**151** E7
Stephens Rd SN3 . . . .**36** A1
Stephens Way SN2 . . . . . .**116** F8
Stephenson Rd
Salisbury SP2 . . . .**145** E1
Swindon SN25 . . . .**35** C7
The Ham BA13 . . . .**108** D5
Steplake La SO51 . . . .**212** F8
Steplake Rd SO51 . . . . . .**212** F8
Sterling Pk 1 SN10 . . . . .**193** C1
Stert Valley La SN10 . . . .**180** A6
Stevenson Rd SN2 . . . .**34** C5
Stewart Cl
Chippenham SN15 . . . .**78** F4
Swindon SN25 . . . .**35** B6
Steway La BA1 . . . .**82** B6
Stibb Hill SN10 . . . .**187** F7
Stickleback Rd SN11 . . . . .**81** B6
Still Man Cl BA14 . . . . . .**101** E8
Stirling Cl
3 Bower Hill SN12 . . . . .**178** B8
Wroughton SN4 . . . .**64** A7
Stirling Rd
Market Lavington SN10 . .**180** A1
South Marston Park SN3 . .**36** C6
Stirling Way BA11 . . . . . .**110** C6
Stobberts Pl 4 SN10 . . . .**179** F1
Stobberts Rd 3 SN10 . . .**179** F1
Stock La
Aldbourne SN8 . . . .**169** D4
Landford SP5 . . . .**212** C7
Stock's Cross SO43 . . . . .**212** D2
Stockbridge Copse
SN5 . . . .**34** A2
Stockham Cl SN6 . . . .**19** E8
Stockley Hollow SN11 . . . .**89** C6
Stockley La SN11 . . . .**89** C6
Stockley Rd SN11 . . . .**89** C2
Stockport Rd SP4 . . . . . .**217** D1
Stocks Bridge La SP5 . . .**151** A1
Stockton Earthworks ★
BA12 . . . .**201** A6
Stockton House ★
BA12 . . . .**195** B1
Stockton Rd SN2 . . . .**35** C4
Stockwell Rd SN10 . . . . .**214** C4
Stockwood Cl SP1 . . . . . .**146** C3
Stockwood Rd SN14 . . . . .**78** B6
Stoke Comm La SN5 . . . . .**19** A2
Stoke Common Mdws Nature
Reserve ★ SN6 . . . .**18** E1
Stoke Mead BA2 . . . .**98** F7
Stokehill BA14 . . . .**106** A8
Stokes Rd SN13 . . . .**85** A8
Stokes' Croft SN11 . . . . . .**81** B4
Stokesay Dr SN5 . . . .**49** C4
Stonar Sch SN12 . . . .**92** B8
Stone (site of King's Elm) ★
SP3 . . . .**142** B1
Stone Ave ★ SN8 . . . .**173** C8
Stone Cl SP5 . . . .**149** C6
Stone La
Lydiard Millicent SN5 . . . .**33** E1
Ramsbury SN8 . . . .**175** D8
Stonebridge Cl SN8 . . . . .**213** F3
Stonebridge Dr BA11 . . .**110** B7
Stonecrop Way SN25 . . . .**34** E5
Stonefield Dr SN6 . . . .**23** A5
Stonehenge ★ SP4 . . . . . .**197** E5
Stonehenge Cursus ★
SP4 . . . .**197** C6
Stonehenge Rd SP4 . . . . .**198** A4
Stonehenge Sch The
SP4 . . . .**217** B4
Stonehill Barn GL8 . . . .**3** C6
Stonehill Gn SN5 . . . .**49** D6
Stonehill La GL8 . . . .**3** C6
Stoneleigh Rise BA11 . . .**110** A6
Stoneover La
Lydiard Tregoze SN4 . . . . .**48** A3
Wootton Bassett SN4 . . . . .**47** F2
Stones La SN6 . . . .**8** B1
Stonewall Terr BA11 . . . .**110** A3
Stoney Bridge BA9 . . . . . .**136** B4
Stoney Cross 20 SP11 . . .**192** A5
Stony Gutter BA14 . . . . .**102** D1

Stony La
Damerham SP6 . . . .**209** E2
Lambourn RG17 . . . .**171** B6
Stonybeck Cl SN5 . . . .**49** D6
Stop St SP3 . . . .**200** C2
Stoppers Hill SN15 . . . . . .**46** B7
Stops Hill SP3 . . . .**200** B3
Stormore BA13 . . . .**111** F8
Storridge Rd BA13 . . . . . .**108** C6
Stour Cl 5 SO51 . . . .**212** F6
Stour Wlk SN25 . . . .**35** B4
Stourhead House & Gdns ★
BA12 . . . .**123** F1
Stourton House Flower Gdn ★
BA12 . . . .**123** F1
Stourton La BA12 . . . .**123** E3
Stourton Rd BA12 . . . . . .**102** B3
Stowell Pk ★ SN8 . . . .**182** A8
Stradbrook BA13 . . . .**186** B7
Straight La Dean SP5 . . . .**207** E3
Lambourn RG17 . . . .**171** C6
Strand The Calne SN11 . . . .**81** B3
Steeple Ashton BA14 . . . .**178** A3
Stranks Cl SN5 . . . .**23** A4
Stratford Cl SN5 . . . .**49** D5
Stratford Rd SN9 . . . .**146** A3
Stratford Sub Castle CE Prim
Sch SP1 . . . .**145** D5
Stratford Tony Rd
SP5 . . . .**150** E2
Stratton Orch 1 SN3 . . . . .**36** A2
Stratton Rd & Marshgate Ind
Est SN1 . . . .**50** E5
Stratton Rd
Pewsey SN9 . . . .**215** C4
Swindon SN1 . . . .**50** F8
The Ham BA13 . . . .**108** D5
Strattons Wlk SN12 . . . . .**94** B4
Strawberry Hill SN10 . . .**187** C2
Strawberry La GL7 . . . .**1** A4
Street La
Brewham BA10 . . . .**122** A4
Sedgehill & Semley SP7 . .**202** C6
Street The
All Cannings SN10 . . . . . .**172** F1
Alvediston SP5 . . . .**204** B2
Bishops Cannings SN10 . .**172** B3
Brinkworth SN15 . . . .**45** F6
Broughton Gifford SN12 . . .**93** B4
Castle Combe SN14 . . . . . .**68** A7
Castle Eaton SN6 . . . .**10** B4
Charlton SN16 . . . .**29** B6
Cherhill SN11 . . . .**166** B1
Chilmark SP3 . . . .**201** A3
Chirton SN10 . . . .**180** F4
Crudwell SN16 . . . .**14** E5
Didmarton GL9 . . . .**24** C3
East Knoyle SP3 . . . .**141** C1
Holt BA14 . . . .**101** D8
Hullavington SN14 . . . .**41** F1
Kilmington BA12 . . . .**123** C4
Latton SN6 . . . .**8** C4
Lea SN16 . . . .**28** F1
Liddington SN4 . . . .**163** A4
Little Somerford SN15 . . . .**44** C5
Luckington SN14 . . . .**39** E4
Lydiard Millicent SN5 . . . .**48** D8
Marden SN10 . . . .**181** A4
Marston Maisey SN6 . . . . . .**9** D6
Milton Lilbourne SN9 . . . .**182** E7
Motcombe SP7 . . . .**202** A5
Nettleton SN14 . . . .**53** B4
Oaksey SN16 . . . .**15** F8
Pitton & Farley SP5 . . . . .**154** E7
Shipton Moyne GL8 . . . . . .**26** B4
Swindon SN25 . . . .**34** E3
West Knoyle BA12 . . . . . .**140** D5
Winterslow SP5 . . . .**149** A5
Yatton Keynell SN14 . . . . .**68** F6
Stroma Way SN6 . . . .**22** E7
Strongrove Hill RG17 . . .**177** A7
Strongs Cl BA14 . . . .**178** C4
Stroud La SN10 . . . .**179** F5
Stroud's Hill SN4 . . . .**65** D4
Stuart Cl 2 Swindon SN3 . .**50** F6
Trowbridge BA14 . . . .**101** E4
Stuart Gn BA12 . . . .**117** A6
Stubbs Cl 3 SP10 . . . .**193** D1
Stubbs La SN14 . . . .**70** A7
Stubhampton Bottom
DT11 . . . .**206** C3
Stubsmead SN3 . . . .**51** C5
Stuckton Rd SP6 . . . .**210** E1
Studio Theatre ★ SP2 . . .**146** A2
Studland Cl SN3 . . . .**51** B3
Studland Pk BA13 . . . . . .**109** B2
Studley Castle ★ SP6 . . . .**211** F3
Studley Gn Prim Sch
BA14 . . . .**105** A6
Studley Hill SN11 . . . .**80** A6
Studley La SN11 . . . .**80** A6
Studley Rise BA14 . . . . . .**105** D6
Styles Ave BA11 . . . .**110** C4
Styles Cl BA11 . . . .**110** B4
Styles Hill BA11 . . . .**110** B4
Styles Pk BA11 . . . .**110** B4
Styles The SP5 . . . .**205** F4
Sudeley Dr GL7 . . . .**6** F6
Sudeley Way SN5 . . . .**49** A5
Sudley Way SN5 . . . .**48** F5
Suffolk Cl SN16 . . . .**29** A7
Suffolk Gl GL7 . . . .**8** D7
Suffolk Rd
Salisbury SP2 . . . .**151** E6
5 Westbury Leigh BA13 . .**108** C1
Suffolk St SN2 . . . .**50** C8
Summer Down Wlk
BA14 . . . .**105** C5

Sou – Swi **241**

Summer La
Castle Combe SN14 . . . . . .**53** F3
Monkton Combe BA2 . . . . .**98** D8
Summer Rd BA13 . . . .**108** F4
Summerdown Ct
BA13 . . . .**109** A4
Summerhouse Rd SN4 . . .**63** F7
Summerleaze BA14 . . . . .**105** A6
Summerlock App 2
SP2 . . . .**146** A1
Summers La SN4 . . . .**167** C7
Summers St SN2 . . . .**49** F7
Sumsions Dr SN13 . . . . . .**76** D1
Sun La BA13 . . . .**108** E1
Sunderland Cl 14 SN12 . .**178** B8
Sunningdale Cl SN15 . . . .**78** F7
Sunningdale Rd SN25 . . . .**35** C4
Sunnyhill SN8 . . . .**191** D8
Sunnyhill La SN8 . . . .**174** C1
Sunnyhill Rd SP1 . . . .**146** A4
Sunnyside SN10 . . . .**187** E8
Sunnyside Ave SN1 . . . . . .**50** A4
Surrendell Cottage
SN14 . . . .**55** B8
Surrey Pl BA14 . . . .**105** B7
Surrey Rd SN2 . . . .**35** A1
Sussex Rd SP2 . . . .**151** E6
Sussex Sq SN1 . . . .**50** E6
Sutherland Cresent
SN14 . . . .**70** B3
Sutherland Ct 5 SP10 . . .**193** D1
Suthmere Dr SN8 . . . .**183** D8
Sutton Benger CE Prim Sch
SN15 . . . .**57** D2
Sutton Bottom SP3 . . . . .**141** B5
Sutton Hill
Sherrington BA12 . . . .**195** A2
Sutton Mandeville SP3 . . .**204** C7
Sutton La
Langley Burrell Without
SN15 . . . .**71** C5
Sutton Benger SN15 . . . . . .**57** D1
Sutton Pk SN26 . . . .**21** C1
Sutton Rd Fovant SP3 . . . .**204** D7
Kington Langley SN15 . . . .**70** F7
Swindon SN3 . . . .**51** C4
Sutton Veny CE Prim Sch
BA12 . . . .**194** A4
Suvla La 6 SP4 . . . .**198** E6
Swaddon St SN11 . . . .**81** B4
Swallet House SN15 . . . . .**58** D5
Swallow Cl
Tidworth SP9 . . . .**216** D6
2 Warminster BA12 . . . . .**116** E5
Swallow Dr
Frome BA11 . . . .**110** B6
4 Trowbridge BA14 . . . . .**105** B8
Swallowdale SN3 . . . .**51** D7
Swallowfield Ave SN3 . . . .**50** F5
Swallowmead 1 SP2 . . . .**152** A5
Swallows Mead 9 SN4 . . .**48** A2
Swan Barton SN16 . . . .**40** C8
Swan Cl
9 Durrington/Bulford
SP4 . . . .**198** C7
Lechlade GL7 . . . .**2** C4
Salisbury SP2 . . . .**152** A6
Swan Dr BA14 . . . .**101** D5
Swan La SN6 . . . .**17** F5
Swan Meadow SN9 . . . . . .**215** D3
Swan Rd Corsham SN13 . . .**76** E1
Pewsey SN9 . . . .**215** C4
Swanage Wlk SN25 . . . . . .**34** E3
Swan's Bottom 7 SN8 . . .**170** B2
Swan's Cl 9 SN8 . . . .**170** B2
Swanborough Cl 6 SN15 . .**78** F4
Swanborough Tump ★
SN9 . . . .**181** F6
Swanbrook SN3 . . . .**51** D8
Swangate RG17 . . . .**177** B8
Swansfield GL7 . . . .**2** B6
Swattons Cl SP4 . . . .**217** E8
Swayne Cl 6 SN15 . . . .**78** F5
Swayne Rd SP2 . . . .**144** C2
Swaynes Cl 1 SP1 . . . . . .**146** B2
Sweet Briar Rd SN12 . . . .**94** C3
Sweetmans Rd SP7 . . . . .**202** C2
Swift Ave SN25 . . . .**35** A7
Swift Mead BA12 . . . .**116** E5
Swiftdown 5 SP2 . . . .**152** A5
Swillbrook Lakes Nature
Reserve ★ SN16 . . . .**16** F8
Swinburne Pl SN4 . . . .**47** E3
Swindon & Cricklade Rly ★
SN25 . . . .**33** F8
Swindon Arts Ctr ★
SN1 . . . .**50** C4
Swindon Coll
Marlborough SN8 . . . .**213** D3
Swindon SN5 . . . .**49** B6
Swindon SN1 . . . .**50** C5
Swindon SN3 . . . .**50** B8
Swindon Mus & Art Gall ★
SN1 . . . .**50** D4
Swindon Rd
Cricklade SN6 . . . .**19** F7
Highworth SN6 . . . .**22** F3
Hilmarton SN11 . . . .**73** F3
Kington Langley SN5 . . . . .**70** F5
Lydiard Tregoze SN4 . . . . .**48** C2
Swindon SN1 . . . .**36** A1
Wootton Bassett SN4 . . . . .**47** F3
Wroughton SN4 . . . .**64** C7
Swindon St SN6 . . . .**23** A5
Swindon Sta SN2 . . . .**50** B7

Swindon Town Football Club
SN1 ....50 D7
Swinley Dr SN5 ....34 A1
Sword Gdns 5 SN1 ....49 F4
Swynford Cl GL7 ....10 D6
Sycamore Cl
Lyneham & Bradenstoke
SN15 ....60 C2
North Tidworth SP9 .....216 E6
Sixpenny Handley SP5 .208 A4
Sycamore Dr
8 Frome BA11 ....110 B7
Salisbury SP1 ....146 C5
Sycamore Gr
Swindon SN2 ....35 C2
Trowbridge BA14 .....105 C5
Westbury BA13 ....108 F3
Sydnalls La SN14 ....115 D6
Symonds SN5 ....49 B3
Syon Cl Corsham SN13 .84 E8
4 Swindon SN25 ....34 F6
Syringa Ct SP2 ....145 D1
Sywell Rd SN3 ....51 C8

T

Tadpole La
Blunsdon St Andrew SN25 .34 C8
Purton SN5 ....33 F8
Talavera Rd SN4 .....168 E8
Talbot Cl
Melksham SN12 ....94 D5
Salisbury SP1 ....146 C4
Talbot Rd BA14 ......105 A7
Talboys (Medieval Hall
House)★ BA14 ......178 B4
Tallis Wlk SN5 ....49 A5
Tallow La 5 SN4 .....163 A6
Tamar Cl SN5 ....35 A4
Tamar Rd SN12 ....94 A6
Tamesis Dr GL7 ....4 F7
Tamworth Dr SN5 .....49 A7
Tan La SP8 ....138 A2
Tanarisk Cl SN11 .....81 C1
Tangmere Cl 18 SN12 .178 B8
Tank La SP5 ....205 B4
Tankard La 15 SN8 ....170 B2
Tankey's Cl 5 BA11 .110 A7
Tanner Cl SN15 ....78 F5
Tanners Cl
Winterbourne SP4 .....133 A1
Wootton Bassett SN4 ..47 D2
Tanners Field SP4 ...217 D3
Tanners Hill SN16 .....40 C8
Tanners La
Sandleheath SP6 ......210 A1
Shrewton SP3 ....196 E7
Winterbourne SP4 .....133 A1
Tansley Moor SN3 .....51 E3
Tanyard La 6 SP7 ...202 B1
Taplow Wlk SN3 ....51 A4
Taramah Gdns 10 SP3 .203 E8
Targetts Mead SP3 ...203 E8
Tarka Cl SN25 ....34 F7
Tarragon Cl SN2 ......34 C4
Tarrant's Hill 24 RG17 .177 B7
Tarters The SN16 ......40 D8
Tascroft BA12 ....116 B5
Tasker Cl SN13 ....84 E8
Taskers La SN8 ....183 D8
Tattershall SN3 ....49 C3
Taunton Cl 2 SN14 ...77 F5
Taunton St SN1 ....50 A6
Tavinor Dr SN15 ....78 E4
Tavistock Rd SN3 .....51 B5
Tawny Owl Cl SN3 ....51 C8
Taylor Cres SN3 ....36 A4
Taylors Gn SN8 ....174 A7
Taylors La SN8 ......168 B1
Taylors View BA14 ...101 D1
Teal Ave SN15 ....60 A1
Teal Cl BA13 ....109 B4
Tealgate RG17 ....177 B8
Tealsbrook SN3 ....51 D7
Teapot St BA12 ......201 E8
Teasel Cl Devizes SN10 .214 E2
28 Ludgershall SP11 .192 A6
Teasels The BA12 ....116 F6
Techno Ind Est SN2 ...35 E1
Tedder Ave SN13 ......84 A8
Tedder Cl SN25 ....35 B2
Tees Cl SN25 ....35 A4
Teeswater Cl SN5 .....49 A6
Teffont Field Bldgs★
SP3 ....201 D4
Teffont Manor★ SP3 .201 D2
Telford Rd SN2 ....151 E8
Telford Way SN1 ....49 E4
Tellcroft Cl SN13 .....84 F8
Tellings Orch SN16 ...16 D3
Tempest Rd 9 SP4 ...217 D3
Templar's Firs SN4 ....61 E8
Temple St SN1 ....50 D4
Ten Acres SP7 ....202 C2
Tenby Cl SN3 ....50 F3
Tennis Cnr Dro BA11 .107 D2
Tennyson Cl BA12 ...116 E6
Tennyson Rd SN4 .....47 F3
Tennyson St SN1 ......50 B5
Tenzing Gdns SN25 ...35 C3
Tern Cl SN11 ....81 D2
Terncliff SN3 ....51 D7
Tetbury Hill SN16 .....27 F6
Tetbury La SN16 ......14 D6

Tetbury Rd SN16 ......25 D2
Tethering Dro SP6 ...211 C6
Tewkesbury Way
Lydiard Millicent SN5 ...48 E7
Swindon SN5 ....49 A6
Thackeray Cl SN3 .....51 D4
Thackeray Cres SN12 .94 B4
Thames Ave SN25 .....34 E5
Thames Cl BA12 .....117 A5
Thames Cres SN12 ....94 A6
Thames La SN6 ....19 E8
Thames St GL7 ....2 C3
Thames View
Ashton Keynes SN6 .....17 F8
Ewen GL7 ....5 C8
Thamesdown Dr
Haydon Wick SN25 .....34 B7
Swindon SN25 ....35 A7
Thatcham Cl SN11 .....81 A4
Thatchers The SN25 ...35 C7
Theatre Sq SN1 ....50 C6
Theobald St SN1 ....50 B6
Thestfield Dr BA14 ..101 D4
Thetford Way SN3 .....34 C5
Thicketts Rd SN8 ...169 C1
Thickwood La SN14 ...75 C6
Thirsk Cl SN14 ....78 A5
Thistlebarrow Rd SP1 .146 A4
Thistledown 6 SN4 ..163 A6
Thomas Byron Rd
SN10 ....214 C1
Thomas Ct SN11 ....81 C1
Thomas Hardy Dr 8
SP7 ....202 D2
Thomas Mead SN15 ...78 E5
Thomas St SN2 ....49 F7
Thomas Wyatt Rd
SN10 ....214 B1
Thompson Cl SP2 ....151 F5
Thompsons Hill SN16 .40 C7
Thomson Way SN8 ...213 B2
Thorley Ct SN25 ....35 A6
Thornbank SN12 ....94 A3
Thornbridge Ave SN3 .51 A4
Thornbury Rd BA13 ..108 F4
Thorne Cl SP5 ....150 F1
Thorne Rd
2 Netheravon SP4 ....190 A4
Swindon SN3 ....51 C4
Thorneydown Rd SP4 .133 C1
Thornford Dr SN5 .....49 C5
Thornhill Dr SN25 ....35 A8
Thornhill Ind Est SN2 .35 E1
Thornhill Rd BA12 ...116 D5
Thorns The SN8 .....213 D5
Thornton Cres SP2 ...144 F4
Threadgill Way 6 SP9 .199 C8
Three Barrows★ SN8 .164 B3
Three Cuppes La 4
SP1 ....146 B1
Three Horseshoes Wlk 3
BA12 ....117 A7
Three Oak Hill Dr
SN8 ....175 D4
Three Shire Stones★
SN14 ....74 D1
Three Sisters Rd 1
SN4 ....163 B6
Thresher Dr SN25 .....35 C6
Thrushel Cl SN25 .....34 E4
Thruxton Motor Racing
Circuit★ SP11 ....192 C1
Thurlestone Rd SN3 ...50 E5
Thurlow Cl 10 SP4 ...217 E3
Thursday St SN25 .....34 D6
Thyme Cl SN2 ....34 C3
Tibb's Meadow SP11 .192 D8
Tiberius Rd 24 SP10 .193 E2
Tidcombe (Long Barrow)★
SN8 ....184 D4
Tidling Cnr SN16 ......16 C5
Tidworth Cl 3 SN1 ....49 F4
Tidworth Coll SP9 ...216 D6
Tidworth Leisure Ctr
SP9 ....216 D6
Tidworth Oval★ SP9 .216 C5
Tidworth Rd
Bulford SP4 ....199 A7
Collingbourne Ducis
SN8 ....191 D7
Ludgershall SP11 .....191 F5
Milston SP4 ....191 B1
Porton SP4 ....133 E7
Tile Hill BA10 ....122 A5
Tilley's La SN3 ....36 A2
Tilshead Wlk SN2 .....35 B5
Timandra Cl 1 SN25 .35 A6
Timber St SN15 ....78 E7
Timberley La SP5 ....211 E7
Timbrell St SN14 .....101 D1
Timbrells The GL7 .....5 C8
Timor Rd BA13 ....108 E2
Tin Pit SN8 ....213 E4
Tinhead Rd BA13 ....186 C8
Tinings The SN15 ......79 A8
Tinkers Field SN4 .....47 D2
Tinkers Mead SN9 ...215 D4
Tinneys Cl SP5 ....211 C6
Tintagel Cl
18 Andover SP10 .....193 E2
Swindon SN5 ....49 B4
Tintern Rd SN25 ....34 E4
Tisbury & District Sports Ctr
SP3 ....203 D8
Tisbury Cl 1 SN2 .....35 C6
Tisbury Rd SP3 ....204 D8
Tisbury Row SP3 .....203 F8
Tisbury Sta SP3 .....203 E7

Tismeads Cres SN1 ...50 C2
Titan Barrow BA1 .....82 C2
Titchfield Cl 5 SN8 ...48 F5
Tittymouse La SP11 .192 F1
Tiverton Rd SN2 ....35 C1
Tobruk Cl 5 SP11 ...193 E4
Tobruk Rd SP11 ......191 F3
Tobys Ct 25 SP7 .....202 C2
Tockenham Cnr SN4 ..60 D6
Tockenham Way SN2 ..35 B6
Toghill Cres SN13 .....76 B1
Tokes La SP7 ....202 E6
Toll Down Way SN14 ..53 A4
Tollard Cl SN3 ....51 C6
Tollgate Cl SP4 ......217 A5
Tollgate Pk SP7 .....202 C3
Tollgate Rd
Andover SP10 ....193 C1
Salisbury SP1 ....152 B8
Tombs Rd SP4 ....198 A6
Toothill Prim Sch SN5 .49 C4
Top La
Atworth/Whitley SN12 ..85 C1
Stourton with Gasper
BA12 ....137 D7
Top Rd GL7 ....10 C7
Top St SN15 ....44 A2
Toppers Cl SN25 ......35 A3
Tormarton Rd
Acton Turville GL9 ....52 E6
Marshfield SN14 ......66 A2
Torno Cl SN10 ......214 D4
Torr Cl SN14 ....70 B2
Torridge Cl SN25 .....34 F4
Torrington Ct SN3 ....51 A5
Torun Way SN25 ......34 D6
Tottenham Ho★ SN8 .175 F2
Tottenham Pk★ SN8 .175 F3
Totterdown Cl SN3 ...51 E7
Totterdown La GL7 .....1 F7
Totts La SN14 ....75 B3
Totworth Rd SN25 ....34 C8
Touchorne La SP3 ...141 A4
Tournament Rd SP2 .145 C3
Tout Hill SP7 ....202 B2
Tovey Ct 3 SP10 ....193 F1
Tovey Rd SN2 ....35 B2
Tow Barrow (Long Barrow)★
SN8 ....184 B4
Towcester Cl SN14 ...77 F5
Towcester Pl 1 SN14 .77 F5
Towcester Rd
North Bradley BA14 ..105 E4
Swindon SN3 ....51 C4
Towell Rd 5 SP4 ....198 A6
Tower Cl Andover SP10 .193 C2
Trowbridge BA14 .....105 A7
Tower Hill
Dilton Marsh BA13 ....112 D7
Iwerne Minster DT11 .206 A1
Tower Mews SP1 ....146 B2
Tower Rd
Melksham SN12 ....94 C5
Stourton with Gasper
BA10 ....122 A5
Swindon SN5 ....34 B2
Tower View SN10 ......96 D2

Town Bridge
Bradford-on-Avon★
BA15 ....100 C6
Town Cl SN14 ....69 F8
Town Farm Pl SP5 ...208 B4
Town Gdns★ SN1 .....50 C4
Town Mill SN8 ....213 D2
Town Path SP2 ......151 E7
Townfield 10 SN8 ...170 B2
Townsend
Chitterne BA12 ....195 D7
Pitton & Farley SP5 .148 C4
Townsend Cl BA12 ..138 F5
Townsend La SP6 ...209 A6
Townsend Pl SN14 ....77 F8
Towpath Rd BA14 ...101 D4
Tracy Cl SN25 ....35 A6
Trafalgar Ho★ SP5 .159 D4
Trajan Rd SN3 ....36 C1
Transfer Bridges Ind Est
SN1 ....50 D8
Travellers Rest SN13 .76 C1
Tree Tops Cl SN15 ....59 C3
Tregantle Wlk SN3 ...51 C6
Tregoze Prim Sch SN5 .49 A6
Tregoze Way SN5 .....48 F5
Trenchard Ave
Box SN13 ....84 A8
Calne Without SN11 ...81 F1
4 Corsham SN13 ......76 B1
Winterbourne SP4 ....133 C2
Trenchard Cl 5 SN14 .78 A6
Trenchard Rd
Lyneham SN15 ....60 A1
Stanton Fitzwarren SN6 .22 B2
Trent Cres SN12 ....94 A6
Trent Rd SN25 ....35 A4
Trentham Cl SN3 ......51 A4
Trevithick Cl 5 BA11 .110 C6
Triangle The SP5 ....161 D4
Trimm's Dro SP6 ....211 A4
Trimnells SN14 ....75 B3
Trinity Cl SN3 ....51 A3
Trinity Pk SN11 ....81 C1
Trinity Rd SP3 ....196 F7
Trinity Rise SP11 ....193 A2
Trinity St SP1 ....152 B8
Tropenell Ct 2 SN13 ..76 E1
Trout La SN13 ....84 B7
Trow La Brinkworth SN15 .59 F8

Trow La continued
Maiden Bradley with Yarnfield
BA12 ....118 E4
Trowbridge Com Hospl
BA14 ....101 D2
Trowbridge Lodge Pk
BA14 ....105 F8
Trowbridge Mus★
BA14 ....105 D8
Trowbridge Parochial Jun
Sch BA14 ....101 E2
Trowbridge Rd
Bradford-on-Avon BA15 .100 E5
Bratton BA13 ....186 A8
Seend SN12 ....178 C7
Trowbridge BA14 .....102 A2
Westbury BA13 ....109 B5
Trowbridge Sports Ctr
BA14 ....105 B6
Trowbridge Sta BA14 .105 C8
Trowle BA14 ....101 A2
Truman Cl SN3 ....51 C4
Truro Wlk SN14 ....77 F6
Tryhorn Dr SP1 ......146 C5
Tryon Cl SN3 ....51 D2
Tubbs Farm Cl 6 RG17 .165 A1
Tucker Cl 6 SP4 .....217 C2
Tuckers La SN4 ......163 D6
Tuckwell Rd GL7 ......10 E6
Tudor Cl SN15 ....79 A4
Tudor Cres SN3 ....36 B1
Tudor Dr BA14 ....101 E4
Tudor Wlk SN3 ....50 F6
Tugela Rd SN15 ....70 E1
Tuggy's La BA12 ......98 E1
Tulip Tree Cl SN2 .....35 C2
Tulse Hill Zeale BA12 .138 A4
Zennor BA12 ....137 F3
Tumlins SN10 ....180 F8
Tunball La SN8 ....184 F4
Tunnel Hill SP5 ......153 C2
Tupman Rd SN13 ......76 E2
Turf Ho La SN11 ....72 D1
Turin St SP10 ....193 E2
Turl St SN1 ....50 C6
Turnball SN4 ....65 D4
Turnberry Cl SN15 ....78 F7
Turner Cl 2 SP2 .....151 E7
Turner Ct SP10 ......193 D1
Turner St SN1 ....50 A5
Turnham Gn SN5 ......49 A4
Turnpike 4 SN8 .....170 A6
Turnpike Rd
Blunsdon St Andrew SN26 .35 C8
Highworth SN6 ....23 A6
Turnpike The
Chippenham SN15 .....79 B5
East Knoyle SP3 .....202 D8
Turpin Way SN14 ......77 F7
Tutton Hill SN14 ......75 B3
Twatley Cotts SN16 ...27 C4
Tweed Cl SN25 ....34 F4
Twickenham Way SN15 .70 E1
Twineham Gdns SP5 .153 F2
Twineham Rd SN25 ...34 C8
Twyford Cl SN3 ....51 A6
Twynham Cl SN5 .....211 A4
Twynnoy Cl SN16 .....28 A5
Tyburn Cl SN5 ....49 B5
Tydeman St SN1 ......35 D1
Tye Gdns SN5 ....48 F5
Tylees Ct SN10 ......214 B3
Tylers Cl SP2 ....151 D7
Tyndales Meadow
SP3 ....201 F2
Tyneham Rd SN3 ......51 B6
Tyning Cl 1 BA14 ...105 A7
Tyning La 9 BA13 ...186 B7
Tyning Pk SN11 ....81 C1
Tyning Rd
Bathampton BA2 ......82 A2
Winsley BA15 ....99 E7
Tyning The BA2 ....99 B4
Tynings The
Biddestone SN14 ......76 D7
Westbury BA13 ....108 F2
Tynings Way BA15 ....99 F3
Tyrone Ave SP4 ......118 A4
Tytherington Rd BA12 .194 C5
Tytherley Rd SP5 ....149 E6

U

Ullswater Cl SN3 ......51 E3
Ulysses Rd SN25 ......34 B7
Umbers Hill 2 SP7 ...202 B1
Underdown Cl 12 SN4 .163 A6
Underhill Mere BA12 .138 F5
Pen Selwood BA9 ....137 D2
Underwood Dr SP4 ...217 D2
Union Rd
Chippenham SN15 .....78 D8
Tisbury SP3 ....203 F2
Union Row SN1 ....50 D4
Union St Melksham SN12 .94 A4
Ramsbury SN8 ....170 B2
Swindon SN1 ....50 C5
Trowbridge BA14 .....101 D1
Unity St SN14 ....78 C7
University of Bath in Swindon
(Oakfield Campus)
SN3 ....51 A7
Up St BA12 ....194 E4
Upavon Airfield SN9 .182 B1
Upavon Ct SN2 ....35 C5
Upavon Prim Sch SN9 .182 A1

Upcott SN6 ....8 C4
Upfield SN3 ....51 D3
Upham Rd SN3 ....50 E5
Upham Village★ SN8 .169 C8
Upland Rise BA13 ...109 B2
Uplands 28 RG17 ...177 B7
Uplands Cl BA2 ....98 F7
Uplands Specl Sch SN5 .35 C4
Uplands The BA14 ...117 C7
Upnor Cl SP11 ....191 F4
Upper Avon Sch SP4 .198 C7
Upper Backway SP3 .196 F7
Upper Broad St BA14 .101 C1
Upper Church Fields
SN8 ....213 E1
Upper Dro SP10 ......193 C1
Upper Eddington
RG17 ....177 C8
Upper Folly SP2 .....144 B1
Upper Garston La 8
BA13 ....186 B7
Upper Isbury SN8 ...213 E2
Upper La SN13 ....84 D7
Upper Lambourn Rd
RG17 ....165 A2
Upper Ley SN13 ....83 D5
Upper Marsh La BA12 .117 A5
Upper Marsh Rd BA12 .117 A4
Upper Noremarsh SN4 .47 F1
Upper North Rd SP5 .207 C5
Upper Pavenhill SN5 ..32 F4
Upper Potley SN13 ....84 E7
Upper Regents Pk
BA15 ....100 D6
Upper St SP2 ....151 D7
Upper Waterhay Nature
Reserve★ SN6 ....18 D7
Upper Wr St BA12 ...139 B5
Uppington La SP3 ...129 E8
Upton Cl Swindon SN25 .34 F5
5 Warminster BA12 ..116 E7
Upton Great Barrow★
BA12 ....194 F5
Urchfont CE Prim Sch
SN10 ....180 B4
Urchfont Manor Coll
SN10 ....180 B3
Urchfont Way SN2 ....35 C4
Utah Cl SN1 ....49 F4
Utterson View SN15 ..78 C7
Uxbridge Rd SN5 ....49 A3

V

Vale Leaze SN15 ......44 C5
Vale Rd Pewsey SN9 .215 B5
Redlynch SP5 ....211 C7
Vale View SN4 ....47 D1
Vale View Rd SP2 ...130 B2
Valens Terr SN13 .....83 C6
Valentia Ct 19 SN12 .178 B8
Valiant Cl 9 SN11 ....178 B8
Valletta Gdns SN14 ...56 B5
Valley Cl SP5 ....211 C7
Valley Rd SN13 ....76 E1
Valley The SP2 ......145 C5
Valley View SN11 .....81 A2
Valley Way SN14 ......75 C6
Valleyside SN1 ....50 A4
Van Diemen's Cl SN8 .213 E2
Vanbrugh Gate SN3 ...50 F1
Vanessa Ave SP1 ....146 D1
Vastern Wharf SN4 ...61 A7
Vasterne Cl SN4 ......33 B5
Vega Cl SN25 ....34 B7
Velley Hill SN13 ....85 C5
Venice Ct SP11 ......193 F2
Venn The 11 SP7 ....202 C2
Ventnor Cl SN2 ....34 E4
Ventry Cl 3 SP1 ....146 B2
Ventry The 4 SP1 ...146 B2
Verden Way 19 SP10 .193 D2
Verney Cl SN3 ....51 C6
Vernham Dean Gullum's Prim
Sch SP11 ....185 C3
Vernon Cl 2 SP4 ....217 E3
Verona Rd SP1 ......145 F4
Verulam Cl SN3 ....51 D8
Verwood Cl SN3 ......51 B4
Vespasian Cl SN3 ....51 C8
Vespasian Rd 19 SP10 .193 E2
Vicarage Cl Calne SN11 .81 B3
Marlborough SN8 ....213 E3
Vicarage Cotts SN15 ..57 F6
Vicarage Gdns 3 SP4 .190 A3
Vicarage La
Charlton SN16 ....29 B7
Colerne SN14 ....75 C3
Easterton SN10 ......179 F2
Hankerton SN16 ......15 B1
Highworth SN6 ....23 A6
Steeple Ashton BA14 .178 A3
Upavon SN9 ....181 F2
Vicarage Mews BA12 .116 F7
Vicarage Pk 1 SP5 ..211 C7
Vicarage Rd
Redlynch SP5 ....211 E7
Swindon SN2 ....34 F1
Tisbury SP3 ....203 E8
Vicarage St BA12 ...116 F7
Vice La SO51 ....212 E2
Victoria Cl
Lyneham SN11 ....73 E8
Wilton SP2 ....144 C4
Victoria Cross Rd SN4 .63 F7
Victoria Ct SP1 .....146 A3
Victoria Dr SN15 ......60 B1

Victoria Gdns
14 Sandleheath SP6 210 C1
Trowbridge BA14 101 E2
Victoria Hospl SN1 50 B4
Victoria Pk SN10 187 B8
Victoria Rd
Devizes SN10 214 B4
Frome BA11 110 A4
Salisbury SP1 146 A2
Sandleheath SP6 210 C1
Swindon SN1 50 C5
Trowbridge BA14 101 E3
Warminster BA12 116 C6
Wilton SP2 144 C3
Victoria St 21 SP7 202 C2
Victoria Terr SN11 81 B3
Victory Rd BA13 108 C6
Vigo Inf Sch SP10 193 F1
Viking Cl SN25 34 F7
Viking Way
Andover SP10 193 E2
Salisbury SP2 152 B5
Vilett St SN1 50 B6
Village Mus the Castle Combe* SN14 68 A7
Village St SN8 173 D1
Villiers Cl
Chippenham SN15 78 F7
Lydiard Tregoze SN5 48 F7
Vimoutiers Ct 16 SP6 210 D1
Vimy Cres 8 SP4 198 E6
Vincent Cl SN12 94 C4
Vincients Rd SN14 69 F1
Vincients Wood Nature Reserve* SN14 77 F7
Viner's La GL9 53 B5
Virginia Cl 1 SP4 217 E3
Virginia Dr BA12 116 E7
Viscount Way SN3 36 C6
Vockins Cl SP9 216 C8
Volpe Cl SN5 48 F4
Volta Rd SN1 50 C6
Vorda Rd SN6 23 A7
Vowley View SN4 47 F1
Voyager Dr SN25 34 B7

W

Wade Hill SN6 22 F5
Wadswick La SN13 84 B3
Waggoner Cl SN25 35 B6
Wagtail Cl SN3 51 C8
Waiblingen Way SN10 214 A4
Wain-a-Long Rd SP1 146 C1
Wains Way SP4 190 A3
Wainwright Cl 4 SN3 51 D4
Wainwright Dr 5 BA11 110 C7
Waite Meads Cl SN5 33 C4
Wakefield Cl
Kempsford GL7 10 E6
Swindon SN5 49 A4
Walbury Hill (Fort)* RG17 185 F8
Walcot Rd SN3 50 E5
Walden Lodge Cl SN10 214 B2
Waldron Cl 3 SN3 51 C4
Waleran Cl SP5 153 E2
Walker Rd BA11 110 A3
Walker's La 3 RG17 165 A2
Wallbridge BA11 110 B4
Wallbridge Ave 2 BA11 110 A4
Wallbridge Gdns 1 BA11 110 A4
Wallbridge Mills BA11 110 B4
Waller Rd SN10 214 E7
Wallingford Cl SN5 49 C3
Wallingtons Rd RG17 177 F4
Wallis Dr SN25 35 A8
Wallsworth Rd 4 SN3 51 A4
Walmesley Chase BA14 102 A1
Walnut Cl
3 Netheravon SP4 190 A4
Pewsey SN9 215 D5
Rowde SN10 96 D1
Sutton Veny BA12 121 F8
Walnut Dr SN14 74 F6
Walnut Gr BA14 105 B6
Walnut Rd BA12 139 B4
Walnut Tree Cl SN3 36 B2
Walnut Tree Gdns SN5 48 D8
Walnut Trees Hill SN6 164 A8
Walnut Wlk 1 BA11 110 B7
Walronds Cl SN8 170 C8
Walsingham Rd SN3 50 F6
Walter Cl SN5 49 A6
Walter Sutton Cl SN11 80 F3
Walton Cl 5 SN3 50 F4
Walwayne Ct Prim Sch BA14 105 B8
Walwayne Field SN2 36 A5
Walworth Rd SP10 193 F1
Wanborough Prim Sch SN4 163 A6
Wanborough Rd
Swindon SN3 36 C1
Wanborough SN4 51 F6
Wansdyke* SN11 172 C5
Wansdyke Cty Prim Sch SN10 214 B1
Wansdyke Dr SN11 81 A3
Wansdyke Rd SN8 176 B4
Wanshot Cl SN4 64 C5
Wantage Rd RG17 165 B2
War Meml Ave 13 RG17 177 B6
Waram Cl RG17 177 C8
Warbeck Gate 11 SN5 48 F5
Warbler Cl 1 BA14 105 B8
Warburton Cl BA14 105 A6
Wardley Cl SN3 51 A4
Wardour Cl SN3 50 E3
Wardour Pl 4 SN12 94 A2
Wardour RC Prim Sch SP3 203 C6
Wardour Rd 4 SN14 78 A6
Wardrobe Mus* SP1 152 A8
Wareham Cl SN5 49 B5
Warleigh Dr BA1 82 A3
Warleigh La BA1 82 B1
Warmer's Inn La SN16 27 D8
Warminster Ave 2 SN2 35 C5
Warminster Coll BA12 117 A7
Warminster Com Hospl BA12 117 A7
Warminster Dewey Museum* BA12 117 B7
Warminster Prep Sch BA12 116 F7
Warminster Rd
Claverton BA2 90 B4
Frome BA11 110 B4
Westbury BA13 108 F1
Wilton SP2 144 D5
Warminster Sch BA12 116 F7
Warminster Sports Ctr BA12 117 D6
Warminster Sta BA12 117 B7
Warneage Gn 2 SN4 163 A5
Warneford Cl 4 SN5 49 D4
Warner Cl 2 SN3 36 B3
Warren Cres SN11 81 C4
Warren Rd BA14 101 D5
Warrener Cl SN25 35 B7
Warrens La SP5 159 A4
Warwick Cl
Chippenham SN14 77 F5
Salisbury SP1 145 F3
Warwick Cres SN12 94 B3
Warwick Rd SN1 50 C5
Washbourne Rd SN4 47 E1
Washern Cl SP2 144 C1
Washers Pit* DT11 206 D3
Washington Rd BA13 108 C6
Washmeres SN14 75 B2
Washpool La GL7 10 E8
Wason Rd 5 SP4 197 E6
Wastfield SN13 84 F8
Water Ditchampton SP2 144 C4
Water Field SN5 33 A3
Water Furlongs 2 SN6 19 D7
Water La
Castle Combe SN14 68 A7
Enford SN9 190 B6
Horningsham BA12 119 A8
Salisbury SP1 152 A8
Water Meadows SN16 28 A2
Water St
Berwick St John SP7 203 E1
Durrington/Bulford SP4 217 D8
Mere BA12 139 B5
Upton Lovell BA12 194 E3
Watercrook Mews 2 SN5 49 D5
Waterdown Cl 2 SN2 34 C4
Waterford Beck BA14 104 F6
Watergate La SP4 217 C7
Watergates SN14 75 C3
Waterhouse La BA2 98 F8
Waterloo Rd SP1 152 C7
Watermead SN3 36 C2
Watermeadow La BA12 195 C1
Watermint Way SN11 80 F4
Waters Bank Rd SN13 84 B8
Waters Edge SN15 78 E5
Waters Rd SP1 146 A4
Waterside Pk Ind Est SN2 49 E8
Waterside Way SN3 51 A1
Watersmeet Rd SP2 152 A6
Waterworks Rd BA14 105 B7
Watery La
Donhead St Mary SP7 203 A3
Shaftesbury SP7 202 C1
Sutton Veny BA12 117 F4
Watling Cl SN2 49 E6
Watson Rd SP4 197 E7
Watt Cl 4 SP10 193 C1
Watt Rd SP2 151 D8
Watt's Way 22 SN10 179 F1
Watts La SN14 41 F1
Wavell Rd
Salisbury SP2 152 A6
Swindon SN2 35 B2
Tidworth SP9 216 B8
Waverley Cl
7 Fordingbridge SP6 210 D2
Frome BA11 110 C6
Waverley Ct SN13 85 A8
Waverley Gdns SN12 94 A3
Waverley Rd
Fordingbridge SP6 210 D2
Swindon SN3 36 C1
Waylands Cricklade SN6 19 E7
Devizes SN10 214 D3
Wayne Cl SN25 35 A5
Wayside Cl
Frome BA11 110 C6
Kington Langley SN15 70 E7
Swindon SN2 49 E7
Weaveland Rd 2 SP3 203 E8
Weavern Ct SN14 78 A7
Weavern La SN13 76 A5
Weavers Cl 3 SN16 28 A5
Weavers Crofts SN12 94 A5
Weavers Dr BA14 105 D7
Weavers La RG17 177 E3
Weavers Mead SN10 179 C1
Weavers The SN3 50 D4
Webb Cl SN15 78 E5
Webbers Ct BA14 105 A6
Webbington Rd SN15 78 E5
Webbs Ct SN15 60 A3
Webbs Way
Burbage SN8 183 D8
Malmesbury SN16 28 A5
Webbs Wood SN5 34 A2
Wedgewood Cl SN2 50 A7
Wedmore Ave SN15 70 C1
Wedmore Cl BA11 110 C7
Weedon Rd SN3 51 B8
Weeke Cl 1 SP5 210 F8
Weir Hayes 7 SN13 76 B1
Weir La SN14 74 A8
Weir The BA13 186 C8
Weirside Ave SN4 64 B6
Welbeck Cl SN3 50 F5
Welcombe Ave SN3 51 A5
Welford Cl SN3 51 C8
Well Cl SN4 65 D4
Well House Cl SP6 210 B6
Well La Godshill SP6 211 A1
Hawkesbury GL9 38 E5
4 Shaftesbury SP7 202 B2
Welle Sley Cl 18 SN12 178 B8
Weller Rd SN13 76 F2
Wellhead Dro BA13 109 A1
Wellhead La BA13 109 A1
Wellington Dr
Bishops Cannings SN10 214 F7
Bower Hill SN12 94 C1
Wellington Pl SN14 55 F8
Wellington Rd
5 Durrington/Bulford SP4 198 F7
South Marston SN3 36 C6
Wellington Sq SN12 94 C1
Wellington St SN1 50 C7
Wellington Way SP2 145 D3
Wellow Dr BA11 110 C7
Wellow La BA2 98 D1
Wellow Wood Rd SO51 212 F8
Wells Cl
Chippenham SN14 78 A5
Durrington SP4 198 A6
Wells Rd SP4 198 A6
Wells St SN1 50 C6
Welsh Way GL7 1 D8
Welton Rd SN5 49 D6
Wembley St SN2 49 F8
Wenhill Hts SN11 81 B2
Wenhill La SN11 81 A1
Wensleydale Cl SN5 49 B6
Wentworth Cl SN15 78 F7
Wentworth Pk 1 SN5 49 A4
Were Cl 3 BA12 116 E7
Werg SN8 175 B8
Wesley Cl BA14 104 E2
Wesley La BA14 104 E2
Wesley Rd BA14 105 C7
Wesley St SN1 50 C4
Wessex Cl Calne SN11 81 C3
2 Hungerford RG17 177 B7
Melksham SN12 94 B3
Semington BA14 102 E5
Wessex Coll BA12 117 C6
Wessex Pl 29 RG17 177 B7
Wessex Rd
Chippenham SN14 78 B8
Salisbury SP1 146 C1
Wilton SP2 144 C1
Wessex Way SN6 23 B7
Wessex Wlk BA13 109 A4
Wessington Ave SN11 81 C1
Wessington Ct SN11 81 C1
Wessington Pk SN11 81 C1
West Allcourt GL7 2 C4
West Ashton CE Prim Sch BA14 106 B4
West Ashton Rd BA14 105 E8
West Bourton Rd SP8 137 D1
West Cepen Way
Chippenham SN14 70 B3
Chippenham Without SN14 77 F5
West Ditch La BA14 106 E4
West End
Bishops Cannings SN10 172 B3
Melksham SN12 94 A3
Westbury BA13 109 A3
West End La
Bishopstone SN6 163 E6
Donhead St Andrew SP7 203 B3
West End Rd
Salisbury SP2 145 E2
Swindon SN3 36 A1
West Ennox La SN13 84 A6
West Hay Gr GL7 4 F7
West Highland Rd SN25 34 F7
West Hill
Broad Blunsdon SN26 21 B2
Melksham Without SN12 85 B1
West Kennett Long Barrow* SN8 173 C6
West La Kemble GL7 4 F7
Melbury Abbas SP7 206 A7
West Manton SN8 174 C7
West Mill La SN6 8 C1
West Par BA12 116 F6
West Pk
Appleshaw SP11 192 E3
Rockbourne SP6 210 A3
West Pk Dr SP6 209 F3
West Pk La SP6 209 F3
West Pk Rd SN13 76 E1
West Portway SP10 193 C1
West St Aldbourne SN8 170 A6
Barford St Martin SP3 143 A4
Castle Combe SN14 68 A7
22 Fordingbridge SP6 210 D1
Great Somerford SN15 43 F2
Great Wishford SP2 129 F4
Lacock SN15 86 D5
4 Malmesbury SN16 28 A4
Salisbury SP2 145 F1
Trowbridge BA14 105 C8
Warminster BA12 116 E6
Wilton SP2 144 C3
West St Pl BA12 116 E6
West Swindon Sh Ctr SN5 49 B5
West View
Everleigh SN8 191 A8
Swindon SN3 51 B7
West View Cres SN10 214 A3
West View Rd BA1 82 A3
West Way GL7 2 C5
West Wilts Trading Est BA13 108 D7
West Wiltshire Craft Ctr* BA13 108 D6
West Wlk SP1 152 A7
Westbourne Cl SP1 152 C8
Westbourne Gdns 6 BA14 105 B8
Westbourne Rd
Trowbridge BA14 105 B8
Westbury BA13 109 A3
Westbrook Cl
Chippenham SN14 78 A7
14 Hungerford RG17 177 B7
Westbrook Gn SN15 95 E8
Westbrook Rd
Bromham SN15 88 A1
Swindon SN2 35 A1
Westbury CE Jun Sch BA13 108 F3
Westbury Com Hospl BA13 109 A2
Westbury Ind Est BA13 108 E5
Westbury Leigh BA13 108 E1
Westbury Leigh CE Prim Sch BA13 108 E1
Westbury Pk SN4 47 D1
Westbury Rd
Bratton BA13 186 A7
Cheverell Magna SN10 179 C1
Heywood BA13 109 A8
North Bradley BA14 105 E3
Swindon SN2 35 B5
Warminster BA12 113 A2
Westbury Sta BA13 108 E5
Westbury View SN12 94 C4
Westbury Visitor Ctr* BA13 109 A3
Westbury White Horse* BA13 109 F3
Westcombe La BA12 195 E1
Westcott Cl 9 BA11 110 C6
Westcott Pl SN1 50 A5
Westcott St SN1 50 A5
Westcroft SN14 78 A5
Westcroft St BA14 101 C1
Westerham Wlk SN11 81 C2
Westerleigh Cl SN14 78 B6
Western Downland CE Prim Sch SP6 210 A5
Western Downland Prim Sch SP6 209 F2
Western St SN1 50 C5
Western Way
Melksham SN12 93 F3
Salisbury SP2 145 B3
Westfield BA15 100 B7
Westfield Chase 13 SN8 170 A6
Westfield Cl
15 Durrington/Bulford SP4 198 B7
Laverstock SP1 146 D2
Trowbridge BA14 105 A6
Westfield Est BA12 137 F4
Westfield Rd BA14 105 A7
Westfield Way SN2 34 D4
Westgrove 17 SP6 210 D1
Westhill Cl SN6 22 F5
Westlake Pl SN15 57 D1
Westland Cl 3 SP4 217 D3
Westlands 2 BA12 194 C5
Westlands La SN12 85 F2
Westlea Campus SN5 49 C7
Westlea Dr SN5 49 C5
Westlea Prim Sch SN5 49 C6
Westlecot Rd SN1 50 B3
Westleigh BA12 116 E6
Westmead Cres BA14 105 B4
Westmead Dr SN5 49 D7
Westmead Ind Est SN5 49 D6
Westmead La SN15 78 D7
Westmead Terr SN15 78 E6
Westminster Cl 1 SP7 202 D2
Westminster Gdns SN14 78 B7
Westminster Meml Hospl SP7 202 B1
Westminster Rd
Salisbury SP2 145 F2
Westminster Rd *continued*
Swindon SN5 49 B4
Westmorland Rd SN1 50 D5
Weston Ct 1 SP11 193 E4
Weston La SP5 149 B5
Westonbirt Arboretum* GL8 25 B8
Westonbirt Sch GL8 25 E8
Westpoint Bsns Pk SN14 70 A1
Westrop SN6 23 A6
Westrop Prim Sch SN6 22 F6
Westside SP4 199 A2
Westside Cl SP4 146 C8
Westview Orch BA2 99 B5
Westwells SN13 84 C6
Westwells Rd SN13 84 B7
Westwood Manor House* BA15 100 A3
Westwood Rd
Corsham SN13 84 B8
Salisbury SP2 145 B4
Swindon SN2 35 C6
Wingfield BA15 100 D2
Westwood St Thomas Sch SP2 145 A4
Westwood with Iford Prim Sch BA15 99 F3
Westwoods BA1 82 B3
Wet La BA12 139 D2
Wet Pits La SN8 168 E3
Wetherby Cl 1 SN14 78 A5
Wexland Ave SP4 189 F3
Wey Cl SN25 35 A4
Weyhill Cl SN3 51 B5
Weyhill Gdns 7 SP11 192 F1
Weyhill Rd SP11 193 A1
Weymouth St BA12 117 A6
Whaddon La
Hilperton BA14 102 B5
Trowbridge BA14 102 A3
Whalley Cres SN4 63 F6
Wharf Ct SN12 94 B3
Wharf Ctr The* SN10 214 A4
Wharf La Kempsford GL7 10 D6
Lechlade GL7 2 D3
Wharf Rd SN4 49 C1
Wharf St SN10 214 A4
Wharf The SN13 83 D6
Wharf Theatre & Ctr The SN10 214 A4
Wharfings The GL7 10 D6
Whatcombe Brow SP3 196 D8
Whatleys Cl SN10 179 A4
Whatleys Orch SN6 163 E6
Wheatlands SN25 34 E4
Wheatsheaf La SN16 16 A8
Wheatstone Rd SN3 51 E4
Wheeler Ave SN2 35 D2
Wheeler Cl SN9 215 B5
Wheelwright's Cl SP5 208 A4
Whelford Rd GL7 10 D7
Whilestone Way SN3 36 C1
Whinyates Rd 2 SP4 197 E7
Whistley Rd SN10 179 C8
Whitbourne Ave SN3 50 F5
Whitbred Cl 2 SN5 49 B7
Whitbred Rd SP2 145 C5
Whitby Gr SN2 34 F1
Whitchers Meadow SP5 153 D4
Whitcombe Cl SN15 73 F8
White Barrow (Long Barrow)* SP3 188 B1
White Beam Ct SN2 35 B2
White Castle SN5 49 C3
White Cliff* BA13 186 B6
White Edge Moor SN3 51 D2
White Ennox La SN13 83 F7
White Farm La SN8 185 C7
White Hart La 12 SP7 202 C1
White Hill
Bishopstone SN4 163 D5
Pitton & Farley SP5 148 C3
White Horse Bsns Pk BA14 105 D4
White Horse Cl BA14 105 D6
White Horse Dr 8 BA11 110 C6
White Horse Rd
Cricklade SN6 19 D8
Winsley BA15 99 E7
White Horse Sports Ctr SN11 81 C1
White Horse Way
Calne SN11 81 B1
Westbury BA13 109 A4
White Lion Pk SN16 27 E4
White Pit La SP7 206 B6
White Rd Mere BA12 139 B6
Savernake SN8 175 A6
White Row Hill BA14 105 A5
White Sheet Castle* BA12 124 E1
White Sheet Hill Nature Reserve* BA12 124 E2
White Sheet La BA12 124 C3
White Shute RG17 171 A8
White St
Easterton SN10 180 A1
Horningsham BA12 119 B8
21 Market Lavington SN10 179 F1
White Way
Broad Town SN4 167 A8

White Way continued
Pitton & Farley SP5 . . . . . .148 C3
White's Hill SN8 . . . . . .169 F2
Whitebridge Rd SP1 . .146 D1
Whitecroft BA13 . . . . . .112 C8
Whitefield Cl BA1 . . . . . .82 B4
Whitefield Cres SN5 . . . . . .34 A1
Whitefriars La SN6 . . . . . . .6 E3
Whitefriars Rd 1 SP1 . .152 B7
Whitegates SN14 . . . . . .68 A8
Whitehead St SN1 . . . . . .50 B5
Whiteheads La BA15 . .100 D7
Whitehill SN8 . . . . . .100 D7
Whitehill Cl 11 SN8 . . .170 B2
Whitehill La SN4 . . . . . .47 B2
Whitehill Way SN5 . . . . .48 F3
Whitehorn Cl SN4 . . . . . .47 E4
Whitehorn Dr SP5 . . . . .212 C5
Whitehouse La GL8 . . . .26 B8
Whitehouse Rd SN2 . . . .50 B8
Whiteland Rise BA13 . .109 B8
Whitelands Rd SN3 . . . . .36 A1
Whitelawn La BA14 . . .106 F4
Whitelocks Piece
RG17 . . . . .171 A1
Whiteman St SN2 . . . . . .50 C8
Whitemarsh BA12 . . . . .139 B4
Whiterow Pk BA14 . . . .105 A6
Whites Cnr SN12 . . . . . .85 D1
Whitesbury Rd SP5 . . . .152 B1
Whitesheet CE Prim Sch
BA12 . . . . .123 E6
Whitesheets Prim Sch
BA12 . . . . .138 A4
Whiteshoot SP5 . . . . . .211 D6
Whiteshoot Hill SP5 . . .211 D6
Whitestone Rd BA11 . . .110 B6
Whitfield Cl BA12 . . . . .117 C7
Whitgift Cl SN5 . . . . . . .48 F6
Whitley Rd 14 SN8 . . . .170 A6
Whitlock Rise SP5 . . . .205 F5
Whitmarsh Cl 7 SP4 . . .190 A4
Whitmore Cl SN5 . . . . . .48 F6
Whitney St SN1 . . . . . . .50 C5
Whittington Rd SN5 . . . .49 C6
Whittle Ave SN11 . . . . .166 A1
Whittle Cl SN14 . . . . . . .78 A7
Whittle Rd
4 Andover SP10 . . . .193 B1
Salisbury SP2 . . . . . . .145 D1
Whitworth Rd SN25 . . . . .35 A3
Wichelstok Cl SN1 . . . . .50 C3
Wick La Devizes SN10 . .214 B1
Downton SP5 . . . . .210 E8
Lacock SN15 . . . . .85 F4
Manningford SN9 . . . . .181 F5
Wanborough SN4 . . . . . .51 F6
Wick Rd SN16 . . . . .16 A8
Wickdown Ave SN25 . . . .34 F3
Wicker Hill BA14 . . . . . .101 C1
Wickfield SN10 . . . . . . .214 B2
Wicks Cl SN25 . . . . .34 E5
Wicks Dr SN15 . . . . .78 F5
Wickwater La GL7 . . . . . . .7 C4
Widbrook Meadow
BA14 . . . . .105 A8
Widbrook View BA15 . . .100 E5
Widhill La SN26 . . . . . . .21 A1
Wigmore Ave SN3 . . . . . .50 F3
Wilcot Ave SN2 . . . . . . .35 D5
Wilcot Cl
Amesbury SP4 . . . . . . .217 D2
Trowbridge BA14 . . . . .105 C6
Wilcot Rd SN9 . . . . . . .215 B5
Wilcox Cl SN2 . . . . .35 C2
Wild Acre 9 SN4 . . . . .163 A6
Wildern Sq SN3 . . . . . . .36 A4
Wilderness The BA15 . .100 C7
Wildmoorway La GL7 . . . .7 B7
Wiley Terr SP2 . . . . . . .144 D4
Wilkins Cl SN2 . . . . .35 F5
William Cl SP1 . . . . . . .146 D1
William Rd SN10 . . . . . .214 D2
William Robbins Ct
SN25 . . . . .34 F3
William St Chippenham SN11 . .81 C4
Swindon SN1 . . . . .50 A5
William Stumpes Cl 7
SN16 . . . . .28 A5
Williams Gr SN15 . . . . . .85 A8
Williamson Cl 3 SP11 . .192 A5
Willis Cl
5 Chippenham SN15 . . .78 F4
Great Bedwyn SN8 . . . .176 C3
Willis Way SN5 . . . . . . .33 B3
Willoughby Cl BA13 . . .108 E2
Willoughby Rd SP4 . . . .197 E6
Willow Ave 5 SP6 . . . .210 D1
Willow Cl
Laverstock SP1 . . . . . . .146 D2
Melksham SN12 . . . . . . .94 A3
Willow Cres
Broughton Gifford SN12 . .93 A5
Warminster BA12 . . . . .117 C5
Willow Dr
Devizes SN10 . . . . .214 E5
4 Durrington SP4 . . . .198 B7
Willow Gr
Chippenham SN14 . . . . . .70 E2
Trowbridge BA14 . . . . .105 B5
Westbury BA13 . . . . . . .108 C4
Willow View BA14 . . . .105 C3
Willow View Cl SN16 . . . .27 F4

Willow Way SP7 . . . . . .202 A4
Willow Wlk SN4 . . . . . . .64 B6
Willowbank SN14 . . . . . .70 A2
Willowbrook SN5 . . . . . .33 C4
Willowbrook End SN15 . .57 D2
Willowherb Cl SN25 . . . .34 E5
Willows Ave SN2 . . . . . .35 C3
Willows The Calne SN11 . .89 E8
Highworth SN6 . . . . .23 A5
Swindon SN5 . . . . .34 A2
Wills Ave SN1 . . . . .50 E8
Wilman Way SP2 . . . . . .151 F5
Wilmot Cl SN5 . . . . .48 F6
Wilsford Group (Tumuli)
SP4 . . . . .197 D2
Wilsford Rd SN9 . . . . . .181 C5
Wilson Rd Larkhill SP4 . .197 A6
Swindon SN25 . . . . .34 F6
Wilson Sq BA12 . . . . . .117 C7
Wilton Carpet Factory★
SP2 . . . . .144 D4
Wilton CE Fst Sch
SP2 . . . . .144 B2
Wilton CE Mid Sch
SP2 . . . . .144 B4
Wilton Dr BA14 . . . . . . .105 D6
Wilton Ho★ SP2 . . . . . .144 D2
Wilton Pk★ SP2 . . . . . .144 D1
Wilton Rd
Barford St Martin SP3 . .143 C3
East Grafton SN8 . . . . .184 A7
Quidhampton SP2 . . . . .144 F3
Wylye BA12 . . . . .201 F8
Wilton Sh Village, SP2 .144 E3
Wilton Windmill★
SN8 . . . . .184 B8
Wilton Wlk SN2 . . . . . . .35 C6
Wiltshire Ave SN2 . . . . . .50 A8
Wiltshire Cl
Bulford SP4 . . . . .217 F8
3 Hungerford RG17 . . .177 B7
Wiltshire Coll
Calne SN11 . . . . .81 D2
Chippenham SN15 . . . . . .78 E8
Chippenham SN15 . . . . . .78 E1
Devizes SN10 . . . . .214 B3
Malmesbury SN16 . . . . . .28 A3
Melksham SN12 . . . . . . .94 A5
Trowbridge BA14 . . . . .105 C8
Trowbridge BA14 . . . . .105 B6
Westbury BA13 . . . . . . .109 A3
Wiltshire Cres SN12 . . . .94 C3
Wiltshire Dr 4 BA14 . .105 D6
Wiltshire Gall The★
SP1 . . . . .145 F1
Wiltshire Heritage Mus★
SN10 . . . . .214 A3
Wiltshire Music Ctr
BA15 . . . . .100 B8
Wiltshire Rd SP2 . . . . . .151 E6
Wiltshire Way BA13 . . . .109 A4
Wimpole Cl SN3 . . . . . . .51 B4
Win Gn View 7 SP7 . . .202 D2
Winchester Cl
Amesbury SP4 . . . . . . .217 D2
2 Chippenham SN14 . . .78 A6
North Bradley BA14 . . . .105 C2
Swindon SN3 . . . . .36 B1
Winchester St SP1 . . . .146 B1
Wincombe Bsns Pk
SP7 . . . . .202 C3
Wincombe La 2 SP7 . . .202 D2
Wincombe Pk★ SP7 . . .202 D3
Windbrook Meadow
SN2 . . . . .36 A4
Windermere SN3 . . . . . .51 D3
Windermere Rd BA14 . .101 E2
Windflower Rd SN25 . . . .34 E5
Winding Way SP2 . . . . .145 B3
Windlass Way SN15 . . . .78 E5
Windlesham Rd SP1 . .146 B4
Windmill Cl
3 Aldbourne SN8 . . . .170 A7
Aldbury SP5 . . . . .153 C2
4 Shaftesbury SP7 . . .202 C2
Windmill Hill (Causewayed
Enclosure)★ SN4 . . .167 A2
Windmill Hill Bsns Pk
SN5 . . . . .48 F3
Windmill Hill Prim Sch
SN5 . . . . .49 A3
Windmill La
Hurstbourne Tarrant
SP11 . . . . .193 B1
Winterbourne SP4 . . . . .133 B4
Windmill Piece SN4 . . . .65 D4
Windmill Rd GL7 . . . . . . .4 F3
Windmill Tump (Long
Barrow)★ GL7 . . . . . . .3 A7
Windrush SN6 . . . . .22 E5
Windrush Rd SN25 . . . . .35 A3
Windsor Ave SN12 . . . . .94 B3
Windsor Dr
Chippenham SN14 . . . . . .78 A6
Lydiard Tregoze SN4 . . . .47 F6
Windsor Cres BA11 . . . .110 A5
Windsor Dr
Devizes SN10 . . . . .214 D3
1 Trowbridge BA14 . . .105 B5
Westbury BA13 . . . . . . .109 B4
Windsor Mews 8 SP4 . .198 B7
Windsor Rd
Calne Without SN11 . . . .81 F1
9 Durrington/Bulford
SP4 . . . . .198 B7
North Bradley BA14 . . . .105 A4
9 Salisbury SP2 . . . . .145 F1
Swindon SN3 . . . . .50 F2

Windsor St 10 SP2 . . . .145 F1
Windwhistle Cnr SP7 . .202 E2
Windwhistle La
Alderbury SP5 . . . . . . .160 B7
Grimstead SP5 . . . . . . .154 B1
Windwhistle Way SP5 .153 F2
Wine St
Bradford-on-Avon BA15 . .100 C6
Devizes SN10 . . . . .214 B3
Wing Rd SP4 . . . . .198 E6
Wingate Par SN2 . . . . . .35 A2
Wingfield SP2 . . . . .36 A5
Wingfield Ave SN2 . . . . .35 C6
Wingfield CE Prim Sch
BA14 . . . . .104 C6
Wingfield Rd BA14 . . . .105 A7
Winifred St SN1 . . . . . . .50 D3
Winkelbury Hill (Hill Fort)★
SP7 . . . . .207 C8
Winkins La SN15 . . . . . .44 A2
Winkworth Cottage
SN16 . . . . .29 C2
Winlaw Cl SN5 . . . . .49 C7
Winscombe Ct BA11 . . .110 B5
Winsley CE Prim Sch
BA15 . . . . .99 E7
Winsley Cl SN2 . . . . . . .35 C4
Winsley Hill BA2 . . . . . .99 B6
Winsley Rd BA15 . . . . .100 B7
Winstanley Cl 8 SN5 . . .49 A4
Winston Ave SN4 . . . . . .93 F1
Winter Gn SN11 . . . . . . .80 F3
Winterbourne Earls CE Prim
Sch SP4 . . . . .133 C4
Winterbourne Stoke Group
(Tumuli)★ SP4 . . . . . .197 C4
Winterslow CE Prim Sch
SP5 . . . . .149 B6
Winterslow Rd
Idmiston SP4 . . . . .198 C1
Porton SP4 . . . . .133 D6
Swindon SN2 . . . . .35 B5
2 Trowbridge BA14 . . .105 B5
Winton Cl SP9 . . . . .216 D4
Winton Rd SN3 . . . . . . .36 B4
Winwick Rd SN5 . . . . . .49 B4
Wirr The SP3 . . . . .128 D7
Wirral Way SN25 . . . . . .34 F7
Wise Cl SN2 . . . . .35 E3
Wise La SP3 . . . . .141 C4
Wiseman Cl 2 SN3 . . . .51 E6
Wishart Way SN15 . . . . .78 F5
Wishford Rd SP2 . . . . . .144 B5
Witan Cl 8 SP10 . . . . . .193 E2
Witchcombe La SN10 . .179 B1
Witchell La SN10 . . . . . .180 B3
Witfield Cl SN5 . . . . .33 B5
Witham Way SN2 . . . . . .35 F4
Witherington Rd
Alderbury SP5 . . . . . . .153 C2
Downton SP5 . . . . .159 C5
Witherington Ring (Field
System)★ SP5 . . . . . .159 D7
Witheys The 10 SN4 . . .163 A6
Withies The SN8 . . . . . .175 D1
Withy Bed SN4 . . . . .61 C1
Withy Cl
Trowbridge BA14 . . . . .101 E3
Wootton Bassett SN4 . . .47 B3
Withybed La RG17 . . . .177 F5
Withymead Rd SN14 . . . .74 A8
Witt Rd SP5 . . . . .149 D5
Wittenham View 7 SP4 .217 C5
Wittensford La SO51 . . .212 F1
Witts La SN5 . . . . .33 B5
Wivenhoe Ct 7 BA11 . .110 C6
Woburn Cl
Swindon SN25 . . . . .34 F6
Trowbridge BA14 . . . . .105 A8
Wolferstan Dr SP1 . . . .146 D5
Wolfhall Rd SN8 . . . . . .183 D8
Wolsely Ave SN1 . . . . . .51 A4
Wolverton Cl SN14 . . . . .77 F6
Wood H Dr SN2 . . . . . . .34 D3
Wood La
Brinkworth SN15 . . . . . .46 D7
Chapmanslade BA13 . . .111 D4
Chippenham SN15 . . . . . .78 C2
Fonthill Bishop SP3 . . . .200 C2
Lydiard Millicent SN5 . . .32 A1
Nettleton SN14 . . . . . . .67 B8
Purton SN5 . . . . .31 C1
Sherston GL8 . . . . .25 B5
Wood Rd SP4 . . . . .198 A6
Wood St Calne SN11 . . . .81 B3
Clyffe Pypard SN4 . . . . .65 D4
Swindon SN1 . . . . .50 D4
Wootton Bassett SN4 . . .47 D2
Woodborough CE Aided Prim
Sch SN9 . . . . .181 C6
Woodborough Cl
BA14 . . . . .105 D5
Woodborough Rd
Beechingstoke SN9 . . . .181 B6
Corsham SN13 . . . . .85 B7
Pewsey SN9 . . . . .215 A5
Woodbury SP3 . . . . . . .165 B1
Woodbury Cl 2 SN5 . . . .49 A8
Woodbury Gdns SP2 . . .152 A5
Woodchester SN5 . . . . . .49 C5
Woodcock Cl SP9 . . . . .216 D6
Woodcock Gdns BA12 . .117 C6
Woodcock Ind Est
BA12 . . . . .117 D7
Woodcock La BA12 . . . .117 B7
Woodcock Pk BA12 . . . .117 C6
Woodcock Rd BA12 . . . .117 C6
Woodcombe SN12 . . . . . .94 C6

Woodcote Rd SN8 . . . . .185 B8
Woodcutters Mews
SN25 . . . . .35 C6
Woodfern SP6 . . . . .210 F1
Woodfolds SN16 . . . . . . .15 F7
Woodford Cl 3 SN2 . . . .35 C6
Woodford Valley CE Prim Sch
SP4 . . . . .131 C5
Woodhayes Rd BA11 . . .110 C6
Woodhenge★ SP4 . . . . .217 A7
Woodhill Ave SN11 . . . . .81 C3
Woodhill Pk★ SN4 . . . .166 E7
Woodhill Rise SN11 . . . . .81 C4
Woodhill Village★
SN4 . . . . .166 D8
Woodhouse Castle (rems
of)★ BA12 . . . . .114 E1
Woodhouse Gdns
BA14 . . . . .102 B2
Woodhouse Rd 3 SN3 . . .50 F5
Woodland Dr SP5 . . . . .149 B6
Woodland Heritage Ctr The★
BA13 . . . . .107 F5
Woodland Ind Est
BA13 . . . . .108 F2
Woodland Pk SN11 . . . . .81 B2
Woodland Rd
Patney SN10 . . . . .180 F5
Woodland View
Westbury BA13 . . . . . . .112 B8
Wroughton SN4 . . . . . . .50 B1
Woodland Way
Devizes SN10 . . . . .214 A1
Salisbury SP1 . . . . .146 E2
Woodlands SN13 . . . . . . .76 E2
Woodlands Bglws SN14 . .78 B7
Woodlands La SP7 . . . .203 E1
Woodlands Manor★
BA12 . . . . .139 A3
Woodlands Prim Sch
SP1 . . . . .145 B4
Woodlands Rd
Chippenham SN14 . . . . . .78 C8
Mere BA12 . . . . .139 B2
Mildenhall SN8 . . . . . . .169 A1
Pewsey SN9 . . . . .215 D6
Woodlands Rd Ind Est
BA12 . . . . .139 B4
Woodlands The BA15 . .113 A1
Woodlea SN14 . . . . .75 C6
Woodlea Grange SP5 . .153 E2
Woodling Cres SP6 . . . .210 F1
Woodman Mead 5
BA12 . . . . .116 F7
Woodmarsh BA14 . . . . .105 D4
Woodpecker Mews
SN14 . . . . .70 B2
Woodroffe Sq SN11 . . . .81 C2
Woodrow SN12 . . . . .94 D7
Woodrow Rd SN12 . . . . .94 C6
Woods Cl SN16 . . . . . . .25 C1
Woods Hill BA2 . . . . .99 A6
Woodsage Way SN11 . . .80 F3
Woods's La SP3 . . . . . . .200 F2
Woodshaw Mead 8 SN4 . .48 A2
Woodside Ave SN3 . . . . .50 E5
Woodside Rd
Salisbury SP2 . . . . .145 C3
South Marston Park SN3 . .36 C7
Woodsman Rd SN25 . . . .35 B6
Woodstock Gdns SN12 . .94 B3
Woodstock Rd SP1 . . . .146 B2
Woodvill Rd SP1 . . . . . .146 D4
Woodway Cotts GL9 . . . .24 E5
Woolands La 1 SP7 . . .202 B2
Woolcott La SP8 . . . . . .137 D1
Wooley Dr BA15 . . . . . .100 E7
Woolford Grange 2 SN4 . .48 A2
Woollaton Cl SN5 . . . . . .49 A5
Woolley Cl BA15 . . . . . .100 E7
Woolley Rd BA15 . . . . . .100 E7
Woolley St BA15 . . . . . .100 E6
Woolley Terr BA15 . . . . .100 E7
Woolmer Dro SN8 . . . . .168 F6
Woolpack Meadows
BA14 . . . . .105 E7
Wootton Bassett Inf Sch
SN4 . . . . .47 C1
Wootton Bassett Mus★
SN4 . . . . .47 D1
Wootton Bassett Rd
SN5 . . . . .49 C5
Wootton Bassett Sch
SN4 . . . . .47 D3
Wor Barrow (Long Barrow)★
SP5 . . . . .208 C4
Worcester Lodge★
GL9 . . . . .24 A3
Wordsworth Cl 1 SN4 . . .47 F3
Wordsworth Dr SN2 . . . .35 F4
Wordsworth Rd SP1 . . .146 B2
Worlidge Dr SN5 . . . . . .49 B8
Wormcliff La SN13 . . . . .83 A4
Worsley Rd SN5 . . . . . . .49 A4
Worsted Cl BA14 . . . . . .105 E7
Wortheys Cl SN16 . . . . . .28 A5
Worton & Marston Prim Sch
SN10 . . . . .179 B4
Worton Rd SN10 . . . . . .179 C4
Wouldham Cl SP11 . . . .191 F4
Wren Cl Frome BA11 . . .110 B7
3 Warminster BA12 . . .116 E5
Wren Ct SN14 . . . . .105 B8
Wrenscroft 8 SP2 . . . . .152 A5
Wrenswood SN3 . . . . . . .51 D8
Wroughton Airfield
SN4 . . . . .63 F2

Wroughton Inf Sch
SN4 . . . . .64 A6
Wroughton Jun Sch
SN4 . . . . .64 A7
Wroughton Science
Museum★ SN3 . . . . . . .64 B1
Wych Elm Rd BA14 . . . .110 C6
Wychurch Rd 4 SN16 . . .28 A5
Wyck Village★ SP3 . . . .203 E2
Wycombe La SN10 . . . . .79 F2
Wycombe La SN10 . . . .172 F1
Wyke Rd BA14 . . . . . . .101 E4
Wyld Ct SN25 . . . . .34 E8
Wyle Down National Nature
Reserve★ BA12 . . . . .201 E7
Wylye Cl Swindon SN25 . .34 F4
Warminster BA12 . . . . .116 F5
Wylye Rd
Steeple Langford SP3 . . .128 B7
Tidworth SP9 . . . . .216 D7
Warminster BA12 . . . . .117 A5
Wylye BA12 . . . . .201 F8
Wyncies The SN6 . . . . .163 E6
Wynd The SN11 . . . . . . .81 B4
Wyndham Cl SN15 . . . . .79 A8
Wyndham La SN4 . . . . .199 A2
Wyndham Pk SP1 . . . . .146 B2
Wyndham Pk Inf Sch
SP1 . . . . .146 B3
Wyndham Rd
Salisbury SP1 . . . . .146 A2
Swindon SN2 . . . . .50 A7
Wyndham Terr SP1 . . . .146 B2
Wynford Rd BA11 . . . . .110 B6
Wynndale Cl SN3 . . . . . .36 A4
Wynsome St BA14 . . . . .104 F3
Wynwards Rd SN25 . . . .35 A5
Wythburn Rd BA11 . . . .110 C5
Wyver Coll SN8 . . . . . . .213 E1
Wyvern Ave SN11 . . . . . .81 C3
Wyvern Cl SN1 . . . . .50 C2
Wyvern Coll SP1 . . . . . .146 E3
Wyvern Rd
Bowerhill SN12 . . . . . . .94 D1
Durrington/Bulford SP4 . .198 E6
Wyvern Theatre & Arts Ctr★
SN1 . . . . .50 C6
Wyvern Wlk BA13 . . . . .108 E3
Wyville Rd BA11 . . . . . .110 C6

Y
Yard Ct BA12 . . . . .117 B6
Yard La SN15 . . . . .96 D7
Yard's La SN9 . . . . .181 C5
Yardley Cl SN2 . . . . .34 F2
Yarmley La SP5 . . . . . . .149 B6
Yarmouth Cl SN5 . . . . . .49 B4
Yarnbrook Rd
Steeple Ashton BA14 . . .102 E1
West Ashton BA14 . . . .105 F2
Yarnbury Castle (Fort)★
BA12 . . . . .196 B3
Yarnton Cl SN5 . . . . . . .49 A8
Yarrow Cl SN2 . . . . .34 C3
Yatton Rd SN14 . . . . . . .68 E1
Yeatmans Cl 6 SP7 . . .202 B2
Yeatmans La 3 SP7 . . .202 B2
Yeats Cl SN25 . . . . .35 A8
Yellow Way Rd BA11 . . .118 A5
Yellowhammer Cl SN3 . . .51 C8
Yeoman
5 Market Lavington SN10 179 F1
Swindon SN5 . . . . .49 A7
Yeoman Way BA14 . . . .105 C7
Yeovil Cl SN3 . . . . .51 B5
Yerbury St 1 BA14 . . . .105 E8
Yew Tree Cl Calne SN11 . .81 A3
Chirton SN10 . . . . .180 F4
The Common SP5 . . . . .149 B6
Yew Tree Gdns SN3 . . . .36 E4
Yew Tree La SN4 . . . . . .167 C7
Yews The BA12 . . . . . . .139 A6
Yewstock Cres W SN15 . .70 C1
Yewtree Cl 8 SP4 . . . . .198 C7
Yiewsley Cres SN3 . . . . .36 B2
Yockney Cl SN13 . . . . . .76 E1
Yonder Way 7 SN4 . . . .163 A6
York Bldgs BA14 . . . . . .101 D1
York Cl
Chippenham SN14 . . . . . .78 A6
Corsham SN13 . . . . .76 F2
York Dro SP5 . . . . .212 C4
York La SN15 . . . . .46 A7
York Rd
7 Hungerford RG17 . . .177 B6
Lyneham SN15 . . . . .60 B2
Salisbury SP2 . . . . .145 F1
Stapleford SP3 . . . . . . .197 B1
Swindon SN1 . . . . .50 D6
Upavon Down SN9 . . . .182 B1
Youngs Paddock SP5 . .149 C6
Yule Hill SP3 . . . . .203 F6

Z
Zakopane Rd SN25 . . . . .34 D6
Zander Rd SN11 . . . . . . .81 B5
Zeals Gn Dr BA12 . . . . .138 A4
Zeals Rise BA12 . . . . . .137 F4
Zig Zag Hill SP7 . . . . . .206 C2
Zion Rd SP11 . . . . .199 F3
Zouch Ave SP9 . . . . . . .216 C7
Zouch Cl SP9 . . . . .216 C7
Zouch Farm Rd SP9 . . .216 C7
Zouch Prim Sch SP9 . . .216 B8

NG	NH	NJ	NK
NM	NN	NO	NP
NR	NS	NT	NU
NX	NY	NZ	
SC	SD	SE	TA
SH	SJ	SK	TF	TG
SM	SN	SO	SP	TL	TM
SR	SS	ST	SU	TQ	TR
SW	SX	SY	SZ	TV

Any feature in this atlas can be given a unique reference to help you find the same feature on other Ordnance Survey maps of the area, or to help someone else locate you if they do not have a Street Atlas.

The grid squares in this atlas match the Ordnance Survey National Grid and are at 500 metre intervals. The small figures at the bottom and sides of every other grid line are the National Grid kilometre values (**00** to **99** km) and are repeated across the country every 100 km (see left).

To give a unique National Grid reference you need to locate where in the country you are. The country is divided into 100 km squares with each square given a unique two-letter reference. Use the administrative map to determine in which 100 km square a particular page of this atlas falls.

The bold letters and numbers between each grid line (**A** to **F**, **1** to **8**) are for use within a specific Street Atlas only, and when used with the page number, are a convenient way of referencing these grid squares.

Example   The railway bridge over DARLEY GREEN RD in grid square B1

Step 1: Identify the two-letter reference, in this example the page is in **SP**

Step 2: Identify the 1 km square in which the railway bridge falls. Use the figures in the southwest corner of this square: Eastings **17**, Northings **74**. This gives a unique reference: **SP 17 74**, accurate to 1 km.

Step 3: To give a more precise reference accurate to 100 m you need to estimate how many tenths along and how many tenths up this 1 km square the feature is (to help with this the 1 km square is divided into four 500 m squares). This makes the bridge about **8** tenths along and about **1** tenth up from the southwest corner.

This gives a unique reference: **SP 178 741**, accurate to 100 m.

Eastings (read from left to right along the bottom) come before Northings (read from bottom to top). If you have trouble remembering say to yourself "Along the hall, THEN up the stairs"!

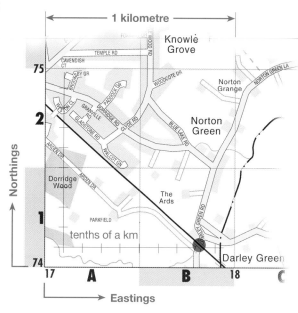

PHILIP'S MAPS

the Gold Standard for drivers

◆ **Philip's street atlases cover every county in England, Wales, Northern Ireland and much of Scotland**

- ◆ Every named street is shown, including alleys, lanes and walkways
- ◆ Thousands of additional features marked: stations, public buildings, car parks, places of interest
- ◆ Route-planning maps to get you close to your destination
- ◆ Postcodes on the maps and in the index
- ◆ Widely used by the emergency services, transport companies and local authorities

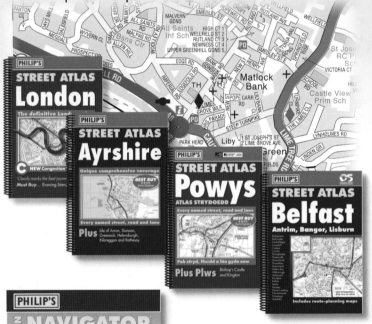

For national mapping, choose **Philip's Navigator Britain** the most detailed road atlas available of England, Wales and Scotland. Hailed by Auto Express as 'the ultimate road atlas', the atlas shows every road and lane in Britain.

Street atlases currently available

England
Bedfordshire and Luton
Berkshire
Birmingham and West Midlands
Bristol and Bath
Buckinghamshire and Milton Keynes
Cambridgeshire and Peterborough
Cheshire
Cornwall
Cumbria
Derbyshire
Devon
Dorset
County Durham and Teesside
Essex
North Essex
South Essex
Gloucestershire and Bristol
Hampshire
North Hampshire
South Hampshire
Herefordshire Monmouthshire
Hertfordshire
Isle of Wight
Kent
East Kent
West Kent
Lancashire
Leicestershire and Rutland
Lincolnshire
Liverpool and Merseyside
London
Greater Manchester
Norfolk
Northamptonshire
Northumberland
Nottinghamshire
Oxfordshire
Shropshire
Somerset
Staffordshire
Suffolk

Surrey
East Sussex
West Sussex
Tyne and Wear
Warwickshire and Coventry
Wiltshire and Swindon
Worcestershire
East Yorkshire Northern Lincolnshire
North Yorkshire
South Yorkshire
West Yorkshire

Wales
Anglesey, Conwy and Gwynedd
Cardiff, Swansea and The Valleys
Carmarthenshire, Pembrokeshire and Swansea
Ceredigion and South Gwynedd
Denbighshire, Flintshire, Wrexham
Herefordshire Monmouthshire
Powys

Scotland
Aberdeenshire
Ayrshire
Dumfries and Galloway
Edinburgh and East Central Scotland
Fife and Tayside
Glasgow and West Central Scotland
Inverness and Moray
Lanarkshire
Scottish Borders

Northern Ireland
County Antrim and County Londonderry
County Armagh and County Down
Belfast
County Tyrone and County Fermanagh

How to order
Philip's maps and atlases are available from bookshops, motorway services and petrol stations. You can order direct from the publisher by phoning **0207 531 8473** or online at **www.philips-maps.co.uk**
For bulk orders only, e-mail philips@philips-maps.co.uk